THE STRATEGIST CODE

THE TIMELESS SYSTEM OF THE TITANS OF STRATEGY

*How the Heroes of History Exploited the Code
to Conquer and Command the World*

Dr. Johnny Welch M.T.S., M.B.A.
By the People Books, San Diego, CA

By the People Books
Copyright © 2023 | All Rights Reserved.

Hardcover Version: ISBN-13: 978-1-7331005-3-3 | ISBN-10: 1-7331005-3-9
Paperback Version: ISBN-13: 978-1-7331005-2-6 | ISBN-10: 1-7331005-2-0

LCCN (Hardcover): 2023907044
LCCN (Paperback): 2023904926
(Library of Congress Control Number)

Library of Congress
US Programs, Law, and Literature Division
Cataloging in Publication Program
101 Independence Avenue, S.E.
Washington, DC 20540-4283

— For Stella Bella and all the friends who became family. —

CONTENTS

PART 1: INTRODUCTION

Think Like a Strategist, Exploit the Proven Power of a Superior Strategic Plan: Napoleon Bonaparte Assumes First Command

"The profoundest truth of war is that the issue of battle is decided in the minds of the opposing commanders, not in the bodies of their men."[1]
—Sir B. H. Liddell Hart, British Military Strategist and Historian

On the fateful day of August 28, 1793, the vibrant city of Toulon, once a bastion of French patriotism, fell victim to a treacherous act of betrayal. In a sinister dance with the enemies of the French Revolution, a band of royalists invited foreign powers in to occupy their beloved city. Soldiers from England and Spain, along with smaller detachments from Sardinia, Sicily and Naples, were crawling all over the city. Like an insidious plague, they swarmed every street and alley, infecting every nook and cranny. They brazenly occupied private homes, indulged in local restaurants, and claimed ownership of bustling stores. Government buildings were transformed into foreign strongholds, while the once serene harbor now groaned under the crowded weight of their imposing ships.

The English and their allies were being led by the formidable British Admiral Sir Samuel Hood who was "famous throughout the Royal Navy for his dramatic clashes with the French during the American Revolution."[2] Hood's occupying forces consisted of nearly 20,000 troops which were all well-supplied and reinforced by the guns of nearly 70 allied warships. These foreign forces were determined to extinguish the flames of revolutionary fervor in France, which was seen as a threat to the rule of monarchs across Europe.

Taking Toulon and its surrounding forts was a major coup. The well-defended, strategically located port city on the Mediterranean coast was France's most important naval base. Along with harboring nearly half of the French Navy,[3] it had "some of the thickest and most advanced defenses…in Europe."[4] "Toulon was considered to be one of the most impregnable fortified cities in the world."[5] It was also the "key to French control of the Mediterranean," writes David Chandler, former Head of the Department of War Studies at the Royal Military Academy at Sandhurst, "and its loss through treachery represented a most damaging blow to the Republic's reputation, both at home and abroad."[6]

France's fledgling revolutionary government was now desperate to take it back. Unfortunately, given its advanced defenses, the daunting task of recapturing Toulon loomed large. The leaders in command of French forces could not see *how* to reclaim the city, particularly given the strategically located fortresses surrounding the landward side of the city.

At last, in the waning days of summer, a young and ambitious figure arrived on the scene—none other than Napoleon Bonaparte, who was still completely unknown at the time. As luck would have it, the political officer tasked with overseeing the French forces outside Toulon, Antoine Saliceti, "happened also to be a fellow Corsican and friend of the Bonaparte family," which led to Napoleon being appointed to replace the artillery officer who had just been severely wounded.[7]

Leaping immediately into action, Napoleon assessed the situation, conducted some initial reconnaissance, and quickly determined what had to be done. Within days, the French army's new artillery officer had a shrewd strategy to retake Toulon and eject the British and Spanish fleets. He recognized that Fort L'Éguillette (Needle Point), located on the heights of Cairo Hill, overlooking the harbor on the opposite side of Toulon, would put the docked enemy warships within range of French artillery. If the French could retake Fort L'Éguillette they would also control access to the harbor. This, Napoleon believed, would force the enemy fleet to evacuate the harbor in order to avoid being burned down by fiery hot cannonballs.

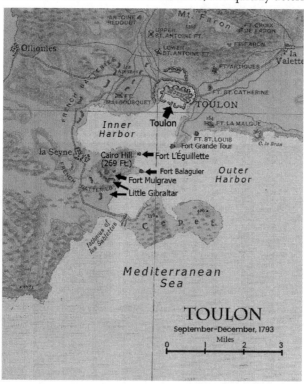

Freedom of access to the harbor was key to the enemy's survival. "If Toulon was impregnable on the landward side, it could not hold out unless it was resupplied by sea, and no ship could approach the harbor if the heights commanding the [inner and outer harbors] were not secured."[8] In effect, Napoleon thought that this one small fort on the cliff was the key to unlocking Toulon,[9] and he quickly began pressing to put his strategic plan into play. After all, he reasoned, "a victory at Toulon could save the Revolution, the rights of man, justice under the law, all the ideals in which Napoleon believed. And he was certain Toulon could be captured—with guns."[10] "Take L'Éguillette," Napoleon told the commanding officer, General Jean Carteaux, "and within a week you are in Toulon."[11]

But the 42-year-old Carteaux, a painter by profession, who had only just recently become a General, "had other ideas and…soon became heartily sick of the young 'know-it-all' planted in [his] midst."[12] At the time, Bonaparte was only 24, and he looked even younger. He had just been appointed as captain— thanks primarily to his political connections in the capital (but, undoubtedly, also his military training at Brienne and the École Militaire in Paris)—and he was still essentially untested and unknown. In other words, along with whatever the strength of his ideas, and the ability of his superiors to recognize the merit of those ideas, he had little more than his personal charisma and persuasion skills to put his strategy into play. This was evidently insufficient for Carteaux.

The other senior officers at Toulon were equally incompetent and indecisive. They were not only unable to recognize the caliber of Bonaparte's strategy, but they also lacked a viable strategy of their own. In fact, Carteaux, who had been hastily promoted, had no strategy at all.[13] Furthermore, "completely unversed in siege warfare and justifiably worried that a disaster might cost him his head,"[14] Carteaux "was clearly not up to the responsibilities and complexities of his present exalted position," which he wasted no time in making frustratingly obvious to Napoleon.[15]

But it was not just a lack of leadership and strategy that was threatening French efforts to retake Toulon. There was also a lack of basic military intelligence and training. "Anyone could see that Toulon was all but impregnable and that only bombardment could yield results, but as Bonaparte quickly realized, Carteaux had no idea how to lay siege to a city. He insisted that he would capture it 'à l'arme blanche,' that is to say with sword and bayonet, and ignored Bonaparte's advice."[16]

Adding insult to injury, Napoleon also quickly learned that the French army's area headquarters was "a nest of political intrigue and infighting."[17] "Everybody thought that he alone knew what needed to be done" to retake Toulon, but, alas, "there was no real direction from the top."[18]

Map Out Your Strategic Game Plan

Bonaparte, however, was unwilling to let his winning strategy sit by the wayside. Despite his limited authority and lack of experience, "he immediately took charge."[19] Indeed, "throughout this period of divided councils and indecision,"[20] Bonaparte was already revealing himself as both a strategist and a leader of men.

While Carteaux and the other leaders waffled and delayed, "Bonaparte quietly continued making his own preparations."[21] "He...was hard at work using every possible means to collect the necessary equipment and cannon."[22] "He fired off flurries of orders to administrative and military leaders across the region to requisition all available artillery, munitions, provisions, drovers, draft animals and wagons."[23] He made requisitions from every corner of the land. Guns were swiftly seized from Marseilles, Avignon and even the Army of Italy itself. Steeds and supplies were secured through ruthless coercion of the reluctant peasantry using whatever crafty course necessary, including manipulation and intimidation. Nothing would be spared in the persistent pursuit of victory.[24]

When Napoleon first arrived, Carteaux had a mere five guns,[25] which he absurdly believed to be enough. Napoleon, in contrast, "by dint of superhuman exertions,"[26] was able to build it up to 194 guns,[27] "including a fair proportion of 24-pounders and long-range mortars."[28]

Filling the ranks was another problem, but Bonaparte was undaunted. At his request, retired artillery officers living in the area dusted off their uniforms and returned to the roar and smoke of the battlefield. Soldiers previously unversed in the art of gunnery now drilled relentlessly under the unforgiving sun and the eagle eye of young Bonaparte, the senior gunner.[29] Starting with a mere handful of soldiers trained in artillery, Napoleon again completely outclassed Carteaux, building up his regiment to 1,600 men.[30]

Napoleon's next step, a masterstroke in the chaos of the siege, was to establish an armory and artillery park at Ollioules. Here, a symphony of industry roared into life as eighty blacksmiths, cartwrights, and carpenters toiled, manufacturing and mending muskets, their sweat glistening on the incendiary cannonballs. From the bustling heart of Marseilles, he summoned skilled workers to build the artillery equipment. A regional foundry, once silent, now echoed with the relentless rhythm of production, birthing case shot, cannon balls, and shells for the mortars. The artillery company, once a disorganized rabble, was transformed into a well-oiled machine. He wrestled with suppliers, wrangling for the precious powder that had been woefully absent upon his arrival. He scoured the surrounding region, unearthing more cannon, like a miner striking gold. Each action, each decision, was a note in the orchestra of war, his leadership the conductor guiding the company to victory.[31]

Bonaparte next began altering the field of battle to suit his purposes. He requisitioned some "5,000 sacks of earth a day from Marseilles to build ramparts."[32] Despite being detested by Carteaux and his staff officers, despite being rudely referred to as either "Captain Cannon" or "the Greenhorn," Napoleon brushed the hostility aside and, focused on the mission at hand, transferred the cannons from Montauban Hill to establish two artillery batteries close enough to quickly send the enemy ships fleeing from the River Seine.[33]

"Bonaparte's dynamism and decisiveness sharply contrasted with Carteaux's lethargy."[34] Where the French troops had previously been at a loss for what to do, Napoleon, writes historian Andrew Roberts, "injected a sense of unceasing activity into his men. Constantly imploring, complaining and raging—there wasn't enough gunpowder, the cartridges were the wrong size, trained artillery horses were being requisitioned for other uses, and so on—he sent scores of letters with demands to Bouchotte and even on occasion to the Committee of Public Safety itself, going over the heads of Carteaux and his immediate superiors."[35]

Stick to Your Guns.

"All the time Bonaparte was chafing at the delays occasioned by his inefficient superiors and their general lack of purpose and decision."[36] In the meantime, he "kept hammering home the necessity of seizing the western promontory forts" on Cairo hill.[37] "Take l'Eguillette," he told Carteaux yet again, "and before eight days you will be in Toulon."[38] Thanks, in part, to the support of Saliceti, "Napoleon's persistence finally caused Carteaux to order the desired attack."[39]

Carteaux, however, "insisted on retaining command of the initial assault against British positions on the high ground,"[40] and, as a result, the September 22 attack on Fort L'Éguillette was "uninspired and ineffective."[41] American military historian and Korean War veteran Captain Robert Asprey put it even more bluntly, "the effort was timid in the extreme, probably on Carteaux's orders, and was easily repulsed."[42] Clearly, the painter turned amateur general "did not share Bonaparte's conviction about the fort's importance and deployed too few men, while the British quickly brought up reinforcements."[43]

But the real disaster was what happened afterwards. The failed attack on Fort L'Éguillette alerted the English to the vulnerability of their fleet if they lost the fort. Carteaux had spoiled the vitally important element of *surprise*.

The following day, the English quickly moved to reinforce the position with two additional earthworks on its flanks as well as a new battery, which they named Fort Mulgrave in honor of the British commander, Lord Mulgrave. Still more, the English then built three *additional*, smaller forts to support Fort Mulgrave, which they christened Saint-Philippe, Saint-Côme, and Saint-Charles.[44] The French now began to refer to the area as "'Little Gibraltar' because it was so heavily fortified."[45]

This was a major setback and Napoleon was furious. The loss of surprise would cost more French lives. What's more, Asprey writes, "this was a real blow to Napoleon's plans for a quick tactical coup. His fury was shared by Saliceti who reported the débâcle in detail to the Committee of Public Safety, glumly adding: 'We consider our joint plan, then, a failure and the expedition of Toulon...becomes a lengthy affair which will succeed only with time and [additional] forces.'"[46]

Rather than backing away from his strategy, however, or allowing it to morph into a more conventional, protracted siege or, perhaps, a direct attack on Toulon, Napoleon, "greatly to his credit," adds Asprey, "stuck to his guns" and doubled down on his original plan.[47] He scoured artillery parks along the coast for still more cannons and mortars, as well as wagons and horses and men. He arranged for an additional 100 sacks of dirt a day to be delivered from Marseilles. He set up forges to repair the cannons, mortars, muskets, and other guns.[48]

Never Lose Your Nerve or Your Head.

As a son of the revolution, Bonaparte was a respecter of talent not titles. He rewarded courage and ability not pedigree or seniority. Not surprisingly, he had "little respect for his nominal superiors,"[49] most of whom, as a result of their political connections and anti-royalist beliefs, had been appointed in haste to fill a near continuous stream of openings caused by revolution and war.

For Napoleon, General Carteaux's weak, failed attack on L'Éguillette was the last straw. He soon wrote a scathing letter to the Committee of Public Safety—the provisional government in France, led by the infamous revolutionary mastermind Maximilien "Reign of Terror" Robespierre—which both explained the problem and offered an easy solution: The appointment of a general to command the artillery, someone who could, "if only by making use of his rank," Napoleon wrote on October 25, "command respect and deal with a crowd of fools on the staff with whom one has constantly to argue and lay down the law in order to overcome their prejudices and make them take steps which theory and practice alike have shown to be axiomatic to any trained officer of this corps."[50]

Napoleon had already expressed his deep dissatisfaction with Carteaux to one French military officer, explaining that he could no longer serve under "this old painter, who manifestly does not possess the least notions of the military art."[51] But now he was at his wits' end. And he was not alone.

"The reports of Saliceti and other [government officials] convinced Paris to replace Carteaux with General François Doppet on 10 November."[52] Napoleon was simultaneously promoted to the rank of major and given tacit approval to take charge of the military efforts at Toulon despite the protests of his senior commanders.[53]

"A physician who dabbled in literature," Doppet, like Carteaux, "had only won high rank by finding himself in the right place at the right time."[54] Alas, Doppet, "proved even more unfit for command than Carteaux."[55] The most frustrating part for Napoleon was not just that Carteaux and Doppet were so reluctant to implement his strategy, but that they were unable to recognize its merit.[56]

After some initial resistance, Doppet gave in to the pressure and agreed to attempt to execute Napoleon's strategy once again. On November 15, the French mounted an attack on Little Gibraltar.

The battle initially appeared to be favoring the French. But then, suddenly, an aide standing next to General Doppet literally "lost his head to a passing cannon-ball."[57] It was a horrific sight that led the old doctor turned amateur general to lose his nerve and order a hasty retreat.[58]

Napoleon, mounted on horseback with "his face bathed in blood from a light wound,"[59] witnessed the spectacle and immediately "lost his temper, shouting within earshot of Doppet, 'The f@c|<er who ordered the retreat causes us to lose Toulon.'"[60]

Of course, he "knew perfectly well who the villain was,"[61] but "Doppet took it well. He was aware of his limitations," and he recognized that Major "Bonaparte knew his business."[62] Unlike Carteaux, Doppet at least realized his inability to lead the army and he soon surrendered to Bonaparte's pressure to resign.[63]

Explore Alternative Views.

At last, on November 16, a professional soldier, a man "who knew how to call the troops to order," the fifty-five-year-old General Jacques Dugommier— a veteran of both the Seven Years' War and the American Revolutionary War—was brought in to lead the Siege of Toulon.[64]

A week later, to hammer out their strategy, Dugommier summoned a war council for November 25, which, among others, included Saliceti and Augustin Robespierre, the brother of the infamous Maximilien Robespierre.

With Bonaparte serving as secretary,[65] three different strategic plans were "presented for consideration,"[66] including Dugommier's own plan, but also a plan drawn up in Paris by the clever mathematician and physicist Lazare Carnot, a member of the Committee of Public Safety who would become the President of the National Convention the following year.[67] The third plan was the one Bonaparte had been advocating since he first arrived, which involved a few feint attacks at various points around Toulon to confuse the enemy and prevent them from swarming the real target, followed by a concentrated attack before dawn on Fort Mulgrave and the three surrounding forts (Little Gibraltar). The final part of Bonaparte's plan was to turn the cannons at Fort L'Éguillette toward the harbor to bombard the British and Spanish fleets with flaming hot cannonballs.[68]

Taking a stand against the other two plans, both of which involved multiple attacks around Toulon, Bonaparte argued that they would disperse their forces too much and, without a *concentration of forces* on Little Gibraltar, they would fail to capture Fort L'Éguillette, which was key to force the enemy ships to evacuate the harbor and ensure the fall of Toulon.[69]

Saliceti was already convinced. Now, Dugommier recognized the superiority of Bonaparte's strategy over his own. In fact, following the meeting,

Dugommier wrote to the Minister of War in Paris, "there is only one possible plan—Bonaparte's."[70] At last, all were agreed and at once committed "to implement the scheme Bonaparte had always had in mind."[71]

Execute Your Strategy, Following All the Way Through.

"Take time to deliberate, but when the time for action has arrived, stop thinking and go in."[72]

—Napoleon Bonaparte (1769—1821)

Finally, at one o'clock in the morning on Tuesday, December 17, 1793, after two days of heavy shelling, Dugommier finally put Napoleon's plan of attack into play.[73] The violent lightning and pouring rain nearly caused Dugommier to delay the attack, but Napoleon urged him on, insisting that it could work to their advantage. It was not the surprise attack for which Bonaparte had originally hoped, but attacking in the middle of the night during a fierce thunderstorm would at least have the strategic advantage of being *unexpected.*

Under the protective cover of heavy fire from the rear, the first French column made it to the second line of defenses, but then faltered.[74] Dugommier then sent in a second column of some 2,000 men, this one led by Bonaparte who boldly galloped into "the teeth of driving rain, high winds...lightning strikes,"[75] and a barrage of bullets from the British lines.

Within minutes, his horse was shot out from under him.[76] Landing on his feet, Bonaparte leapt into the ranks of the foot soldiers who were pressing forward at a speed that alarmed the enemy forces who were defending the fort. After intense hand-to-hand fighting, Napoleon was slashed in the thigh with a bayonet, but managed to continue fighting.

At last, at three o'clock in the morning, "after a couple of hours' bitter fighting...the fort fell..."[77] Wasting no time, Napoleon then quickly "proceeded to pour heated cannonballs onto the Royal Navy vessels across the harbor below."[78] "The memory of the explosion of two Spanish gunpowder-ships stayed with him for the rest of his life."[79] Recalling the Siege of Toulon decades later, he could still see, he said, "the whirlwind of flames and smoke from the arsenal resembled the eruption of a volcano, and the thirteen vessels blazing in the [harbor] were like so many displays of fireworks: the masts and forms of the vessels were distinctly traced out by the flames, which lasted many hours and formed an unparalleled spectacle.'"[80]

As the sun soon began to rise on Toulon, pandemonium ensued. Following the success of the French army, "just as Napoleon had foreseen, the neighboring forts were evacuated."[81] With the French now in control of Cairo hill, including Fort L'Éguillette and Fort Balaguier, Admiral Hood needed no Jewish dream interpreter to read the writing on the wall. "It was clear that the fleet's position was no longer tenable, and Admiral Hood ordered the evacuation of the port."[82]

Knowing that the sea was their only means of escape, the mere sight of so many ships going up in flames caused the troops of the English and their allies to panic. "The twenty-nine-year-old English sailor Sidney Smith, already knighted for feats of gallantry, and Hood's right-hand man in Toulon, remarked that troops 'crowded to the water like the herd of swine that ran furiously into the sea possessed of the devil.'"[83]

All those royalist citizens of Toulon who were responsible for delivering the city into British hands in the first place were also now frantic to escape. Leaving all of their possessions behind, they fled their homes and raced toward the harbor. "While rearguard troops set fire to the arsenal, powder magazines and anchored French ships, small craft jostled with each other in carrying panic-stricken royalists through burning waters to the departing vessels."[84] The French took back control of the city that same day.

|PROBLEM|

Skirt the Perils and Pitfalls
of the Aimless, Undisciplined Mind

"Death is nothing, but to live defeated and inglorious is to die daily."[85]
—Napoleon Bonaparte, First Emperor of France (1804—1814, 1815)

We all want more out of life. We all have unmet desires and unfulfilled dreams. We all want to do more, achieve more, give more, and be more. To envision a brighter future, an age of peace and prosperity, is part of what it means to be human and what separates us from every other species on Earth.

The challenge is we live in trying times. We live in a warp-speed world of cut-throat competition, limited resources, and finite time. We are surrounded by rapid, often tumultuous and sometimes even overwhelming change. We face uncertainty and volatility and complexity in virtually every realm—from international relations and domestic affairs to our relationships, health, businesses and careers. Even in the realms of science, education, dating, and sports we face an increasingly ambiguous and unpredictable world.

Given so much uncertainty and rapid, unpredictable change, it is easy to imagine that success in today's world is mostly a matter of the birth lottery, privilege, or luck.[86] No doubt, life is not always fair, and it can be intensely difficult at times. Your greatest goals and aspirations will often be harder and take longer than you expect. Circumstances, careers, and entire industries can all change overnight. And there are sometimes a surprising number of opposing forces or obstacles to overcome. This leads many people to doubt themselves, their luck, or the goals they set. Some will become cynical or lash out at others. Many others will slowly lower their sights, convincing themselves that they are just being more realistic and mature.

But the real problem is not vigorous competition, limited resources, or the madness of the modern world. The real problem is not a lack of time, privilege, or luck. The real problem is not "out there" at all. The real problem is in your thinking. "Remember," writes Stephen Covey, "that every time you think the problem is out there, that very thought is the problem."[87]

Avoid the Trap of Unquestioned Patterns of Thinking and Unexamined Habits of Mind.

> *"The unexamined life is not worth living."*
> —Socrates, Ancient Greek Philosopher,
> At his trial as recorded in Plato's *Apology*

Unfortunately, without an adequate understanding of the type and quality of the thinking that success requires, the great majority of people fall back on any number of futile or ineffective defaults, including, most commonly, one or more of the following 8 thinking traps:

(1.) <u>No Thinking: The Default Bias</u>. The first group is like General Doppet, they simply surrender or submit, letting people and circumstances or their own emotions blow them around like a feather whirling in the wind. When the revolutionaries wanted to promote Doppet, he accepted even though he was a doctor with no experience as a military leader, never mind a general. When Napoleon, a soldier well below Doppet's rank, insisted that he resign, Doppet, once again, surrendered to circumstance. Unfortunately, going with the flow may seem like a spiritual or enlightened approach to the river of life, but it eventually leads to getting raked over the rocks or pushed over the falls.

(2.) <u>No New Thinking: The Status Quo Bias</u>. A second group is like General Carteaux, they keep doing what they have always done. This group essentially ignores the need for change and seeks to maintain things as they are. Rather than rejecting or growing beyond the status quo, they embrace it.[88] People in this group may be open to small, incremental adjustments to strategy, or efforts to move more quickly or efficiently, but they still fundamentally stand for the status quo. The problem is they miss out on opportunities or fail to avoid looming threats. Carteaux, for example, did his best to ignore and even ridicule Napoleon, despite his training and evident knowledge. He disregarded the power and obvious advantages of artillery, and instead wanted to storm Toulon with bayonets. He also wanted to do this despite the fact that the British had guns, they controlled all the forts with guns, and they had some 70 heavily armed warships which could easily be brought to bear on any approaching French column.

(3.) <u>Reactive Thinking: The Strategy of Wait, React and Defend</u>. The third group is like Admiral Hood, they have some idea of the direction they want to go, but their only real strategy is to react. When Hood was sent to France in support of the royalists, he stationed his fleet outside of Toulon. When royalists in Toulon invited him to occupy the harbor, he obliged.

When the French attacked Cairo hill, he built Fort Mulgrave. When the French rained down cannon on the ships, Hood sailed away. At no point, did Hood appear to take any real initiative. In fact, weeks before they were forced to evacuate, in reaction to the French building up batteries around Toulon, Hood had already issued plans to evacuate to his captains. In other words, he recognized what was happening far in advance, but still merely waited to react. To be clear, strategists must *respond* to events. This may even require, on *rare* occasions, a change in strategy rather than merely an adjustment to tactics. Nevertheless, you cannot succeed as a strategist if all you can or ever do is react.

Not surprisingly, given the rapid pace of change, this reactive approach is exceedingly common today. To be sure, as strategy consultants Lafley and Martin write in *Playing to Win: How Strategy Really Works*, "The world is changing so quickly, some leaders argue, that it's impossible to think about strategy in advance and that, instead, a firm should respond to new threats and opportunities as they emerge."[89] Perhaps to comfort themselves or add legitimacy, they even came up with a name for it, "emergent strategy." But surrendering the initiative and reacting to others has never been a long-term strategy for success. "Unfortunately," referring to this so-called "emergent strategy," Lafley and Martin conclude, "such an approach places a company in a reactive mode, making it easy prey for more-strategic rivals. Not only is strategy possible in times of tumultuous change, but it can be a competitive advantage and a source of significant value creation."[90]

(4.) <u>Subjective Thinking: The Cognitive Corruption of the Echo Chamber</u>. A fourth group is like the officers surrounding Carteaux, rather than thinking for themselves and helping to sharpen Carteaux's thinking, they simply followed his lead, repeated his views, and ridiculed Bonaparte as a know-it-all greenhorn. Today, the internet makes it easy to get trapped in a toxic echo chamber. Social media sites work hard to fill your feed with whatever you already believe, perpetuating beliefs and biases that inhibit your best thinking. The internet itself can begin to corrupt your thinking, depending on how you use it and where you go. Returning to the same partisan sites or sensationalized, ill-informed sources can quickly lead to extremist thinking and dangerous, self-sabotaging views. If, on the other hand, you actively limit information that only reinforces what you already think or believe and, instead, seek to inform yourself by reading a range of views on a topic, then you can greatly strengthen your understanding and sharpen your thinking and improve your life as a result. This was Abraham Lincoln's approach long before he became president. He used to read a number of rival newspapers every morning because he said that it was the only way to get some general idea of the truth of what was happening in the world.

(5.) <u>Short-Term Thinking: The Flawed Fixation on Only Immediate Results.</u>

A fifth group is like those among France's revolutionary leaders who put such absurdly unqualified generals in command in the first place. They had a gap in the command structure that needed to be filled so they appointed men they knew who shared their political convictions, regardless of their job qualifications or ability to lead. This certainly solved the immediate problem of the gap in command, but with disastrous long-term consequences, including the unnecessary loss of untold lives.

This sort of short-term thinking is another terribly common trap. Of course there are times when a tactical approach to problems makes sense, but a short-term focus on results must never be detached from the long-term strategic plan. Short-term thinking is painfully common in the corporate world, particularly in the midst of economic and political uncertainty. "Executives tend to shift their focus from a strategic horizon to a short-term, immediate, operational success,"[91] Columbia professor Julia Sloan writes in *Learning to Think Strategically*. "In some companies, those responsible for strategy have actually stepped back from their strategic responsibility in an effort to perform operational triage."[92] The problem, however, is the long-term consequences of such a short-term approach. "Such a panicked emphasis on emergency, short-term results, coupled with obsessiveness about short-term financial strength," writes Sloan, "can eventually sever the companies' lifeline to a competitive future."[93]

(6.) <u>Half Way Thinking: The Perils of Acting on Impulse or a Superficial Assessment</u>. A sixth group is like General Carteaux when he finally agreed to lead an assault on the fort on Cairo hill. It seems evident that he wanted the attack to fail, perhaps to make it look like Bonaparte's plan was flawed all along. But it also seems clear that he failed to think about the consequences of that failure which not only alerted the British to the importance of L'Éguillette and, thus, led to the conspicuous reinforcement of their defenses, but which also resulted in the removal of Carteaux himself from command. Most people are lazy thinkers. It's not necessarily difficult to think more than a couple of steps ahead. The challenge is that it can take time because each new step can usually be met in more than one way. To fail to think through the potential ramifications of your actions, however, can have career-changing consequences, as it did for Carteaux.

(7.) <u>Wishful Thinking: The Problem of Fantasizing Without Facing the Brutal Truths and Difficult Facts</u>. A seventh group is like General Doppet. It's not clear what Doppet was thinking when he ordered a retreat after his aid literally lost is head, but it seems his idea about how war would unfold did not include those close to him losing their lives. Perhaps this writer of poetry and romances had a more fantastical vision of war, but it came to an abrupt end when it made its inevitable contact with a harsh reality. Ordering a retreat was also a sort of wishful thinking, at least from the perspective of the French, particularly since their assault was actually unfolding reasonably well.

Wishful or aspirational thinking certainly has its place, particularly at the stage of idea generation. Hopes, dreams, and visions of the future are actually vital. Indeed, the whole point of strategy is to improve the probability of achieving your grand vision and goals. "Without vision, the people perish," Proverbs tells us. However, to engage in wishful or far-fetched thinking without ever tempering your ideas or grounding yourself in reality—including the truth about where you are now and what difficult obstacles lay ahead—can become a significant threat to your success.

(8.) <u>Thinking Without End: The Curse of Indecisiveness</u>. An eighth group is like the French army's area headquarters when Napoleon first arrived on the scene in Toulon. Lots of ideas continued to be thrown about by lots of people with lots of plans, but there was still a critical lack of direction and decisiveness from those at the top.[94] This last trap amounts to a failure to finally decide upon, communicate, and execute the strategy.

People often get trapped in planning and strategizing because they are unable to make a final decision or commit to the decision they make. Indecision is about doubt and fear of the unknown. If you always had perfect and complete information, you would never struggle to decide. Decisions entail certain risks and risks can create doubt, apprehension, and fear. But not making a decision is still a decision; it is just accompanied by a different set of risks. You may not face the consequences of your indecision right away, but the consequences will come (e.g. a lack of confidence, failing to achieve your objective, deterioration in morale, the pain of mediocrity, and on and on).

Management legend Peter Drucker once said, "People who don't take risks generally make about two big mistakes a year. People who do take risks generally make about two big mistakes a year."[95] In other words, being indecisive is not making your life or career better or more secure. It's really just narrowing your options. The difference is that decisiveness gives you much greater control. Rather than reacting to others or waiting to see what happens, you influence events and force people to react to you. "Indecisiveness entails letting decisions, and their accompanying consequences, be determined for you."[96] To lead is to decide. As Napoleon himself advised, "Take time to deliberate, but when the time for action has arrived, stop thinking and go in."[97]

Think to Rise, Think Strategically to Outperform and Excel.

"No problem can withstand the assault of sustained thinking."[98]
—Voltaire, French Enlightenment Writer and Historian

What all of these groups have in common is a failure to think strategically. Arguing that humans are slaves to the narrow circumstances, rigid attitudes, common prejudices, and practical necessities of their lives, Martin Heidegger, one of the foremost philosophers of the 20th century, concluded that "the most thought-provoking thing in our thought-provoking time is that we are still not thinking."[99] Only through thinking, Heidegger said, can we be free. American revolutionary leader Thomas Paine, author of *Common Sense*, put it this way: "When men yield up the privilege of thinking, the last shadow of liberty quits the horizon."[100]

Only through thinking can we transcend the artificial boundaries and unfounded fears that limit our actions and hold us back. Only through thinking can we uncover the flawed assumptions and false beliefs that hinder our strategies, and derail our plans. Only through thinking can we discover our purpose and realize our potential. "Everything begins with thinking," writes Brian Tracy.[101] "The highest paid and most valuable work in America is thinking. This is because of all of the things people do, thinking has the greatest possible consequences. The better you think the better decisions you make, the better decisions you make the better actions you will take, the better actions you take the better results you get, and the better will be the quality of your life and work."[102]

People fail to think because thinking is hard. It takes effort and time. In fact, Henry Ford said, "thinking is the hardest work there is, which is probably the reason why so few engage in it."[103] Martin Luther King Jr. similarly said, "Rarely do we find men who willingly engage in hard, solid thinking. There is an almost universal quest for easy answers and half-baked solutions. Nothing pains some people more than having to think."[104]

But if *thinking* is uncommon, than thinking *strategically* is exceptionally rare—but also even more richly rewarded as a result. This is precisely what was happening when Napoleon Bonaparte arrived in Toulon and, because he did not have final authority, this is what continued to happen until he was able to leverage his connections and personal power to have both Carteaux and Doppet replaced.

On the other hand, because Napoleon was a *strategist*, because he did *think strategically*, not only did he succeed in retaking Toulon, standing head and shoulders above the two generals and the other high ranking "crowd of fools" in the officer corps, but he also preserved the strength and momentum of the French Revolution and sent some of the greatest powers in Europe at the time home to lick their wounds.

Master the Art of the Strategist

"Take a close look at great heroes of history and you see that they're all very different, except for one thing: They're all great strategists."[105]

—William Duggan, Columbia Business School Professor,
Napoleon's Glance: The Secret of Strategy

Learning to think strategically and formulate and execute effective strategy is more than a vital part of the solution to the problems of fierce competition, limited resources, and rapid, volatile change. It is key to the vast majority of the challenges of life. Strategy is practical wisdom of the highest form.[106] Time and again, thinking strategically proves the defining difference between struggle and success. To develop the ability to think, plan, and operate as a master strategist is to possess a kind of cognitive superpower.

But what does it mean to *think strategically*? What is *strategy*?

Strategic thinking is the process of thinking critically and creatively, proactively and systematically about how to achieve your chief purpose; all with an eye on context, history, resources, opportunities, and threats. To put it more succinctly, the essence of the idea is thinking with the big picture in mind about how to get what you want.

Strategy is a firm but flexible course of action which involves the formulation, execution, and ongoing adaptation of plans, methods, and maneuvers in the efficient and effective use of resources in pursuit of your overarching vision and long-term goals. In a word, strategy is *how—how* you employ what you have or can acquire, to achieve what you desire. If your vision is "where you are going," then your strategy is "how you get there." If the dream is "what you want," then your strategy is "how you attain it." Strategy, in essence, is the plan of action for how to achieve your ultimate chief aim.[107]

Serving as an advisor to John F. Kennedy during his 1960 campaign for president, political consultant Joseph Napolitan (the man who coined the term "political consultant") once said that, "Strategy is the single most important factor in a political campaign. This," he said, "is the most important lesson I have learned in 30 years. The right strategy can survive a mediocre campaign, but even a brilliant campaign is likely to fail if the strategy is wrong."[108]

Naturally, strategy goes well beyond politics. In fact, it is equally important in business. According to *Harvard Business Review*, "If you aren't working with a strategy, you're wasting your time."[109] But strategy also goes beyond business, sports, and war. Wherever resources are limited, wherever competition is stiff, strategy reigns supreme.

Most important is the *strategist, one who thinks strategically and who possesses the knowledge, characteristics, and competencies necessary to effectively formulate and execute strategic plans, as well as the wisdom to know if, when, and how those plans need to change to achieve the desired end.*[110] "The real heart of strategy is the strategist. Becoming a strategist is about getting better at shaping events."[111]

Study Strategy to Win.

> *"In its purest, most straightforward expression, strategy is the art of winning. It is a theory of victory; it is how to win."*[112]
>
> —Alan Stephens and Nicola Baker, *Making Sense of War: Strategy for the 21st Century*

While the roots of strategy can be traced back to the ancient Greeks, it was the astonishing success of Napoleon Bonaparte around the turn of the 18th century which served as the catalyst to the scholarly study of strategy.[113] As a matter of fact, what is perhaps most remarkable about the Siege of Toulon is not that Napoleon was appointed as general while he was still only 24. Indeed, Joan of Arc, an unknown, illiterate peasant farm girl with no experience fighting anyone for anything—never mind any *training* in leadership, strategy, or tactics—became the supreme commander of French military forces at only age 17. Not incidentally, Joan of Arc was officially recognized as a national symbol of France in 1803 by none other than Napoleon Bonaparte.

What stands out about the Siege of Toulon is the extent to which Bonaparte was already demonstrating every single one of the key factors of strategic leadership. Perhaps this helps to explain why it was Napoleon Bonaparte's surprising success in Europe as a military and political strategist that led to the study of strategy as a discipline.

The term *strategy* comes from the Greek word *strategia*, meaning "office or command of a general," and *strategos*, meaning "army leader"[114] or "general, commander of an army." But the word *strategy*, as in "the art of a general," did not come into use until the beginning of the 19th century, and it came into use as a direct result of Napoleon and the Napoleonic Wars.[115] As Columbia Business School professor William Duggan explains, the word strategy "entered the English language…in 1810 because that was the height of success of Napoleon Bonaparte, who won battle after battle across Europe."[116]

The other key figure here is Carl von Clausewitz, who, as a young Prussian army officer, fought against Napoleon and lost. Earlier, Clausewitz had graduated from the Berlin War Academy at the top of his class. Also in 1810, not coincidentally, Clausewitz "returned to the academy as a professor of strategy."[117]

At the time, "Napoleon ranked as the most successful battlefield general in recorded history."[118] Even in the face of larger armies, he was victorious in one battle after another.[119] "His victories took him from a modest background in Corsica, with a thick accent that the French elite laughed at, to emperor of Europe in less than a decade."[120] Clausewitz wanted to understand why Napoleon was so successful. So he started to study his strategy. In fact, all of Napoleon's "enemies started studying his strategy, especially the English and Prussians, so that they could defeat him. And in 1815, at Waterloo, they did.

From then on, "strategy" became a formal discipline, taught in universities,"[121] where it grew and spread beyond "military science...to other fields, especially business."[122]

"Clausewitz went on to become the leading theorist on strategy in the Western world and remains so to this day," according to Duggan[123] and others.[124] Clausewitz' study of Napoleon eventually became his celebrated book, *On War*, published in 1832. Still to this day, Columbia Business School professor Willie Pietersen writes, "*On War* is regarded by military experts...as the definitive study of warfare. His ideas remain widely taught in military schools, and are, more than ever, essential to the modern strategist." *On War*, essentially, "distilled Napoleon into theory."[125] "Napoleon won more battles than any other general in history, before or since. *On War* explains how he did it."[126]

Master Napoleon Bonaparte's 4-Part, 16-Factor Framework for Strategic Mastery

So, what can today's aspiring strategists learn from Napoleon Bonaparte? Napoleon's success as a strategist can be divided into four core components or stages, which we can use as a framework for thinking about and developing strategic mastery. Within this 4-part framework are a total of 16 different strategic factors. Serving as a prelude to the chapters in this book, the following is concise summary of each of these 16 strategic factors, with a brief illustration of how each one contributed to Bonaparte's success at the Siege of Toulon.

|INSPIRATION—Thinking About What You Want.|

The first stage, inspiration, is about how strategists think about what they want and how to approach it, and it includes 4 key strategic factors: thinking strategically, thinking with a purpose-driven, future focus, thinking proactively, and thinking critically.

(1.) Appropriate the Extraordinary Secret Psychology of Strategic Mastery. *Strategists rule the world.* By thinking strategically about how to get what they want, by formulating and executing strategy effectively, strategists expand their options, leverage their opportunities, and multiply their probability of success.

To succeed as a strategist, you must spurn the short-term, status quo, subjective, and reactive thinking that plagues the modern world. Instead, maintain a big-picture, long-term, purpose-driven perspective of the broader context, external forces, and conflicting tensions at play and you will immediately begin to change what you see and improve how you think. Rather than letting a fragile ego, fleeting emotions, or false urgency control your focus, dictate your decisions, and define your future, adopt the mindset of the master strategist. Stop and reflect and elevate your thinking, find your leverage points, and force your mind to focus on how best to achieve your grand purpose and goals. Master the practice of thinking strategically and resourcefully, with purpose and agility, about how to exploit available resources, overcome inevitable obstacles, and navigate competing priorities and you will increase exponentially your prospects for success.

In the case of Napoleon, strategic thinking is what set him apart from the moment he arrived on the scene at Toulon. Even the most primitive soldier understood that the goal was to eject or destroy the English and their allies. But it was Napoleon who took the time to think, formulate, and implement an effective strategy to achieve that goal; including identifying their optimal point of leverage, determining how to acquire and concentrate the available resources, anticipating the reaction of the enemy, working to ensure the effective execution of his strategy, and rapidly adapting when circumstances changed.

(2.) Be Future-Focused and Purpose-Driven. Tap the Power of Your Purpose to Perform. *The dream is everything.* There is no point to strategy if there is no goal. Strategy is about how to achieve your vision. But the big dream, your definite chief purpose and corresponding goals, this is the ultimate point of it all and where the strategist begins. Strategists, therefore, are future-focused and purpose-driven almost by definition. To think strategically is, first and foremost, to think with the desired end goal in mind.

In the case of Napoleon at Toulon, his future focus was saving the French Revolution. Naturally, as a soldier, Napoleon was there to do a job. And, furthermore, already intensely ambitious, his future focus necessarily included advancing his own military career. Nonetheless, he also believed in the vision and values of the revolution—liberty, equality, fraternity—and was at least as eager as the revolutionary leaders in the capital to bring Toulon back under French control.

(3.) Think Proactively. Seize, Sustain, and Exploit the Initiative. Prepare to Play an Offensive Game. *Winning requires thinking and being proactive. It requires seizing the initiative and playing a predominantly offensive game.* To fail to take the initiative and think only reactively is to play a defensive game, but to succeed as a strategist, to multiply your chances of success, you must think proactively, and plan and prepare to play the offense again and again. Seizing the initiative is often harder, but more valuable and abundantly rewarded. "Opportunities multiply as they are seized," wrote Sun Tzu.[127] When you seize the initiative, you force others to respond to you. Rather than taking their own proactive measures or executing their own offensive plans, they must first figure out how to react to yours—which can take time, energy, and resources they did not anticipate. This is true in war, in politics, in business, and in sports, but also in everyday leadership and life. To be proactive, to assume ownership and seize the initiative is to exercise leadership. To maintain and consistently exploit the initiative is to win.

Seizing the initiative was the very first thing Napoleon did at Toulon. Despite his limited authority and lack of experience, he immediately set out to survey the situation and create a plan. The plan itself was designed to regain control of the situation and retake Toulon. He then maintained the initiative as he went about acquiring the resources to implement his plan. When his strategy was rejected or poorly executed, he again took the initiative to remove the obstacles, and, when necessary, adjust his plans. The English and their allies, in contrast, virtually never seized the initiative. They simply reacted to various maneuvers and pressure from the French. Even when they took over Toulon it was only in response to the French royalists who invited them in.

(4.) Champion Critical Thinking to Devise Informed and Incisive Decisions, Craft Cunning Solutions, and Achieve Superior Success. "*No problem can withstand the assault of sustained thinking*," said Voltaire.[128] To become a master strategist is to become an effective, critical thinker. Develop an ability to break down and objectively analyze, interpret, and evaluate complex facts, evidence, arguments, and information to form reasoned, unbiased judgments and you will multiply your odds of success. On the other hand, few things will lead to disaster faster than flawed, biased, emotional, or irrational thinking.

In terms of critical thinking, the best example we have from Napoleon at Toulon is when he invited input on his strategy from the other officers, but also how he analyzed prior campaigns,[129] and how he compared and contrasted Toulon with earlier campaigns and battles fought on similar terrain.[130] He would later become known for wanting to explore with his generals both sides of an argument for every available option.[131] He also sought to consider his options from the perspective of his opponents.[132]

|EXPLORATION—Investigating How to Get What You Want.|

The second stage, exploration, is about how strategists research, investigate, and explore how to get what they want. The exploration stage also includes 4 strategic factors: cultivating curiosity, reaping the wisdom of history, exploiting new advances and breakthroughs, and identifying leverage points.

(5.) <u>Cultivate the Hidden Power of Concentrated Curiosity.</u> *Curiosity is the strategist's secret sauce.* The most effective strategies are invariably formulated by the most inquisitive minds. Curiosity is the engine of creativity, innovation, possibility thinking, and continuous learning and growth. Curiosity enhances adaptation and reduces surprise. Curiosity drives the strategist to understand the competition, context, and terrain, but also to explore the past and discover the future.

In Napoleon's case, he has been described as "among history's most curious men."[133] Furthermore, his uncommon curiosity consistently proved to be a critical characteristic of his success, particularly in regards to gathering intelligence, uncovering assumptions, and exploring alternative perspectives. At Toulon, curiosity is what drove him to survey the city when he first arrived. It's what pushed him to explore what resources he might discover in nearby towns. And, as he advanced, it was curiosity that spurred him to read and study everything he could about his enemy, prior relevant battles, local politics, and the history, culture, weather, and terrain. Later, he would go on campaign with a miniaturized library of thousands of books.

(6.) <u>Reap the Wisdom of History. Profit from the Power of the Past to Influence the Future.</u> *Strategists are historians in action. Strategists shape the future by being steadfast students of the past.* Even the most mediocre mind can learn from its own experience, wrote Bismarck. What sets strategists apart is their ability to learn from the experience of others. "History is universal experience," wrote military theorist and historian Captain Liddell Hart, "the experience not of another but of many others under manifold conditions."[134]

In Napoleon's case, history was by far one of his greatest strengths, including as time went on, his own personal history or accumulated experience, but, initially, the experience of "the great commanders," as he called them, going as far back as Julius Caesar, Hannibal, and Alexander the Great. Both Joan of Arc's focus on outlying forts and George Washington's use of cannon in the American Revolutionary War helped to inform Napoleon's strategy at Toulon.[135]

(7.) <u>Spy Swiftly New Breakthroughs to Advance.</u> *As with mankind's discovery of fire, the smallest spark of innovation can sometimes lead to the most revolutionary advantages.* Whoever dominates the cutting edge first wins. New breakthrough technologies, processes, and innovations can give you a massive competitive advantage. Sometimes something as simple as a stirrup can enable much smaller armies to conquer the world.

It is not always a new technological breakthrough or innovation that leads to a strategic advantage, however. It is just as often an existing technology adapted to a new context, or exploited in a surprising new way.

Unlike General Carteaux who wanted to charge the enemy with sword and bayonet, it was Napoleon's readiness to exploit new technological advances that helped him to see how mobile artillery would be key to successfully forcing the enemy ships out of the harbor at Toulon.

(8.) <u>To Escalate Your Influence, Locate Your Leverage Points</u>. *Leverage is power*. Leverage is about achieving more with less. The legendary quests for the Golden Fleece, the Holy Grail, the Lance of Longinus, and the Fountain of Youth; the enduring myth of the time machine, the magic carpet, and the philosopher's stone; the persistent pursuit of the miracle cure, the secret elixir, and the silver bullet; rather than the whims of fanciful minds, what humankind's everlasting search and obsession with these ideas reflects above all is an intuitive understanding of the power and possibility of leverage.[136] In the realm of strategy, leverage is about gaining a strategic advantage. Because not all actions are equal, the key is to identify the specific actions, exact methods, or particular tools, resources, knowledge, or capabilities that will require the *least* time, effort, or investment, but will lead to the greatest, lasting strategic advantage. Rather than focusing solely on *what* you can leverage, to maximize your strategic advantage you must also think critically about *where* to focus—including where on the *hierarchy of leverage points*. Identifying your ideal leverage point will save more time, money, and effort than anything else you can do.

Regarding leverage points, this is what was brilliant about taking Fort L'Eguillette, particularly before Carteaux screwed it up by triggering additional, reinforced fortifications. Rather than trying to tackle the whole city at once, by taking this one point across the harbor they could control the city—that's leverage. Bonaparte also identified key leverage points in dealing with the incompetent senior officers, such as the expedient, albeit risky, decision to write letters critical of the siege to his political connections in Paris.

|IMPLEMENTATION—Planning and Preparing to Get What You Want.|

The focus of stage three, implementation, is about how strategists plan and prepare to get what they want. The 4 strategic factors here include: exploiting the power of surprise, simplicity, concentration, and collaboration.

(9.) <u>Profit from the Supremacy of Strategic Surprise</u>. *Surprise can overcome even the greatest strategic advantage.* The sudden and unexpected can allure, engage, and enthrall, or it can disorient, distract and confuse—changing the dynamic, upsetting the balance, and increasing your power, influence or control. No matter what field of endeavor—prevailing over an opponent in politics, launching a new innovation to crush the competition, executing an upset play in sports, destroying an enemy in warfare, or even pursuing a potential mate—there are remarkable rewards to be reaped from surprise. There is power in being unpredictable. The opposite is equally true. As soon as others have you figured out, you surrender power. The spell is broken.[137] You lose the initiative and fade into the background, increasing your risk of irrelevance, obscurity, or defeat.

Whether out of spite or incompetence, Napoleon's first plan for surprise at Toulon was spoiled not by the stealthy intelligence gathering of his enemy (a constant risk in business, politics and war), but by General Carteaux's feeble and timid attack on Fort L'Éguillette. Napoleon was then forced to settle for an inferior form of surprise—attacking the fort at an unexpected time (in the middle of the night) and under unexpected circumstances (during a violent lightning storm). Napoleon's use of surprise also included a few feint attacks at various points around Toulon to confuse the enemy and further obscure the fact that the mass of French forces were concentrated on Fort L'Éguillette. As Napoleon said himself, to gain the "advantage" you must "attack the enemy unexpectedly, to take him off his guard, to surprise him, and let him feel the thunder before he sees the flash…"[138] What's more, he added, "While a general should adhere to general principles, he should never lose the opportunity to profit by these surprises. It is the essence of genius."[139]

(10.) <u>Exploit the Unexpected Genius of Simplicity</u>. *The simplest strategies are the best strategies.* Chaos, complexity, and confusion are threats to success in virtually every realm, though they are particularly prevalent in large organizations, competitive landscapes, or domains in the midst of rapid or revolutionary change. The antidote is simplicity. Because strategy has such a sweeping influence over the organization, simplicity is an especially critical principle of strategic success. As more and more people, layers, and divisions are involved, the probability of confusion, miscommunication, misunderstandings, and mistakes swiftly escalates. Keep your strategy simple and you increase your odds of success. With each new element or level of complexity, on the other hand, your probability of failure expands. Simplicity does not mean easy, however. In fact, simplicity can be hard, and, yet, once you "make it simple," said Steve Jobs, "you can move mountains."[140]

Simplicity was, for Napoleon, a guiding principle of strategy. And his "his extraordinary taste for simplicity, worthy of the heroes of classical antiquity,"[141] according to Talleyrand, was readily apparent in his plan to retake Toulon. "Take L'Éguillette," Napoleon told the commanding officer, General Jean Carteaux, "and within a week you are in Toulon."[142] He also emphasized the importance of simplicity to others. As he wrote in his criticism of the plans of the Directory: "War being a practical profession, all complex schemes must be excluded from it."[143] "What is appropriate to war," Napoleon wrote on another occasion, "is simplicity and reliability."[144] "The art of war is," he said, "like anything beautiful: it is simple. The simplest maneuvers are the best."[145]

(11.) <u>Focus Your Forces, Amass Your Resources, Concentrate on Just One Thing</u>. *"Success demands singleness of purpose."*[146] You can reach the moon, but only if you amass and concentrate your forces on just one carefully chosen strategic point at a time. Many strategy theorists, including Antoine Henri de Jomini, the renowned Swiss strategist, believe that concentration is the essence of strategy, but it is not enough to maximize your limited resources through force concentration, you must also focus them on the key point where you can have the greatest strategic advantage. As Clausewitz wrote, "the talent of the strategist is to identify the decisive point and to concentrate everything on it, removing forces from secondary fronts and ignoring lesser objectives."[147]

From the outset, Bonaparte had devised a strategy that involved concentrating a mass of French forces on Fort L'Éguillette located on the heights of Cairo hill. This is part of why he was furious with General Carteaux's attack on the fort, which was anything *but* a mass concentration of French forces. Later, at the first strategy meeting with the Siege of Toulon's third and final commander, General Jacques Dugommier, Napoleon again emphasized this key strategic factor. Dugommier wanted to go wide with multiple attacks, but Bonaparte convinced him of the importance of concentrating their forces in a massive attack on Fort L'Éguillette. "The essence of strategy," Napoleon said, "...is always to have more force at a crucial point than the enemy."[148] However, Napoleon was also careful to use a small contingent of forces in a few feint attacks around Toulon to fool the enemy into thinking it was a dispersed attack and, thereby, conceal their true strategic intent. As the famed British strategist and historian Captain Liddell Hart explains, "True concentration is the fruit of calculated dispersion."[149]

(12.) <u>Catapult Your Power through Mutually Assured Success</u>. *The fittest may survive, but it's the collaborators who thrive.* No matter how strong or brilliant you are as a strategist, as long as you continue to work predominantly as a solo-operator, you will continue to place decisive limits on your success. When you develop a tight inner circle, however, people you can count on and trust, your likelihood of success increases exponentially. Indeed, there is extraordinary, synergistic power in banding together and forging unbreakable bonds with other like-minded people and groups. This is how you build the kind of power which is categorically greater than any single leader could ever realistically imagine.

In terms of strategic alliances and collaboration, this was a critical part of what enabled Bonaparte to round up the guns and supplies he needed from surrounding areas. His existing alliances were also key not just to getting his placement as the artillery officer in Toulon in the first place, but also getting the incompetent generals over him replaced. He also later relied on the alliances he built at Toulon—including, surprisingly, Carteaux, the general Napoleon worked to have replaced (when Napoleon became First Consul he appointed Carteaux as an administrator over the French lottery), but also his aide de camp, Jean-Andoche Junot, who became one of Napoleon's generals.[150]

|ACTUALIZATION—Executing Your Strategic Plan Until You Get What You Want.|

The fourth and final stage, culmination or actualization, focuses on how strategists carry out their plans until they get what they want. This stage includes the final four strategic factors: belief, agility, reflective action, and execution.

(13.) <u>Believe Absolutely to Inspire Absolute Belief</u>. *There is no greater power in the world than belief.* Your beliefs about the world tell you what is possible or impossible. Your beliefs about yourself tell you what you can or cannot do. What you believe about whether or not you ought to enlist and persist in a quest will determine whether or not you do. Belief is the bedrock of courage, tenacity, resilience and grit. To succeed, the ancient Chinese military strategist Sun Tzu once said, "you must believe in yourself."[151] To find victory, you must, he said, "believe in what you are doing."[152] No matter what it is, your greatest aspirations and goals will require the buy-in, assistance, and support of others. Develop a deep, unflinching, unshakeable sense of belief in yourself and what you are doing and it will have an unmistakable, often decisive influence on the beliefs of others.

Napoleon had a profound sense of self-belief, which was vital to assuming command, generating buy-in, and both formulating and executing his strategy. Even at Toulon, the untested 24-year-old captain exuded a powerful sense of self-belief. "In war, as in any other critical situation, people quickly rally to the person who gives the impression of knowing what they are about, and Bonaparte's self-confidence was magnetic."[153] On full display at Toulon, he said things and took actions that both communicated his own calm sense of self-assurance, but also built up the confidence of others, effectively creating a virtuous feedback loop, a tremendous resource in trying times.

(14.) Model the Masters of Strategic Agility, Engineer the Flexibility and Mobility to Quickly and Cleverly Adapt. *Agility is the linchpin to future success.* We live in a quickly changing, constantly evolving world. To thrive, therefore, you must be willing to continuously learn, grow, and adapt. Strategic agility is about being flexible and swift to respond and adapt optimally to a dynamic, changing environment. The key words are flexibility and adaptation, but agility is also about speed and mobility, and using good intelligence and swift, accurate communication in order to rapidly respond, successfully adapt, and, ultimately, maximize the benefits of change. Agility is not the opposite of rigidity, however. The agile leader is grounded in a solid inner core and, thus, stands as a balance between the extremes of rigidity and anarchy.

In Napoleon's case, agility was one of the early secrets of his success, and what set him apart from so many of the stodgy, old-fashioned generals of the day. There are a number of instances where Napoleon quickly adapted as needed to developments at Toulon, including working around weak leaders to get the job done, building his own foundry when he discovered they didn't have the cannonballs they needed, and working to have Carteaux relocated when he proved too incompetent to continue. Furthermore, when the British built Fort Mulgrave to reinforce L'Éguillette following Carteaux's failed attack, Napoleon quickly adapted by redoubling his troops. When his troops shied away from defending the dangerous main battery, Napoleon simply named it with a sign that read "The Battery of Men Without Fear," which led to a constant supply of men ready to serve and, simultaneously, demonstrated his understanding of human psychology and group dynamics, as well as his strategic agility and leadership ability.

(15.) <u>Wield Power with Wisdom, Get Both In and Out of the Game</u>. *You can never effectively apprehend what is happening in the arena until you step back and get outside of the game, and get the immediacy of the game outside of your head.* Success on the field requires a certain level of self-discipline and self-restraint. You must be able to shut out the outside world as you narrow your focus to the direct, pressing concerns of the game. Operate in this mode for too long, however, and your thinking becomes increasingly tactical, your focus almost completely short-term. Only when you get sufficient mental distance from the drama, only when you elevate yourself above the arena are you free to process your experience in fresh, resourceful ways, consider the big picture, and place circumstances and events in their broader context. Only then can you reexamine priorities, make new comparisons, recognize recurring themes and patterns, and reassess key factors and prevailing forces. All of this better enables you to generate new ideas and insights and see things through new frames, leading to improved decisions and more effective action.[154]

With respect to Napoleon's reflective action or balancing action with critical reflection, perhaps the best evidence we have here is in the letters he wrote to various political leaders in Paris about the situation in Toulon. And while he may not have intended to take time out to detach and reflect on what was happening on the ground in Toulon, that is precisely what happened in the process of writing those letters. But this was only the beginning of Bonaparte's inclination to stop and write about what was happening while on campaign. In fact, Bonaparte was a writer before he was a soldier and he continued to send a constant stream of letters and dispatches from the front. Furthermore, within five years of Toulon, Napoleon had either established or gained control of no less than six newspapers, to which he was himself a regular contributor. While this was primarily for purposes of propaganda, including countering the effect of negative propaganda aimed at him, it provided Napoleon with more than ample time to get outside of the arena and reflect on the big picture and broader context of each battle or campaign. To be sure, writing is one of the best tools leaders can use to get some distance or get outside of the arena and reflect on what's happening on the ground. Whether you choose to write, however, consult with a coach or mentor, or engage in reflective dialogue with your mastermind, inner circle, or team, this practice of getting outside of the arena is vital to maximizing your effectiveness as a strategist.

(16.) <u>Execute from the Vital Center of the Action, Master the Secrets of Strategy Execution at the Front</u>. *Strategy is worthless without successful execution.* There can be no triumph, no victory, no achievement, or success unless you can effectively execute the plan. No matter how brilliant your strategy, execution is where the dream becomes reality. Never content to simply send orders down from on high, history's greatest strategists have all been intimately familiar with the implementation and execution of their plans, often from the front lines. The great strategist is the one who is "actually in the arena," as Theodore Roosevelt put it, with a face "marred by dust and sweat and blood."[155] The vital center is where the strategist must be because this is where the action happens, events emerge, disruptions arise, surprises occur, and plans must change. Here is where the strategist seeks to peer through the fog, make meaning of volatility, uncertainty, and chaos. Here is where the strategist reinterprets and, if necessary, reformulates the strategy to adapt.

Napoleon demonstrated his mastery of execution and leading from the front throughout the siege of Toulon, including when he helped load the cannons when another gunner was struck down, when he led the charge on Fort L'Éguillette even after his horse was shot out from under him, and when, after Fort L'Éguillette fell, he immediately began firing the cannons on the ships in the harbor. No matter what was happening, Napoleon was right there either directly involved in the action or closely monitoring and supporting the performance of trusted lieutenants, which enabled him to ensure the effective execution of the strategy, or quickly adjust course and communicate the changes if and when required. The point is not necessarily to be on the front lines, however—which is not always possible anyway (as Napoleon realized when his army's grew and he had multiple fronts[156]). The point is to have instant access to accurate, unfiltered intelligence from the front that you can trust. The point is to be able to immediately communicate your response to any new developments at the front or, when necessary, have trusted lieutenants which you have trained to do the same.

Be the Mastermind Behind the Success.

"Strategy is an exercise in power."[157]
—Richard Rumelt, *The Crux: How Leaders Become Strategists*

For the ongoing revolution in France, the retaking of Toulon was a vitally important victory.[158] "It expelled the combined forces of four nations from French soil."[159] It also brought the royalist rebellion in the South to an end.[160] The retaking of Toulon, writes former British historian Vincent Cronin, even "became the subject of patriotic songs and of 'a heroic and historical drama.'"[161]

The successful Siege of Toulon was also "a great triumph for Napoleon's nascent military genius," British historian Frank McLynn explains.[162] "It was during the siege of Toulon that Bonaparte first revealed the dimensions of his genius."[163] "Although technically he was never more than artillery adviser to a succession of commanders in chief, Major Bonaparte was generally recognized as being the mastermind behind the success."[164]

Following the successful siege, General Dugommier wrote to the Minister of War, "I have no words to describe Bonaparte's merit: much technical skill, an equal degree of intelligence and too much gallantry, there you have a poor sketch of this rare officer..."[165]

The successful execution of his strategy also led to "his first brush with national fame." His cool and thorough command of the siege was subsequently "rewarded with a great leap forward in rank, promotion to brigadier general at the age of only 24."[166] "Great and deserved benefits flowed to Napoleon from the victory at Toulon. On December 22 he was appointed...inspector of coastal defenses from the Rhône to the Var."[167]

What's more, impressed by his leadership during the siege, "Saliceti brought him to the attention of the senior politicians Paul Barras and Louis-Stanislas Fréron..."[168] "Napoleon had now made his reputation among elite circles, even if he was still a long way from being a household name."[169]

"After Toulon, Napoleon rose quickly through the ranks of the French army. In 1796 he took up the same command as the general [Carteaux] who laughed in his face at Toulon. He now led the army in open battle across the Italian border, against a larger force of Italians and Austrians."[170] The retaking of Toulon "was the presage of ruin to our enemies," Napoleon later said in an address to his troops.[171] "But best of all, as he later put it, Toulon 'gave him confidence in himself.' He had shown that he could be trusted with command."[172]

The Siege of Toulon was only the beginning of Napoleon's big reveal as a master strategist, and, furthermore, Napoleon was only just beginning to reveal how and why the most masterful strategists rule the world. This sentiment was captured by the French politician Paul Barras, who had official oversight of the Siege of Toulon and who two years later became the main executive leader of the French Directory. Barras was so impressed with Bonaparte's actions at Toulon that he became his professed patron. Barras subsequently sent Napoleon to Paris with a letter to Count Carnot, one of the Ministers of War, which read, "I send you a young man who has distinguished himself very much during the siege, and earnestly recommend you advance him speedily: If you do not, he will most assuredly advance himself."[173]

PART 2: OVERVIEW

|PURPOSE|

REAP THE REWARDS, RULE YOUR WORLD

History is clear: Strategists rule the world. Modern warfare, politics, business, and entrepreneurship all continue to reinforce this historic, universal truth: Those who think strategically and who formulate and execute strategy most effectively are the ones who consistently come out on top. To become a *master* strategist is to learn to effectively command unruly forces, conquer unyielding problems, overcome insurmountable obstacles, and accomplish improbable aims.

In the last two decades, the skills and abilities of the strategist have repeatedly ranked among the five most prized executive leadership skills.[1] More recently, the demand for learning and development solutions focused on strategy or strategic thinking has regularly ranked at the top.

"In study after study," *Harvard Business Review* (HBR) reports, "strategic thinkers are found to be among the most highly effective leaders."[2] One study, HBR further reports, "found that a strategic approach to leadership was, on average, 10 times more important to the perception of effectiveness than other behaviors studied. It was twice as important as communication (the second most important behavior) and almost 50 times more important than hands-on tactical behaviors."[3] Of course, there are many other crucial leadership competencies, but, unlike the strategist, "they don't differentiate the highly effective leaders from everyone else."[4]

Master the Strategist Code.

Strategy and strategic thinking are vital to virtually every realm of human affairs. Whether you are a military commander or a corporate executive, a politician or a preacher, an entrepreneur or a teacher, or whether you simply want to think more strategically, tap more of your potential, and find greater success, mastering the code of the strategist is key. Your ability to think strategically, your ability to formulate and execute strategy, in short, your ability to think and act like a strategist is indispensable to getting the outcomes you desire.

As a timeless system anchored in the wisdom and insights of history's titans of strategy, the purpose of *The Strategist Code* is to equip you with the paradigms, principles, and practices, but also the key action strategies, tactics, and tools necessary to become a master strategist. The ultimate aim of this book is to help you unlock your potential as a strategist. It will teach you how to structure and streamline your thoughts and actions around the effective formulation and execution of strategy. It will also help you to calibrate and accelerate your development as a strategic thinker and leader. All of this will, ultimately, better enable and equip you to increase the influence and power you need to realize your chief purpose and goals.

As you learn to master the art of the strategist you will discover a surprising number of benefits. In fact, as you grasp the timeless wisdom and insights of history's titans of strategy as revealed throughout the pages of *The Strategist Code*, you will gain a number of decisive advantages. In the 1st of the 4-part framework (Chapters 1-4), you will:

(1.) DISCOVER the secrets of the *strategist mindset* and how to marshal it to outmaneuver and outshine those with deeper pockets, greater resources, and better intelligence;

(2.) LEARN how to unlock the power of a *future-focused, purpose-driven* time horizon to eliminate wasted effort, foster resilience and think in more far-reaching ways;

(3.) BUILD a more practical, applicable understanding of the link between victory and *thinking proactively*, winning and *playing the offense*, and seizing and *sustaining* the *initiative* until you succeed; and

(4.) GAIN greater awareness and insight into the power of disciplined thinking and how to *think critically* under pressure, improving decisions, actions, and results.

In the 2nd stage of the framework (Chapters 5-8), if you commit to learning and applying the wisdom and insights outlined in the pages ahead, you will:

(5.) UNDERSTAND the nexus between strategy and concentrated *curiosity* and discover the seven proven methods to cultivate a *concentrated curiosity* in order to better think strategically, strengthen effective strategy formulation, and expand your possibilities for success;

(6.) GRASP the powerful role of the past in shaping the future and how to use past experience, historical analogies and the *wisdom of history* to explore options, gain insights, improve decisions, and influence people, outcomes, and events;

(7.) DEVELOP a deeper understanding and new insights into the connection between *un*learning, creative *re*thinking, and game-changing strategy, and how early adopters and *innovative,* pioneering, and experimental thinkers invariably accrue decisive strategic advantages;

(8.) EXPLORE the power of *leverage points* and learn how to use systems thinking and the six levels of *leverage* to optimize the effectiveness of your strategy and elevate the impact of your influence, power and strength.

In the 3rd stage of the framework (Chapters 9-12), if you resolve to maintain a learner's mindset, and set aside your internal critic, you will:

(9.) APPREHEND the fundamental power of *surprise* and its essential role in strategic mastery, as well as the 8 key types of surprise and how to exploit them to maximize your potential success;

(10.) RECOGNIZE the surprising power but, often, imprudent resistance to *simplicity*; why it is a critical success factor in war, politics, business and sports and how best to exploit the power of *simplicity* without losing what is essential, meaningful, or distinct;

(11.) DISCOVER the cardinal principle of strategic success, why Napoleon Bonaparte was obsessed with *concentration*, and how, when, and where to *amass* and *focus* your forces to maximize your impact and minimize your risks;

(12.) UNCOVER the code to developing the synergistic strength of *collaboration* and discover how to tap the power of unified, unbreakable bonds for a level of *mutually assured success* and power beyond what any independent leader or solo operator could ever hope to expect.

Finally, in the 4th stage of the framework (Chapters 13-16), if you remain resolved to master the art and science of *The Strategist Code*, you will:

(13.) EXPAND and enhance your understanding of the unparalleled power of unflinching *self-belief,* and how to discover, develop, and tap the power of belief to achieve the unbelievable;

(14.) IDENTIFY the pivotal importance of *agility* to the success of great strategists, how to best optimize and reap its power, and the critical tactics to employ and integrate it into your strategic operations and the execution of your strategic plans;

(15.) LEVERAGE the game-changing power of *reflective action,* how to develop a *reflective practice* that suits your preferences, and discover a simple approach that you can immediately put into play to bring about more strategic and effective results; and, finally,

(16.) UNDERSTAND the supreme importance of effective strategy *execution* and discover the seven keys to successfully execute your strategy and ensure the realization of your ultimate chief purpose and goals.

Learn from the Legends

"The ideas I stand for are not mine. I borrowed them from Socrates. I swiped them from Chesterfield. I stole them from Jesus. And I put them in a book. If you don't like their rules, whose would you use?"[5]

—Dale Carnegie, *How to Win Friends and Influence People*

The Strategist Code is grounded in a simple premise: There are timeless lessons we can learn from history. There are indispensable insights, there is invaluable wisdom that that we can reap from the pages of the past.

No doubt, to avoid the pitfalls of *survivorship bias*, we must remember that history is written by the winners and the losers often lose their voice (and may even be erased). Remember that luck, external factors, and environmental forces can occasionally play a leading role. Remember that context matters and confirming evidence across different accounts is key. And we must remember that we can learn as much—perhaps more, at times—from defeat.

Nevertheless, there is no question that the legends and heroes of history are also distinguished by recurring characteristics, competencies, and cognitive frames. History itself teems with repeating patterns, principles, and themes. There are ancient secrets of strategic mastery revealing themselves over time. There are applicable lessons rising across the ages. There are strategy rules, laws, and codes which both echo through time and reverberate throughout the social sciences and beyond to this day—all of which confirm this irrefutable fact: History repeats. This is largely because human behavior is predictable and human nature does not change, but also because the past has a profound collective influence on the present and, therefore, the future. What we discover in history is not new thoughts or novel ideas, but endless wisdom and timeless truths. This is part of what gives authority to the themes discussed throughout this book, but it also helps explain why these concepts are often just as applicable across a variety of different domains, situations and times— regardless of the inexorable advance of technology and innovation.

After years of rigorous research, reading through hundreds of articles and books—from biography, history, and social science to business, politics, sports, and war—*The Strategist Code* was ultimately distilled from the historical record of a number of the greatest strategists in history; including many of the great military strategists (e.g. Alexander the Great, Hannibal Barca, Genghis Khan, Joan of Arc, and Napoleon Bonaparte) and naval strategists (e.g. Admiral Horatio Nelson, Captain Henry Morgan), as well as a number of political strategists (e.g. Cleopatra, Catherine the Great, Charlemagne, Isabella of Castile, Mary Tudor, John F. Kennedy, and Martin Luther King), but also strategists in business (e.g. the Rothschilds, Andrew Carnegie, Henry Ford, Steve Jobs, Jack Welch), strategic thinkers in science (e.g. Albert Einstein, Marie Curie) and strategic coaches in sports (e.g. Vince Lombardi, John Wooden).

To build a more rigorous, substantive case for the key concepts and themes, *The Strategist Code* also draws on the works of a selection of history's greatest strategic theorists (e.g. Polybius, Sun Tzu, Niccolò Machiavelli, Napoleon Bonaparte, Antoine Henri de Jomini, Carl von Clausewitz, and Basil Liddell Hart), ancient historians (e.g. Arrian, Thucydides, Plutarch, Livy), modern historians (e.g. David Chandler, Kirstin Downey, Andrew Roberts, Robert Greene, Frank McLynn, Vincent Cronin, Linda Porter, Laurence Bergreen, Anna Whitelock, Colin Woodard, Janet Nelson, Walter Isaacson, Sarah Gristwood, Paul Strathern, Marcus Rediker, Robin Lane Fox, Niall Ferguson, Kenneth Harl, David McCullough), as well as a handful of leadership theorists and social scientists (e.g. James MacGregor Burns, Peter Drucker, Edward Banfield, Robert Cialdini, Leslie Ian, Charles Duhigg, William Duggan), business thinkers (Stephen Covey, Brian Tracy, Anthony Robbins), and presidential scholars and political scientists (e.g. David Gergen, Richard Neustadt, H.W. Brands, Robert Dallek).

|STRUCTURE|
Master the Core Components of the Strategist Code

The Strategist Code consists of 16 chapters, one for each of the 16 key strategic factors (i.e. the essential paradigms, principles, and practices of the strategist) which are divided into the 4 core components of the code—inspiration, exploration, implementation, actualization. These 16 factors were identified using the leading research methods of qualitative research (i.e. predominantly case study and grounded theory), and, as such, represent the patterns, key concepts and themes that most frequently surfaced in the research literature and historical record and which best explain the key success factors of the individual cases included, given the particular research questions behind this book. This is an important part of what, hopefully, sets this book apart from the scores of other strategy books. Rather than relying on one individual's experience, genius, or expertise, this book is a synthesis of a broad sweep of many of the greatest strategists and strategic theorists in history.

In reading the biographies and historical accounts of the greatest strategists and strategic leaders in history, the primary research question was: In regards to their strategies and tactics, strategic thinking, or strategic leadership, what was the key factor or set of factors that led to their success, or, when they failed or made a major misstep, what critical factor or set of factors was missing?

In reading other books, articles, and research papers on strategy and strategic thinking, the primary research question was: What does this author, thought leader, theorist, journalist or historian, etc. believe to be the most critical factor or set of factors in effectively formulating and executing strategy?

What also, hopefully, helps to differentiate this book is the use of stories and anecdotes combined with a focus on application. The whole point and purpose of this book is to help you become a more effective strategist and, thereby, improve your prospects and possibilities for achieving some of your more challenging aspirations and goals.

The best way to tackle this—through a book, video, or podcast at least (i.e. without the ability to interact)—is through storytelling. As humans have known since the dawn of time and research in neuroscience now confirms, the best way to capture attention, maintain interest, increase recall, create connections, change behaviors, and alter outcomes is through storytelling. In *The Leadership Challenge*, Kouzes and Posner argue that storytelling is central to leadership. "A story is not only easier to remember and recall than a set of facts, it translates more quickly into action....Stories are better able to accomplish the objectives of teaching, mobilizing, and motivating... Well-told stories reach inside us and pull us along. They give us the actual experience of being there and of learning what is really important about the experience."[6]

"Storytelling is the most powerful way to put ideas into the world today," writes USC professor Robert McKee, Hollywood's most sought-after storytelling consultant.[7] "If history were taught in the form of stories," Rudyard Kipling once said, "it would never be forgotten."[8] "Storytelling is how people pass along lessons from generation to generation, culture to culture."[9]

It is worth noting that, in some respects, this book goes beyond the what, when and how-to of the strategist. Grounded in qualitative research methods and principles, the findings of this research are presented so that the stories and anecdotes of the various different historical figures take center stage of the overarching narrative of the section or chapter. In other words, the stories selected were those that best suited the topic or theme, weaving the insights together into a rich tapestry rather than providing isolated snapshots. However, the lessons and insights drawn from each story—while still applicable to the overall theme—often touch on a wealth of other topics and themes. Rather than ignoring those lessons and insights because they were not immediately related, they were included with the belief that they help to paint a greater and more nuanced portrait of what it meant to be an effective strategist in that particular situation and context and, thereby, forming a mosaic of perspectives. This book, as a result, is primarily about learning to become a master strategist. But it is also, secondarily, a book about ultimate triumph, high achievement, excellence, and success.

Read to Learn, Absorb to Apply

The recommended approach to *The Strategist Code* is to read straight through from beginning to end in order to gain a solid grasp of the material, its most essential elements, and, given your specific circumstances and context, the various potential areas of application. It's unlikely that every one of the 16 different strategic factors will apply directly to your unique circumstances or situation at the moment. Nevertheless, by absorbing this material at once you will gain a greater grasp of the code of the strategist which will enable and prepare you to more effectively and skillfully deal with whatever relevant scenarios arise.

The other advantage is that this will give you a more accurate and complete conceptual framework for examining and, perhaps, reexamining past successes and failures in order to gain new insights, perspective and wisdom for the future, all of which will better enable you to make wiser and more strategic and resourceful decisions going forward and, thereby, increase the speed and improve the likelihood of achieving your chief purpose and goals.

Created to further enable you to master this material, this book was created with a supplemental resource, *Mastering the Strategist Code: A Guidebook* (available for free at www.classicinfluence.com/strategist, no credit card required. If you prefer a hardcopy, a paperback version of *Mastering the Strategist Code: A Guidebook* is forthcoming at Amazon and Barnes & Noble). If you are committed to becoming an effective strategist, working through the various exercises included in this guidebook is essential. For those interested in true mastery, the guidebook also includes sets of discussion questions and exercises that you can use to deep dive into this topic with a book study club or mastermind group. Actually working through the exercises in this guidebook can be a powerful way to further comprehend, integrate and apply the wisdom, insights, and lessons learned from this book, and, as Theodore Roosevelt once said, "It is of little use for us to pay lip-loyalty to the mighty men of the past unless we sincerely endeavor to apply to the problems of the present precisely the qualities which in other crises enabled the men of that day to meet those crises."[10]

Put the Master Strategist Pre-Game Plan into Play

Master strategists tend to be marked by a particular operational code. They share certain instrumental beliefs, values, and frames that filter how they perceive, process, and respond to people, situations, and events. Meaningful research reveals that strategic mastery stems partly from shared higher-order cognitive strategies rather than just innate talents. There are distinct mental models and methods of mastery the aspiring strategist needs to succeed. To master the strategist code is not something you can accomplish in a few days or weeks. Even if that was possible, the fact is that the world's greatest strategists never stop learning and growing and developing their core competencies. They never cease from striving to further master their craft. If you aspire to become a master strategist, begin by building the basis for strategic mastery. Start by integrating the following five foundational mental models and methods of action into your strategic arsenal, as summarized here (each of which is expanded into a full chapter in *Mastering the Strategist Code: A Guidebook*). Think of these core concepts as initial building blocks to begin to develop your strategic acumen, to explore, experiment, refine, and follow through on your journey from apprentice to master strategist.

(1.) ***Compound Learning to Develop Mysterious Power***. Knowledge is *not* power. "Knowledge is only potential power," said Anthony Robbins.[11] The real power is in practical wisdom and strategic insight effectively applied. Wisdom and insight come from reflecting on and learning from experience—both your own hard won experience, but, more importantly, the historical record which, for the strategist, goes back thousands of years. The best way to maximize this power is to put the principle of compound learning into play. Operating much like compound interest (which has been called "the most powerful force in the universe"[12]), compound learning is one of the key secrets of the success of everyone from Napoleon Bonaparte to Warren Buffett. In Napoleon's case, his learning about strategy and tactics began when he was a young child, and his extraordinary lifelong love of knowledge and reading never stopped.[F1]

(2.) ***Think Big, Believe Big, Be Big, Achieve Big***. There is little point in learning the art of strategy if you have only limited vision and mediocre goals. To succeed on a grand scale, in contrast, requires becoming a master strategist and more. Great achievements begin with big bold thoughts, actions, and beliefs. Strategy is how you get there, but the vision is what, where, and why. To echo Nietzsche, if you have a strong enough why, you will figure out the how. If you have a big, bold inspiring vision, a grand aspiration or goal that you believe you can achieve, then you will become the strategist you need to succeed.[F2]

(3.) ***Sacrifice. Delay Gratification. Let Your Long Game Reign Supreme***. Effective strategists are masters of the long game. They remain calm and cool under pressure. They check their impulses and control their emotions, resisting the temptation to gratify their interests or satisfy their desires whenever it might undermine their long-term plans. Your future demands sacrifices. "The successful among us delay gratification. The successful among us bargain with the future,"[13] writes Peterson.[F3]

(4.) ***Assume Ownership, Take Command of the Situation at Hand***. Assume ownership. Take responsibility. Be proactive. Grab the bull by the horns. These parallel principles of success go beyond the realm of strategy, leadership, and power. For strategic mastery, however, seizing command of the situation at hand is practically a prerequisite of success. There can be no implementation and execution of strategy if the leader

---

F1. To learn more about the surprising power of compound learning see the accompanying workbook, *Mastering the Strategist Code: A Guidebook*, Chapter 1. "Compound Learning to Develop Mysterious Power: Napoleon Bonaparte's Coup d'Oeil Militaire."

F2. To learn more about the importance of your thoughts, actions, and beliefs see the accompanying workbook, *Mastering the Strategist Code*, Chapter 2. "Think Big, Believe Big, Be Big, Achieve Big: President Kennedy Puts Man on the Moon."

F3. To learn more about the power of playing the long game see the accompanying workbook, *Mastering the Strategist Code: A Guidebook*, Chapter 3. "Sacrifice. Delay Gratification. Let Your Long Game Reign Supreme: Isabella of Castile Lays the Groundwork for the Largest Empire on Earth."

does not first step up and take command.[F4]

(5.) ***Follow All the Way Through***. Finishing is everything. "There is no value in anything until it is finished,"[14] said Genghis Khan, one of history's greatest strategists; "the merit of an action lies in finishing it to the end," he said.[15] You can't win if you never finish the race. You can't succeed if you fail to see the venture all the way through. You can't become a master strategist or a master of anything else if you don't follow through and persist in mastering the field. In the words of the great American inventor Charles F. Kettering, the holder of 186 U.S. patents, "because it is so easy to stop," he said, "it is the 'follow through' that makes the great difference between ultimate success and failure."[16] Successful people are people who finish. They see things through to the end and they are trusted and respected and more successful as a result. As Napoleon Hill once put it, "The real thing upon which most great fortunes were built—the thing that helps men and women rise to fame and high position in the world—is easily described: It is simply the habit of completing everything one begins, first having learned what to begin and what not to begin."[17, F5]

Fulfill Your Promise

It is difficult to overstate the power and influence or overinflate the magnitude and significance of the master strategist. The most effective strategists truly do rule the world. The more you learn to think like a strategist, the more accomplished you become at formulating and executing strategy, the more power and influence you will gain too. In fact, it is hardly an exaggeration to say that you can have more of the things you want in life, and you can avoid more of the things you don't want, simply by learning, integrating and mastering the 16 strategic factors found in this book, paradigms and principles grounded in the wisdom and insights of history's heroes and titans of strategy.

But this is also the catch. It is not enough to simply *skim* through the pages of this book or any other book on strategy or the strategist code. Success also requires identifying areas where you can and will consistently *apply* the wisdom, insights, and lessons learned.

It is a select group of people that makes reading books a regular part of their daily lives. Sticking with this habit over time, this group ends up with a number of distinct advantages over another group—the great mass of people who read less than a book a year. As a matter of fact, research reveals that, on average, this select group of regular readers tends to be significantly healthier, wealthier, happier, and less stressed.[18]

F4. To learn more see the accompanying workbook, *Mastering the Strategist Code: A Guidebook*, Chapter 4. "Assume Ownership, Take Command of the Situation at Hand: Catherine the Great Usurps the Russian Throne."

F5. To learn more about the secrets and significance of effective follow through see the accompanying workbook, *Mastering the Strategist Code*, Chapter 5. "Follow All the Way Through: Hannibal Rattles the Gates of Rome."

But there is a third group that is even more rare and, on average, across every dimension, even more richly rewarded. This group spends even more time reading—averaging 10 hours or more per week (but 3 hours a day if you're Mark Cuban,[19] and 80% of your working day if you're Warren Buffet[20]). In essence, in the long run, reading pays enormous dividends.

However, this third group is also more selective about what they read, preferring books for education and self-improvement rather than entertainment,[21] and when they make a decision to read something, they are much more likely to follow through to the end of the book.

But what truly sets this group apart is that they actively engage with the things they read, highlighting key passages, making notes in the margins, sometimes wrestling with and reflecting on key concepts, and often writing out lists of the key takeaways or lessons learned. *Most importantly*, this group actively seeks to *apply* the wisdom and insights gained.

This is what you must do if you hope to become a master strategist. It is only when you take action and work to apply the code of the titans of strategy—implementing and mobilizing their wisdom and insights, their strategies, tactics, and tools for success—and only when you *learn from your experience* working with the strategist code that you begin to think like and become a strategist and, thereby, reap the real rewards of increased influence and power, the real magic of the strategist code. That is the promise at the heart of this book.

PART 3: THE STRATEGIST CODE

|1|

Appropriate the Extraordinary Secret Psychology of Strategic Mastery: The Strategist Mindset as the Cornerstone of Alexander the Great's Empire Building Success

*"I am sometimes a fox and sometimes a lion. The whole secret
of government lies in knowing when to be the one or the other."*[1]
—Napoleon Bonaparte, Emperor of France

In 336 B.C., to celebrate the marriage of his daughter, Cleopatra, Philip II of Macedonia invited friends, leading nobles, and influential people from across the land. The guests marveled at the elaborate festivities and sumptuous feasts of the royal wedding. Outdoors on a beautiful sunny day, the setting was surrounded by statues of the twelve Greek gods, as well as a statue of Philip himself, enthroned among the lofty Olympians. Eager to forge this new alliance, this was the day that Philip might well have been the happiest man in all of Greece.

As he walked out of the theatre to greet the guests, Philip suddenly heard his bodyguards cry out. Seconds later he felt the searing pain of sharp, cold steel radiate throughout his body as Pausanias, a former bodyguard and spurned lover, thrust his dagger deep into Philip's upper body. The once mighty Macedonian King collapsed helplessly to the ground.

Standing mere steps away, his twenty-year-old son, Alexander, overcome with intense emotion, fell to his knees as Philip's assassin attempted to escape. Tears streamed down his face as he cradled his father in his arms. Calling his name helplessly, Alexander could only watch as Philip's blood poured out, and his life slipped away.

Ever on guard for just such an event, Alexander's friends quickly rushed in to aid their new king. Knowing that he was backed by both the army and many leading nobles, Alexander, with raging tears in his eyes and his father's blood dripping down his arms, slowly stood up and stepped in to fill the void and assume the throne, as his friends placed the crown of the fallen king on Alexander's head.

Despite the shock of watching his father's assassination, Alexander was not completely unprepared. Ever the strategist, always thinking and planning ahead, Alexander had undoubtedly considered this gruesome possibility many times before. After all, the threat of assassination went beyond Philip. Indeed,

The Strategist Code | 39

given the risk that he might be the next to die by the dagger of an assassin, particularly given the persistent questions surrounding his own legitimacy as the rightful heir to the throne of Macedonia, Alexander, along with the help of his ever-scheming mother, Olympias, moved swiftly to eliminate his potential rivals.

"His powerful opponents may well have thought they could dispose of this upstart boy without trouble. They were wrong: he showed himself absolutely ruthless from the start and had good reason to be," writes historian Peter Green.[2] "He knew that both his cousin Amyntas, and Cleopatra's newborn son, Caranus (named, ostentatiously, after the dynasty's mythical founder), represented a direct threat to his rule and had powerful backers."[3]

Nor was resistance to his rule limited to Macedonia. In fact, as soon as word spread that Philip was dead, other Greek city-states—known for their democratic ideals and aversion to monarchy—began to rebel against this young, inexperienced "barbarian king," and his authority over them as the hegemon or leader of the League of Corinth.

Model the Strategic Surprise and Agility of the Strategic Mind

In response, Alexander quickly rode south with 3,000 cavalry to squash the rebellion. He soon found Thessaly's army occupying the pass at Mount Olympus. When the Thessalians awoke the following morning to find that Alexander and his men had boldly and cunningly outmaneuvered them in the dark of night, and were now in their rear, they immediately surrendered and joined Alexander's ranks.

After defeating several Thracian tribes in the North, Alexander next turned his attention to Thebes who, much more aggressive in their resistance to Alexander's rule, had rashly declared their independence from Macedonia. Thebes had a history of betraying their Greek neighbors, including siding with the Persian conqueror King Xerxes when he invaded in 480 B.C.[4] When they refused to reverse their ill-conceived plan, showing no mercy, and with full support from the League of Corinth,[5] writes historian Graham Wrightson, "Alexander razed Thebes to the ground and sold the entire city into slavery,"[6] with the exception of the priests and poets, including the descendants of his favorite poet, Pindar.

When the sun came up on the captured city the following morning, order was swiftly restored as Alexander called off his dogs. Following a night of violence, all butchery was now banned by decree. Many were liberated from fear of further bloodshed, "and a large number of Thebans—guest-friends, pro-Macedonian politicians, priests, and any who could show that they had opposed the uprising—were set free together with their families. Of the thirty thousand prisoners it appears that...twenty thousand were sold."[7]

News of the destruction of Thebes sent shockwaves throughout the Greek world. After reversing course once already, Athens soon sued for peace a second time, which Alexander graciously accepted. He had already clearly demonstrated both his capability as a military general, and his capacity for ruthlessness. With Athens, he would demonstrate restraint.

Maintain Your Vision, Adapt Your Strategy, Tactics, and Tools

"If you only have a hammer, you tend to see every problem as a nail."[8]
—Abraham Maslow, American Psychologist, Creator of Maslow's Hierarchy of Needs

Without a doubt, Alexander could be brutally unforgiving, but he never saw force as the only means at his disposal. Furthermore, once he had brought the various rebellions to an end, he understood that the strategic value of force was severely curtailed. He could never lead the Greek states through the threat of "brute force alone," at least not effectively.[9] In fact, "one of Alexander's key attributes," writes historian David Lonsdale, "was his awareness of the limits of force."[10] While he was driven by a deep, unquenchable desire, he was never so foolish as to imagine that he could build an empire with a hammer alone.

He used force when he felt it was necessary, as with Thebes and the Thracian tribes, but he used tactical maneuvers, diplomacy and alliances, as with Thessaly and Athens, whenever and wherever he could. Indeed, rather than force, it was his friendships, close connections with the army, and strategic alliances with leading nobles that enabled him, despite questions surrounding his legitimacy as heir, to ascend to the throne of Macedonia in the first place.

Within a period of several months, Alexander the Great had effectively consolidated his power over the confederation of Greek nations with a range of strategies, tactics, and tools. By this time, he had earned Greece's respect—not just for his military prowess, but for what they perceived to be his magnanimity, his lack of petty vindictiveness, as well as his capacity for being ruthless toward his enemies. To further solidify his leadership, however, Alexander had yet another key strategic endeavor in mind, a plan to unite all of Greece around a common cause. Now he would do something *for* the Greek city-states, and for his own ambitions.

With roots in his early youth, Alexander's vision had never changed; he wanted to lead Greece to new frontiers. He wanted to build the greatest empire on earth, and spread Greek culture around the globe. With this vision fixed firmly in mind, Alexander, a virtual archetype of Plato's *philosopher king*, understood that to achieve this dream would require *adapting* and *adjusting* his strategy along the way, tailoring his tactics to circumstances, and applying different stratagems, clever tricks, and psychological tools.

His ascension only gives us a glimpse of the range of Alexander's aptitude as a master strategist, and it tells us virtually nothing of his mastery of strategy in warfare, or tactics in the field. But this was also just the beginning of Alexander's journey to conquer the known world.

In time, he would reveal himself to be both a brilliant military tactician, and a master of grand strategy. Always adopting a long-term perspective with an impressively broad scope, he was never thinking solely of how to outmaneuver an enemy on the battlefield. Along with the strategic use of military force, Alexander was also thinking of the relevant geopolitical and economic factors, the diplomatic means at his disposal, the intelligence assets he could exploit, how he would navigate the cultural differences and lead the people he conquered, what influence his actions would have on Greece, and how to maintain both the morale of his men, and the loyalty of the rebellious Greeks back home.

In essence, Alexander demonstrated a remarkable multi-dimensional grasp of strategy, which was essential to his grand vision of cultural exchange within what would become his global, cosmopolitan empire.

In the end, Alexander failed to achieve his dream. And, yet, as the Greek historian Ptolemy said, "What failure! His failure towered over other men's successes."[11] Across a wide array of different terrains, facing a range of diverse enemy forces, often two or three times the size of the Macedonian army, Alexander, always leading from the front, not once defeated in battle, ultimately, after campaigning for a staggering 22,000 miles, conquered the known world, and built an empire the likes of which no one had ever before seen. What's more, he did all of this a long, long way from home. And he did it all before age 33.

Master the Discipline of Strategic Thinking

Since his death over twenty-three centuries ago, many of history's greatest strategists have carefully studied his example, looking to learn from the leadership wisdom and strategic genius of Alexander the Great. The list of those who considered themselves students of Alexander includes exemplary leaders across a range of different domains, from ancient military leaders such as Hannibal Barca and Julius Caesar to medieval merchants and monarchs such as the Medicis and the Hapsburgs. The list of self-proclaimed students of Alexander includes the renowned Renaissance political strategist Niccolò Machiavelli and the influential military theorist Frederick the Great, but also military leaders such as Napoleon Bonaparte and George Washington, strategists from both sides of the American Civil War—Robert E. Lee and Ulysses S. Grant—as well as business titans such as J.P. Morgan and Ted Turner, and even the celebrated American educator Edith Hamilton.[12]

What each one of these leaders learned from Alexander is the extraordinary power of the strategist mindset and, furthermore, the vital importance of strategy in the attainment of your grand aspirations and goals. To be sure, as history's greatest military, political, and business leaders have demonstrated again and again, with the exception of your grand purpose and guiding principles—your vision and values—*nothing* is more important than strategy. Strategy is indispensable to the attainment of your goal. As Bolman and Deal put it in *Reframing Organizations*, "A vision without a strategy remains an illusion."[13]

The problem for most leaders is that they consistently fail to think strategically. They fail to grasp the central importance of strategy, and, as a result, they fail to effectively formulate and execute the strategies and tactics they need to achieve their purpose and goals.

But this is also part of why mastering the discipline of strategic thinking can give you such a tremendous edge. As Irish playwright and political activist George Bernard Shaw once wryly observed, "Most people don't take the time to think. I made an international reputation for myself by deciding to think twice a week."[14]

Ply the Tools of the Strategist

"Key to the success or failure of much strategic action,
regardless of the venue, is the mindset of the strategist."[15]
—Stanley K. Ridgley, Former U.S. Military Intelligence Officer,
Professor of Management, Drexel University

Strategy is basically about taking a broader, strategic perspective on how to use the power and resources you have to achieve the vision and goals you desire. For the strategist, part of the challenge, but also the adventure, comes in tackling the various sets of roles and responsibilities involved in effectively formulating, planning, implementing, and executing strategy. What makes this even more challenging is the addition of complexity, unpredictability, and the many different, often conflicting forces and ambiguous demands placed on the strategist. Fortunately, there are some powerful tools you can use to significantly improve your probability of success.

Exploit the Power of Models and Frameworks.

One of the best ways to tackle challenges like this is through the use of models or frameworks. Models are like maps. By *representing* reality, maps make it easier to visualize and conceptualize the area and main features the map represents. Maps give us a much more clear and powerful sense of where we are, what we are dealing with, and how to get where we want to go. A good map will help us get oriented, provide direction, depict shape and size, represent relationships and relative proportion, point out the pitfalls and roadblocks, give us a sense of the terrain, and provide alternative paths we might take to the top.

A good model or framework is very similar. It essentially provides a system and structure for thinking more strategically. It serves as a tool for organizing and streamlining your thoughts and actions, helping you explore, investigate, and understand the world. This book, *The Strategist Code*, for example, with its 4 parts and 16 factors is a model for understanding and effectively navigating the world—your life, business, career—as a strategist. There are a number of other useful strategy frameworks (see notes for a list of 12 of the most popular strategy frameworks in business[16]).

There is a balance, however. If the map or model is too simple, it's often less useful, but if it's too complex its more difficult to use and less widely applicable. The usefulness of frameworks comes not from being a perfectly accurate representation of reality (which is impossible anyway), but from exploring the world through it and using it as a source of creative tension.

As we will explore further below and in the pages ahead, Alexander often found ways to use history as a framework. He also used the legends, myths, and heroes of history as both models and maps for making meaning of the world and his experience in it. He also exploited both history and mythology as a source of creative tension for pushing himself and his men to achieve the seemingly impossible.

Adopt the Navigator Mindset: Think in Terms of Tensions, Then Navigate, Manage, or Resolve—The 7 Paradoxes of the Strategist.

> *"The test of a first-rate intelligence is the ability to hold two opposed ideas in the mind at the same time, and still retain the ability to function."*[17]
>
> —F. Scott Fitzgerald, "The Crack-Up"

This leads to another useful tool for thinking through the complex challenges of formulating, planning, and implementing strategy: Framing the challenges in terms of various *tensions*, opposing sets of priorities, or disparate demands. According to Newton's Third Law of Motion, for every action you take there is an equal and opposite reaction. Similarly, the more time and energy you focus in one area, the greater the lack of time and energy you will tend to focus in some conflicting or opposite area. Sometimes this is good and healthy. In most cases, however, it leads to a potentially perilous imbalance. Think, for example, of what happens when you spend all of your time and energy focused on work; it almost invariably comes at a cost to your family or social life.

People often find similar conflicts (but also clever solutions, fortunately) between working *on* your business versus working *in* your business; enjoying life *today* versus creating a compelling *future*; *creating* art versus *selling* art; engaging people with *familiarity* (known, comfortable) versus *innovation* (unknown, stimulating);[18] strategy *formulation* versus strategy *execution*; and so on.

Much of the stress we face and problems we confront in business and life come from a failure to effectively manage *or even notice* these competing demands. Simply recognizing that the challenge you are confronting or the stress you are dealing with is the result of a critical conflict, paradox, or tension—or, perhaps, a whole set of conflicts and tensions (such as the 7 outlined below)—can go a long way toward helping you better understand and constructively *resolve* the challenges you face. *Identifying*, *naming*, and *clarifying* the tensions you are dealing with can make it much easier to generate new, creative ideas or "third alternatives;" solutions that you never could have imagined if you had not first recognized and gotten clear about the conflicting priorities or competing demands that you face. Once you have clarity and understanding, it is so much easier to better manage or navigate a course between the two competing forces, desires, or demands.

In some cases, the tension or pair of competing demands you identify is not directly connected to the problem you must address. Nevertheless, the tension you identify may still be causing headaches and stress because it is *preventing*, distracting, or derailing you from dealing with the real problem. In these cases, identifying and acknowledging and even naming, or *accurately labeling*, the tension can help to clear the fog or turmoil so that the real challenges can be clearly identified and addressed.

What made Alexander the Great such a brilliant strategic thinker was not just that he had a superior mental framework or superior models for thinking about strategy, or that he easily grasped the apparently conflicting, often paradoxical demands placed on the strategist. What stands out about Alexander is how skillfully he was able to navigate the tensions between so many competing demands. Rather than trafficking in absolutes or being pulled apart or derailed by the tensions, he recognized the importance of the opposing priorities and plotted a path between the two that best suited the circumstances and environment in which he was operating. Indeed, in some measure, his genius was revealed by his calm and collected confidence and even *comfort in contradiction*, successfully navigating a course through some of the most extreme, volatile, and uncertain situations and circumstances imaginable.

This is the extraordinary secret psychology of strategic mastery. It takes a certain level of psychological development to recognize the inherent paradoxes the strategist must confront. It takes another level to understand and accept them. But to hold and embrace and even thrive in the midst of such an array of competing, often contradictory, demands is something entirely different. This is a key part of where the core power of strategic mastery is found, in learning to effectively identify, navigate and even profit from these prevailing tensions. The following are seven of the most persistent tensions the strategist must learn to effectively navigate:

(1.) The Visionary Tactician.

The first and most fundamental tension strategists must navigate is between the need for a grand, sweeping vision of a distant future and the need to be grounded in the immediate tactical priorities of the day. To excel as a strategist, playing the long game is essential, but to do that effectively requires focusing on the closely aligned short-term tasks and objectives you need to accomplish in order to successfully realize your ultimate purpose and goals. (Discussed further in Chapter 2.)

In Alexander's case, constantly leading his army from the front, he spent a great deal of his time thinking as a tactician, focused on maneuvers and logistics, grounded in the objectives and priorities of the day. However, he also had to continually consider the impact these measures would have on his long-term vision. To illustrate, following his ascension to the throne of Macedonia, he had to fight to preserve the leadership his father held over the League of Corinth. He had to suppress the rebellion and discipline the defiant Greek city-states. At the same time, however, he knew that he would need to build a great, loyal army from the same city-states he was now subduing if he hoped to achieve his grand vision of conquering the world and advancing Greek civilization. He would also need the loyalty of the elites from these same Greek city-states once he was out on campaign in order to ensure his place over Greece in his absence.

Part of the solution was in being firm, but fair and generous whenever possible. Another part of the solution (discussed further below) was in how he worked to reshape the identity of his army at the beginning of the campaign and how he worked to gain their respect, leading by example and sharing in their burdens. Suffering a number of severe wounds by lance, sword, arrow, stone, club, and knife, Alexander once said to his soldiers, "There is no part of my body but my back which has not a scar; not a weapon a man may grasp or fling the mark of which I do not carry upon me...again and again I have been struck...and all for your sakes: for your glory and your gain. Over every land and sea, across river, mountain, and plain I led you to the world's end, a victorious army."[19]

The third part of the solution—and the most important part of leadership—was found in Alexander's vision. A clear and compelling shared vision will *inspire* people to work long and hard, day in and day out, to bring it about. Inspiration, in other words, can play an important, galvanizing part of ensuring adequate tactical execution. In the case of Alexander's vision, as his friend, advisor, and general, Ptolemy, said, "I've lived long life, but the glory and the memory of man will always belong to the ones who follow their great visions. And the greatest of these is the one they now call...*Megas Alexandros*. The greatest of them all."[20]

(2.) The Democratic Autocrat.

There is another important tension between transformational and authoritarian leadership. Master strategists are eager to listen and solicit input, ideas, and constructive feedback from trusted advisors, particularly in the early stages of strategy formulation and implementation, but ultimately they assume extreme ownership and responsibility for the decisions and the successful execution of the strategic plan. They understand the value and importance of sharing information, power, authority, and credit, and they seek to delegate to reliable lieutenants (i.e. those trusted for both their character and competence), but they also understand the need for control and coordination,[21] they are equally capable of dictating orders in a crisis or under significant pressure or time constraints, and they are perfectly willing to withhold power and information if and when necessary to ensure secrecy, surprise, or success.

Throughout *most* of his career, Alexander balanced this tension exceptionally well. In some sense, it seems that Greek culture and tradition as well as his own premiere education (his tutor was none other than Aristotle) helped to ensure that he sought counsel from his top generals and worked to ensure sufficient "external dialogue assessing the strategic rationale of decisions."[22] Not until late in his campaign, while in India, did he start to increasingly disregard the counsel of his generals, losing some of his prized "strategic focus and subtlety" as a result.[23]

(3.) <u>The Vigilant Hustler.</u>

The strategist must also strike a balance between being an enterprising go-getter who is eager to exploit *opportunities* and seize the initiative (i.e. hustling) while also being continually on guard against potential *threats* (i.e. being vigilant). It often makes sense to be heavily biased toward discovering opportunities to triumph and excel. Referred to as the *strategic offensive*, one of the key principles of strategy is the idea that 'the best defense is a good offense.' Seizing and maintaining the initiative can keep your opponents from mounting an offense, making defensive measures unnecessary. It's a mistake, however, to ignore the need for continuous environmental scanning in order to spot potential risks and hazards that could lead to disaster, or simply losing the initiative, which could make it more difficult to succeed. Keeping a watchful, enterprising eye on potential hazards and threats might also lead to the discovery of unexpected opportunities or hidden benefits. (Discussed further in Chapter 3.)

Alexander's reign began with a thunderstorm of violent internal and external threats. Triggered by the assassination of his father, he was literally surrounded by rebellion and competing claims to the throne, each one of which required a rapid, decisive response. Not until he restored order and secured power would he be free to turn his attention to his grand aspiration of conquering the world. Even before this, however, even before he could seize the overall initiative in a war against Greece's age-old enemy, the Persians, Alexander was on the lookout, scanning for opportunities to gain the initiative over the individual city-states of Greece. When he saw the opportunity to outmaneuver the Thessalians at night by showing up in their rear, for example, or when he took the opportunity to destroy Thebes completely, with support from the Hellenic League,[24] which would not likely have been supported against another city-state, but which still sent an unmistakable warning to

Athens and the other rebellious city-states, Alexander was taking initiative and exploiting opportunities to achieve his aim.

(4.) The Futuristic Historian.

Another important tension is between the past and the future. Strategists both learn from history, including the immediate past and personal experience, but they also continually turn their attention to the future and how best to shape it. Strategists both tap the wisdom of history and pioneer new technological advances and tactical innovations. They understand how the past shapes the future in many hidden and unhidden ways and, therefore, they study the past to better anticipate and influence the future. In searching for the *optimal* strategy, the strategist will invariably *investigate* and critically *evaluate* what's working for others, as well as what worked in the past, but they are also perfectly willing to innovate, experiment, and explore. Rather than looking in one direction or the other, they look both to the past and the future (Discussed further in Chapters 6 & 7.)

Beginning early in his youth and continuing on throughout his life, Alexander was a devoted student of history. He was even known to travel with history books and he slept with his favorite "history" book (a papyrus scroll of Homer's *Iliad*) under his pillow. Alexander was not just wistfully daydreaming of a bygone era, however. He was looking to the future. And he often found clever ways to exploit history as a tool to shape the future (see Chapter 6). On the other hand, Alexander was also forever at the forefront seeking to do what had never been done before, and many of his victories were the result of new innovations in warfare, such as at the Siege of Tyre, which involved building a causeway (which still exists today) from the mainland out to the well-fortified island nation. He is also said to have created innovations in troop maneuvers and formations, such as arranging his troops in levels to confront an enemy with greater numbers, as he did against Darius at the Battle of Gaugamela.

(5.) The Collaborative Competitor.

Typically, people think of business success as beating the competition. History's greatest conquerors are likewise remembered for their triumphs in battle. Master strategists understand, however, that defeating one's opponent is just *one* of the potential paths to success, and it is not usually the best and certainly not the most predictable one. The ancient Chinese military strategist Sun Tzu went as far as saying that "the supreme art of war is to subdue the enemy *without fighting*."[25] Many of history's greatest military strategists embraced this idea, as did Alexander, but so too did the Golden Age pirates, such as Blackbeard, the Vikings, and Genghis Khan, who were all loathe to lose their own men.

It's important to remember that victory is rarely, if ever, the ultimate goal. Victory is the means to some other end. Even in competitive sports, where competition is required by definition, the ultimate goal is not necessarily victory over any particular opponent, or even to be the reigning champion.

Named by ESPN as the "Coach of the Century," UCLA's John Wooden explains: "Success is peace of mind which is a direct result of self-satisfaction in knowing you made the effort to become the best of which you are capable."[26] What's more, rather than emphasizing winning or victory, John Wooden's definition of "competitive greatness" was as follows: "Perform at your best when your best is required. Your best is required each day."[27]

The challenge for the strategist is to navigate or resolve the tension between struggling *against* those who *seem* to be standing in your way and working together *with* them. The correct path is the one most likely to lead to your chief purpose. And given its unpredictable nature, a *violent* conflict or *vicious*, malicious competition might well be considered the method of last resort.

Compete to Bring Out Your Best. It's also true, however, that vigorous, healthy competition can help to bring out your best. For the ancient Greeks, competition was a virtue and the gymnasium was a central part of Greek life. In fact, the ancient Greeks were the first to formally celebrate competition; the Olympic Games we still celebrate around the world today were born in Olympia, Greece in 776 B.C.

But these were much more than mere games. The Greeks believed that the supreme Grecian virtue was *aretas*, which means "attaining excellence through competition."[28] "*Aretas* was something that the gods had and mere mortals sought to achieve,"[29] and the Olympic Games began as "a religious festival—a way to demonstrate one's *aretas*."[30] "Sports were not merely an entertainment, or a distraction, or a mimicry of war...The human competitors were hoping to demonstrate traits associated with the gods: through the events, the athletes were following the path of the gods to the divine."[31]

The Greeks believed that, as one historian put it, "competition was the outlet for all other virtues—courage, loyalty, trustworthiness."[32] "Competition brought out the best and taught athletes to be their absolute best."[33] "The Ancient Greeks did not fear that competition bred immoral behavior. They believed that competition *taught* moral behavior...*Aretas* meant that competing had shaped you into a better person: competition challenged you to become the best you could be."[34]

"In the heat of battle," Bronson and Merryman write in *Top Dog: The Science of Winning and Losing*, "someone with *aretas* had proven himself to be a fearless opponent and brilliant strategist. When tested, he was a leader, masterfully skilled, knowledgeable, and persuasive...He had...a cunning intelligence. He was...fast...and agile...He was brave and steadfast in character."[35]

In essence, the ultimate goal of competition was not to triumph over your competitor. Competition was a means of tapping your unrealized potential, drawing out your hidden reservoirs of energy, intelligence, and grit.

Seeing competition in this way is more congruent with the original meaning of the term. The Latin root of the word *compete* is "*competere*," which comes from "com" ("with, together" or "in the company of another") and "petere" ("to seek" or "to strive after"). Thus, the term *competere* translates as "to seek together" or "to strive after in the company of another." (Discussed further in Chapter 12.)

In Alexander's case, true to his own Greek upbringing and education, he craved more than victory. His vision was about spreading Greek civilization and ruling over the known world. But a critical part of what drove Alexander was *pothos* a longing to emulate the gods (Discussed further in Chapter 6). Ultimately, he was a peace-seeking militarist, a collaborative competitor; he wanted peace, but he was perfectly willing to fight to get peace on his terms. He was willing to use force, but he also recognized its risks and limits. Alexander is often remembered as a conqueror, but, throughout his life, he frequently preferred to form alliances with the peoples of foreign lands, co-opting rather than destroying them,[36] and these alliances helped to change the world he left behind.

(6.) The Agile Anchor.

The master strategist is also both flexible and firm, both responsive and resolute. Strategists are unpredictable. In fact, with respect to their opponents or competitors, being unpredictable is a principal part of how they operate (Discussed further in Chapter 9). They can be surprisingly flexible in some ways and unexpectedly firm in others. In regards to the pursuit of their goals, they are able to easily maneuver and adapt to respond to inevitable change. At the same time, however, strategists remain grounded by a stable core, which at the very least includes a persistent purpose and principles or a hard and fast vision and values (Discussed further in Chapter 2.) which allows them to adapt to a rapidly evolving environment without losing their way.[37] (Discussed further in Chapter 14.)

Agility was one of Alexander's greatest strengths. He repeatedly demonstrated the ability to swiftly adapt both weapons and ideas to new contexts and unfamiliar environments. He also made maximum use of mobility and flexibility on the field of battle, enabling his army to maneuver and respond to sudden developments that often surprised his enemies. On the other hand, Alexander was also guided by a number of *enduring* Greek values (honor, respect, courage, generosity) and *unyielding* principles of war (e.g. speed, boldness, discipline, surprise), but also proven operational doctrines, as well as certain trusty tactics that he used on the battlefield again and again, such as the Macedonian phalanx formation, and the deployment of cavalry in a wedge.

(7.) The Reflective Practitioner.

The final tension the strategist must navigate is between action and reflection, between strategy formulation and strategy execution. As leaders, strategists are rightly eager to get into the center of the action, or "the center of the center of the action," as President Kennedy put it, "in the very thick of the fight."[38] But action is not enough. To be all about action means to be without strategic thinking, which leads to poor decisions and predictable mistakes. The strategist, therefore, must also make time to get perspective, get on the balcony, and think.[39] "That is why," former French president Charles De Gaulle wrote in *The Edge of the Sword*, "great men of action have always been of the meditative type."[40] The key, management pioneer Peter Drucker wrote, is to "follow effective action with quiet reflection. From the quiet reflection will come even more effective action."[41] (Discussed further in Chapters 15 & 16.)

As regularly recurring as these seven strategic tensions appear in the realm of strategy, your success as a strategist is *less* about the exact set of tensions or the precise equilibrium you need to navigate your course, some of which will almost invariably change depending on your particular context, environmental conditions, and competitive pressures. Your success, instead, is far *more* about adopting the mindset of the strategist—which includes learning to think in terms of these and other *strategic tensions*. Furthermore, adopting the mindset of a strategist is also about making use of *models and frameworks* for strategic thinking, as well as *key success factors*, recurring *principles and patterns*, and a number of other powerful strategic tools (as we will explore in the chapters ahead).

Determine to Develop a More Cunning and Strategic Mind.

To learn to think like a strategist is to greatly improve the probability of achieving your goals. To master the strategist mindset is to gain a powerful competitive advantage. No question, it can take time to learn to think strategically; it takes effort to develop a more cunning and strategic mind. But it is possible. "There is no doubt," writes Switzerland's IMD Business School professor Michael Watkins, "that strategic thinking, like any other skill, can be improved with training."[42]

Despite the time, effort, and determination it may take—as with any craft worth developing—the good news is that whatever time and effort you invest in learning to think like a strategist will be richly rewarded in return. Furthermore, rather than becoming stale, dated, or obsolete, learning to think strategically is a timeless, irrevocable power that can strengthen your decision-making, heighten your capacity to persuade, increase your power and influence, and lead to superior results in virtually every area of your life.[43]

Resist the tendency to default to the same old, tired approach to your problems, purpose, and goals. Instead, resolve to take a more strategic approach. Follow the lead of Alexander. Fill your mind with the strategies, tactics, and mental tools that keep your thinking fresh, fluid, adaptive, resourceful, unpredictable, and sharp.

Study and Learn from History, Adopt the Long-Term Point of View.

With a blend of alliance-building, diplomacy, and force, once Alexander had tamed the rebellious city-states of Greece, he immediately pivoted to his ultimate purpose. This grand aspiration of building a great empire and spreading Greek civilization to the edge of the world, including conquering the Persian Empire (Greece's age-old enemy), would not only help to satisfy his own unquenchable ambition, but it also held great appeal for the Greeks, and, therefore, would help to further solidify Alexander's leadership over Greece.

The conflict between Greece and Persia first began when Cyrus the Great began invading Greek settlements in Asia Minor. When the Greeks began to revolt against Persian rule, it led to the Greco-Persian Wars, which included the first failed invasion of Greece by Persia under Darius the Great in 492 B.C. This invasion ended at the Battle of Marathon—a watershed in the Greco-Persian wars, and a pivotal event in the rise of Classical Greek civilization.[44]

The other key historical conflict was the second failed invasion of Greece by Persia under the leadership of Darius' son, Xerxes I. This invasion is most famous for the Battle of Thermopylae, in which the king of Sparta, Leonidas, and 300 brave, selfless Spartans took a bold, "heroic last stand against tens of thousands of Persian"[45] soldiers at the narrow mountain pass of Thermopylae and, in defending all of Greece from the invaders, made the ultimate sacrifice. After sacking a handful of cities in Greece, including an evacuated Athens, the Persians were ultimately defeated in 479 B.C.

By the time Alexander came to power, the Greeks remained rightly concerned that the Persians would once again attempt to invade Greece. Alexander's father, Philip II, had long dreamed of punishing the Persians for their unprovoked invasions. But Alexander was destined to do it.

"Always the savvy strategist," Alexander carefully "framed" the campaign against Persia as a just and long overdue "patriotic retaliation."[46] He would heal past pains, restore Greek honor, free the Greek cities still ruled by Persian tyrants, and create the general sense of safety and security that is so essential to the development, prosperity, and advance of civilization. "If his study of history had taught him anything—and, with the philosopher and scientist Aristotle as his teacher, he [was] certainly…well schooled—it would have been that nothing unites states and their people more than having a reviled common enemy."[47] By framing the campaign in the interests of Greece, he was cleverly navigating the tension, so often faced by strategists, between maintenance and growth. In business this often manifests as a conflict between protecting market share versus growing market share, or servicing your existing clients versus selling to new ones. In Alexander's case, expanding his empire by conquering Persia (growing market share), he was simultaneously strengthening the power of Greece (protecting market share).

After his success over the Persian satraps at the Battle of Granicus in May 334 B.C., Alexander briefly turned his attention back to Greece. Alexander's next step would be to bring all of Asia Minor under his control. He wanted to liberate the Greeks who were living under Persian despotism in these important coastal cities. This would serve to strengthen his leadership and the loyalty of Greece, "leaving a stable political structure in his wake," but it would also deprive the Persians of key naval bases which served his larger "strategic purpose...allowing him to push farther inland."[48]

Before he would continue to conquer Persia, however, Alexander had yet another shrewd strategic maneuver in mind. Designed to reinforce his power and influence at home, Alexander was essentially navigating yet another key strategic tension—that is, between growing his empire and maintaining the empire he had.

One of the most popular gods in Athens was Athena, the Olympian goddess of wisdom, strategy, and warfare. "In all these roles she was especially valued because she was always accessible, unlike many gods who kept their distance from humans."[49] As a result, the Athenians put images of Athena and her sacred symbol, the owl, on their coins. What's more, in order to worship Athena, the Athenians built the Parthenon on the Acropolis, the high hill overlooking the city.[50]

Following his triumph at Granicus, as a symbol in honor of Sparta's King Leonidas and the brave 300, Alexander "had 300 sets of Persian armor sent to Athens as a dedication to Athena on the Acropolis as a reminder that he had avenged the Persian destruction and sacrilege to the older Parthenon in 480 B.C."[51] With this victory over the Greeks age-old enemy, and the powerful symbolism of this dedication to Athena, the city-states of Greece were now more certain than ever that Alexander was destined to be their leader.

Even as Alexander's leadership echoed Plato's philosopher king,[52] it also reflected the mythology of Athena. When the Greek goddess Athena sprang fully formed from the forehead of Zeus she was clad in armor. And although she was the goddess of strategy, wisdom, and war, she did not like fighting without a purpose. What's more, whenever possible, she preferred to use wisdom and strategy to advance her purposes. While Alexander the Great is often remembered as a conqueror, the truth is that he was far more a leader in the mold of Athena, drawing not solely on the use of force, but on a wide array of strategies, tactics, tricks, and psychological tools to achieve his aims. Thus, far more than a great conqueror, Alexander the Great should be remembered above all as a master strategist.

To achieve your own bold aspirations and goals, becoming an effective strategist is key. Learn from the example of Alexander the Great. Draw on Alexander's strategic genius to inspire and inform your decisions and you will almost certainly find yourself driving to go further than ever before, reaching beyond whatever limits you now see, and, with a little luck and a lot of grit, achieving more than most men and women even imagine. As the renowned scholar of classical antiquity Edith Hamilton once wrote, "There is something breathtaking in Alexander the Great. Like everything stupendous—the pyramids, the Grand Canyon, Mount Everest—one can never get quite used to it. It drives us out beyond the everyday limits we set for ourselves of the possible."[53]

2

BE LONG-TERM FUTURE-FOCUSED AND MISSION-DRIVEN; TAP THE POWER AND PROMISE OF YOUR PURPOSE TO PERFORM: CHARLEMAGNE BECOMES THE FATHER OF EUROPE

"Sound strategy starts with having the right goal."[1]
—Michael Porter, Harvard Business School

On April 25, 799 A.D., in celebration of St. Mark's Day, Pope Leo III was leading the annual procession across a piazza in the heart of Rome. Suddenly, the Pope was attacked by a band of armed thugs. Brandishing their weapons, they threw the Supreme Pontiff to the ground. The Pope's entourage and onlookers all fled the scene in fear for their lives. The vicious attackers then ripped off the Pope's robes and attempted to pull out his tongue and gouge out his eyes, leaving him bleeding in the street. After dark, they dragged him off to San Silvestro in Capite, "a monastery...firmly in rebel hands,"[2] and again attempted to blind him and root out his tongue in order that he would be unfit to rule as pope.[3] They then "beat him with clubs and left him half-dead" before the alter, under armed guard, soaking in his own blood.[4] Later, his attackers returned again, imprisoned him in the monastery at St. Erasmus,[5] and declared him deposed.[6]

The brutal and alarming assault of the Supreme Pontiff, the Vicar of Christ on Earth, was seen in some quarters as a shocking, apocalyptic sign.[7] The reality was that the ringleaders of the revolt were part of a rival faction, "one of the old established aristocratic Roman families,"[8] which was intent on toppling the Pope from the apostolic throne simply because they regarded Leo as an outsider whose humble origins made him unworthy and unfit to be pontiff.

The fierce, "chaotic fighting between opposing factions" was not a new development; the "old struggles for supremacy" had also "dogged" the reign of Leo's predecessor, Pope Adrian I.[9] Nor, unfortunately, was this sort of vicious violence entirely uncharacteristic of the day.[10] In fact, in the centuries following the collapse of the Western Roman Empire—a period popularly known as the Dark Ages—before the Renaissance and the Age of Reason, some scholars have estimated the levels of *interpersonal violence*, including homicide, to be "at least 10 times what they are today" (other experts calculate the figures to be far higher).[11]

Fortunately, in the case of Pope Leo, he survived the brutal assault. Rumors soon spread of his miraculous recovery and escape. Still able to both see and speak, Leo fled Rome to seek sanctuary with the King of Francia, Charles the Great, known today as Charlemagne.

Charlemagne was born circa 742 A.D., a few centuries after the fall of the Western Roman Empire. It was a period marked by chaos and instability. All of Rome's laws, the trade networks and systems of commerce, the education system and the civil service, and even most of the roads and bridges and aqueducts of the Roman Empire were long gone. Without this overall order, stability and structure, without society and the civilizing functions provided by the Roman Empire, the whole continent of Europe struggled to adapt.[12]

Unlike the vastness of Rome's "empire without end," the Europe of the Dark Ages was divided into the tiny territories of trifling barbarian warlords and the piddling provinces of small squabbling kingdoms, all of which were constantly battling one another.[13] Striving merely for supremacy, the lack of vision and limited horizons of their leaders left the great masses of people focused foremost on simple survival, desperate to avoid the pillage, plunder, slaughter, and rape that ran rampant across the land. Living in a state of chaos, for many people, life was not unlike what English political philosopher Thomas Hobbes would later describe as "war of all against all," where people live in "continual fear, and danger of violent death," where life is, "solitary, poor, nasty, brutish, and short."[14]

Within Europe, a land now "broken up into a collection of independent and constantly fighting kingdoms," was Francia, one of "the biggest and most powerful"[15] of the kingdoms, a territory which included present-day France, but also western Germany, and the much smaller nations of Belgium, Switzerland, the Netherlands, and parts of Holland.

Charlemagne inherited the kingdom of Francia from his father, Pepin the Short, when he was just twenty-six. Francia was not immune to the problems faced throughout Europe. The many diverse peoples of Francia were divided. The lack of unity, further separated by the lack of a common language, made ruling over the legal, political, and cultural divisions of the kingdom complicated and difficult.

As with most leaders of the time, Charlemagne started out in the mold of a warrior king. In fact, he was an accomplished and highly capable military commander, a crucial ability for surviving as a king in this era. His greatest troubles were in Saxony, the large northern region of Germany. Believing pagans to be backwards and superstitious, Charlemagne battled the tribes of Saxony, in what came to be known as the Saxon Wars, for a grand total of "eighteen campaigns, the first in 772, and the last in 804."[16]

Beyond the Saxons, Charlemagne was also forced to confront the brutal Avars, Eurasian nomads in Eastern Europe, as well as the tribes of Slavic pagans in both the Northeast and Southeast.

Strategize with Your Vision in Mind

"Outstanding people have one thing in common: An absolute sense of mission."[17]

—Zig Ziglar (1926—2012), American Author & Speaker

Despite being a great military leader, and well-accustomed to violence and war, Charlemagne was looking beyond the tip of his sword. He was driven by something deeper and more enduring, something far different than endless conflict and war. Unlike the other tribal chiefs and the "do nothing" kings of the day, Charlemagne had a dream. He wanted to bring his kingdom out of the darkness and ignorance of the Medieval Era. His vision was not to dominate other tribes or conquer foreign kingdoms to satisfy his own selfish interests. His vision was to advance civilization and bring people together in a united, culturally diverse nation-state. In essence, Charlemagne envisioned recreating the mighty Roman empire and making himself into a powerful Christian emperor like Constantine the Great.[18]

To achieve this vision, Charlemagne embarked with a full slate of new developments across the kingdom, including engaging in public works, creating massive construction projects, setting up schools throughout the realm, increasing literacy around a common language, calling councils of bishops, ramping up the reproduction of ancient books and religious texts to make them widely available, and creating programs of standardization that would ensure governance would be the same anywhere in the kingdom, from the laws and the standards of offices, to the use of equal and exact weights and measures in commerce and trade.[19] Along with military advancements, developments in centralized governance, and economic reforms, Charlemagne also supported architectural and artistic endeavors, and he actively "encourage[d] a cultural, scholarly and intellectual awakening that had been missing in Europe during the Dark Ages."[20]

In effect, Charlemagne instituted a "cultural, political, and military renaissance," which later became known as the Carolingian Renaissance, and which largely came about because of Charlemagne's vision. Of the various characteristics we can point to in order to explain Charlemagne's success—including his leadership and military prowess—his ultimate impact would have amounted to very little without his exceptional vision. It was his vision, above all else, that directed his focus, shaped his decisions, fueled his efforts, and, ultimately, helped to ensure he would achieve all that he did.

His vision was not about the size, wealth, or power of his kingdom so much as the progress, civilization, and enlightenment of its people. As one medieval court poet put it, in the midst of the Dark Ages, Charlemagne was the "lighthouse" of Europe.[21]

Today, Charlemagne is often remembered as "a symbol of European unity" and the "Father of [the] European Union."[22] As *The Wall Street Journal* recently put it, "Charlemagne…was patron of the first renaissance of classical antiquity and thus a savior of Western culture."[23]

Discover and Live Your Purpose

"The two most important days in life are the day you are born,
and the day you discover the reason why."[24]

—The Apocryphal Mark Twain

There is virtually nothing in life more important than the purpose of your life. In fact, for those who are inclined to think that perhaps health and relationships are more important, a growing field of research reveals the many benefits of maintaining a purpose in life—including improved relationships, health, and well-being, as well as reduced "all-cause mortality and cardiovascular problems," "reduced incidence of sleep disturbances," and even "increased longevity."[25] University researchers in South Korea have even found that maintaining a clear purpose for one's life acts "as a protective factor against cognitive decline."[26] A definite chief purpose has also been associated with a lower allostatic load (i.e. wear and tear on the body, which is generally attributed to chronic stress), which is also linked with a reduced "risk of diseases, mortality and cognitive decline."[27] In short, "if you want to live a happy life,"[28] Albert Einstein once said, "you should tie your life to a goal, not to other people and not to things."[29]

"A 1986 Harvard study revealed that outstanding people have one thing in common—an absolute sense of mission. They don't go to work every day— they go on a mission. They have something they really want to do. I believe," writes Zig Ziglar, "that *desire* is the great equalizer."[30] If you have enough desire to do something you can surpass all those who have greater advantages, but who lack the intense desire.

We are all goal-striving beings by nature. Setting and achieving goals is part of what it means to be human. In the words of the Columbia-trained physician Dr. Maxwell Maltz, author of *Psycho-Cybernetics*, "We are built to conquer environment, solve problems, achieve goals, and we find no real satisfaction or happiness in life without obstacles to conquer and goals to achieve."[31] Robert Schuller put it even more emphatically, "Goals are not only absolutely necessary to motivate us. They are essential to really keep us alive." "The greatest tragedy is not death," said Rick Warren, "but life without purpose."[32]

Purpose is also indispensable to strategic thinking. In fact, your purpose is the *sine qua non* (Latin for "without which not") of thinking strategically. In other words, there is no point to thinking strategically if you have no purpose, no vision or ambition or goal. Strategy, after all, is *how* you propose to achieve your goal, and as Harvard's Michael Porter writes, "*sound* strategy starts with having the *right* goal."[33]

In a study of history's greatest strategists (e.g. Napoleon, Clausewitz, Sun Tzu, Jomini, Hart, etc.), 14 of the 24 strategists included "objective" as the *number one* principle of war. The other 10 did not include it at all—perhaps because they deemed the chief objective or purpose (i.e. "winning") as too obvious to include or, even more likely, they neglected to consider it because the goal or purpose is the *starting point* out of which strategy begins.[34] As Sun Tzu authority Gerald Michaelson put it, "Some strategists believe that the objective is the most important principle because without an objective, all of the other principles are pointless."[35]

In arguing that "the object of war, as of all creative activity, was the employment of the available means for the predetermined end,"[36] Clausewitz made strategy relevant to virtually every other "creative" realm of life. Indeed, as Andreas Kluth argues in his book on strategy, *Hannibal and Me: What History's Greatest Military Strategist Can Teach Us About Success and Failure*,

> *"By equating strategy in war with strategy in the rest of life and defining it as the alignment of means to desired ends, Clausewitz made himself relevant to all of us. He was the first to see that war was not an exception to ordinary life but a part and continuation of it. ...Clausewitz knew that tactics was about winning battles, but strategy was about something much, much larger. It was about winning wars...about winning the peace...about achieving the ultimate objective, whatever that may be."[37]*

Regardless of how obviously important it is (i.e. "the number one principle"), the problem is that people too often fail to adequately define their ultimate purpose, objective, or goal; they are unable to describe, in sufficient detail, a clear and compelling vision of the future which they truly, deeply desire. Mark Twain was hardly exaggerating when he said, "I can teach anybody how to get what they want out of life. The problem is that I can't find anybody who can tell me what they want."[38]

The best strategists in the world are useless without a clear and compelling end in mind. As the first century Roman stoic philosopher and statesman Seneca observed, "To the person who does not know where he wants to go there is no favorable wind."[39]

"Regardless of the area of endeavor, the key to any successful strategy is an overall sense of mission, what business strategists Hamel and Prahalad called 'strategic intent.' Far from an empty exercise, crafting a clear and meaningful mission statement shapes the entire strategic planning process."[40] And, consequently, for the strategist, purpose is paramount and indispensable.

Let the Dream Do the Heavy Lifting,
Let Your Vision Frame, Structure, and Shape the World

With the seed of his vision firmly planted the first time "the boy's astonished eyes" witnessed the sheer splendor and "magnificence" of "the miracle of Rome,"[41] Charlemagne would be driven throughout his life by his dream of rebuilding the mighty Roman Empire. Consequently, his vision for Francia, and the future of Europe, had a powerful influence over virtually every aspect of his life, his leadership, and his reign, including how he approached the people and situations he faced, how he dealt with various opportunities and threats, and the strategies and tactics he adopted to achieve his aims. In short, as with most every great leader in history, his vision framed his thoughts, influenced his decisions, shaped his actions, and, in the end, significantly impacted his results.

A great vision can be an exceptionally powerful force, but very few know how to put it into practice in a way that maximizes and mobilizes its potential power and, in effect, sends it into battle.[42] What follows are seven of the most important ways Charlemagne's long-term, future-focused, purpose-driven approach helped to make him a more effective strategist.

Start with and Sustain a Purpose-Centered Approach.

Strategy is essentially about how to achieve your vision and goals. Strategy is the path to the dream. But the big dream, your definite chief purpose and corresponding goals, this is where it all begins. "Early and accurate selection of an appropriate overarching goal is the critical keystone for creating and executing successful strategy."[43]

To be an effective strategist is to be purpose-driven, focused on the long-term dream. To think strategically is, first and foremost, to think with the desired end in mind. Without purpose, without a definite end in mind, strategy is meaningless. With purpose, both strategy and performance improve significantly. "With adequate focus on the appropriate goal, much can be accomplished with little; but absent a specific, clear, attainable, and unifying goal, little may be accomplished despite great exertion."[44] In fact, Stanford University research reveals that those with an explicit purpose and supporting strategy outperform those without a purpose by six-to-one.[45] Leaders who are purpose-driven, waste less time, conserve more resources, and are far more likely to achieve aims which once seemed too far out of reach.

As Malnight et al write in the *Harvard Business Review*, "Leaders need to constantly assess how purpose can guide strategy, and they need to be willing to adjust or redefine this relationship as conditions change. That demands a new kind of sustained focus, but the advantages it can confer are legion."[46] "By putting purpose at the core of strategy, firms can realize three specific benefits: more-unified organizations, more-motivated stakeholders, and a broader positive impact on society."[47]

In Charlemagne's case, catching his vision early in life, upon his first visit to Rome, his vision was the lens through which he looked out at the world. It framed his thinking and helped shape his experience throughout his life. It also better enabled him to evaluate and effectively respond to the considerable challenges he faced. According to Belgian medievalist François Louis Ganshof, "this vision…animated much of what Charlemagne tried to do, even as the king and his men scrambled to respond to the succession of everyday events and frequent crises."[48]

Identify a Clear and Compelling Purpose.

"Great leadership requires a great vision, one that inspires
the leader and enables him to inspire the nation."[49]

—President Richard Nixon, *Leaders*

More than 50 years ago, America landed the first man on the moon. To this day, no other nation on Earth has achieved the same feat. That remarkable triumph began with John F. Kennedy's bold vision. It began with thinking big and believing it was possible—even before all of the necessary technologies were invented—and then taking consistent action on those beliefs.

The most effective visions are big, bold and inspiring. Your purpose must be clear, crystal clear, but also compelling. "Dream no small dreams," Goethe said, "for they have no power to move the hearts of men." Lofty dreams inspire hard work. Big dreams force new ways of thinking from our minds, new actions and habits from our lives.[50] "A vision has no power to inspire or energize people and no ability to set a new standard or attract commitment unless it offers a view of the future that is clearly and demonstrably better for the organization, for the people in the organization...or for the society within which the organization operates...The vision, in short, must be manifestly desirable, a bold and worthy challenge for those who accept it."[51]

Moreover, highly capable, competent people are not drawn to mediocre leaders with mediocre dreams. Highly effective people want to continue to learn and grow and achieve great things. "The greater your dream is," writes John Maxwell, "the greater the people who will be attracted to you."[52]

From the earliest histories of leadership we can discover examples of the great significance of a bold and bright vision. In Charlemagne's case, rather than having to intentionally strive to keep his vision at the forefront of his mind, it happened naturally. Because he was so was completely captivated with his vision of restoring the Roman Empire, he was a visionary leader from the very beginning of his time in power, and, explains British historian Janet Nelson, his "sense of mission" was a powerful and continuous influence throughout his entire reign.[53] This is the power of a clear and compelling vision. The more intensely you desire something the more you think about it, the more it influences how you see and interpret the world, and what you think, say, and do as a result. No doubt, if it is effectively employed to shape and guide your strategy, a clear and compelling purpose can become a remarkable form of power in itself.

Play the Long Game, Operate with a Long-Term Point of View.

The first to be referred to as the "Queen of Spain," Isabella I of Castile and León, was a cunning, iron-willed woman who defied the odds. Painting a portrait of Isabella with words such as "calm,"[54] "steady,"[55] "reserved,"[56] and "cool,"[57] historians describe Isabella as a clever strategist surviving and thriving in a world of dynastic feuds dominated by men. With her eyes focused on the throne, Isabella of Castile outwitted and outlasted her rivals, rising to become the iconic queen who united Spain.

Seeing beyond the borders of her kingdom, and the limited vision of her husband, King Ferdinand II of Aragon, Isabella was the only one among her monarchical peers in Europe who, looking to Spain's future, was willing to risk funding Christopher Columbus and his perilous voyage across the Atlantic in 1492. "I...am ready to pawn my jewels," she told Columbus regarding his proposed voyage, "to defray the expenses of it..."[58] Her bold, independent actions and piercing long-term vision ultimately helped to launch the Age of Exploration, laying the foundation for the Golden Age of Spain.

Like Isabella of Castile—the inspiration behind the most powerful piece in the game of chess, the Queen—strategists are without exception long-term thinkers. "Strategy tends to be long term in its development, its execution, and its effects."[59] Rather than surrendering to the urgency of the moment or yielding to short-term pressures, strategists make their decisions and behave in ways that are congruent with their long-term vision and goals, and they greatly increase their probability of success as a result.

The strategic importance of adopting a long-term orientation to time is an enduring, universal principle which can be traced back to ancient Greece. In fact, for the ancient Greeks, this long-term orientation was central to the role of the strategist; strategy for them, writes Columbia University's Julia Sloan, was "about detached long-term forethought, planning, and ordering in advance of action."[60]

Decades of research on upward mobility has repeatedly confirmed that those who work from longer time horizons rise higher in society. As a matter of fact, on average, the most successful people operate according to the longest time horizons, often thinking and acting in accord with plans that are mapped out five, ten, twenty or more years into the future.

In contrast, those who were found to be the least successful, or financially impoverished, worked from the shortest time horizons. Harvard professor of political science Edward Banfield explains that those who are unable to discipline themselves "to sacrifice a present for a future satisfaction," or who had no compelling personal vision or even a "sense of the future," were inevitably governed by their impulses instead.[61] Unfortunately, the habits and behaviors that bring immediate pleasure are very often those that bring harmful outcomes in the long run.[62]

Constantly operating from a limited time horizon makes it impossible to take a more strategic and, therefore, more effective approach to your ultimate purpose and goals. Your long-term success demands that you play the long game, including thinking strategically, developing a winning strategy, and taking action on decisions aligned and congruent with your long-term vision and goals. Rather than continually giving in to what you desire in the moment, or within the next hour, day, or week, start making decisions based on what you want to see in your life in the months, years, and decades ahead. As U.S.

Army War College strategy professor Harry Yarger writes, "The strategist must reject the expedient, near-term solution for the long-term benefit."[63]

The best way to begin operating from a long-term time horizon is to create an image of your future that is so completely inspiring and so crystal clear and compelling that you can't help but want to work toward achieving it every spare moment you can. Your ultimate purpose, Napoleon Hill said, "must be a burning desire, and it must become so definitely an obsessive desire that you are willing to pay whatever price its attainment may cost."[64]

But don't stop at the vision; be sure to break the dream down into a number of specific, *achievable* goals which, like stepping stones, will take you directly down the path toward your ultimate burning desire. "If you have built castles in the air," wrote Thoreau, "your work need not be lost; that is where they should be. Now put the foundations under them."[65]

In Charlemagne's case, operating from a long-term time horizon, he made considerable investments in education and learning, building schools, translating and reproducing countless books and sacred texts, knowing that it would be many years before his kingdom would reap the rewards of these investments. With his long-term strategic vision in mind, Charlemagne also embarked on massive years-long building projects, including rebuilding the ancient Roman city of Aachen into the capital of his empire, with works that continued on for more than a decade *after his death*.

Maintain Strategic Alignment, Ensure Goals are Congruent, Consistent and Clear.

Your strategic purpose is more than a beacon or guidepost. It is not intended to hint, insinuate, or suggest what goals you set; it is the key, fundamental factor to determine, define, and direct them. The strategist must work to ensure that the strategy and goals are tightly aligned and congruent with the vision.

Furthermore, just as the goals you pursue must always be aligned with and subordinate to your ultimate purpose or vision, the tactics you use to pursue your goals and objectives must be aligned and synchronized with the strategy you employ to realize your dream. Nothing you do, in other words, should be disconnected from anything else, but rather must be situated within an overriding strategic framework, all of which is geared toward accomplishing your ultimate chief aim. As the management consultant and celebrated futurist Alvin Toffler wrote, "You've got to think about big things while you're doing small things, so that all the small things go in the right direction."[66]

Writing in *Making Sense of War: Strategy of the 21st Century*, Stephens and Baker place considerable emphasis on this principle, "The time any decision-maker, from a president to a commanding general to a private soldier, spends on two critical considerations will never be wasted. First, they must clearly understand what, in the prevailing circumstances, they mean by winning. And second, the importance of establishing and maintaining a logical relationship between winning and ends, ways and means cannot be overstated."[67]

No doubt, many of the world's largest empires have been built largely by brute force. In fact, Charlemagne himself, "a skilled military strategist," was forced to spend "much of his reign engaged in warfare in order to accomplish his goals."[68] But Charlemagne's vision went beyond great power and control. His dream was not about an absolute dictatorship and, therefore, "no matter how much his greatness rested on the point of the sword, the king had long since realized that force alone was not enough to keep any empire together."[69] Because Charlemagne's vision went well beyond the notion of empire, or even his own individual needs and interests, rather than a strategy based exclusively on the use of force or military might, he required a more comprehensive, multifaceted strategy which better suited his soaring vision and goals. In other words, in order to achieve his vision of rebuilding the Roman Empire, Charlemagne needed a more suitable and congruent grand strategy, of which the use of force, however important, was only one part.

One of the key ways in which his vision shaped his strategy was in regards to standardization. To effectively build and manage such a huge empire, Charlemagne focused on implementing various sets of consistent standards throughout the empire. "For example," Nelson explains, "by initiating Latin as a common language, Charles made it easier for people to communicate. This led to new ways of collaborating, particularly when it came to projects like building schools."[70]

This strategy also helped to keep his expanding empire unified. Rather than allowing the people to continue operating however they saw fit, "Charlemagne unified his newly conquered territories by introducing common political, social, and business reforms,"[71] standards and norms which were universally shared across the realm. He was also careful to submit "himself to the same code of ethics that he expected of his magnates," which, naturally, further reinforced the *alignment* and *congruence* of his strategic vision.[72]

Work to Ensure the Vision and Values are Shared.

Master strategists recognize *shared vision* as one of the most powerful forces in human affairs.[73] Nothing will inspire courage and commitment like a great vision that is grounded in the shared interests, hopes and dreams of the people with which it is shared. As an effective champion of a shared vision, you also make it much easier to build beneficial long-term alliances with those who share the vision, values, and interests involved.

As a devout Christian, Charlemagne naturally shared the beliefs and values of the Pope. As a ruler, he was also well aware of the power and influence of the church, and how the church could either become an obstacle to his ambitions or a source of tremendous support. If his vision had focused merely on rebuilding the Roman Empire, he might still have counted on the church for some support. However, by also connecting his vision to the rule of

Constantine the Great, the 4th century Roman emperor known for being the first Roman emperor to convert to Christianity, Charlemagne ensured his vision would be shared with the church. Like Constantine, the prevailing force behind the Edict of Milan (313 A.D.), a proclamation that declared tolerance for Christianity across the Roman Empire, Charlemagne would be a fierce defender of the faith, and protector of the church—in other words, another *Christian* emperor of Rome.

The failure to articulate a shared vision for the future was the number one reason that Winston Churchill fell from power in 1945. As much as the British people loved and respected Churchill and knew that they would not have survived the war with Nazi Germany without his leadership, he failed to articulate a shared vision following the end of the war. He failed to cast a captivating common purpose which could capture the hopes and dreams of the British people. In May of 1945, *Life Magazine* wrote: "England no longer needs his V sign to signal the common purpose. What concerns England now is the size of the refrigerator in the postwar house."[74]

Churchill, however, was still at war. After the Germans surrendered, he turned his attention to Stalin and the Soviets and the hazard of Hitler's hold over Europe slipping into the hands of the Red Army (who already occupied much of Eastern Europe) which, Churchill feared, would cut off the Eastern bloc of the Continent behind an "Iron Curtain." And though events would soon vindicate Churchill's warnings regarding Stalin, this was clearly not the direction in which the British people were interested in October of 1945.

And, thus, as a result of Churchill's extravagant rhetoric and ramblings about Russia and Japan, he was seen as a beloved, but unbefitting leader who was out of step with the British people. In the end, this was the chief cause of Churchill's challenges in the post-war campaign. Embroiled in the immediate situation, he missed the much more fundamental change in context. He neglected to take time to step back and take in the bigger picture. He had gotten so used to the day-to-day intensity of war, of giving direct and decisive orders that he neglected to stop and spend time listening carefully to the British people.

This is not to suggest that leaders must always take their cues and direction from the people. The people are often uninformed, frequently misguided, and sometimes just plain wrong. Leaders are at their best when they bring out the "better angels" within the people—but only after they do their utmost to listen to and understand the needs and interests of the people, their hopes and dreams, and their plans and ideas for the future.

Establish a Crowning Commitment.

> *"Finis coronat opus." ("The end crowns the work.")*[75]
> —Latin Proverb

By the time of the attack on Pope Leo, Charlemagne, with his kingdom now covering most of Western Europe, was at the height of his power. When Leo fled Rome for safety, he first headed for Spoleto, 80 miles north, accompanied and under the protection of the Duke of Spoleto, who was appointed by Charlemagne.

Leo then traveled up to Paderborn in Saxony where Charlemagne was planning a campaign.[76] After staying as Charlemagne's guest for a fortnight, Leo, now apparently ensured of Charlemagne's support and protection, returned to Rome accompanied by a retinue of some 200 men,[77] including "Frankish royal messengers," in order that he might "occupy the apostolic throne once more."[78] "When he reached Rome, the populace greeted him and his accompanying contingent of foreign troops, comprising Franks, Frisians, Saxons, and Lombards; brandishing crosses and flags and singing hymns."[79]

Finally, Charlemagne entered Rome on November 25, 800,[80] "with a sizeable (and no doubt fairly threatening) entourage."[81] He summoned a hearing with the religious authorities of the city and listened patiently as Pope Leo was accused of various crimes by his rivals, including perjury and fornication. The council then heard from Leo, who maintained his innocence. Charlemagne sided with Leo and ordered the execution of his attackers, but Leo intervened on their behalf, suggesting they might be banished instead.[82] Charlemagne then exiled the murderous thugs, and restored Leo to his rightful place on the apostolic throne. Charlemagne then restored the lands that had been lost, putting the Papal States on a firm footing for the first time.

However sincere, Charlemagne was not acting solely out of devotion to God and Church. He was also acting strategically, in alignment with his vision for Europe. Ensuring the legitimate power and smooth functioning of the church was a critical part of Charlemagne's big dream, his grand aspiration of reviving the Roman Empire.

A month later, while Charlemagne remained in Rome, Leo secretly began to take steps toward his own contribution to their *shared* vision for Europe. Suddenly, on Christmas Day in 800 A.D. at St. Peter's Basilica in Rome, while Charlemagne knelt at the altar in prayer, Pope Leo III surprised Charlemagne with a beautiful gold crown, declaring him Holy Roman Emperor.

In some ways, after decades of struggle and strife, the event marked the crowning of his vision. For many, the event also marked the unification of western Europe, and the restoration of the Roman Empire; "Charlemagne was now the rightful successor to Augustus Caesar."[83] "He was the first Western emperor for three centuries, and his lands became known as the Holy Roman Empire."[84]

"That moment on Christmas Day—the coronation of Charlemagne (or Charles the Great) as the first Holy Roman Emperor—has since been described as one of the most seismic events in European history,"[85] laying "the foundation for modern-day Europe,"[86] "the political base of Western Civilization,"[87] and helping to ensure that the legend of the "King of the Franks, conqueror of Saxony, founder of the Holy Roman Empire, and one of the foremost rulers in European history"[88] "would never be forgotten."[89]

Today remembered as "the Father of Europe," at the time of his death in 814 A.D., Charlemagne's empire, which included most of western Europe, was the biggest the world had seen since the fall of the Roman Empire nearly 400 years before. Furthermore, it would endure for more than a thousand years,[90] that is, until the last Holy Roman Emperor Francis II abdicated in 1806, following French Emperor Napoleon Bonaparte's greatest victory, the Battle of Austerlitz in December 1805.

Determine Your Definite Chief Purpose.

"Make no little plans. Make the biggest one you can think of,
and spend the rest of your life carrying it out."[91]

—Harry Truman, 33rd U.S. President

Whether in war, politics, business, or sports, your definite chief purpose is both the starting point of your success and the most essential element of your strategic vision (i.e. vision, strategy, and goals). As a strategist, whether flying solo or leading a great empire, of all the possible actions you could take to become 'the master of your fate,' there is virtually nothing more important than establishing a clear and compelling purpose. "Definiteness of purpose," wrote W. Clement Stone, "is the starting point of all achievement."[92] If you hope to live an extraordinary life, you must begin with an extraordinary purpose. "All who have accomplished great things have had a great aim, have fixed their gaze on a goal which was high, one which sometimes seemed impossible."[93]

The point is not that it will be easy. Indeed, a great vision will undoubtedly require great effort and sacrifice. But this is precisely why a clear and *compelling* vision is indispensable to your success. Reflecting on his experience living in the woods at Walden Pond, Henry David Thoreau wrote this: "If one advances confidently in the direction of his dreams, and endeavors to live the life which he has imagined, he will meet with success unexpected in common hours."[94]

If you think this is mere motivational claptrap, stop and consider the reason why this is true. The operative word here is *dream*. It's the big dream, the "why," that gets you through the "how." In fact, the more clear and compelling the dream, the greater its power. As the German philosopher Friedrich Nietzsche wrote, "he who has a *why* to live can bear almost any *how*."[95] There is, in other words, remarkable power in your purpose. And you increase your power when you actively, consistently, and persistently pursue your purpose.[96]

Today, social science research is beginning to bear this out in a number of surprising ways. "In a recent study, the American Psychiatric Association concluded that the principal cause of fatigue in the world today, and most particularly the United States, is the failure of people to have something that seems bigger and more important than themselves to live for."[97] In essence, to echo Nietzsche, it's a compelling, inspiring vision that can help to get you through the inevitable challenges and setbacks that you need to achieve something great. The greater the obstacles you face, the greater must be the vision and your belief in it.

3

THINK PROACTIVELY. SEIZE, SUSTAIN, AND EXPLOIT THE INITIATIVE. WIN BY PLAYING AN OFFENSIVE GAME: MARY TUDOR'S BLOODY FIGHT FOR THE ENGLISH THRONE

"Behind every pulsating, vibrant successful strategy is a leader who seized the initiative and made it happen."[1]
—Cynthia Montgomery, Strategy Professor, Harvard Business School

By July 1553, the 15-year-old King Edward VI of England was fighting for his life. He was coughing up a "greenish yellow and black, sometimes pink" matter from his lungs, according to one eyewitness.[2] "Scabs and sores covered his body, and his hair had fallen out in clumps. His fingernails and toenails had turned black and come off. He couldn't sleep, could barely breathe, and vomited everything he ate."[3] Clearly, the son of King Henry VIII was deathly ill, possibly from tuberculosis, but rumors of poisoning were running rampant.

King Edward summoned his 37-year-old half-sister Mary Tudor to London. Mary was uncertain what to expect. The two had once been close, but religious differences had been threatening to tear them and the kingdom apart.

Mary was a devout Catholic, and Edward, a determined Protestant, was still greatly influenced by his father's Privy Councilors, who also carried the Protestant banner, and who had benefited immensely[4] from King Henry VIII's split with the Catholic Church more than 20 years earlier, a break which led to the English Reformation.

As much as Mary may have wanted to visit her dying brother, she had good reason to be concerned. Still in the thick of the Protestant Reformation, her steadfast commitment to her Catholic faith had long been a thorn in the side of her brother and his councilors.

Religious turmoil had been the dominant theme of Mary's life. At the heart of her father's break with the Catholic Church was the Pope's refusal to annul his marriage to Mary's mother, Catherine of Aragon—another devout Catholic, and the daughter of Queen Isabella and King Ferdinand, who were famously christened "The Catholic Monarchs" by the Borgia Pope, Alexander VI.

When King Henry VIII defied the Supreme Pontiff, Pope Clement, and ended Papal Supremacy over the English Crown, he "appointed himself supreme head of the English Church and deemed his union to Catherine void."[5] This made their daughter, Mary, illegitimate and, thereby, "no longer the heir apparent to the throne."[6] Henry restored both Mary and her younger half-sister Elizabeth to the line of succession nearly a decade later, and while the reinstated claims were approved and "put on the statute books by Parliament in 1543,"[7] the two princesses both remained legally illegitimate.

When Mary's half-brother Edward became king, following the death of King Henry VIII in 1547, Mary's brazen commitment to her Catholic faith became an issue of defiance of the law and leadership of King Edward's Protestant England. Her bold disobedience helped ensure that she "would always serve as a figurehead for loyal papist plotters,"[8] and, indeed, "she remained a trump card of many a Catholic plot…"[9]

The conflict was rapidly becoming a test of wills between Edward, a sheltered, impressionable boy in his early teens who was now the King of England, and his older, loving, but bossy sister Mary—a mature woman with deep religious convictions, now in her early thirties, who was also supported by her powerful cousin, Charles V, the Holy Roman Emperor, another fierce defender of the Catholic faith.

By 1550, the young king and his councilors were not at all certain that Mary, should *she* ever become queen, would preserve the changes in support of the Protestant Reformation for which they had all been working—and profiting greatly.

By *January* 1553, Edward was resolved to remove Mary from the line of succession, and he penned a plan to do it entitled "My Devise for the Succession." Soon afterwards, he became ill. By June, now gravely ill, he told his councilors outright, "My resolve is to disown and disinherit Mary together with her sister Elizabeth."[10]

In one stroke, the son of King Henry VIII disowned his only two sisters.[11]

The throne would pass instead to his *cousin*, Lady Jane Grey, who *just so happened* to be married to the son of King Edward's chief minister, the powerful, scheming John Dudley, Duke of Northumberland. Lady Jane Grey was also exceptionally well-educated and, of course, "staunchly anti-Catholic,"[12] and, at just sixteen, the Duke of Northumberland's daughter-in-law would be easy for him to control.

Despite the weak resistance of a small minority of his councilors, with the aggressive support of Northumberland (who imagined that, upon Edward's death, *he* would become king in all but name), "using a mixture of persuasion and threats, Edward was able to stage his own coup d'état in the final weeks of his life."[13]

On June 21, Edward had his new succession plan written into his will and issued as an official document with the support of his entire Privy Council, as well as peers, bishops, and judges. It was not, however, made public, or passed by parliament—this would require time, and much more support, neither of which was on Edward's side.

Meanwhile, Northumberland continued to attempt to deceive Mary about the succession. "He needed to ensure that Mary did not become suspicious of his intentions for the succession and sought to lull her into a false state of security, regularly sending her news of the king's health and promising that if he should die she would be queen with his assistance."[14]

Gather Intelligence, Seek to Anticipate Pitfalls, Opportunities and Threats

This was the context within which Mary had been summoned in Edward's final hours. "The princess knew from her own sources that her brother's illness was fatal. She was also well aware of the steps that had been taken to deprive her of the crown."[15] But what could she do? What should she do? If she went to London, she would be completely under his power, or, if word of his imminent death was accurate, the power of his chief minister, the devious double-dealing Northumberland.[16]

Mary's cousin, Holy Roman Emperor Charles V, who had been keeping up regular correspondence with Mary, also feared for her safety. He too had gotten word of all the succession scheming happening behind the scenes. Furthermore, regarding his "assessment of her situation," writes historian Linda Porter, "he gave her little chance of success. Everything he heard made him think she would be lucky to survive, let alone become queen."[17]

After all, what power did she really have? Northumberland "had control of the fleet as well as the treasury;" he also "commanded the fortresses and garrisons of the land."[18] In possession of the Tower, effectively securing the capital of England, Northumberland also had "warships...dispatched to the [River] Thames, and 'troops were stationed everywhere to prevent the people from rising in arms or causing any disorder.'"[19]

Anticipating a trap, rather than responding to the summons and visiting her brother on his deathbed, Mary fled. In fact, she left her residence in Hunsdon on July 4th, two days before her brother's death. Traveling at night under the cover of darkness, Mary and her entourage made their way to a series of "safe houses, owned by trusted sympathizers" that had been prepared to aid in her escape.[20] Fearing for her life, she even adopted a disguise, riding behind her own people, "dressed as a servant."[21] On July 6th, King Edward finally succumbed to his illness (or, as some historians argue, the poisoning carried out by Northumberland).[22] Northumberland, meanwhile, who hoped Mary would have already been under his "power by now, deliberately concealed the king's death for two days."[23]

"...Despite his precautions, the news was difficult to suppress."[24] By July 9th, all lingering doubts had disappeared. The rumors were confirmed. King Edward was dead. Mary had "escaped Northumberland's clutches," effectively foiling the first part of his plan; she was now prepared to seize the initiative and put her own plan into play.[25] But she was by no means out of the woods. "The powerful Duke of Northumberland—supported by a well-provisioned army—was preparing to make his move for the throne."[26]

Mary, meanwhile, had little *apparent* power, or "sufficient funds."[27] To be sure, at this point, she had little more than the members of her staff.[28] "She commanded no army, no backers of any importance among the nobility, and," writes Porter, "Charles V had all but abandoned her."[29] According to all *outward* appearances, "the only people who *believed* in Mary were her household, and even they, no matter how much affection they bore her, must have been apprehensive."[30]

"She was," essentially, writes British historian Anna Whitelock, "an isolated figure in East Anglia, surrounded only by her household servants. The ambassadors sent by the emperor were pessimistic about her safety. Believing Northumberland had secured French support, they feared nothing could be done to prevent Jane's accession and considered Mary's chances 'well-nigh impossible.'"[31]

Risk Bold Action to Seize the Initiative and Win the Day

"Freedom lies in being bold."[32]
—Robert Frost (1874—1963), American Poet

Tap the Power of the Past.

What Mary Tudor did have, however, was a bold conviction about her claim to the throne. "The throne of England was hers by right of law and of descent."[33] She also had her sublime self-confidence, her faith in God, and the Tudor heritage, and "everything in Mary Tudor's heritage told her the crown was a prize worth fighting for."[34] "She was the daughter of Henry VIII and Catherine of Aragon," she was the granddaughter of Isabella of Castile, "and she *would* prevail."[35] And, so, "rather than bowing down," she resolved to stand up and fight.[36]

To be sure, history can be an immensely powerful resource. Understanding the past helps to both see possibilities in the present, and shape the future. In the words of Lord Byron, "The best prophet of the future is the past."[37] History can also serve as a rich source of wisdom, insight, and inspiration. In Mary's case, history provided a compelling personal example of what was possible, and the motivation to do it. Decades earlier Mary's maternal grandmother, Isabella of Castile, had become the first woman to assume the throne in Castile. As with Mary, controversy surrounded Isabella's claim to the throne as well.

Isabella had defied her half-brother, King Henry IV of Castile, and married the man of her own choosing, Ferdinand II of Aragon, a man far more suitable to her own future ambitions, rather than a man that suited King Henry's desperate attempt to hold on to power. When King Henry died, with Ferdinand away in Aragon, Isabella immediately took bold action on her own behalf. Rather than accepting Henry's (alleged) daughter, Joanna, as the rightful heir apparent to the throne of Castile, Isabella, despite being disinherited and removed from the line of succession by Henry (because of her unsanctioned marriage to Ferdinand), immediately jumped into action. She assembled a public ceremony in the center of the town of Segovia, placed a crown on her own head in what, essentially, amounted to a self-coronation, and transformed herself into a queen. "Inspired by the example of Joan of Arc," revealing not the slightest "trace of fear or hesitation," she then moved to reassure her subjects, and perhaps herself, and proceeded straight to Segovia's cathedral where she "prostrated herself in prayer before the altar, offering her thanks and imploring God to help her rule wisely and well."[38]

In a world of dynastic feuds dominated by men, with her eyes focused on the throne, Isabella of Castile outwitted and outlasted her rivals, rising to become the iconic queen who united Spain. No doubt Isabella's story was a powerful motivating factor for Mary. As Tudor historian Sarah Gristwood writes, "Isabella of Castile represented a precedent that must have been ever-present in her granddaughter Mary's mind"[39]

Take Bold, Sudden Action.

Sequestered with a handful of counselors, Mary quickly concluded that there was really only one clear course to the crown: She must take bold, immediate action; if no one would proclaim her queen, then she would do it herself.

But this meant preparing for *armed* conflict. "Much of her adult life had been passed in opposition," writes Porter, "but now there was a need for clear thinking and boldness, not protests and tears."[40] There was a need for playing an offensive game with uncommon courage, not defense and fear.

Despite her daring readiness to fight, many found it ridiculous "to tackle a powerful and well-prepared enemy..."[41] "Most of her contemporaries thought she was mad when she unfurled her standard at the castle of Framlingham in Suffolk..."[42] Indeed, "to cooler observers," Mary's plan to seize power "seemed impossible. The Habsburg ambassadors reported that all the country's forces were in the hands of the men who had proclaimed Jane Grey."[43]

To really grasp the audacity of her bold action, you have to consider what was at stake for those Protestants in power. With a Catholic on the throne of England again, they stood to lose *everything*—their power and position, their wealth and lands. In truth, for those who had been openly opposed to Mary, their very lives were at stake. Without a doubt, history remembers her as "Bloody" Mary for good reason.

Of course, these men were no fools; they were all well aware of the possibilities. In fact, if not directly implicated, they had all bore witness to the far more murderous religious reforms of Mary's father, King Henry VIII, the tyrant who executed two of his own wives.

Naturally, they were eager to avoid such a fate. Thus, by reaching for the throne, Mary was undoubtedly putting her own life in jeopardy. She knew "...she had good reason to fear the Duke of Northumberland...If she stayed, he would come for her and she would almost certainly be imprisoned, perhaps worse."[44]

Still, if there was *ever* a chance to seize the initiative, this was it. "She had a chance to act. To act as her mother Catherine had wanted; and act as her grandmother Isabella had done"[45] when she seized the throne of Castile in 1474 under her own uniquely perilous circumstances.

Seize the Initiative, Then Stand Firm.

Immediately upon learning of the death of her brother, Mary wrote a letter to the "most prominent noblemen of the kingdom."[46] She was civil, but firm, demanding what she said was her "right and title to the crown and government of this realm," and that it was to be proclaimed in London.[47]

The following day, July 10, 1553, *before* Mary's letter had been received, "the royal council proclaimed Jane queen"[48] and the herald-at-arms announced the accession of Queen Jane Grey in the public square. Rather than cheering at the news, however, the crowds were silent, and visibly discontent. One boy, Gilbert Potter, the son of a wine merchant, cried out that Lady Mary had a better claim to the throne. The nobles had the boy seized, and, the following morning, they cut off his ears.[49]

When they received her message, Northumberland and the king's councilors were completely surprised by Mary's bold action.[50] Her determination to seize the initiative had not ended there, however. She had also sent out "letters and proclamations announcing her accession," calling on her "loyal subjects to proclaim her," and, far more importantly, and definitively, requesting armed "forces to come to her aid."[51] Clearly, Mary was preparing to play an offensive game. She had seized the initiative with her letter, forcing Northumberland and the council to react to her, and she was now taking steps to retain the initiative.

The council's surprise quickly collapsed into deep concern, apprehension, and, for many, fear.[52] "It is reported that the lords looked into one another's faces uneasily, and that their wives sobbed. A reply was sent ordering Mary not to 'vex and molest' the people of England with her false claim."[53]

Mary, meanwhile, still without an army, "found herself firmly on the back foot,"[54] at least according to all outward appearances. If Jane's claim was declared legitimate, then Mary's proclamation would be an act of treason, and conviction would mean death.

"Northumberland had decided to detain Mary, by force, and bring her to London."[55] "The following morning," as his own anxiety grew, "Northumberland set out from Durham Palace with munitions, artillery, field guns, and more than 6,000 men. The imperial ambassadors wrote to Charles V, 'We believe that my Lady will be in his hands in four days' time unless she has sufficient force to resist.'"[56]

"Mary stood her ground. She was," writes historian Peter Ackroyd, "resolute and defiant on the model of her father; she had a stern Tudor sense of majesty, allied with an awareness of her religious mission..."[57] She was now at Framlingham Castle, a well-fortified stronghold in Suffolk, East Anglia, "where she was a major landowner, and incredibly popular; this proved to be a wise move."[58]

From here, "she might repel any armed force."[59] "From this defensive position, Mary was able to rally"[60] what came to be a startling number of supporters—many Catholics, not surprisingly, but also "those with different religious views," who, despite their differences, supported a *civilized* England, the rule of law, and the *legal* transfer of power.[61] These folks all "flocked to her banner in the coming days."[62] With growing hope and anticipation, "careful plans were made to evade and outwit the authorities, to wrestle the initiative from the preoccupied council in London."[63]

"Yet she was still in the utmost danger. If she had been defeated and come to trial," writes Ackroyd, "she would have been declared guilty of treason. The fate of the nation, and of her religion, was now at stake."[64]

Build a Bastion for Bold Action

Meanwhile, the plans of Northumberland and the council were crumbling before their eyes. "Some of the councilors secretly doubted [Northumberland]. Others were confused and uncertain. William Cecil armed himself and made plans to flee the realm."[65]

People continued to flock "to what they saw as the true Tudor monarchy. As the Genoese merchant Baptista Spinola reported: 'The hearts of the people are with Mary, the Spanish Queen's daughter.'"[66]

Before long, droves of supporters were turning to Mary, "with the earl of Sussex and the earl of Bath among the first of them. The people from the towns and villages of the region took up their weapons. It seemed that the whole of East Anglia had risen for her. The city of Norwich proclaimed her as rightful sovereign. A small navy of six ships, sent out by Northumberland to guard the seaways off the Norfolk coast, *defected* to Mary's camp. When she went out to review her new troops the cry went up 'Long live our good Queen Mary!'"[67]

In the end, writes Ackroyd, "all Northumberland's power was not enough in the face of her determined opposition and the evident fury of her supporters. The lawful succession to the throne of England could not be compromised by double-dealing."[68]

Hated as an upstart usurper, Northumberland's power rapidly evaporated. "His mission proved to be fruitless. Rather than gaining support as he had hoped, Northumberland's forces began to desert him in favor of Mary. As soon as he left London, sensing the mood of the people and hearing of the increased support for Mary, the Privy Council finally decided to abandon Jane."[69]

By this time, Mary was joined by some 15,000 men, far surpassing the divided and deteriorating numbers that Northumberland had been able to muster. In the words of one historian, "Northumberland's puny force was no match for the thousands who, in the greatest mass-demonstration of loyalty ever accorded to a Tudor, flocked to Mary's camp...."[70]

By July 19, 1553, "Mary had won the day without a drop of bloodshed."[71] Lady Jane, now remembered as the "Nine Days' Queen," was ousted, and "Mary was proclaimed queen to the great joy of her subjects."[72] Indeed, according to one contemporary chronicler, "It was said that no one could remember there ever having been public rejoicing such as this."[73]

Take Initiative, Gain Power and Control.

Initiative is central to success of all kinds. "The greatest of all success secrets is initiative," wrote Robert Collier in *The Secret of the Ages*. "It is the one quality which more than any other has put men and women in high places."[74] For the strategist, initiative is indispensable. You cannot execute your strategy or achieve your purpose without taking action to implement your plan. As renowned British historian David Chandler put it, "to implement no initiatives means to achieve no results."[75]

"Taking the initiative," therefore, writes Major General William Cohen, "is always critical for any strategy."[76] In the words of Harvard Business School professor Cynthia Montgomery, "behind every...successful strategy is a leader who seized the initiative and made it happen."[77]

To take initiative is to assume responsibility, exercise leadership, and stand apart from the pack. In competitive situations, there are a number of critical advantages to seizing the initiative and, furthermore, Cohen writes in *The Art of the Strategist*, "the advantages of seizing the initiative are well documented throughout military history, as well as in countless business success stories."[78]

By far the most important advantage is in how seizing the initiative increases your probability of success. When you seize the initiative, for example, you force others to react to you. If, in contrast, you fail to seize the initiative, you will almost invariably find yourself *reacting* to the actions of others, *instead of taking actions to achieve your goal*. In fact, William Johnsen, military history and strategy professor at the U.S. Army War College, takes it even further, arguing that "strategists who passively wait for an opponent to act can make no strategic decisions of their own, and eventually will be at the mercy of their adversary."[79] In contrast, he continues, "seizing, retaining, and exploiting the initiative allows one to set the strategic agenda, to shape the strategic environment in directions of one's choosing, and to force an opponent constantly to react to changing conditions that concomitantly inhibit his ability to regain the initiative."[80] In turn, with this greater control comes less friction, increased efficiency, greater autonomy, and a tighter, more certain link between your strategy, purpose, and goals.[81]

Seize, Exploit, and Maintain the Initiative to Win

To encourage taking decisive action and seizing the initiative is not to advocate bold, *reckless* action, however, or jumping without thinking ahead. Along with taking carefully *calculated* risks, the way in which Mary Tudor skillfully seized the English throne illustrates a number of critical factors worth contemplating before you boldly act.

Gather Intelligence, Survey the Landscape Before You Act.

Only fools barrel ahead without thinking. The clever strategist, in contrast, is careful to survey and assess the situation first. There are a number of useful strategy tools that you can employ here (e.g. trend analysis, environmental scanning, force field analysis, benchmarking, SWOT analysis, etc.), but one of the most important things you can do is simply talk to people, ask good questions, and *listen* between the lines. If its a high stakes situation, this might also include interviews and focus groups, or even teams of researchers, investigators, and spies. If this seems like a lot of work or a big expense, keep the following ancient military maxim in mind: "Time spent on reconnaissance is never wasted."[82]

In the case of Mary Tudor, she had sources inside her brother's household that kept her abreast of various developments. In fact, she was well aware of the machinations taking place to deprive her of the throne. Her advisors were also able to gather intelligence from leading nobles and Catholic supporters outside of London, such as Sir John Huddleston of Cambridgeshire, who had his house burned down by Northumberland for his loyalty to the Princess.[83] Mary also had connections with powerful figures outside of England, such as her cousin, Charles V, the Holy Roman Emperor, who had his own spies and informants which were an additional source of valuable intelligence.

Map Your Mission, Plot Your Purpose, Begin with an Exemplary End.

To be effective, your actions must be aligned with your ultimate purpose and goals. The challenge comes in crafting the optimal course among multiple possibilities. In Mary's case, for example, she could have seized the initiative by leaving England and returning with an army funded by Catholic supporters. Perhaps she might also have visited her brother on his deathbed while accompanied by a substantial guard. She might also have made her intentions to ascend the throne more public while her brother was still alive. In retrospect, it's easy to argue that she made the right choice given that we know it turned out to her advantage, without a drop of blood. At the time, however, Mary undoubtedly felt like she faced nothing but impossible choices to achieve her goal.

There are two key guideposts in a situation like this. The first is strategic thinking and planning. "The strategic element comes in the planning: Setting an overall goal, crafting ways to reach it, and thinking the whole plan through in intense detail."[84] The idea is to think beyond the first action and reaction, and instead think several moves ahead, including various different scenarios if necessary. "This means thinking in terms of a campaign, not individual battles. It also means knowing the strengths and weaknesses of the other side, so that you can calibrate your strikes to its vulnerabilities."[85] In general, provided you don't face too much unexpected friction or a game-changing surprise, "the more detailed your planning, the more confident you will feel as you go into battle, and the easier it will be to stay on course once the inevitable problems arise."[86]

The second key touchstone is justification. The stronger your belief in and rationale for an action the better. Nothing will undermine your actions more than if you *or those you are leading* lack faith in your cause or the action itself. Think, for example, of how easily the Privy Council abandoned Northumberland and Queen Jane Grey as soon as they sensed a shift in the mood of the people. Another more recent example is Vladimir Putin's war in Ukraine. Putin's lack of a clear and compelling rationale has led to a dangerous lack of support among the Russian soldiers, many of whom struggle to understand how Ukrainians, particularly innocent non-combatants, have suddenly become enemies deserving to die.

Furthermore, the more you believe in your mission, the more you can lean on it in the midst of difficulty or doubt. The more your supporters believe in what you're doing, and the more they believe that what you're doing is in their own best interests as well, the more likely they are to take steps and make sacrifices to help make it work (explored further in the section on Joan of Arc, see Chapter 13).

In Mary's case, she genuinely believed she was fighting not just for all Catholics everywhere, but for the legitimacy of the English monarch and the rule of law. Northumberland, in contrast, was an opportunist fighting only for himself. Not surprisingly, not only were his doubts often shared among his conspirators, but his duplicity and doubts about his dealings occasionally gave him away. At his execution, after acting as a *Protestant* all along, he looked out at the crowd and said, "I beseech you all to bear me witness, that I die in the true *Catholic* faith." He then turned to the executioner, who "wore a white apron, like a butcher," and said, "I have deserved a thousand deaths."[87]

Prepare to Play Offense: Stay Focused on Your Strategic Plan.

Seizing the initiative is about playing an offensive game. You cannot win the game or even obtain your objective by strictly playing defense.[88] "No matter how well developed your ability to counter the actions of rivals," to win you must initiate your own actions.[89] "This is the form of warfare practiced by the most successful captains in history."[90]

The challenge here comes when you are facing a tough competitor or a fierce enemy. The more you fear your opponents or worry about your competitors, the more attention they will occupy in your mind. This is natural and, to a certain extent, it makes sense—you never want to underestimate your competitors. However, there is a limit. The more attention they occupy, the more likely you are to obsess over what they might or might not do instead of the far more important matter of thinking about what *you need to do*.

During the American Civil War, Confederate General Robert E. Lee was proving to be a masterful tactician. After suffering a series of Lee's treacherous surprises, the Union generals in charge of the Army of the Potomac started obsessing over what Lee was likely to do next. "The Union senior commanders had become extremely cautious as a result."[91]

Meanwhile, Union General Ulysses S. Grant was operating in the western theatre, where the Union army under his command was engaging in one successful offensive maneuver after another. Once President Lincoln appointed him General-in-Chief, Grant moved his headquarters to the east where he was alarmed by the Army of the Potomac's lack of confidence and failure to be proactive.[92] Finally, in one strategy meeting, after listening to yet another extended monologue about what General Lee was likely to do next, Grant snapped. "I am heartily tired of hearing about what Lee is going to do," he said. "Some of you always seem to think he is suddenly going to turn a double somersault and land in our rear and on both of our flanks at the same time. Go back to our command and try to think what we are going to do ourselves, instead of what Lee is going to do."[93]

Nearly a century later, the heroic World War II general, George S. Patton, who was celebrated for his rapid and aggressive offensive actions, took it even further, perhaps to the point of extreme, when he said, "I don't care what the enemy intends to do. I only care about what I intend to do."[94]

Arnold Schwarzenegger defeated more than a few of his rivals in competitive bodybuilding by tricking them into adopting a *defensive* approach. Rather than building the best physique that they possibly could, maximizing their own unique genetic and psychological strengths, Arnold, as the reigning champion, made his competitors believe that their best hope for victory was based entirely on how they measured up to him. As a result of becoming obsessed with Arnold, and whatever weaknesses they had in comparison—a defensive strategy, which Arnold hammered into them relentlessly—they consistently failed to unseat him from the bodybuilding throne (beginning in 1970, Arnold was the reigning Mr. Olympia for 6 consecutive years, and again in 1980).

Take Bold Action: Resolve to Pay the Necessary Price, Then Do Whatever Has to Be Done.

Initiative is about taking intelligent action. Action triggers a cascade of consequences which advance you inescapably toward your intended target.[95] Action signals to others the seriousness of your intent, which then gains the attention of like-minded people and attracts the interest, community, and support of those with similar or overlapping goals.[96] Action sets you up to learn from your experience, including your missteps, but also the feedback of others.[97] You gain insights into your own, perhaps previously unknown, strengths, as well as areas where you will need to learn more, or further develop your knowledge or skill.[98] Action makes much of what once seemed challenging or confusing, to seem far more simple and clear, which boosts your confidence and increases your appetite for more and greater action.[99] Indeed, as Jack Canfield writes in *The Success Principles*, "All manner of good things begin to flow in your direction once you begin to take action."[100] The ancient Chinese military strategist Sun Tzu put it this way, "Opportunities multiply as they are seized."[101]

Despite the many benefits and, indeed, the *necessity* of taking bold action to seize the initiative, people come up with all sort of excuses for their lack of action—most of which amount to some form of procrastination, perfectionism, or fear. It is unlikely that taking bold action will ever require you to put your life on the line, as Mary did when she defied the ruling nobles to claim the English throne. Nevertheless, the more bold and daring the action, the more likely you are to face internal and external resistance of some, perhaps multiple kinds.

This is why commitment is so critical. If you cannot commit completely, then do not act at all. Otherwise, your wavering, lukewarm commitment may very well undermine your effort, and spoil the desired result.

If you want to succeed, however, you must make up your mind to pay whatever the necessary price. Then, kill the delay and execute the play.

In Mary's case, she was willing to go to war to secure the throne. She was also willing to put her own life in jeopardy. Despite the obvious risks, however, because she was committed, others were willing to commit to her, both of which greatly increased her probability of success.

Ultimately, if you are going to succeed, you must assume responsibility, recognize the urgency of opportunity, be decisive, and act. As Theodore Roosevelt liked to say, "Get action! Seize the moment. Man was never intended to become an oyster."[102]

Win the Psychological Game: Project Confidence, Surprise Conviction, and Ultimate Success.

Fear and self-doubt are two of the most formidable enemies of success.[103] In competitive situations, your fear gives your opponent untold advantages.[104] "The other side has endless possibilities for using your fear to help control you, keep you on the defensive. Those who are tyrants and domineering types can smell your anxiety, and it makes them even more tyrannical."[105]

No doubt, there are times, particularly when the risks are high, when it is difficult to summon the courage you need to boldly seize the initiative. But what is the alternative? In the process of surrendering to fear, whether consciously or unconsciously, you may convince yourself that you are merely taking the easy way out or the less risky route, but is that really true in the end? Think about what all will be lost. Consider the *long-term* cost.

In Mary's case, she could just as easily have accepted the will of her brother, and let Northumberland rule. But as the figurehead of Catholic resistance, would she ever really be safe?

In contrast to Mary's boldness, King Edward's cowardice set his plan up for failure. If he wanted to change the line of succession, why did he not make that desire public while he was still alive? Instead, by leaving it in his will, he ensured that the public would not find out until after he was dead, effectively ensuring it would come off as a coup, undercutting his potential support. Only the most extreme anti-Catholic fanatics could support such a perversion of the transfer of power.

"To control the dynamic, you must be able to control yourself and your emotions."[106] When you control your emotions and boldly act to seize the initiative in spite of your doubts, apprehensions, and fears, you start to nudge people and circumstances in your favor. When you act boldly and project unmistakable confidence and conviction in your action, it becomes a positive feedback loop and, ultimately, a self-fulfilling prophecy.

"By acting boldly, before others are ready, by moving to seize the initiative, you create your own circumstances rather than simply waiting for what life brings you. Your initial push alters the situation, on your terms. People are made to react to you," writes Greene, "making you seem larger and more powerful than may be the case. The respect and fear you inspire will translate into offensive power, a reputation that precedes you."[107]

"Before anything else you must lose your fear—of death, of the consequences of a bold maneuver, of other people's opinion of you. That single moment will suddenly open up vistas of possibilities. And in the end whichever side has more possibilities for positive action has greater control."[108]

The *desire* to thrive is in our nature as human beings. We are all instinctively drawn toward success. An important part of succeeding and engaging people, therefore, whether in relationships, business, politics, or war, is about confidently *projecting* success. Coming across as a winner, radiating victory, casting the impression of success increases the likelihood that you will indeed win. Confidence, conviction, and success come, first and foremost, from your *beliefs*. *Believing* in the actions you take, *believing* that you can get what you really want, significantly increases the likelihood that *you will get it.*

Retain the Initiative, Maintain the Momentum, Keep Forcing Them to Think About and React to You.

As important and powerful as it can be, rarely is it enough to simply seize the initiative. Winning requires seizing and *retaining* the initiative *until* you succeed. Seizing the initiative will generate that initial momentum you need to succeed, it will also push your opponents back on their heels, forcing them to react to you, but the key is to build on that momentum to keep up a relentless pressure while you still have freedom of action (i.e. before you're being forced to *react* to your opponent's action).

As with seizing the initiative, retaining the initiative is about taking *offensive* action. "In war, sports, business, and politics, this is fundamentally true across all levels of operations," writes Ridgley, "We 'play defense' only as a temporary necessity and only as a respite before we can seize the initiative and continue our offensive actions. The reason for this should be clear: The side that retains the initiative through offensive action forces competitors to react rather than allowing them to act."[109]

Strive to Retain Rather than Regain the Initiative. Far better to work hard to *retain* the initiative rather than trying to *regain* it once it is lost. Not only will this allow you greater freedom to chart your course, but it will also force your competitors to continue playing catch-up,[110] while spending valuable time and resources trying to anticipate and get the jump on your next move.

If you lose the initiative, as is often the case when grappling with a worthy competitor, you must act quickly and do whatever is necessary to take it back before your opponent gains momentum, takes greater control, wins increased support, or gains market share. In *The Book of Five Rings*, the renowned 17th century strategist and swordsmen Miyamoto Musashi writes, "in battles based on martial strategy, it is taboo to let your opponent take the initiative, thus putting yourself on the defensive. You must try at all costs to lead your opponent by taking complete control of him."[111]

In Mary's case, she had generally been reacting to the initiative of the royal court her entire life. It was not until her brother's illness that she first took initiative and began taking steps to prepare to ascend to the English throne. After securing herself within a stronghold in East Anglia, she then seized the initiative when she sent her letter to the leading nobles of England demanding the immediate proclamation of her ascension to the throne. Completely surprised by her letter, Northumberland and the nobles were forced to react, which led Northumberland to muster forces. But Mary had also already sent out her own letters and proclamations, she also called on her loyal supporters to proclaim her. She had established herself at the well-fortified Framlingham Castle and sent out what was in effect a clarion call-to-arms.[112] In fact, as a result, the entire region seemed to rise up on her behalf.

She also went out to personally visit the navy's troops, effectively locking in their support. She sent out servants to win over powerful lords and prominent noblemen, in some cases warning of the consequences of forsaking her cause.[113] Finally, after winning over Lord Wentworth and "a multitude of other gentlemen," she appointed field commanders and began preparing her forces for battle. "Wherefore, good people," she said in an address to her mustered army, "prepare yourselves in all haste with all power" to defeat Northumberland, the "most errant traitor to God and to the realm."[114] "Within days an unskilled and disorganized mob had been turned into a disciplined army, obedient to order and eager to meet the enemy."[115]

In essence, rather than simply writing to the nobles and waiting for a response, she had essentially taken every step necessary to successfully secure the throne. She had even prepared herself mentally for civil war.[116]

Depending on the particular situation and context, there are undoubtedly a range of possible actions you might take to maintain the initiative. Regardless of the specifics, the general idea is to keep shifting or changing the competition or battle to an area or domain where you will continue to have a clear advantage or greater control. You want to engage on your terms, with those who you choose, at a time of your choosing, on terrain with which you are familiar, and in a place where you have an advantage.[117] The key in every situation is to manage your emotions and "plot your moves in advance, seeing the entire chessboard."[118]

Frame and Maintain the Initiative, Demand Secrecy, Speed and Surprise. To do this most effectively will often require one or more of the following four factors: (a.) *secrecy*—hiding your preparations and keeping your actions covert to prevent your opponents from anticipating your intent and stealing the initiative (b.) *surprise*—doing the unexpected to catch your opponents off guard and help ensure they are unprepared (c.) *speed*—moving swiftly to prevent your opponents from catching up or seizing the initiative before being forced to respond to yours and (d.) *framing*—being first to define, interpret, and shape what your opponents think, see, and understand, and what they say and do as a result.

In the case of Mary successfully seizing power from Northumberland, each one of these four factors had a part to play. First, she and her entourage relied on *secrecy* and stealth, traveling to a series of safe houses at night and under disguise to escape to the fortified castle in Suffolk. Second, while it was undoubtedly unintentional, she also profited significantly from *surprise*. When the deceased King's councilors received her letter demanding they proclaim her queen in London, they were so shocked by her daring initiative that it essentially sent the whole conniving cabal into an emotional tailspin. Clearly lacking in their own efforts to gather intelligence, they apparently never even got a whiff of an idea that she might seek to secure the throne on her own. In fact, to some extent, this one surprise act of seizing the initiative had such a tremendous impact that it alone helped to ensure that the initiative would remain in her hands until the end. Third, the *speed* with which everything came together—from her swift escape and her letter to the councilors to the rapid response by her supporters and the speed with which her supporters "flocked to her banner"[119]—ensured that Northumberland had no real time to prepare a more significant military response, perhaps even allying with the

French, as he had already been planning. Fourth, Mary also benefitted significantly from how the struggle was *framed*. Northumberland, Queen Jane Grey, and their councilors were all diehard Protestants intent on keeping the crown out of a Catholic's hands. Their primary frame, in other words, was to see the legitimacy of succession through a religious lens. And, to be sure, Mary was equally fanatical about her own religious beliefs. It is also true, moreover, that a great many of the English viewed the succession through a religious lens. However, rather than trying to frame the succession as a matter of Catholics before Protestants, Mary very cleverly focused on her legitimacy as the rightful, legal heir. This frame ensured she had the support of all of the Catholics, but also all those English subjects who believed in the rule of law, which included a great many Protestants as well.

Achieve Startling Success; Take Bold Action In Pursuit Of Your Goal.

Undoubtedly recognizing the extent to which Mary had cleared a potential path for *her own* future, Mary's sibling, her half-sister Elizabeth, a Protestant, and the daughter of Anne Boleyn, "wrote to Mary, offering her congratulations."[120] On October 1, 1553, accompanied by Elizabeth and some 800 leading nobles, Mary rode to Westminster Abbey in London where she was crowned Queen of England.

As the first English queen to reign over the realm in her own right,[121] Mary I had become the first legitimate queen *regnant* of England. Unlike a queen *consort* (the wife of a reigning king), or a queen *regent* (the guardian of a child monarch who rules until the child comes of age), Mary ruled England with all the rank, titles, and sovereign powers of a king.

One contemporary, aware of the powerful resistance she faced, was in awe of her achievement, describing the feat as one "of Herculean...daring.'"[122] "As queen she had asserted her authority as the first female monarch to reign supreme."[123] Just as Isabella had served as a powerful example and source of inspiration for Mary, Mary's success, in turn, became a powerful example for Elizabeth. In fact, according to historian Samson Alexander, "Ultimately...Mary's greatest achievement may have been to provide a model for her younger sibling, Elizabeth, to follow. Mary and Elizabeth had a troubled relationship...Yet the older sister set down the statutory foundations of female rule on which the younger sister built, offering a prototype of strong, independent, royal government, and an assiduous and involved monarch, unswayed by the powerful male courtiers who surrounded her."[124]

Mary, of course, known by her enemies as "Bloody Mary," is rightly criticized for her barbaric crackdown on religious dissent, which included burning nearly 300 people at the stake. But she was also an "intelligent, politically adept...trailblazer, a political pioneer whose reign redefined the English monarchy."[125]

|4|

CHAMPION CRITICAL THINKING TO CRAFT CUNNING SOLUTIONS AND ACHIEVE SUPERIOR SUCCESS: PRESIDENT JOHN F. KENNEDY TRANSFORMS HIS DECISION-MAKING SYSTEM FROM THE BAY OF PIGS FIASCO TO THE MISSILE CRISIS IN CUBA

"If everyone is thinking alike, then no one is thinking at all."[1]
—John F. Kennedy, 35th President of the United States

On October 15, 1962, President John F. Kennedy learned that Soviet Premier Nikita Khrushchev had placed medium-range ballistic missiles in Fidel Castro's Cuba, a mere 90 miles off the coast of Florida and well within range of all but the northwest corner of the continental United States. Kennedy was livid. As the central figure responsible for protecting the United States, allowing the threat of nuclear missiles in our own backyard was unthinkable. Publicly, Khrushchev and the Soviets had been making a case for nuclear disarmament. Privately, however, they were secretly installing nuclear weapons, dramatically escalating Cold War tensions, and increasing the very real possibility of nuclear war.

Refusing to accept the presence of nuclear missiles so close to U.S. shores, Kennedy's first thought was an immediate air strike to wipe the missile base off the map.[2] After all, a Russian nuclear missile base in Cuba presented a number of grave risks. Along with the threat to the lives of countless Americans, it would almost certainly increase the stature and confidence of Khrushchev and Castro, as well as America's other enemies. It would also undermine Kennedy's standing at home and erode the power and influence of the United States around the world.[3]

Fortunately, Kennedy's cooler, more pragmatic approach to problems soon followed. Kennedy began meeting with his Executive Committee of the National Security Council (known as ExComm), where a consensus soon emerged: Despite America's overwhelming missile advantage, a Soviet missile base in Cuba was "at the very least, psychologically and politically intolerable."[4]

Within days, Kennedy went public, explaining to the American people that they had discovered Soviet nuclear weapons in Cuba, and why they could not allow the situation to stand. Speaking to the American people from the Oval Office in what would later be called, "probably the most dramatic and most frightening presidential address in the history of the republic,"[5] Kennedy went straight to the heart of the matter: "This secret, swift, and extraordinary build-up of Communist missiles...in violation of Soviet assurances, and in defiance of American and hemispheric policy...is a deliberately provocative and unjustified change in the status quo which cannot be accepted by this country if our courage and our commitments are ever to be trusted again by either friend or foe..."[6]

President Kennedy addressed his television audience, publicly demanding that the nuclear missiles be dismantled and returned. He also explained that he had ordered a naval "quarantine" of the island nation[7]—a term intended to downplay the fact that the action was effectively a naval "blockade," which was a term reserved for a state of war. While Kennedy spoke, the U.S. Armed Forces were put on DEFCON 3 (high alert and increased readiness).

Kennedy then delivered an unmistakable warning to the Russians, "Should these offensive military preparations continue...further action will be justified...It shall be the policy of this nation to regard any nuclear missile launched from Cuba against any nation in the Western Hemisphere as an attack by the Soviet Union on the United States, requiring a full retaliatory response upon the Soviet Union."[8]

It was a bold stand filled with grave risks and potential peril.

As the world held its breath, Kennedy continued, "My fellow citizens, let no one doubt that this is a difficult and dangerous effort on which we have set out. No one can foresee precisely what course it will take or what costs and casualties will be incurred."[9] Kennedy ended his address with a call for "sacrifice and self-discipline" to confront the unknown peril ahead.[10]

The world was suddenly on the precipice of nuclear war.

While Kennedy spoke, the U.S. military was implementing his response to the crisis: A military blockade at sea to prevent the completion of the missile base. With the U.S. naval blockade in place, and the Soviet ships sailing to Cuba full steam ahead, the world continued to hold its breath.

Following the shocking announcement, billions of people around the world immediately leapt into action, taking steps that they hoped would help ensure the survival of their families in the event of a global nuclear holocaust, including, in some cases, building elaborate underground bunkers.

While protests broke out in opposition to the world's only two superpowers, people everywhere worked themselves into a frenzy—stockpiling food, water, and supplies all while hanging on every scrap of information in the news. Families came together to make emergency plans, and ready any means of shelter or escape. Many people felt helpless and panicky as they scurried aimlessly through crowded streets with no real clue where to turn. "I'm here because I feel completely hysterical about the world situation," admitted one young woman; "I don't know what else to do."[11]

Learn from Experience, Profit from Stupid Mistakes: Kennedy, Castro, and the Fiasco in the Bay of Pigs

This was not the first time the U.S. and the U.S.S.R. had tumbled into a treacherous confrontation. Transpiring only 18 months earlier, it was the Bay of Pigs fiasco between the U.S. and Cuba (a close Soviet ally) that led to the Cuban Missile Crisis.

First conceived under President Eisenhower, the Central Intelligence Agency's plan to help Cuban exiles overthrow Fidel Castro's communist government in Cuba was already well underway by the time John F. Kennedy came to power in 1961. This should have been Kennedy's first red flag. Why had Eisenhower not pulled the trigger on the plan? Even before learning about the specifics of the plan, Kennedy might have immediately assumed that it would be difficult to oppose the clandestine operation given certain basic facts: (a.) it was already in the works, (b.) it had apparently been tacitly approved by President Eisenhower, the former five-star general, as well as (c.) the CIA, arguably the world's greatest intelligence agency, (d.) against Cuba, an unruly neighbor that was known to be a thorn in Uncle Sam's side, but also (e.) a communist dictatorship and (f.) a satellite of the U.S.S.R.

And, indeed, despite the fact that Kennedy's top advisors were all esteemed, educated men from Harvard, within three months, his entire Executive Committee (ExComm) supported the CIA's invasion plan. The virtually unanimous support should have been Kennedy's second red flag. Unfortunately, as leadership authority James MacGregor Burns explains, the CIA played right into "JFK's bias for action and eagerness to project strength."[12]

The covert invasion plan, however, turned out to be a complete catastrophe. According to Irving Janis, author of *Groupthink*, "The Kennedy administration's Bay of Pigs decision ranks among the worst fiascoes ever perpetrated by a responsible government."[13] JFK himself said, "How could I have been so stupid to let them go ahead?"[14] Privately, he told friends he wanted to "splinter the CIA in a thousand pieces and scatter it to the winds."[15]

The failed invasion was President Kennedy's first major mishap and it was a whopper. Lacking proper air cover, the invading force was attacked and crippled by Cuban planes. Once on the beach at the Bay of Pigs, "most of the invaders were taken prisoner" by troops loyal to Castro.[16] Contrary to the CIA's expectations, there was no internal uprising in Cuba. Further, contrary to Kennedy's most important requirement, American involvement was also readily apparent. Worse still, 4 Americans died in the invasion, along with 118 Cuban revolutionaries.

Internationally, U.S. involvement in the invasion was a diplomatic disaster. Domestically, the failed invasion was a political catastrophe. As president, Kennedy knew that he was at fault for approving the flawed plan, but, as he said to Richard Bissell, the CIA's mastermind behind the Bay of Pigs invasion,

"In a parliamentary government, I'd have to resign. But in this government I can't, so you and Allen [Dulles] have to go."[17]

Before the invasion, Kennedy said of Bissell, "You can't beat brains."[18] After the invasion, he was angry with himself for having been seduced by the aura of intelligence. Humiliated by his own naiveté, Kennedy said to Cord Meyer, "You always assume that the military and intelligence people have some secret skill not available to ordinary mortals."[19] He was determined to never make such a stupid assumption again.

Speaking at a press conference the day after the failed invasion was over, Kennedy said, "There's an old saying that victory has 100 fathers and defeat is an orphan. [...] Further statements, detailed discussions, are not to conceal responsibility because I'm the responsible officer of the Government..."[20]

Take Time to Carefully Communicate, Contemplate, Deliberate, and Think.

Chastened by the Bay of Pigs fiasco in April 1961, President Kennedy made a number of critical changes to his decision making apparatus to ensure their mistakes would not be repeated. By the time of the Cuban Missile Crisis in October of 1962, Kennedy had adopted a far more strategic and deliberative approach to his foreign policy problems.

Ten days and many sleepless nights after CIA analysts first spotted the missile launchers in Cuba, the intense internal deliberations of Kennedy's advisors and the delicate, unstable negotiations between the President and the Soviet Premier seemed to reach a tentative resolution. And, yet, the Russian ships continued to sail full steam ahead, charging directly toward the U.S. naval blockade, all while being shadowed by four nuclear-armed Soviet submarines.[21]

As they held their breath, many wondered if Khrushchev had been bluffing. Had the hawks in his circle pushed him closer to the precipice of war? Was a rebellious commander acting alone? Had there been some breakdown in communication? "The great danger and risk in all of this," Kennedy said to his brother, "is a miscalculation—a mistake in judgment."[22]

But then, suddenly, the Soviet ships stopped.

A tidal surge of relief washed over the men.

Still, the ships remained in position.

Several minutes later, Khrushchev ordered the Cuba-bound ships to turn tail and head home.

The crisis was over. The prospect of nuclear war was at last at an end.

The military blockade, framed as a "quarantine," turned out to be precisely the right balance between a direct attack—which might easily have devolved into a global nuclear exchange—and doing nothing—which would have severely undermined American power and prestige around the world.

Today, the 13-day period that followed the discovery of the Soviet's secret deployment of nuclear missiles a mere 90 miles off the coast of Florida is still widely regarded as "...the closest the world has come to World War III," and, according Joseph Nye, former Dean at Harvard's John F. Kennedy School of Government, the closest humans have come to our own extinction.[23]

Arthur M. Schlesinger Jr., the former Harvard historian and Special Assistant to President Kennedy, called it "the most dangerous moment in human history."[24]

Make Smart Choices: 8 Key Critical Thinking Practices to Employ

Despite the demands of the modern world, educational systems continue to graduate students who lack critical thinking skills. According to a 2019 report from the Society of Human Resource Management (SHRM), critical thinking remains at the top of the list of missing skills among job applicants. A recent survey of more than 60,000 managers and 14,000 college graduates, as reported in *Harvard Business Review (HBR)*, ranked "critical thinking [as] the number one soft skill managers feel new graduates are lacking, with 60% feeling this way."[25]

The good news is that critical thinking is a skill that can be cultivated, sharpened, and refined. It may require some extra time and effort on the front end, but the time, money, and resources that you will save with more intelligent, resourceful, and strategic decisions and actions will almost always outweigh your initial investment, sometimes dramatically. Think, for example, of the considerable costs the country endured as a result of President Kennedy's failure to think critically in the run up to the Bay of Pigs Fiasco, or, in contrast, the unthinkable costs and consequences that were successfully averted as a result of the vigilant, critical thinking he deliberately facilitated during the Cuban Missile Crisis. Indeed, the differences in how he handled these two events could scarcely be more stark.

In fact, the clear, critical thinking and effective decision-making that took place throughout the Cuban Missile Crisis stands today as a preeminent example of the power of critical thinking and also offers a number of crucial lessons and clear practices for how to effectively engage in and facilitate critical thinking that go well beyond the American presidency, foreign relations, conflict resolution, or war.

Critical thinking can be defined as *the process of objectively analyzing, interpreting, and evaluating information in order to make a sound judgment or determine future action*. To reap the tremendous potential rewards of critical thinking, see how easily you can learn to put the following 8 key practices into play:

(1.) *Bridle and Saddle Your Mind:*
Stop and Think About Your Thinking.

The biggest failure in regards to critical thinking is the failure to think at all. Of course, we are all thinking virtually all the time. But rarely do most people stop to *think about their thinking*. Instead of being purposeful or intentional about their thinking, most people simply drift along with whatever thoughts pop into their mind or whatever mental scripts are triggered by the people and circumstances of their lives.

President Kennedy's Bay of Pigs decision-making process failed not because he wasn't *capable* of thinking critically. It failed because he didn't *bother* to think critically. Instead, as is so often the case, he was operating on autopilot. He defaulted to his habitual decision-making routines.

After his initial outburst following the failed invasion, however, Kennedy immediately turned toward taking ownership of the fiasco. By assuming full responsibility, Kennedy drove himself to stop and examine the fatal decision, including the context and conditions that prevented him from seeing what, in retrospect, was clearly a reckless, foolhardy plan. This also set him on the path to rethinking his decision-making *process*, making a number of critical changes, and greatly improving the quality of his future decisions as a result.

Your willingness to stop and think before making important decisions has a tremendous influence on the quality of your decisions. Your mind is easily your greatest, most powerful asset, but only *if* you take time to put it to work. As Eckhart Tolle writes in *The Power of Now*, "The mind is a superb instrument if used rightly. Used wrongly, however, it becomes very destructive. To put it more accurately," he said, "it is not so much that you use your mind wrongly—you usually don't use it at all."[26]

(2.) *Solve the Right Problem. Identify the Underlying Cause.*

"There is nothing so useless as doing efficiently that which should not be done at all."[27]
—Peter F. Drucker (1909—2005),"The Founder of Modern Management"

Regardless of the challenge you face, critical thinking begins with getting clear about the core problem. But only an idiot would go about solving the wrong problem, right? Wrong! It is deceptively easy to focus on the wrong problem. Organizations do this all the time. If you have a tough problem and not one of the many solutions you have tried seems to work, the chances are good that you are trying to solve the wrong problem, usually a painful or prominent *symptom* of the *root* problem or the real, *underlying* cause. Virtually everyone has a tendency, at times, to be distracted or misled by the most painful or salient *symptoms* of problems, rather than focusing in on the root cause. This is particularly true in healthcare. And, yet, while addressing the symptoms may help to bring some relief (though often with a hidden cost), it will do nothing to alleviate the underlying cause.

It is also possible to redefine or *reframe* the problem to open up the possibilities or potential solutions. When the Disney theme parks started receiving criticism about the length of the lines to get on the rides inside, the leadership team immediately started trying to figure out how to make the lines shorter. The only two solutions they could come up with, however, were to add more rides, or to admit fewer people into the parks. Both of these solutions, however, would cost them tens of millions of dollars. In exasperation, they finally decided to hire a consultant to fix the problem. Rather than accepting the problem as the Disney leadership team defined it, however, the consultants thought that the problem was not necessarily that the lines were too long. The real problem, the way they framed it, was that people were bored while waiting in line. If there was a way to make the guests comfortable and content or even entertained while they waited, then they would not perceive the lines to be too long. When Disney then refashioned the entrances to the rides by adding stories to the waiting areas, including theme music and videos, the complaints evaporated overnight. The lines were now a part of the experience, helping to *build anticipation* for the ride at the end.

As simple as this sort of reframe or redefining of the problem often is, the costs of failing to do so can be severe. In fact, failing to accurately define the problem has destroyed countless successful businesses and careers. To better avoid this fate, avoid rushing to the solution and instead use the problem solving process below to ensure you are solving the *right* problem rather than just your most salient point of pain.

A. *Write Out a Clear and Concise Definition of the Problem*: The first step is to clearly define the problem, actually writing out the definition. In some cases, the solution will emerge after this one step alone. This often happens because once you are sufficiently clear about the problem, the solution becomes obvious. Getting it down on paper, surprisingly, can also help you get perspective. Be careful not to hold on to this definition too tightly, however. "If you are too attached to your initial answer, you may refuse to let it go, no matter where the data leads. But if you treat your own answer as a strawman," John Coleman writes in *Harvard Business Review* (HBR), "holding your assumptions loosely, you'll be willing to totally abandon it if the situation calls for it."[28]

B. *Question Your Assumptions About that Definition*: The next step is to challenge the assumptions behind your written definition of the problem. In other words, what must you assume or what would you have to believe in order for that definition to be a truly accurate representation of the problem? If previous solutions to the problem have failed, there's good reason to believe one of your assumptions or beliefs is wrong. Identifying your assumptions may help you realize that this is not actually the right problem, or it may at least help to loosen your attachment to it and, thereby, make space for other possibilities.

C. *Explore Other Problem Possibilities:* The next step is to ask yourself this question: If the current problem you are trying to solve is not the real problem, then what might the real problem be?[29] At this point, you will likely need to consider a broader range of possibilities. The challenge here is to effectively navigate the tension between opening your mind or broadening your scope enough to consider what you have so far missed, while at the same time being careful not to get distracted by irrelevant information, or issues and concerns that may be important but are not actually critical to the current concern. One way to do this is to keep your mission or end goal in mind, and let that guide your thoughts and direct your focus. You can also make a list of all the various factors that you believe to be important and then rank them in order of how relevant they are to your desired end.

D. *Test Out New Solutions:* The final step is to test your solutions against your new understanding of the problem. The process of actually testing out new solutions can also help to reveal new insights or trigger new ideas about the problem or alternatives for how to solve it. As Peter Bregman writes in HBR, "There's an additional advantage to redefining your problem: it frees you to experiment with "beginner's mind." You get to start over, trying different solutions, assessing their effectiveness, learning from failures, and trying again."[30]

Albert Einstein once reportedly said, "If I were given one hour to save the planet, I would spend 59 minutes defining the problem and one minute resolving it."[31] Alas, in a culture obsessed with quick fix, the problem solving process outlined above is too often given short shrift. "Indeed," Dwayne Spradlin writes in HBR, "when developing new products, processes, or even businesses, most companies aren't sufficiently rigorous in defining the problems they're attempting to solve and articulating why those issues are important."[32] And, yet, without sufficient rigor, they waste time and resources on the wrong problem, miss the opportunities connected to the right problem, and may even put the future of their organization at risk.[33]

In light of the crucial significance of getting this right, investing time in solving the right problem will invariably prove to be time well spent. As research repeatedly reveals, people and organizations that invest the time and "...develop the skills and discipline to ask better questions and define their problems with more rigor can create strategic advantage[s], unlock truly groundbreaking innovation, and drive better business performance."[34] The brutal truth, Spradlin concludes, is that "many organizations need to become better at asking the right questions so that they tackle the right problems" and, ultimately, "deliver...better results."[35]

(3.) *Avoid Being Driven By Ego and Emotion.*

> *"Whoever is slow to anger is better than the mighty,*
> *and he who rules his spirit than he who takes a city."*[36]
> —Proverbs 16:32

Emotion is another chief obstacle to critical thinking. Attempting to think clearly and make smart decisions while in a charged emotional state is a fool's errand. Whether negative *or positive*, imbalanced or unchecked emotions undermine measured, rational thinking. The stronger the emotion, the greater the risk it will lead you astray. Irrational exuberance, impulsiveness, and overconfidence can be just as detrimental to your decision-making as unbridled anger, desperation or fear. It is a calm, stable mind and a cool, steady hand that enables clear, critical thinking. It is emotional stability that facilitates smart choices and wise decisions.

In his book, *Thirteen Days: A Memoir of the Cuban Missile Crisis*, Robert F. Kennedy discusses his brother's leadership and decision-making style during the crisis. He recalls being surprised by how the men that made up the President's Executive Committee all shied away from voicing an opinion different from that of the President. These intelligent, educated, and accomplished men, all leaders in their own right, were more concerned with pleasing Kennedy and being liked and accepted by the group, than helping the President make the best decision possible for the nation and the world. Kennedy writes, "Personalities change when the President is present, and frequently even strong men make recommendations on the basis of what they believe the President wishes to hear."[37]

In order to counter this bias, Kennedy took different steps, including deciding "not to attend all the meetings of our committee," writes RFK.[38] Along with having these *leaderless meetings* as well as *private discussions*, he also *mixed up the group participants at different times*, and had *subgroups meet together on their own*.[39]

President Kennedy also made good use of *questions*. Rather than responding to disagreements with his own thoughts or opinions, he used questions to *probe deeper*, or even gently *push back* on positions or arguments that on the surface seemed weak, rather than getting sucked into an emotional debate. This enabled him to think more critically and rationally, rather than making decisions driven primarily by emotions.[40]

The pressures you face in pursuit of your own aims will likely never be as severe as they were for Kennedy and Khrushchev during the Cuban Missile Crisis, and, yet, unchecked emotions can derail effective decision-making all the same. Everyone has certain emotional triggers which can disrupt their thought processes and prevent clear, critical thinking. The key is *awareness*. If you can recognize *when* you are experiencing heightened emotions, then you can either immediately initiate a process to return to a state of emotional equilibrium, or, at the very least, take steps to avoid making any final, lasting decisions. As the 17th century Spanish Jesuit and philosopher Baltasar Gracián writes in *The Art of Worldly Wisdom*, "Don't act when moved by passion: you will get everything wrong. You cannot act for yourself if you are beside yourself, and passion always sends reason into exile. [...] When prudence feels emotion coming on, it is time to beat a hasty retreat."[41]

When President Kennedy first met with leaders in Congress to tell them about the discovery of missiles in Cuba, there was a general sense of outrage. "The President," writes Robert Kennedy, "after listening to the frequently emotional criticism"[42] of their plans for a naval blockade, "was upset by the time the meeting ended."[43] However, he added, "when we discussed it later he was more philosophical, pointing out that the Congressional leaders' reaction to what we should do, although more militant than his, was much the same as our first reaction when we first heard about the missiles the previous Tuesday."[44]

In other words, with a chance to decompress and reflect, Kennedy recognized their anger as a natural response to a severe existential threat, a response that echoed their own, and, as a result, rather than taking it personally and responding in kind, he avoided saying or doing anything that might damage his relationship with congressional leaders or worsen the ongoing crisis. While the emotional outrage they all felt when they first received news of the missiles is completely reasonable, making any lasting decisions in that heightened emotional state could easily lead to unreasonable actions and unnecessary mistakes.

Meanwhile, emotions were running equally high on the other side. In fact, one of Nikita Khrushchev's messages during the crisis led to "the allegation that at the time Khrushchev wrote it he must have been so unstable or emotional that he had become incoherent."[45] In the midst of a crisis that required flawless communication, which still might not have been enough, incoherence was a recipe for disaster. Fortunately, almost certainly by putting himself in Khrushchev's shoes, Kennedy had a different take, arguing that "there was no question that the letter had been written by him personally. It was very long and emotional. But it was not incoherent, and the emotion was directed at the death, destruction, and anarchy that nuclear war would bring to his people and all mankind. That, he said again and again and in many different ways, must be avoided."[46]

Even more fortunate was the fact that Kennedy was aware of and thinking about the emotions of the actors involved—including, perhaps most importantly, his *own*—and how to make allowance for those emotions without being triggered or carried away by them. This is the essential thing: Being aware of and effectively regulating your emotions and keeping your ego in check, which is also equally important to putting all of the other critical thinking practices into play. In the words of Lao Tzu, the 5th century B.C. Chinese philosopher, "He who controls others may be powerful, but he who has mastered himself is mightier still."[47]

(4.) *Identify and Challenge Your Assumptions.*

"Incorrect assumptions lie at the root of every failure.
Have the courage to test your assumptions."

—Brian Tracy

Shortly after midnight on September 26, 1983, in the midst of heightened Cold War tensions, lieutenant colonel Stanislav Petrov of the Soviet Air Defense Forces was observing the Soviet Union's nuclear early-warning system when the satellite suddenly detected 5 incoming intercontinental ballistic missiles from the United States. With the warning lights flashing and sirens blaring, Petrov had just one simple job to do and less than ten minutes to do it. If the satellite system showed incoming missiles he only had to press a single red button which would immediately transmit the information to Jurij Votincev, the Commander in Chief of the Russian missile defense, and Soviet leader Yuri Andropov, who was virtually certain to launch a counterattack.

Dozens of panicked military personnel sat frozen behind Petrov, staring at the giant screen waiting to see what he would do.[48] "Everyone jumped from their seats looking at me," Petrov recalled later.[49] "What could I do? There was a procedure that I had written myself."[50]

Naturally, nowhere in his job description did it say anything about challenging assumptions or critical thinking. If the early-warning system showed incoming missiles, he was to assume it was a legitimate attack. Based on the doctrine of Mutually Assured Destruction (MAD), Soviet policy dictated an immediate and compulsory nuclear counter-attack. Due to recent U.S. ballistic missile installations in Europe, as well as the greatly deteriorated relationship between the nations, the Soviets believed the U.S. was preparing a secret nuclear attack and were on hair-trigger alert. Only three and a half weeks earlier, the Soviets shot down a South Korean passenger jet that had inadvertently strayed into Soviet air space, killing all 269 passengers, including U.S. Congressman Larry McDonald and 61 other U.S. citizens. Was this attack an attempt at "just revenge?"

Fortunately, when the nuclear missile warning system was triggered, Petrov stopped to think. To begin with, Petrov thought, despite strained relations, it was highly unlikely that the U.S. would suddenly launch an unprovoked nuclear war. Furthermore, it was a relatively small attack, a mere five missiles. If the U.S. was going to attack, it was highly unlikely that they would start with such a small payload. In his training, he was taught to expect a massive attack. Finally, the satellite detection system was still relatively new and, yet, its reliability had already been questioned before. Perhaps, Petrov reasoned, it might still have a few bugs to work out.

As a result, with the window of opportunity to retaliate rapidly evaporating, rather than launching "an irreversible chain reaction in a system geared to launch a counter-strike without human interference,"[51] Petrov immediately began questioning his assumptions. In fact, as his mind raced through various scenarios, Petrov was, remarkably, challenging the chain of logic behind the protocol that he himself had helped to create. After several minutes passed, the ground radar detection system failed to confirm the satellite's early-warning, validating Petrov's decision to disobey orders, notifying his superior only after the incident was over.

Fortunately, for Petrov and the world, he made the right decision. The satellite system was triggered by the reflection of a high atmosphere cloud. It was a false alarm. And Petrov's willingness to challenge the assumption that the warning of incoming missiles was accurate saved the U.S. from a massive, unprovoked attack, and, quite possibly, the entire planet from nuclear annihilation. Although his bold heroism was never rewarded in Russia, Petrov was recognized by the international community following the publication of previously classified documents in 1998. Along with winning the World Citizen Award and the Dresden Peace Prize, Petrov was hailed in newspapers around the globe as "the man who saved the world" from nuclear war.[52]

> *"...We do not have knowledge of a thing until*
> *we have grasped its why, that is to say, its cause."*[53]
> —Aristotle, *Physics* 194 b 17–20

<u>Ask Lots of Questions, Both the Obvious and the Deep</u>. We all operate from a base of assumptions all the time. Assumptions are part of the mental frameworks through which we look out at the world. But this is part of the problem. Rather than seeing our assumptions, we see the world based on the assumptions we already hold. As a result, embedded in the frames we use to make sense of the world, assumptions can easily go unrecognized. Indeed, the mental scaffolding (i.e. series or cluster of mental frameworks or mental maps) that you use to construct meaning, or make sense of a situation will inevitably contain *multiple* assumptions. Your hidden assumptions are often operating when problems are created. Hidden assumptions may have even *contributed* to the problem. And hidden assumptions may actually preclude or prevent you from *seeing* the *solution*. As Albert Einstein once said, "The significant problems we face cannot be solved at the same level of thinking we were at when we created them."[54] As a result, like a fish that sees everything in the ocean but the water itself, recognizing your mental frames and their various elements—including your assumptions, but also your beliefs, values, personal theories, hidden and unhidden rules, etc.—often requires a degree of self-awareness and a willingness to pause and reflect and introspect (i.e. think about your thinking).

Thus, the difficult part of the task is not so much questioning or challenging assumptions. In the case of the Bay of Pigs invasion, Kennedy could simply have asked the members of ExComm if it was safe to *assume* that their collective lack of opposition was, in actual fact, unanimous support for the plan, or might there be some other reason for the *unusual* consensus.

The greater challenge, in other words, is *noticing* what key assumptions are operating at any given time. Once you begin to identify the assumptions operating, then you can easily begin to take them apart.

The key to identifying assumptions is asking yourself and others lots of questions, including those that may seem obvious as well as those that go deep. Questions are the depth charges a patrol ship drops to surface an enemy submarine. The more questions you drop the more likely you are to surface your hidden or submerged assumptions. Similarly, some questions will need to go deep in order to get to the bottom of the issue.

One approach is to use the *Five Whys Technique*; keep asking *why-in response to each new answer*—about the relevant perceptions, perspectives, understandings, and beliefs and you will likely peel away new layers, revealing additional insight.

Another approach, known as the *Fishbone Diagram*, assumes there are multiple potential causes and, therefore, starts by identifying some number (usually 5 to 8) of categories of potential root causes to further investigate. Typically, after sufficient exploration of the potential root causes, the list of possibilities is ranked and prioritized or further investigated.

In the case of the Cuban Missile Crisis, for example, potential categories to further explore might include the following possible contributing factors: people factors (e.g. Kennedy as a new young president, Khrushchev and pressure from the politburo), foreign policy factors (America's nuclear weapons in Turkey, the Bay of Pigs fiasco, communists' need for allies), historical factors (WWII, President Truman's use of nuclear weapons against Japan, the Korean War, the roots of the Cold War), ideological factors (communism versus capitalism, dictatorship versus democracy), economic factors, et cetera.

The point, in essence, of these and other tools (e.g. Socratic Method, Aristotle's Four Causes, etc.) is to get beyond the surface level thinking and superficial analysis. The key is to get in the habit of thinking more about your thinking, including probing your assumptions and perceptions, and questioning your perspectives and beliefs.

Have the Courage to Ask. Questions are also one of the best ways to keep from making misguided assumptions in the first place. Focus on communication that is explicit and clear. "If you don't understand, ask. Have the courage to ask questions until you are clear as you can be, and even then do not assume you know all there is to know about a given situation."[55]

Anytime you *know* something you can be sure there are certain assumptions operating that may or may not be true. And the stronger the knowing the more those assumptions are likely to be hidden from view. But this is precisely where problems crop up without warning, making them even more difficult to resolve. As the immortal Yogi Berra reportedly said, "What gets us into trouble is not what we don't know. It's what we know for sure that just ain't so."[56]

When the Kennedy administration was planning the Bay of Pigs invasion, there were a number of flawed assumptions operating, including, most importantly, the assumption that helped to keep all of the other assumptions from being identified. Kennedy *assumed* that the absence of open opposition signified unanimous support for the CIA's plan. Rather than raising the alarm, Kennedy assumed the lack of resistance was consensus to charge ahead. Tragically, this single, curiously casual assumption led to the deaths of 4 Americans, 118 Cuban allies, and hundreds of Cubans.

Kennedy might easily have challenged his assumption regarding the lack of opposition to the plan. The problem is that he *never stopped to identify his assumptions*; he never paused to consider whether this particular assumption might be dangerously flawed.

Following the failed invasion at the Bay of Pigs, however, Kennedy identified strategies to avoid repeating the same mistakes, including *designating a rotating devil's advocate*. In this way, in every critical meeting going forward, someone would be assigned to offer counter arguments and challenge whatever ideas, assumptions, and beliefs that were deemed to be flawed, deficient, or weak. To be clear, the point is not to derail every good idea that comes up. The point is to poke and prod, push back, and think through in order to sort out the flawed ideas and identify or improve the best ones.

Of course you cannot question every assumption or challenge every belief. Nevertheless, the higher the stakes, the more important it is for your thinking to be increasingly grounded, accurate, and complete. The key is to ask yourself and others lots of questions. The more thoughtful questions you ask, the more you probe assumptions, perceptions, perspectives, and beliefs, the more likely you are to strengthen your thoughts and ideas, and improve your decisions and results.

(5.) *Contemplate Both the Short-Term and Long-Term Effects.*

Another key element of effective critical thinking is ensuring due deliberation of both the short-term and long-term effects. Most people think only of the short-term consequences of their actions. Even young children are capable of considering what might be the immediate result of what they say or do. Far fewer people, however, are ready and willing to think through the logical long-term consequences of their decisions (particularly politicians, apparently, but also all those CEOs obsessed with quarterly earnings reports). But it is impossible to succeed as a strategist without looking at both the next few immediate moves and the long-term vision and goals, as well as the bridge between the two. In fact, based on the research of former Harvard political scientist Edward Banfield, the most successful strategists, indeed the most successful people, tend to be those who are operating from the longest time horizon. In stark contrast to those operating from a time horizon of five, ten, twenty years or more, the least successful people overwhelmingly tend to be those operating from the shortest time horizon, often an hour or less. No doubt, to be governed predominantly by impulse, seeking only the instant gratification of desires and needs, is a proven formula for strategic disaster.

In the case of President Kennedy, more than once he had to push back on his military advisors for failing to think through the potential consequences of their recommended actions. In one instance, prior to Kennedy taking office in 1961, the nation of Laos, a U.S. ally, was in the midst of being overrun by communist insurgents. Convinced that Laos was the key to preventing the spread of communism in all of Southeast Asia, President Eisenhower warned Kennedy that "it would be fatal for us to permit communists to insert themselves into the Laotian government."[57] We would have to "write off all the area," Eisenhower said to the President-elect.[58]

Once in office, Kennedy began exploring his options. Writing in *Thirteen Days*, Robert Kennedy explains what happened next. "I remember an earlier meeting on Laos, in 1961, when the military unanimously recommended sending in substantial numbers of U.S. troops to stabilize the country. They were to be brought in through two airports with limited capability. Someone questioned what we would do if only a limited number landed and then the Communist Pathet Lao knocked out the airports and proceeded to attack our troops, limited in number and not completely equipped. The representatives of the military said we would then have to destroy Hanoi and possibly use nuclear weapons."[59] The alarming escalation left the impression of an embarrassing lack of foresight. "President Kennedy did not send in the troops and concentrated on diplomatic steps to protect our interests."[60]

The point is not that Kennedy was right to avoid increasing the presence of U.S. military in Laos; it was a complex situation with no good options. The point is that his military advisors had obviously not considered either the short-term or long-term consequences if the implementation of their preferred plan failed. It seems absurd that, at the highest levels of government, there could be such an appalling lack of planning and forethought, even just thinking more than one or two steps ahead. Going forward, Kennedy made it clear that "he wanted to hear presented and challenged all the possible consequences of a particular course of action. The first step might appear sensible, but what would be the reaction of our adversaries and would we actually stand to gain?"[61]

(6.) *Get Perspective, Explore Alternative Frames and Points of View.*

Succeeding as a strategist begins with awareness of your own perspectives, perceptions, and beliefs, but it must also include a curiosity about what others see and how they see it. By working diligently to understand the perspectives and beliefs of others you help to clarify and expand your own. You may also uncover hazardous gaps and limits in your own perspective, errors in your understanding, or you may better develop, clarify, and enlighten your own point of view.

Chastened by the Bay of Pigs fiasco in April 1961, John F. Kennedy made a number of critical changes to his decision making apparatus to ensure their mistakes would not be repeated. By the time of the Cuban Missile Crisis in October of 1962, Kennedy had adopted a far more strategic approach to his foreign policy problems.

Perhaps the most decisive change, the factor that enabled the U.S. and the U.S.S.R. to avoid a global nuclear holocaust, was both his and Robert Kennedy's insistence, throughout the crisis, of exploring alternative perspectives, including repeatedly striving to see the situation from Nikita Khrushchev's point of view. As Robert Kennedy writes in *Thirteen Days*, "The final lesson of the Cuban missile crisis is the importance of placing ourselves in the other country's shoes. During the crisis, President Kennedy spent more time trying to determine the effect of a particular course of action on Khrushchev or the Russians than on any other phase of what he was doing."[62]

But Kennedy's interest in alternative perspectives went beyond the Soviets and the missile crisis. Attempting to anticipate the consequences of various courses of action by examining a range of different, often conflicting points of view had become a part of how he made decisions.

The point is not to discount or disregard your own perspective, or undervalue your own background and experience. The point is that, no matter how intelligent and well-informed your perspective may be, it is impossible to make the wisest most strategic decisions if you can only ever see the world from one point of view. In order to maximize the usefulness of this decision-making tool, there are a number of additional points to consider, including the following:

(A.) Consider the Context. First, consider each source in its context. It should come as no surprise that certain groups can be expected to have certain biases. Rather than dismissing their input or perspective out of hand, however, the solution is to seek their input, but to receive it within its proper context.

In the case of the missile crisis, Kennedy rightly expected the military to have a bias toward putting their knowledge, training and skills to the test. As RFK writes of the President, "...he said we had to remember that they were trained to fight and to wage war—that was their life. Perhaps we would feel even more concerned if they were always opposed to using arms or military means—for if they would not be willing, who would be?"[63]

However, even after the Russians agreed to remove the missiles, there were those in the military who still wanted to attack.[64] Now, even in a military context, this sort of unchecked belligerence ought to raise alarms, and, as a matter of fact, it did. "President Kennedy was disturbed by this inability to look beyond the limited military field."[65] Fortunately, writes RFK, "this experience pointed out for us all the importance of civilian direction and control and the importance of raising probing questions to military recommendations."[66]

(B.) Entrust Judgment, Not Position. Second, avoid relying on the perspective of someone just because of their power, position, experience, or rank alone. Instead, look to include those with good judgment and a willingness to express opinions that differ from the group. As Robert Kennedy writes of his brother, "President Kennedy wanted people who raised questions, who criticized, on whose judgment he could rely, who presented an intelligent point of view, regardless of their rank or viewpoint."[67]

(C.) Be Mindful of Group Dynamics. Third, pay attention to group dynamics and how they can encourage or stifle the sharing of alternative points of view. Splitting into subgroups is one way to change group dynamics and allow other perspectives to get a fair hearing. To account for the potential pitfall of group dynamics, President Kennedy made an effort to "enlarge the meetings to include other opinions. At the missile-crisis conferences he made certain there were experts and representatives of different points of view."[68]

(D.) Establish Collaborative Rules of Engagement for the Group. Fourth, establish meeting guidelines that foster open, uninhibited dialogue, regardless of position or rank. This was another method adopted by President Kennedy during the Cuban Missile Crisis. "During all these deliberations, we all spoke as equals," Robert Kennedy recalled; "there was no rank, and, in fact, we did not even have a chairman [i.e. "leaderless meetings"] [...] As a result, with the encouragement of [U.S. Secretary of Defense Robert] McNamara, [National Security Advisor McGeorge] Bundy, and [Under Secretary of State George] Ball, the conversations were completely uninhibited and unrestricted. Everyone had an equal opportunity to express himself and to be heard directly. It was a tremendously advantageous procedure that does not frequently occur within the executive branch of the government, where rank is often so important."[69]

(E.) Understand the Agenda of Your Source. Fifth, beware of how agenda-driven sources can distort perceptions or even mislead and corrupt. Most so-called "news" sources today, for example, are generally unreliable; some are downright deceptive. Unfortunately, even scientific research by major universities and non-profit research institutions or think tanks can be heavily biased by industry sponsorship or political ideology. The best sources are peer-reviewed, disclose any potential conflicts of interest, and undergo a rigorous review process. Sources that present both sides of an argument or different points of view also *tend* to be more reliable. But if you are unsure if you can trust the source, the best alternative is the final recommendation:

(F.) <u>Seek Independent Verification</u>. Sixth, avoid relying on a single source. Instead, seek a range of different sources with different agendas. Even the most trusted sources are imperfect and, therefore, should be corroborated by other, independent sources. If that is not possible, then perhaps key parts of the report can be confirmed by alternative, independent sources. Also, beware of multiple sources all drawing on or being directed by a single source, or influenced by the same agenda.

When the Cuban Missile Crisis was finally, successfully resolved, Kennedy's aides were jubilant. President Kennedy, in contrast, was far more reserved. As pleased as he was with the outcome, he realized that the tensions between the two nations were still at an all-time high and, therefore, he was *still* considering Khrushchev's perspective. He was now imagining what sort of embarrassment, dishonor, and distress he might be experiencing in light of the Russian retreat. Determined not to see their fragile resolution reversed, Kennedy immediately turned his attention to how he and his administration would be seen to respond. Recognizing the gravity of the crisis they had only just barely averted, Kennedy called for humility and warned his jubilant aides not to gloat.[70]

(7.) *Facilitate Debate, Then Use Critical Input to Recalibrate.*

In direct contrast to the failed decision making behind the Bay of Pigs fiasco, during the Cuban Missile Crisis President Kennedy deliberately sought to encourage vigorous discussion and debate. Rather than having his aides present their arguments to him or respond to each position or argument himself, he directed the meeting participants to respond to one another. He even went as far as scheduling meetings with members of ExComm who he knew had conflicting perspectives, and then he played them off of one another to see how their different arguments would fare. He essentially adopted the role of a facilitator, leading his advisors through an intelligent, rational dialogue and reasoned debate. As Erwin Hargrove explains in *The Effective Presidency*, "He did not so much manage the process as guide it. He asked hard questions and gradually felt his way to a decision."[71]

Given that some people feel more relaxed and candid in different, perhaps less formal, settings, Kennedy also scheduled changes in the group atmosphere in an attempt to stimulate more open and frank dialogue.[72] The point of these debates had nothing to do with the individual advisors themselves. The point was to sharpen his own thinking about the crisis and the various courses of action available in order to optimize his decision-making and, ultimately, avert a nuclear war. As Kennedy himself once said, "Without debate, without criticism, no Administration and no country can succeed—and no republic can survive."[73]

(8.) *Seek Conflicting Information, Rational Criticism, and Constructive Feedback.*

Speaking to the troops on the eve of D-Day during World War II, General Dwight Eisenhower, the Supreme Commander of the Allied forces and a consummate military and political strategist, said, "Here we are on the eve of a great battle. The Force Commanders will brief you on their plans. I would emphasize one thing: I consider it to be the duty of anyone who sees a flaw in the plan not to hesitate to say so. I have no sympathy with anyone, whatever his station, who will not brook criticism. We are here to get the best possible results..."[74]

The key idea with seeking constructive criticism and feedback is to be open and receptive to evaluation and challenge so that you can improve your strategic plan and, thus, your results. To be clear, you are *not* looking for the agreement or support your ego may desire. You are looking for relevant information and knowledge that the effective execution of your strategy may require. In this regard, feedback and even criticism can be immensely useful. "Criticism may not be agreeable," Churchill said, "but it is necessary. It fulfills the same function as pain in the human body; it calls attention to the development of an unhealthy state of things. If it is heeded in time, danger may be averted; if it is suppressed, a fatal distemper may develop."[75]

Along with whatever relevant objective data, information, and reports you can get your hands on, what is essential here is receiving critical input and feedback, ideally from independent, disinterested or impartial sources. In Kennedy's case, though his sources were not necessarily independent or impartial, he did have a number of specific advisors, experts that he trusted to be sufficiently objective and detached. As Robert Kennedy explains in *Thirteen Days*, "It was to obtain an unfettered and objective analysis that he frequently, and in critical times, invited Secretary of the Treasury Douglas Dillon, for whose wisdom he had such respect; Kenny O'Donnell, his appointment secretary; Ted Sorensen; and, at times, former Secretary of State Dean Acheson, former Secretary of Defense Robert Lovett, former High Commissioner of Germany John McCloy, and others. They asked the difficult questions; they made others defend their position; they presented a different point of view; and they were skeptical."[76]

Getting good quality, accurate, and objective information can be a challenge in large organizations where there are many layers of individuals and filters between the leader and the source. "There is also the risk that as information is sifted through a number of different hands up to him or to the President," Kennedy writes, "vital facts may be eliminated or distorted through an error of judgment. Thus it is essential for a President to have personal access to those within the department who have expertise and knowledge. He can in this way," Kennedy continues, "have available unfiltered information to as great a degree as is practical and possible. During the Cuban missile crisis, the President not only received information from all the significant departments, but went to considerable lengths to ensure that he was not insulated from individuals or points of view because of rank or position. He wanted the advice of his Cabinet officers, but he also wanted the opinion of those who were connected with the situation itself."[77]

Between the Bay of Pigs Fiasco in April 1961 and the Cuban Missile Crisis in October 1962, John F. Kennedy's decision-making apparatus underwent a dramatic transformation. Still less than 90 days into his presidency, Kennedy's deliberation and decision-making around the Bay of Pigs was riddled with limits, weaknesses, pitfalls and traps. He neglected to control the data-gathering and decision-making process of his committee and, as a result, he failed to ensure he was receiving the knowledge and information necessary to critically assess their perspective, challenge their assumptions, and question their perspectives, perceptions, biases and beliefs.

The belief or assumption that Kennedy would look with disfavor on any criticism or dissent, along with Kennedy's own failure to seek constructive feedback or solicit alternative perspectives or conflicting interpretations, resulted in his executive committee's failure to think critically and analytically about the strategy, tactics, and logistics behind the CIA's invasion plan, never mind pausing to consider the legitimacy of the objective, or other potentially more viable and justifiable options for achieving their broader aims.[78]

Fortunately, the failed invasion plan was an embarrassing, yet transformational, learning experience for President Kennedy.[79] By the time of the missile crisis eighteen months later, successfully bringing the world back from the brink of a nuclear holocaust, Kennedy had developed a process and approach that was worthy of emulation. No doubt, the more volatile, uncertain, complex and ambiguous the situation, the more urgent the need for intelligent leadership. Employing every one of the eight critical thinking and effective decision-making practices outlined above, John F. Kennedy's handling of the Cuban Missile Crisis stands today as a textbook example of how to effectively deal with complex problems in the midst of extreme pressure, potentially dire consequences, and limited time.

CULTIVATE THE HIDDEN POWER OF CONCENTRATED CURIOSITY: THE SECRET SUCCESS FACTOR OF MARCO POLO AND KUBLAI KHAN

"Ideas come from curiosity."[1]
—Walt Disney

The door of the Genoese prison slammed shut with a loud clang. It was September 1298, the Italian city-states of Genoa and Venice had resumed hostilities. And Marco Polo was now a prisoner of war.

This was not the first time Marco Polo found himself trapped in a treacherous situation. After traveling across Europe and Asia for nearly a quarter of a century, the 44-year-old Venetian explorer and merchant had escaped more close calls than a jackrabbit living in a field of foxes. He had survived everything from Mongol wars and insurrections to hostile Tartar tribes, from blinding blizzards to catastrophic floods, from the sweltering heat of the Earth's driest deserts to the piercing cold of her highest mountains.[2]

Nor was this the first time that Marco Polo would turn a difficult situation to his considerable advantage. Indeed, Marco Polo seemed to have an intuitive understanding of Napoleon Hill's notion that "every adversity brings with it the seed of an equivalent advantage."[3]

Marco Polo had only recently returned to Venice, but he quickly got caught up in the military conflict with Genoa. Driven by their commercial interests, the two Italian Republics had been fighting for dominance of the Mediterranean Sea for nearly four decades. In fact, it was this same conflict that threatened the commercial interests of the Polo family and, in search of new trade routes, it was this same conflict that first drove Marco Polo's father and uncle (Niccolò Polo and Maffeo Polo) to the Silk Road, in what would become a prelude to the Age of Discovery.

Upon his return, Marco Polo found himself in command of a ship in defense of his native Venice. Unfortunately, following nearly nine hours of nonstop combat, "the Genoese finally overwhelmed the Venetian fleet, eventually capturing or destroying eighty-four of their original ninety-six galleys, and taking prisoner no fewer than 8,000 men," including Marco Polo.[4]

Let Curiosity Roam

Unsure of what was to come, Marco soon "reverted to character."[5] "Displaying the same ability he had deployed to survive in the Mongol Empire...he charmed and ingratiated himself with strangers."[6] He entertained his fellow prisoners with fantastic tales of his adventures traveling the Silk Road across the continent, and working closely with the great Mongolian emperor, Kublai Khan, the grandson of Genghis Khan, one of history's greatest conquerors and most brilliant strategists.

Marco Polo's stories had a way of capturing the attention of his audiences, and both prisoners and guards gathered around to hear of his exploits in this strange, distant, and exotic land. "Eventually," writes American historian Laurence Bergreen, "the Genoese, his natural enemies, came to hold the distinguished and entertaining Venetian in high regard."[7] As a matter of fact, according to Renaissance scholar and travel writer Giovanni Battista Ramusio, who recorded one of the first accounts of Marco Polo's odyssey, "The whole city gathered to see him and to talk to him, not treating him as a prisoner, but as a very dear friend and greatly honored gentleman, and showed him so much honor and affection that there was never an hour of the day that he was not visited by the most noble gentlemen of that city, and presented with everything necessary for his daily living."[8]

Marco Polo was not the first European to travel the Silk Road into the heart of the Mongol lands, or return with compelling tales to tell. Nor was he necessarily a gifted storyteller, at least not according to the man who would later help him write his celebrated book. Of course, he *did* have a remarkable story to tell, but that too was due in no small part to the real secret of his success: Marco Polo was a man of "boundless curiosity,"[9] *and* he knew how to arouse and sustain the curiosity of others.

Moreover, relative to the other explorers, what stood out about Marco Polo's account was the depth of his understanding of the people and places he visited, all of the rich, relevant, and intriguing detail, and, perhaps most importantly, what about his unique experiences *would be of greatest interest and appeal.* In essence, Marco Polo's stories *engaged the interests and fed the curiosity of others* because, throughout his two-and-a-half-decades-long trip, he had been relentless in satisfying his own unquenchable curiosity.

It was this same insatiable curiosity that drove him to travel in the first place. It was this same curiosity that helped him to recall what he saw in such detail that he could paint a vivid, visual picture in his listener's minds. It was this same curiosity, this same hunger to see and understand, to observe and absorb all he could, which first caught the attention of Kublai Khan, and which made him such a valuable resource to the Mongolian emperor—Polo could be the eyes and ears that Khan needed to more effectively rule his vast kingdom—so valuable, in fact, that Kublai Khan repeatedly refused Marco Polo's pleas to return to his home in Venice.

Reap the Rich, Proven Rewards
of the Relentlessly Curious Legends

*"The race will go to the curious, the slightly mad,
and those with an un satiated passion for learning and daredeviltry."*[10]
—Tom Peters, *In Search of Excellence*

Along with ambition and courage, a hunger for adventure and an appetite for risk, few would be surprised to discover *curiosity* among the chief characteristics that launched history's great explorers into the unknown. As historian William Goetzmann writes, "explorers have always been…people of vision and, most of all, people of curiosity."[11] In fact, the Age of Discovery was itself largely driven by humankind's curiosity.

But it's not just the great explorers or the Age of Exploration; the Renaissance, the Reformation, the Age of Reason, these periods were all clearly marked by curiosity—a culture of inquiry and innovation, critical thinking, probing questions, and a quest for understanding and truth. As with the life of Marco Polo, these periods were also marked by the *fruits* of their curiosity. Indeed, in the case of the Enlightenment alone, the result was the greatest eruption of philosophical ideals, political modernization, and scientific progress in the entire history of human civilization.[12]

Without a doubt, *concentrated in a profitable direction*, Marco Polo's relentless curiosity served him exceptionally well. But this was perhaps even more true for Kublai Khan.

Slake Curiosity, Slay Leadership.

Unlike his grandfather, Genghis Khan, who relied on horse and arrows, "Kublai was not a barbarian," writes Venetian historian Alvise Zorzi," but "a monarch pursuing high standards of governance, dedicated to learning and implementing the most efficient means to that end," including "constantly seeking better ways to govern and apply spiritual pressure points that would serve his aim of authority better than force."[13] This was no easy task to be sure. As Genghis Khan himself once said, "Conquering the world on horseback is easy; it is dismounting and governing that is hard."[14]

Fortunately, like Marco Polo, like all great strategists, Kublai Khan was surprisingly curious.[15,16] Rather than a general curiosity about everything, however, Kublai Khan kept his focus and narrowed his scope, effectively *concentrating* his curiosity on those areas most pertinent to his principal purpose and goals, particularly in regards to how he might more effectively and efficiently rule.

Known for his curiosity about and openness toward other cultures, Kublai Khan regularly surrounded himself with foreign diplomats, religious figures, and leaders from distant lands. During his feasts with Marco Polo's father and uncle, for example, "Kublai Khan probed his exotic visitors for intelligence about the 'western parts of the world, the Emperor of the Romans, and other Christian kings and princes.' In particular," historian Laurence Bergreen writes, "the Mongol leader wished to be informed of those rulers' 'relative importance, their possessions, the manner in which justice was administered in their kingdoms, and how they conducted themselves in warfare. Above all, he questioned them about the pope, the affairs of the Church, and the religious worship and doctrine of the Christians.'"[17]

"The merchant brothers were hardly experts on such complex subjects, but according to Marco, they supplied 'appropriate answers on all these points in the Mongol language, with which they were perfectly acquainted.' Kublai Khan was so gratified that he summoned them repeatedly for conferences on the state of Christendom."[18]

As much as these conversations with foreigners and other notables from across his realm may have gratified his curiosity, Kublai Khan was also operating as a master strategist, searching for ideas and insights, probing for opportunities and threats. In essence, he was curious because he understood the power of reliable, timely intelligence. In fact, after developing considerable rapport with Niccolò and Maffeo, he sought to employ them as double agents, "they would serve him as ambassadors to the West."[19]

Unlike his grandfather, Genghis Khan, Kublai Khan sought to build a secure and prosperous kingdom without incessant war. To do this he relied on commerce, a series of vast trade routes, which later became known as the Silk Road, as well as an extensive postal system, known as the Yam, first developed by Genghis Khan. Whereas Genghis relied on brute force, Bergreen writes, "Kublai's most potent weapon was not the sword or spear, fire or poison, but commerce with the world beyond the borders of his empire. Indeed, the Mongols needed European, Persian, and Arab goods and technology to survive in the new world order they had created."[20]

To effectively manage this vast empire and ensure the safety and security of trade,[21] Kublai found that swift, accurate intelligence, and reliable allies were key. This strategic focus on quality intelligence, trusted allies, and foreign trade perfectly suited the interests of the well-traveled merchant family from Venice, who found in Kublai Khan "a man whose curiosity about the West matched theirs about the East."[22]

In the case of the Polo's, their years of roaming curiosity, travel, and trade increased their value and influence with Kublai Khan and, in turn, as a result of their relationships with the Mongol leader, the Polo's became "pioneering intermediaries, a conduit through which knowledge of Europe and [Asia] could travel in both directions."[23]

Years later, back home in Venice, with the help of an expert storyteller, Marco Polo's ambitious, adventure-filled, curiosity-fueled travels also led to considerable fame and fortune. Polo happened to be imprisoned with a popular writer known as Rustichello of Pisa, who had written a number of stories of "courtly love and knightly valor, specializing in Arthurian romances."[24] Rustichello, who had once "enjoyed the patronage of Edward the Confessor," had also written a book about the Trojan War, "and a biography of Alexander the Great, paying as much attention to the romance as to the history."[25] The two prisoners soon began to collaborate on a book that "would become one of the best-known works in Europe."[26]

Known as *The Travels of Marco Polo*, the book was a detailed account of Marco Polo's remarkable, 24-year round trip from Venice through Persia to Xanadu and Beijing, down to Sumatra and along the coast through the Arabian Sea, the Mediterranean, and back to Venice, ultimately covering over 20,000 miles of adventure, a territory conquered by Genghis Khan, and now under the control of "his enlightened grandson, Kublai Khan."[27]

While he was still in prison, the 13th century Venetian explorer was treated like royalty. When the hostilities between Venice and Genoa ended in 1299, Marco Polo, Rustichello, and the other prisoners of war were all released. "His book became a best seller, spreading throughout the Italian Peninsula in a matter of months—a remarkable feat in an age before Gutenberg's invention of the printing press around 1439."[28]

"Marco Polo's account of his journey became a best seller partly," explains *National Geographic's* Antonio Ratti, "because of its new insights into a faraway part of the world: Although travelers' tales from the lands of the Silk Road had been distributed before, the wealth of information Marco Polo provided on China and its surrounding lands was unprecedented in its time."[29] "Polo's book reawakened Europe to the possibilities of international trade and expansion, and became a text that heavily influenced the age of discovery that dawned in Europe two centuries later."[30]

Tap the Hidden Powers of Curiosity.

"Through hundreds of thousands of years, man's intellectual curiosity has been essential to all the gains we have made."[31]

–Margaret Mead (1901—1978), American Cultural Anthropologist,
Author of *Some Personal Views* (1979)

It is in our nature as humans to be curious about the world. Since the beginning of human history, curiosity has been a dominant driving force in the development of civilization. Curiosity has driven us to the highest peak of Mount Everest and the lowest depth of the Mariana Trench. Curiosity drives us to explore the oceans and the deserts, the jungles and the plains. It compels us to dig into the past, land on the moon, explore the surface of Mars, and untangle the complexity of the brain. Curiosity pushes us to fly like the birds, and it urges us to reach for the stars.

Naturally, curiosity is not valued the same by all cultures. For some groups, such as the Vikings, curiosity played a defining role in who they were and what they were about. According to Norse and Germanic mythology, Odin, the supreme god in the pagan pantheon,[32] "was the god of curiosity."[33] He was so eager to gain wisdom and understanding that he "sacrificed one of his eyes"[34] in order to look into the well of knowledge. The Vikings also believed that Odin once pierced his own side with his indestructible spear, Gungnir, and then hung himself from Yggdrasil, the immense sacred World Tree, for nine days and nights all in order to discover the secrets of the runes and unlock wisdom from other worlds.

In contrast, demanding absolute order, submission, and control, high authoritarian cultures disdain and actively discourage curiosity and inquisitiveness.[35] Authoritarian leaders may even strive to stamp it out, calling it a corrosive poison to culture, society, or the soul. As Russian novelist Vladimir Nabokov once said, "curiosity in its turn is insubordination in its purest form." Unfortunately, beyond authoritarian regimes, this sort of anti-inquisitiveness can just as easily infect the culture of organizations and political parties, and it dominates political and religious cults.

For those cultures that do cultivate curiosity, however, there are frequently remarkable and recurring rewards. Whatever temporary investments in time and other resources might be involved, they are far outweighed by the considerable, wide-ranging benefits of curiosity. Consider how any one of the following 5 factors could be a game-changer in the pursuit of your own strategic purpose and plans.

(1.) Curiosity Helps Facilitate Discovery and Adventure.

In the case of the great Viking leader Ragnar Lothbrok—who, not incidentally, believed he was a direct descendent of Odin—his curiosity led him to venture far away from the shores of Scandinavia, sailing across the open ocean, and discovering the kingdom of West Francia, the Irish plains, and Anglo-Saxon England, where he led a series of successful raids.

Contrary to the popular, "one-dimensional" myth about the Vikings, Ragnar was not primarily interested in raiding or finding treasure, explains Michael Hirst, the writer and creator of *Vikings* (2013), the Emmy Award-winning television series.[36] "Ragnar was an extraordinary leader," explains Hirst, he traveled to "far-away countries" because he wanted "to find out what was there. He was curious."[37]

Curiosity drove other Viking leaders to defy freezing oceans, treacherous icebergs, and violent storms to discover other foreign lands and conquer frigid frontiers;[38] including Erik the Red, who discovered Greenland, Naddodd, who discovered Iceland, and Leif Erikson,[39] who first landed in North America circa 1000 A.D.,[40] predating Christopher Columbus by more than 500 years.

An Old Norse text, *The King's Mirror* (circa 1250), answers the question of why their people were willing to make such treacherous expeditions: "One motive is fame and rivalry," the author explains, "for it is in the nature of man to seek places where great dangers may be met, and thus to win fame. A second motive is curiosity, for it is also in man's nature to wish to see the things he has heard about...The third is desire for gain; for men seek wealth wherever they have heard that gain is to be gotten, though…there may be great dangers too."[41]

Driving your hunger to explore, curiosity can be a tremendous asset for the strategist, leading to the discovery of new resources and potential allies or, in contrast, emerging competitors or looming threats. In either case, curiosity's desire to discover, explore, and unearth can lead to a significant jump on how, when, and where to make your next strategic move.

(2.) Curiosity Can Enhance Cognition.

While quenching your curiosity can be satisfying in itself, and it can be a potent elixir to boredom, sadness, and, gloom, it can also help to guard against groupthink by motivating the exploration of alternative perspectives. Curiosity can also increase retention and recall, and accelerate learning and growth.[42] What's more, in time, and particularly relevant for the strategist, curiosity can even improve your ability to think. As author Ian Leslie explains, "Highly curious people, who have carefully cultivated their long-term memories, live in a kind of augmented reality; everything they see is overlaid with additional layers of meaning and possibility, unavailable to ordinary observers."[43] "The wider your knowledge," he continues, "the more widely your intelligence can range and the more purchase it gets on new information."[44] In other words, as recent research experiments have repeatedly revealed, curiosity does not just lead to increased knowledge, it can both accelerate your learning, and actually improve your thinking.[45]

Indeed, in his carefully researched biography of Albert Einstein, the quintessential genius of the 20th century, Walter Isaacson writes, "*curiosity*…is perhaps the best place to begin when sifting through the elements of his genius."[46] "The explanation that Einstein himself most often gave for his mental accomplishments was his curiosity."[47] As Einstein wrote, for instance, to Carl Seelig in 1952, "I am not more gifted than anybody else. I am just more curious than the average person, and I will not give up on a problem until I have found the proper solution."[48] Einstein repeated this sentiment toward the end of his life, when he explained, "I have no special talents, I am only passionately curious."[49]

(3.) Curiosity Cultivates Creativity and Innovation.

Playing directly into another key strategic competency (further explored in Chapter 7), curiosity is also the engine of creativity and innovation. From the perspective of former University of Chicago psychologist Mihaly Csikszentmihalyi, author of *Creativity*, "the first step toward a more creative life is the cultivation of curiosity…"[50] It was, for example, one of the essential ingredients of Walt Disney's remarkable success. Noted Disney historian and Brigham Young professor Paul Anderson argues that curiosity was the *number one source* of Walt's *genius*.[51] "Walt wanted to know about everything."[52] "He had this relentless curiosity, and everything was interesting to him. He didn't sit back and wait for reports to cross his desk. He was constantly pursuing information by talking to people at the park, or at WED [Walt Disney Imagineering, Inc], or on the set at the studio."[53] "Walt believed that brilliant ideas were all around, just waiting for someone to ask the right questions," writes Pat Williams in *How to Be Like Walt*.[54] "Around here..." Disney himself said, "we keep moving forward, opening new doors, and doing new things, because we're curious...and curiosity keeps leading us down new paths."[55]

(4.) Curiosity Spurs Progress and Generates Prosperity.

Well beyond the world of business, innovation, or entertainment, the power of curiosity penetrates a wide range of diverse realms, including the political sphere, and broader society itself. In contrast with the Dark Ages in Western Europe (i.e. the Early Medieval Era), the Renaissance and the Reformation witnessed a major shift in thinking about the world and society, about power and authority, as well as knowledge and wisdom. Rather than being chastised or stigmatized, people began to better appreciate the value of being curious and asking questions. They began to better understand the critical significance of inquiry and investigation. By the Age of Reason, or the Enlightenment, these practices and characteristics were increasingly held in high regard. "European societies started to see that their future lay with the curious..."[56] The ultimate upshot was one of the greatest periods of intellectual and philosophical advancement in human history. In essence, Leslie writes in his book, *Curious: The Desire to Know and Why Your Future Depends On It*, "The great unlocking of curiosity translated into a cascade of prosperity for the nations that precipitated it."[57]

(5.) Curiosity Enhances Adaptation and Reduces Surprise.

Perhaps most immediately relevant to the strategist, curiosity leads to a greater understanding of the world around us, both reducing unexpected developments and making it easier to adapt. Well beyond the strategist in fact, according to neuroscientist Mario Livio, curiosity has played an important role in the success of our entire species. In his book, *Why? What Makes Us Curious*, Livio writes, "Human curiosity has clearly evolved at least partially to aid survival. An understanding of the world around us, its causal connections, and the sources of changes have helped humans to reduce prediction errors, cope with the environment, and adapt."[58]

The two greatest threats to curiosity are success and fear. Success can lead to overconfidence and the tendency to think you already know all you need to know. Success can also distort your perception of the image you think you need to project. To be curious and ask questions is to admit you don't have all the answers, which can be surprisingly difficult for leaders who are insecure. As Warren Berger explains in *HBR*, "Advising business leaders to 'be more curious' sounds simple enough, but it may require a change in leadership style. In many cases, managers and top executives have risen through the ranks by providing fixes and solutions, not by asking questions. And once they've attained a position of leadership, they may feel the need to project confident expertise."[59]

Curiosity can also get stifled or suppressed by fear—fear of change, fear of the unknown, fear of losing power, influence, or control. It takes confidence and courage to be curious, to ask questions, to investigate unknowns and explore. After all, not everything you discover will be positive or welcome news. Some revelations will require you to rethink your strategy, revise your tactics, or change your goals. Nevertheless, to paraphrase presidential speechwriter Robert Orben, 'If you think knowledge and understanding comes at a cost, try ignorance.'[60]

It takes even greater confidence to encourage curiosity and inquisitiveness in the people you lead. Nevertheless, courage is wisdom in the end. It is a mistake, therefore, to let fear, success, or anything else crush your curiosity, or undermine your impulse to investigate, discover, and explore.

Profit from the Surprise Power of Concentrated Curiosity

In contrast to authoritarian leaders who seek submission and control, strategists prize wisdom and insight, innovation, and creativity. They understand the powerful benefits of unfettered, inquiring minds, and the need to research, investigate, and explore. They seek to cultivate curiosity and they make space for it to take root and bear fruit.[61]

Fortunately, we can all learn to become more curious; as one researcher explains, curiosity is "more of a state than a trait."[62] But how do you go about cultivating and encouraging curiosity? The following are 7 proven tactics you can employ to cultivate curiosity and reap its rewards:

(1.) Map Your Knowledge Gaps: Know What You Don't Know.

To cultivate your curiosity, begin by increasing your awareness and clarity around what it is you do not know, or would like to learn, particularly in regards to your vision, strategy, and goals, but also the general field or your ideal area of expertise. Increased awareness of your knowledge gaps alone can help to spark a certain level of curiosity. Identifying and defining a knowledge gap can also create an open loop in your brain and strengthen your desire to close the loop and fill the gap.

When Kublai Khan succeeded to the office of the Great Khan in 1260, he was holding the reins of a vast multinational Mongol Empire made up of a "patchwork of faiths, languages, and ethnicities."[63] In contrast to his grandfather, Genghis Khan, rather than winning such an empire, the task for Kublai Khan was to hold it together.

Kublai understood that there was a great deal he did not know about the people in his empire, including the multitude of differences between the various cultures, religions, and beliefs. He was also clear that his lack of knowledge and limited understanding of these differences could create blind spots and put his leadership in jeopardy. This undoubtedly fueled his interest in finding solutions, such as his practice of surrounding himself with advisors of different ethnicities and faiths.

This, in part, helps to explain how a curiously young foreigner like Marco Polo could become an important part of the Mongolian court. Less than two years after he first met the Mongolian Emperor, Marco Polo, still only about twenty-one, was appointed as an envoy of Kublai Khan.[64] "In this role, he served as a representative of the Mongol ruler and his court. The Khan sent Polo throughout his empire to visit various provinces to gather information...Anything that might be considered useful for the Khan to know—how taxes were collected, how taxes were spent regionally, how local governments ruled—was fair game for Polo's observant eye."[65]

The celebrated Scottish physicist James Clerk Maxwell once said that, "thoroughly conscious ignorance is the prelude to every real advance in science."[66] "Companies, and rulers, who learn to cultivate their conscious ignorance—to be fascinated, even obsessed, by what they don't know—are the ones least likely to be caught unaware by change."[67] This was a key part of how Kublai Khan was able to effectively manage his massive kingdom for more than 30 years; he remained conscious of, and curious about, what he did not know.

(2.) Start in the Vicinity of Curiosity.

A third useful tactic for fueling curiosity is to first identify a relevant area where you already are curious or deeply interested (e.g. some part of your chief purpose and goals), and then look for ways to connect or incorporate it into the area where you would like to boost your curiosity. You might, for instance, increase your mild or somewhat *less* intense interest in learning French by linking it with your intense passion for travel. By imagining, for example, what specific French words and sentences, questions and answers you would need to learn to navigate from the Charles de Gaulle Airport in Paris to your hotel on the coast in southern Brittany on the day of your arrival, your curiosity for travel in France gets extended to the rigors of learning a new language.

The reason this approach works is because, as research experiments reveal, "curiosity puts [y]our brain in a state in which it absorbs everything in the vicinity of the object of curiosity."[68] In other words, if you can identify a reasonably convincing connection, you can exploit the energy and enthusiasm you have for one thing to help generate interest in another.

When Pope Julius II invited Michelangelo to paint the twelve apostles on the ceiling of the Sistine Chapel, the Florentine artist was not interested. He preferred *sculpting* to painting frescoes. As a deeply devout Christian, however, Michelangelo did not want to refuse the Pope's request. Thus, rather than declining the work, he chose to do it in a way in which he *was* much more interested. "He chose to fill every inch with dramatic scenes from Genesis, from the creation of Adam and Eve to Noah. Prophets, sibyls (female oracles of Ancient Greece) and the ancestors of Christ would line the ceiling."[69] He also indulged his curiosity in art as narrative, "with the paintings growing more complex as he went along."[70] In other words, feeling obligated by his faith, he transformed his lack of interest in painting the Sistine Chapel by connecting the work with something he *was* interested in and curious about.

(3.) *Capture Curiosity at Work.*

"Describe the tongue of the woodpecker," Leonardo Da Vinci wrote on his to do list for the day. The next item: "Inflate the lungs of a pig and observe whether they increase in width and in length, or only in width.""[71] Leonardo Da Vinci's persistent habit of taking notes, making lists, and keeping journals—described by Walter Isaacson as, "the greatest record of curiosity ever created"[72]—not only helped to reveal the Renaissance polymath's relentless curiosity, but also helped to nurture and channel it.

As with Da Vinci, who was "seldom without charcoal, pen or brush in his hand, compulsively noting in detail flowers, birds, animals, human faces—whatever at the moment attracted his attention"[73]—this practice was also critical to Marco Polo's success. Other Europeans had returned with news of the Mongol Empire, but a key part of what set Marco Polo apart was the scope, depth, and detail of the information and knowledge he had collected. He was, writes historian John Man, "the ideal reporter, roaming widely, curious, always gathering information."[74]

Like Leonardo da Vinci, Marco Polo was "a keen observer of everything around him. He noted the exotic animals, birds, and fish they encountered."[75] Sent by Kublai Khan to "remote regions on certain business of his realm," Polo himself noted, "I observed all things diligently which came to my attention either in going or in returning."[76]

Through his long trips and regular, detailed notes, Marco Polo "soon acquired a unique knowledge of what to Europeans were still the secrets of the East."[77] By noticing what captivated his attention, and capturing the most interesting details of what he saw, Marco Polo also developed an eye for bringing these fantastic legends and the fabulous new things of these far-off places to life.[78] Indeed, for Medieval Europe, "more than bring[ing] Kublai and his court to life," the Venetian explorer "brought a whole unknown country to life."[79]

By keeping a record of the ideas that interest or surprise you—new developments, discoveries, or innovations, interesting people, topics, or stories that capture your attention, or that you would like to further explore—and by periodically reviewing that record, you can get a much better sense of where your interests lie, and the depth and scope of those interests.[80] In fact, over time, keeping a curiosity journal may help to uncover themes and patterns of interest, revealing hidden passions that you might not otherwise discover.[81]

(4.) Schedule Time to Follow Your Curiosity Wherever It May Roam.

To further cultivate curiosity, one of the most productive approaches is to intentionally block off time to let your curiosity roam. When Leonardo Da Vinci began pursuing his interest in human anatomy, he took a number of extraordinary steps to better understand the human form and how it worked, including dissecting cadavers. But he also scheduled time to do it. One of the entries in his notebook, for example, reads as follows: "Go every Saturday to the hot bath where you will see naked men."[82] Commenting on this "oddest of all...entry," Da Vinci biographer Walter Isaacson asks, "We can imagine Leonardo wanting to do that, for reasons both anatomical and aesthetic. But did he really need to remind himself to do it?"[83] Evidently, yes, even Leonardo Da Vinci—described by art historian Kenneth Clark as "the most relentlessly curious man in history"—needed to *schedule time* to let his curiosity roam.[84]

This undoubtedly makes perfect sense to people who are extremely busy. As important as it is to cultivate curiosity, we can all imagine more urgent matters clamoring for our time. Nevertheless, for the strategist, carving out time to follow your curiosity, particularly along the lines of inquiry concentrated around your vision and goals, can pay enormous dividends in the end.

(5.) Reap the Returns of Quality Questions.

"The power to question is the basis of all human progress."[85]
—Indira Gandhi, First Female Prime Minister of India (1966—1977, 1980—1984)

A telling sign of a curious mind, thoughtful questions can also help to awaken curiosity or deepen interest, particularly when unexpected answers lead you in the direction of your needs, interests, or goals. In the case of Leonardo Da Vinci, his notebooks are filled with lists of questions he planned to ask others. "...Ask Maestro Giovannino as to the mode in which the tower of Ferrara is walled without loopholes..."[86] "Ask Maestro Antonio how mortars are placed on bastions...Ask Benedetto Portinari [an agent of the Medici bank] how the people go on the ice in Flanders..."[87] And he often sought out the person most knowledgeable about each particular topic. "Get the master of mathematics to show you how to square a triangle," writes Da Vinci; "find a master of hydraulics and get him to tell you how to repair, and the costs of repair of a lock, canal and mill in the Lombard manner."[88]

Provided you take time to critically reflect on the possible answers, stopping to ask yourself clear, calculated questions can also stir curiosity and increase interest. Nevertheless, whether you look to yourself or others, "the important thing," said Einstein, "is to not stop questioning. Curiosity has its own reason for existing."[89]

This is also where knowing what you don't know can be especially useful, better enabling you to ask better questions, which is "the first step to getting better answers."[90] As Sir Francis Bacon put it, "a prudent question is one-half of wisdom."[91]

In fact, in many cases, to get to the best questions and, therefore, the best answers, requires beginning with "thoroughly conscious ignorance." Wisdom begins with knowing what you don't know. As management authority Peter Drucker once confessed, "My greatest strength as a consultant is to be ignorant and ask a few questions."[92]

Being "thoroughly conscious" of what she did not know and continuing to ask thoughtful questions were key parts of what set the pioneering physicist and chemist Marie Curie apart from the pack. Never content to merely wonder, her "insatiable curiosity" drove her to "work late into the night" confronting the unknown through relentless questioning.[93] Intrigued by the discovery of Becquerel rays, Curie began by asking herself if other elements might have measurable rays of energy as well. She then proceeded to examine and measure "all the elements then known, either in their pure state or in compounds,"[94] coining the term radioactivity in the process, and setting the stage for the field of atomic science.

As her daughter, French journalist Ève Curie wrote in her critically acclaimed book, *Madame Curie*, "Curiosity...the first virtue of a scientist, was developed in Marie to the highest degree. Instead of limiting her observation to simple compounds, salts and oxides, she had the desire to assemble samples of minerals from the collection at the School of Physics, and of making them undergo almost at hazard, for her own amusement, a kind of customs inspection..."[95]

This new method of discovering elements may well have been Marie Curie's greatest contribution, but the fruits of her relentless questioning did not end here. After mapping out "not only simple compounds, salts and oxides, but also a great number of minerals," she was still unable to explain the abnormal radioactivity of "certain ores containing uranium and thorium" which she said, "was much greater than...I had been led to expect."[96]

"At the crossroads where Marie now stood, hundreds of research workers might have remained, nonplussed, for months or even years."[97] No doubt, "after examining all known chemical substances," many "would have continued to ask themselves in vain whence came this mysterious radioactivity. Marie, too, questioned and wondered."[98]

Rather than surrendering to the seemingly impossible mystery, however, she started asking herself different questions, better questions, questions now informed by a much clearer understanding of what was known and unknown about the elements, about radiation and the atom. The better questions she asked, the more the answers she discovered further fueled her curiosity. "She had used up all evident possibilities. Now she turned toward the un-plumbed and the unknown."[99]

"When I had assured myself that it was not due to an error in the experiment," she said, "it became necessary to find an explanation. I then made the hypothesis that the ores of uranium and thorium contain in small quantity a substance much more strongly radioactive than either uranium or thorium itself. This substance could not be one of the known elements, because these had already been examined; it must, therefore, be a new chemical element."[100]

Working at a feverish pace, she soon discovered not one, but two new elements—Polonium, which she named for her home country of Poland, and Radium. In 1903, jointly awarded to her husband, Pierre Curie, and Henri Becquerel, Marie Curie became the first *woman* to win the Nobel Prize in Physics. When she won the Nobel Prize in Chemistry in 1911, she became the first *person* to receive the Noble Prize *twice*. "In the next decade,", largely thanks to Marie Curie's work, which shifted the paradigm of the atom as "indivisible" (the original meaning of the word *atom*), "scientists who located the source and composition of radioactivity made more discoveries concerning the atom and its structure than in all the centuries that had gone before."[101]

(6.) *Immerse Yourself in New and Diverse Worlds.*

Humans are creatures of habit. Most everyone has a tendency to slip into and drift along in the bubble of family, friends, and colleagues with which we surround ourselves, and some limited number of particular places we like to go. This is often especially true for leaders who are also surrounded by gatekeepers, security staff, and any number of key personnel or insiders which can easily consume any leftover scraps of the leader's limited time.

The most infamous example is the presidential bubble, a tightly controlled network of people, communications, and transportation systems that surround and protect presidents, enabling them to move freely (within the bubble) around the world.[102]

While they may help make us efficient and keep us safe, the problem with bubbles is that they cut us off from new people and experiences, limiting our awareness of the rest of the world, leading to a sort of cloistered echo chamber. Particularly for powerful leaders like A-list celebrities, presidents, and CEOs, these bubbles ensure that "you're surrounded by people who are pre-screened and see the world the way you do."[103] This is what led President Harry Truman to call the White House "the great white jail,"[104] and the sociable Bill Clinton to describe the Oval Office as the "the crown jewel of the federal penal system."[105]

Getting outside of this bubble can be a challenge; as President Obama's communications director Anita Dunn said, "Presidents have to work to stay in touch. That's a very real challenge of the job."[106] As President Clinton explained soon after winning the presidency in 1992, "Goodness knows my life is more restricted now than ever before," but, he said, "you can't let the security bubble shut you down. I mean, it's hard enough to stay in touch with people as it is…but there, where most people assume they should not see the president…you could just live your whole life in that bubble. I mean, you live in the White House, you just go to Camp David where there's nobody else and you go around in an armored car and you fly in Air Force One…"[107]

There is significant value in being exposed to different people, places, and ideas. This is especially true for strategists and, in fact, all those who rely on creative, innovative, or divergent thinking to one degree or another. Finding ways to get outside of the bubble, to submerge yourself in new and diverse worlds can help leaders stay grounded and informed, but it can also help stir curiosity and stimulate learning and growth.

Abraham Lincoln kept an open-door policy for these precise purposes. "For myself," he said regarding his open office hours, "I feel—though the tax on my time is heavy—that no hours of my day are better employed than those which thus bring me again within the direct contact and atmosphere of the average of our whole people."[108]

Faced with a somewhat overwhelming, "heterogeneous crowd of men and women, representing all ranks and classes,"[109] Lincoln eventually curtailed the sessions to two, three-hour sessions per week (i.e. *six hours a week*—can you imagine the President of the United States dedicating such time to meeting with everyday Americans?), and he remained committed to the practice, insisting that his open office hours "serve to renew in me a clearer and more vivid image of that great popular assemblage out of which I sprung. I tell you," he said to Major Hay, who was questioning the wisdom of the practice, "that I call these receptions my 'public opinion baths,'"[110] and, furthermore, he added that the effect on him was both "renovating and invigorating."[111]

In the case of Kublai Khan, his mother, Sorghaghtani, was a practicing Christian who understood the value of learning about the diverse worlds of the Mongol empire. "Sorghaghtani ensured Kublai was taught Mongol traditions. She encouraged toleration of other faiths, including Islam, and employed Chinese tutors so that Kublai could learn the local traditions and the foundations of Buddhism and Taoism."[112]

When he came to power, in order to effectively rule his vast multinational empire, Kublai Khan filled his government with a rich diversity of appointees. "He appointed former nomads and Muslims from Central Asia, the Middle East, and even Europeans to positions of power."[113] Kublai also collaborated with Persian Muslims, including Moiz al-Din, "who proposed the creation of the Persian Academy, to educate interpreters. The astronomer Jamal al-Din developed a new calendar for Kublai in 1267, and provided the Mongol state with astronomical instruments such as an astrolabe and an armillary sphere."[114]

Kublai also took a strong interest in Tibetan Buddhism, and he "appointed several lamas, Buddhist priests of Tibet, to direct religious affairs in China."[115]

Europeans also gained some significant influence within Kublai's court, including Marco Polo, who "was sent by Kublai on many missions throughout Asia…"[116] Marco Polo, in fact, became a sort of "roving ambassador."[117]

This practice of surrounding himself with representatives of these diverse worlds not only helped him to better understand the many different needs and interests of his realm and, further, "gratify...his curiosity."[118] By hearing from his officials "all the gossip and detail of the manners and customs of faraway places," by reading the "extensive notes of everything [they] saw and heard," it also helped to further *cultivate* his curiosity and sustain his interest in their plight.[119]

If you cannot travel or visit new places, try bringing new people and places to you. At the very least, surround yourself with curious people, and immerse yourself in their mental worlds. This helps explain why Marco Polo was so valuable to Kublai Khan. He was not only from another world, but he was also exceptionally curious himself, a double win for Kublai.

You can also immerse yourself in the world of other curious people. As leadership authority John Maxwell writes, "Being around people with great curiosity is contagious. I know of few better ways of cultivating and sustaining curiosity."[120]

Of course you don't have to travel, or socialize with diverse people to immerse yourself in diverse worlds. It is easy to become oblivious to our surroundings, but if you are mindful and alert you will notice rich new worlds all around. "One cannot help but be in awe when one contemplates the mysteries of eternity, of life," Einstein once said, "of the marvelous structure of reality."[121] "It is enough if one tries merely to comprehend a little of this mystery each day. Never," Einstein concluded, "lose a holy curiosity."[122]

(7.) Discover Your Source of Inspiration.

Finally, you can further cultivate your curiosity by identifying a source or wellspring you can return to over and again for inspiration, stimulation, and renewal. In the case of Leonardo da Vinci, he found an endless supply of inspiration in nature, and the mysteries of nature never ceased to stir his curiosity.

Albert Einstein, similarly, was in awe of the world. He marveled at mysteries, but he also marveled at the more familiar, those concepts that, as he put it, "the ordinary adult never bothers his head about."[123] In the words of the great French mathematician Blaise Pascal, "Small minds are concerned with the extraordinary, great minds with the ordinary."[124] To put it differently, what most people see as ordinary can actually be extraordinary if you can just learn to see it in a new way. This practice is known as *defamiliarization* and Leo Tolstoy's use of it heightened interest in his writing (Rather than defaulting to customary names for familiar objects, Tolstoy essentially used a distorted perspective to make the ordinary seem strange.).[125]

As useful as this mental maneuvering can be, the world is strange and interesting enough if you just get past the superficial, look below the surface, go deeper and explore. Nature, history, science, psychology, people, sports, music, architecture, art, sometimes simply submerging yourself in an area you find inspiring can help fuel your curiosity and stir your sense of wonder and discovery. But don't stop there. Follow the lead of Leonardo and Einstein, Curie and Kublai, and look deeper into the well. Investigate what about it inspires you. What questions does it elicit? How might you begin to more intentionally explore this area in greater detail? How might you tie it back to your work or your purpose, strategy, and goals?

You may also find that the greatest source of inspiration or means of triggering your curiosity will vary depending on your specific project, area, or job. When Walter Isaacson set out to write a biography of Leonardo da Vinci, he found himself drawn to Leonardo's journals, some 7,200 pages of "glorious notebooks," each volume famously "rich in maps, doodles, anatomical drawings, schema for new machines, models for new weapons, proposals for city redesigns, geometric patterns, portraits...[and] scientific observations of uncanny prescience."[126] Both inspired and curious, Isaacson soon began making what he calls "pilgrimages" so that he could "see the originals in Milan, Florence, Paris, Seattle, Madrid, London, and Windsor Castle,"[127] but also because he was compelled by what he calls "Leonardo's injunction":[128] This idea of going back to the source was both one of the secrets of Da Vinci's mastery, and a fountainhead for his unquenchable curiosity. As Da Vinci himself said, "He who can go to the fountain does not go to the water-jar."[129]

Counter-Punch: Bridle Your Curiosity.

Curiosity is a critical strength for the strategist. And it can be cultivated. But it must also be concentrated, checked, and refined. There are limits to how far and wide you can effectively let your curiosity roam before it begins to undermine your chief purpose and goals. As *Harvard Business Review* put it, "unbounded curiosity can lead you astray...You may get drawn down a rabbit hole and lose sight of your original purpose."[130]

Leonardo da Vinci's 1498 painting, *The Last Supper*, is a case in point. This mural painting of Jesus sharing his last meal with his apostles in Jerusalem eventually deteriorated into a disaster because Da Vinci could not reign in his unquenchable hunger to experiment and explore. Rather than using the proven fresco techniques of the period, Da Vinci's curiosity about different painting techniques ensured that *The Last Supper* would begin to flake and deteriorate in less than twenty years. By 1532, Italian polymath Gerolamo Cardano described it as "blurred and colorless compared with what I remember of it when I saw it as a boy."[131] As a result, we will never see the full, authentic glory of *The Last Supper*.[132]

As unmistakably brilliant as he was, as much as his brilliance was nurtured by his curiosity, his inability to keep it in check also came at a cost. Too often Da Vinci was more interested in learning about new things than getting the job done. His unrelenting inquisitiveness frequently derailed his success. "He irked his patrons with incessant delays, and many of his works went unfinished, including "The Adoration of the Magi" and "The Virgin and Child With Saint

Anne." Scholars have attributed this to his exuberance for new subjects and his perfectionism. It was also because the challenge of doing outweighed the expectation of getting it done. For Leonardo, it's all about process, says Carmen Bambach, curator of drawings and prints at the Metropolitan Museum of Art in New York. "It's not really about the endgame.""[133] "He was an inveterate deadline misser, more beguiled by starting projects than finishing them. He abandoned a 23-foot equestrian statue intended for a prince; he gave up on paintings and murals intended for wealthy patrons; he sketched 'flying machines that never flew, tanks that never rolled, a river that was never diverted.'"[134]

There is a reason that many of the oldest stories about curiosity are intended as warnings. In Greek mythology, curiosity drives Pandora to open what became known as "Pandora's box," unleashing untold curses on humankind. Unable to control their curiosity, Adam and Eve are tempted into taking a bite of the forbidden fruit, leading to untold hardships for humankind. Greek mythology also tells of how men, unable to control their curiosity, are turned into stone for stealing a glance at the monstrous, but mesmerizing Medusa and the live, venomous snakes that had replaced her hair. In Genesis, God instructed Lot and his fleeing family not to look back on Sodom as the city was destroyed for its unrepentant pride, greed, rape, and murder. Alas, overcome with curiosity, Lot's wife looked back and was instantly turned into a pillar of salt.

Clearly, curiosity "doesn't like rules," writes Leslie, "or, at least, it assumes that all rules are provisional, subject to the laceration of a smart question nobody has yet thought to ask. It disdains the approved pathways, preferring diversions, unplanned excursions, impulsive left turns. In short, curiosity is deviant. Pursuing it is liable to bring you into conflict with authority at some point, as everyone from Galileo to Charles Darwin to Steve Jobs could have attested."[135]

But these stories are about something more than curiosity. There are also elements of pride and losing site or one's priorities and purpose.

No doubt, the story of the fall of Icarus was, in part, about his curiosity and desire to experiment and explore. But it was also about the hubris of ignoring the desperate warnings of his father, and the shortsightedness of putting in jeopardy their primary purpose—making it safely away from the labyrinth of King Minos and the man-eating Minotaur.

The tragic myth of Orpheus tells of how he attempted to rescue his lost wife, Eurydice, from the Underworld. After playing the most beautiful melody, Pluto agreed that Orpheus could take Eurydice back on one condition, that he not gaze upon her even once until they were completely out of the Underworld and back in the light. Mere steps away from successfully rescuing his wife—his one and only purpose in life ever since she had been taken—curiosity overcame him. Suddenly, the Roman poet Ovid writes in *Metamorphoses*, "When in fear he might again lose her, and anxious for another look at her, he turned his eyes so he could gaze upon her. Instantly she slipped away. He stretched out to her his despairing arms, eager to rescue her, or feel her form, but could hold nothing save the yielding air."[136]

Do not misunderstand: The moral of these stories is not about the inherently evil or secretly sinful nature of curiosity. In fact, for the strategist, curiosity is key. The highly influential Saint Augustine was sadly mistaken when he claimed that "God fashioned hell for the inquisitive,"[137] as was the humanist philosopher Erasmus when he referred to curiosity as just another form of greed.[138]

In contrast, the moral of these stories is about purpose and priorities, self-discipline and self-control. The message for the strategist is to actively cultivate and nurture curiosity, but to keep it focused and centered around your chief purpose and goals.

Likewise, the lesson the strategist learns from Leonardo is not to kill curiosity, quite the opposite. As Walter Isaacson writes in his biography of Da Vinci, "Above all, Leonardo's relentless curiosity and experimentation should remind us of the importance of instilling, in both ourselves and our children, not just received knowledge but a willingness to question it—to be imaginative and, like talented misfits and rebels in any era, to think different."[139]

It was this more than anything that drew Kublai Khan to Marco Polo and it is what led to their 24-year-long connection, "one of history's great encounters between East and West."[140] For his own part, Kublai Khan found Marco Polo's ability to capture and convey the information and insights he gathered so useful that it was not until 1291, twenty years after leaving Venice, that Kublai Khan at last granted Marco Polo permission to embark on a final journey, accompanying the Mongol princess Kököchin to Persia to be married, after which he would be permitted to return home. Less than 3 years later the depressed and ailing Kublai Khan died at the age of 78.

Meanwhile, Marco Polo's writings spawned a new generation of explorers. Many travelers were inspired to follow in his footsteps, some even retraced his journey to China "bringing back yet more information on these lands. This knowledge fueled a growing curiosity about the world as Europe moved into the Renaissance and the age of discovery toward the end of the 1400s. Better navigation enabled eastward as well as westward trade in that feverish period of exploration."[141]

Finally, in 1324, on his deathbed, still being pressed to confess what some considered his many exaggerations, if not outright falsifications, Marco Polo remained firm. In fact, he said, "I have not written down the half of those things which I saw!"[142]

Throughout history, in business, politics, statecraft, and war, the great strategists have virtually all been marked by unquenchable curiosity. Curiosity is key to learning and development. It is the precursor to discovery and insight, invention and innovation. And, ultimately, curiosity is the key to wisdom, growth, progress and change. To become a master strategist, cultivate a spirit of curiosity, and a hunger for understanding and wisdom. Practice indulging your curiosity. Become your own personal private investigator. Survey and assess your environment. Allow yourself to be driven by bold inquiry. Develop your skills as a researcher, and a passion for relentless trial and error. Learn to ask better questions, and listen far more than you speak. Question your assumptions. Test your theories. Research. Investigate. Explore. Be hungry to learn all that you can and watch how curiosity opens up the possibilities of your world.

REAP THE WISDOM OF HISTORY: PROFIT FROM THE POWER OF THE PAST TO INFLUENCE THE FUTURE

"The great thing about history is that....it can stand in for personal experience. Most of all, thinking historically accustoms the mind to critical analysis." [1]
—Andrew R. Wilson, *Masters of War: History's Greatest Strategic Thinkers*

"Strategists are able to see the past, present and future as connected." [2]
—Max McKeown, *The Strategy Book*

TAP THE POWER OF HISTORY TO ILLUMINATE, ILLUSTRATE, AND INSPIRE: ALEXANDER THE GREAT EMULATES THE GREEK LEGENDS, HEROES AND MYTHS

"To be ignorant of the lives of the most celebrated men of antiquity is to continue in a state of childhood all our days." [3]
—Plutarch (46-119A.D.), Ancient Greek Historian

Alexander III of Macedon was determined to be the first to set foot on this new land. The moment his ship beached, dressed in full armor, Alexander leapt over the side, waded through the shorebreak, and then threw his spear into the dry sand. Claiming ownership of the continent, he cried out, "From the gods I accept Asia, won by the spear." [4]

It was May 334 B.C., and Alexander's flotilla of some 60 warships had just crossed the Hellespont (known today as the Dardanelles), the dividing line between the continents of Europe and Asia. They had landed at the same spot where Alexander believed that Achilles, King Agamemnon and his fleet of Greek ships had landed centuries earlier during the Trojan War. [5]

Claiming to have "won" Asia was clearly a cocky, symbolic play. After all, he had yet to win a single battle on the continent of Asia. [6] Nevertheless, after subduing the rebellious Greek city-states following his father's assassination, Alexander, not yet 22 years old, was now the undisputed leader of the Greeks. What's more, he was now leading an army totaling some 65,000 men. [7]

Rather than consisting entirely of Macedonians, however, Alexander's army was a fragile federation of forces from across the Greek city-states, some of which, only months earlier, had taken part in rebellions against his leadership. Furthermore, many of the men looked down on Macedonians, believing them to be barbarians from the north, and not true Greeks.

The lack of unity and camaraderie amongst the troops was cause for concern. Indeed, some of Alexander's friends thought he was starting his military campaign against the Persians far too early, and with insufficient support. "...Many Macedonian aristocrats had tried to dissuade him from invading Asia. They were convinced that the best course of action was to remain in Macedon, for now, to solidify his hold over Greece and the Balkans and to ensure that recent troubles would not rear their heads again. But Alexander would not be deterred."[8]

Despite his decision to embark at once, however, he was aware that his "troops had very little in common with each other," or so they believed; he also knew he needed a means to bind them together in "a meaningful, commonly held purpose."[9]

Eager to get underway, and given his considerable military acumen, along with his deep sense of self-belief, Alexander might simply have sought to rely on victory in battle—and, without a doubt, winning can be incredibly inspiring and unifying.[10] And, yet, it is often morale which determines who wins. As Napoleon Bonaparte said, "An army's effectiveness depends on its size, training, experience, and morale, and morale is worth more than any of the other factors combined."[11]

Consequently, rather than launching headlong into battle, to unify his men, and, moreover, to help shape their collective identity and common purpose, Alexander first turned to history.

It was no accident that they were landing in the same place where the Greeks had landed during the Trojan War. The detour to the legendary city of Troy was more than just a "deeply felt pilgrimage."[12] It was a masterstroke of leadership. It was the beginning of Alexander's transformation from a "barbarian" to the "New Achilles." It was the beginning of his army's transformation from a fragile federation of Greek forces to a unified body engaged in the "New Trojan War," committed to destroying their shared enemy, the Persians, and conquering the known world.

After landing on the coast, Alexander took his troops on a tour of the legendary city of Troy and the stone sepulcher of Achilles, where Alexander left a commemorative wreath on the fallen hero's tomb. Then, reflecting the tone and manner of the Olympic Games, Alexander stripped naked, covered himself in olive oil, and ran circles around Achilles' memorial. "It was a remarkable tribute, uniquely paid," writes historian Robin Lane Fox.[13] "The symbolism of this action would not have been lost on any who witnessed it. A new Achilles had come to Troy, one who believed himself to be descended from the great hero on his mother's side and one who had every intention of seeing the great cities of Asia fall before him as they had to his ancestor."[14]

To truly grasp the import of Alexander's actions in Troy, you have to understand the context in which he was operating. "Homer's poems were widely known in Macedonia."[15] In fact, Homer's *Iliad* and *Odyssey* were *cornerstones* of classical Greek education, and Alexander and his peers were "deeply immersed"[16] in these works. They would often quote from Homer as a kind of shorthand,[17] some fluently and at length.[18] What's more, explains Indian management consultant Partha Bose, "So steeped did the boys get in the Greek classics that even their actions in battle would resemble episodes from the great works."[19] More to the point, in Homer's "world of heroes...no figure [was] more compelling than...Achilles..."[20] Achilles stood out above all. All young Greeks had heard of his heroic exploits, and, no doubt, many young men hoped to one day emulate his actions.

Alexander's next stop was to pay his respects to the goddess Athena. This too echoed the actions of Achilles. Inside the Temple of Athena, Alexander removed his armor, and "offered it as a gift to the goddess. On the temple walls were a shield and armor that Achilles had reportedly worn. Alexander, with the utmost respect, peeled these and other [trappings] off the walls and handed them to a bodyguard to carry."[21] "Homer's Achilles, too, had received divine armor of his own before going out to battle, none more famous than his shield..."[22] From that point forward, Achilles' sacred armor would be carried into battle for Alexander.[23] "...All the better to make clear who he was and whom he emulated and revered."[24]

Alexander's final stop was the altar of Zeus where "the theme of the new Achilles was stressed [yet] again."[25] "Alexander sacrificed and prayed to Priam, legendary king of Troy, begging him to stay his anger from this new descendant..." of Achilles.[26]

"Throughout," his tour of Troy, "Alexander's purpose was written large in his detailed behavior."[27] "Alexander's visit...turned on a link with the Trojan war and, above all, in its every tribute it had evoked the hero Achilles, his fellow seeker for fame and glory."[28] "Alexander was already seeing himself as a young Achilles and intended his invasion to put him on a par with the Homeric warriors—a desire that underscored many of his personally risky actions in Asia."[29]

Beyond Achilles, Alexander also went to some length "to spin the invasion of Persia as a new Trojan War, which had been immortalized in Homer's *The Iliad*."[30] Indeed, dating back long before the births of Alexander and his father, Philip, "the Trojan War had been cited by Herodotus as the first cause of the ancient enmity between Greece and Asia's monarchies..."[31] "...In Philip's highland Macedonia, pottery has been found painted with scenes of the sack of Troy."[32] What's more, "Philip had already been compared with King Agamemnon, leader of the Greek allies who fought for ten years round Troy, and the style of his infantry was likened to Agamemnon's..."[33]

In short, Fox writes, "past history bore witness that...the Trojan War [was a] worthwhile theme...for a Greek invader of Asia to evoke and imitate."[34] "The mythic link was clear: Like the Greeks in *The Iliad* who resolved to burn Troy to ashes, and did so, with the help of Achilles, the invincible Greek warrior, the Macedonians and Greeks would seek vengeance on Persia for its 150 years of wars against Greece."[35]

At the end of their tour, Alexander met with a seer who reported that the goddess Athena said she would assist Alexander in the upcoming battle against the Persians. This too echoed their shared history. As Bose writes in his book, *Alexander the Great's Art of Strategy*, "The constant subliminal or even direct connections to Homer's *Iliad*, which most of his troops would have read, were impressive. Achilles' final victory over the greatest of the Trojan warriors, Hector, in *The Iliad* was made possible only by the intervention and manipulation of the goddess Athena."[36] Now, Athena was promising to give victory to Alexander, and his "gathered troops cheered such portentous omens."[37]

Along with boosting morale and cultivating camaraderie among the men, Alexander's trip to Troy proved to be a lasting inspiration.[38] With the troops increasingly unified by their shared vision and values, increasingly loyal to the leadership of the New Achilles, Alexander was now more ready than ever to lead his army into the first battle of the New Trojan War.

Days later, after marching from Troy to the Granicus River, the Greeks encountered the forces of Darius III's Persian satraps for the first time. Holding the advantage of being positioned on higher ground on the opposite river bank, the Persians waited for the Greeks to attempt to cross. Wasting no time, and disregarding the advice of his generals, Alexander and his army quickly plunged into the water and across the river. According to the ancient Greek historians Arrian and Plutarch, Alexander had Achilles' shield and armor carried into the battle.[39]

After a feint from the left, Alexander, always at the front, led the cavalry charge directly into the center of the Persian line. As the center collapsed, both of the Persian flanks retreated. With Greek losses totaling some 300 to 400 men to the Persians 4,000 men, Alexander's first battle in Asia, the Battle of Granicus, was a decisive triumph.[40] His next battle against the Persians a year and a half later, the Battle of Issus, proved to be an even more humiliating defeat for Darius. Alexander was already leveling up to the legend of his hero, Achilles.

Gain Vicarious Experience, Knowledge, and Wisdom

Recognition of the vital importance of history can be traced back to our earliest ancestors. In his celebrated book, *The Histories*, the great ancient Greek historian Polybius writes, "the knowledge gained from the study of true history is the best of all educations for practical life."[41] A favorite of America's Founders, as well as Renaissance thinkers such as Niccolò Machiavelli, Polybius also argued that, "the soundest education and training for a life of active politics is the study of History."[42]

At Harvard's John F. Kennedy School of Government, professors Richard Neustadt and Ernest May taught a course on the power of history for decision-makers. Out of that popular, long-running course came a text in which Neustadt and May summarize the driving rationale and purpose behind the course, "Vicarious experience acquired from the past, even the remote past," they write, "gives such guidance to the present that history becomes more than its own reward. Knowledge conveys wisdom; ignorance courts trouble. Persons of good sense," they continue, "are bound to study history in sheer self-interest, reaching out for reference points of likely future relevance and cramming in vicarious experience from each."[43]

Tap the Accumulated Wisdom of History, a Distinguishing Factor of Our Evolutionary Success.

The ability to learn from and build on the lessons learned from the past, to accumulate the knowledge and wisdom gained from our predecessors, is one of the key factors that differentiates us from every other species on Earth. What's more, as Duke University professor of neuroscience Brian Hare explains, this is a critical part of what enabled *homo sapiens* to beat out the other species of *humans* (including Neanderthals and homo erectus), some of which were bigger, and had bigger brains. In their book, *Survival of the Friendliest*, Hare and co-author Vanessa Woods write, "What allowed us to thrive while other humans went extinct was a kind of cognitive superpower: a particular type of friendliness called cooperative communication."[44] "We are experts at working together with other people, even strangers. We can communicate with someone we've never met about a shared goal and work together to accomplish it."[45] Not only does this allow us to "synchronize [our] behavior," and "coordinate different roles," but it also allows us to "pass on [our] innovations."[46] "We develop all of these skills before we can walk or talk, and," Hare and Woods conclude, "they are the gateway to a sophisticated social and cultural world. *They allow us to plug our minds into the minds of others and inherit the knowledge of generations.*"[47][e.a.]

It would be foolish not to take full advantage of this vast generational knowledge, the collected wisdom of history. As Harvard philosophy professor George Santayana reminds us, 'to fail to know history is to doom yourself to repeat its mistakes.'[48]

Draw on History to Identify, Illuminate, and Inspire

In one of Aesop's *Fables*, "The Lion, the Fox, and the Beasts,"[49] he writes of the lion who had a long history of projecting strength and power, taking his food by force, but who had now become too old, weak, and slow to hunt. The lion determined that he would have to use artifice to eat, tricks and ploys to trap his prey. He soon made it publicly known that he was sick. The other animals felt sorry for the great, majestic beast and, one by one, they went to his den to check up on him, only to immediately disappear.

Before long, the short but strange history of disappearing animals caught the attention of the inquisitive fox. Curious as to where the other animals had gone, the fox went to check up on the lion. As he cautiously approached the lion's den, however, he noticed that there were many different hoofprints and pawprints going into the lion's den. He then stopped and studied the prints and quickly realized that not one set of animal tracks could be traced back out.

Still lying down pretending to be sick, when the lion noticed the fox standing outside the entrance, he called out to him, "Hello, old friend. You are so kind to come check up on me. But why do you stand out there, why not come in and chat?" But the clever fox, now hip to the ploy, resolved to expose his devious old friend. He shouted back, "I see that many animals have made their way in to visit you, but I will tell the others that not one has come back out." With that, the lion leapt up as fast as his old bones would allow, hoping to devour the fox before he could expose the trap. But it was too late. The curious and clever fox was too quick for the old lion to cover the distance, and he saved the lives of his friends in the forest as a result.

In his infamous political treatise, *The Prince*, Niccolò Machiavelli describes how leaders must be capable of acting as both the lion and the fox, but the prince must also, he writes, "understand how to avail himself of the beast and the man."[50] "...Half beast and half man...it is necessary for a prince to know how to make use of both natures," Machiavelli writes, "and that one without the other is not durable. A prince...being compelled knowingly to adopt the beast, ought to choose the fox and the lion...a fox to discover the snares and a lion to terrify the wolves."[51]

We can extend Machiavelli's metaphor to Alexander who, in a sense, used history as both man and beast and, as beast, both lion and fox. As a man, he used history as a resource for identifying and reinforcing his identity and ideals. But he also used history as a tool he could wield for strength and power, like the lion, as well as to navigate the world and outfox his opponents.

History for the Man: Identify Your Heroic Ideals.

"Lives of great men all remind us
We can make our lives sublime,

And, departing, leave behind us

Footprints on the sands of time..."
—Henry Wadsworth Longfellow, "A Psalm of Life"

Alexander's visit to Troy was no mere passing amusement. In fact, writes Oxford historian Robin Lane Fox, "no gesture could speak more clearly of his personal ideals."[52] "In all Alexander's career," Fox adds, "there is no behavior more memorable, none more eloquent of his personal ideals."[53]

But it was also an act of leadership. Through these carefully orchestrated actions, Alexander was linking his ideals with those of his troops. He was drawing on more than a common history to strengthen their common bonds, but a deeply shared history with shared heroes and shared values, and a common enemy. This, in essence, was a history that cut to the heart of their identity as Greeks. This seemingly simple detour to Troy provided a deeper sense of who they were, what they were about, and how they would go about it.

Now, together in a new land, rather than seeing him as a barbarian from the north, Alexander's troops could easily identify with him, and, importantly, his sacred, historical vision for their campaign. They were about to face a fierce enemy—indeed, what at the time was "the mightiest empire on earth"[54]—and despite whatever differences they had back home, they would now operate as one.

Establish Your Heroic Ideal, Use It to Shape Your Future. The German philosopher Friedrich Nietzsche argued that "history belongs above all to the man of deeds and power, to him who fights a great fight, who needs models, teachers, consolers and cannot find them among his contemporaries."[55] As we learn from the example of leaders like Alexander the Great, Julius Caesar, Napoleon Bonaparte, and countless others, looking to the leaders of the past can serve as a valuable guide, a powerful source of inspiration, identification, and illumination. Their stories remind us that even the great leaders—perhaps, as Nietzsche argued, *especially* the great leaders—need the heroes of history.

In Alexander's case, one of the key takeaways from this early episode in his life is the power of a compelling identity and self-concept, and how you can draw on the heroes of history to shape and reinforce your identity and ideals, as well as the shared identity and ideals of those you lead, but also how this can help shape your shared future as a result. "Whom we admire, openly," writes management consultant Lance Kurke, "speaks *volumes* about us. It helps establish our identity (i.e., who we are)."[56] Who you are and how you see yourself will then effect what actions you take and, in turn, how others see you, and, ultimately, what results you achieve.

Read, Study, and Learn from Your Heroic Ideals. "Everyone needs a hero, even heroic figures such as Alexander,"[57] who looked not only to Achilles, but, as we'll explore below, a number of other legendary and even mythical figures from history. "Alexander," in turn, "was hero to Caesar, Augustus, Napoleon, Frederick the Great, Louis the XIV (the Sun King), and untold others."[58]

The real value, however, is not simply in identifying those figures whom you most admire. The real value is in studying and learning from their lives, and, importantly, applying the wisdom you extract and the lessons you learn.

"Success leaves clues…If you want to achieve success," writes Anthony Robbins, "all you need to do is find a way to model those who have already succeeded."[59] This is where the stories of the legends and heroes of history can prove invaluable. From recent reporting, modern scholarship, and contemporary biographies to ancient manuscripts, historical records, and sacred texts; the stories of our predecessors in virtually every field offer powerful lessons, wisdom and insight, recurring patterns, and timeless principles and practices that you can still study, learn from, and apply today.[60]

Throughout recorded history, many of the classics bear witness to this endless quest to learn from the past—from Homer's epics and Plutarch's *Lives* to Herodotus' *Histories* and Machiavelli's *Prince*; from Carlyle's *Heroes and Hero Worship* to Emerson's *Representative Men*. "The search after the great man is the dream of youth and the most serious occupation of manhood," wrote Emerson.[61] "We travel into foreign parts to find his works, if possible, to get a glimpse of him."[62]

In Alexander's case, a lifelong student of history, his deep, abiding interest in the life and leadership of Achilles did not end with his visit to Troy. In fact, throughout his early campaign, Achilles and Homer's *Iliad* continued to serve as a resource guide and source of inspiration. Years earlier, Alexander's tutor, Aristotle, had created a personally annotated set of papyrus scrolls of the epic poem for Alexander as a gift.[63] Alexander kept this special copy of the *Iliad* "constantly at his bedside,"[64] and read from it "every night."[65] After the Battle of Issus in 333 B.C., he kept it in a gold chest, which was found among the personal effects of the fleeing, defeated Darius III.[66] "Indeed, he was so attached to it," writes Paul Cartledge, Professor of Greek Culture at Cambridge University, "that at night he allegedly slept with it—and a dagger—under his pillow."[67,68]

One of his own officers reports that Alexander called *The Iliad*, his "journey-book of excellence in war."[69] In historian Paul Johnson's book, *Heroes: From Alexander the Great and Julius Caesar to Churchill and de Gaulle*, he writes that Alexander "read Homer all his life and knew passages by heart. It was, to him, a Bible, a guide to heroic morality, a book of etiquette and a true adventure story."[70]

History for the Lion: Tap the Power of History to Motivate, Mobilize, and Inspire.

"Read Plutarch, and the world is a proud place peopled with men of positive quality, with heroes and demigods standing around us who will not let us sleep."[71]

—Ralph Waldo Emerson

Beyond helping to shape their shared identity and ideals, Alexander also looked to history as a source of motivation, inspiration, and power. While their "trip to Troy remained a lasting inspiration,"[72] Fox reports, Alexander nevertheless looked to a number of *other* legends and heroes from history as well, and he did not hesitate to evoke their names, or recall their accomplishments as a means of motivating and mobilizing his men. While Alexander's admiration for these heroes and legends was authentic, he also understood the need to publicly express his admiration and focus on certain figures at certain times and in such a way that would benefit him as the leader and king.[73]

When his situation or circumstances changed, he used other, more relevant role models to inspire. "Since Achilles never made it past Troy," writes Patrick Garvey of Ancient Heroes, "Achilles became a less useful symbol as his campaign took his army farther from Greece. In Africa and the East, the myths of the far-ranging Heracles and Dionysus became more relevant, both in the minds of Alexander and his soldiers. It is no surprise, then, that he invoked their stories more often."[74]

In one case, for example, after the Battle of the Hydaspes in 326 B.C., Alexander called to mind the exploits of Heracles, a divine hero in Greek mythology, known as Hercules in ancient Rome. The Greeks believed that Heracles was an actual historical figure, and Alexander even claimed to be a descendent of this paragon of heroism and masculinity.

By this time, several years into their historic military campaign, many of his soldiers were weary and began to yearn for home. The Battle of the Hydaspes, where they fought against scores of war elephants and hundreds of thousands of tough Indian soldiers proved to be a draining, Pyrrhic victory. Some historians argue that Alexander faced what amounted to a practical *mutiny*.

Alexander understood their concerns, and he empathized with his aged and disabled veterans. He had also "reached the eastern edge of the territories he had already laid claim to…"[75] At this point, historian Hugh Bowden argues, he was also beginning to focus on "the consolidation of his rule over the territory he had won from Darius III, rather than an endless quest for new conquests."[76]

Nevertheless, he was not ready to head back home yet. And, so, in an attempt to inspire his army to forge ahead, he delivered a speech in which he again turned to their shared history. "I observe, gentlemen, that when I lead you on a new venture you no longer follow me with your old spirit. I have asked you to meet me that we may come to a decision together: are we, upon my advice, to go forward, or, upon yours, to turn back? [...] Are you not aware," Alexander continued after citing their many accomplishments thus far, "that if Heracles, my ancestor, had gone no further than Tiryns or Argos—or even than the Peloponnese or Thebes—he could never have won the glory which changed him from a man into a god, actual or apparent? Even Dionysus, who is a god indeed, in a sense beyond what is applicable to Heracles, faced not a few laborious tasks; yet we have done more: we have passed beyond Nysa and we have taken the rock of Aornos which Heracles himself could not take."[77]

Inspired by what was clearly a remarkable run of historic victories, and satisfied that their concerns had been heard, the soldiers were resolved to stand by Alexander, who, for his own part, "was ready to turn south and march towards the ocean. He was not turning back homewards yet."[78]

<u>Expand Your Horizons, Move Yourself and Your Team to Achieve the Dream</u>. The lives and leadership of the legends and heroes of history can be a surprising source of motivation and inspiration. "We all know how completely

changed we sometimes are after reading a book which has taken a strong, vigorous hold upon us. Thousands of people have found themselves through the reading of some book, which has opened the door within them and given them the first glimpse of their possibilities. I know men and women," writes Orison Swett Marden, the founder of *Success* magazine, "whose whole lives have been molded, the entire trend of their careers completely changed, uplifted beyond their dreams by the books they have read."[79]

As was the case with Homer's *Iliad* and the Greeks, "there are books that have raised the ideals and materially influenced entire nations," Marden writes in *Pushing to the Front*. "Who can estimate the value of books that spur ambition, that awaken slumbering possibilities? Are we ambitious to associate with people who inspire us to nobler deeds? Let us then read uplifting books, which stir us to make the most of ourselves."[80]

Reading the biographies and autobiographies of the great men and women of the world can be a powerful, "perennial inspiration."[81] "We work largely from suggestion. High ideals and splendid models kept constantly before the mind become character makers, life-shapers. We must," therefore, Marden concludes, "learn through the old 'books' about 'men [and women] of higher stature, the only [ones] who speak aloud for future times to hear.'"[82]

<u>Use History to Overcome Obstacles, and Bolster Your Aims</u>. The legends and heroes of history can also be a potent source of energy and determination for dealing with difficulties, overcoming obstacles, and achieving ambitious aims. There are few things more inspiring than a soaring saga of high achievement in spite of immense challenges.[83] If you hope to make your mark on the world, saturate your mind with the inspiring stories of history's heroes. Nothing can take the place of the powerful life story of a great historic legend.[84] "Think of the influence of holding these inspiring models constantly in the mind, of having these magnificent characters actually living in the mind's gallery!"[85] Few things are as helpful as a continuous source of powerful, relevant inspiration, "nothing else will give this so effectively...nothing else will prove so ambition-rousing as the life-stories of those who have accomplished things under great difficulties."[86]

Particularly as a young man dealing with serious health issues and physical weakness, John F. Kennedy drew on the English politician and poet Lord Byron; not because of ancestry, but because of the many parallels—both strengths and weaknesses—he saw between himself and Byron. A close friend of President Kennedy's recalled how "he'd read everything about him and read most of the poetry too. There were a lot of similarities. Bryon too had that conflict between irony and romanticism; he too wanted the world to be better than it was; he also had the disability—the club foot—and the conviction of an early death; and most of all he had the hunger for women and the realization that the hunger was displaced, which led to a fedupness too."[87]

President Richard Nixon, on the other hand, chose role models based on action and ambition.[88] Despite his tragic flaws, Nixon was a visionary. He had an agenda. And he was eager to do great things. He desperately wanted to carve out a place for himself in history and when he read history, he looked to study leaders that could help him achieve his ambitions. Nixon looked to men like Theodore Roosevelt, Woodrow Wilson, Benjamin Disraeli and, above all, the French statesman Charles de Gaulle.

Along with acknowledging action hero John Wayne as a role model,[89] Ronald Reagan looked to the leadership of Franklin Roosevelt for inspiration. Reagan even admitted that he attempted to borrow and build on Roosevelt's style, confessing that "he had carefully studied Roosevelt's gestures and inflections and tried to make them his own."[90] Franklin Roosevelt looked to his distant cousin, Theodore Roosevelt, as a source of inspiration and a hero to emulate.[91] Theodore Roosevelt looked to Abraham Lincoln and George Washington as his personal heroes. Martin Luther King looked to Mahatma Gandhi and Henry David Thoreau, and, of course, as a pastor, the leadership of Jesus Christ. President Bill Clinton modeled himself after John F. Kennedy and Elvis Presley.

Winston Churchill drew inspiration and insight from his ancestor, the Duke of Marlborough. Diving deep into his study of Marlborough, Churchill even produced a 4-volume biography entitled *Marlborough: His Life and Times*, which the preeminent political philosopher Leo Strauss described in 1965, after hearing of the death of Churchill, as "the greatest historical work written in our century, an inexhaustible mine of political wisdom and understanding, which should be required reading for every student of political science."[92]

Russian Empress Catherine the Great's hero was Henry IV of France. She reportedly connected with his religious tolerance and how he put wise pragmatism over ideological dogmatism, but also his genuine concern for the welfare of his subjects.[93] Catherine also found considerable wisdom and inspiration in *Parallel Lives*, a series of 48 paired biographies of famous Greek and Roman leaders written by the ancient Greek historian Plutarch (c. 45—120 A.D.). "Catherine found endless guidance in it. Reading about the careers of those who had made their mark upon the world long before she made hers gave the empress both insight and comfort. She felt less alone as a leader."[94] In an April 1790 letter to her secretary, Alexander Khrapovitsky, Catherine said of Plutarch's *Parallel Lives*, "It fortifies my soul."[95] Catherine turned to Plutarch "particularly in times of crisis," Alan Axelrod explains, "as when Sweden's Gustav III brought war to her very doorstep in St. Petersburg in the spring of 1790. She did not seek escape in her reading, but rather inspiration in the experience of those who had ruled before her."[96]

The immense and inestimable wealth of experience of the acclaimed captains of antiquity awaits willingly in the pages of the past, a vast record of their stories echo across the ages with timeless wisdom and insights into human nature, lessons on leadership and strategy with compelling accounts of those men and women who have fallen from pride and folly.[97] Their power is filed away in the archives, ready to be discovered by those who are able to learn from the experience of others and who are willing to invest the time to do it. "You can slog through life, making endless mistakes, wasting time and energy trying to do things from your own experience. Or you can use the armies of the past," Robert Greene writes in *The 48 Laws of Power*.[98] "Who is wise?," asks Benjamin Franklin in his widely celebrated *Poor Richard's Almanac*, "He that learns from everyone."[99] Time is the most precious and scarce resource of all. You must take every reasonable step possible to quicken your efforts and leverage your time. Learn from and build on the ideas of others, honor and acknowledge them, and give credit when and where due, but do not endeavor to go it alone, or build on or borrow from just one. Your highest achievements and most daring dreams demand that you learn from, build on the pages of the past before you can hope to transform the future.

History for the Fox: Use the Past to Illuminate Your Future.

> *"When the past no longer illuminates the future, the spirit walks in darkness."*[100]
> —Alexis de Tocqueville

Finally, along with helping to shape their *shared identity* and *ideals*, as well as using history as a source of *inspiration*, Alexander also used history as a means of *illuminating the future*.

Using the past to help illuminate the future may be one of the most important ways of tapping the power of history. "Over two thousand years ago, Polybius, the soundest of ancient historians,"[101] argued that there is "no more ready corrective of conduct than knowledge of the past."[102] "We should," Polybius wrote in his celebrated work, *The Histories*, "regard as the best discipline for actual life the experience that accrues from serious history; for this alone makes us, without inflicting any harm on us, the most competent judges of what is best at every time and in every circumstance."[103]

Learn from Both the Successes and Failures, the Sinners and Saints. As surprisingly useful as it is to identify a few worthy role models in your chosen field, it is important to learn from both their successes as well as their failures. Balanced alongside their successes, learning from the misfortunes, miscalculations, and mistakes of history's heroes can help keep you grounded, inspire you to persevere, or bring some much needed perspective. As the ancient Roman historian Livy argued, "history is the best medicine for a sick mind, for in history you have a record of the infinite variety of human experience plainly set out for all to see, and in that record you can find for yourself and your country both examples and warnings: fine things to take as models, [and] base things rotten through and through to avoid."[104]

It is important not to ignore the failures. To be sure, you may find even greater lessons in the failures and mistakes found in history. "History is the best help," wrote military theorist and historian Captain Liddell Hart," because it is "a record of how things usually go wrong."[105] Furthermore, Polybius adds, "the most instructive, indeed the only method of learning to bear with dignity the vicissitude of fortune, is to recall the catastrophes of others.'"[106]

Use History in Three Ways: From Alexander to Nietzsche.

These three themes—*identification, inspiration,* and *illumination*—echo the three practical uses German philosopher Friedrich Nietzsche cited as a rationale for leaders to study history. The first way leaders use history, he argued, is as a source of grounding. This is akin to the way in which Alexander relied on the shared history of the Greeks to help foster a shared sense of *identity, beliefs, and ideals.* According to Nietzsche, writes leadership authority James MacGregor Burns, "knowing where you come from anchors you and helps stabilize you."[107]

The second use of history, according to Nietzsche, is as a source of *inspiration.* By identifying noteworthy predecessors, leaders can become inspired to heroism and high achievement. "Their fame makes people want to imitate them."[108]

Nietzsche's third practical use of history for leaders is found in learning from the successes and failures of the past to better *illuminate the future.* According to Burns' take on Nietzsche, "the third use is to expose and remedy past errors, as the first step toward reform. A person cannot transcend what he or she does not even know."[109]

There is no question that the past can be a powerful tool for improving your present decisions in order to create a more desirable future. As Aesop plainly illustrates in his fable, "The Lion, the Fox, and the Beasts,"[110] this is the fox examining the footprints leading into the lion's den and using that record of the past to decide how to act in the present, and, thereby, altering the future for himself and his friends.

Today, Alexander the Great is remembered as one of the greatest military strategists of all time. An exceptionally courageous and charismatic leader, he conquered the known world, created the largest empire on earth, and laid the foundations for the Hellenistic world without ever losing a single battle. Throughout it all, history was a powerful, unmistakable part of what grounded, guided, and inspired Alexander to succeed.

Rather than longing for some detached, aimless, or uninspired success, Alexander's hunger, writes historian Andrew Stewart, "was a driving appetite to surpass the deeds of the heroes, an indomitable will to succeed where others had failed, and a supreme confidence in his unique ability to do so. It was his route to the center, and the channel for his charisma."[111] Emulating his first hero, Achilles, it was Alexander's yearning (i.e. *pothos*) to achieve his full potential and fulfill his divine purpose (i.e. *arête*) that drove Alexander to cross the Hellespont, besiege Tyre, conquer Egypt, take Gaza, defeat the Persian Empire, and declare himself King of Asia. Seeking to surpass the mighty Heracles, Alexander was further inspired to conquer the allegedly impregnable Aornos Rock. Attempting to rival the god Dionysus, Alexander was then driven into India where he triumphed over King Porus at the Battle of the Hydaspes in May 326 B.C.

Modeling himself after Achilles, Heracles, Dionysus and others, where in the pages of history would Alexander be without the heroes of history? History fed and nurtured his ambition. History grounded and heightened his charismatic appeal. And history informed and sharpened his judgment. And, as one historian put it, "only this extraordinary conjunction of vaulting ambition, spellbinding charisma, and unrivaled grasp of military realities could have enabled him to undertake the longest military campaign in the history of the world, and to emerge from it invincible...to the end."[112]

MAKE HISTORY WORK: NAPOLEON BONAPARTE TAPS THE POWER OF THE PAST TO SHAPE THE FUTURE

"One may teach tactics, military engineering, artillery work, about as [well as] one teaches geometry. But knowledge of the higher branches of war is only acquired by experience and by a study of history of the wars of the great generals. It is not in learning grammar that one learns to compose a great poem, to write a tragedy."[1]
—Napoleon Bonaparte (1769—1821), French Emperor

"Read over and over again the campaigns of Alexander, Hannibal, Caesar, Gustavus, Turenne, Eugene and Frederick. Make them your models. This is the only way to become a great general and to master the secrets of the art of war. With your own genius enlightened by this study, you will reject all maxims opposed to those of these great commanders."[2]
—Napoleon Bonaparte (1769—1821), French Emperor

"How much better to get wisdom than gold, to get insight rather than silver!"[3]
—Proverbs 16:16

On Christmas Eve in 1800, just before eight o'clock, Napoleon Bonaparte and his wife, Josephine, were set to travel in separate carriages to attend the opera to hear *The Creation*, an oratorio written by the celebrated Austrian composer Joseph Haydn.[4] While Josephine lingered behind fussing over her new shawl, Napoleon's carriage left the Tuileries Palace first. His coachman, César, who was slightly intoxicated,[5] raced through the streets of Paris to the opera house several blocks away.

A trip by carriage through the busy streets in the district surrounding the capital was a potentially hazardous prospect for Bonaparte, who was then serving as the First Consul of France. Napoleon had the support of a great majority of the French people, but he also had a number of dangerous enemies, particularly among the royalists who had opposed the French Revolution from its inception, including radicals who were desperate to restore the Bourbon monarchy, and who saw Bonaparte as the chief obstacle to their ambition. By this point, a number of death threats had been received and assassination plots uncovered.

But there was one particular group of assassins who were far more determined than most, and who were being financed by the British government. Under the direction of the royalist leader, Georges Cadoudal, three of the conspirators went to Paris, bought a horse and cart, and then packed a giant wine barrel with gun powder and shrapnel. Within days, they were ready to execute their assassination plot.

On the evening of December 24, they drove the wine barrel bomb to rue Saint-Nicaise, a street just north of the palace, and waited for Napoleon and his entourage to ride through the narrow street on his way to the opera. Rather than tying the horse up, one of the spineless assassins, Robinault de Saint-Régant, paid a 14-year-old girl, Marianne Peusol, to hold the reins of the horse, which together with the cart, nearly barred the narrow street.[6] When the first conspirator spotted Napoleon's carriage fast approaching he gave the signal to Saint-Régant who then quickly lit the fuse before making his cowardly escape.

Despite the traffic and commotion, Napoleon's carriage continued barreling down the street at full speed as the bomb's fuse continued to burn. Josephine and her entourage were now following not too far behind. Just seconds after Napoleon's coachman swerved around and raced past the young girl with the horse cart—KABOOM!—the giant bomb exploded. It killed instantly Marianne and four others. The explosion also maimed dozens more, including the owner of a café, "whose breasts were severed by a piece of one barrel's metal hoops."[7] A handful of nearby buildings and homes were damaged to the point that they had to be demolished.

Napoleon and his entourage, "by a singular chance,"[8] had just barely escaped with their lives. Arriving at the site of the explosion mere seconds later, Josephine and her entourage also just barely escaped with their lives. This "case of double good fortune" Napoleon said was, "God's Providence."[9]

Unharmed, but aware that they might still be in danger, Napoleon and Josephine soon continued on to the opera. The audience, meanwhile, already informed of the assassination attempt, was anxiously awaiting further news. When Napoleon and Josephine arrived at the opera house, clearly intent on continuing with their evening as if all was well with France, the audience erupted in vigorous applause and cheers.

Already wildly popular, the French were now beginning to see Napoleon as a national treasure that needed to be shielded from such nefarious plots. As Napoleon's chief of police, Joseph Fouché, later wrote, it was just "about two seconds," a "scarcely perceptible fraction of time," which "sufficed to save the life of the First Consul, and consolidate his power."[10] To be sure, support for Bonaparte was now "more enthusiastic than ever…"[11]—not at all the outcome the assassins were seeking.

Known as "the infernal machine plot," this assassination attempt "came the closest to success,"[12] but it was not the first or the last. In fact, in "an official report," Police Minister Fouché, "listed no fewer than ten separate conspiracies against Napoleon's life since he had come to power."[13] Offering a stern warning to Napoleon, Fouché concluded, "the air is full of daggers."[14]

Along with the risks to his life, these assassination plots were also strengthening Napoleon's hold on power.[15] As a matter of fact, by 1802, as a direct result of these plots, "the assemblies had declared Napoleon Consul for life."[16] Napoleon then called for "a plebiscite to approve the…constitution," which would also make the Consulate, and thus Napoleon, "a permanent governing entity."[17] "With overwhelming approval from the people,"[18] "three and a half million votes against eight thousand,"[19] the plebiscite effectively reinforced France's determination to make Napoleon's position as First Consul a lifetime appointment.

Meanwhile, despite his popularity, "police reports began to indicate that the public assumed Napoleon would indeed be assassinated sooner or later."[20] The problem for them was not simply a matter of losing a popular leader, the French people needed Napoleon. Napoleon, more than any other leading figure, "embodied in a unique way not only the Revolution but the Republic which had been hammered out of the Revolution."[21] What's more, following years of chaos, murder, and revolution, they were at last desperate for the peace and stability that Napoleon's leadership had brought to France. "The bourgeoisie, and the peasants who now enjoyed the nationalized lands of the Church," as well as the returning émigrés, who had fled France during the revolution, they were all dependent on Napoleon, and they "could never feel safe so long as the survival of the regime depended solely on Napoleon's life."[22]

What if, asked the French people, Napoleon's coachmen had been driving at his normal speed?[23] What if the popular French General, Jean Moreau, an enemy of Napoleon, had actually agreed to work with the royalist leader, Georges Cadoudal, and his assassins?[24] "Suppose Napoleon were to fall in battle or fall to another assassin's dagger? The Republic would then collapse: it would be either the Bourbons, a military dictatorship, or the Jacobins with their guillotine. The problem, then, was how to make the Republic more secure, and in particular, should the thin thread of one man's life be cut, how to achieve continuity."[25]

More than one of Napoleon's advisors argued that "hereditary succession" was "the only possible solution."[26] "If he established a dynasty with hereditary succession, it would be pointless in the future for royalists to try to kill *him*."[27] "This step," writes historian Felix Markham, "was the logical culmination of the Life Consulate not only because it accorded with Napoleon's ambition, but because it safeguarded the gains of the Revolution."[28]

No doubt, Napoleon was ambitious. Napoleon loved power. "But still, Napoleon hesitated."[29] He had always believed in the principles of the revolution—particularly liberty and equality over nobility, merit over privilege, ability over birth. Furthermore, it was, in part, these same principles that enabled his own rapid rise to power in the first place, and which he relied on to ensure he had the best, most talented and capable leaders in place throughout his army and government. As Napoleon, the "Corsican outsider," said himself, "It is I who embody the French revolution."[30]

A little too reminiscent of the monarchy that the French Revolution had overthrown, many others were even more resistant to "hereditary succession." Of course, Napoleon, well aware of France's enduring discontent with the Bourbon monarchy, was not about to let his own head end up in a basket. At the same time, however, "given that the Bourbons launched a series of assassination attempts on him—30 in all," he was also convinced that some "provision for continuity was prudent."[31] Something had to be done.

Use History to Broaden Your Scope, and Expand Your Options.

As is so often the case, answers to the present dilemma lie in the past. And, as he so often did, Napoleon Bonaparte turned to history for the solution—in this case, the historical record of ancient Rome. Even before his meteoric rise, Napoleon had looked to history for answers and ideas, and he had used history as a tool of influence. As a military leader, he naturally looked to the lessons and insights of the great military commanders, men like, as he said, "Alexander, Hannibal, [Julius] Caesar…and Frederick [the Great]."[32]

Napoleon again turned to history when he and his co-conspirators first assumed political power. Drawing on the model of ancient Rome, they established the French Consulate, and Napoleon maneuvered to become First Consul of the new triumvirate executive in 1799. *Consul* had been the highest elected political office in the ancient Roman Republic. With initial help from Pompey and Crassus (The First Triumvirate), *consul* was also the title Julius Caesar held before becoming "dictator for life," setting the stage for Rome's first *emperor*. A great admirer of Julius Caesar, Napoleon appeared to be following in his hero's footsteps.

Napoleon clearly understood that history can be used not only to stir thinking, spark ideas, warn of potential pitfalls, and offer options about how to move ahead, but it can also be used as a tool of influence. He could use history to enhance his legitimacy, build support for his actions and plans, and reduce resistance, doubt, apprehension, and fear. Napoleon, for example, acknowledged that "the present head of the government was…a dictator," but, calling on the selfless heroes of ancient Rome, Napoleon explained, it was a dictatorship "in the same sense in which Fabius, Camillus, and Cincinnatus" were dictators.[33] He was a citizen of France first, in other words, and his supreme power was a *provisional* measure, taken only out of necessity, to achieve a specific purpose—in this case, saving France from the upheaval of the revolution, and the threats and influence of foreign powers.[34] By echoing ancient Rome, at a time when the French people were desperate for an end to the years of violence and chaos, Napoleon's words and actions were evoking images of the sort of strength, order, and stability that France now craved.

Evoke the Echoes of History.

Neither the title of First Consul, nor the lifetime appointment, however, solved the problem of assassination. When the Pichegru plot was uncovered in 1804—a scheme which, beyond assassination, amounted to a new, British-backed revolution—Napoleon knew it was time to make another move. "The incident was too good an opportunity for Napoleon to waste politically"[35] and, again, turning to the history of ancient Rome, he used this assassination plot as justification for the creation of an imperial system—which would make Napoleon the Emperor of France, but also which, as with the Roman Empire, "allowed Bonaparte to nominate his successor as Emperor."[36] Transitioning France to an imperial system of government also echoed the transition of ancient Rome from a Republic to an Empire under Julius Caesar and his chosen successor Augustus, which led to a 200-year period of relative peace known as *Pax Romana,* another useful historical reference for promoting Napoleon's plan.

"As for the term 'emperor,' originally the Roman emperor had been the man who exercised the imperium on behalf of the people of the republic: hence coins displayed the emperor's head on one side, and on the other the word *respublica.* Napoleon, then," writes Cronin, "saw nothing objectionable to republican feeling in the word 'emperor'. It was merely a change of title which would establish in the eyes of the world the legality and continuity of the Republic."[37]

By creating a government based on the model of ancient Rome, Napoleon, a clever political operator, was not only avoiding any unnecessary, objectionable association with kings and monarchs, but he was also creating a framework for the future, and something beyond and bigger than France. "To Napoleon's own ear, the word King might sound as if it restricted his power within the limits of the ancient kingdom; while that of Emperor," writes one historian, "might comprise dominions equal to the wide sweep of ancient Rome herself, and the bounds of the habitable earth alone could be considered as circumscribing their extent."[38] In short, given his extraordinary military successes throughout Europe, for Napoleon Bonaparte, the title of emperor was also seen to be far more fitting than king.

Select the Suitable Crown.

After he had risen to the height of his power in France, Napoleon continued to draw on history as a means of influence. Recognizing the preeminent importance of his coronation as emperor, for example, and the subtle but surprising power of symbolism, suggestion, metaphor, and motif, Napoleon gave careful consideration to every aspect of the coronation ceremony, particularly the crown itself. Instead of a closed crown, "worn by the hereditary—and, as Napoleon thought, degenerate—kings of Europe,"[39] Napoleon chose an open crown, a gold laurel wreath,[40] which was "reminiscent of the Caesars of Ancient Rome."[41] In this way, by evoking the mighty Roman Empire and the victorious Roman conquerors, Napoleon was relaying his own power and glory, status and authority.

The ancient Romans were themselves drawing on history; the laurel wreath (which might be substituted with an olive wreath) was originally awarded to the victors of the ancient Olympic games held in Olympia, Greece, beginning in 776 B.C. Still more, the Olympians were drawing on ancient Greek mythology, and the story of Heracles using the laurel wreath as a prize for the winner of a running race. Heracles, in turn, chose the laurel wreath in honor of his father, Zeus, who had sided with his daughter, Athena, over his brother, Poseidon, in a dispute over their conflicting claim to the city of Athens. Zeus sided with Athena because she had given Athens their greatest gift, the first olive tree.

Clearly, as Napoleon well understood, the regal and enduring laurel wreath has an exceptionally long history of use as a powerful, crowning emblem of victory, glory, and success. And Napoleon continued to use a gilded laurel wreath as an emblem of his empire. Exactly as Julius Caesar had done, Napoleon also commissioned a number of sculptures and paintings and coins of himself, all crowned with a laurel wreath (see book cover[42]).

By this time, rather than relying on the history of ancient Rome alone, however, Napoleon was also beginning to draw on more recent European history, specifically Charlemagne, who had ruled most of Europe around the turn of the 8th century, and who, furthermore, had himself sought to *reestablish* the Roman empire (see Chapter 2).

At his coronation as Emperor Napoleon I, at the Cathedral of Notre Dame in Paris on Sunday, December 2, 1804, Napoleon used two separate crowns. Calling to mind ancient Rome, he wore the gilded laurel wreath throughout the ceremony. For the official crowning, however, Napoleon sought to "emphasize his link with Charlemagne."[43] Symbolic of the revolutionary principle of rising by merit, and the republican principle of self-rule, rather than being crowned by the Pope, Pius VII, who stood nearby as a mere spectator, Napoleon, in a symbolic gesture, raised a replica of Charlemagne's crown, and briefly held it over his own head.[44]

Known as the "Father of Europe," and crowned Emperor of the Romans in 800 A.D., Charlemagne's title and success in reviving the idea of the Roman Empire clearly appealed to Napoleon's own ambitions for Europe. At another coronation, when Napoleon had himself crowned King of Italy in Milan, he again turned to the history of Charlemagne. "On this occasion," writes author Andrew Knighton, "he was crowned with the Iron Crown of Lombardy, one of the most ancient royal relics in Europe, with a heritage and mythology stretching back to Charlemagne's Kingdom of Lombardy. Once again, Napoleon was taking on a title associated with Charlemagne. This time, he did so wearing a crown that many believed Charlemagne himself had worn. To hammer the point home, he marked the occasion by giving a painting of Charlemagne to the city of Milan."[45]

Learn from the Past: History as Master.

"The art of what works is the secret of strategy,
a timeless truth for success in business or any other field."[46]

—William Duggan, Columbia Business School

Napoleon Bonaparte was a faithful student of history, and history served his purposes and aided his efforts in a number of important ways. Napoleon's use of history can be divided into the following two frames: History as master and history as servant. In the first frame, history is the wise teacher offering an endless source of wisdom and insight to uncover, "rules and principles"[47] to conform to, as Napoleon put it, and themes and patterns to understand, orient around, adapt to, or exploit. In this case, we see Napoleon, the strategist, using history as a decision-making tool, or as part of his decision-making process. It was from this frame that Winston Churchill said, "Study history, study history; in history lie all the secrets..."[48] Within this frame, three key themes emerge:

Study History to Gain a Greater, More Expansive Scope.

There are few things more valuable to leaders and their ability to make wise decisions than their understanding of the big picture, or their ability to take a long-term perspective. History is indispensable in this regard. In fact, according to Winston Churchill, "The farther backward you can look, the farther forward you can see."[49]

"Learn all you can about the history of the past," Churchill wrote to his grandson, "for how else can one even make a guess at what is going to happen in the future?"[50]

Being steeped in history provides *perspective* on current events. It assists in identifying parallels and points of comparison. It aids in recognizing trends and patterns. Being steeped in history even helps foster critical thinking, sparking insights into the future. To be "steeped in history," writes Harvard Kennedy School professor David Gergen, "is a priceless asset for a leader."[51]

Naturally, your own hard won experience can be exceedingly valuable. And, no doubt, so long as you actively reflect on and learn from your experience, the more years of experience you have, the wiser you may become. Nevertheless, as military theorist and historian Captain Liddell Hart contends, unless you are three or four thousand years old, there is no good excuse for not studying history, and learning from the experience of others. Even "fools learn from experience," wrote the 19th century Prussian statesman Otto von Bismarck, "the wise learn from the experience of others."[52]

"History...is universal experience"[53] writes Hart, only it is "infinitely longer, wider, and more varied than any individual's experience,"[54] and, therefore, writes the ancient Greek historian Polybius, "the knowledge gained from the study of true history is the best of all educations for practical life."[55]

Do not just look back to the immediate past, however. Remember what Churchill said: "The farther backward you can look, the farther forward you can see."[56] In Napoleon's case, he looked to the leadership of the 18th century Prussian king and military leader Frederick the Great, as well as more recent military commanders such as Eugene of Savoy, and the 17th century French general Turenne. But he also looked to the example of Charlemagne, who ruled during the Early Middle Ages, Julius Caesar in the first century A.D., and Alexander the Great who lived in the fourth century B.C.

Study History to Spur Thinking,
Explore Options, and Gain Insight and Ideas.

The second theme relates to how history can be a powerful tool for generating ideas, and exploring options. Even in seemingly simple matters, such as choosing his personal emblem, Napoleon would often consult with an historian. "He was trying to build up the future," explains historian Andrew Roberts, "but to do so he had to find roots in the past..."[57] Regarding his personal emblem, and whether to use a lion, a rooster, an eagle or a bee, "he wanted something ancient,"[58] he wanted something that echoed a glorious past. But he was also careful to ensure that it was before the time that France was ruled by kings.[59]

Study History to Learn What Worked, What Failed, and Why.

The third key theme to emerge is how we can learn from the successes and failures of the past and, from this collective experience, how we can begin to generate timeless principles and practices, and applicable lessons learned. Cataloging the exploits of the great Carthaginian general, Hannibal Barca, Napoleon asks, "Can it be supposed that Hannibal's glorious career and achievements were the mere result of chance, and fortune's favors?"[60] Certainly not, he argues. "All the great captains of antiquity, and those who in modern times have successfully retraced their footsteps, performed vast achievements, only by conforming with the rules and principles of the art; that is to say, by correct combinations, and by justly comparing the relation between means and consequences, effects and obstacles."[61]

They succeeded, in other words, through their mastery of history. "They succeeded only by the strict observance of these rules," Napoleon said, "whatever may have been the boldness of their enterprises, or the extent of the advantages gained. They invariably practiced war as a science. Thus they have become our great models, and it is only by closely imitating them that we can hope to approach them."[62]

Use the Past to Influence the Future: History as Servant.

In terms of the application of history, another key frame is to think of history as your servant offering itself as a source of motivation, inspiration, and even power. In this case, we see Napoleon using history as a tool of influence. In other words, rather than using history to improve his own thinking and decisions, he used it to shape the opinions and decisions of others. It was from this frame that Winston Churchill said, "History will be kind to me, for I intend to write it."[63] Of course, the idea is not to write history, but to draw on it, to mobilize and marshal it, and "send it into battle."[64] In regards to Napoleon's example, consider a few of the different ways he used history as a tool of influence.

Echo History to Increase Legitimacy
and Improve Your Image and Appeal.

As we know from studies in psychology and neuroscience, we are all biased toward what is familiar. Known in the research as the "mere exposure effect," this is "one of the sturdiest findings in modern psychology...Across hundreds of studies and metastudies, subjects around the world prefer familiar shapes, landscapes, consumer goods, songs, and human voices."[65] Our bias for what is familiar is so persistent and "universal that some think it must be written into our genetic code from back when our ancestors trawled the savanna. The evolutionary explanation for the exposure effect is simple: If you recognize an animal or plant, then it hasn't killed you yet."[66] What's more, while we are often "curious to discover new things," most people are also anxious about "anything that's too new."[67]

This prevented a challenge for Napoleon, particularly given his sudden emergence on the national stage following a violent revolution. Napoleon was born outside mainland France, on the Island of Corsica, which did not become part of France until 1768 (one year before Napoleon's birth). Raised speaking Corsican and Italian, Napoleon also continued to struggle with the French language and was still seen in some circles as an outsider. While this did help to make some people curious about him, and added to his charismatic appeal (i.e. charismatic leaders often have some foreign element that creates an aura of mystery and intrigue), it also made many anxious and uncertain. Given the fact that France had just thrown off nearly a thousand years of monarchy, perhaps an even greater challenge was settling on the right form of rule.

As a result of these and other challenges, finding ways to make himself more *familiar* went a long way toward increasing his appeal. By echoing the heroes of history, he added to his perceived legitimacy. In fact, Knighton contends, "the connections he drew between his own life and that of great figures from history," was "one of the most powerful tools in Napoleon Bonaparte's intellectual arsenal...By linking himself to these great men...he could improve his public image, win support and provide legitimacy for his regime."[68]

"For the most part, we like things that are familiar to us," Robert Cialdini writes in his classic book, *Influence*; "...because of its effect on liking, familiarity plays a role in decisions about all sorts of things, including the politicians we elect."[69] Cialdini gives the example of the politician who was expected to lose the race for attorney-general in Ohio. When the politician suddenly changed his legal name to Brown, just before the election—a name with much political tradition in Ohio (similar to the Kennedys in Massachusetts)—he was swept into a surprising victory.[70]

In Napoleon's case, by strategically drawing on a familiar history and echoing cherished ideals and esteemed leaders of the past, he succeeded in making himself a hit with the French people. In effect, from a marketing perspective, Napoleon had struck just the right balance between the new and the old, the fresh but familiar. As Derek Thompson writes in his book, *Hit Makers: The Science of Popularity in an Age of Distraction*, "The best hit makers are gifted at creating moments of meaning by marrying new and old, anxiety and understanding. They are architects of familiar surprises."[71]

Virtually every culture has their heroes and villains, figures from the past who are widely admired or reviled, respected or detested. The key is to avoid association with the villains and instead identify ways of echoing the heroes, sages and saints. When your words, actions, or appearances, or the symbols and images you associate yourself with, call those influential figures to mind for your audience, you benefit from this natural preference for what is familiar and liked. Be careful, however, to avoid *mimicking* or copying outright the legends and heroes of the past and, instead, find _new_ and _fresh_ ways to *blend* with a past that is _familiar_ and _liked_.

Use an Inspirational Past to Reduce Resistance to Your Plan for the Future.

Associating yourself or your plans with an inspiring past can also help to facilitate acceptance or reduce resistance to your vision for the future. In Napoleon's case, he wanted to unify all of Europe, and given his "vast knowledge of history," he believed this vision was within reach.[72] "I wished to found a European system, a European Code of Laws, a European judiciary," Napoleon wrote on St. Helena, "there would be but one people in Europe."[73] And while it was not achieved in his lifetime, the European Union did begin to take shape following World War II, and, consisting of 27 member states, it includes a single market, a single, primary currency (the Euro), and a standardized system of laws (interestingly, as it was in Napoleon's day, Britain remains the most resistant to this union).

Do not misunderstand: The point has nothing to do with whether or not Napoleon was right to try unify Europe. Nor is the point about how surprisingly close he came to achieving his aim, though that is getting closer to it. The point is how effective an inspiring past can be in helping to shape the future.

In regards to his grand vision for Europe, Napoleon could not have found a more perfect exemplar than the medieval emperor, Charlemagne, a heroic figure throughout Europe. It was Charlemagne that had first sought to revive the Roman Empire (renamed the Holy Roman Empire), and it was Napoleon's Grand Empire which "...replaced the ailing Holy Roman Empire" and which itself was "basically a continuation of the ancient Roman Empire."[74]

"Napoleon worked tirelessly to push the name of Charlemagne into the forefront of people's minds when they saw him."[75] Further, given that Charlemagne was a zealous defender of Christianity, and protector of the popes, Napoleon's efforts to associate himself with Charlemagne was also a clever part of how he maneuvered to win the support of the church. "He regularly spoke about the medieval emperor, telling papal representatives in 1809 that "In me you see Charlemagne. I am Charlemagne, me!'"[76]

"Even Charlemagne's capital of Aachen was incorporated into this grand work of propaganda. A portrait of the new emperor was displayed there, and in 1811 an effigy of Charlemagne was paraded through the city, with a message inscribed upon it in both German and French: "I am only surpassed by Napoleon.""[77]

Of course, associating himself with Charlemagne carried more weight with some than others. Nevertheless, given Charlemagne's unquestionable accomplishments and general esteem, the steady stream of both subtle and direct comparisons communicated something of Bonaparte's grand aspirations not just for himself, but for all of those under his rule.

Exploit the Subtle Power of Symbols, Signs, Emblems, Icons and Art.

Napoleon also made extensive use of symbols, emblems, icons, and other more artful links with history as a means of influence. In one instance, when discussing which animal would be used on the official badge to represent the Empire, a number of recommendations were made. The special committee unanimously selected the cock, but Napoleon rejected their recommendation. "The cock belongs to the farmyard," he said, "it is far too feeble a creature."[78] Other recommendations from his Council included the elephant, the lion, the eagle, and the bee; an oak tree and even an ear of corn had some supporters.[79] Napoleon finally chose the lion and they moved on.

Soon after the meeting, however, all too aware of the power of history and its symbols, "Napoleon changed his mind from the lion to an eagle with spread wings," because, he said, "it 'affirms imperial dignity and recalls Charlemagne.'"[80] What's more, adds historian Andrew Roberts, "It also recalled Ancient Rome."[81]

"Not content with having just one symbol, Napoleon also chose the bee as a personal and family emblem…"[82] The bee had been the emblem of the fifth-century King Childeric I of France. Thus, by also using Childeric's bee, "Napoleon was consciously connecting the house of Bonaparte with the ancient…dynasty that [had] created the sovereign" nation of France in the first place.[83]

Some of the connections Napoleon sought to make with Charlemagne were a "little more subtle, though not much, as when he travelled aboard the boat Charlemagne in 1811."[84] Napoleon also commissioned the artist "Jacques-Louis David, who famously painted propaganda pieces for the Emperor's reign, to connect him with Charlemagne."[85] In his most famous work, *Napoleon Crossing the Alps*, Charlemagne's name is written in Latin ("Karolus Magnus") on one of the rocks under Napoleon's horse, alongside the names "Hannibal," and, of course, "Bonaparte."

It is easy to overlook the power and importance of symbols. After all, we are not always *consciously* aware of their influence, or how they can subtly stir memories, elicit emotions, fuel imagination, and direct behavior. In fact, more often than not, we are influenced by symbols, emblems, and icons without conscious, rational thought. Whether we are always aware of their influence or not, "symbols are powerful conveyors of meaning," and they may serve as potent spurs to action.[86] National symbols such as flags and standards, for example, can evoke profound emotions and lead to heroic exploits.[87] Religious symbols, similarly, can lead to powerful, personal transformation, and may lead some people to lay down their lives.[88] Even without national flags or religious faith, however, symbols can be a powerful force. When you use symbols associated with an inspiring past or heroic history, these powerful visual representations can help to reinforce values, fortify beliefs, strengthen connections, and inspire, motivate and push people to superhuman effort and personal sacrifice. Symbols can even give life meaning and as Carl Jung wrote, "He can withstand the most incredible hardships when he is convinced that they make sense."[89]

Put the Past on a Pedestal, Make It Work for Your Future.

Napoleon Bonaparte was very much a self-made man. Indeed, according to one historian, Napoleon was "perhaps the finest example of the self-made man of the 19th century."[90] Unable to rely on an inherited fortune, hereditary rank, powerful family connections, or the social, political, and economic privileges of the French aristocracy, Napoleon was largely left to his own devices.

The far more powerful resource that Napoleon *did* have, however, was history—an extensive knowledge of and a deep and abiding understanding of the power of history. Where he lacked personal mentors and influential connections, he instead had the legends and heroes of history, from Alexander and Hannibal to Julius Caesar and Charlemagne. Along with his driving ambition and relentless determination, "by standing on the shoulders of [these] giants,"[91] as Isaac Newton put it, Napoleon was able to see further, work smarter, and achieve more than any of the high-born, well-connected, privileged elites of Europe, including the most powerful monarchs and scores of other nobles of hereditary title he would later defeat in battle.

What's more, with a strategic and enterprising mind, Napoleon learned to master history, making it work for him in various different ways. Throughout his reign, in fact, he tapped the power of history to his considerable advantage, using it to spur his ambition, explore his options, enrich his perspective, inform his decisions, enhance his judgment, inspire his actions, increase his legitimacy, and, perhaps most importantly, Napoleon deployed history as a tool of influence.

If there was ever a man capable of placing history on a pedestal, that man was Napoleon Bonaparte. After defeating the larger Russian and Austrian armies at the Battle of Austerlitz in 1805, widely regarded as his greatest victory, Napoleon created the Vendôme Column, a 145-foot monument inspired by Roman emperor Trajan's Column. Spiraling around from the base to the top are scenes of Bonaparte's military triumphs. At the top of the column is a statue of Napoleon, depicted as an emperor of ancient Rome, crowned with a laurel wreath. In one hand is a sword, in the other a globe on top of which stands a statue of Victoria, the Roman goddess of victory. Napoleon's column still stands today as a striking reminder of the power and influence of history, a lasting inspiration towering above the pages of the past.

Build an Arsenal of Analogies, a Foundation of Relevant History, Recurring Patterns and Themes: President Harry Truman Taps History to Navigate the U.S. Ship of State

"The only thing new in the world is the history you don't know."[1]
—Harry S. Truman, 33rd U.S. President

"What has been will be again, what has been done will be done again; there is nothing new under the sun."[2]
—Ecclesiastes 1:9

Construct a Foundation to Accelerate Learning, Wisdom, and Growth: Harry Truman Takes the Reigns of the Presidency Following the Death of FDR

"Readers of good books, particularly books of biography and history, are preparing themselves for leadership. Not all readers become leaders, but all leaders must be readers."[3]
—Harry S. Truman

"I have a terrific headache," President Franklin D. Roosevelt said to an aid while on retreat at the "Little White House" in Warm Springs, Georgia. Suddenly, Roosevelt lost consciousness and slumped forward in his chair. Within hours, one of the greatest[4] presidents in U.S. history and one of the most influential figures in the 20th century was dead.

It was April 12, 1945, and America was still fighting in the final days of World War II. Chosen to be Roosevelt's running mate for his 4th term, Harry Truman had been serving as Vice President for less than 90 days when Roosevelt died. Truman had served Missouri as a United States Senator for 10 years, but he had absolutely no executive experience, never mind any mentoring from FDR. In fact, Truman knew virtually nothing about what Roosevelt was up to behind the scenes. When Truman first heard the news from First Lady Eleanor Roosevelt, he immediately asked her if there was anything he could do for her—to which she immediately replied, "Is there anything *we* can do for *you*? For you are the one in trouble now!"[5]

Indeed, Truman was in trouble. From the very moment he was first thrust into the presidency by the death of Roosevelt, almost no one thought he could handle the job. Without a doubt, "President" Harry Truman was the second big bombshell about FDR's death. As Pulitzer Prize-winning historian David McCullough writes,

> "To the country, the Congress, the Washington bureaucracy, to hundreds of veteran New Dealers...to much of the military high command, to millions of American men and women overseas, the news of Franklin Roosevelt's death, followed by the realization that Harry Truman was President, struck like massive earth tremors in quick succession, the thought of Truman in the White House coming with the force of a shock wave. To many it was not just that the greatest of men had fallen, but that the least of men—or at any rate the least likely of men—had assumed his place."[6]

Not only had Roosevelt led the nation through the Great Depression and World War II, but, after being elected an unprecedented four times, Roosevelt had also been America's president for just over twelve *years*. To consider the notion that some unknown common man from Missouri would now take over the most powerful nation on Earth in the midst of a global war was, for most folks, to defy imagination. Everywhere, people were asking in disbelief, 'Good God, Harry Truman is President?'[7] "'If Harry Truman can be President, so could my next-door neighbor.' People were fearful about the future of the country," writes McCullough, "fearful the war would drag on longer now. 'What a great, great tragedy. God help us all,' wrote David Lilienthal, head of TVA. The thought of Truman made him feel physically ill. 'The country and the world don't deserve to be left this way...'" he said.[8] Many people from his own party thought that Truman should resign the presidency.

Sadly, even Truman himself harbored deep doubts about whether he was up to the task. "Only gradually would he reveal his own feelings, making plain that if anyone was stunned by the turn of fate, or worried over the future, or distressed by the inadequacies of the man stepping into the place of Franklin Roosevelt, it was Harry Truman."[9]

The day after he was sworn in as President, Truman encountered a crowd of reporters who had gathered to greet him and shake his hand. "Boys," he said, "if you ever pray, pray for me now. I don't know whether you fellows ever had a load of hay fall on you, but when they told me yesterday what had happened, I felt like the moon, the stars, and all the planets had fallen on me."[10]

Despite his unease and understandable concerns, Truman had already hinted at how he would get along. Earlier that morning, just after leaving his apartment for the White House, Truman happened to see Tony Vaccaro of the Associated Press and asked him if he wanted a ride. As they headed downtown, looking ahead stoically, Truman said, "There have been few men in all history the equal of the man into whose shoes I am stepping."[11] Turning to face Vaccaro, he added, "I pray God I can measure up to the task."[12] This was no idle compliment of America's fallen hero. With his reference to the great "men in all history," Truman knew precisely what he was talking about, and, given his inner resources and vast knowledge of history, he undoubtedly had a few specific leaders in mind.

Notwithstanding the tide of naysayers, doubters, and critics, there were those few who, "facing the prospect of a Truman presidency, felt confident the country was in good hands. They knew the man, they said. They understood his origins. They had seen how he handled responsibility and knew the inner resources he could draw on."[13] "As before and later in his life," writes McCullough, "confidence in Harry Truman was greatest among those who knew him best."[14]

"'Truman is honest and patriotic and has a head full of good horse sense. Besides, he has guts,' wrote [FDR's first Vice President] John Nance Garner to [Speaker of the House] Sam Rayburn, who was himself assuring reporters that Truman would make a good, sound President 'by God,' he said, because 'he's got the stuff in him.'"[15]

No matter what the pressure, no matter how widespread the misgivings and doubts, including his own, Harry Truman was determined to do his duty, serve his country, and uphold his oath of office as president of the United States. "When Franklin Roosevelt died," Truman later recalled, "I felt there must be a million men better qualified than I, to take up the Presidential task. But the work was mine to do, and I had to do it. And I tried to give it everything that was in me."[16] Days later, speaking before Congress about his responsibilities as president he said, "that is my duty and I shall not shirk it."[17]

Lean on the Wisdom of History.

"A good decision is based on knowledge."[18]
—Plato, Father of Political Philosophy

In order to handle the enormous burden of the presidency, Harry Truman would turn again and again to the wisdom of history. In fact, within *hours* of FDR's death, Truman's mind had already turned to history to deal with the challenges he faced, searching for precedents and possibilities about how best to move ahead. As he later wrote in his memoirs, "during those first few hours, painful as they were because of our tragic loss, my mind kept turning to the task I had inherited and to the grave responsibilities that confronted our nation at that critical moment in history. From my reading of American history," he continued, "I knew there was no cut-and dried answer to the question of what obligations a President by inheritance had in regard to the program of his predecessor—especially a program on which a *great* President had recently been *re-elected* for the *fourth* time."[19]

Even if history could never offer precise, pre-packaged solutions to the problems he faced, it remained for Truman a constant guide, a check on his actions, and a source of insight, ideas, and inspiration. At the very least,

Truman found solace in knowing that his actions were not flying in the face of the wisdom of history.

As the new president began to face more specific questions, he found himself looking to history over and over again. In what amounted to his first formal decision, for example, Truman was asked if he planned to keep the U.S. involved in the United Nations (UN). He immediately replied, based on his understanding of history, arguing for a "strong and lasting" United Nations. Truman admired FDR, but his favorite president was Woodrow Wilson. Wilson had tried desperately to start the League of Nations, the predecessor of the UN. Truman was also familiar with the potential power of alliances, not just the Allied forces in WWI and WWII, but also the League of Corinth, under the leadership of Alexander the Great, which helped the Greeks put an end to the Persian invasions. Truman was also familiar with the various military alliances of the great European powers of the late 18th and early 19th century and how those coalitions eventually defeated the seemingly invincible Napoleon Bonaparte.

President Truman identified a number of great American presidents which he looked to as guides for navigating the turbulence of his own presidency, a few of which served as lasting examples. "I've been asked which presidents served as models for me when I was president myself," Truman once said, "and the answer is that there were three of them. Two were Jefferson and Jackson, and the third was Woodrow Wilson."[20]

Of course Truman was unmistakably his own man. He was true to himself and his core beliefs. But he also recognized the value of having guides. "Every president has to act on his own," Truman wrote, "no matter what the situation may have been before he came along, but he has to have that background, that knowledge of past history, to be sure that he's doing what's right. And Woodrow Wilson served as a constant example to me of how to operate and function as president of the United States."[21]

"Truman's study of history proved indispensable."[22] Within the first few months, as Truman adjusted to the presidency, his plain-spoken manner and sound decision-making began to win people over. In fact, his approval rating hovered above 70% for the remainder of his first year. But Truman was not out of the woods, and his occasional failure to learn from the lessons of the past, or apply those relevant, timeless principles to the present, occasionally surrendering to his emotions instead, would hover over his presidency like a dark cloud.

Study the Past to Shape the Future.

Since time immemorial, many of the most celebrated leaders and their advisors, both practitioners and theorists, have recognized the importance of understanding history. The sophisticated politics of the Renaissance, the rise of the merchant class and the non-noble upper class, out of which came families like the Borgias and the Medicis, put a premium on political savvy and intrigue, artful persuasion and influence, and leaders who could be crafty and cunning, but also insightful and wise.

It was in this context that an understanding of the value and importance of history began to accelerate, particularly among leaders, aspiring leaders, and those who were ambitious to gain power or maintain the power they had. "It was in this context that Machiavelli wrote his book *The Prince*, a late example of the medieval genre called *specula principum*, meaning 'mirrors for princes.'"[23] Similar books in this genre include *Maxims and Reflections* (c. 1537) by Francesco Guicciardini, a friend of Machiavelli, and Antonio de Guevara's *Dial of Princes* (1529), a major bestseller at the time, and Baltasar Gracián's *The Art of Worldly Wisdom* (1647). "These were early self-help books aimed at rulers, prescribing advice for rulership and effective governance. Many early texts used history as an illustration, providing advice for how to avoid historical calamities and how to emulate historical successes."[24]

In his *Discourses on Livy*, Niccolò Machiavelli himself explains, "Wise men say, and not without reason, that whoever wishes to foresee the future must consult the past; for human events ever resemble those of preceding times. This arises from the fact that they are produced by men who ever have been, and ever shall be, animated by the same passions, and thus they necessarily have the same results."[25]

Widely recognized as an invaluable resource for decision-making and analysis, today numerous disciplines seek to benefit from the study of the past. Case studies of significant business scenarios from the past are the cornerstone method of instruction at Harvard Business School. West Point cadets continue to study the writings of Sun Tzu, Clausewitz, and Jomini, and the military exploits of Alexander, Hannibal, Napoleon and Frederick the Great. Legal precedents, market analysis, diplomacy, military strategy, political leadership— all of these fields are deeply reliant on the past.[26] The idea that there are not lessons that we can learn from history is equivalent to the belief that humankind is incapable of learning from its successes and mistakes.[27] Of course history does not offer "final answers,"[28] but, writes Yale historian Donald Kagan, "the careful analysis of past situations and experiences similar to those of our time can provide useful indications of the opportunities and dangers that lie before us."[29] "Look back over the past…" wrote the ancient Roman emperor Marcus Aurelius, "and you can foresee the future too…"[30]

> *"If you don't know history, then you don't know anything.*
> *You are a leaf that doesn't know it is part of a tree."*[31]
> —Michael Crichton, American Author and Filmmaker

Unfortunately, what we see far too often today is leaders who ignore history. Usually with a fair share of both arrogance and ignorance, these people imagine that the past has no part to play in the future. But the exact opposite is true. The notion that history is somehow irrelevant is irrational and doctrinaire. "We cannot escape history," said Lincoln.[32]

From historian David McCullough's perspective, "History is who we are and why we are the way we are." Carl Jung put it this way, "Who has fully realized that history is not contained in thick books but lives in our very blood?"[33]

If you hope to shape the future, you must first understand the past. The great Enlightenment philosopher Spinoza similarly said, "If you want the present to be different from the past, study the past."[34] And, sure enough, as we will see in the case of President Harry S. Truman, it is when leaders fail to look to the lessons of history that they are most likely to fail to shape the future the way they want.

Study History, Study History

"Study history, study history—in history lie all the secrets..."[35]
—Winston Churchill (1874—1965), U.K. Prime Minister

"The future is unknown and the present is fleeting, which means that everything is history. The skills acquired from studying the past provide an excellent foundation for navigating the present and preparing for the future."[36]
—Mark Bailey, University of East Anglia

Without a college degree, very limited exposure to the world, or even the country, and no executive experience whatsoever, Harry Truman might have been expected to fail miserably as president. Instead, though far from perfect, he is remembered as one of the near greats, consistently ranked by scholars across the political spectrum in the top ten of *all* American presidents—usually seventh.[37]

No doubt, along with his character and capacity for leadership, Truman had a number of admirable qualities that were well suited to the American Presidency (e.g. vision, character, social intelligence, leadership capacity, ability to communicate, willingness to take risks, etc.). Yet, regarding his effectiveness as leader of the free world, what Truman himself pointed to was history. In fact, as American historian Michael Beschloss reports, "Harry Truman said he could never have functioned as President had he not read his eyes out about the leadership qualities of his predecessors."[38]

From the very beginning of his political career, according to Samuel Rushay, lead archivist at the Truman Presidential Library, "history...provided him ethical and moral guidance and was a tool that he used to make decisions, most notably as President of the United States during his two terms of office...Truman 'internalized' history and looked to the past almost reflexively whenever a problem or issue arose."[39]

But how did he draw on history and what did he gain? And what can we learn from his example? President Truman's experience reveals four core themes, paradigms and practices you can employ to exploit the power of the past.

(1.) Study History to Accelerate Your Growth.

In 1894, when Harry Truman turned ten, his mother presented him with a birthday gift that he would later mark as one of the key turning points in his life.[40] It was a large series of illustrated articles from leading American and British magazines published as a 4-volume set entitled, *Great Men and Famous Women.*[41] Covering hundreds of heroic historical figures, the volumes in the set included, *Soldiers and Sailors, Statesmen and Sages, Workmen and Heroes,* and *Artists and Authors.* Even "while still a boy," Truman said, "I could see that history had some extremely valuable lessons to teach."[42] The budding young historian "would eventually plow his way through all of them, *Soldiers and Sailors* appealing especially. He dreamed of becoming a great general. He loved best the story of Hannibal, who had only one eye."[43]

As he grew, "history became a passion"[44] and he read his way through shelves of books "on ancient Egypt...Greece, and Rome, the exploits of Genghis Khan and the stories of [Eastern] civilizations...and particularly the history of America."[45] "I became very interested in the men who made world history," Truman said, "...and I soon learned that the really successful ones were few and far between. I wanted to know what caused the successes or the failures of all the famous leaders of history. The only way to find the answers was to read."[46]

And, so, that is exactly what Truman did. He read page after page of history day after day. "Reading history, to me," he said, "was far more than a romantic adventure. It was solid instruction and wise teaching which I somehow felt that I wanted and needed."[47] No doubt, it was an ideal instinct for a future president. As Truman later wrote in his *Memoirs,* "My debt to history is one which cannot be calculated. I know of no other motivation which so accounts for my awakening interest as a young lad in the principles of leadership and government."[48]

"Especially in reading the history of American Presidents did I become aware of the value of knowing what has gone before...These lessons were to stand me in good stead years later, when I was to be confronted with similar problems. There were countless other lessons which history taught that would prove valuable to me."[49] "The one great external influence which, more than anything else, nourished and sustained" his interest in leadership, inspired his actions, and informed his judgment was "the endless reading of history"—an activity which, he said *after* leaving the White House, "I began as a boy and...have kept up ever since."[50]

To profit from the power of history begins with grasping its value and committing to its study. This is the first key lesson learned from Truman, which is captured in the counsel Winston Churchill once offered to a young

American scholar, James Humes. When Humes met Churchill in 1953 while an exchange student at Stowe in England, Churchill told Humes, "Study history, study history—in history lie all the secrets..."[51] Truman, likewise, found such tremendous value in studying history that he emphatically recommended the discipline to all leaders. "Not all readers become leaders," Truman said, "but all leaders must be readers." "There is nothing new in the world except," he said, "the history you do not know."[52]

(2.) <u>Focus on Learning from the Experience of Predecessors.</u>

"The nearest thing to having experience of one's own,
is to have other people's affairs brought before us in a shape that is interesting."[53]

—Benjamin Franklin, *Autobiography*

Closely related to the study of history is the idea of learning from the experience of others. According to the ancient Greek historian Dionysius of Halicarnassus, "History *is* experience teaching through examples."[54]

Particularly useful is learning from the experience—both the successes and failures—of the leading figures in your field. No matter how advanced you are in your career, regardless of whether you are the president, prime minister, or CEO, your own personal experience will always have distinct limits and, therefore, you can always benefit from the study of others' experience as a supplement to your own. As Harvard's Richard Neustadt writes in his book, *Presidential Power and the Modern Presidents*, "If Presidents cannot count on their own experience...they can try to ride on other people's experience, whether direct through observation or indirect through study."[55]

There are numerous advantages to this practice. For one thing, "you can accelerate your growth by learning from the experiences of others in your field."[56] This was the approach of the brilliant German statesman Otto von Bismarck, who once said, "Even fools learn from experience. I prefer to learn from the experience of others."[57]

In Truman's case, along with reading general history, he "particularly liked biography," writes McCullough, and "George Washington, Andrew Jackson, Robert E. Lee; they were his heroes and he wanted to be like they were."[58] Beyond serving as role models, however, what Truman found on a number of different occasions is that being sufficiently familiar with the experience of others can also help you dodge comparable pitfalls and avoid making similar mistakes. This alone proves well worth the time invested in learning about the experience of others.

As our own specific backgrounds and experiences shape the way we view the world, a deep understanding of the background and experiences of others can also help us step outside of our own frames to see the world through different lenses. The more different backgrounds and experiences you collect, the greater your perspective, the more imaginative your ideas, and the more resourceful your thinking, all of which can be a tremendous advantage to the strategist. In his essay, "Wealth," in *The Conduct of Life* (1909), Ralph Waldo Emerson put it this way: "He is the rich man who can avail himself of all men's faculties. He is the richest man who knows how to draw a benefit from the labors of the greatest number of men, of men in distant countries and in past times."[59]

(3.) <u>Exploit the Matthew Effect.</u>

> *"For whoever has will be given more, and they will have an abundance.*
> *Whoever does not have, even what they have will be taken from them."*[60]
> —Jesus on the Parable of the Talents, Matthew 25:29

Known in the Book of Matthew as the "Parable of the Talents," Jesus tells of the master who was leaving on a journey to become king. Before he left, he entrusted each of his three servants with a number of talents or bags of gold, each according to his ability. Each talent was worth a small fortune. To the first servant he gave 10 talents, to the second he gave 5 talents, and to the third he gave 1 talent. When he returned he found that the first two servants had each doubled the number of talents. The master, who was now king, was very pleased and, in response, he gave the first servant 10 cities to oversee, and the second servant five cities. The third servant, however, with only the single talent to return, tried to explain:

> "'Master,' he said, 'I knew that you are a hard man, harvesting where you have not sown and gathering where you have not scattered seed. So I was afraid and went out and hid your gold in the ground. See, here is what belongs to you.'

> "His master replied, 'You wicked, lazy servant! So you knew that I harvest where I have not sown and gather where I have not scattered seed? Well then, you should have put my money on deposit with the bankers, so that when I returned I would have received it back with interest.'

> "'So take the bag of gold from him and give it to the one who has ten bags. For whoever has will be given more, and they will have an abundance. Whoever does not have, even what they have will be taken from them.'"[61]

Known today as the *Matthew Principle* or the *Matthew Effect of Accumulated Advantage*, a term coined by Columbia University sociologist Robert Merton in 1968, this concept is often simplified with the saying "the rich get richer and the poor get poorer."[62] The effects are not limited to economics, however. In fact, the idea that an initial advantage often leads to further advantages can be found at work in all manner of different areas, including making money, accumulating power, gaining influence, and increasing popularity, confidence, and fame. It is, for example, far easier for those who are slightly famous to become even more famous, but it is very difficult (yet still possible) for those who are completely unknown to gain even a little fame.

This principle is also at play in the realm of dating. Desirability, in essence, is *partly* a function of what others desire (also known as social proof). We are more *likely* to desire what many others desire, and we are more *likely* to lack attraction for what many others reject or avoid.

In the animal kingdom, or even biology, a tiny advantage in terms of access to resources often leads to a greater ability to gain even greater resources and, thereby, further dominance and control. A slightly taller or wider plant will receive more rainfall and sunlight, throwing shade on the thirsty plants nearby.

In regards to knowledge, whether in history, leadership studies, psychology, or some other field, it is also true that the more you learn, the easier it will be to absorb even more and, in many cases, the more you will want to learn, and the better you will be able to think about and within that discipline. In short, knowledge is also subject to the principle of accumulated advantage. "Start off with a small net, and you'll always be playing catch-up. …In other words, the knowledge rich tend to get richer, while the knowledge poor get poorer."[63]

You don't have to know a great deal about a topic to greatly increase your ability to learn more and think well. "Knowledge, even shallow knowledge—knowing a little about a lot—widens your cognitive bandwidth. It means you get more out of a trip to the theater or a museum or from a novel, a poem, or a history book."[64]

Knowledge helps you to grasp the essence of what you read more quickly; it makes it easier and more enjoyable for you to engage with others around a greater range of issues.[65] Knowledge enables you to make more meaningful contributions to discussions. Knowledge also makes you less vulnerable to questionable claims. It helps you ask more astute questions and, thereby, receive more helpful answers. "Whoever you are and whatever start you get in life, knowing stuff makes the world more abundant with possibility and gleams of light more likely to illuminate the darkness. It opens the universe a little."[66]

In order to best exploit the Matthew Effect, think in terms of the following three key themes:

(A.) *Build a Foundation of Fundamental Facts.*

One of the best ways to begin to take advantage of the power of the Matthew Effect is to begin building a foundation of fundamental facts and information, which, along with being useful in themselves, can also serve as mental hooks to help you group and organize and recall your memories. Fact-based learning or learning by memorizing facts has its critics, and not without reason. Learning certainly must go beyond mere memorization. However, in most every field of endeavor, memorizing key facts, concepts, and theories is indispensible to chunking information together in memory, drawing connections between ideas and networks of ideas, and building a foundational understanding—each of which, in turn, is critical to deeper learning, higher-level thinking, and more thoughtful analysis.

"Critics of fact-based learning will sometimes ask, 'Why does it matter if a child knows the date of the Battle of Hastings?' It matters," explains Ian Leslie in his book, *Curious: The Desire to Know and Why Your Future Depends On It*, "because facts stored in long-term memory are not islands unto themselves; they join up with other facts to form associative networks of understanding."[67]

Once you know that the Battle of Hastings, a pivotal event in English history, was in 1066, for example, and that that same date also marks the end of the Viking Age (793—1066), then you can begin to grasp connections between the two (e.g. how centuries of onslaught by migrating Viking raiders ultimately led to the consolidation of the weak, warring kingdoms of England, which culminated in the Battle of Hastings). In other words, once important dates like this are chunked and locked in your long-term memory, they can serve as a chronological scaffolding which can help to categorize, contextualize, organize, and recall a great many other important people, places, and events. This scaffolding also provides your brain with the structure and freedom to begin grappling with more critical and creative questions such as the impact of migration and the evolution of nations.[68]

Memorizing important facts and information helps to free our minds to focus on other, more critical tasks. "The less we know in the first place, the more brain power we have to expend on processing, comprehending, and remembering what we've read and the less we have left over to reflect on it."[69]

In 1946, the Dutch chess master and psychologist Adriaan de Groot published a groundbreaking study that showed that it was not analytical thinking or raw computing power that marked the masters of chess, as was typically assumed. De Groot's study, which had a profound influence on the study of expertise in general, found that what stood out about the best chess players was pattern recognition.[70] In other words, compared with the weaker players, the expert players had a superior knowledge of typical chess positions, which they had acquired through memorization. This study has since been replicated across various different fields.[71]

One study even found that those who were considered "poor" readers outperformed "good" readers on scores of reading comprehension whenever the "poor" readers had greater *prior knowledge* of the subject matter.[72] In essence, as Natalie Wexler writes in *Forbes*, and "as cognitive scientists have long known—memorization isn't antithetical to critical and analytical thinking, it's what lays the foundation for it."[73]

It's no surprise that improving your recall of relevant facts will improve your score on questions about those facts. What is surprising is that improving recall of relevant facts also improves scores on questions that require *analysis* related to those facts. What is even more surprising is that scores on questions that require analysis increase *even higher* than questions about the basic recall of those facts. In essence, memorizing relevant facts can be a powerful way to *improve your ability to think.*[74] As Leslie so sardonically put it, "The emptier our long-term memories, the harder we find it to think. Anyone who stops learning facts for himself because he can Google them later [or ask ChatGPT] is literally making himself stupid."[75]

Memorization also helps to prepare our minds for a more nuanced understanding and more thoughtful discussions. This, in turn, can help to spark new insights, spawn creative thinking, and foster more fortuitous effects. As Louis Pasteur said, "Chance favors only the prepared mind."[76]

Brilliant new insights and ideas rarely, if ever, spring fully formed like Athena from the forehead of Zeus the moment you determine to create one. In contrast, brilliant new insights and ideas are far more likely to have roots that reach back across many months or years of study, perhaps even "decades into their author's life; they are products of long-formed habits of mind as much as they are of flashes of brilliance."[77]

As the American Advertising Federation Hall of Fame inductee James Webb Young wrote in his book, *A Technique for Producing Ideas,* "To some minds each fact is a separate bit of knowledge. To others it is a link in a chain of knowledge. It has relationships and similarities. It is not so much a fact as [an] illustration of a general law applying to a whole series of facts."[78]

The general principle, in essence, is that "new knowledge is assimilated better, and has more creative possibility, the bigger the store of existing knowledge it is joining. Knowledge loves knowledge."[79]

None of these ideas will come as a surprise to historians. Nor should it come as a surprise to effective, experienced leaders "whose leisure reading is [typically] dominated by history and biography. In many ways business leaders," writes *Harvard Business Review (HBR),* "regardless of their educational background, must think like historians."[80] This includes more than merely starting with an "insistence on basing any serious decision on facts," or "treating facts with intellectual integrity."[81] "To be a good historian" also requires investing time in gathering, organizing, and understanding the facts, gaining command over the facts in their proper context, "viewing them with an open mind and a willingness to be surprised"[82] and, ultimately, seeking to transform facts and information into practical knowledge and wisdom.

In Truman's case, with scarcely a sprinkling of college courses under his belt, even if he was not always making overt comparisons or drawing on explicit analogues, we know that Truman had amassed a giant catalog of facts and insights and lessons learned from history all of which helped to improve his judgment and make him a more resourceful thinker and, therefore, a more effective leader. With today's intense time pressures and pressing demands, it is easy for future-focused leaders to dismiss this vitally important, but non-urgent activity. "We also know, however," Seaman and Smith write in HBR, "that leaders with no patience for history are missing a vital truth: A sophisticated understanding of the past is one of the most powerful tools we have for shaping the future."[83]

(B.) *Recognize Recurring Patterns, Phases, Cycles, and Themes.*

In an effort to overcome the challenges of predicting the weather, meteorologists[84] have identified a number of weather patterns, meteorological principles and processes, and various other recurring phases and cycles which, taken together, make weather forecasting an indispensable part of protecting life and property from a severe weather event. Similarly, though studies in the social sciences repeatedly reveal the predictability of human behavior, like the weather, human history rarely repeats itself exactly. Yet, as with weather forecasts, there are repeating patterns and recurring themes which allow the steadfast student of history to make wiser and more informed choices. As Mark Twain observed: "History doesn't repeat itself, but it can rhyme."[85] One of the key tasks for strategists is to understand these historical rhythms.

Many of the great political philosophers have alluded to the recurring themes and repeating or expanding patterns of history. Plato wrote in *The Republic* that, "...everything that comes into being must decay...All plants that grow in the earth, and also all animals that grow upon it, have periods of fruitfulness and barrenness of both soul and body as often as the revolutions complete the circumferences of their circles."[86] In the end, Plato writes, "all forms of government [eventually] destroy themselves by carrying their basic principles to excess."[87]

In *Politics*, Aristotle spoke of different regimes (monarchy, aristocracy and democracy), each of which devolves into its own degenerate form (tyranny, oligarchy and anarchy; respectively) until a revolt is brought on as a result.[88,89]

Similarly, Hegel, in his lectures on *The Philosophy of History*, spoke of a "disturbing historical pattern—the crack and fall of civilizations owing to a morbid intensification of their own first principles."[90]

Machiavelli wrote in the *Discourses* of the perennial "renewal" of civic life and the "restoration" of "wholesome laws."[91] Hobbes identifies the "circular motion of the Sovereign Power."[92] Locke describes the "dissolution of government" and a return to the original body.[93]

In the case of the 33rd U.S. President, writes historian Samuel Rushay, "Truman saw cycles in American history," and he repeatedly referred to them. Recognizing the recurring principles, patterns and themes early in his study of history, President Truman himself said, "I began to see that the history of the world has moved in cycles and that very often we find ourselves in the midst of political circumstances which appear to be new but which might have existed in almost identical form at various times during the past 6,000 years."[94]

In another instance, meeting with presidential historian Arthur Schlesinger in the last month of his presidency, Truman shared his fear of the "hysteria" that would follow the end of the Korean War. Hoping the pattern could be interrupted this time, "Truman cited the Citizen Genêt episode after the Revolutionary War, the rise of the Ku Klux Klan after the Civil War, and the A. Mitchell Palmer raids after World War I."[95] Meeting again with Schlesinger in 1954, right around the time Senator Joseph McCarthy's communist witch hunt was at a fever pitch, Truman told the Harvard historian that he had just written a monograph on the "periods of hysteria in American history"[96] expressing his certainty that America would soon emerge from the Red Scare.

Later, in his post-presidential lectures at Columbia University in April 1959, Truman referred to the progressive cycles in American history, including the "witch-hunting" cycles—from the Salem witch trials, to the Alien and Sedition Act of 1800, to the 1830s Anti-Masonic movement.[97]

Despite competing metaphors and differences in time and scope, the central shared idea is that—beyond sheer facts and figures—the study of history reveals vital recurring phases and cycles, repeating principles, patterns, and themes, and that identifying, exploring, and understanding them can prove exceptionally useful. In fact, for the strategist, it can be an invaluable resource, if not a strategic advantage, for better navigating the present and influencing the future. (*See Notes for 6 benefits.*[98])

It is difficult to overstate the value of being able to recognize the repeating patterns and recurring themes of history, particularly the history most relevant to your specific context or domain. Rather than floundering in the muck of short-sighted, disconnected, linear, one-way thinking; master strategists take time to reflect, grasp the big picture, and identify the recurring principles, patterns, cycles, and themes of history to make the wisest and most informed choices possible. To be sure, your future depends on your ability to learn from the past.

(C.) *Build an Arsenal of Analogies, Timeless Principles, Reliable Rules, and Exemplars to Emulate.*

Beyond building a foundation of important information and key facts, there are a handful of other useful ways to approach history and build a base of historical knowledge.

Historical analogies, for instance, which are the basis of the case study method, can be another powerful tool in the strategists arsenal (as we will explore further below). Pinpointing an apt historical analogy can be an illuminating way of making sense of what appears to be a novel event, particularly if there are sufficient similarities. No analogy is perfect, however, and it is important to be aware of assumptions, knowledge gaps, and key differences between the current situation and the historical analogy. Nonetheless, as President Truman argued in his *Memoirs,* "I was beginning to realize—forty years before I had any thought of becoming President of the United States—that almost all current events in the affairs of governments and nations have their parallels...in the past."[99]

Identifying the *relevant sets of timeless, universal principles* can be equally worthwhile in both understanding the past and shaping the future. Aristotle wrote at length about the importance of this subject, arguing that it was impossible to really understand anything without knowing its causes and principles.[100] This too is an area where Plato placed considerable emphasis and, in *The Republic,* he outlined the principles by which he thought political leaders must govern (i.e. by reason, virtue and wisdom).[101]

In the words of celebrated American author, educator and businessman Stephen Covey, "The lesson of history is that to the degree people and civilizations have operated in harmony with correct principles, they have prospered. At the root of societal declines are foolish practices that represent violations of correct principles. Whether or not we believe in them, they have been proven effective throughout centuries of human history."[102]

Referring to a particular set of principles, President Truman himself said, "History showed me...ideas of government that are imperishable and fundamental to any society of people living together and governing themselves."[103]

"All the great captains of antiquity," Napoleon Bonaparte said, "and those who in modern times have successfully trodden in their steps, performed vast achievements, only by conforming with the *rules and principles* of the art; that is to say, by correct combinations, and by justly comparing the relation between means and consequences, effects and obstacles. They succeeded only by the strict observance of these rules, whatever may have been the boldness of their enterprises, or the extent of the advantages gained."[104]

Despite the power of proven principles and reliable rules, most leaders prefer a good analogy. What's more, as Axelrod and Forster write, "although the abstraction of general principles and rules is often treated as the highest form of intellectual accomplishment, there is substantial and wide-ranging evidence that human reasoning is heavily grounded in previous examples or cases to make sense of novel situations encountered in the world."[105] Rather than one or the other, however, the ideal is "both and..." Build an arsenal of analogies and a pool of proven principles and reliable rules as well.

As discussed in above, it is also possible to benefit from the study of key historical figures and worthy exemplars. In Truman's case, it was frequently through the stories of the leading legends and heroes of history that he approached the topic and, over time, developed his *accumulated advantage*. As he read history and biography, writes McCullough, "his list of heroes advanced. To Andrew Jackson, Hannibal, and Robert E. Lee were added Cincinnatus, Scipio, Cyrus the Great, and Gustavus Adolphus, the seventeenth-century Swedish king."[106]

(4.) Develop Effortless Recall.

At the 1948 Democratic National Convention in Philadelphia, President Harry Truman found himself waiting for hours in a room at the hotel, biding his time until it was his turn to take the stage. As he stood on the balcony looking out over the city, he reflected back on America's history of political conventions. "It hardly seemed possible to me," he said, "in the early-morning hours of July 15, 1948, that so much had happened since that 1944 convention at which I was nominated for the vice-presidency and that shortly I was to take my place before the 1948 Democratic National Convention to accept the nomination for President of the United States. Into this situation," Truman continued, "as into every major experience which I went through in that high office, I went with a consciousness of the history of American government and politics. The caucuses and conventions of the forty national elections which had preceded that of 1948 were as real to me as the one before which I was about to make my appearance."[107]

It was an interesting choice of words. He didn't say, 'I had a book on the shelf I could refer to if needed,' or, as one might today, 'I could go and look them all up online.' No. He said these 40 prior conventions "were as real to me" as the one in which he was about to actually participate.[108]

In regards to strategic thinking, this was an immensely resourceful place to be. Indeed, because they were so real to him, Truman, in effect, had far more than his own experience to draw on while navigating a convention that was not without its challenges, particularly given that Truman was widely expected to lose his bid for reelection.

This is the power of *effortless recall*. When you understand something so well, when you are so familiar with its various key elements and determining factors that you can instantly recall them without effort, this is what transforms the experience of others into something approaching, and akin to, your own experience. What's more, as we know from cognitive psychology, the more available (or salient) your knowledge or experience, the more "readily it will be recalled and used in judgment."[109]

In other words, your brain will give more weight to what you can easily recall, even if what you easily recall is not nearly as useful or relevant as whatever you might struggle to recall—never mind all the useful and relevant history of which you are completely unaware and incapable of recalling.

In essence, your judgment, the effectiveness of your decision making, is significantly dependent on the breadth and depth of the historical facts, the recurring patterns and themes, and the analogies and principles which you are able to effortlessly recall.

In short, the quality of your decisions depends on the *accumulated knowledge* you can *effortlessly recall*—regardless of whether that knowledge is based on personal experience or from learning about the experience of others.

As Napoleon Bonaparte put it, "Knowledge of grand tactics is gained only by experience and by the study of the campaigns of all the great captains." The task then, he said, is "to read and *reread* the campaigns of Alexander, Hannibal, Caesar, Gustavus, Eugene and Frederick. This is the only way to became a great captain."[110] "Thus, Napoleon, like many others, regarded the combination of experience plus reflection upon the immediate and distant past as essential guideposts…"[111]

Once described as "a thorough, dedicated, deeply *read* professional solider,"[112] perhaps it was U.S. General George S. Patton who explained it best. In his last year at West Point,[113] the 24-year-old Patton wrote in his cadet notebook, "I believe that in order for a man to become a great soldier…it is necessary for him to be so thoroughly conversant with all sorts of military possibilities that whenever an occasion arises he has at his hand *without effort on his part* a parallel. To attain this end," Patton continued, "I think that it is necessary for a man to begin to read military history in its earliest and hence crudest form and to follow it down in natural sequence permitting his mind to grow with his subject until he can grasp *without effort* the most abstruse question of the science of war because he is already permeated with all its elements."[114]

The Spanish-American philosopher George Santayana famously said, "Those who cannot remember the past are condemned to repeat it."[115] What we learn from Patton, Napoleon, Truman, and countless others is, for the strategist, equally important: Those who can effortlessly recall the past are best equipped to shape the future.

Discover Your Love of the Sport of History.

Years later, even after Truman was well adjusted to his role and responsibilities as president, he continued to turn to history to deal with the challenges he faced. He continued to accumulate knowledge, cultivate insight and wisdom, and unearth leadership lessons he had not yet learned.

Given the office and his infectious enthusiasm for history, it's no surprise that Truman frequently discussed history with others in his administration. Reflecting back on his numerous trips with Truman "to Key West or Shangri-La (later [renamed] Camp David) or aboard the *Williamsburg*," one assistant to the President, Joseph Feeney, recalled the impressive scope of Truman's historical knowledge.[116]

"...The thing that amazed me," Feeney said, "was his very complete knowledge of history; he was an expert on military history. And I said to him one time, 'How do you ever remember so many facts and details about military history?'"[117]

"Because I love it,'" Truman said.[118]

Indeed, Feeney recalled in an interview later, "He had a great love for history—great love for history. And I always felt that when he left the Presidency, and I asked him one time if he wouldn't like to become a professor of history at a university, and he said, 'That's the one thing in my life that I'd like.' He said, 'I hope when I leave the White House some university will offer me a professorship.'"[119]

After a lifetime of leadership experience, ten years in the U.S. Senate, and nearly eight years as Commander-in-Chief, Harry S. Truman believed that a thorough and scrupulous study of the leaders of the past was an unparalleled advantage, an indispensable way to prepare to meet the leadership challenges of the future—even as the President of the United States. "I think every one of our past presidents who made great names for themselves," Truman wrote, "were men who knew history..."[120]

"It was the same with those old birds in Greece and Rome as it is now..." Truman declared; "the only thing new in this world is the history that you don't know."[121] In his book, *Where the Buck Stops*, Truman adds: "In a sense, that's one of the main reasons for writing this book: To get people, perhaps some future presidents among them, interested in history and make them realize how important an understanding of the past is in dealing with the present and the future."[122]

As dedicated as he was to the sport of history, however, Truman did not always hit the mark. As we will explore below, there were also those times when he failed in his efforts to draw on history, and there were other times when he foolishly disregarded the lessons we know he learned from the past.

Exploit the Power of Analogy to Sharpen Decisions, Expand Options, and Increase Your Probability of Success: President Truman Draws the Line on Military Aggression in Korea

"Whoever considers the past and the present will readily observe that all cities and all peoples are and ever have been animated by the same desires and the same ferments; so that it is easy, by diligent study of the past, to foresee what is likely to happen in the future...and to prepare those remedies that were used by the ancients, or, not finding any that were employed by them, to devise new ones from the similarity of events."[1]

—Niccolò Machiavelli (1469—1527), *Discourses on Livy*

Suddenly, an emergency call came in for President Harry S. Truman while he was on vacation at his home in Missouri. It was just after ten o'clock at night on Saturday, June 24, 1950, and Secretary of State Dean Acheson was on the line. "Mr. President," he said, "I have very serious news."[2]

North Korea, the infamously oppressive, Soviet-backed communist regime which occupies the northern part of the Korean Peninsula, had just invaded the U.S.-backed South Korea with a force of nearly 100,000 men. Once united but ruled with an iron fist by the Empire of Japan, the Korean Peninsula was divided down the 38th parallel in 1945, following the U.S. victory over Japan at the end of World War II, creating a boundary between Soviet and American occupation zones.

Now, without warning, trained and sustained by Soviet arms and aid, North Korean forces swept across the 38th parallel, inciting what some considered a civil war. Unprepared for such a massive surprise onslaught, the South Korean forces were easily overwhelmed, and soon surrendered Seoul, the capital of South Korea, to the communist forces.

Believing that Soviet leader Joseph Stalin was behind the communist invasion of South Korea, President Truman was furious. But what should he do? Was this really only a civil war? A conflict to be sorted out by the Korean people? Could the U.S. justify *inaction* given that the conflict was contained on the Korean Peninsula? What's more, given the recent world wars and the history of isolationism, would American citizens tolerate U.S. intervention in what was perceived by some to be just another foreign war?

To Realize Your Vision of the Future, Turn to and Learn from the Past.

Truman immediately cut his vacation short. Flying back to D.C. on *Independence* (his presidential plane, named after his hometown), Truman turned his mind to previous acts of military aggression to help him make sense of the situation he was facing now.[3] "The plane left the Kansas City Municipal Airport at two o'clock, and it took just a little over three hours to make the trip to Washington. I had time to think aboard the plane," Truman recalled in his *Memoirs*.[4] "In my generation, this was not the first occasion when the strong had attacked the weak. I recalled some earlier instances: Manchuria, Ethiopia, Austria. I remembered how each time that the democracies failed to act it had encouraged the aggressors to keep going ahead."[5]

In other words, from Truman's *initial* vantage point, informed by the record of the past, this was no mere civil war. This was the spread of something more sinister. This was an unmistakable part of a mighty clash between what he called the "totalitarian regimes" and the "free peoples" of the world. "Communism," he continued, "was acting in Korea just as Hitler, Mussolini, and the Japanese had acted ten, fifteen, and twenty years earlier."[6]

In what became known as the Truman Doctrine, President Truman had already taken a strong stand against the spread of communism in a March 12, 1947 speech, which marked the start of the Cold War. Pledging to "support free peoples who are resisting attempted subjugation by armed minorities or by outside pressures," Truman stated that it was the policy of the United States to contain Soviet geopolitical expansion.[7]

Now, reflecting on the current crisis in Korea, he said, "I felt certain that if South Korea was allowed to fall Communist leaders would be emboldened to override nations closer to our own shores. If the Communists were permitted to force their way into the Republic of Korea without opposition from the free world, no small nation would have the courage to resist threats and aggression by stronger Communist neighbors. If this was allowed to go unchallenged it would mean a third world war, just as similar incidents had brought on the second world war. It was also clear to me," Truman continued, "that the foundations and the principles of the United Nations were at stake unless this unprovoked attack on Korea could be stopped."[8]

While in flight, Truman radioed Acheson to set up a dinner conference at the Blair House.[9] After a full briefing and recommendations, Truman opened the meeting up for discussion. He asked everyone of the thirteen officials to state whether they agreed or disagreed on any point and to share any other views they might have.

At this point, Truman was surprised and encouraged by the fact that, as he later recorded, there was "complete, almost unspoken acceptance on the part of everyone that whatever had to be done to meet this aggression had to be done. There was no suggestion from anyone that either the United Nations or the United States could back away from it."[10] Rather than being a case of groupthink (e.g. see the Bay of Pigs fiasco in Chapter 4), Truman saw this as confirmation that they had learned one of the key lessons from World War II: The need for "collective security."[11] Following an emergency session at the United Nations, Secretary Acheson also reported that the U.N. Security Council "had, by a vote of 9 to 0, approved a resolution declaring that a breach of the peace had been committed by the North Korean action and ordering the North Koreans to cease their action and withdraw their forces."[12]

There *was*, however, some lukewarm opposition in the U.S. Senate. But Truman had made his decision; "the United States President had to stand firm."[13] "I'm not going to tremble like a psychopath before the Russians," he told one worried senator; "I'm not going to surrender all our rights, or the rights of the South Koreans."[14] Rather, Truman vowed privately, "By God, I am going to let them have it."[15] The only big question remaining was precisely how was he going to do it.

As soon as the U.N. Security Council approved the use of force, Truman approved a bombing campaign against North Korea below the 38th parallel.[16] At this point, Truman was still reluctant to commit ground troops but also still confident that the communists could be defeated by air and naval power alone.

Unfortunately, the bombing proved insufficient. After capturing Seoul, North Korean forces continued to progress southwards.

On June 30, Truman committed ground troops to South Korea. Unified under U.N. command, headed by U.S. General Douglas MacArthur, the U.S. troops were accompanied by fighting forces from 16 additional nations tasked with expelling the communists from South Korea.

After an initial stumble around the southern port city of Pusan, General MacArthur executed a daring rescue plan. After cutting off North Korean supply lines, MacArthur's U.S. and U.N. forces retook Seoul and began driving what was left of the largely eviscerated North Korean army back into the North, beyond the 38th parallel. President Truman was elated, and General MacArthur was a war hero once again. Unfortunately, this was only the beginning of the Korean War.

Exploit History's Recurring Patterns, Rhythms, and Rhymes.

"History does not repeat itself, but it often rhymes."[17]
—Mark Twain, Samuel Clemens (1835—1910), American Writer, Lecturer, Humorist

Thucydides, a military general of Ancient Athens, is generally recognized today as the most influential historian of all time. Known as both the "father of scientific history" and "the father of political realism," Thucydides is still studied at military academies around the world. In the introduction to his most famous work, the *History of the Peloponnesian War*, written over 2,500 years ago, Thucydides argued that his history would equip future leaders to make wiser decisions when they face "comparable choices."[18] History was, he wrote, for "those who want to understand clearly the events, which happened in the past, and which (human nature being what it is) will at some time or other and in much the same ways be repeated in the future."[19]

Vice Admiral James Bond Stockdale, the former President of both the Naval War College and The Citadel, believed that the disciplined study of history was indispensable to effective leadership. In fact, according to

Stockdale, a three-star naval officer who spent seven years as a prisoner of war in Vietnam, "The single most important foundation for any leader is a solid academic background in history. That discipline gives perspective to the problems of the present and drives home the point that there is really very little new under the sun."[20]

This is exactly what President Truman believed, as he said himself again and again with both his words and actions. "I believe that people in positions of responsibility in government should know the historical background of these periods...and the events which have led to them," Truman said on another occasion, referring to the recurring historical patterns around mass hysteria.[21]

Of course, Truman's use of history was no guarantee that he would always get the decision right. After all, "thinking historically," Seaman and Smith write in *Harvard Business Review (HBR)*, "is not easy. It requires an appreciation of the dynamic nature of change in a complex human system. It demands an understanding of the particularity of problems and the often unintended consequences of their solutions. Emphasizing the contingency of cause and effect, it rejects formulaic approaches, because no two situations are ever identical in detail or in context."[22]

Fortunately, it is not an identical situation or duplicate context that we require. As Twain suggested, it is the detection and discernment of history's rhymes and rhythms that strategists desire.[23] "That is why we also search for useful analogues in history. For it is in the rhyming, the patterns, that we can find perspective on the dimensions of our challenges and on the questions we must pose in order to progress."[24]

Reason by Historical Analogy

In the matter of going to war against North Korea in defense of South Korea, Truman's use of history is generally applauded by historians today. Unlike Vietnam and other U.S. military debacles, write Neustadt and May, "along with the American Revolution and World War II, Korea is an exception. Few historians write it off as a blunder or an avoidable tragedy. Nor do we."[25] Instead, the authors of *Thinking in Time* continue, "Truman's way of using history in June 1950 had much to commend it."[26]

But what exactly was Truman's way of using history in 1950 and when, where, and how did it go wrong? The following are the three (3) key lessons we can learn from the 33rd President's use of history in this early stage of the Korean War:

Draw on Historical Analogies to Explore, Strategize, and, with a Little Luck, Make Fewer Mistakes. The first and most obvious way in which Truman used history was through the use of analogy or analogical reasoning. Considered "fundamental to human thought,"[27] the idea of reasoning by analogy is that when faced with an unknown situation, we can draw on a known situation which is similar in order to better understand what might otherwise remain unknown. Because two situations are similar in some important respects, we may reasonably infer that some additional similarities exist as well.

According to the *Stanford Encyclopedia of Philosophy*, "Analogies are widely recognized as playing an important *heuristic* role, as aids to discovery. They have been employed, in a wide variety of settings and with considerable success, to generate insight and to formulate possible solutions to problems."[28] In the words of pioneering political theorist and philosopher Joseph Priestley, "analogy is our best guide in all philosophical investigations; and all discoveries, which were not made by mere accident, have been made by the help of it..."[29]

"Benjamin Franklin," for example, "conducted his kite experiment to test an analogy he drew between lightning and [static] electricity."[30] Galileo used the analogy of the moon's orbit around the Earth to make the case that the Earth orbited the sun (and therefore, that the sun was the center of the universe—a highly controversial idea at the time).[31] Isaac Newton relied on analogy in "his hypothesis that the orbits of the planets are governed by gravitational force."[32]

The list goes on and on, well beyond science and innovation.[33] Whether we realize it or not, we all reason by analogy all the time. "Faced with an unfamiliar problem or opportunity," writes HBR, "senior managers often think back to some similar situation they have seen or heard about, draw lessons from it, and apply those lessons to the current situation."[34]

Thus, the key to improve your decision-making is to recognize this fact and, more importantly, to recognize it while it is happening. The problem is that very few leaders ever stop to think about their thinking, they neglect to "realize that they're reasoning by analogy. As a result, they are unable to make use of insights that psychologists, cognitive scientists, and political scientists have generated about the power and the pitfalls of analogy."[35] The good news, Gavetti and Rivkin conclude in "How Strategists Really Think: Tapping the Power of Analogy," is that leaders who *do* "pay attention to their own analogical thinking will make better strategic decisions and fewer mistakes."[36]

In Truman's case, he recognized the power of this mental tool early on. As he said himself, decades before he even entertained the notion of national office, "almost all current events...have their parallels and precedents in the past. It was obvious to me even then that a clear understanding of administrative problems presupposes a knowledge of similar ones as recorded in history and of their disposition. Long before I ever considered going into public life, I had arrived at the conclusion that no decisions affecting the people should be made impulsively, but on the basis of historical background and careful consideration of the facts as they exist at the time."[37]

When Truman suddenly ascended to the presidency upon the death of FDR, his mind immediately turned to historical parallels. From his earlier reading, he said, "I learned of the unique problems of Andrew Johnson, whose destiny it was to be thrust suddenly into the presidency to fill the shoes of one of history's great leaders. When the same thing happened to me, I knew just how Johnson had coped with his problems, and I did not make the mistakes he made."[38]

When it came to the matter of Korea, Truman again turned to historical analogies. "Truman said in his memoirs that three events of the 1930s had come to his mind: the Manchurian incident of 1931–32, when Japan seized Manchuria from China; Italy's aggression against Ethiopia in 1935; and Hitler's forcible annexation of Austria (the Anschluss) in 1938."[39]

When Truman spoke to Congress about why he decided to send troops into Korea, he again turned to historical analogy, speaking of the "fateful events of the nineteen-thirties, when aggression unopposed bred more aggression and eventually war."[40]

Given his lifelong study of history, Truman had a great many sources he could draw on to help generate insight and better inform his decisions. But he also had his favorites which he returned to again and again. When he was asked in an interview, for example, about reading Plutarch's *Parallel Lives* (a favorite of Catherine the Great as well[41]), Truman said,

"I've read Plutarch through many times since. I never have figured out how he knew so much. I tell you. They just don't come any better than old Plutarch. He knew more about politics than all the other writers I've read put together. When I was in politics, there would be times when I tried to figure somebody out, and I could always turn to Plutarch, and nine times out of ten I'd be able to find a parallel in there."[42] In one case, Truman continues,

> "In 1940, when I was running for reelection to the Senate, there was this big apple grower named Stark trying to beat me. I'd started him out in politics, but in 1940 he was out to lick me, and I couldn't figure it out. But the more I thought about him, the more he reminded me of what Plutarch said about Nero. I'd done a lot of thinking about Nero. What I was interested in was how having started as well as he did, he ended up in ruin. And Plutarch said the start of his troubles was when he began to take his friends for granted and started to buy his enemies. And I noticed some of those same traits in old Stark. That's how I decided I could lick him, and I did, of course. Nobody thought I could, but I did. I'll tell you about that campaign at another time....But about Plutarch. It was the same with those old birds in Greece and Rome as it is now. I told you. The only thing new in the world is the history you don't know."[43]

Recalling a handful of the countless lessons he learned from history, America's 33rd President makes a compelling case for the study of history as the foundation for effective leadership. "History taught me," Truman writes in his *Memoirs*, "that the leader of any country, in order to assume his responsibilities as a leader, must know the history of not only his own country but of all the other great countries, and that he must make the effort to apply this knowledge to the decisions that have to be made for the welfare of all the people."[44]

"These lessons," he acquired from his reading of history were, he said, "...to stand me in good stead years later, when I was to be confronted with similar problems. There were countless other lessons which history taught that would prove valuable to me."[45] Truman continues,

"There was the miserable performance of the Committee on the Conduct of the War in the 1860s, which did such a poor job for the federal government that Douglas Freeman, talking about his biography of Robert E. Lee, told me the committee was worth several divisions to the Confederacy. I was thoroughly familiar with the antics of that committee, and as chairman of the Senate special committee to investigate the defense effort in the 1940s, I avoided every pitfall into which my predecessors had fallen."[46]

"By nature not given to making snap judgments or easy decisions," Truman added on another occasion, "I required all available facts and information before coming to a decision. But once a decision was made, I did not worry about it afterward, I had trained myself to look back into history for precedents, because instinctively I sought perspective in the span of history for the decisions I had to make. That is why I read and re-read history. Most of the problems a President has to face have their roots in the past."[47]

Identify Alternative Historical Analogies. As powerful as analogical reasoning can be, it would be a mistake to simply identify the first suitable analogy that comes to mind and then latch on like a leech, sucking the host dry until it dies. In most cases, it is better to have at least one good working analogy than none at all. At the very least, this will give you a point of contrast and comparison, something with which to wrestle and reflect. However, getting too caught up with one comparable set of circumstances or historical analogy will also likely present certain pitfalls and traps.

Avoid Fighting Only the Last War. Winston Churchill once said that, "Generals are always prepared to fight the last war."[48] In most cases, the generals in the upcoming or current conflict are the ones who lived through the last war. The generals personally experienced the successes and failures of the last war. In the last war, the generals witnessed some of their own men die. Not surprisingly, they are exceptionally eager to both do what they know worked in the last war, and avoid repeating any of the same mistakes. The problem is that, as with drawing on a *single* analogy, from the perspective of the long history of warfare, the last war offers only a limited range of lessons to learn and apply. "The terrible losses of the American Civil War, the Boer War, the Russo-Japanese War, and, above all, the First World War are part of the reason 'fighting the last war' has become shorthand for murderous folly. The blood price paid on the Somme and at Verdun is seen as eloquent condemnation of military rigidity, of generals who couldn't understand that old tactics were suicidal against new weapons."[49]

Do not misunderstand: The point is not that the last war is necessarily a weak analogy. The last war may actually turn out to be a surprisingly suitable analogy. "If military technology is stable—as was the case, for example, in the long age of black powder and fighting sail—the lessons of the last war probably retain their authority."[50] What's more, as Fredric Smoler writes in *American Heritage*, "Alexander, Hannibal, Caesar, Marlborough, Eugene of Savoy, and the Duke of Wellington are famous for having very effectively fought the last war."[51]

The point is to avoid holding the last war—or any other compelling analogy—too tightly. There is a fair chance that more than a couple of key factors are significantly different, particularly in terms of technology, but you could easily overlook those key differences if you are too attached to your analogy.

Sadly, this is far more common than you might imagine. The generals and politicians involved in World War II were practically obsessed with "the beginnings, conduct, and aftermath of World War I."[52] As Holyoak and Thagard write in their book, *Mental Leaps: Analogy in Creative Thought*, "It often seems as if some single source analog dominates the decision making of a generation of leaders, who apply it profligately and uncritically to whatever crises arise on their watch."[53]

Perhaps the most ridiculous example of this—the inclination to become too reliant on an analogy simply because it is most salient—is one that has been given its own name, Godwin's law, which the *Oxford English Dictionary* defines as, "a facetious aphorism maintaining that as an online debate increases in length, it becomes inevitable that someone will eventually compare someone or something to Adolf Hitler or the Nazis."[54]

The fact is that, no matter how timely or sufficiently similar, the more you rely on one analogy alone, the more likely you are to make some mistake. Somewhere, somehow that one analogy will not match up the way you imagined. We live in a world of continuous change. "There is nothing permanent except change,"[55] the ancient Greek philosopher Heraclitus wrote more than 2,500 years ago. "You cannot step into the same river twice; for it's not the same river, and it's not the same man."[56]

In C.S. Lewis' *The Chronicles of Narnia*, Lucy asks the lion Aslan, who represents Christ, "Why couldn't you come roaring in to save us like last time?" To which Aslan replies, "Things never happen the same way twice."[57]

Likewise, looking back over just the last few wars reveals one of the most critical, timeless and universal lessons: War is always changing. Particularly in the last century and a half, the rapid and near constant evolution of technology and "successive revolutions in tactics," continuously changes the way we wage war.[58] This holds true in business, politics, science, entertainment, and virtually every other field. This does not make analogical reasoning irrelevant, however. In fact, continuous change makes useful analogies all the more important, but also all the more critical to use well. "Every historical analogy must be carefully examined to see if it really sheds light on the situation at hand. Even if it sheds some light, it will not provide a ready-made solution.

When it comes down to it, there is simply no substitute for actually thinking through all the options in a given situation."[59]

Answer the Problems of History with More History. We study history to learn the lessons, avoid the disasters, shorten the learning curve, and make wiser, more strategic decisions. And, yet, as with all of the social sciences, the historical record is complete with inherent biases, inaccuracies, distortions and, in some cases, downright deception. Winston Churchill, an outspoken believer in the need for leaders to study history, also openly confessed to his own bias. "History is going to be kind to me," Churchill said, "for I intend to write it."[60] Napoleon Bonaparte, another unabashed supporter of the study of history, once asked rhetorically, "What is history but a fable agreed upon?"[61]

However, to conclude that history is somehow unimportant, insignificant, or irrelevant to the challenges of today would be foolish, unreasonable, and unsound. Business, law, political science, international relations, leadership studies, sociology, economics—numerous disciplines use history as a primary resource for decision-making and analysis.

The solution to the challenge of bias and inaccuracy is not to neglect the study of history—quite the opposite. The solution is to read *multiple* accounts across a range of alternative perspectives. In the words of one historian, "practical realism dictates that the sum of interpretations, the common efforts, of objective scholars can and does reveal a reasonably accurate picture of the past."[62]

In essence, rather than employing a *single* historical analogue to *determine* your course, far better to selectively use *multiple* alternative analogies, "often in piecemeal fashion,"[63] through which to *explore, analyze,* and *assess* the many possible courses of action. "History offers appropriate, plausible analogies, not final answers."[64] Yes, there are biases. Yes, there are distortions. "History does not repeat itself precisely, and all historical analogies are imperfect," writes Yale historian Donald Kagan, and, nevertheless, the careful study of historical analogues can still prove immensely useful in exploiting the opportunities and avoiding the perils in the path ahead.[65]

Be Aware of the Analogies at Work. No doubt, Harry Truman was steeped in history and his knowledge and understanding of history served him at nearly every turn. What's more, Truman often did identify multiple alternative analogies. In the case of his own transition to the presidency following the death of FDR, for example, Truman recalled other difficult transitions including John Adams to Thomas Jefferson, William Howard Taft to Woodrow Wilson, Woodrow Wilson to Warren Harding, and Herbert Hoover to Franklin Roosevelt. Likewise, in the matter of North Korea, the Red Scare, and other domestic issues, Truman often had a number of historical analogies in mind.

Truman also surrounded himself with advisors who could *supplement* his historical knowledge and propose alternative analogies from their own accumulated knowledge of history. In the case of North Korea's border-crossing aggression against South Korea, not surprisingly, there were a number of other useful historical parallels. One compelling example might have been the civil war in Spain, "when the great powers pretended to leave Spain alone while in actuality the Germans and Italians helped the Nationalists, the Russians aided the Republicans, and all were disappointed by the ultimate outcome."[66] "He could equally well have called to mind the Rhineland crisis of 1936, when Hitler suddenly marched troops into that presumably demilitarized area, or the Czech crisis of 1938, when Britain, France, and Italy bought temporary peace at the Munich Conference by giving Hitler crucial portions of Czechoslovakia."[67] Fortunately, Neustadt reports, "others in his circle made reference to those events,"[68] but it was only because Truman was wise enough to surround himself with others who studied history.

But how well did Truman use the historical analogies that came to his attention? It is impossible to know exactly what Truman was thinking in each case. We may get some idea based on what he said, both publicly and privately, but the challenge is distinguishing between the analogies he used to *justify* his actions and the analogies, beliefs, and values he *actually used* to make his decisions. As Chris Argyris and Donald Schön point out with their *theories of action*—Truman himself may not have recognized any difference between his *espoused theory*—the mental frames, analogies, perspectives, beliefs, principles, et cetera that people *claim* to follow or which they *believe* guide their actions— and his *theory-in-use*—the mental frames, analogies, perspectives, beliefs, principles, et cetera that *actually drive* people's actions. Few people are aware of their *theories-in-use*, never mind that they are often surprisingly different from their *espoused theories*.

But the point is not that they must always be the same. There certainly may be times when you need to rely on one particular historical analogy as a means of rationalization or as a tool of persuasion and advocacy. The point, however, for strategists, is that you must be aware of the theories, analogies, or frames that are *actually operating* (i.e. theory-in-use) so that you can understand your thoughts and actions and question or even challenge your relevant mental models, perspectives, or beliefs. It makes little sense to test the analogy you are merely *espousing* or challenge the theory or worldview that is *not actually guiding or determining your actions*, while failing to notice the one that is.

Similar risks arise when you use a compelling historical analogy merely to justify what you have already made up your mind to say or do. The point is that it is difficult if not impossible to take the wisest actions or adopt the most strategic course if you are not clear and honest with yourself about the theories behind your decisions.

Likewise, it is equally unwise to disregard a fitting analogy simply because it does not serve your predetermined purposes. Just because you "do not wish to use it," does not mean that it is safe to ignore.[69] "The unwillingness of Lyndon Johnson and his advisers to pay close attention to the French defeat in Indochina when deciding to Americanize the war in Vietnam is a case in point.

The Johnson administration did produce a memorandum called "France in Vietnam, 1954, and the U.S. in Vietnam, 1965—A Useful Analogy?" But the document was not taken seriously. For obvious reasons," Robert Dallek writes in *The New Republic*, "it emphasized the differences rather than the similarities, and it was used for advocacy rather than analysis…"[70] The U.S. war in Afghanistan offers another stark warning. A number of foreign powers have proven unable to secure a lasting victory in Afghanistan, including major powers such as the Soviet Union and the British Empire, which failed on three separate occasions. And, yet, more than a few American presidents imagined they could somehow succeed where so many others have failed. As of President Joe Biden's disastrous 2021 withdrawal, lasting victory in Afghanistan continues to prove elusive.

This leads us to the third crucial step in reasoning through historical analogy.

<u>Look Beyond Superficial Similarities and Differences. Inspect the Historical Analogy in Depth.</u> When you are faced with a difficult situation filled with unknowns, there is undoubtedly some sense of reassurance in identifying a compelling historical analogy. But herein lies the trap. A little familiarity can create a false sense of security which can keep you from looking beyond superficial similarities and differences. What's more, the real value is found in the enhanced perception and insights gained from a more thorough analysis or thoughtful comparison of the similarities and differences between the present situation and the past.[71]

The human brain evolved to recognize patterns. In fact, our ability to recognize and process patterns is one of the key distinguishing factors of the brain and which makes us superior to other species.[72] Problems arise, however, when we start to base decisions on superficial similarities and differences, or when context and conflicting information is ignored. To be seduced by the superficial is to significantly increase the probability of poor decisions, unexpected outcomes, and, ultimately, the failure of your intended aims. The risk is particularly acute if the similar situation is close in time, location, or to the individuals involved. The following three key steps can help to lessen the risk:

(1.) *Surface the Analogy in Mind, Make Explicit Your Use.* The key to avoid being led astray by false analogies is first and foremost awareness. In other words, simply stop to explicitly acknowledge the fact that you are employing an analogy and that—despite the similarities and because of the differences—the present situation may not play out the way you think. This alone will help to open your mind to more careful inspection and more critical and reflective use of that analogy.[73] The crucial advantage with being explicit is that you are much more likely to avoid a bad analogy. This awareness should lead directly to the second key to avoid being led astray by a false analogy.

(2.) *Make a Deeper Comparison.* By far the best way to make use of analogical thinking is to make the time to carefully analyze the analogies you are using. This includes, at the very least, getting clear about the similarities and the differences. Given that our brains evolved to recognize patterns, the similarities between two situations often spring to mind easily. In order to make effective decisions, however, it is important to also think about the relevant differences and how and where the analogy breaks down. Neustadt and May recommend listing the similarities and differences between the historical analogy and the current situation in two columns which, they argue, "can help block misleading analogies."[74] They are also quite clear on the need to *write it down*; as Lee Iacocca once said, "In conversation you can get away with all kinds of vagueness and nonsense, often without even realizing it. But there's something about putting your thoughts on paper that forces you to get down to specifics. That way, it's harder to deceive yourself-or anybody else."[75]

(3.) *Review the Context, Trace the History.* Reviewing the issue in context can also be critical to assessing the effectiveness of the analogy. As part of analyzing the context, Neustadt and May recommend "tracing how the specific concerns arose."[76] Rather than simply noting similarities, it can be immensely helpful to identify the catalyst, trigger, causal factors, or preceding events that led to the issue in question in the first place.

This was one of the key practices that set apart Under Secretary of State George Ball, the sole internal dissenter of the escalation of the Vietnam War, the man Holyoak and Thagard refer to as "the greatest American political analogist of his time."[77] Serving in the administrations of both John F. Kennedy and Lyndon Johnson, Ball was outspoken in his opposition to the war in Vietnam. Pleading with John F. Kennedy to recall France's failure in Vietnam, Ball once said to the President, "Within five years we'll have 300,000 men in the paddies and jungles and never find them again."[78] Kennedy reportedly laughed and replied, "Well, George, you're supposed to be one of the smartest guys in town, but you're crazier than hell. That will never happen."[79]

Tragically, Ball's prediction proved remarkably prescient. Unlike other key advisors in the Johnson administration, Ball took a more contextual view of relevant historical analogues. "Using multiple analogies, selectively and often in piecemeal fashion," Ball, the authors of *Mental Leaps* write, "was able to contrast the situations in Korea and Vietnam without entirely dismissing the Korean precedent. He focused on specific causal factors linked to the outcomes in each situation, such as the contrast between the stable government and strong leader of Korea and the shifting, unpopular figures who headed the government of South Vietnam. Ball's opponents in the debates often seemed to confuse the causal relevance of similarities and differences."[80]

In the case of the Truman administration and North Korea, to their credit, they were clearly drawing on a number of relevant historical analogies. Focused primarily on superficial similarities, however, what Truman and his advisors apparently failed to do was scrutinize those various alternative analogies in any real depth.

As we will examine in the following section, this lack of sufficient rigor and precision almost certainly contributed to Truman's failure to adequately define the final strategic objective or exit strategy he had in mind when he made the decision to enter the war.[81] Unfortunately, failing to *firmly and explicitly* establish a clear end game allowed Truman's successful military intervention to rapidly escalate, but ultimately devolve into its own disastrous undoing.

Think in Time to Influence the Future, Make the Most of the Power of the Past with a Systematic Plan: General MacArthur and President Truman Blunder Across the Korean Rubicon

"History is a vast early warning system."[1]
—Norman Cousins, American Author & Professor

Raising a shot glass full of whiskey to his lips, the President jerked his head back and gulped down the smooth, slightly musky bourbon. A warm feeling of excitement settled in his stomach that matched his mood. President Truman had gathered together with a few friends and close members of his staff to celebrate General Douglas MacArthur's successful amphibious landing at Inchon, South Korea, a daring masterstroke that helped turn the tide of the Korean War.

When the war first broke out, Truman's goal was to push North Korea back across the 38th parallel. Of course, he wanted to teach the invaders a lesson and, as he said soon after he learned of the invasion, "By God, I am going to let them have it!"[2] The goal was not, however, to obliterate North Korea entirely. Nor was the goal to unify the Korean peninsula under the leadership of South Korea. "That was not the intent at all," Assistant to the President George M. Elsey recalled later.[3] And the goal was certainly not to provoke the Chinese or the Russians into another major war. In fact, another one of Truman's clear goals from the very beginning was to take whatever reasonable actions were necessary to avoid World War III.

The problem now, however, was that Truman, in his excitement over MacArthur's success, was giving way to his emotions rather than sticking with his original goal—a rational, strategic, historically well-informed plan to restore the Korean peninsula to its post-World War II status quo.

To be sure, explains historian David McCullough, "the prevailing wisdom around the president was that the last thing in the world that the United States should do would be get involved in a major land war with the Chinese."[4] But Truman and his advisors were all tempted by "the chance to drive the communists once and for all from the peninsula by crossing the 38th parallel and pursuing them into North Korea."[5]

The 38th Parallel was the original boundary established by the U.S. and the Soviet Union at the end of World War II. With the formation of the two nations in 1948, it became a de facto international boundary, an ideological line between communism in the North and democracy in the South, and one of the hottest fronts in the Cold War. In effect, the 38th Parallel had become the Rubicon of Korea. To be sure, Chairman Mao Zedong had used diplomatic channels to issue *explicit* warnings to President Truman that China *would* enter the war if he crossed the 38th Parallel.

Truman, however, was temporarily trapped in a state of irrational exuberance. High on MacArthur's stunning initial victory, Truman was no longer looking to historical precedent. He was no longer adhering to his original objectives, which were grounded in his assessment of a handful of historical parallels.

Truman was also now ignoring the reality that Russia and China would intervene. Despite the fact that the Chinese army was already amassing troops on the border of North Korea, Truman allowed himself to be fooled into believing that the warnings were just a bluff. With a presidential approval rating below 40%, he was desperate for a big win, and "with the enemy in retreat, Truman's native optimism took over."[6] He approved the ambitious General MacArthur's request to cross the 38th parallel, and on September 27th the general "received a memorandum from the Joint Chiefs of Staff, approved by the President, 'Your military objective,' it read, 'is the destruction of the North Korean armed forces.'"[7] And across the 38th Parallel MacArthur went.[8]

Before long, to Truman's humiliating surprise, the crossing of the 38th Parallel did indeed trigger the entry of the Chinese army which was also backed by deadly air support from the Soviet Union. China's *massive* invasion force hammered the United Nations forces, headed by U.S. General Douglas MacArthur, ensuring a costly continuation of the war.

After an even more massive buildup of some 420,000 Chinese and North Korean regulars, an avalanche of communist troops proceeded to drive MacArthur and the allied forces back across the 38th Parallel in what is often referred to today as "the longest retreat in U.S. military history."[9] Puffed up with pride and overconfidence, the retreat was a great source of humiliation and outrage for MacArthur, and it would soon cause him to begin exceeding subsequent orders in direct defiance of the President of the United States.

President Truman, meanwhile, was devastated. "Victory in Korea would have been the crowning achievement of his presidency—proof that his determination to hold the line against communism was working."[10] "If he had ordered MacArthur to halt at the 38th Parallel, a status quo ante bellum would have been established and the Chinese would not have had to intervene to save Kim-Il-sung's regime. The Korean War would have ended two and a half years earlier. Millions of lives would have been spared."[11] "Instead, Truman faced disaster."[12] Among his many years in the White House, these were the darkest of all his days.[13]

Listen, Learn, and Let Go: Use the Wisdom of the Past to Shape the Future.

"I have but one lamp by which my feet are guided, and that is the lamp of experience. I know of no way of judging the future save by the past."[14]

—Patrick Henry, U.S. Founder, 1st Governor of Virginia

Among the different ideas about what constitutes good judgment and how to develop it, the following are two of the most critical, commonly-cited themes which repeatedly surface in the research:

(1.) <u>Identify Patterns, Discern Order</u>. The first theme states that good judgment amounts to an ability to recognize patterns and parallels, or otherwise perceive order. Intelligence experts Fatmi and Young of the University of London, for example, famously describe it as, "that faculty of mind by which order is perceived in a situation previously considered disordered."[15]

In terms of development, *experience* is widely understood to be the most critical factor for increasing and enhancing your ability to recognize patterns and perceive order and, thereby, improve your judgment. Of course, this is only true if you are actually paying attention to and *learning* from your experience. In fact, if you are actively reflecting on and drawing insights and wisdom from your experience then you can easily *accelerate* your learning and surpass those with more years of experience under their belts.

What is even more important, however, is being able to learn from the experience of *others*. Naturally, this is includes reading and learning from history. It also explains why listening is such a critical skill for leaders. As Sir Andrew Likierman writes in *Harvard Business Review*, "I've found that leaders with good judgment tend to be good listeners and readers—able to hear what other people actually mean, and thus able to see patterns that others do not. They have a breadth of experiences and relationships that enable them to recognize parallels or analogies that others miss—and if they don't know something, they'll know someone who does and lean on that person's judgment."[16] This ability to lean on the judgment of another person or persons, at times, or under certain circumstances, leads to the second most critical factor.

(2.) <u>Learn to Step Back and Detach</u>. The second factor crucial to good judgment is making decisions without the undue interference of your own biases and emotions (including ego or pride). The key in this case is developing a certain level of self-awareness and cool detachment. The more aware you are of the emotions you are experiencing and the subjective biases you tend to bring to your decisions, the easier it is to see how these things are shaping your decisions. Good judgment requires being able to acknowledge your limitations and assume ownership over your mistakes, but this takes self-awareness and self-control. To be an effective strategist, consequently, you must be able to step back and detach, and recognize your own biases and emotions and have the wherewithal to "take them out of the equation."[17] But the next step is equally important—bringing others (advisors, analysts, experts, etc.) into the equation, including those, for example, with the analytical skills, relevant experience, or creative idea-generating, option-expanding talents you need in order to optimize your decisions.[18] "The ability to detach, both intellectually and emotionally," writes Likierman, "is therefore a vital component of good judgment."[19]

Be Wary of the Whiskey.

"The appearance of weakness often brings out people's aggressive side, making them drop strategy and prudence for an emotional and violent attack."[20]

—Robert Greene, *The 33 Strategies of War*

Historians, political scientists, and leadership scholars across the political spectrum all generally agree that Harry Truman was a "great" (1st quartile) president.[21] He made a number of good decisions that history views favorably (e.g. the Truman Doctrine, the Marshall Plan, the Berlin Airlift, establishing the NSC, the NSA, and the CIA, and ending racial segregation in the armed forces). In many cases, drawing on the wisdom of history was a critical part of his decision-making process.

There were also times, however, when he neglected, misused, and abused history. In the case of Korea, given his uncharacteristic neglect of the factors *critical to good judgment*, it is perhaps no surprise that his hasty and haphazard escalation of the war in Korea proved to be one of his worst decisions.

To be clear, the argument is not about whether or not allied forces should have crossed the 38th Parallel, destroyed the regime in North Korea, or even taken the conflict into China. Truman's failure was in falling back on his emotions and, in the process, ignoring history—including isolating the incident, rather than viewing it in context or as "part of an historical sequence,"[22] relying on untested assumptions, giving way to "excessively hasty action," and disregarding the rational, well-informed goals for the initial intervention which he himself established in the first place.[23]

Regardless of how much he loved history or understood its unparalleled value for leaders, Truman, in this case—widely unpopular at home and overeager for a big win abroad—let his emotions get the best of him. Rather than using his better judgment, informed by history, as he so often did, Truman fell prey to a number of the most common mistakes leaders make in regards to historical decision making.

To Avoid Emotional Decisions, Stick with a Rational, Strategic Plan.

Reading and learning about the relevant history of an issue is the bedrock of good judgment. More than a sweeping knowledge of history, is the importance of "using" history well. We all draw on history, including our own personal experience, all the time. The question is are you doing it explicitly and strategically, with the aid of a proven, systematic approach, or carelessly and haphazardly with little to guide you but your ego and emotions? Are you using history with a rational and open mind in order to logically explore the current situation, or are you just using history to back up the emotional decision you have already made?

One of the most critical steps you can take to improve your decisions is simply having a rational, strategic decision-making plan in place before the crisis arrives. To avoid the most common decision-making mistakes leaders make when drawing on history, use the following 7 guidelines (amended and adapted from Neustadt and May's *Thinking in Time*[24]):

(1.) <u>Avoid Deciding in Advance, Get Answers to Key Questions First</u>. The first mistake is to make a decision without sufficient intelligence and analysis of the available facts. Unfortunately, perhaps because this step seems so elementary, it is frequently forgotten or ignored. At the very least, *before* making any preliminary decision, the classic questions of a journalist ought to be answered.[25] Referring to these questions in his poem, "Six Honest Serving Men," the English writer and journalist Rudyard Kipling wrote,

"I keep six honest serving-men

(They taught me all I knew);

Their names are What and Why and When,

And How and Where and Who."[26]

But, ideally, this step would also include writing down[27] the following five (separated) factors: (a.) a clear and concise definition of the issue, (b.) a short list of key concerns, (c.) a list of what is known, (d.) a list of what is unknown or unclear,[28] and (e.) what is the background story, how did this issue arise?[29]

Truman (largely) avoided this trap with his initial decision to enter the Korean War (although he was apparently immediately resolved to "let them have it"[30]). When it came to the decision about whether or not to cross the 38th parallel, however, not only did Truman fail to adequately analyze the available facts (e.g. that Chinese troops were amassing on the border, for starters), but he also neglected to stop and question and, perhaps, admit to himself why he was now going against his initial decision to not cross the 38th parallel.

(2.) <u>Prevent Hasty, Thoughtless Action</u>. The second common mistake is to rush into action. When a crisis emerges, the tendency is to assume that the problem is obvious and, therefore, the first question usually is, "What do we *do*?" But this question creates an impulsive and imprudent rush toward action. Far better to first get clear about the situation by asking questions such as, "What is the issue?" and, equally significant, "*Why* is a decision necessary?"[31] Importantly, rather than rushing in with impetuous action, as Neustadt and May point out, taking time to stop and think and "figure out *why* action is called for helps in defining the objectives of action."[32] "History thus becomes useful in determining what the issue is, whether and how the situation has changed from the status quo ante [e.g. Have the costs or stakes changed?], and what action has been taken in similar situations, in pursuit of what objectives, and to what effect."[33]

(3.) Challenge Prevailing Stereotypes. Mindlessly relying on prevalent stereotypes is another common factor in flawed decision-making. While stereotypes *may* have an element of truth and they can certainly help to speed decisions (albeit often at the price of accuracy), in the great majority of cases they are grossly exaggerated characterizations or far too simplistic to aid in effective decision-making. Thus, rather than relying on stereotypes, far wiser to surface any stereotypes operating or involved in decision-making. Then, explicitly challenge their accuracy and usefulness, and question and explore how they may be leading to flawed decisions.

(4.) Question Key Assumptions. We all make and rely on assumptions all the time. The problem is that our assumptions are often wrong, not just about minor concerns, but sometimes about matters of grave importance. The difficulty lies not with *challenging* potentially flawed assumptions, however. Because our assumptions are so often operating outside of our conscious awareness, the difficulty is in *identifying* the relevant hidden assumptions that are operating. The secret to surfacing hidden assumptions is to ask lots of questions, including seemingly simple questions. The idea is to think more about your thinking. As you or the group of decision makers becomes more self-aware, the less likely you are to be undermined by hidden assumptions. Once you have listed out your key assumptions, be sure to question each one in turn. You may also find it useful here to ask the following hypothetical question: *What new knowledge or bit of intel would change your assumption?*[34]

(5.) Refrain from Overreliance on Unclear Analogies. That everyone can easily see why a particular analogy is being drawn says nothing about how accurate or useful it is. As discussed in greater detail above, to avoid an "overdependence on fuzzy analogies"[35] or flawed parallels, look for additional analogies, and get clear about where the analogy is weak, unclear, or breaks down. Rather than rushing to a decision based on any one particular analogy, decision makers would do well to explicitly identify the *similarities* and *differences* between the current situation and the dominant analogy.[36] "Compare 'now' with 'then' before turning to what should be done now."[37]

(6.) Avoid Isolating the Incident, Narrowing Your Options. Another leading contributor to flawed decision making is the tendency to isolate incidents rather than seeing them as part of the bigger picture or broader context.[38] Not only can this lead to an inaccurate or incomplete understanding of the issue, but it can also cause you to narrow your perceived options for how best to address the issue or move ahead.

Rather than looking to a singular event in isolation, effective decision making includes considering other related factors that may have contributed to that event. This might include various environmental factors, the business or economic outlook, the status of the political system, the role of culture or ideology, or some other external factor, underlying structure, or causal loop. Of course, it is vitally important to avoid complicating the situation with unnecessary information, factors that are only weakly relevant, or just too much detail to tackle in time.

One of the best examples of this is President Kennedy's leadership during the Cuban Missile Crisis and his unmistakable focus on the history and context of the issue (which was in stark contrast to his handling of the Bay of Pigs Fiasco).[39] For starters, the people that Kennedy chose to be a part of the top secret Executive Committee (ExComm), had various different backgrounds and "long and wide-ranging experience."[40] In fact, Neustadt and May write, "he had around him men whose memories of dealing with the Soviet Union reached all the way back to World War II. He also called in Charles Bohlen and Llewellyn Thompson, two of the most senior serving members of the State Department's Russian service, and Edwin Martin from the State Department's Latin American bureau. Those three had memories, the first two of Russia and the third of Cuba, which also went far back."[41] Along with a richer context and a deeper, more nuanced understanding, this allowed for multiple different accounts.

Kennedy also sought to determine when exactly the Russians made the decision to place the missiles in Cuba, hoping that this would provide "some clue to their possible motives."[42] Moreover, he sought a better understanding of the context; for example, asking an ExComm subcommittee to focus on a report on "the Cuban base problem in perspective."[43]

Further, rather than limiting the discussion to Russia's installation of missiles in Cuba, there was also a fair amount of attention paid to the nuclear "Jupiter" missiles the U.S. had in Turkey (i.e. Russia's backyard) since 1957.[44] With respect to *expanding your options*, the missiles in Turkey proved to be one of the factors that helped resolve the missile crisis in Cuba. Although he refused to allow the deal to be made public (and it remained secret for more than 25 years[45]), Kennedy promised Khrushchev that the U.S. would remove the missiles in Turkey at some future date (a promise he fulfilled in April 1963[46]).

(7.) <u>Understand the Historical Context, Trace the History of the Issue</u>. The final common contributor to flawed decision making is the failure to understand the history of an issue, including its roots, evolution, and previous treatment.[47] It is easy to misunderstand why something is happening if you are unaware of how the situation progressed to its present point. Ignorant of the solutions that others have tried, it is also easy to inadvertently repeat their same mistakes.

To avoid this issue, stop asking yourself, 'What's the problem?,' and start asking, 'What's the story?' The idea here, known as "Goldberg's Rule"[48] is that by asking for the *story* rather than the *problem*, you will discover "what the problem *really* is."[49] Just be sure the story starts at the beginning (which reduces the likelihood the story will be shaped by advocacy).[50]

Tracing the history of an issue also better enables you to understand the origins and purpose, possible motives, causation, the significance and interests at stake, and trends through time. Without this step, you may assume the wrong cause of an event, or, without a point of comparison, you may misinterpret its significance. *A trend will always reveal more than a snapshot in time.* By "placing" an issue and the individuals and organizations or institutions involved in their context and particular stream of time, decision makers gain a greater appreciation for what, if anything, has changed and what remains the same.[51] "Furthermore, since the future emerges from the past, this process allows decision makers to employ the predictive value of the past in shaping the future."[52]

As an avid reader of history, President Truman was well aware of the importance of historical context. In one instance, in his *Memoirs*, Truman recalled the challenge of dealing with isolationists in America, "I could never quite forget the strong hold which isolationism had gained over our country after World War I."[53] For support, he said, the isolationists would often point to George Washington's Farewell Address. But, Truman argued, to view Washington's Farewell Address *outside of its historical context* was to miss the *real* message and key lesson learned.[54]

"Throughout my years in the Senate," Truman recalled, "I listened each year as one of the senators would read Washington's Farewell Address. It served little purpose to point out to the isolationists that Washington had advised a method suitable under the conditions of *his* day to achieve the great end of preserving the nation, and that although conditions and our international position had changed, the objectives of our policy—peace and security—were still the same. For the isolationists," Truman continued, "this address was like a biblical text. The America First organization of 1940-41, the Ku Klux Klan, Pelley and his Silver Shirts—they all quoted the first President in support of their assorted aims."[55] But they also all quoted the first President *out of context*.

Truman usually tried to avoid making this same mistake himself. He had a deep appreciation for the importance of the origins and historical context of an issue. It's true that he would often tackle problems by immediately making a snap, *preliminary* decision, but then he would hold off on his *final* decision until he had time to think it over. Looking back over his presidency, Truman recalled, "I was always thinking about what was pending and hoping that the final decision would be correct. I thought about them on my walks. I thought about them in the morning and the afternoon and thought about them after I went to bed..."[56] After he had mulled over an issue, he would then do, he added, "...a lot of reading to see if I could find some background of history which would affect what had to be done."[57] Only then would he be prepared to make his final decision.

Today, for example, Abraham Lincoln's reputation is under fire from certain groups for some of the things he once said about race. But these people are ignorant of the historical context and they are liable to make critically flawed decisions as a result (e.g. removing statues of Lincoln, or renaming parks and schools). To illustrate, when Lincoln was running for office in 1858, he once said to an audience, "I have no purpose to introduce political and social equality between the white and black races. ...I...am in favor of the race to which I belong having the superior position."[58] Of course, to even think along these lines today would be completely inappropriate. When you consider the historical context, however, you come to a much better understanding of the situation Lincoln was in and *why* he said what he said. In brief, Lincoln was already taking a dangerously divisive stand—so divisive, in fact, that it led to civil war. If Lincoln had let it be widely known what he *really* believed—that the races were equal and deserved to be treated as such—he would have alienated a great many of his supporters (people that nevertheless agreed that slavery was an abomination that had to be abolished) and, most importantly, he would have utterly destroyed his chances of being elected as the 16th President of the United States. In other words, what we learn from the historical context is that Lincoln said only what he believed he had to say in order to get elected, so that he might then bring slavery to an end (and since he is the one who abolished slavery, a cause for which he lost his life, perhaps we ought to give him the benefit of any lingering doubt).

Formulate a Plan to Put History to Work.

Riding high on General MacArthur's initial victory in Korea, President Truman stopped listening to history, and his emotionally-driven decision to cross the 38th parallel turned what might have been a brief, limited conflict into his greatest foreign policy blunder—a much longer and far more devastating war, with an estimated 2.5 million lives lost.

In time, MacArthur regained much of the ground he had lost. But the war stalemated soon after and Truman, now desperate to get out of Korea, started sending feelers for peace.

As much as Truman was an outspoken advocate for the value of history and the vital need for leaders to learn from the past, his own reliance on history suffered from one major flaw: It was selective and haphazard rather than systematic. As much as he believed in the *why*, he had no real consistent, structured *plan* for *how* and *when* to use history.

When Truman initially decided to enter the Korean conflict, he did well in drawing on the analogies of the 1930s, which clearly illustrated "how the failure of the democracies to halt aggression in Manchuria, Ethiopia, and Austria emboldened the fascists and led to a world war."[59] But the lessons learned from these experiences, writes Columbia University historian Robert Dallek, "hardly justified the attempt to conquer the whole country."[60]

Alas, in making this decision, Truman was no longer looking to history. "In making this decision," Dallek adds, "Truman and his advisers failed to 'ask why the analogues of the 1930s came so irresistibly to mind,' and what 'lesson' they actually taught."[61] If Truman and his military advisors had at least worked their way through the process outlined in step one above (i.e. Writing down answers to questions such as, How are we defining the issue? What are the top few concerns? What is known, unknown, and unclear? What is the background story? What about this situation is similar to and different from relevant historical analogues?) they almost invariably would have chosen a less emotional and more fruitful and effective way forward.[62] As Dallek writes, "had the Truman administration followed this procedure when it began its deliberations on Korea, it would have seen how little need there was for crossing the parallel, or how well a restoration of the status quo ante would have served its purposes. More precisely," he continues, "had the administration thought matters through more systematically, it would have recognized that the objective was not to destroy the adversary, but rather to enforce a system of collective security constructed to prevent aggression."[63]

Unfortunately, while Truman had only temporarily let his emotions get the best of him, General MacArthur seemed to slip even more dangerously out of control. After being seriously scorched by communist forces, the prima donna General desperately wanted to restore his reputation and teach the Chinese a lesson. He was now calling for "total war" on China, including the use of the atomic bomb. In fact, apparently on the brink of a meltdown, MacArthur had drawn up plans (which he later denied) to drop an astonishing 30 to 50 atomic bombs on China.[64]

Lean on History as a Guide,
Mine the Wisdom of History to Decide:
General MacArthur vs. President Truman
and the Threat of a Third World War

"He is the rich man who can avail himself of all men's faculties. He is the richest man who knows how to draw a benefit from the labors of the greatest number of men, of men in distant countries and in past times."[1]

—Ralph Waldo Emerson, "Wealth," *The Conduct of Life* (1909)

On March 20, 1951, when he first learned that President Harry Truman was actively maneuvering to find a peaceful resolution to the war in Korea, General Douglas MacArthur was livid. The five-star general who had previously bragged of his plans "to get the Eighth Army back by Christmas" and, writes the *Chicago Tribune*, "who fancied that he understood 'the Oriental mentality,'"[2] had completely, catastrophically miscalculated China's willingness to enter the war, and he suffered "the longest military retreat in U.S. history" as a result. After being forced hundreds of miles back below the 38th parallel by a flood of hundreds of thousands of Chinese soldiers, MacArthur, as General Matthew Ridgway said at the time, "had been made a fool of by the Chinese communist armies."[3]

"Here was a classic case of hubris and overreach: Having achieved a tremendous victory with the Inchon landing, MacArthur felt invincible."[4] Now, unfortunately, as General "Lightning Joe" Collins put it, "MacArthur…was like a Greek hero of old, marching to an unkind and inexorable fate."[5]

But how did the great General MacArthur "blunder so badly?"[6] "How could he miss more than 300,000 Chinese soldiers"[7] amassing on the border?

"Once the intelligence finally came in loud and clear," American historian Hampton Sides explains, "[MacArthur] and his staff of sycophants continued to dismiss it, suppress it, or willfully misinterpret its import. In so doing, they recklessly put tens of thousands of American and other United Nations troops in mortal danger. The result was catastrophic: One of the worst defeats, and one of the most ignominious withdrawals, in American military history."[8]

Worse still, Sides writes in his book, *On Desperate Ground*, "MacArthur…had been outwitted and outflanked by a guerrilla army with no air force, crude logistics, and primitive communications, an army with no tanks and precious little artillery. He was responsible for one of the most egregious intelligence failures in American military history."[9] As a result, writes David Halberstam in *The Coldest Winter*, MacArthur had "lost face not just before the entire world, but before his own troops, and perhaps most important of all before himself."[10] "All of this happened because MacArthur was almost criminally out of touch with reality."[11] He had created his own isolated universe, sealed off and complete with "a top-down structure that maintained a stubborn hostility to facts."[12]

"MacArthur, meanwhile, was being taken to task by the press, as he had never been. An editorial in the conservative New York *Herald-Tribune* referred to his 'colossal military blunder,'"[13] as "one of the greatest military reverses in the history of American arms."[14] *Time*, which had long glorified him, now charged him with being "responsible for one of the greatest military catastrophes of all time, 'the worst the United States ever suffered.'"[15]

"To no one's surprise," MacArthur failed to take personal "responsibility for the defeat..."[16] Once referred to by President Franklin D. Roosevelt as, "the most dangerous man in America," MacArthur was now desperate for a scapegoat.[17] "Unused to such criticism, his immense vanity wounded, MacArthur started issuing statements of his own to the press. He denied that his strategy had precipitated the Chinese invasion and said his inability to defeat the new enemy was due to restrictions imposed by Washington that were "without precedent.'"[18] "MacArthur...spoke as if he had been the principal victim of Washington's policies."[19] "He had never responded gracefully to faultfinders, and now they had multiplied tenfold."[20]

The flamboyant, egotistical General was also now desperate to exact revenge on the Chinese. On March 24, just three days after MacArthur learned of Truman's cease-fire proposal, the General sought to steal the initiative from the President. Without warning, MacArthur issued his own proclamation to the Chinese, "in effect threatening them with full-out war."[21] "All Truman's careful preparations of a cease-fire proposal were now in vain. MacArthur had cut the ground out from under him."[22] MacArthur had "perpetrated a major act of sabotage,"[23] according to U.S. Secretary of State Dean Acheson, who described it as "insubordination of the grossest sort to his Commander in Chief."[24] In the words of 1st Chairman of the Joint Chiefs of Staff Omar Bradley, one of only a handful of other five-star generals in U.S. history, it was an "unforgivable and irretrievable act."[25]

Naturally, President Truman was furious.[26] But the way he chose to respond made all the difference.

In stark contrast to MacArthur, the disastrous experience in Korea triggered in Truman a desire to reground himself in reality.

Meanwhile, something had to be done about this renegade general, but what should he do? And when and how should he do it? As he began contemplating his next move, Truman turned back to history.

Lean on History as a Guide

There were two particular historical parallels that came easily to Truman's mind. In the first case, Truman turned to "the relationship between President Abraham Lincoln and General George B. McClellan during the Civil War, in the autumn of 1862, when Lincoln had been forced to relieve McClellan of command of the Army of the Potomac."[27] Like MacArthur, General McClellan had repeatedly ignored the orders of his Commander-in-Chief. "Also like MacArthur, McClellan occasionally made political statements on matters outside the military field."[28] Truman was already familiar with the confrontation, but, hoping to gain some additional insight, "Truman...sent one of his staff to the Library of Congress to review the details of the Lincoln-McClellan crisis and give him a report."[29]

After reviewing the report, Truman reflected on how, despite the difficulty, President Lincoln was able to maintain a certain detached patience. At the time, Governor Andrew had asked Lincoln about his thoughts on the matter and "Lincoln, according to a story Truman loved, said it reminded him of the man who, when his horse kicked up and stuck a foot through the stirrup, said to the horse, 'If you are going to get on, I will get off.'"[30] Lincoln, in other words, was eager to avoid getting himself and the nation caught up in McClellan's foolish self-sabotage.

President Truman had always, he said, "found the teachings of history to be valuable in my approach to current problems."[31] Reflecting on the historical analogy, he added, "Lincoln was patient, for that was his nature, but at long last he was compelled to relieve the Union Army's principal commander. And though I gave this difficulty with MacArthur much wearisome thought, I realized that I would have no other choice myself than to relieve the nation's top field commander..."[32]

It was certainly a delicate situation; a situation that *required* patience. In Lincoln's case, he "feared that the army would mutiny if he relieved McClellan of command; the troops were quite fond of the little general..."[33] Truman, likewise, had to consider the potentially serious consequences of relieving a widely popular general, particularly given his own historic lack of popular approval.

The other historical parallel that Truman mined during this time was President James Polk's experience dealing with Major General Winfield Scott, known as "Old Fuss and Feathers," another excessively prideful war hero with presidential ambitions who was using his influence in Congress in opposition to his Commander-in-Chief. President Polk eventually removed Major General Scott from command as well.

Truman was also familiar with MacArthur's personal history. Douglas MacArthur's father, General Arthur MacArthur Jr., was another successful military leader who also had a mind to defy authority. In fact, he once told his son, "There are times when a truly remarkable soldier must resort to unorthodox behavior, disobeying his superiors to gain the greater glory."[34] And, as early as his time as a West Point cadet, that is apparently what the son set out to do. Indeed, Douglas MacArthur continually defied the orders of his superior officers throughout his career in the military. As Commander-in-Chief, Truman was the end of a long line of superior officers who had to deal with MacArthur's disobedience, including two other U.S. Presidents (Herbert Hoover and Franklin Roosevelt).

As Truman could clearly see, there were a number of recurring themes running through these various different incidents: All three of the generals were distinguished war heroes, but all three were also vain, prideful, politically ambitious, and insubordinate. What each situation also seemed to require was a strong and decisive president who was willing to be patient, but who was also prepared to do what was unpopular.

If Truman had acted too hastily to fire MacArthur his action would not have had sufficient support from the top military brass. Instead, like Lincoln, Truman proved exceptionally patient, biding his time, waiting for the right time to act. That time turned out to be April 5.

The final straw came when Congressman Joseph Martin read a letter from General MacArthur on the House floor. In a highly inflammatory statement, Martin had previously said that "if we are not in Korea to win, then this administration should be indicted for the murder of American boys."[35]

In MacArthur's reply, which Martin was now making public, MacArthur was shown to be in agreement with these seditious remarks. Furthermore, while Truman was actively maneuvering for peace, MacArthur was desperate to continue the war. "As you pointed out," MacArthur wrote in support to Martin, "we must win. There is no substitute for victory."[36]

Of course the problem had far less to do with MacArthur's military objectives in Korea. Truman had had high hopes for victory too. The problem, an enraged Truman wrote in his diary in caps was that this was "Rank insubordination."[37]

At last, Truman was done with this American Caesar. "This looks like the last straw," he wrote.[38] For the President of the United States to be publicly challenged on his grand strategy in the middle of a major war by his own leading general—this, for Truman, was unthinkable. Leaning on history yet again, Truman wrote, "He's going to be regarded as a worse double-crosser than McClellan. He did just what McClellan did—got in touch with minority leaders in the Senate. He worked with the minority to undercut the administration when there was a war on."[39]

"Dean Acheson caught a whiff of coup d'état in MacArthur's collaboration with Joseph Martin."[40] There was no longer any doubt about what had to be done. Truman's top military advisors were now in agreement: General Douglas MacArthur had to be removed from command.

Within days, MacArthur was dismissed.

"Harry Truman's decision to fire Douglas MacArthur at the height of the Korean War in April 1951 shocked the American political system and astonished the world," writes American historian H.W. Brands.[41] "Much of the world didn't realize the president had the power to fire a five-star general; much of America didn't realize Truman had the *nerve*."[42]

To be sure, it was an audacious move, even for Truman. "And he did it very abruptly. And he did it knowing full well what would happen."[43] Reading about Lincoln and Polk provided Truman with the guidance and understanding he needed, but also the confidence and conviction to take such historic action.

Nevertheless, Truman was predictably vilified across the country. "In Worcester, Massachusetts, and San Gabriel, California, Truman was burned in effigy. In Houston, a Protestant minister became so angry dictating a telegram to the White House that he died of a heart attack."[44] Truman no longer had to "worry about a coup," but it did look like he might be impeached.[45] "Sixty-nine percent of the American people supported MacArthur."[46]

MacArthur, meanwhile, was treated like a national hero. Parades were held in his honor in several cities across the nation. "A TV audience of 30 million watched the general's farewell address to Congress."[47] "We heard God speak here today!" a ridiculous lickspittle congressman screeched after his speech.[48] "Seven million came out for his tickertape parade in New York."[49]

The criticism Truman faced after firing MacArthur was intense. Although he knew it was coming before he made the decision, the scale and intensity of the blowback was not easy to bear. He, nevertheless, continued to stand by his decision. He knew that there was nothing in history that could rescue him from this situation, but it did give him the solace and strength to do what he knew he had to do in spite of the harsh consequences.

Recalling the public anger President Thomas Jefferson faced following the Louisiana Purchase, Truman found comfort in thinking about how, in the end, it turned out to be a wise decision for which Jefferson was justly applauded. As former Princeton professor of politics Fred Greenstein argued, Truman's reading of history emboldened him beyond his own limitations, and it provided him "with the rationale for such bold presidential actions as relieving Douglas MacArthur as commander in Korea in 1951," but also, for example, "placing the steel industry under federal control in the face of a threatened strike in 1952."[50]

Despite the political fallout, "Truman would regard the decision to fire MacArthur as among the most important he made as president."[51] Steeped in history, Truman understood he was doing what any reasonably responsible leader had to do—not just avoiding WWIII or an unnecessary nuclear holocaust, but also preserving civilian control of the military and, thus, freedom and democracy in the United States.

Ground Your Ego, Mind History to Decide

Naturally, Truman's decision-making process went well beyond his reliance on history. Yet, by turning to history, Truman gained a few critical advantages which better enabled him to effectively navigate multiple crises during his term, including the debacle with General MacArthur. Consider the following five keys:

(1.) <u>Maintain a Grounded Perspective</u>.

Part of what made the situation with MacArthur so difficult was that MacArthur's own *superior* officers were cowered by the great five-star, World War II hero, and they feared going against him. As Manchester writes, "The fact is that America's high command appears to have been afraid of the General. Acheson tells us that Bradley and Collins 'defended MacArthur and said that a war could not be run by a committee.' If that was true, the Joint Chiefs should have been disbanded. It was their job to supervise theater commanders, and the only explanation for their negligence in this instance is that SCAP's [MacArthur's] fame had intimidated them."[52]

The 1st Chairman of the Joint Chiefs of Staff, General Omar Bradley likewise described MacArthur as "awesomely brilliant;" however, Bradley also admitted that "MacArthur was a megalomaniac," adding that "as a leader he had several major flaws: an obsession for self-glorification, almost no consideration for other men with whom he served, and a contempt for the judgment of his superiors."[53]

Even President Truman was not immune to MacArthur's towering reputation. When he visited MacArthur at Wake Island (a location far more convenient for MacArthur) on October 15, 1950, still in the early days of the escalating conflict, Truman presented MacArthur with his fifth Army Distinguished Service Medal. In their private meeting, rather than taking time to build rapport, ask probing questions, and gain a deeper understanding, Dean Rusk noticed that the President was rushing. He passed a note suggesting that Truman slow down, but Truman wrote back, "Hell, no! I want to get out of here before we get into trouble!"[54] It was a ridiculous perspective to take.

Still, as he learned more about what he was dealing with, and after he had a chance to reorient and reground himself in history, Truman became far less flattering and deferential. The Joint Chiefs, in contrast, continued to defer to MacArthur's "experience, rank, and reputation, to his intense emotional involvement in the Far East…and to his unmeasured but possibly dangerous political potency as a man cultivated and admired by Republican party leaders."[55] Unfortunately, Manchester continues,

> "Acheson—and Marshall—were equally wary. [General Matthew] Ridgway describes a Pentagon conference during which his suggestion that the General be bluntly told to toe the line was followed by 'a frightened silence' on the part of the secretary of state, the secretary of defense, and the Chiefs. Leaving the meeting, Ridgway told Hoyt Vandenberg, a close friend, that he didn't understand why they didn't tell MacArthur exactly what to do. Vandenberg replied: 'What good would that do? He wouldn't obey the orders. What can we do?' Ridgway said: 'You can relieve any commander that won't obey orders, can't you?' He recalls that Vandenberg looked 'puzzled and amazed' and walked away."[56]

The military's top brass were so absurdly deferential, in fact, writes R. F. Weigley in *History of the United States Army*, and "so reluctant were they to interfere with MacArthur on a matter of military judgment that they urged Secretary of State Dean Acheson to intervene with the President, so that Truman might instruct MacArthur..."[57] And, not surprisingly, as he often demonstrated throughout his career, Truman rose to the occasion.

One of the greatest gifts history gave to Truman was the sense of calm groundedness and perspective that came from a general, big-picture understanding of what was happening. The historical parallels, the repeating patterns and themes, the timeless recurring principles, and even the unrelenting reality of human nature; Truman's knowledge and understanding of these things helped to ensure he was never completely in the dark. History provided Truman with the touchstones and guideposts he needed to navigate and the beacons and lodestars that helped to illuminate his path. His considerable knowledge of history also gave him a certain level of self-confidence and the self-assurance that he could successfully plot a course through the unique particulars of any situation he faced as president. As the celebrated military theorist and historian Captain Liddell Hart once wrote, "a long historical view not only helps us to keep calm in a "time of trouble" but reminds us that there is an end to the longest tunnel. Even if we can see no good hope ahead, an historical interest as to what will happen is a help in carrying on. For a thinking man," Hart adds, perhaps a bit dramatically, "it can be the strongest check on a suicidal feeling."[58]

(2.) Manage Your Emotion, Be a Model of Self-Control.

Despite being swamped with bad news, it is perhaps no surprise that, in what was later described as his political cunning,[59] Truman refused "to act impulsively or irresponsibly, whatever his own feelings."[60] Historian David McCullough describes Truman here, in the midst of the MacArthur showdown, as "a model of self-control."[61] "...Those close to Truman knew that 'uncontrolled passion' was never a problem."[62] "Under the pressures of this tensest of times, with so much of his own stature and political welfare riding on his every move, he was at his steadiest."[63] For this was when his mind was most saturated in and, thus, best supported by history. "For the next several days an air of unnatural calm seemed to hang over the White House."[64] Even House Minority Leader Joe Martin, who was intentionally trying to provoke Truman,[65] was surprised by Truman's calm; "the wind died down," Martin remembered, "the surface was placid...nothing happened."[66]

MacArthur, in contrast, following the ignominious retreat back below the 38th parallel, was trapped in a toxic tailspin. So focused on protecting his fragile ego, MacArthur wrote frantically to the press to "correct" the record about why he was failing so badly. He "lashed out," writes Manchester, "at the 'disaster school of war reporting,'" denouncing what MacArthur said were "irresponsible correspondents at the front, aided and abetted by other such unpatriotic elements at home."[67] "Then he began giving his version of what had happened to friendly journalists."[68]

At the time, quoting Euripides, Secretary of State Acheson said of MacArthur, "whom the gods would destroy they first make mad." Bradley's aide, Colonel Chester Clifton, later said, "What really counted was that MacArthur had lost confidence in himself and was beginning to lose the confidence of his field officers and troops. There is nothing in the book that more seriously undermines a commander's effectiveness than this. When it happens, he's through…"[69]

(3.) Keep Your Ego in Check. Put Purpose Before Pride.

No doubt, like General MacArthur, President Truman's ego was also badly bruised by the catastrophic miscalculation and subsequent setback in Korea following the intervention of the Chinese. For various additional reasons, Truman was also doing terrible in the polls.[70] A March 14 Gallup poll "reported the president's public approval at an all-time low of 26 percent. And soon there were appalling new statistics: U.N. forces had now suffered 228,941 casualties, mostly South Koreans but including [36,574[71]] Americans."[72]

In stark contrast to MacArthur, however, rather than obsessing over himself, or being preoccupied with repairing his reputation or ensuring his reelection, President Truman, always with an eye to history and, in this case, all too familiar with the ease with which precipitating forces brought about World War II, still wanted nothing more than to avoid another catastrophic world war. And, furthermore, he was certainly not about to hazard a nuclear war with China and Russia "merely to placate MacArthur's wounded pride."[73]

Conversely, rather than giving his undivided attention to winning the war within the prescribed boundaries, MacArthur, whose judgment was often "clouded by his gargantuan ego,"[74] remained obsessed with his public image. Even after Truman demanded that he stop issuing public statements, he repeatedly requested permission from the Pentagon to reply to various media outlets to correct factual inaccuracies.[75]

Regardless of the knowledge, wisdom, or intelligence of others, MacArthur always "knew better," writes McCullough, "which in a way was part of the problem: He always knew better than his commanding officers, whether they were the Joint Chiefs of Staff or the president of the United States, and always felt free to question, circumvent, countermand or just flat-out disobey the orders of his superiors whenever it suited him. And it suited him more often than not."[76]

In contrast to Truman, for MacArthur this was deeply personal. As historian William Manchester writes in *American Caesar*, "He simply could not bear to end his career in checkmate. It would, in his view, be a betrayal of his mission, an acknowledgment that MacArthur was imperfect."[77] The war in Korea was not about Truman or the men who fought under him. It was about *him*. Sadly, as was often the case with MacArthur, "the men who fought under him, and the civilians who happened to get in his way, often paid a terrible price."[78]

(4.) <u>Assume Ultimate Ownership, Take Complete Responsibility as a Rule.</u>

Perhaps the biggest problem with pride, and the greatest difference between "Dugout Doug"[79] MacArthur and Harry "The Buck Stops Here" Truman was the willingness to take responsibility. Truman never blamed MacArthur for the intervention of the Chinese. In fact, Truman said that MacArthur was "no more to be blamed for the fact that he was outnumbered than General Eisenhower could be charged with the heavy losses of the Battle of the Bulge."[80]

MacArthur, however, as Truman said to his advisers, was making it "quite plain that no blame attached to himself or his staff."[81] MacArthur was also actively casting blame on others, and, worse still, he was doing it through the press. As Truman said to his staff at the time, again relying on past experience, "Every second lieutenant knows best what his platoon ought to do. He thinks the higher-ups are just blind when they don't see things his way. But General MacArthur—and rightly too—would have court-martialed any second lieutenant who gave press interviews to express his disagreement."[82]

Truman wanted to run for reelection, and he knew that firing MacArthur would hurt his already abysmal approval rating. But he also understood the danger and the harm that MacArthur's actions, left unchecked, would cause. Fortunately, in this case, drawing strength from history, Truman put the interests of the United States before his personal pride and career. "I have always found comfort and guidance in the lessons of history, and," as he had said earlier, "I realized that my position...was, historically, nothing new."[83]

(5.) <u>Align with the Long-Term.</u>

Finally, being steeped in history better enabled Truman to adopt a long-term perspective on the problems he faced. And, therefore, rather than surrendering to his immediate impulses or short-term emotional needs, he was able to make more strategic, enduring decisions that were in the best interests of the American people.

The study of history naturally encourages greater perspective-taking and long-term thinking. Perhaps this is unsurprising given that, as Hart explains, "the study of history...is universal experience—infinitely longer, wider, and more varied than any individual's experience."[84] *Harvard Business Review* similarly concludes, "as the study of change over time, history...impels us to think about the long term," and this, authors Seaman and Smith argue, is "another strength of the best leaders, whose well-developed, long-range perspective on the companies they manage may be the only antidote to the pressures of quarterly earnings reporting and the need to react to one crisis (real or perceived) after another."[85] As Winston Churchill said, this greater perspective, in turn, leads to wiser, more strategic decisions and effective long-term thinking. In fact, Churchill said, "The farther back you look, the farther forward you can see."[86]

Lean on the Long-Term, Trust in the Wisdom of Time

The public backlash against President Truman, including a flood of mail and telegrams pushing for impeachment, quickly led Congress to hold hearings to investigate the firing of General MacArthur. As Truman continued to effectively weather the storm, the full story began to emerge. When the Joint Chiefs of Staff testified that they fully supported President Truman's decision to fire General MacArthur, public sentiment began to cool.[87] As the Joint Chiefs pointed out their disagreements with the General, MacArthur's reputation began to suffer while Truman's *slowly* started to recover.

The real clincher came when Chairman of the Joint Chiefs of Staff Omar Bradley "flatly rejected MacArthur's call for a wider war" with China and Russia.[88] In one of the most widely quoted comments from the proceedings, Bradley, referring to MacArthur's policies, said that, "In the opinion of the Joint Chiefs of Staff, this strategy would involve us in the wrong war, in the wrong place, at the wrong time and with the wrong enemy."[89] As American historian H.W. Brands put it, "Bradley's categorical conclusion proved the most compelling public statement by any official at the committee hearings. For a soldier of Bradley's stature, with no history of politics, to contradict MacArthur so completely caused even the most ardent of MacArthur's supporters to pause and reconsider."[90]

As the story unfolded, MacArthur quickly lost a level of credibility not just in politics, but as a military strategist.[91] Even his most stalwart supporters quietly began to back away from "MacArthur and the belligerent course he favored."[92]

At first it appeared that the move cost Truman a great deal of political capital, but "bringing MacArthur home was one of Truman's finest moments. It reminded the top brass that a constitutionally elected civilian outranked them all."[93] "Eventually, Americans came to understand the importance of the principles of civilian control of the military and the danger of insubordination in a world with nuclear weapons."[94]

When Truman left office in January 1953, he had one of the lowest approval ratings in U.S. history. With the passing of time and increased perspective, however, Truman's reputation began to rise dramatically.

The release, in the 1970s, of previously classified testimony into MacArthur's firing helped further boost Truman's reputation and further discredited MacArthur's. Perhaps the greatest damage came when the public learned what both Truman and MacArthur knew at the time; that considerable Russian forces had also amassed along the border—including 35 Russian divisions and 500,000 troops, with massive naval and air support—all of which made it increasingly, devastatingly clear that a broader war with China and

Russia would have led to even more catastrophic losses,[95] and, almost certainly, the third even more horrendous global war.

Learn from Success and Failure, "Employ History for the Purpose of Life."

Historians today frequently cite Truman's firing of MacArthur as one of his most important and courageous moments. From his own perspective, Harry "Give 'Em Hell" Truman said that, "courage didn't have anything to do with it."[96] "I fired him because he wouldn't respect the authority of the President. I didn't fire him because he was a dumb son of a bitch, although he was, but that's not against the law for generals. If it was," Truman added, with obvious exaggeration, "half to three-quarters of them would be in jail."[97]

Regarding MacArthur's "grandiose foreign policy" ideas, Truman concluded, "I've given that a lot of thought and finally decided that there were times when he wasn't right in his head. And there was never anybody around him to keep him in line. He didn't have anyone on his staff who wasn't an ass kisser. Why, hell, if he'd had his way, he'd have had us in the Third World War and blown up two-thirds of the world."[98]

Fortunately, Truman had the wherewithal to stand up to MacArthur. Though he was not immediately rewarded by the American people, Truman, a "man of action," leaning on history in his time of need, has come to take his "place of honor in the temple of history."[99] Today, President Truman is consistently placed among the top ten greatest American presidents.[100]

In a very real sense, echoing the example of President Lincoln, Harry Truman eventually came to characterize a passage from the celebrated German philosopher Friedrich Nietzsche's writings on the uses of history for life.

> "...The man of action," Nietzsche writes, "avoids despair and disgust by turning his gaze backwards and pausing for breath in his march towards the goal. His goal, however, is some happiness, perhaps not his own but often that of a nation or of mankind as a whole; he flees from resignation and needs history as a means against it. Mostly there is no reward beckoning him on, unless it be fame, that is, the expectation of a place of honor in the temple of history, where he in turn can be a teacher, comforter and admonisher to those who come after him."[101]

Clearly flawed and imperfect, but also, in many respects, great; today both Truman and MacArthur occupy a place of honor in the temple of history. So long as we commit to learning from both their successes and failures, they both stand as teachers, comforters, and admonishers. And, in putting their hard won wisdom into practice, we hold fast to Nietzsche's greatest command: "Let us at least learn better how to employ history for the purpose of life!"[102]

EXPLOIT TO EXCEED THE EXAMPLE OF THE EXEMPLARS: ALEXANDER THE GREAT AND THE SIEGE OF AORNOS ROCK

"Deep within each one of us there is an inner longing to live a life of greatness and contribution—to really matter, to really make difference. We may doubt ourselves and our ability to do so, but I want you to know of my deep conviction that you can live such a life. You have the potential within you. We all do.
It is the birthright of the human family."[1]
—Stephen R. Covey, *The 8ᵗʰ Habit*

Suddenly, on his third and final attempt to conquer Aornos Rock,[2] the hot-tempered hero felt a sharp jolt followed by a great and loud rumbling of the Earth. He looked up to see a massive landslide in the distance. Boulders burst before his eyes as towering trees fell at his feet. After witnessing these and "other divine signs," writes Diodorus[3] Heracles decided that the "mighty mass of rock" was "impregnable."[4] Laying siege to Aornos Rock must be forbidden by the gods of Mount Olympus, perhaps Zeus himself.

The divine hero in Greek mythology had failed. Known as Hercules in Roman mythology, Heracles "was of uncommon strength and unaccustomed to the taste of defeat."[5] This, after all, was the son of Zeus and the half-brother of both Perseus and Dionysus.

In the time of Alexander the Great, Heracles, who was believed to be an actual historical figure, as well as an ancestor of Alexander, was most famous for his Twelve Labors, a series of punishing challenges that were so difficult they seemed impossible. As a result of his spectacular success in accomplishing the Twelve Labors—which included slaying the Nemean lion, defeating the nine-headed Hydra, capturing a mad bull, killing the monstrous man-eating birds of the Stymphalian marshes, and fetching the hound of Hades, the triple-headed dog, Cerberus, who was the guardian of the gates of the underworld— Heracles was revered as the greatest of all of the Greek heroes.

In contrast to the gods of Mount Olympus, what fascinated the Greeks most about the heroes was the epic battles they were forced to fight, often against all odds, and, despite their mortality, how they were able to achieve greatness.[6] Not merely to entertain, these fantastic tales of danger and adventure helped to highlight certain qualities and character strengths that the Greeks prized, such as courage, ambition, risk-taking, resilience, and grit.[7]

In 327 B.C., when Alexander the Great was on campaign in India, he was passing nearby Aornos Rock. Given that his army's supply line had become stretched thin back across the Hindu Kush mountain range and was, thus, dangerously vulnerable to attack from raiders in nearby towns, he questioned whether or not he needed to take the settlement atop Aornos Rock to ensure the safety of his supplies. When he was told by the locals that the people were out of his reach and that Aornos Rock was famously impregnable, Alexander's ambition began to fire.[8] When he further learned that even the god known in India as Krishna was unable to take Aornos, Alexander immediately recognized the story as the local, equivalent version of the story of Heracles, and the feat that he *failed* to accomplish during his Twelve Labors.

Upon hearing this, the ancient Greek historian Arrian of Nicomedia writes, Alexander was seized with "a passionate desire to capture it."[9] To tell him that it was impregnable was already alluring enough. To tell him that not even a Greek hero or a Hindu deity could take it, this was something entirely different. This was practically what Alexander lived for. This, writes Arrian, "made Alexander even more eager to capture the stronghold...'"[10] and, thereby, "surpass his illustrious ancestor by taking it himself."[11]

When he learned from Craterus, one of his closest generals, that certain rebels in the region had "retreated to the fortress of the Aornos Rock," the same "precipitous and sheer wall [that] had baffled even the great Heracles," his mind was made up.[12] "Alexander eagerly seized the chance to outdo Heracles, setting the scene for another spectacular siege."[13]

Known today as Mount Pir Sar, a mountain spur in the Hindu Kush in northern Pakistan, the challenge of Aornos Rock went beyond scaling its massive sheer walls which "become narrower as they rise higher...into a sharp point."[14] In fact, according to Bose, the defenders had to be "let down and hauled up with ropes and chains from the top, but once these accoutrements of mountain climbing were gone there was just no way for any human to climb the steep slopes surrounding three-fourths of the seven-thousand-foot mountain."[15]

Furthermore, the summit of the rock is flat, nearly a mile long and some 200 yards wide—wide enough to grow crops and mount a large defense.[16] It is also well supplied with timber and natural springs. The citadel atop the rock was built beside a volcanic lake.[17] The rebellious tribes, therefore, could not be starved into submission either.

What's more, at 7,000 feet[18,19] above the Indus River, towering "over forests of fir and pine...as far as the eye can see,"[20] "its elevation alone would make an attack difficult.[21, 22] Indeed, alluding to its height, the Greek term *aornos* literally means *without birds*.

But all of this only further seized Alexander with a fierce determination to take it.[23]

With three of the four sides surrounded by deep gorges and sheer rock cliffs, there was really only one possible approach for an attacking army. But this side too, rapidly descending into a deep ravine, was unusually easy to defend. The tribes could simply pick off any would-be invaders with arrows or roll large rocks and logs down upon them as they attempted the long, steep, and difficult ascent. Covered in armor and forced to carry a shield in one arm as protection from a shower of arrows and rocks, invaders had little hope of mounting a successful attack while they climbed.

In order to overcome these obstacles and take the fortress atop the summit, Alexander devised a nearly impossible flanking maneuver.[24] Under the command of Ptolemy (Egypt's future king), Alexander sent a detachment of his army to scale the sheer wall and attack the citadel from one side of the rock. "The climb took two days because the defenders could fire off arrows and other missiles at them and so impede their progress."[25]

"While they were preoccupied defending themselves against an attack from Ptolemy, Alexander led the rest of the troops around the other side of the mountain," the side with the deep ravine.[26] Alexander then split the troops into three groups—one group cut down trees, a second hauled the logs and large rocks to the ravine, and a third hammered the trees into place, packing them with dirt and rocks.

Working in relay teams day and night for nearly a week,[27] Alexander filled the 500 yard ravine and covered it with a flat surface. As the bridge began to take shape, Alexander had his troops roll the large siege engines into place to begin their assault. Consumed with Ptolemy's attack, by the time the Indians realized what Alexander was up to, it was too late. The Indian's more primitive weapons could not reach Alexander's troops unless they came down from the protection of their citadel. In contrast, the citadel was now within range of Alexander's siege weapons, which included catapults and giant crossbows.[28]

The Indians were astonished by this massive earth-moving endeavor and engineering feat. "Just the sight of these fearsome machines trained on their walls panicked the defenders, who sent an envoy to Alexander asking for terms."[29] After agreeing to Alexander's terms, the Indians, assuming they would be slaughtered, attempted to retreat down the mountain in the night.

"Unfortunately for them, Alexander had anticipated their action. As soon as they made their move, he and 700 men crossed the bridge and took the citadel."[30] After seizing command of the fortress atop the summit, Alexander established a garrison "to watch over the land all around."[31] He then erected an altar to Athena, the ancient Greek goddess of wisdom and strategy.

Alexander had once again achieved what was believed to be impossible. He had conquered Aornos Rock, succeeding where even the mighty Heracles had failed. "The capture of Mount Aornos again revealed how physical advantages like a mountain could not stand against the will and guile of a determined leader like Alexander."[32]

Strive for Greatness, Seek to Surpass the Myths, Legends, Titans and Demigods

Not one of us really knows to what heights we might soar. Not one of us really knows what untapped potential we might unleash. Not one of us really knows for sure what great miraculous thing we might achieve if we would but resolve, no matter what, to achieve it.

What we do know is the great *many* remarkable things that have already been achieved, and the names and stories of the great men and women who achieved them. We know the story of Hannibal crossing the Alps, Columbus crossing the Atlantic, Mandela ending apartheid, and the Wright brothers conquering the sky. We know the works of Leonardo da Vinci, Michelangelo, Shakespeare, Beethoven, and Bach; the achievements of Amelia Earhart, Albert Einstein, Marie Curie, Harriet Tubman, Simón Bolívar, Napoleon Bonaparte, and Joan of Arc.

But rather than standing helplessly in awe of their achievements or, in contrast, foolishly imagining them as somehow irrelevant, why not see them as markers, as beacons or lodestars, of what humans can achieve? Why not see them as something that someone will someday surpass? Better still, why not use their collective stories as both a means and a reminder to discover your own power, your own potential greatness in your own unique voice?

"The power to discover our voice," Stephen Covey writes in *The 8th Habit,* "lies in the potential that was bequeathed us at birth. Latent and undeveloped, the seeds of greatness were planted. We were given magnificent "birth gifts"—talents, capacities, privileges, intelligences, opportunities—that would remain largely unopened except through our own decision and effort. Because of these gifts, the potential within an individual is tremendous," Covey continues, "even infinite. We really have no idea what a person is capable of. A baby may be the most dependent creation in the universe, and yet within a few short years, it becomes the most powerful. The more we use and magnify our present talents, the more talents we are given and the greater our capacity becomes."[33]

This is the most lasting lesson we learn from Alexander. As we know from ancient Greek historians Arrian, Diodorus,[34] and Plutarch, while it's true that Alexander seemed to model himself after one hero or another at different times, it's also true, as host of Ancient Heroes Patrick Garvey writes, "the whole of his life suggests that his greatest similarity to them was in wishing to establish his own immortal legacy—one that was uniquely his."[35]

Alexander the Great learned from the heroes of history, he emulated their actions at times, not as an end in itself, but as a means to a much greater end. And he stands today as a powerful example of the importance of benefiting from and building on the past.

History played a powerful role in Alexander's longing to be great. But he was not alone in harboring this desire. "Deep within each one of us," Covey writes, "there is an inner longing to live a life of greatness and contribution—to really matter, to really make a difference."[36] What sets Alexander apart from so many others is the extent to which he exploited history in pursuit of greatness; how he used the heroes, titans, and demigods; how he profited from their stories, even when those stories were often little more than legend and myth.

But how did he do this? And, more importantly, how can we use history in pursuit of a life of greatness? How can we exploit the example of the legends and heroes of history to better maximize the tremendous potential we all have within us? The following are six lessons strategists can learn from Alexander's success in surpassing the myths, legends, and gods of ancient Greece.

(1.) Believe to Achieve, Achieve to Believe: Put the Power of Expectations into Play.

History can have a powerful influence over what you believe and, therefore, what you achieve. What you achieve, in turn, influences what you believe and what you expect to achieve in the future. The deeper your understanding of the great exploits of history, the greater the possibility those stories will help shape your values, perspectives, and beliefs and, consequently, the more likely they are to influence your thoughts, words, and actions.

This is why the Vikings told and retold the stories of the greatest Viking leaders in history—men and women like Ragnar Lothbrok, Lagertha the Shieldmaiden, Rollo of Normandy, and Cnut the Great—over and over again, generation after generation: They were making these bold, adventurous leaders a part of what it meant to be a Viking, a part of who they were as a people. Through the telling and retelling of the stories of Bjorn Ironside, Freydis Eiríksdóttir, Ivar the Boneless, and others, the mindset that Vikings do extraordinary things had a profound effect on Viking culture, and went a long way toward cultivating ambition and courage and self-belief.

The ancient Greeks went even further. They believed that, through the performance of superhuman exploits, it was possible to rival or even surpass the gods. In fact, this idea was so commonplace that the Greeks had a word for it, *pothos*, which meant *a longing to surpass even the gods.*

It's easy to imagine this as a contributing factor in Alexander's success. He was not merely ambitious in the way that a typical leader might be ambitious. Like all Greeks of his day, Alexander believed that it was possible to surpass the gods. Rather than imagining the ordinary limits of mortal man, Alexander believed it was possible to do what no man had ever done before.

So much of his life was influenced by the legends, myths, and heroes of history that it is difficult to imagine what, if anything, Alexander's life would have amounted to *without* the stories of Achilles, Heracles, Dionysus, and Zeus. Even the heroic exploits of his father, Philip II, one of the greatest leaders in Macedonia's history, helped shape Alexander's beliefs about what was possible for him and what he would or would not achieve. In the words of one historian, "Philip was descended, according to legend, from Heracles and his military skills prepared the way for his son to achieve greatness."[37]

In addition to his father's claim of divine ancestry, his mother, Olympias, "claimed to be a direct descendant of Achilles, the hero of the Trojan Wars and the *Iliad*."[38] Olympias also claimed that Zeus, the chief god of Mount Olympus, was Alexander's real father. Is it any wonder, then, that they became benchmarks or yardsticks for his own ultimate potential, or that Alexander fully expected that he would one day rival the greatness of these and other Greek heroes and gods? Given the historical context, was this not a perfectly rational and, yet, still exceptionally empowering way to think?

Their stories helped him believe that he could achieve greatness and, in time, his own actions helped him develop the expectation that he would. And, yet, it's not that Alexander actually was a descendant of Heracles, Achilles or Zeus. What made the difference was that he *believed* that he was and, therefore, he believed that he could surpass their heroic deeds. In short, it's what you *believe* that has such a powerful, decisive influence on what you achieve—often regardless of the extent to which those beliefs are grounded in reality.

(2.) Unleash the Driving Force of a Crowning Desire.

Beyond his *belief* that it was possible to achieve the unachievable was Alexander's intense *longing* to do it. This was the other key part of *pothos*; along with the implicit belief was the deep *desire* to surpass the gods. This pothos, this "craving, yearning, longing or powerful desire," explains British historian Paul Cartledge, comes up again and again "throughout Arrian's historical account" of "Alexander's more adventurous undertakings."[39]

Alexander's *desire* to surpass the gods was at least *as* important as the *belief* that he could. It was "*pothos*," writes Andrew Stewart in *Faces of Power*, that "drove Alexander to cross the Danube, to sever the Gordian knot, to found Alexandria, to consult Ammon at Siwah in emulation of his ancestors Perseus and Heracles, and to initiate the exploration of the Persian Gulf, the Indian Ocean, and the Caspian Sea. It even drove him to surpass the gods themselves: to take the Rock of Aornos where Heracles had failed, and to advance into India beyond Dionysos' birthplace at Nysa."[40]

These were not mere random achievements. Alexander was driven to do what no one else could do—not man, not the heroes, not even the gods. Alexander was, essentially, driven to do the impossible. Indeed, Alexander the Great's heroic ambition, "tempered by brilliant and rational calculation, led him to conquer the world."[41] This, explains Tulane historian Kenneth Harl, "was the driving force behind all of Alexander's actions."[42] "He was not subject to personal ambition as ordinarily conceived so much as to a need to achieve the impossible. That was true glory, he believed."[43]

This is what drove him to conquer India in the first place. "This nation was the last frontier before the world ended in a vast ocean—that is what Aristotle had told him. Now that he had every nation from Greece to the farthest eastern outposts of Persia under his rule, Alexander resolved to stand on the sands of the ocean and proclaim himself 'Ruler of the World'—a world unifier."[44]

Naturally, you do have to get the lay of the land and map the terrain. You have to know where those perceived limits are in order to exceed them. But knowing history, knowing what others have and have not achieved can also help to fuel your own internal fire. In the case of his campaign into India, "Alexander had one other reason for wanting to invade India: It was a challenge he couldn't pass up. No foreign invader had conquered India, and the experience of some of the greatest rulers who ever lived but failed to conquer India was the stuff of legends. Heading the list," writes Partha Bose, author of *Alexander the Great's Art of Strategy*, "was the legendary eighth-century B.C. Assyrian queen Semiramis. In her long reign she had accomplished such remarkable feats as rebuilding the city of Babylon, destroyed by the Hittites almost a thousand years before. In her attempt to conquer India, however, her troops foundered in the desert crossing through Afghanistan."[45]

In the 6th century B.C., Nebuchadnezzar the Great, king of Babylon, also tried and failed to conquer India.[46] "Cyrus the Great, the founder of the Achaemenid Empire, who had conquered [large parts] of Asia and even Greece, could only reach the outskirts of India—no more. Even the divine Heracles, who came through India in his quest to complete his 'Twelve Labors' failed to conquer the nation. That's how stacked the decks were against Alexander."[47]

But this was exactly the sort of challenge that spurred Alexander on. Not only would he surpass three legendary leaders of ancient history, conquering India would also mean rivaling a god, Dionysus, another son of Zeus, who had succeeded in conquering India.[48] "If this son of Zeus could succeed, Alexander, who by now was convinced of his divinity, believed so could he. In the spring of 327 B.C. Alexander's army crossed over the Hindu Kush from northern Afghanistan into the Kabul Valley. There, after resting awhile, he persuaded his troops to undertake the arduous journey into India."[49]

Of course, Alexander's greatest desire went beyond India, Persia, or any other land. "It went much deeper than that."[50] Alexander's crowning desire, the driving force behind it all was to be able to "conclude by his lifetime that by his great and glorious deeds, he would enter the company of the gods."[51] He would transform himself from a heroic, but mortal man, into an immortal god.

(3.) Break It Down to Build Belief.

Great achievements begin with great beliefs. To achieve something remarkable you must first believe that you can. The problem is that when you first look at the great achievements of others, they often seem impossibly difficult. Imagining what it might take, most people quickly conclude that they don't have the time, money, connections, or talent to attain such a remarkable accomplishment. The secret is to get a much closer look.

The ancient Greek historian Diodorus tells us that when Alexander first surveyed the "deep gorges and sheer cliffs" of Aornos Rock, he "decided that its forcible capture was impossible."[52] It was not until he learned more, by getting a closer and more complete look, that he began to change his mind.

Soon after his survey, Diodorus explains, Alexander was approached by an old man who had lived in the region for many years in extreme poverty, occupying a cave, and living off the land. "Here the old man camped with his sons, and had come to know the country intimately. When he appeared before the king, he told his story and offered to guide the king through the hills and bring him to a point where he would be above the people who occupied the rock."[53] This was the side with the deep ravine, the only place where Alexander's army could possibly have constructed the bridge they used to place their siege weapons within range. "Alexander promised him rich gifts," and, in exchange, the old man guided Alexander to "the path which led up to the rock," to the place where Alexander could mount an effective offense.[54]

Understanding is key to building the beliefs you need to achieve great deeds. But the goal is not a superficial understanding. The goal is to gain a higher level of understanding,[55] to the point that you can see the details, distinctions, and nuance that most others miss. The more you study and explore what others did, the paths they traveled and the steps they took, the easier it is to understand precisely how they did what they did, and, thus, to see how you can do it too. In the words of Harvard psychologist Ellen Langer, "People can imagine themselves taking steps, while great heights seem entirely forbidden."[56] From a distance, greatness looks like magic and luck, but the closer you get the more you see hard work and pluck. As the great Renaissance artist Michelangelo reportedly said, "If people knew how hard I had to work to gain my mastery, it would not seem so wonderful at all."[57]

(4.) Do the Necessary Work, Pay the Necessary Price.

"We will achieve greatness only through an enormous
amount of hard work over many years."[58]

—Geoff Colvin, Talent is Overrated

Perhaps the most practical advantage of Alexander's yearning to exceed the exploits of the heroes and gods of Greek history was how it fueled and fortified him with the will and grit to do whatever work was necessary or pay whatever the necessary price.

Conquering Aornos Rock certainly involved good intelligence and a clever, creative strategy, but it was mostly a matter of Herculean effort and hard work. It was the 500-yard land bridge that enabled Alexander to best Heracles. And it was the history of Heracles and his failure that drove Alexander to succeed.

Alexander showed little concern for *how* he bested the gods, so long as he succeeded where they failed. To be sure, Alexander the Great was a brilliant strategist and tactician and, yet, he also understood that it is effort and persistence that so often leads to success. As effective strategists must understand today, it is hard work and deliberate practice, not talent, that so often makes people great. "If the activities that lead to greatness were easy and fun, then everyone would do them and they would not distinguish the best from the rest."[59]

History provided Alexander with one other major advantage. Unlike most world religions today, ancient Greeks did not imagine an impassable chasm between the gods and men. The difference between the gods and the heroes, or the heroes and men was even more narrow, Paul Johnson explains in his book, *Heroes: From Alexander the Great and Julius Caesar to Churchill and De Gaulle*.[60] "The chasm could in fact be bridged by superhuman virtue, by the displaying of what the Greeks called *arete* (i.e. excellence or virtue). Alexander's own heroic ancestors, Heracles and Achilles, had done just this..."[61] In the case of Heracles, for example, according to what the Greeks saw as part of their history, through his heroic deeds, the hot-tempered hero had gained full immortality, taking his place among the gods of Mount Olympus.[62]

For Alexander and his contemporaries, the meaning of the story of Heracles was that mere mortals could attain immortality by virtue of the many heroic deeds they performed as mortals.[63] "Great men were able to cross [the line] and become *isotheoi*, equals of the gods or demigods."[64] We know that Alexander was thinking along these lines because at one point, while in Egypt, he embarked upon "a dangerous and difficult mission to see the oracle in the Siwa Oasis in the Western Desert, to ask if he had, or would have, divine status."[65]

Of course, with the possible exception of some lunatic cult leader, no one today looks to exceed the exploits of Greek heroes or pagan gods as a means of attaining immortality. On the other hand, the legends and heroes of history continue to fire the imagination and fuel the determination of countless men and women around the world, driving and inspiring them to do whatever work is necessary to live a life that matters and leave a legacy that lasts. History compels them to accept, even *welcome* the words of the ancient Roman poet Horace who said, "Life grants nothing to us mortals without hard work."[66]

(5.) Be Action-Oriented, But Purpose Driven.

As ambitious as Alexander was to exceed the example of the heroes of Greek history, he was careful to avoid losing sight of his supreme purpose. Above all else, the story of Alexander is the story of a mortal man with an impossible dream—to conquer and rule the whole world—a dream he would never waver from and which he would pursue by any means necessary, including leadership, alliances, diplomacy, marriage, and war.[67]

When you look at the many great achievements in Alexander's life, there is no question that they share "the common element of seeking to do or to see the unusual, the daunting, that which is beyond the normal ken of most ordinary mortals."[68] To be sure, there were times when Alexander seemed to find greater satisfaction in these more superhuman exploits, and he continuously felt the driving desire to rival history's heroes, myths, legends, and gods.[69] Nevertheless, as Cartledge explains, "this does not mean that there were not also perfectly good secular or humanly rational motives for the various actions" he took or objectives he set.[70]

In other words, as much as he enjoyed pushing his limits, as much as he yearned to surpass the gods, there was *almost* nothing that would deter or derail him from the pursuit of his ultimate dream. He benefitted considerably from his knowledge and understanding of history, but he never let it take him away from his purpose. If anything, it was the opposite: Everything was brought into service of his dream, including history. Just as Nietzsche urged, Alexander learned to "employ history for the purpose of life!"[71]

The point, for the strategist, is to let history guide and drive, not dictate and decide. Leaders must never cease from taking action toward the future. "The study of history," writes Nietzsche, "is something salutary and fruitful for the future only as the attendant of a mighty new current of life, of an evolving culture for example, that is to say only when it is dominated and directed by a higher force and does not itself dominate and direct."[72]

In the case of Aornos Rock, for example, contrary to what some historians have argued, this was no mere "meaningless diversion."[73] In fact, beyond the immense personal satisfaction Alexander gained from succeeding where Heracles failed, conquering Aornos had a couple of direct practical advantages as well.

For starters, as historian Miles Doleac argues, "Aornos Rock...was defended by the leaders of several recalcitrant tribes from the Bajaur and Swat Valleys. Taking it would, no doubt, have had strategic significance as well, at least as Alexander might have seen it, namely the collapse of further resistance north of the Indus. Who would dare challenge the man who conquered the Rock that bested even Heracles?"[74] Or Krishna? Indeed, confounding the Indian defenders, "Aornos was the most remarkable of his sieges," and, therefore, writes Everitt, "His reputation as a military leader was now such that many thought twice before opposing him."[75]

The other practical purpose for conquering Aornos was the military advantage it provided. At 7,000 feet and strategically located, Aornos Rock made for the perfect "natural observation post."[76] As a matter of fact, with his own garrison now established atop Aornos, Alexander "controlled the entire Cophen Valley"[77]

Unfortunately, there *was* at least one notable occasion when Alexander went off track—embarking on an expedition for no other reason than to succeed where other legendary historical figures had failed. Perhaps it is fitting, then, that it ended in disaster. It was the fall of 325 B.C. and Alexander and his army were finally circling back to return home from India when Alexander decided that he wanted to take the route through the Gedrosian desert—a dry, treeless, barren, mountainous desert region along the Southern coast of what is today Iran and Pakistan.

Alexander had heard the horrific tales of extreme heat and hardship and how no one had ever succeeded in bringing an army through the wild desert wasteland. He knew the story of the legendary Assyrian queen, Semiramis, and her retreat from India and how her army had been decimated by the blazing heat, reduced to a mere twenty survivors. Cyrus the Great, another legendary figure whom Alexander had long looked to as a rival, also attempted to invade India by leading his army through the Gedrosian. The army of Cyrus, the founder of the first Persian empire, was reduced to a mere seven survivors. "According to legend, Heracles, who appears to have visited everywhere...had [also] tried and failed to cross Gedrosia."[78] Naturally, these tales of history's heroes suffering disastrous defeat were enough to fire Alexander's ambition. The ancient Greek historian Arrian of Nicomedia writes, "Alexander heard these old stories; they inspired him to go one better than Cyrus and Semiramis, and that was the reason...why, according to Nearchus [the head of Alexander's navy], he marched by that route."[79] In Everitt's words, "The king, always competitive, would be delighted to outcompete them."[80]

"Alexander recognized that guiding his men through the desert would be one of his greatest challenges and he took great pains over his preparations."[81] Despite Alexander's enthusiasm for the excursion, however, there was no strategic or practical purpose for taking such a perilous path home. It was pure hubris. And, tragically, the two-month long trek through the Gedrosian desert was the single "greatest disaster in Alexander's career. Of more than 30,000 men only a quarter survived."[82]

Without exception, the most successful strategists stay focused and purpose-driven. While there are often considerable advantages in setting your aim high, or aiming to better the best, master strategists avoid pursuing goals that may bring some temporary ego satisfaction, but offer no strategic significance toward the achievement of their ultimate dream.

No doubt, we are today often surrounded by a continuous barrage of tempting prospects and alluring distractions. And even Alexander the Great was, on rare occasions, side-tracked by a daring challenge. But to succeed in the long run, to succeed on a grand scale, sticking to your purpose is key. To do that, your vision must be so clear and compelling that it constantly remains your highest priority. "You have to decide what your highest priorities are and," writes Covey, "have the courage—pleasantly, smilingly, non-apologetically, to say 'no' to other things. And the way you do that is by having a bigger 'yes' burning inside."[83]

(6.) Do More to Increase Your Capacity to Do Still More.

Alexander the Great did not start out trying to surpass the exploits of the gods. In the beginning, Alexander used the legends and heroes of ancient history and Greek mythology as a source of wisdom and insight, as well as a source of inspiration and personal identification. Achilles, Hercules, Dionysus, Zeus—these figures inspired and encouraged Alexander and pushed him to excel. The harder and further he pushed himself, the more he grew as a result. As the American aviation pioneer Amelia Earhart once said, "The more one does and sees and feels, the more one is able to do..."[84]

In time, however, something more happened. There was an evolution to his relationship with these eternal titans and immortals. As he took action and began to *rival* the heroes, his appetite, confidence and capacity all increased, making it possible for him to achieve still more. As Covey explains in *The 8th Habit*, "the more we use and magnify our present talents, *the more talents we are given and the greater our capacity becomes.*"[85]

According to Austrian scholar Fritz Schachermeyr, Alexander's "spiritual progression can be measured in terms of his choices of ancestral heroes and gods to emulate or surpass at successive stages in his career."[86]

Alexander began his military conquest by emulating Achilles, a hero of the Trojan War who was regarded in Alexander's time as the greatest of all the Greek warriors. Achilles was also a central character of Homer's *Iliad*, and he may have been an actual historical figure.

Emulating Achilles took Alexander "up to the first phase of Asiatic conquest," writes Cartledge, "including the symbolic visit with Hephaestion to Troy."[87]

"Achilles' humanity made him an easier figure for a young Alexander to relate to," writes Garvey, "especially if he could not yet imagine equaling the feats of Heracles and Dionysus."[88]

"Then, before and after the Battle of Gaugamela, he took on Heracles, until it came to the invasion of India and beyond the Achaemenid frontier, where Dionysus finally came into play."[89]

But it was not only where they were so much as what Alexander had achieved. As Garvey explains, "after visiting the Oracle of Ammon and defeating the Great King Darius, Alexander grew far more comfortable comparing himself to the gods. The more he accomplished, and the bigger his ego grew, the more he was drawn to the immortal Heracles and Dionysus."[90] As Alexander's military campaigns and foreign conquests continued to accumulate, he took to rivaling or outstripping Heracles, Dionysus and even Zeus.[91]

Understand: Alexander didn't start out seeking to surpass the gods of Mount Olympus. Rather than starting by striving to rival or surpass the leading figures in *your* field, focus first on learning from and emulating their worthwhile achievements. With each increasing achievement you increase your capacity for still greater achievements. Not only does every new achievement increase your own ambition, momentum, and sense of self-belief, including confidence in your capacity for greater achievements, but it can also influence those around you, increasing your capacity further still.

In Alexander's case, in an attempt to spur his men on to still greater achievements, he explicitly highlighted their collective achievements, intentionally noting how they had surpassed the heroes and gods. When Alexander reached "Nysa, a town near the Indus," he discovered that it had allegedly "been founded by Dionysus and was reputed to be his birthplace."[92] To Alexander's way of thinking, this was excellent news because it meant that "he himself had already traveled as far as Dionysus and would yet go beyond him."[93] Equally important, however, as Everitt writes, "Alexander calculated that the Macedonians would not be so reluctant to follow him on grueling campaigns in still more distant places if the ambition to surpass Dionysus's achievements spurred them on."[94] "Arrian and Curtuis both suggest that Alexander's men were indeed inspired by the sight of the Ivy and the rumored connection of the place to Dionysus."[95]

To better emphasize the point and make the connection with Dionysus more memorable, Alexander used their achievement of reaching Nysa as a cause for celebration. "He announced a ten-day holiday and led his entire army up the mountain overlooking the town. There he sacrificed to Dionysus and held a lavish banquet. It must have been quite a party, for even senior Macedonians in his inner circle 'became possessed by Dionysus, raised the cult cry of euoi, and fell into a Bacchic frenzy.'"[96]

In India, at the Hyphasis River, when Alexander's troops—battle weary and aching for home—refused to march any further into India, Alexander again invoked the achievements of both Heracles and Dionysus. Recall Alexander's words as recorded by the ancient Greek historian Arrian:

> "Are you not aware that if Heracles, my ancestor, had gone no further than Tiryns or Argos—or even than the Peloponnese or Thebes—he could never had won the glory which changed him from a man into a god, actual or apparent? Even Dionysus, who is a god indeed, in a sense beyond what is applicable to Heracles, faced not a few laborious tasks; yet we have done more: we have passed beyond Nysa and we have taken the rock of Aornos which Heracles himself could not take. Come, then; add the rest o fAsia to what you already possess—a small addition to the great sum of your conquests. What great or noble work could we ourselves have achieved had we thought it enough, living at ease in Macedon, merely to guard our homes, accepting no burden beyond checking the encroachment of the Thracians on our borders, or the Illyrians and Triballians, or perhaps such Greeks as might prove a menace to our comfort?"[97]

Celebrate Success, Make Your Mark on the World.

In the end, Alexander's efforts to surpass the legends, heroes, and gods of Greek history succeeded on an epic scale. He certainly achieved greatness, and, in the process, "came to be regarded as a god by the 40,000 men who, for eight long years, were prepared to follow him to the ends of the Earth."[98] Even Athens, the Greek city-state that had initially rebelled against Alexander's leadership following the assassination of his father, Philip, was now celebrating Alexander as something beyond a mere heroic conqueror.

In fact, in 324 B.C. when he emerged from the Gedrosian desert at the head of his army, "victorious from his campaign in Pakistan," it was treated as a great cause for celebration across the Greek world.[99] Embassies were sent from the cities to Babylon to congratulate Alexander on his great unprecedented conquering of the known world. "In Athens a decision was taken to honor Alexander with a statue bearing the inscription 'King Alexander, Invincible God.'"[100]

What's more, writes King's College historian Hugh Bowden, "There is no reason to believe that this did not reflect the popular view of Alexander at that point as more than a conquering hero, and there was no significant objection to the proposal, which is known from a fragment of a contemporary speech."[101] This "rather extravagant description of Alexander," Bowden explains, "could be justified by the claims made, amongst others, that in Pakistan Alexander had travelled further than the god Dionysus, and captured places that even Heracles had failed to capture."[102]

Since his time, Alexander's reputation has hardly diminished. "His conquests, in fact, made the subsequent Roman Empire possible, and it can be said that, as a result of Alexander's imperialism, the world took a giant step forward, to civilized unity and globalization."[103] With Alexander the Great, together with Julius Caesar, Johnson writes in *Heroes*, "we come to the two principal actors of antiquity who operated in the theater of the entire known world and became prototypes of the heroic character for the next thousand years. They carved out vast empires for themselves and hammered their names into the history of the earth. Each was brave, highly intelligent, almost horrifically self-assured, whose ambitions knew no bounds. [...] But they were admired, inevitably, more perhaps than any other two men of their kind. They were giant-like, almost superhuman in every respect."[104]

Strive to Better the Best.

There will never be another Alexander the Great. Indeed, the age of glorifying conquerors has long passed. And, yet, in many ways, the timeless leadership and strategy lessons we can learn from Alexander's example endure to this day. Perhaps the simplest lesson is also the most profound: To strive to do something great, something that will be remembered, to strive to better the best, and to make use of the stories of the heroes of history toward that end.

In Alexander's case, beginning with the Homeric stories of the heroic Achilles, "he...went on to Heracles the universal hero who becomes a god, and climaxed with Dionysus the universal god of wine, transformation and spiritual release. Perhaps all that was left was to compete with himself as a god presiding over a universal empire? That would certainly have been 'striving to better the best,' a thoroughly modern version of the age-old Homeric aristocratic ideal."[105]

Indeed, had he not died of fever so young, just short of age 33, Alexander would have kept on striving. Whatever his plans for the future, writes the ancient Greek historian Arrian in *Anabasis*, "I can say one thing without fear of contradiction, and that is that none was small and petty, and he would not have stopped conquering even if he'd added Europe to Asia and the Britannic Islands to Europe. On the contrary, he would have continued to seek beyond them for unknown lands, as it was ever his nature, if he had no rival, to strive to better the best."[106]

History can be a powerful tool to help you draw out and maximize your potential and, thereby, leave your own unique mark on the world. In his book, *The Art of Worldly Wisdom*, the 17th century Spanish Jesuit Baltasar Gracián writes that everyone ought to choose a heroic ideal; not to imitate or replicate, but rather to transcend and eclipse. "There are examples of greatness, living texts of renown. Select the best in your own area, not so much to follow as to surpass," Gracián explains.[107] "Alexander wept, not for Achilles in his tomb, but for himself, not yet risen to universal fame. Nothing so incites ambition within the spirit as the trumpeting of another's fame: it demolishes envy and inspires noble actions."[108] "Maybe we can't expect most people to achieve greatness. It's just too demanding. But," Geoff Colvin writes in *Talent is Overrated*, "the striking, liberating news is that greatness isn't reserved for a preordained few. It is available to you and to everyone."[109]

7

Spy Swiftly New Breakthroughs and Innovations to Advance: Rothschild's Run on Wellington's Win at Waterloo

"Game-changing strategies...are born of creative thinking: a spark of intuition, a connection between different ways of thinking, a leap into the unexpected. [...] The recipe for the successful strategist is: Think differently from other players."[1]
—Adam Brandenburger, *Harvard Business Review*

On June 19, 1815, a warm, windy, and unusually wet weekday afternoon in London, Nathan Mayer Rothschild, the most prominent member of the Rothschild banking dynasty, received a message of monumental importance. At long last, French Emperor Napoleon Bonaparte, known throughout England as "the Scourge"[2] of Europe, had been defeated by British commander Arthur Wellesley, Duke of Wellington at the Battle of Waterloo in Belgium. As the man responsible for financing England's war against France, Rothschild knew instantly what he had to do next.

Recognizing the vital strategic value of swift communication, the Rothschilds had long ago implemented a courier and communications system that was second to none. Along with an extensive network of trusted couriers and informants, and some of the fastest riders in Europe, the Rothschilds made good use of prized racing pigeons which, naturally, are able to take the most direct and uninhibited route and which can reach speeds of up to 100 miles per hour.[3]

In a period well before the sending of text messages by telegraph, first used in 1844, the Rothschilds extensive and superior private communication system allowed them to receive critical news and information ahead of all others, including governments and markets,[4] providing them with significant political and economic advantages—which further rendered the Rothschilds invaluable to European powers.

In this particular case, with virtually everyone in England eager for news of the war, Nathan Mayer Rothschild got wind of Wellington's victory at Waterloo a full 48 hours (according to some historians[5]) before anyone else in London. Within moments of first receiving the dispatch, Rothschild raced off to Whitehall to make maximum use of this prized information. Compelled to first report the news to the British government, he initially headed to Downing Street. Rothschild's next move has become the source of both legend and conspiracy. To be clear, Napoleon Bonaparte represented a very real, existential threat to Britain. Napoleon saw himself as a great conqueror in the mold of Julius Caesar or Alexander the Great, and, as with Charlemagne, his vision was to unite all the nations of Europe, "under one law and one set of political values."[6] This included England which had a long history of conflict with France, going back at least as far as the Norman Conquest of 1066.

The British, meanwhile, were doing everything in their power to defeat Napoleon, including tripling their national debt. In fact, as Niall Ferguson writes in *The Ascent of Money*, "Never had so many bonds been issued to finance a military conflict."[7] This was also an instrumental part of what kept England's allies in the fight against Napoleon.

Behind those bonds was none other than Nathan Mayer Rothschild. If Napoleon won, the London branch of the Rothschilds bank would be finished. If, on the other hand, Wellington won, British bonds would soar.

In response to the historic news of Wellington's win at Waterloo, Rothschild headed to London's Royal Exchange. What he did next is a matter of some debate.

According to his *supporters*, he simply invested in bonds and, as a result, particularly given the Napoleon predicament, Rothschild set himself up to make a sizeable fortune.

According to his *critics*, however, Rothschild's next move was much more crafty. Knowing that no one else had this information, and, moreover, knowing that his moves on the market—given his wealth and influence—were always closely watched, rather than investing in British bonds, he *sold*.[8] He dumped as many bonds as he could as fast as he could.

Whispered rumors began rippling through the Royal Exchange.[9] "Rothschild knows…Waterloo is lost."[10] As word spread, and the bonds dropped, "Nathan kept on selling," writes historian Frederic Morton, "his round face motionless and stern, his pudgy fingers depressing the market by tens of thousands of pounds with each sell signal."[11]

Rothschild's unusual selling spree sparked a panic and drove the bonds toward rock bottom. Then, suddenly, "a split second before it was too late," when Rothschild satisfied himself that they had reached their low, he immediately reversed course, and started buying British bonds for a tiny fraction of the day's opening price.[12]

When the dust settled, and the news of Wellington's victory at Waterloo was widespread, Nathan Mayer Rothschild had made an absolute killing. According to one historian, within just a few short years, the Rothschilds were "worth nine times more" than they were before Napoleon's last war.[13]

With the end of the Napoleonic wars, Rothschild continued to profit by providing "loans to help rebuild the nations crippled by fighting."[14] Further bolstering their banking empire, after "having helped to finance the struggle against the French Empire, the Rothschilds became financiers to the Holy Alliance" (i.e. Russia, Prussia, and Austria).[15] Meanwhile, the Rothschilds' courier and communications network had gained an enviable reputation for its unrivaled speed and reliability.

Avoid Waiting Until the Signal is Strong.

Sometimes the smallest spark of innovation can lead to the most tremendous advantages. Imagine, for instance, when our early ancestors first began to use fire. In addition to providing a source of warmth and a method of cooking and, thereby, a better way of preserving food, fire also became a means of protecting themselves from predators. Along with helping them to clear land and work past dark, fire also helped humans fashion tools for hunting the most mighty and menacing animals, fierce beasts such as cave lions, dire wolves, saber-toothed tigers, and bears.[16] Fire became one of the defining developments and signs of intelligence that separated humans from other animals.

The invention of the wheel was another seemingly simple, yet powerful development, enabling humans to transport large, heavy objects, and increasing the speed, maneuverability, and distances they could move. The invention of the compass—using lodestone, a naturally magnetized rock mineral, and a bowl of water—revolutionized navigation, travel, and trade. "The compass provided explorers with a reliable method for traversing the world's oceans, a breakthrough that ignited the Age of Discovery and won Europe the wealth and power that later fueled the Industrial Revolution."[17]

The printing press, the steam engine, penicillin, electricity, the internet and AI, automobiles, computers, and planes—these were some of the greatest breakthroughs in human history. And, yet, such transformational innovations are not always quickly or easily adopted. Following the invention of the wheel during the Bronze Age, for example, hundreds of years elapsed before it was widely adopted as a means of travel.

Even recognizing the significance of a new innovation can be a challenge. The world laughed at the Wright Brothers and their perilous, impossible pursuit. "Leave flying to the birds,"[18] they were repeatedly told. When they finally succeeded in 1903, the press barely mentioned the world-changing event. "It wasn't until seven years later, when people actually saw a photograph of President Theodore Roosevelt in an airplane that the average American finally realized that flight was possible."[19]

When the benefits are not immediately obvious, adoption can be even slower. To be sure, the signals and indicators are not always strong.[20] Moreover, along with whatever *first mover advantages* exist, there may also be certain *risks* and prohibitive costs involved in being an early adopter. At the very least, it will require money and time to adapt and learn.

On the other hand, writes *Harvard Business Review (HBR)*, "failure to pay attention to external signals—or waiting until a signal becomes strong before acting—can have harsh consequences."[21] And in some cases, being an "early" adopter may still be too late, particularly if a rival is able to use the new process or technology to win a sustainable competitive advantage, transform the landscape to their benefit, build up the barriers to entry, or change the rules of the game.

Adapt Swiftly to Survive and Thrive.

*"It is not the strongest of the species that survives,
nor even the most intelligent; the species that survives
is the one most responsive to change."*[22]

—Charles Darwin

Through his brutal conquests, Genghis Khan first unified the rivaling nomadic tribes of Mongolia becoming the 1st Great Khan of the Mongolian Empire in 1206 A.D. With his Mongolian horde of ferocious warriors, Genghis then took the world by storm, first by conquering Asia, and then most of Eurasia, building what eventually became the largest contiguous empire in history.

Key to Khan's success were two critical breakthroughs, one a tactical innovation, and the other a technological breakthrough. The focal point of the Mongolian warlord's success was his horse-mounted archers who were trained for warfare from an early age. But what led historian Frank McLynn to refer to the horse-mounted archers as a "quantum leap in military technology,"[23] was more than just years of rigorous training in archery and horsemanship. The first vital innovation was metal stirrups.

The stirrup, a simple loop hanging from the horse's saddle, was one of the most important inventions in the history of warfare and had an "immense influence" on the global balance of power.[24] Some historians have argued that the stirrup led to the system of knights which, in turn, led to Europe's feudal system. Medieval historian Lynn White explains, "Few inventions have been so simple as the stirrup, but few have had so catalytic an influence on history. The requirements of the new mode of warfare which it made possible found expression in a new form of western European society dominated by an aristocracy of warriors endowed with land so that they might fight in a new and highly specialized way."[25]

As with the knights in Medieval Europe, "the metal stirrup allowed Mongolian riders unrivaled mobility, stability, and balance thus giving them a great advantage in any fight."[26] The metal stirrup also better enabled the horse-mounted archers to stand and twist around to the side or even ride backwards, allowing them to continue attacking even while in retreat. In this way, a tactical retreat could, in effect, amount to an offensive maneuver.[27]

Genghis Khan's second key innovation was a technique his warriors were trained to master. By releasing their arrows just at the moment when "all of their horse's hooves left the ground" his archers were able to significantly increase their accuracy.[28] The combination of these two innovations, made the Mongolian cavalry the most fierce fighting force on Earth, ensuring the devastation of his enemies, who proved unable to match the Mongolian's rapid tactical and technological advances.

Beyond the realm of military conflict and war, the failure to recognize the importance of a new technology, process, or innovation is also one of the most common reasons market leaders fail. Kodak, for example, founded in the 1880s, held a virtual monopoly on photography for nearly a century, but somehow failed to recognize the disruption of digital cameras and, consequently, went bankrupt in 2012 nearly $7 billion in debt.

How could they have missed the market for so long? Apparently a single word had something to do with it. When a Kodak engineer, Steven Sasson, built a device in 1974 to capture images and display them digitally he presented it to his boss, calling it "filmless photography." But inside the world of Kodak in the mid 1970s, the word "filmless" was something akin to "profitless," or "bankruptcy." Selling film for their cameras was a vital part of their business model. As *HBR* writes, "that positioning clashed with the very raison d'être of his audience—executives whose careers depended on the sale and processing of film—all but guaranteeing a tepid response. Instead of seizing an advantage in the consumer market, Kodak held off for nearly two decades, by which time several competitors were contesting the market space."[29] Sasson himself later said of his flawed framing, "It never occurred to me that I was at odds with the fundamental mission of the company for the last 100 years."[30]

Seek the Advantages of the Pioneer.

After founding Carnegie Steel in 1875, Andrew Carnegie became America's leading steel supplier. His approach to the market amounted to "a vertically-integrated manufacturing process" along with a commitment to "consistently incorporate...the latest technological innovation."[31] This, in fact, was a foundational component of Carnegie's strategy. "Amid the Vanderbilts, Rockefellers, and Morgans of his day, Andrew Carnegie understood he could not rely on being the premier capitalist," and, therefore, he "embraced technology as the key driver of operational and financial success. He continually reinvested profits into the mills and frequently ordered even modestly outdated equipment torn out and replaced."[32] When he finally sold Carnegie Steel for $480 million in 1902, Andrew Carnegie was the richest man in the world.

Throughout history we repeatedly see the often tremendous advantages that accrued to early adopters and pioneers. Alexander the Great mastered the use of the Phalanx—a mass military formation composed of long spears—giving him a lethal advantage over his enemies.

Possessing the latest weapons of war, Charlemagne's enemies were terrified when they first set eyes on his "iron army." Beyond the *psychological* advantage, with his soldiers "wearing chain mail and scale armor for protection—highly sophisticated equipment for the time," this also gave Charlemagne a decisive *technological* advantage.[33]

The Protestant Reformation was made possible almost entirely due to the invention of the printing press. As Martin Luther said himself, "Printing is the ultimate gift of God and the greatest one."[34]

Napoleon Bonaparte gained considerable power through his effective use of the press, due in large part to establishing or gaining control over a total of six newspapers in France.[35] Of course, newspapers were nothing new and primitive forms of propaganda can be traced back to the beginning or recorded history (e.g. see Behistun Inscription, circa 515 B.C.). By controlling six newspapers, however, Napoleon was pioneering something more akin to a modern mass media conglomerate.

Louisiana Governor Huey Long also gained a controlling advantage over his opponents by establishing his own newspaper, *The American Progress*, but Long also used automobiles and newfangled sound trucks, with giant loud speakers attached to the corners of the roof, like no Southern politician had ever done and like most Louisiana voters had never *seen*.

Many politicians have won or strengthened their hold on high office by capitalizing on the latest technology. With his "fireside chats," President Franklin Roosevelt was one of the first political figures to exploit the power of radio, effectively bypassing the media, speaking directly to Americans in the comfort of their own homes.

As a runner in World War I, Adolf Hitler was well aware of the crucial advantage that could be gained by rapid and reliable communication on the battlefield. As a result, the Nazis focused the necessary resources on putting radios in every tank, plane, and platoon possible. This gave them a major communications advantage over the allies who had not yet fully appreciated the tactical advantages of an entire battalion being able to adapt to sudden developments in the field almost instantly. The Germans later extended their communications advantage with the invention of Enigma, an encryption machine that kept their communications secret.[36]

In his 1948 race for the U.S. Senate, Lyndon Johnson was one of the firsts to campaign in a helicopter, leaving an unforgettable impression on all those voters so far out in the boonies that they had never even heard of, let alone seen, such a novel contraption.[37]

In the first ever televised presidential debate, a rested and tanned Senator John F. Kennedy used his understanding of the new medium to beat the sweaty, unshaven Vice President Richard Nixon in 1960.

Barack Obama was the first to effectively exploit social media to emerge as the victor in 2008.

And Donald Trump bypassed the media and wiped out an entire field of GOP candidates in 2016 due in no small part to his near-continuous stream of rash, attention-seeking, headline-grabbing Tweets on Twitter.

American computer scientist Alan Kay once said, "The best way to predict the future is to invent it."[38] Fortunately, to succeed as a strategist, you do not have to invent the future or even predict it in order to profit from it. But you do have to prevent your head from getting stuck in the sand. You do have to be quick to spot the technological innovations or breakthrough developments, processes, inventions, or apps.

Scan Far. Scan Deep. Scan Wide. Monitor Movement Worldwide.

If you do not learn about a new technology, tool, or innovation until everyone is already talking about it, then the chances are high that you've already missed the greater part of that opportunity. By the time Genghis Khan's enemies learned about the metal stirrup, for example, they had already either been conquered or sworn their allegiance to him.

To spy new breakthroughs or technological advances before the signal is strong requires *intentional monitoring* of trends, issues, or developments in the external environment. It requires continuous *horizon scanning* or *environmental scanning*—which goes beyond innovation and includes monitoring for both opportunities and threats.[39]

Regardless of how you go about keeping your eyes and ears open, you are essentially looking for emerging trends, developments, breakthroughs, paradigm shifts, or relevant information that could overturn assumptions, invalidate existing technologies or tactics, disrupt markets, make current products or services obsolete, or otherwise have a profound effect on your team or organization's future. "It's important to draw from a broad array of sources. Doing so will likely unearth a trend faster than relying on one stream of information alone."[40] According to Harvard Business School professor Francis Aguilar, "70 percent of the information on which strategists operate comes from outside of their organizations and 50 percent comes through informal channels."[41]

Swiftly Assimilate the Advantage of New, Relevant Breakthroughs, Advances, or Tech.

The task is not simply to keep your finger on the pulse of innovation, but to carefully *think through how* new developments can be applied in a way that gives you a competitive or worthwhile *advantage*. While some historians argue that Nathan Rothschild's run on Wellington's win at Waterloo was the source of Rothschild's fabled wealth, this is almost certainly an exaggeration. There is no question, however, that the Rothschilds' advanced communication network, along with their ongoing ability to discover or swiftly capitalize on new developments and emerging technological advances, played a vital role in amassing an unparalleled fortune.

Rarely is it necessary to be the *first* to adopt a new technology or innovation in order to win big; just don't wait too long to be convinced. A recent *HBR* study found that the "pioneers" (those organizations who "believe strongly in the benefits of adopting new technologies and that pursue first-mover advantage") experience more than twice the revenue growth of the "followers" (those who watch the pioneers, and wait until benefits are proven), and more than three times the revenue growth of the "cautious" (those who wait until a technology is well-established before adopting it).[42] Pioneers are also correlated with "better business outcomes," including maintaining a leading position in their market.[43]

To be clear, the point is not to adopt every new innovation, technology, or breakthrough that comes along. Instead, strategists stay focused on building competitive strengths, exploiting opportunities, and eliminating weaknesses and threats. Thus, the best approach is to use your strategic vision as a filter to screen out all those ideas that are impractical, unnecessary, misaligned, or out of reach.

Take an Experimental Tack:
Six Practical Proven Approaches

"Along with thinking differently to come up with revolutionary new ideas or products, there is also seeing differently. Great creators, innovators, and entrepreneurs look at the world in ways that are different from how many of us look at things. This is why they see opportunities that other people miss."[44]

—Adam Brandenburger, *Harvard Business Review*

Rather than waiting for a new technology, tool, process, or innovation to emerge, there are also countless different ways you might go about creating your own. And while there may be no full-proof *formula* for creativity or innovation, you can certainly create the conditions that help to cultivate and nurture the creative process.[45] Below is a list of six (6) practical, proven approaches to help spur your thinking and generate powerful, game-changing strategic ideas or new, innovative strategies and tactics of your own.

(1.) *Start with a Bold, Audacious Goal.*

Regardless of which approach or combination you adopt, the first logical step is to get clear about what you hope to achieve with this innovation. Are you looking for a solution to a problem? Is there an unmet need or desire, or an unfulfilled demand in the market? What is it that's not working well or quickly or cheaply enough? And what do you envision happening as a result of your innovation?

Along with casting a clear vision and establishing a clear direction, this step can also be used to spur creativity. If you start with a big, audacious goal, something that seems slightly out-of-reach, a goal you cannot accomplish with the actions and plans currently in place, then you force yourself to do things differently, boosting the odds of innovation as a result. In other words, creative energy rolls when you set stretch goals.

The use of walls as a means of protection can be traced back to the very beginning of human history. The earliest known example is the wall of the Theopetra Cave in Thessaly, Greece, which was built around 21,000 B.C. and still stands today. When the Roman Emperor Constantine moved the capital of the empire to Byzantium, which he renamed Constantinople, he wanted to transform it into the greatest city in the world and, moreover, he wanted Constantinople to be impervious to foreign assault. His attention soon turned to the walls of the city. Lots of cities had walls around the perimeter as a means of protection. Constantine's innovation was to make the walls of Constantinople impenetrable. To do this, he strengthened the existing walls and added military towers and fortified gates. When Theodosius the Great reigned (378-395), he took Constantine's idea even further, adding a moat with a low wall and an additional inner wall around the entire perimeter. The system of walls eventually consisted of four walls and a moat, complete with 96 towers. Despite numerous sieges, including by the Avars, the Arabs, and the Bulgarians, the walls were never breached. For more than 1,000 years they protected the city from all would-be invaders.

No doubt, in the Middle Ages, the idea of building a city that was completely impervious to outside attack must have seemed like a fantastic dream. And, yet, it is also undoubtedly true that bold, inspiring visions and fantastic dreams can be a powerful part of fostering the creative and innovative thinking we need to achieve them. In fact, research in organizational psychology has repeatedly revealed that pushing people "to commit to ambitious, seemingly out-of-reach objectives can spark outsized jumps in innovation and productivity."[46] As author and *New York Times* columnist Charles Duhigg writes in *Smarter, Faster, Better*, "Stretch goals can spark remarkable innovations, but," he cautions, "only when people have a system for breaking them into concrete plans."[47]

The reason stretch goals can be so effective is that they jolt you out of your current mode of operating, challenging complacency, and shaking up the status quo with new ways of thinking and working.[48] By substantially elevating your aspirations, Duhigg writes, "…stretch goals can shift attention to possible new futures and perhaps spark increased energy…prompt[ing] exploratory learning through experimentation, innovation, broad search, or playfulness."[49]

To be effective, stretch goals must be a bit outrageous, slightly unrealistic, but *not* ridiculously impossible—to *you* (they can seem impossible to outsiders, so long as *you* are convinced there is a way). Goals that are believed to be impossible risk undermining motivation and morale. The key here is to situate stretch goals within the SMARTER goal system (Specific, Measurable, Ambitious, Relevant, Time-bound, Exciting, and Results-based). As Duhigg explains, "It's often not clear how to start on a stretch goal. And so, for a stretch goal to become more than just an aspiration, we need a disciplined mindset to show us how to turn a far-off objective into a series of realistic short-term aims. […] Stretch goals, paired with SMART thinking, can help put the impossible within reach."[50] "Don't bunt," said David Ogilvy, the "Father of Advertising;" aim out of the ball park. Aim for the company of immortals."[51]

As important as it is to be bold, it is also important to be self-aware. Rather than suppressing any doubts and fears you may feel, stop and reflect and take a more critical look. "Fear isn't just an inhibiting force; it can be a powerful teacher, signaling that you are underequipped or underinformed. So pinpointing the source of your angst is critical to addressing it."[52]

(2.) *Interrupt the Pattern, Disturb the Status Quo.*

If something is not working the way you would like, rather than sticking with the status quo, one of the first things to do is interrupt the pattern. New or more challenging goals can help interrupt patterns, but there are other ways as well. You might, for example, try adding someone or something, or taking someone or something away. During the Civil War, for example, when President Lincoln was struggling with how his senior commanders were prosecuting the war in the eastern theatre, he appointed Ulysses S. Grant as General-in-Chief, who immediately assumed a far more proactive, offensive approach in dealing with Confederate General Robert E. Lee.

You might also find a way to rearrange the order, break the process apart, or just take a hiatus to work on something else. President Kennedy adopted a number of effective pattern interrupts during the Cuban Missile Crisis to better ensure critical thinking and creative problem solving, including mixing up group participants, scheduling meetings in new and different places, having leaderless meetings, and assigning a rotating devil's advocate.[53]

The key is to break out of the pattern that is not working to make space to think and see differently. The point here is not to completely change everything, however. When you break the pattern, or create a disturbance, you make space for something new to develop.[54] If you completely obliterate the pattern, in contrast, you risk being too disruptive, destroying much that is good, or forcing an unnecessary, wasteful start from scratch. "When strong ideas take root, they can sometimes crowd out competitors so thoroughly that alternatives can't prosper. So sometimes the best way to spark creativity is by disturbing things just enough to let some light through."[55]

Although it is difficult to give Charles VII of France any credit for her success, the reality is that he *was* willing to take a chance on an unknown, illiterate, teenage peasant girl who had no experience or military training whatsoever because, clearly, after more than 90 years into the Hundred Years' War, nothing else was working. Meanwhile, the English continued to strengthen their hold over France. By taking a stand against his advisors and giving Joan of Arc a chance to lead the French troops to lift the siege of Orléans, he not only helped to ensure his coronation as King of France, but he also played his small but important part in bringing an end to the Hundred Years' War.

(3.) *Alter the Level or Direction.*

Adjust the Scope. Another approach to the creative process is to alter the way you are approaching the problem or potential opportunity. It may help, for example, to *step back* and examine the issue in its larger context. Virtually every issue or topic you consider is just one part of a larger set of interrelated factors. Identify the larger set and, from that perspective, redefine the challenge or need.

In other cases, it may help to narrow the scope, sometimes literally. Think, for example, of the world of possibilities that opened up with the invention of the microscope. Sometimes you have to focus in on the finest of details to develop the game-changing strategic idea you need. In the case of Genghis Khan and the Mongolian warriors, for example, it was just a quick flash of space, barely more than a second, when their horses were completely off the ground, that led to the game-changing accuracy of their archers.

Strip It Down to the Essence. Most every problem or need can also be broken down into its constituent parts. Try breaking your problem or need apart and redefining each part. You might also try stripping the issue down to its most basic essence. In her article, "Break Free from the Product Life Cycle," Harvard Business School professor of strategy and innovation, Youngme Moon, makes the case for what she terms *reverse positioning*, which amounts to stripping away "sacred" product attributes as a way of repositioning the product in the market.[56] In this way, rather than marching along in the endless parade of product augmentation, innovation is achieved by "boldly limiting…the features offered."[57] Consider, for example, how Trader Joe's was able to carve out an unusually lucrative space in the highly competitive grocery store industry not with another giant supermarket or huge big box food store, but by significantly *limiting* the number of items offered. Related concepts discussed below include the Pareto principle (80/20 rule), Minimum Viable Product, and the power sweep.

Change the Direction. You might also consider the *direction* that is *driving* the identification of the problem or need. In other words, is there some external force or new development or trend that is creating this situation, or defining the problem or need? If so, how might thinking about the influence of this external factor change the way you are thinking about the problem or opportunity at hand? And is this driving you or your team or organization toward one thing, perhaps a misguided or short-sighted solution? Or away from something else, perhaps a viable solution?

In the beginning of the Viking Age (793-1066 A.D.), for example, the way the English responded to the ruthless Viking raiders was by relying on local militias. Nearly a century passed before they began to rely on a standing, mobile field army, strategically located forts, and a budding navy. And, yet, the Vikings continued to come. It was not until they began thinking about how to seduce and convert the Vikings to their culture, religion, and way of life that the senseless slaughter of innocents finally started to end.

Whatever new, creative strategy or tactical innovation you ultimately adopt, the key to get there is to think differently. "What these approaches have in common is the goal of moving strategy past the insights delivered by analytic tools (which are close at hand) and into territory that's further afield, or—to use a bit of academic jargon—cognitively distant. They take their inspiration more from how our thought processes work," Adam Brandenburger writes in *HBR Guide to Setting Your Strategy*, "than from how industries or business models are structured. For that reason they can help strategists make the creative leap beyond what already exists to invent a genuinely new way of doing business."[58]

The goal with each one of these approaches is to see the same old thing in a new, unfamiliar way. "When we look at the world, we should not just *examine*, but examine with a deliberately different perspective. Not just name what is around us, but come up with new names. Not just consider the whole, but break things up (or down) into pieces."[59] Simple tactics and techniques like this can be a surprisingly powerful way for strategists to spy new, revolutionary ways of achieving their purpose and goals.[60]

(4.) *Increase Your Exposure. Absorb and Apply Insights and Ideas from Different Domains.*

In 1888, Mohandas K. Gandhi decided that he wanted to go abroad for law school in London, the biggest and most cosmopolitan city on the planet at the time. Not content to learn about it from others, the shy, sheltered 18-year-old wanted to see the world with his own eyes. Unfortunately, his family was against the idea, particularly his mother who did not approve of him being so far away from home, or leaving his new bride. Gandhi's caste was also staunchly opposed, and they refused to give him permission.

Nevertheless, with "all of his characteristic stubbornness and resourcefulness,"[61] despite the fact that he was formally *excommunicated by his caste*, Gandhi sailed from Bombay to London determined to experience the world for himself and learn all he could about life outside the narrow confines of his circle in Porbandar.

The first time in a big city, Gandhi had never seen such luxury and grandeur, strange contraptions like an elevator, and lights everywhere powered by electricity.[62] So impressed with his room at the Victoria Hotel, he said, "I thought I could pass a lifetime in that room."[63]

"I was quite dazzled by the splendor," he wrote of his first time in the heart of the mighty British empire, "all the time smiling within myself."[64]

Beyond the technological developments of the big city, Gandhi was also gaining exposure to an entirely different culture. As he wrote in his autobiography, "Everything was strange—the people, their ways, and even their dwellings. I was a complete novice in the matters of English etiquette and continually had to be on my guard."[65]

"…He soon began to soak up many new experiences. He experimented with ballroom dancing classes, tried elocution lessons and learned Latin. While studying law, he also became attracted to London's radical politics, meeting freethinkers, theosophists (who believe that knowledge from the distant past offers a route to enlightenment), artists, politicians and writers, many of whom were highly critical of Victorian society. […] He also made excursions, including to Paris and to Brighton. He found a modest foothold as a committee leader of the Vegetarian Society, where he honed his journalistic and campaigning skills."[66]

In essence, the wealth of diverse experiences outside of his small coastal hometown in India broadened and enriched Gandhi's perspective and greatly expanded his network of friends and colleagues. It also gave him a chance to mature and reinvent himself, and it opened up a whole new world of possibilities for his future.

Of course, Gandhi's decision to leave India and study abroad, in defiance of his family and caste, was not some masterstroke of a grand strategist. Regardless of the underlying motivation, however, the result was the same. He gained a whole new understanding and appreciation for, and access to, the wider world. Nor was the tremendous value of this exposure lost on Gandhi. In fact, in the decades ahead, he would put the general principle into practice again and again. Indeed, along with the lasting relationships he forged, Gandhi's experiences in England would later prove invaluable to his leadership of the independence movement back in India. As Oxford historian Yasmin Khan writes, "…as an outsider, with time on his hands, he came to understand the British from afar, and was able to use these insights to develop a unique analysis of imperial and racial injustices."[67] Perhaps most importantly, while Gandhi was "in London, he learned how British political systems operated— and, conversely, how he might subvert them."[68]

Furthermore, Gandhi also "developed a deep fondness for British people during these years, which he would retain all his life."[69] His experiences, in turn, helped make it easy for him to see the British people as an important *ally*. If Gandhi had not lived among the British people he might never have recognized the role they could play in winning India's independence.

Blend the New with the Old. Understand: Exposure can be an immensely powerful input to innovation. Thus, the essential idea with this approach is to recognize "creativity as an import-export business."[70] The point is not to go abroad (though that may very well prove the right move for some). The point is to increase your exposure to new experiences, places, and people as a way of boosting creative thinking and innovation.

"Fostering creativity by juxtaposing old ideas in original ways isn't new. Historians have noted that most of Thomas Edison's inventions were the result of importing ideas from one area of science into another."[71] As Stanford engineers Hargadon and Sutton explain, "Edison and his colleagues used their knowledge of electromagnetic power from the telegraph industry, where they first worked, to transfer old ideas that were new to the lighting, telephone, phonograph, railway, and mining industries."[72]

This process of "taking proven, conventional ideas from other settings and combining them in new ways...is remarkably effective, it turns out. It's a tactic all kinds of people have used to spark creative successes."[73] "Scientists, artists, management consultants, and others involved in creative problem-solving efforts often build innovative new ideas by recombining existing ideas. It is an old notion that innovations are built from existing works, but the image often remains of the lone genius inventing ideas from scratch."[74]

Think Beyond Category, Context, and Time. The Rothschilds wealth was built on one of the most important breakthroughs in history—international banking. By the early 1800s, with branches of the Rothschild banking empire in five major cities—Frankfurt, London, Naples, Vienna, and Paris, each one headed by one of Mayer Amschel Rothschild's five sons—the bank as a whole was largely impervious to political and economic threats faced by any of the individual branches. With eyes and ears spread across Europe, the Rothschilds also had a more complete view of important social, political, military, and economic developments. This enabled them to share valuable information that could prove highly profitable, and help to safeguard their power and influence.

But, yet again, the general idea was not altogether new. Long before the beginning of the Rothschilds banking empire, the Borgia Pope, Alexander VI (1431—1503), who has been called "the father, almost the creator, of modern diplomacy,"[75] consolidated his power by having trusted members of his inner circle permanently stationed as ambassadors in other major cities across Europe. "He introduced the practice of stationing the prototypical ambassadors at the city-states to live there, and then he started doing that with major north European capitals."[76] Each of the Pope Alexander's numerous ambassadors lived at the heart of the various seats of European power, regularly reporting back to the Vatican, effectively "consolidate[ing] his power across Europe."[77]

What often appears to be a brilliant new insight is really just an old idea applied in a new way or place. As Kellogg School of Management professor Brian Uzzi said, "a lot of the people we think of as exceptionally creative are essentially intellectual middlemen...They've learned how to transfer knowledge between different industries or groups. They've seen a lot of different people attack the same problems in different settings, and so they know which kinds of ideas are more likely to work."[78]

As Steve Jobs famously put it in 1996, "Creativity is just connecting things."[79] Referring to his experience working with the creative minds inside Apple and Pixar, Jobs went on to reveal that, "when you ask creative people how they did something, they feel a little guilty because they didn't really do it, they just saw something. It seemed obvious to them after a while. That's because they were able to connect experiences they've had and synthesize new things. And the reason they were able to do that," Jobs concluded, "was that they've had more experiences or they have thought more about their experiences than other people."[80]

In his book, *Smarter, Faster, Better*, Charles Duhigg put it this way, "the building blocks of new ideas are often embodied in existing knowledge...Combinations of existing material are centerpieces in theories of creativity, whether in the arts, the sciences, or commercial innovation."[81] "Researchers have consistently found that labs and companies encourage such combinations to spark creativity."[82] "If you reflect on how a problem similar to yours was solved in an entirely different context, surprising insights may emerge."[83]

Great strategists tend to have a wide swath of experiences to draw on. Equally important, great strategists continue to create new experiences, and voraciously consume new, creative content in a variety of forms—from books, articles, videos, and podcasts, to conferences, workshops, lectures, documentaries, and shows.[84] Exposure to a boundless flow of creative stimuli helps strategists generate interesting, alternative perspectives and fresh approaches to old problems, helping them to see new parallels, identify emerging opportunities, and frame existing challenges in new ways.[85]

Borrow and Build On The Ideas of Others. As a strategist, you do not necessarily need to develop a new technology or innovation yourself. You don't even have to be the first to recognize the potential advantages. Nathan Rothschild did not invent the courier system. Andrew Carnegie did not develop the Bessemer steel-making process. In fact, steel plants in England had adopted Henry Bessemer's method long before Carnegie incorporated the superior process into his mills in America.[86]

The Medicis did not devise the bill of exchange,[87] though their clever use of them to skirt usury laws was key to their becoming the wealthiest family in Europe. Instead, writes historian Paul Strathern, "their success was based almost exclusively on the use of tried-and-trusted techniques pioneered by others."[88]

Bill Gates and Paul Allen did not create the original operating system (OS) that became MS-DOS and then Windows. When these two founders of Microsoft were first approached by IBM to submit a proposal for an OS to go with the first IBM personal computer, they did not even have an operating system. Nor did they have the time to develop one to meet IBM's deadline. Regardless, Gates' response to IBM was, "Sure, right away!" He then immediately started hustling to find an operating system he could sell. He quickly found one in Seattle, but the company already tried to sell it to IBM and failed. Nevertheless, Gates bought it for $50,000 and turned around and sold it to IBM, eventually making *billions* of dollars as a result.[89]

The key is to find the innovation, recognize its crucial value, and rapidly put it into play, ideally before it goes mainstream. The ability to quickly assimilate new military technologies and innovations into his massive war machine was a key part of what enabled Genghis Khan to become one of the greatest conquerors in history. Along with metal stirrups, composite bows, and leather armor, Genghis Khan appropriated other key military technologies from his enemies and subjects, including the use of gunpowder, horse armor, and siege weapons such as the catapult. The Mongolian conqueror did not stop with technological innovations, however. He also developed or adopted "a complex new military structure and new military tactics, like arrow storms, amassing huge arsenals, engaging in repeated hit-and-run barrages, delayed sieges, and psychological warfare."[90]

Naturally, the notion of borrowing and building on new technologies goes well beyond the battlefield. Indeed, rather than conflict or even competition, it is just as often the fruit of partnerships and collaboration, or the simple act of networking or talking with your customers or clients, or followers and fans. In the words of now billionaire businessman Bill Gates, "innovation requires the ability to collaborate and share ideas with other people, and to sit down and talk with customers and get their feedback and understand their needs."[91]

(5.) *Exploit the Power of Analogy.*

> *"Analogical reasoning is a key implement*
> *in the toolbox of the typical real-world strategist."*[92]

—Giovanni Gavetti and Jan Rivkin, Harvard Business School

Metaphors, similes and analogies are powerful conceptual tools. They are fundamental to both how we make meaning of the world,[93] and how we communicate meaning to others.[94] "We may not always know it," writes cognitive linguist George Lakoff, "but we think in metaphor. A large proportion of our most commonplace thoughts make use of an extensive, but unconscious, system of metaphorical concepts, that is, concepts from a typically concrete realm of thought that are used to comprehend another, completely different domain."[95]

Metaphors, similes and analogies all make use of *comparison* to better understand or communicate something. But analogies are slightly different in that they are more of a logical argument and, thus, may require some elaboration or explanation. In other words, rather than merely using one thing to represent another—as we do with metaphor (e.g. "I am sometimes a fox and sometimes a lion," Napoleon said.[96]) and simile (e.g. "Bonaparte flies like lightning and strikes like a thunderbolt,"[97] Napoleon wrote about himself in a propaganda piece.)—with an analogy, you are making a logical comparison as a means of deciding what to do or how to handle it (e.g. 'This is just like that time when…or that case where… And, therefore, the logical thing to do here is…').

Whether we realize it or not, we all do this all the time. When confronted with an unfamiliar problem or opportunity, we will often think back to some previous experience we've had or learned about in an attempt to "draw lessons from it, and apply those lessons to the current situation."[98] This is what it means to reason by analogy.

Not surprisingly, when used correctly, these conceptual devices can significantly improve strategic thinking, decision making, and persuasion. The opposite is also true. If you are stuck or struggling, it may be because you are operating, perhaps unconsciously, according to a weak, flawed, incomplete, or unresourceful analogy.

Along with being "a source of remarkable insight," a useful analogy can also help break stale thinking and become a powerful input to the creative process.[99] As Harvard Business School professors Gavetti and Rivkin write, "Analogies lie at the root of some of the most compelling and creative thinking in business as a whole, not just in discussions of strategy."[100]

Nonetheless, in the realm of strategy, the value of reasoning by analogy is well established, and with good cause. Reasoning by analogy is well-suited to the needs of strategists and the limits they face. Analogies, for example (as discussed further in Chapter 6, Section 3, Subsection 2), can be exceptionally useful even when the information available is incomplete.[101] What's more, the power of analogical reasoning is heightened by greater experience, which strategists often possess, but which they can also reap from history, as Clausewitz said, or, as Bismarck said, learn from others.[102] The strategist's need for creative solutions and innovative strategies is also well met by the creativity generated through the use of analogy.[103] "Reflecting these matches, business schools typically teach strategy by means of case studies, which provide an abundance of analogies from which the students can draw. [...] Similarly, some of the foremost strategy consultants are famed for their ability to draw lessons from one industry and apply them to another. Thus," Gavetti and Rivkin conclude, "we have ample reason to believe that analogical reasoning is a key implement in the toolbox of the typical real-world strategist."[104, 105]

(6.) *Always Be Experimenting. Explore. Investigate. Test It Out and See.*

Few capture the essence of this approach to innovation better than America's greatest inventor, Thomas Alva Edison. "Everything he achieved was the result of persistent trials and experiments," wrote Edison's former rival, Nikola Tesla, the celebrated Serbian-American inventor.[106] According to Tesla, Edison's experiments were "...often performed at random but always attesting extraordinary vigor and resource. Starting from a few known elements, he would make their combinations and permutations, tabulate them and run through the whole list, completing test after test with incredible rapidity until he obtained a clue. His mind was dominated by one idea, to leave no stone unturned, to exhaust every possibility."[107]

In essence, the path to groundbreaking innovation, Edison believed, was rigorous and relentless experimentation. As Edison himself said, "The real measure of success is the number of experiments that can be crowded into 24 hours."[108] Ralph Waldo Emerson similarly said, "All life is an experiment. The more experiments you make the better."[109]

The thrust of this approach, therefore, is to get good at concocting experiments. Figure out ways to conduct more tests and trials. Get aggressive about trial and error. Collect feedback and data to measure your results. "Pay attention to negative feedback and solicit it, particularly from friends," Elon Musk said in a TED talk.[110] "Hardly anyone does that, and it's incredibly helpful."[111]

Then, make the necessary adjustments and begin again. Not everything has to succeed. In fact, you may only need one good idea or breakthrough advance. As Mark Cuban writes in his book, "In business, to be a success, you only have to be right once. One single time and you are set for life. That's the beauty of the business world."[112]

Key to this approach is skirting any sort of emotional investment in the result. If your idea or experiment fails, just move on to the next one—and fast. Imagine yourself as a scientist methodically conducting experiments, one after another, logically eliminating any idea that doesn't work.

This idea of seeing yourself as a scientist conducting experiments, rather than a businessperson trying to earn a profit, has proven to be a more profitable and effective approach. Wharton Business School professor Adam Grant writes about a study on entrepreneurship in Milan which found that economic performance was significantly improved when the subjects were trained to think like experimental scientists actively testing hypothesis.

In the study, both groups were taught about the importance of creating a strategy, interviewing customers, creating a minimum viable product or service, and then offering a prototype to customers. The control group was taught about these key concepts from the perspective of a traditional entrepreneur. The other group was taught about these same key concepts from the perspective of an experimental scientist. "From that perspective, their strategy is a theory, customer interviews help to develop hypotheses, and their minimum viable product and prototype are experiments to test those hypotheses. Their task is to rigorously measure the results and make decisions based on whether their hypotheses are supported or refuted."[113]

The results of the study were remarkable. In less than a year, the average revenue for those subjects in the entrepreneurship group was a meager $300. The average revenue for those subjects trained to think like experimental scientists, in contrast, was more than $12,000. They also began attracting customers twice as quickly. The reason for the surprising difference is that, as Grant put it, "the entrepreneurs in the control group tended to stay wedded to their original strategies and products. It was too easy to preach the virtues of their past decisions, prosecute the vices of alternative options, and politick by catering to advisers who favored the existing direction. The entrepreneurs who had been taught to think like scientists, in contrast, pivoted more than twice as often. When their hypotheses weren't supported, they knew it was time to rethink their business models."[114] In short, as the authors of the study conclude, "using genuinely rigorous investigation techniques is likely to produce better results."[115]

"It is critical to maintain some distance from what we create. Without self-criticism, without tension, one idea can quickly crowd out competitors," writes Duhigg.[116] "But we can regain that critical distance by forcing ourselves to critique what we've already done, by making ourselves look at it from a completely different perspective, by changing the power dynamics in the room or giving new authority to someone who didn't have it before."[117] This was part of the approach to decision-making President Kennedy adopted with his Executive Committee following the disastrous Bay of Pigs invasion, which helped to generate more fruitful dialogue and critical thinking and, ultimately, more creative problem solving.

Emulate the example of Thomas Edison, who maintained the optimal mindset for innovation. "I never allow myself to become discouraged under any circumstances," he once said.[118] "After we had conducted thousands of experiments on a certain project without solving the problem...we *had* learned something," he told an interviewer at the time.[119] "For we had learned for a certainty that the thing couldn't be done that way, and that we would have to try some other way. We sometimes learn a lot from our failures if we have put into the effort the best thought and work we are capable of."[120]

Though we often remember Thomas Edison as one of the world's greatest inventors, we might not remember him at all if not for his practical, hard working, no-nonsense business approach to innovation. In the words of another great American inventor, business magnate Bill Gates, "In the pantheon of American innovation, Thomas Edison holds a unique place. He became a symbol of American ingenuity and the conviction that inspiration and perspiration could lead to remarkable things."[121]

Avoid Overlooking the Obvious, or Blowing Off Hot Air

Above all else, it was innovation that helped the Rothschilds build one of the greatest private fortunes in the history of the world. Their unrivaled communications network of secret routes, swift riders, and fast ships afforded them with a major competitive advantage, an advantage that proved especially profitable in times of war. This included, most significantly, the epic economic advantage Nathan Rothschild gained by being the first to receive word of Wellington's win over Napoleon at Waterloo. Nathan Rothschild clearly understood that opportunities to create and innovate were often found in more chaotic and unpredictable environments.[122] Perhaps not surprisingly, it was also Nathan Rothschild who once noted that "great fortunes are made when cannonballs fall in the harbor, not when violins play in the ballroom."[123]

To be sure, the Rothschilds have never been celebrated as innovators. They certainly embraced innovation and supported it, but they were always bankers first. Rather than innovating themselves, or being directly involved in the creative process, they simply borrowed and built on the best ideas of others.

Curiously, it was, in part, Napoleon Bonaparte's *failure* to recognize and capitalize on the best ideas of others that led to his career-ending defeat. Shortly after Napoleon became First Consul, without explanation, he ordered the disbandment of the French army's one and only unit of balloonists. At the time, these hot air balloons were the only means available for any sort of aerial reconnaissance. What's more, the unit had already proven its value in France's victory over the Coalition Army at the Battle of Fleurus in 1794.[124] And, yet, somehow Napoleon still failed to appreciate their worth, effectively dismissing the unit as a lot of hot air. In the words of British historian David G. Chandler, former professor at the Royal Military Academy at Sandhurst and Marine Corps University in the U.S., "This ill-judged decision—which well illustrates that there were distinct limits to even Napoleon's powers of intellectual vision—is hard to comprehend."[125]

Unfortunately, the decision would lead to his downfall at the Battle of Waterloo. "Walking the battlefield today," writes historian Andrew Roberts, "it's all too easy to understand why he lost. From the 140-foot-high Lion's Mound, which was built in the 1820s on top of Wellington's front line, one can see what Napoleon could not: the woods to the east from which 50,000 Prussians started to emerge at 1 p.m. to stave in the French right flank..."[126] Had the French army's balloonists still been operating, "such an instrument of intelligence gathering (the equivalent, perhaps, to modern satellite surveillance)," would have easily alerted Napoleon to the presence of Prussian troops at least as early as "10 a.m. instead of 1.30 p.m.," writes Chandler, "with possibly incalculable results on the outcome of the...Battle of Waterloo."[127] Instead, however, Napoleon's generals were unable to keep the Prussians in check, and by the time "German reinforcements finally arrived to help Wellington, Napoleon's last charge collapsed, and the French army disintegrated."[128]

While he was a brilliant strategist and tactician who furthered the development of the art of warfare, Napoleon Bonaparte, as an innovator, had distinct limits. "Napoleon's genius," writes military historian Francis Petre in *Napoleon at War*, "was not that of a creator. Indeed, he made few practical reforms or innovations in the military art."[129] What's more, Chandler adds, "He distrusted novel ideas;" not only did he disband the balloon companies, but he also rejected "Roger Fulton's offer of submarines and naval mines."[130]

"His talents lay elsewhere."[131] To be sure, despite his lack of imagination as an innovator, Napoleon excelled in a number of other areas, including his mastery of military history—which proved an exceptionally powerful tool (as examined in chapter 6.2). "His genius was essentially practical, and his military concepts evolved from the close study of earlier commanders, particularly Frederick the Great. He made the fullest use of the ideas of his predecessors and breathed life into them."[132]

8

To Unlock Unparalleled Power, Target Your Peak Leverage Points: The Legend of Lady Godiva and Her Naked Ride

"People with leverage have dominance over people with less leverage.
In other words, just as humans gained advantages over animals by creating
leveraged tools, similarly, humans who use these tools of leverage have more power
over humans that do not. Saying it more simply, Leverage is power."
—Robert Kiyosaki, *Rich Dad's Retire Young, Retire Rich*[1]

The young and famously beautiful Lady Godiva was stark naked when she mounted her horse. Living in 11th century England, the highly respectable Anglo-Saxon noblewoman did her best to cover her breasts with her long flowing black hair, but there was no hiding the fact that she was riding without clothes. What was far less clear was the motive of the man, Leofric, that drove the honorable Lady Godiva to dare to ride her horse naked through the heart of a crowded market in her hometown in the middle of the day.

Lady Godiva was a kind and compassionate woman who empathized with the people of Coventry who were suffering grievously under excessive taxation, and she was determined to do what she could to lessen their struggles and ease their financial burdens, including making generous donations and, oftentimes, giving away her own expensive jewelry. Now she seemed to be risking her well known reputation as a chaste and virtuous woman. But why?

The problem was that Lady Godiva was the wife of Leofric, Earl of Mercia, the very man responsible for imposing the oppressive taxation on the people. Lady Godiva had already repeatedly appealed to her husband to lower their taxes and relieve their burdens, but it was all to no avail. Leofric sternly refused her pleas again and again. In fact, Leofric had begun to lose his patience with his wife.

Lady Godiva was not some submissive wife pestering a powerful husband, however. She was "a clever and assertive wife"[2] who appears to have calculated with the craftiness of a campaign strategist that her "relentless advocacy"[3] would exasperate her husband, pushing him enough that "he might give a rash answer that she can capitalize on."[4]

And, indeed, this is exactly what happened next. Leofric at last responded with a rhetorical device known as an *impossibilia*—in other words, he said "yes," but attached a condition that he assumed would still make it impossible or at least "unthinkable to carry out (e.g. "over my dead body")."[5]

"Mount your horse naked," he said, "and ride through the town's marketplace from one end to the other when all the people are gathered, and when you return you will get what you demand."[6]

With this, Leofric thought he had succeeded in silencing his wife. When she then explicitly asked, "And if I am willing to do so, will you give me permission?,"[7] Leofric assumed that she was merely challenging whether he would even permit such a thing in the first place and, thus, he immediately said "yes."

But now Lady Godiva had her husband cornered. Not only was this whole public nudity idea his, but because he gave her his permission, and "because he has legal rights over her body, her nakedness would be socially humiliating to him as well as to her."[8] This effectively transforms his hasty pledge to eliminate the oppressive taxes in return for her nude ride into a sort of sacred promise. To refuse to lower taxes after she completed the public spectacle would be to risk ruining both his own reputation and that of his wife.

Still smugly satisfied with his "impossible" condition and still assuming his wife would recoil at the prospect of revealing her body in public,[9] Leofric sat in stunned amazement once he grasped that his chaste wife was prepared to exploit his careless bargain. And, at last, we see, writes Harvard's Daniel Donoghue in his book, *Lady Godiva*, "There is an element of cunning in the successful manipulation of her husband."[10]

When the people learn of the bargain she struck on their behalf, they agreed to go into their homes at the appointed time and shutter their windows so that Lady Godiva's nakedness would be unobserved and her honor preserved. When Lady Godiva completed her spree through the village, "she returned rejoicing to her husband, who considered it miraculous."[11]

Leofric, for his part, honored his word to his wife, released the people from their "servitude" and "confirmed [Coventry's] charter with the stamp of his own seal."[12] "The highborn Lady Godiva became an instant heroine to the common people of Coventry."[13]

Get Leverage, Gain Power

"Leverage is everything...don't begin to pry
till you have got the long arm on your side."[14]

—Oliver Wendell Holmes (1841—1935), U.S. Supreme Court Justice

Leverage is power. Leverage is about achieving more with less. It's about getting greater results with less effort or fewer resources. "The law of leverage," as Brian Tracy puts it, states that "certain things you do enable you to accomplish vastly more than you would if you spent the same amount of time in other activities."[15]

By turning your attention away from low leverage activities and focusing instead on those few things, or even that *single* thing, that will have an extraordinary impact on the results you desire, you can greatly increase your influence and power.[16] Indeed, the degree and extent to which you are able to put the principle of leverage into practice will determine your ultimate level and scale of success. As Robert Kiyosaki, author of *Rich Dad, Poor Dad*, writes, "Leverage is the reason some people become rich and others do not become rich."[17]

Exploiting the power of leverage begins with this simple premise: Not all actions are equal.[18] Some actions you take will make no difference at all; other actions will radically transform your world. This is why leverage is so critical to the strategist code. It is these game-changing actions that will enable you to achieve your greatest goals.[19] As MIT's Peter Senge writes in *The Fifth Discipline*, "tackling a difficult problem is often a matter of seeing where the high leverage lies, a change which—with a minimum of effort—would lead to lasting, significant improvement."[20]

The genius American architect, engineer, and systems theorist Buckminster Fuller often used the metaphor of a trim tab to explain the power of leverage. Think of a titanic ocean liner such as the RMS *Queen Mary* (1,019 feet). To turn such a massive ship requires a giant rudder.[21] But to turn such a rudder is difficult, requiring considerable power, due to the depth and volume of the water flowing around it. A trim tab, in contrast, which is a "miniature rudder" on the rudder of a ship, requires very little power, in fact, Fuller said, "almost no effort at all."[22] Even though it is "only a fraction of the size of the rudder," by disrupting the smooth flow of water across the rudder, the trim tab makes it much easier and more efficient "to turn the rudder, which, then, makes it easier to turn the ship."[23] This is leverage.

Leverage is everywhere and in everything. As direct response marketing pioneer Jay Abraham put it, "Everything you do, in every way you do it, with everyone you do it with, internally and externally, has within it [and] is replete with leverage...usually underrecognized leverage...underutilized leverage"[24]

The problem is that leverage often remains invisible, hidden, or ignored. The problem is that high-leverage actions are not always obvious.[25] Lady Godiva had for some time been acting to pressure her husband to reduce the excessive taxes on the people. She had even given away her own precious jewelry on occasion to help relieve the burden on the poor. But it was not until she provoked his rash retort that she uncovered the leverage point she needed to achieve her goal.

Because high-leverage actions are rarely obvious, people tend to focus on low-leverage changes, such as focusing on symptoms and short-term effects rather than underlying causes and long-term results. But the greatest power comes from identifying high-leverage changes.

Explore Your Options for Leverage

*"The main benefit of leverage is that you can do more with less,
maximizing achievement in every area of your life."*[26]
—Anthony Robbins

In thinking about *how* to get leverage, it's important to distinguish between *what* to leverage and *where* to focus or intervene. In business, the most common example of *what* to leverage is *other people's money* (OPM). Other typical examples include *other people's knowledge* and *other people's labor.* "By developing your ability to pull together other people's efforts, other people's knowledge and other people's money, you can accomplish vastly more in the same period of time than someone who is forced to rely on his or her own personal energy and resources."[27]

Technology, including the internet and AI, can also be a powerful tool to gain leverage. Other categories to explore in your search for leverage include the following:

(1.) *Leverage Your Time.*

With the possible exception of money, time is undoubtedly the greatest limiting factor in achieving your goals. In fact, the whole reason we need strategy in the first place is because of limits on time and money. Leveraging time is about multiplying the speed with which you can get things done. This includes delegating or outsourcing whatever others can do better, faster, or cheaper. Grant Cardone, author of *The 10X Rule*, writes, "The wealthy know that time is the only truly scarce resource. You can't buy more of it. So they maximize their time by letting go of the need [to] control every small detail of their business or portfolio, and learn to effectively outsource and delegate to good, smart people who will trade their time for money."[28] Effectively leveraging your time also includes creating systems and processes, finding methods or learning tactics to leapfrog steps, or grouping or batching similar tasks or jobs. Utilizing coaches and mentors (other people's knowledge) are additional ways to speed the learning curve and save time. Finally, leveraging time can include using technology to streamline and automate as much of your work as possible, or accomplish more than one thing at once.

(2.) *Leverage Your Opportunities.*

Opportunities can also be employed to bypass steps or accelerate effort. Think, for example, of the impact of effective partnerships, collaborations, and affiliate relationships. We all make choices everyday about what we are going to do, or which opportunities we are going to pursue. You can either squander those opportunities that present themselves, or you can focus on leverage and choose to pursue high impact opportunities. The key is to avoid giving in to your moods, feelings, or fears and instead think carefully about which opportunities will have the greatest impact on your future success.

(3.) *Leverage Your Assets and Strengths.*

Start with what you have now. Take an inventory of your assets and strengths to see what you might put to better use. *"It is far more lucrative and fun to leverage your strengths instead of attempting to fix all the chinks in your armor,"* writes Tim Ferriss in *The 4-Hour Workweek.*[29] "The choice is between *multiplication* [high leverage] of results using strengths or incremental improvement fixing weaknesses that will, at best, become mediocre. Focus on better use of your best weapons instead of constant repair."[30]

Your assets and strengths can include everything from past experience, education, accomplishments, or awards to your background, culture, memberships, affiliations, and networks. This can also include any useful knowledge, skills, or abilities you might possess. The key is to think about how you might get better use out of your assets, how you might spread them around, use them to spur new developments, open some new door, or propel yourself to new accomplishments or a higher level of success. "Another form of leverage, which can also cost nothing, is simply knowing the right people."[31] Networking at an alumni event, for example, might lead to a powerful mentoring relationship that transforms your business or career. According to Mark Victor Hansen and Robert Allen, "having a top mentor is the quickest way to climb the millionaire mountain. You will also begin to appreciate the leveraging power of networks. Most people think that strong, close relationships are key in business. However, Hansen and Allen suggest, it is the "weak ties," friends of friends or acquaintances in your field, who can make all the difference. The more you have of these, the more leads, sources of ideas, or potential champions you will have."[32]

(4.) *Leverage Your Liabilities.*

Rather than wasting time trying to make up for them, sometimes it is even possible to leverage your so-called "liabilities" or "weaknesses," as the German-born Catherine the Great was able to do with her status as an outsider in Russia.[33] At a time when men ruled the world, Queen Elizabeth I also cleverly exploited her sex (as well as her status as a maiden or single woman) to enhance her power in England. Rather than tying herself down, for example, by keeping her options open, and the throne beside her empty, she ensured that many men would work harder to win her favor. What supposed "liability" do you have that is actually a strength? With the right mindset or clever reframe, you can uncover leverage in all sorts of surprising places.

The key with all of these resources is to start with what you have, where you are now. Instead of trying to build, create, or earn something you can leverage in the future, identify what you can use as leverage now. Think, for example, of how, in 2005, the Canadian blogger Kyle MacDonald traded his way from a single red paperclip to a two-story farm house in Kipling, Saskatchewan in less than a year. He was able to do this in just 14 trades because he was able to find people who wanted what he had more than they wanted what they had. In other words, in each case, he found a trade in which his current possession had sufficient leverage with the trader.

No doubt, the publicity his project received as it gained momentum made it easier to find willing traders. But that too is leverage at work. In one of the trades, for example, a Montreal radio personality, Michel Barrette, traded a keg of beer for a used snowmobile. Presumably, the reason he was willing to make this trade, in part, at least, was because of the free publicity that he would gain (which is evidently still working).

It's important to keep in mind that MacDonald didn't need to find the greatest possible leverage for each trade. He only needed to find a trade a little bit better (i.e. perceived value to the next trader) than his last trade (e.g. a paperclip to a pen, a pen to a doorknob, etc.). There is an ancient Japanese folk tale known as the "Straw Millionaire" that tells of a peasant who traded his way up to become a millionaire. In one instance, he trades three oranges for an expensive piece of silk cloth. The reason the successful silk merchant was willing to part with one of her many expensive silks was because she was so dehydrated at the time. That is, with the thirsty rich merchant, the peasant's three juicy oranges had considerable leverage.

In the case of Lady Godiva, she didn't have any additional resources once she finally figured out how to get what she wanted. Her husband's reputation and her own honor had been a part of their story all along. She simply found a wily way to reveal an existing resource along with an expedient way to exploit it—she found, in other words, a way to do more with what she already had.

Furthermore, since the people also wanted taxes lowered, their shared goal was another potential resource she could leverage. Because they supported her efforts, they were more than happy to go inside during her naked ride. And, therefore, with her honor thereby preserved, the sacrifice and risks required of Lady Godiva were significantly reduced.

Identify the Optimal Leverage Point

"This idea of leverage points is not unique to systems analysis—
it's embedded in legend: the silver bullet; the trim tab; the miracle cure;
the secret passage; the magic password; the single hero who turns the tide of history;
the nearly effortless way to cut through or leap over huge obstacles.
We not only want to believe that there are leverage points, we want to
know where they are and how to get our hands on them.
Leverage points are points of power."[34]
—Donella Meadows, American Environmental Scientist,
Author of *Thinking in Systems*

Beyond thinking about *what* you might use as leverage, it is even more critical to think about *where* to focus. This is where systems thinking can prove especially useful. If we adopt a mechanical lever as a metaphor, we can think of *what* we leverage as the *beam* (i.e. the rigid board, bar, or lever), and *where* we intervene as the *fulcrum* (i.e. the axis or point of support about which the lever pivots). To be clear, *where* the fulcrum is located has a pivotal impact on how much leverage you gain. The closer the fulcrum is to what you want to move, the less effort you will need to apply to the beam.

Leverage *points* are the places where a "small shift in one thing can produce big changes in everything."[35] In order to better identify crucial leverage points, consider the following leverage points framework (adapted and modified from the systems thinking work of Donella Meadows' *Thinking in Systems* and Peter Senge's *The Fifth Discipline*).[36] To be clear, leverage points exist at every level of this framework. However, as you can see from the following 6-step progression of leverage points, the leverage you gain generally increases as you progress to higher levels:

> *"There are no simple rules for finding high-leverage changes,*
> *but there are ways of thinking that make it more likely."*[37]
>
> —Peter Senge, *The Fifth Discipline*

(1.) LEVEL 1—EVENTS.

    a. This includes what happens on the surface level that everyone can easily see.

    b. The central focus here is an event or a snapshot in time.

    c. The core question here is: What happened?

    d. The leverage points focus on the symptoms, evidence, or outcomes.

    e. In the case of Lady Godiva and the people of Coventry, notable events may have included a poor citizen being forced to sell a goat to survive or perhaps Lady Godiva donating an expensive necklace to a wife who lost her husband and was unable to care for her children.

(2.) LEVEL 2—PATTERNS OF BEHAVIOR.

    a. This includes what is happening just below the surface, and it is more difficult to see (particularly if you are new or have only recently begun to pay attention).

    b. The central focus here includes multiple events or incidents, over a certain period of time.

    c. The core questions here are: What has been happening? What are the apparent trends? Patterns? Or recurring themes?

    d. The leverage points at this level are focused on practices, behaviors, norms, and rules.

    e. At this level, Lady Godiva may have found herself attempting to help multiple families from falling into poverty. She is now beginning to notice a pattern of financial troubles.

(3.) LEVEL 3—SYSTEMS.

    a. This includes what is happening well below the surface and remains hidden from all but the careful observer.

    b. The central focus here is the system, particularly the "key interrelationships that influence behavior over time."[38] "These are not interrelationships between people, but among key variables"[39] Senge refers to these "interrelationships that control behavior" as "underlying structures."[40]

    c. The core questions here are: Why is this happening? What explains it? What is causing or influencing the patterns we see? What are the relationships between the parts?

    d. The leverage points at this level are focused on the key interrelationships between the key variables, which can include everything from physical objects (roads, bridges, buildings, mountains, rivers, terrain) and organizations to laws, regulations, and policies.

    e. At this level, by looking at the economic system in Coventry, Lady Godiva recognizes that the high taxes are the root cause behind the pattern of economic struggles.

(4.) LEVEL 4—GOALS.

    a. This includes what is happening on the surface, but also often well below the surface where their influence is less obvious. The goal or purpose of a system often remains hidden behind assumptions such as the following: 'This is just the way it has always been done,' or 'This is just the way things are,' or 'This is the natural order of things.'

    b. The central focus here is "the purpose or function of the system."[41]

    c. The core question here is: What is the purpose of this system?

    d. The leverage points at this level are focused on the intended beneficial consequences or positive outcomes of the system.

    e. Here Godiva sees that the goal or driving force behind the excessive taxation on the people is her husband's greed or maybe his goal of amassing wealth and power, perhaps to rival that of her father or other rulers across England. Even if his motives are good (e.g. to have the means to hire soldiers to protect the people in a time of war), the goal or purpose of the system of taxes is the same: to accumulate wealth.

(5.) LEVEL 5—LEADER.

    a. Those leaders with the power to change the system tend to remain hidden below the surface. While it is usually easy to recognize who occupies formal positions of power, it is not always so easy to see who has the power to change the system or its purpose. In fact, it is often the case that leaders are just another interchangeable part of the system itself and, therefore, they too are essentially powerless to bring change. In this case, "changing the players in the system is a low-level intervention, as long as the players fit into the same old system."[42] To be a higher level point of leverage, the intervention must focus on those leaders who *do* have the power or wherewithal to adjust the system or its goal.

b. The central focus here is the leader, actor, or player who has "the power to change the system's goal."[43]

c. The core question here is: Who benefits? Who stands to gain from the intended outcome of this system? The person or group who gains the *greatest* benefit is almost always the one with the power to change the system.

d. The leverage points at this level are focused on the specific leader or leaders or power brokers who are benefiting from the status quo.

e. In Godiva's case, once she recognizes that the goal of amassing wealth is behind the high taxes, it is just a small step to see that it is her husband, the Earl of Mercia, who is the greatest leverage point for her efforts. Unfortunately, identifying the leader behind the goal or system is not always so simple. In the case of Lady Godiva's husband, Leofric, for example, perhaps he was himself being pressed to contribute to the common defense by England's king, Edward the Confessor (assuming Godiva's story is more than mere legend).

(6.) LEVEL 6—MENTAL MODELS.

a. This includes what is happening in deep water, often in the unconscious mind. Mental models are invisible and are generally only inferred or deduced.

b. The focus at this level centers around the mental models that allow the system or some subset of key interrelationships to continue functioning.

c. The core questions here are: What are the underlying assumptions, perspectives, and beliefs? What are the values, expectations, and personal theories that are operating behind or supporting this system?

d. The leverage points at this level are focused on the mental models or paradigms (i.e. "the mind-set out of which the system—its goals, structure, rules, delays, parameters—arises"[44]). Paradigms or mental models or frames can include beliefs, perceptions, values, traditions, perspectives, personal theories, assumptions, attitudes, morals, or hidden rules.

e. While Leofric was undoubtedly compelled to reevaluate his priorities as a result of Lady Godiva's efforts, it is unclear if she succeeded in changing one or more of her husband's mental models about the oppressive taxes on the poor. It is certainly possible that he gained an increased understanding of power in the aftermath of Lady Godiva's naked ride and subsequent status as a hero to her people. Nonetheless, from what little we know of the legend, Lady Godiva's leverage point was centered around pressuring the leader, her husband, to change—not one or more of his mental models.

Nevertheless, given that there are only six levels of increasing leverage, focusing her efforts on the leader who actually possess the power to change the system was a level five point of leverage, and far higher than her initial level-1 efforts focused on rescuing a single mother by selling an expensive bracelet or ring.

In summary, as you move through these six levels—events, patterns of behavior, systems, goals, leaders, and mental models—you increase your potential leverage. The key, therefore, is to think carefully about what you want within the context of the bigger picture—to see the patterns and relationships of the whole system, its purpose and who controls it—before you decide when and where to intervene. *What* you leverage or *how much* leverage you gain can change dramatically depending on *where* you intervene.

Whatever the historical truth behind the legend of Lady Godiva's clever use of leverage, such a bold action might very well have saved a people from more than mere poverty and hardship. In fact, it was around this same period of time, in neighboring Worcester, England, that King Harthacnut's similarly burdensome taxation led to the 1041 riot in which the people of Worcester killed two of his tax collectors. In response, Harthacnut plundered the town and burned it to the ground, killing several people and, thereby, eliminating one of his significant sources of tax revenue. A man of extremes and excess, Harthacnut died a year later at a wedding after drinking too much alcohol.[45]

9

PROFIT FROM THE SUPREMACY OF STRATEGIC SURPRISE: THE TRIUMPH OF THE VIKINGS—THE SONS OF RAGNAR LOTHBROK, OLEG, ROLLO, CANUTE THE GREAT, AND OTHER SEAFARING WAR WOLVES OF THE VIKING AGE

"War is composed of nothing but surprises.
While a general should adhere to general principles,
he should never lose the opportunity to profit by these surprises.
It is the essence of genius."[1,2]
—Napoleon Bonaparte

Sailing in the Mediterranean Sea along the coast of Northern Italy, the Vikings were stunned when they first caught sight of the shimmering white, marbled city. They stood up in their ships to get a better look. Could this be Rome? Had they somehow, serendipitously stumbled upon the richest and most renowned city in the world?

It was 860 A.D. and two of the most famous Vikings in history, Björn Ironside and Hastein Ragnarsson[3]—both believed to be sons of the legendary Viking leader Ragnar Lothbrok[4]—were sailing at the head of a fleet of 62 Viking longships. In the thick of their four-year long southern odyssey (circa 858—862), one of the longest, most impressive Viking expeditions in history,[5] these two Viking leaders and their mass pack of seafaring war wolves sailed down the Atlantic, along the coast of Brittany and West Francia, "and on through the stormy seas of Biscay."[6] Ripping past the rocky cliffs of the Iberian Peninsula,[7] they sailed through the Straits of Gibraltar, past the Pillars of Hercules, and into the Mediterranean, leading raids and capturing cities along the North African coast.[8] Pushing onward, they sailed into Spain, Italy, and possibly farther still.[9] "One Arab source even puts them credibly in Alexandria, raising the extraordinary possibility that the Vikings reached Egypt."[10] And, yet, the Vikings had never seen a city quite like this before; "so big, so white, so splendid, so marbled."[11]

With its Roman architecture and fortifications, according to one contemporary account, Björn and Hastein assumed it was the ancient city of Rome, the birthplace of the mighty Roman Empire and the most famous city in history. Given Viking culture and the fierce ambition of these two glory-driven, profit-seeking, celebrated "Sons of Ragnar," they were suddenly overcome with a determination to sack this historic, treasure-laden Italian city and, thereby, leave their own indelible imprint on the world.[12]

The problem was that, unlike the soft targets the Vikings had often encountered along the coasts and rivers of Europe (i.e. defenseless villages, churches, abbeys, monasteries, and even nunneries[13]), this city—while it was Luna, not Rome—had indeed been established as a military stronghold by the ancient Romans and, thus, its "defenses were so strong" and well-fortified that, lacking adequate siege weapons and experience, Björn and Hastein quickly "judged it impervious to assault."[14]

They were not about to give up, of course, but they recognized that sacking this city would require something more than brute force. An alternative "time-honored tactic"[15] would be deployed instead: Surprise.

After spending a calm, quiet evening outside the city, the following morning Hastein and Björn and a few other Vikings approach the gates of the city unarmed. They claim to be exiles passing through and ask to speak with the leaders of the church. They explain that their brave and noble leader, Jarl Hastein, is gravely ill, dying in fact, and he fears what may await him in the afterlife. "Recognizing the power of the Christian faith and wishing to protect his immortal soul as it went on its perilous way into another world,"[16] Hastein then asks if he could be permitted entry in order to be baptized and receive last rites.

Given Hastein's apparent illness, his status as a Viking jarl (earl or chieftain), and their own sense of Christian duty, the leaders of the city decide to grant his request. Indeed, W.B. Bartlett writes in *Vikings: A History of the Northmen*, "the authorities in the city rejoiced at such a gesture and the prestige it brought to their religion."[17]

Afterwards, believing that they had earned the town's trust, Hastein, Björn, and the others leave peacefully as the town breathes a collective sigh of relief.

A day later, a solemn Björn and two others return to the gate with terrible news. Hastein had suddenly died in the night. With tears in his eyes, an emotional Björn explains that Hastein's dying wish was to receive a proper Christian burial, which the Vikings were not equipped to handle.

Recognizing the prospect of a Christian funeral for a prominent Viking leader as a major public relations coup, the bishop immediately agrees. The great Viking leader's deathbed conversion would be honored with a funeral service in the magnificent Luna Cathedral.

The following morning, as the church bells tolled and the city gates were opened, a procession of some 50 Vikings adorned in loose-fitting robes proceeded with great ceremony through the giant iron gates of the citadel to the cathedral, carrying the pine box casket containing their fallen leader's body on a bier.[18]

As they were welcomed into the cathedral by the monks in their vestments, the wailing, grief-stricken Vikings humbly took seats in various places carefully stationed around the church. Still preoccupied with the message he would share, the bishop waited patiently for the casket to be placed at the altar as the priests and monks, along with a great many curious and finely dressed men, women and children from the town, all took their seats.[19] "It was a day such as the city had not seen for centuries."[20]

Just as the bishop was about to begin, Björn suddenly flipped a large gold coin high into the air. The moment the coin came down with a loud clang on the stone floor beside the catafalque, the Vikings knew it was time to reveal their terrible surprise: The city's leaders had fallen straight into a crafty Viking trap.[21]

Suddenly, perfectly alive and well, dressed in full battle gear, Hastein burst open the coffin, tossing the wood lid to the floor.

The congregation erupted in a collective gasp. The bishop froze, still not sure what was happening.

With his sword already in hand, Hastein swung and cut the unsuspecting bishop down with one slash.

Björn and the other Vikings immediately leapt into action, throwing off their cloaks to reveal their carefully concealed knives, axes, and swords. Some rushed to bar the church exits while others ran toward the casket to seize additional weapons.

Unleashing a barrage of bloody, sword-swinging chaos on defenseless men and women, young and old alike, the Norse warriors slaughtered everyone within the walls of the church. "The Viking horde streamed out of the church and onto the city streets. Some fought their way to the city's closed gates cutting down any resistance in their way."[22] They swung the gates open letting the remaining mass of Vikings storm inside. "The inhabitants who tried to defend their city were caught between the two groups of warriors and stood no chance—the city quickly fell into Viking hands."[23]

Within hours, the Vikings sailed off into the sunset with the cargo holds of their dragon-headed longships stuffed with treasure, provisions, and supplies. For these two pioneering explorers, Hastein Ragnarsson and Björn Ironside, along with those among their many maritime marauders who survived, the long and perilous expedition was a massive success. When the cunning and resourceful raiders returned home in 862 A.D., they became instant Viking celebrities. Stories of their daring adventures deep into foreign lands would be told and retold by the skalds for centuries until at last their names were immortalized in Viking legend and lore.

Profit from the Power of the Unexpected and Unforeseen.

Surprise is power. Whether for offense or defense, good or ill, enemies or friends; there is power in being unpredictable. The sudden and unexpected can allure, engage, and enthrall, or it can disorient, distract and confuse. No matter what field of endeavor—prevailing over an opponent in politics, launching a new innovation to crush the competition, executing an upset play in sports, destroying an enemy in warfare, or even pursuing a potential mate—there are remarkable rewards to be reaped from surprise. The opposite is equally true. If you lose the ability to surprise, you surrender power, influence, and control. To surprise is to gain the initiative. To be predictable and lose the initiative is to lose control and magnify the probability of defeat.

The element common to virtually every definition of surprise is the *unexpected*. In one way or another surprise disrupts, derails, reverses, or overturns expectations. To surprise is to do that which is unanticipated, unannounced, unsuspected, and unforeseen.

In situations where you are facing a challenger, competitor, rival, or foe, such as those found in sports, business, politics, and war, surprise is very often *vital* to success. A study of the top strategy theorists in history (Napoleon, Clausewitz, Sun Tzu, Jomini, Liddell Hart, Montgomery, etc.) found that 18 of the 24 theoreticians included in the research explicitly identified surprise as one of the key principles of strategy.[24] What's more, 9 of those 18 ranked surprise as one of the top 3 principles. "Surprise is such an important principle in warfare that some writers consider it the single most important principle of strategy."[25] Julius Caesar once said that "the most potent thing in war is the unexpected." General Douglas MacArthur similarly said that "surprise is the most vital element for success in modern war." Alexander Suvorov, one of the greatest military strategists in Russian history, basically equated surprise with success. "To surprise is to conquer," he said.[26]

Research into the military strategy "based on a data set of 93 cases of Western strategic military battles from 1914 to 1973 and covering all the large-scale wars of the major powers during that period" found that if surprise is achieved, the probability of victory is 93%.[27] If there is no surprise, however, the probability falls to 50%.[28] In essence, the author of the study concludes, "achieving surprise contributes significantly to victory."[29] The highly decorated German General Waldemar Erfurth, author of *Surprise*, a widely cited military treatise, concluded that "the history of war shows that through the centuries, almost all decisive victories have been preceded by successful surprises..."[30]

But the importance of surprise goes well beyond war. Regardless of your field of endeavor, surprise can make a game-changing difference in the implementation of your strategic plans. In competitive situations, surprise is essential. Being surprised, in contrast, can spell the end.

History is clear: In the arsenal of strategies for survival and success, surprise can be an exceptionally powerful tool. The calculated, clever execution of strategic surprise can result in a number of significant advantages, including the following: (1.) Surprise can help to capture attention and create attraction.[31] (2.) Surprise can spark curiosity, and deepen interest.[32] (3.) Caught in a state of curiosity, confusion or indecision, surprise can reduce or even eliminate unconscious, programmed resistance. (4.) Surprise can disrupt equilibrium, unsettle your opponent or competitor, and create confusion, hesitation, apprehension, and fear. (5.) Surprise can boost recall and subsequent recognition. (6.) A series of small surprises can create sustained interest. (7.) Finally, positive or desirable surprise can increase loyalty, and stimulate sharing and word-of-mouth.

Disparage the Power and Importance of Surprise at Your Own Peril.

The most common error is to overlook or underestimate the importance of strategic surprise. The strong and powerful are often at the greatest risk of making this mistake. Scrappy underdogs, in contrast, are often quicker to grasp the value of a well-timed, well-executed strategic surprise and how it can be a game-changer in the pursuit of their goals. Recorded in the *Military Maxims of Napoleon*, the French Emperor argued that "a leader has the right to be beaten, but never the right to be surprised."[33] And, yet, when Napoleon, at the peak of his power, marched into Russia in 1812 with an army of more than half a million men, not only did he fail to surprise his enemy, but he repeatedly, publicly announced his intentions beforehand.[34] What's more, when the Russians boldly burned Moscow[35] to the ground to deprive his army of the food and shelter they badly needed to survive, it was Napoleon who was surprised—*profoundly, catastrophically surprised.* "This fire demolished everything," Napoleon told a British doctor years later.[36] "I was ready for everything but not this. Who could think that people would burn their own capital? If not for that fateful fire, I would have had everything for the army."[37]

In a letter to Alexander I, Emperor of Russia, Napoleon further reveals how such tactics were to him unexpected and unthinkable,

> "The superb and beautiful city of Moscow no longer exists...Such conduct is atrocious and useless...why destroy one of the most beautiful cities in the world, the work of centuries, for so paltry an end? It is the same line of conduct that has been followed from Smolensk, and has left 600,000 families homeless. [...] If I imagined for an instant that such a state of affairs was authorized by your Majesty, I should not write this letter; but I hold it as impossible that, with your Majesty's principles, and heart, with the justice of your Majesty's ideas, you could authorize excesses that are unworthy of a great sovereign and of a great nation."[38]

The Russians' scorched-earth strategy in Moscow came us such a shocking surprise to Napoleon that he was forced into a humiliating retreat, a retreat in the middle of a brutal Russian winter that devastated his army, a retreat that triggered the beginning of the end of Napoleon's otherwise astonishingly successful military career.

The second most frequent mistake is to fail to understand how to create and capitalize on the power of strategic surprise. Fortunately, gaining a better understanding of strategies for creating surprise can also better enable you to anticipate, prepare for, and deal with surprises when they happen to you.

Play the Offense, Leverage the Power of Strategic Surprise.

"Let your plans be dark and impenetrable as night,
and when you move, fall like a thunderbolt." [39]

—Sun Tzu, *The Art of War*

Surprise enabled the Viking Age to happen. There were multiple factors driving the attacks upon western Europe—primarily the Vikings' unquenchable curiosity and yearning to explore, the love of celebrity, and the lure of wealthy towns and weak, warring kingdoms. [40] "The deeper causes of the Viking movement overseas were rooted in human nature: the northern peoples had needs and ambitions, were prepared to make demands, and had the will, strength, and technical means to enforce them. They wanted land to farm, wealth to make life splendid, or bearable, and some of them wanted dignity and fame." [41]

But it was the *success* of their raids that transformed these ordinary needs and desires into a movement and, in time, a mass migration and, eventually, an era. And it was *surprise* that was so often critical to their success. [42] In fact, the beginning of the Viking Age (793—1066) is marked by the Vikings' surprise attack on the abbey at Lindisfarne. Surprise also happened to be instrumental in the success of William the Conqueror [43]—a descendant of the great Viking leader Rollo—in the Battle of Hastings in 1066, which marked the end of the Viking Age.

Exploit the Seemingly Superhuman Power of Persistent Surprise.

Contrary to what was frequently written about the Vikings at the time, there was obviously nothing devilishly supernatural or superhuman about the Scandinavian raiders. The problem was that "the raiders came unannounced and unsuspected." [44] The warring lords and nobles of Northumbria, East Anglia, Mercia, Wessex, and the Frankish Empire (England, France, and Germany today) did not anticipate and, therefore, were not prepared to fend off an enduring onslaught of Viking raiders. It took many decades before they had any significant success at all in defending against the Vikings and their surprise attacks.

If they had not been so thoroughly and repeatedly *surprised* by the Vikings, three centuries of large-scale raiding, colonizing, and conquest might never have gotten off the ground. In fact, as Bartlett writes in *Vikings*, "When, over the course of a very long time, the areas being raided improved their defenses and their general state of preparedness, the raiders would often be on the wrong end of a defeat; but that situation would take time to come about in many regions." [45] Indeed, in the words of Nordic historian Gwyn Jones, "once the period of surprise and unpreparedness was over, the Vikings...were in a position of much peril." [46]

In the beginning, however, the sudden, surprise attacks proved exceptionally profitable for the Vikings, both in terms of gold and glory. What made matters worse was that, given their love of fame, word of their successful exploits traveled swiftly throughout Scandinavia, sparking the ambitions of waves of future raiders. "As the ninth century dawned, all the pieces of the Viking Age were in place. The Scandinavians had an advantage at sea that was impossible to defend against, knowledge of the major trade routes, and an unsuspecting world in full view."[47]

Pursue Surprise, Elude Surprise.

Given the wealth of potential benefits, master strategists are often willing to make great sacrifices of time and money in order to ensure the successful execution of strategic surprise. Given the potential consequences, they are likewise willing to go to great lengths to avoid *being* surprised. But what can we learn from the Vikings about the power and importance of surprise and, more importantly, what can we learn about how strategists think about and put the principle of surprise into play?

The following eight (8) sections cover the many ways the Vikings created or triggered surprise, and how they leveraged or capitalized on its power, as well as how you might use one or perhaps some combination of these different types of surprise to exploit its power toward your own strategic purpose and goals.

[POSITIONAL SURPRISE]
Tap the Power of the Unanticipated Location, Position, or Place: The Vikings Surprise Attack on the Lindisfarne Monastery

On a clear and cold day in January 793 A.D., a fleet of Viking longships suddenly appeared on the horizon. The unmistakable cluster of large, square sails and fearsome dragon heads on the prows of the ships caught the monks of the monastery at Lindisfarne completely by surprise. Most of the young men had never seen such a menacing sight.

Given that English merchants had traded with the peoples of Scandinavia before, the monks were yet hopeful that it was a trading expedition that had gone astray and lost its way. Lindisfarne was certainly no international trading hub. It was also more ships than they expected for a group of traders. But what other reason could there possibly be for foreigners to travel so far and to such an isolated place?

Unfortunately, this group of sheltered, scholarly, innocent, and unsuspecting monks was in for a terrible surprise. Sailing their ships straight up on to the beach, the Viking warriors disembarked with weapons in hand. They quickly descended upon the monastery and, without provocation, proceeded to butcher the brothers like a flock of guileless, unguarded sheep.

Medieval chronicler Simeon of Durham describes how the Vikings, "laid everything waste with grievous plundering, trampled the holy places with polluted steps, dug up the altars and seized all the treasures, killed some of the brothers, some taken away in fetters, many driven out naked and loaded with insults, and some they drowned in the sea."[48] Alcuin of York (735—804), an influential Northumbrian scholar, further describes how the church itself was "spattered with the blood of the priests of God, despoiled of all its ornaments,"[49] and how the ruthless Viking raiders "trampled on the bodies of saints in the temple of God, like dung in the street."[50]

That first sudden assault left a searing imprint on the imaginations of men and women beyond Northumbria, beyond even England. As Gwyn Jones writes in *A History of the Vikings*, "The unexpectedness, the swiftness, and the savagery of the Viking raid on the monastery at Lindisfarne in 793 came as a bolt from the blue not only to the monks surprised and slaughtered there but to Alcuin over in Charlemagne's court."[51]

Alcuin himself writes, "'It is some 350 years that we and our forefathers have inhabited this lovely land, and never before in Britain has such a terror appeared as this we have now suffered at the hands of the heathen. Nor was it thought possible that such an inroad from the sea could be made.'"[52]

"Later accounts describe how the monks were killed outright, thrown into the sea to drown, or enslaved, and the church plate was carried off. Alcuin returned to the Lindisfarne raid several times in his letters and notes, but one theme emerges consistently—the idea of surprise, the sense that this had never happened before."[53] As Bartlett put it, "It was an outrage made worse because it was so unexpected."[54]

Positional Surprise (Where): Appear Suddenly Out of the Blue in an Unexpected Position or Place. As with most animals, humans are instinctively territorial. Because our safety and security may depend on it, we are at times hyper-aware of our location and position and what constitutes our personal space. A threat to our territory or position is a threat to our power and, therefore, our future. But we also tend to become quickly habituated to our environment, position, and place, often with certain emotional attachments and underlying assumptions and beliefs. The longer we are in a certain place or position, the more comfortable we become, the more entrenched our assumptions and beliefs, the less guarded and prepared and more vulnerable to surprise.

Together these factors create a multitude of opportunities for surprise. When you disrupt your target's expectations about their position, place, or space, you immediately gain the initiative, trigger a flood of emotion, and force them to mull a response. The greater the difficulty or courage required to gain the position or place, *or* the greater the disruption to your target's expectations, the greater attention you will gain and either interest and engagement from supporters or, from rivals, confusion, frustration, doubt, anger, or fear.

The vicious Viking raid and senseless slaughter of the defenseless monks at Lindisfarne was one of the first and most famous examples of the Vikings suddenly appearing out of nowhere in a surprise attack, but it was only the beginning of a long, recurring pattern of raids in one unsuspecting, unprepared location after another. Because they came by sea, it was impossible to know where they would strike next, giving them both the advantage of surprise and a swift, safe means of retreat.[55]

Not all targets were as soft as Lindisfarne, particularly as the Anglo-Saxons slowly began to wise up and adapt. And, yet, the Vikings continued to profit from this type of surprise, simply by sailing on by whenever they encountered sufficiently prepared resistance. As John Haywood writes in *Northmen: The Viking Saga*, "The Viking way was always to move on if resistance proved too strong in one place, knowing that they would eventually catch somewhere off-guard."[56]

Beyond attacking unsuspecting cities and towns, the Vikings found other ways to use positional surprise to their advantage. The tales of the well-traveled, noble-born Harald "Hardrada" ("Hard Ruler" or "Ruthless") Sigurdsson, for example, tell of how he would dig tunnels under the walls of a "besieged city and burst through the floor to surprise their enemies.[57] Before becoming King of Norway (1046—1066), while working undercover and using the alias Nordbrikt ("North-Bright"), Hardrada became so well-known for his sudden surprise maneuvers and prowess in war that he came to be called the "Thunder Bolt of the North."[58]

It is also possible to surprise your target by controlling a position or restricting space. In 862, for example, a Viking fleet destroyed a bridge at Trilbardou in West Francia as they raided their way up the Marne river. Rather than chasing after the Vikings, Charles the Bald (grandson of Charlemagne) quickly rebuilt and refortified the bridge. When the they sailed back down on the return trip it was the Vikings who were surprised when they suddenly discovered they were trapped. With additional troops deployed along the river banks, the Vikings soon sued for terms and agreed to depart in peace.[59] Demonstrating a "keen understanding of what gave the Vikings their strategic advantages and how they could best be countered," Charles then embarked on an extensive, fortified bridge-building plan, seriously hindering the Vikings easy access to treasured sites along the rivers of his realm.[60]

During World War II, in an deception campaign known as Operation Bodyguard, the Allied forces successfully fooled Adolf Hitler into believing they were planning a later invasion for northwest Europe around Calais. This allowed the Allied forces, led by U.S. General Dwight Eisenhower, to succeed in landing at Normandy on June 6, 1944. Known as Operation Overlord or simply D-Day, the successful invasion of German-occupied Western Europe was the largest amphibious assault in history, and it provided the Allies with an urgently needed foothold in France which, in less than a year, led to the end of the Third Reich.

Whether entering a new market or niche in business, inventing a new category for your product or brand,[61] running a political campaign in an atypical neighborhood or district, gaining the higher ground on the field of battle, occupying the open position on the playing field, or simply seizing center stage in a meeting at work, there are often considerable benefits to be gained, including increased influence, power, or control, when you suddenly occupy an unexpected location, position or place.

When thinking about positional surprise, do not limit yourself to the physical realm. You can also create surprise by suddenly changing the position you occupy in the mind of your target audience. An unexpected achievement could reposition how an employer thinks of a member of his or her staff. A change in branding could reposition a product in the market. A change in messaging could reposition a candidate in an electoral race. Surprise position and proximity also play a role in dating. No doubt, in numerous domains, a sudden change in location, position, or appearance can trigger surprise, transform the dynamic, and alter the calculus in your prospect's or opponent's mind.

[TEMPORAL SURPRISE]

Exploit the Advantage of an Unexpected Time, Day, or Season, or a Startling, Unforeseen Speed: The Vikings and the St. John's Day Surprise Sack of Nantes.

Profit from the Disruption of the Day. On June 24, 843 A.D., the ancient city of Nantes was bustling with activity in celebration of St. John's Day, a popular Christian holiday of feasting and remembrance of John the Baptist. It was a beautiful Sunday morning and people from the surrounding villages and nearby towns had all made their way to the city to join in the festivities. The streets were lined with vendors selling their goods, friends in conversation, and children at play.

As the leaders of the city busied themselves with running the events, activities, and affairs of the holiday, the church leaders prepared for the main service in the cathedral at the heart of the city.

Meanwhile, a fleet of 67 Viking longships quietly sailed up the Loire river, making their way to the city entirely undetected and unopposed. Suddenly, within minutes of their swift arrival, the Vikings swooped down on their prime target, the wealth and treasures inside the magnificent cathedral of Nantes.

Bursting through the large, ornate doors, the vicious raiders proceeded to slaughter the unsuspecting congregation, unleashing an assault of "surpassing brutality,"[62] slaying Bishop Gunhard at the altar.[63] As one historian described it, "they slew in the streets, they slew in the houses, they slew bishop and congregation in the church."[64]

According to one *eyewitness* account, "the heathens mowed down the entire multitude of priest, clerics, and laity...except those" who would later be ransomed or sold into slavery.[65] "They did their will till nightfall, and the ships they rowed downriver were deep-laden with plunder and prisoners."[66]

As random and unexpected as it all seemed to the people of Nantes, the Vikings had purposely planned and carefully coordinated their attack to occur at that hour on that particular day. They knew that a popular Christian holiday meant that the city would be filled with merry celebrants with money to spend, church leaders who might be ransomed, wealthy merchants, and scores of potential slaves. By choosing to attack during a religious festival, "among the most profitable times to attack,"[67] a time when the people would be distracted by the various events and festivities of the day, a time when the leaders would be off-guard and unprepared, the Vikings helped to ensure their attack came as a complete surprise.

Timing their attacks to such opportune moments was, according to one historian, "a stratagem the Vikings used more than once."[68] Nordic historian Gwyn Jones similarly explains that the surprise sack of Nantes on St. John's Day is "a classic example of Viking tactics and the conditions which ensured their success."[69]

After decades of dealing with Viking raiders, the abbeys, villages, and towns of the Anglo-Saxons—some of which were attacked multiple times—could no longer claim to be surprised that their location along the coast or river was a target. However, because they didn't know *when* or even *if* the Viking raiders would return, the sudden appearance of a swarm of square sails and sinister serpent heads on the horizon was still certain to trigger sufficient surprise if not sheer panic, pandemonium, and fear.

Exploit Seasonal Assumptions to Gain an Edge. In the beginning of the Viking Age, the Vikings had become known for carrying out their attacks during the late spring and summer. "The winter did not lend itself so well to war and travel, whether by sea or land."[70] "By September the Vikings were heading home to avoid getting caught at sea by autumn gales."[71] In essence, raiding was seasonal and the Vikings wintered at home.

In time, however, they began establishing fortified camps in England, which allowed them to raid and plunder year round. Thus, at least initially, a surprise attack midwinter would be even more unexpected. As a matter of fact, the Vikings' infamous assault on the monastery at Lindisfarne was originally reported in the Anglo-Saxon Chronicle with a date of January 793 A.D. Subsequent editors of the Chronicle, however, found the month so far-fetched that they thought it was an error and changed it to June. It was inconceivable that the Vikings could launch an attack in the middle of winter. "In fact it *had* been January, a time when their assault would provide the maximum surprise."[72]

The extreme winter conditions with which the Scandinavians were accustomed were a world apart from the English. In a lecture entitled, "Warfare and Society in the Viking Age," Tulane University's Kenneth Harl explains, "Scandinavians were extremely good in determining logistics, what were the food requirements, in foraging, and, above all, in campaigning in winter. Much of the transportation in Scandinavia in the winter time is done by skis. It's done over frozen rivers and by sleds. Campaigning in winter in a place like France and England was a cake walk for most of these people. And repeatedly English armies get caught short because the Scandinavians show up in a winter campaign."[73]

When the Viking leader Guthrum led a surprise attack on Alfred the Great on January 6, 878, the day of feasting known as Epiphany, he was effectively doubling the odds that Alfred and his men would be surprised and unprepared. And, sure enough, writes Jones, Guthrum's "midwinter attack from his base at Gloucester...took the West Saxons completely by surprise."[74] "All of the favorite Viking tactics were on display. Not only did Guthrum attack Alfred's stronghold of Chippenham during the winter, but he waited until Twelfth Night—a time when most of Alfred's army would be either home celebrating Christmas with their families, or deep into their wine."[75]

Once again, attacking on a holiday proved surprisingly profitable. As Lars Brownworth writes in *The Sea Wolves*, "The lightning blow caught the king completely by surprise. He had dismissed the field army for the holiday, and was protected only by his personal guard. They were quickly overpowered, and Alfred himself barely escaped."[76]

Alfred was forced into hiding in the maze of swampy trails in the marshes of Somerset along with just a handful of his guards who had survived the Viking's surprise attack. Guthrum, who later became King of East Anglia, "had shattered the power of Wessex, bringing almost all of England under Viking domination in the process."[77]

Mind the Time to Surprise. The Vikings did not have to wait for a holiday to catch their targets at a surprise time; any special event—such as a wedding, coronation, or memorial—would work just as well. Even just an unusual hour could help to heighten the surprise. Rögnvald Brusason, the Earl of Orkney, for example, attacked his brother, Thorfinn the Mighty (aka Thorfinn Skull-Splitter), late one night when he was drinking with his men in his hall. Rögnvald's far-flung attack also came during an unexpected season, after the autumn equinox, a time when "Vikings rarely made long sea voyages...for fear of storms."[78] Because he did not know his brother was anywhere around, Thorfinn's guard was down. This made it much easier for Rögnvald to simply sneak up and barricade the door to the hall and burn the wood building down (though Thorfinn was clearly surprised, he managed to hack his way through a wall in the back to make his escape).

In another incident, as recorded in *The Legendary Saga of St. Olaf*, Olaf II Haraldsson, King of Norway from 1015 to 1028, got word of a rebellion planned against him by five minor kings from Uppland. Profiting from the advantage of an unexpected time, Olaf responded by surprising the conspirators while they slept. "One had his tongue cut out and another was blinded. The rest were sent into exile."[79]

Act with Unexpected Speed. Whether on an unexpected day, season, or time, the key was that the Vikings' victims didn't see them coming. In this respect, along with secrecy, speed was often a contributing factor to the Vikings' surprise success. To be sure, some historians see speed, primarily due to their ships, as one of the key factors that gave the Vikings the critical advantage of surprise. "The surprise attack [was] made possible by their fast ships," writes Swedish historian Anders Winroth, "which made them infamous and feared."[80]

Compared to armies of the day, which "lumbered slowly across land, providing plenty of advance warning for civilians to hide themselves and their valuables before the armies' arrival," the Vikings seemed to appear "as if from nowhere, although, in fact, they came from the sea on their fast ships."[81] "Sea trials with reconstructed Viking ships confirm the impression that they were very seaworthy and fast. *Helge Ask*, a modern copy of the Viking Age ship *Skuldelev*, for example, has sailed at speeds of more than fifteen knots and it can be rowed at almost six knots."[82]

Unmistakably aware of the advantage, "the Vikings used the speed of their ships to good effect, to show up in force suddenly and without warning and to disappear just as quickly without risking a fight with the well-armed and powerful but slow regular army..."[83]

"Contemporary chroniclers often emphasized the surprise element in Viking attacks, describing the Northmen"[84] in terms depicting speed (e.g. "'rushing in,' 'falling upon,' or 'bursting in' with their ships").[85] "The Nantes eyewitness," for example, "gives us the impression that the Vikings attacked suddenly and unexpectedly. Everything was fine, and then, all of a sudden, armed Vikings swarmed everywhere."[86]

According to the great Prussian military strategist, Carl von Clausewitz, successful surprise is a product of secrecy and speed.[87] Whether in war, politics, business, or sports, if a key strategic or tactical plan is "executed with the utmost speed, the chances are that the enemy will be surprised."[88]

Temporal Surprise (When): Arrive, Execute, or Effect at an Unsuspected Time, Season, or Speed. Even the most vigilant and prepared among us have days and times when they drop or lower their guard. The more distant or remote the potential surprise, the more likely our attention is to drift to more pressing concerns. However rational this may be, it also makes us more susceptible to surprise. Whatever significant actions you take or maneuvers you make, timing is key. The right time or moment can significantly heighten the surprise. The wrong time can spoil the effect or the whole endeavor. Your task is to put yourself in your target's shoes and consider how to use the calendar or the clock to intensify surprise and amplify the impact of your actions as a result.

Win the Edge with Unexpected Numbers or an Unanticipated Size: The Sons of Ragnar Lothbrok and the Vikings' 'Great Heathen Army.'

"Pagans from the northern regions came with a naval force to Britain like stinging hornets and spread on all sides like fearful wolves."[89]

—Simeon of Durham

In the spring of 851, when the West Saxon's King Aethelwulf got wind that a fleet of 350 Viking longships was at the mouth of the Thames in Kent he was so alarmed that he sent his son Alfred to Rome to plea for God's support.[90] Clearly, this was no ordinary Viking menace. In fact, by far the largest Viking fleet to attack England in its history,[91] the sheer size alone signaled something far more sinister. The arrival of this massive Viking fleet teeming with fierce Viking warriors signaled a major shift in Viking strategy. No longer were the Vikings a lethal, but seasonal and sporadic, nuisance primarily interested in raiding and which could occasionally be paid to leave. Aiming for outright conquest, the Vikings were now an existential threat.

The Vikings first descended upon Canterbury, the center of the church's power in England. Next, they sailed on to London, a growing port town which they set ablaze.[92] By this time, King Beorhtwulf of Mercia mustered his army to face the Vikings in the first pitched battle. "Normally, the Vikings avoided pitched battles, but this time they had the numbers to feel confident."[93] When the Vikings burst through the Mercian shield wall, Beorhtwulf and his army fled the battlefield.

Buoyed by their victories, the Vikings then turned their attention back to Wessex, crossing the Thames to face Aethelwulf, the devout West Saxon king and his sons.[94] Only this time it was Aethelwulf who proved the master of surprise. And it was the Vikings who were greatly outnumbered, and who "suffered a crushing defeat" as a result.[95] *The Anglo-Saxon Chronicle* reports that it was "the greatest slaughter of a heathen host that we have heard tell of up to the present day."[96] The somewhat less dramatic reality was that the Vikings were itching for another battle within the year.[97]

As was typical with most armies throughout history, when they were significantly outnumbered, the Vikings took a serious beating, but they also learned that "a Viking force could stand against a royal army in the field and come out the victor. They had failed only because they had lacked a unified strategy, and had been severely outnumbered," Brownworth writes in *The Sea Wolves.*[98]

Several years later, the Vikings remained as determined as ever. "The aim of the army was to occupy and conquer the four English kingdoms of East Anglia, Northumbria, Mercia, and Wessex."[99] This is also the point at which the sons of Ragnar Lothbrok arrive on the scene.

Legend has it that the Viking Great Army was initially led by the five sons of Ragnar Lothbrok—Björn Ironside, Sigurd Snake-in-the-Eye, Halfdan (or Hvitserk, "Whiteshirt"), Ivar the Boneless, and Ubba —who were determined to exact revenge on the king who brutally tortured and murdered their father.

As recorded in the legendary sagas, it was not until his twilight years that Ragnar Lothbrok was finally defeated. When the Anglo-Saxon King Ælla II of Northumbria captured the Viking legend, he viciously stabbed and tortured him, leading Ragnar to famously say, referring to his sons who would be honor-bound to seek vengeance, "Oh, how the little piggies will grunt when they hear how the old boar suffered."[100]

When King Ælla finally hurled him into a pit filled with poisonous snakes,[101] Ragnar Lothbrok met his horrendous end as only a Viking legend could: Singing a song in celebration of the Viking afterlife. "Neither does the hero cry at this death in the wonderful Valhalla," Ragnar shouted out in song loud enough for Ælla and his soldiers to hear. "Nor do I go in sorrow to Odin's great hall,"[102] Ragnar sang as dozens of fangs pierced his flesh, and the venom took its lethal effect.[103]

But Ivar the Boneless wanted more than mere revenge. Like his father before him, Ivar had a dream; he wanted to settle in England and rule as a king.[104] And he had a plan to do it. It was around this time that the legendary Viking leader began to reveal himself as a master tactician.

Understanding the power of superior numbers, but also the vital importance of keeping the army well-fed and well-supplied, Ivar would not repeat the mistakes made when the Vikings were outnumbered and defeated by Aethelwulf.[105] In fact, Ivar was determined to build the greatest Viking army that the world had ever seen. He recruited male as well as female warriors, known as "shieldmaidens," from across the Viking world—from Denmark and the western Baltic to the Frisian islands and the Norwegian fjords.[106] "Tremendous planning had gone into the creation of the army," writes Brownworth.[107] "Unlike previous Viking forces, this was not just a collection of war bands, but was under the unified command of a single leader and his ruthless lieutenants."[108]

By 865, Ivar was in command of a Viking army *so* massive that the *Anglo-Saxon Chronicle* took to calling it "the Great Heathen Army."[109] Together with Olaf the White, three of the sons of Ragnar Lothbrok—Ivar, Ubba, and Hvitserk—"launched the largest invasion of the British Isles in recorded history."[110]

When the Great Heathen Army (known to the Vikings as the *Viking Great Army*) finally landed at East Anglia in 865, the locals were so stunned and overwhelmed by its sheer magnitude that they didn't even attempt to resist. Instead, they gave the Vikings the horses "from the well-stocked royal studs,"[111] supplies, and the money they needed to become an even more swift and menacing threat.

Continuing their campaign of conquest, the Viking army then proceeded to take the kingdom of Deira and accept a payment from Mercia for peace before heading back to East Anglia. "The campaign was a step up for the Vikings, with smaller, hit-and-run raids having been replaced by a thirst for something entirely different, namely long-term political conquest."[112]

In the ensuing years, "detachments of this army and its allies enjoyed a remarkable series of victories."[113] "Like most battles of the time, victory was achieved as much by the weight of numbers as by superior generalship."[114] "It should be stated clearly: in just nine years, an invading Scandinavian force had effectively destroyed all but one of the English kingdoms."[115] In the end, the Viking Great Army came as a shocking surprise to Anglo-Saxon England. Though not always successful, the Viking Great Army "won most of the battles,"[116] and irrevocably altered British history.[117]

Mass Surprise (What): Use Numbers or Size to Create Strategic Surprise. A sudden, significant change in numbers or size can trigger a powerful sense of surprise. This can help to capture attention and deepen the interest of your target audience or, in the case of a rival or opponent, it can disrupt equilibrium and trigger confusion, chaos, apprehension, and fear.

Building a mass surprise in numbers or size is not necessarily an easy task, of course. But you may not need the numbers you imagine either. As much as historians make of the "Great Heathen Army," for example, some experts argue that it was no more than 500 to 1,000 men.[118] Other experts put the figure in the "low thousands," and Logan puts it "between about 500 and 2000 Vikings." In *Vikings at War*, Kim Hjardar supports the 2,000 to 5,000 range arguing that it was "surely never more than 5,000" as "there were no lines of supply, either from Scandinavia or from a central base in England, from which the army could draw replenishments to support such large numbers."[119]

Regardless of the exact numbers, what matters is *perspective* and *proportion*. The Viking army was clearly large enough to shock some towns into immediate submission and prompt other armies to flee in fear. In terms of proportion, at least initially, it was also larger than the armies that the kings of England could muster. The size of the Viking army surprised King Ælla, for example, who actually fled York when the Vikings arrived only to join forces and return with another Anglo-Saxon king. But by then it was too little, too late.[120]

What's more, numbers do not necessarily have to be permanent. Sometimes a temporary show of mass is enough to trigger the surprise effect you desire. Nor does the size or the numbers always need to be real. Depending on the context and ethics, there may be times when appearing bigger, stronger, or more popular can help create an important strategic advantage. There is a long history of military generals going to considerable lengths to make their armies appear larger in order to intimidate an enemy or to draw their attention away from their intended point of attack.

You can also use smaller numbers or size to trick your target into making a mistake. Think, for example, of the way that the Philistine giant, Goliath, underestimated and, thus, failed to adequately defend himself against David, the small shepherd with a simple sling, "five smooth stones," and wicked precise aim.

In the case of the Carthaginian general Hannibal Barca, prior to the Battle of Lake Trasimene, his forces outnumbered the Romans by two-to-one. The problem was that these were not the sort of numbers that made the Romans eager to attack, which is what Hannibal wanted. So what did he do? He hid the bulk of his army on the edge of the forest on the hills of Mt. Cortona. He then set up his camp further down the road along the lake in plain sight, effectively luring the Roman consul, Gaius Flaminius, into a trap. Leading the Roman army in a single column along the lake's shore directly toward Hannibal's camp, Flaminius, who had failed to send scouts to do reconnaissance beforehand, was stunned when the hidden army emerged from the forest to attack the flank of his column. Flaminius would almost certainly have avoided attacking Hannibal if he only had known he was outnumbered two-to-one, particularly since he could have waited to team up with his colleague, Servilius.

In essence, numbers and size often speak volumes and when strategically employed can easily alter the calculus of a conflict, competition, or campaign. But they are also frequently manipulated and, therefore, can be an important function of tactical surprise.

[TACTICAL SURPRISE]

Gain the Advantage with Unanticipated Methods, Maneuvers, Tricks, Plots, or Ploys: Ivar the Boneless the Tactician and the Treacherous Trap at York.

The Vikings violent "out of the blue" surprise assault at York on All Saints' Day, November 1, 866 was so brutal and overwhelming that "the streets were made slippery by the blood of slaughtered residents and visitors."[121] "With their usual surprise attack,"[122] the Vikings were yet again exploiting a religious holiday in order to maximize their potential plunder and increase the impact of their surprise.

"It was packed with people," Bartlett writes in *Vikings*, "and therefore wealth. Probably it was weakly guarded given the distraction of the holy festival..."[123]

"Masters of intelligence gathering,"[124] the Vikings were also making timely use of the warring political divisions within the walls of York. "Inside the city at the time was not only Ælla but the rival king of Northumbria with whom he remained in competition, Osberht (the *Historia de Sancto Cuthberto* says that the two men were actually brothers). Northumbria had descended into political chaos because of the fighting between the two factions; or, as Asser put it, it was in 'a great dispute, fomented by the devil.'"[125]

The strategically located, easily defended city of York, known as Jorvik by the Vikings, was established by the Roman Ninth Legion in 71 A.D. and had been an important political and economic center long before becoming the capital of the Anglo-Saxon Kingdom of Northumbria.[126] Along with a number of ancient Roman buildings and fortified walls, the people of York also had one of the finest cathedrals in medieval Europe, "a monastery famous for its learning, and merchants from many countries."[127] Now, in command of the Viking Great Army, Ivar the Boneless and his brothers were determined to keep York for themselves.

But the Northumbrians were equally determined to keep York in Anglo-Saxon hands and King Ælla and King Osberht had both somehow escaped York during the mayhem of the massacre on All Saints' Day. Far more clever than the Anglo-Saxons cared to admit, the Vikings were well aware of the advantages of internal strife and how, for example, men like Ælla and Osberht would be too preoccupied with their own petty squabbles to pay attention to the pagan peril on the horizon. Now, however, the Viking occupation of York put their differences in perspective. Before long, the two former rivals agreed to combine their two armies in one joint effort to rid York of the vicious Viking invaders.

"Unfortunately for York, it took more than four and a half months for the joint army to reach the city, and by that time the Vikings had firmly dug in."[128] In fact, well aware that the two kings could return with a larger army, Ivar, a cunning strategist, had immediately begun making plans for just such an assault.

Given the natural defenses of its position, with reinforced walls, York could be made into an ideal stronghold.[129] The old Roman fortifications surrounding the city were still standing; the defenses had been maintained by the Anglians,[130] but they were in disrepair. The Vikings used their winter in York to repair the fortifications and add some new sections and fortifications of their own.[131] "They actually rebuilt part of the Roman wall."[132] With a keen understanding of logistics, Ivar had also undertaken to ensure the Viking army had sufficient water and food within the walls.

The plan was not to prepare for a long siege, however. What Ivar had in mind instead was a clever deception and a trap.

"The Vikings were expert at building fortifications."[133] Skilled at using fortresses in both defensive and offensive maneuvers, Hjardar and Vike write in *Vikings at War*, "They could be used to stop an enemy, or to lure an opponent into making an unwise tactical choice. They could also be launch points for counterattack. Sometimes they were used for pure trickery."[134] And pure trickery is precisely what Ivar the Boneless had in mind that winter in York.

On March 21, 867, known today as the Battle of York, the two rivals to the throne of Northumbria, Ælla and Osberht,[135] finally arrived to cast the Viking invaders out of York.[136] Despite the size of the Great Heathen Army, it was now the two combined armies of the Northumbrians who had the numerical advantage.[137] Rather than leaving the protection of the city's defenses to meet the two armies in the field, where the Northumbrians' greater numbers would be the biggest threat, Ivar put his treacherous plan into play.

His first step was to give the Northumbrian scouts time to discover the most vulnerable point in their fortifications, a weak section of the old crumbling Roman wall that the Vikings *intentionally* neglected to reinforce. Once the Northumbrian forces began to position themselves nearby, Ivar sent a small force of Vikings out to meet the threat. He wanted to maintain the initiative and ensure Ælla and Osberht took the bait.

Recognizing their superior numbers, the Northumbrians raced forward to attack. Within minutes, the Vikings were routed and sent fleeing back into the city. Thrilled to be suddenly retaking York, Ælla and Osberht sent the rest of their joint forces in after the heathens. What the Northumbrians found on the other side of that wall, however, was not at all what they expected.

The narrow streets of York had been reconfigured into a puzzling maze of passages, a "labyrinth of carefully prepared traps, and confusing dead-ends,"[138] with groups of Viking warriors hiding around corners, behind walls, or perched overhead with bows, arrows, and spears. The numerical advantage the Northumbrian forces would have had in the field suddenly vanished[139] as one tightly packed group after another was easily surrounded and slaughtered. At other turns, the farmers and peasant laborers who were recruited to join the Northumbrian army found themselves forced to combat fierce Viking warriors in single combat in the narrow streets.[140]

Within hours, the Northumbrian army was annihilated, along with 8 ealdormen and King Osberht.[141] "According to the account of Asser, this was a crushing Viking victory."[142] The *Anglo-Saxon Chronicle* reports "an excessive slaughter made of the Northumbrians."[143]

Ragnar's sons also caught up with their father's murderer, King Ælla. According to the Old Norse saga, "*The Tale of Ragnar's Sons,*" Ivar inflicted on Ælla a horrific execution as a sacrifice to Odin. Known as a "blood eagle," the ritual purportedly involved slicing open the victim's back, separating each of the ribs from the backbone with an axe, and pulling out the lungs and letting them quiver on the shoulders like a set of blood-soaked eagle's wings.

With both kings dead, the Vikings were now free to establish their own kingdom in Northumbria,[144] an historic first in England.[145] Revealing his cunning as a strategist,[146] it was Ivar the Boneless, with his wily tactical surprise at York, who gave the Vikings "their first firm foothold in England."[147] Following his death in Ireland in 873 A.D., the "normally reliable" *Annals of Ulster* described Ivar as "the king of the Northmen in the whole of Ireland and Britain."[148] "By 875 AD, a Viking kingdom centered upon Jorvík (York) was well established,"[149] with Halfdan (Hvitserk), the brother of Ivar the Boneless, as the king.[150] Jorvík flourished under the Vikings. Rapidly doubling in population, the Vikings transformed Jorvík into one of Europe's thriving economic centers, a major trading hub,[151] a gateway to Scandinavia,[152] and "for almost a century afterwards...*the* main Viking stronghold of the north."[153]

Tactical or Methodological Surprise (How): Devise a Surprise Method, Tactic, Trick, Plot, or Plan. Most people are not at all reflective. They take what they see at face value, rarely stopping to think about what might be happening below the surface or behind the scenes. They also tend to hold on to old frames and beliefs even as they are proving obsolete. This failure to stop and think, or question their assumptions and challenge their beliefs, creates another opening for surprise.

Think about what people will naturally assume given the situation, context, and history as well as what they are and are not able to see or perceive, and you will begin to identify numerous possibilities for surprise. The challenge here is for you to break free from *your own* habits of mind or mental scripts regarding the situation, context, and history in order to imagine a tactical surprise. One approach is to list the relevant assumptions and beliefs from which your target is likely operating, or which you would likely be operating from if you were in their shoes, and then identify which of those assumptions might be most effectively overturned. Start by keeping it simple and just think about what they might naturally *expect*, given the situation. Next, think about ways you might disrupt those expectations or otherwise turn them to your advantage.

In the case of Ivar the Boneless at York for example, the key assumption was likely the idea that they needed to identify the weakest section of the wall to attack. Ivar then overturned this assumption by transforming the perceived weakness of the crumbling section of the wall into a trap.

The Northumbrians, given their superior numbers, also undoubtedly *assumed* or *believed* that they could beat the Vikings if they could just goad them to come out and fight. Ivar also played to this impulse by pretending to send a contingent of Vikings out to do battle, but which were actually used as bait to lure the blundering Northumbrians inside. This tactical retreat played to yet another typical assumption in warfare, that is, that the enemy retreats when he is beaten or afraid.

Closely related, but perhaps even more fundamental, was the Northumbrian's perception that this was a siege. In other words, the Vikings were believed to be in the defensive position and, thus, the goal of the Northumbrians was to break through the defenses. The reality, however, was that the Vikings were not trying to defend the city. Seizing the initiative, Ivar was on the offense, and, rather than attempting to hold the city, he had transformed it into a giant trap. Finally, many of the Northumbrians were from York. This was their city and, unlike the Vikings, many of them knew the streets like the back of their hands and, thus, undoubtedly entered the city with flawed maps of the streets in their minds.

Disrupt Prevailing Norms, Defy Assumed Doctrines, Gain a Game-Changing Edge: Alfred the Great, Guthrum, and the Ring of Thor.

Where was Alfred and his army? The Viking chief Guthrum was surprised by the strange lack of resistance. In command of the Viking's Great Summer Army in 875 A.D., the Viking leader and Danish earl expected a battle with Alfred of Wessex. Instead, he marched south across one of the four great kingdoms in England virtually unopposed.

But why? Was Alfred unable to find the forces he needed to muster an army and continue the war?[154]

Or was this some kind of trap?

Following the Great Heathen Army's "stunning" conquest of the Northumbrians at York, "the Vikings immediately established a client king in York and invaded Mercia in the Midlands, seizing the royal center at Nottingham."[155] Next, they overthrew King Edmund in East Anglia. News of their startling successes spread like wildfire across Scandinavia and "by 870—871, large numbers of new recruits were joining the Great Army..."[156]

By the time Guthrum was marching on Wessex with the Great Summer Army in 875 A.D., the Vikings had all but conquered three of the four major kingdoms of England—East Anglia, Mercia,[157] and Northumbria.[158] Wessex was in effect "the last kingdom" still in Saxon hands.

But now, Guthrum and the other Viking leaders were determined to have it all. "The ultimate goal of the action was to force the English king to submit to the supremacy of the Viking sea kings."[159]

But Alfred of Wessex (later known as Alfred the Great) had thus far been doing everything in his power to stop the Viking assault, including, in the fall of 871, paying the Vikings a *danegeld* (i.e. a large ransom or tribute) to leave Wessex in peace.[160] This would at least give Alfred more time to build a bigger army.

A few short years later, however, while Alfred imagined they were still at peace, Guthrum's forces were marching across Wessex. Rather than laying a careful trap, however, "Alfred appears to have been taken completely by surprise."[161]

After making it clear across the kingdom without incident, Guthrum established his headquarters in Alfred's royal stronghold at Wareham on the southern coast of Wessex. "From this secure base they began to raid the surrounding countryside."[162]

Once he learned that Guthrum had taken over the royal fort, "Alfred promptly laid siege to Wareham."[163] His army soon had the Vikings completely surrounded, which came as a surprise to Guthrum, who lacked the provisions to endure a long siege. With the Vikings unable to escape,[164] Alfred would now seek to starve the Vikings into submission.

But then, Alfred suddenly received discouraging news. Before he left his winter quarters in Cambridge, Guthrum had split his forces. As he led half of his army in a march to Wareham, a fleet of 120 Viking warships, crewed by the other half of the Viking's Great Summer Army, was sailing along the coast making its way to Wareham through the English Channel.[165]

At this point, recognizing that a siege was futile, Alfred sought to negotiate a truce while he still had the upper hand. Eager to leave his "beleaguered encampment"[166] at Wareham, Guthrum grudgingly agreed to meet.

Alfred had already been burned by Guthrum once before. He knew the Vikings were unlikely to honor the promises they made, at least not for long. He, therefore, determined that this time would be different. First, he agreed to pay another *danegeld*. Without this payment, Guthrum would likely have never agreed to meet. Second, as "a demonstration of good faith,"[167] he persuaded Guthrum to exchange hostages, who, according to the *Anglo-Saxon Chronicle*, "were the most important men next to their king in the army."[168] Finally, in order to seal the deal, Alfred initiated a sacred oath ceremony. As U.S. Naval Academy historian Richard Abels explains in *Alfred the Great*, "sacred oaths played a critical role in resolving disputes in ninth-century England. Sworn on holy relics, they drew upon a force more powerful than any wielded by an earthly king, the shared Christian belief that divine retribution would visit oathbreakers."[169]

Alfred was obviously aware that Guthrum was not a Christian, never mind English. But the Vikings were also known to swear oaths. Rather than swearing over Christian relics, however, the Vikings would seal agreements "with oaths sworn on a sacred ring dedicated to Thor."[170] In fact, this was a fairly common practice in Scandinavia. Historian John Haywood, an expert in Dark Age Europe, explains, "Pagan Scandinavians kept such rings, reddened with sacrificial blood, in temples specifically for the swearing of oaths."[171]

The only uncommon part of this agreement was that Alfred, a devout Christian, "was willing to sanction a pagan ceremony."[172] No doubt, Alfred believed Guthrum would be more bound by an oath sworn before Thor than Jesus Christ. And Guthrum's respectful participation in the sacred oath ceremony apparently confirmed his belief.

Alas, Guthrum had no intention of honoring his oath; he "simply used the peace agreement to lull Alfred into a false sense of security."[173] By nightfall, soon after Alfred and the Saxons withdrew, Guthrum had slit the throats of Alfred's hostages and abandoned his own Viking hostages to their fate.[174] He then set off for the far more defensible fort at Exeter in Devon.[175] "The Vikings had slipped out of Alfred's trap."[176]

Beware of the Refusal to Quit. When Alfred learned of the betrayal and the brutal massacre of his hostages, he was furious. He, undoubtedly, also felt like a fool. Despite his usual caution against a rash pursuit of an apparently fleeing foe,[177] he immediately led his army in pursuit. But it was too late. Guthrum's army made it to the safety of the fortress at Exeter, where they could not be overcome.[178]

"The Vikings were now established in the heart of Wessex. If they could hold that position, commanding the Thames River valley, they would dominate both the economic and spiritual heart of the English kingdom."[179] Still in command of the Viking Great Summer Army, Guthrum soon set about laying waste to Wessex from his fortified base at Exeter while his fleet continued to pillage and plunder their way along the Wessex coast.[180] "If the two linked up, there was little hope for Wessex of avoiding a Viking triumph. Alfred would be forced to his knees, Danegeld would be paid, and Wessex would be compelled to admit the supremacy of a Viking overlord."[181]

When Guthrum suddenly lost half of the Great Summer Army (upwards of 3,600 warriors[182]), after his fleet foundered during a violent storm off the coast of Swanage Bay in 877 (not long after breaking his oath to Thor), Alfred once again, astonishingly, sought to negotiate a peace treaty with Guthrum the oathbreaker. For his part, Guthrum once again happily accepted a large bribe to leave Wessex. New oaths were sworn and this time Guthrum actually did leave the Kingdom of Wessex. But not for long.

After wintering in Gloucester, Mercia, however, Guthrum returned on January 6, 878 A.D. with yet another surprise assault. Attacking Alfred's stronghold at Chippenham in winter, during a Christmas holiday (Twelfth Night), a time when most of his army was home with their families, Alfred was, *unbelievably*, once again caught by surprise—this time a triple (during winter, on a holiday, by the same man who had thrice sworn an oath for peace). After barely escaping with his life, now forced to become a fugitive in his own land, Alfred had at last run out of room for mistakes.

This was Alfred the Great's lowest point. And it was very nearly his end. It was also the high point for the Vikings thus far; the heathen invaders were now in control of most all of England. From the time the sons of Ragnar Lothbrok began building the Viking Great Army, descending on England circa 865 to the standoff with Alfred in 878, the Vikings had achieved what Tulane historian Kenneth Harl describes as "a *stunning* piece of campaigning."[183] In a little more than a decade, with several thousand veteran warriors, the Viking army "showed a remarkable knowledge of logistics, the political situation, fortified bases, winter campaigns, seizing towns, setting up defensive positions, forcing ill-trained levies to make these attacks, counterattacking, all the advantages of Viking warfare is seen in this campaign in microcosm. And it shows the type of determined and violent foes the Vikings could be."[184]

The Vikings were not victorious in every battle and skirmish, but their dominance over this period remains undisputed. Indeed, in less than 15 years, the Vikings had conquered three of the four kingdoms of England and very nearly the fourth. All told, the Viking Great Army "had conquered an area which took 150 years for the Anglo-Saxons to master," and Harl concludes, "no army has done this in Britain since the Roman age."[185]

Doctrinal Surprise (Why): Disrupt Norms, Defy Doctrines, or Upset Assumptions and Beliefs. Most people are largely oblivious to how their own cultural and religious norms, values, and beliefs shape the way they see the world and even what they are *able* to see. Like a fish in the ocean, they see everything in the water except the water itself, or how the water effects and distorts what they see. This makes them vulnerable to another type of surprise. The less aware you are of how you are thinking and operating according to your own worldview and mental frames, including religious and cultural norms, values and beliefs, the more likely you are to be surprised by the actions of those who are operating according to a different worldview or set of mental frames, values, and beliefs.

Know Your Enemy. Regardless of whether you are taking an offensive or defensive position, the key is to *understand* your target well enough to reassess the situation from their perspective and beliefs. That the churches and monasteries of Anglo-Saxon England left such tremendous wealth completely unguarded is a case-in-point. Even when they were at war with one another, the Anglo-Saxons generally understood that the church was above politics and war. They also believed that raiding a church or murdering a priest would have consequences beyond this world.

The Vikings, in contrast, operated from an entirely different worldview, including some very different values and existential beliefs. "They followed very different rules from their victims."[186] They appeared to have "no regard for anyone's religion, including their own."[187] In fact, it was not just the men of the monasteries, or the priests and monks who were attacked by the Vikings. "Nunneries in England were [also] devastated; at least forty-one such establishments were destroyed and there were very few remaining. Nuns were almost as likely to perish as monks; when Vikings attacked the nunnery at Barking back in 870, the women inside were burned alive."[188] These extreme differences in beliefs and values made the Anglo-Saxons unexpectedly vulnerable to the Vikings and susceptible to devastating surprise.

Another illustration of this type of surprise (as discussed above) is the time when the Viking leader Hastein Ragnarsson faked his death in order to be granted a proper Christian burial service in the church and, thereby, gain access to the city. What made the devilish deception so clever (albeit vile) was that it was virtually inconceivable to the church leaders. In other words, it was so far outside of their beliefs and values, as well as their collective lifetime of experience, that they likely never even imagined something so horrific actually taking place.

Get Beyond Superficial Understanding. In the case of King Alfred of Wessex, he certainly attempted to see things from the perspective of the Vikings. He was also wise enough to avoid thinking the Vikings would be bound by an oath made on Christian relics. He also grasped the importance of the Viking god Thor. Unfortunately, he assumed that an oath sworn before Thor was binding regardless of to whom the oath was sworn. The reality, however, was that the pagan ceremony with an oath sworn to a Christian meant nothing to the Vikings.[189] "Guthrum felt himself no more bound by an oath sworn on a hallowed pagan object than he would have been by a promise made on a Christian relic..."[190] In essence, as much as he may have *wanted* to understand his enemy, Alfred knew very little about the Vikings and their gods. Rather than betraying his own values, Guthrum was actually acting in accord with his religion. He was following the counsel as it was written in the Viking god Odin's sacred text, *The Sayings of the High One*. In this text, Odin writes, "If there's a man whom you don't trust, but from whom you want nothing but good, speak fairly to him but think falsely."[191] In essence, Guthrum may have easily justified his deception and betrayal simply because he believed Alfred to be untrustworthy.

Refrain from Feeding Crocodiles. There are scores of examples of this type of surprise throughout history. Over 1,000 years after Alfred, another English leader would make a similar mistake, but with even more devastating consequences. When Neville Chamberlain met with the German dictator in Munich in 1938, Adolf Hitler promised the British Prime Minister peace. Hitler even signed a document, known as the Munich Agreement, promising "never to go to war with one another again." Chamberlain went home imagining he was a hero, claiming to have "returned from Germany bringing peace with honor," Chamberlain said, "I believe it is peace for our time." Winston Churchill remained unconvinced. "An appeaser," Churchill said, "is one who feeds a crocodile hoping it will eat him last."

When Hitler walked out of that same meeting with Chamberlain, he turned to a worried aid and said that that little "scrap of paper" isn't worth the ink used to write it.[192] Eleven months later the United Kingdom was forced to declare war on Germany following Hitler's invasion of Poland.

Beware of Imagining Your Mindset or Mental Models are Shared. During the Vietnam War, U.S. leaders were repeatedly surprised by Ho Chi Minh's lack of regard for the lives of the Vietnamese people. Part of why President Lyndon Johnson and later President Richard Nixon continued to escalate the bombing, known as Operation Rolling Thunder, is that it was entirely unthinkable to them that Ho Chi Minh could continue to tolerate the annihilation of his own people on such a devastating scale. American leaders kept insisting that there had to be a breaking point, but that was their value system, not Ho Chi Minh's.[193]

Change the Norms or Rework the Rules of the Game. When Napoleon Bonaparte was first coming to prominence in Europe his enemies discovered that he was not operating in accord with the customs and traditions of warfare as they knew them. Instead, in stark contrast, he seemed to be reinventing the rules right before their eyes. Prior to Napoleon's Italian campaign, war had been a gentleman's game. Military historian Owen Connelly explains, "In the

18th century there were nobles commanding on both sides and they had a certain 'code.' The armies would maneuver, and, very often, if one had the other 'in check,' that would be the end of it. There would be *no* fight."[194] This immediately set Napoleon apart. Connelly adds, "Napoleon was, in a way, the first modern general. He did *not* accommodate those old codgers on the other side *at all*."[195] Regardless of the position or maneuvers of his opponent, Napoleon would continue his relentless assault, driving himself and his men beyond his opponents' comprehension. "He attacks every day. He attacks when it snows. He attacks at night. He attacks when it's cold. It's not the way the game is played," historian Jacques Garnier explains.[196] "He looks for the enemy, fights it, and when they assume he is going to stop, he continues. The next day he fights again. It *surprises* them."[197] Bonaparte triumphs again and again in no small part because his opponents are again and again surprised as a result of their own flawed beliefs.

Raise the Standards. This type of surprise does not have to come as a perceived lowering of norms and standards or a degrading of values. In fact, it can be the opposite. Surprise can come from an appeal to our "better angels," which is most effective when you are operating from a position of strength, or a willingness to make certain sacrifices for the good of the whole (e.g. Lincoln's "team of rivals," Christ's servant leadership, etc.) or a long-term goal (e.g. George Washington diffusing a coup, known as the Newburgh Conspiracy).

Forge Common Ground to Reduce Surprise. This also helps to explain Alfred's behavior in regards to Guthrum and what drove him to give Guthrum multiple chances. Although he very nearly lost his life, Alfred was playing the long game. After escaping to the marshes of Somerset, Alfred was quickly able to rebuild his army. When he faced the Vikings at Edington in 878, Alfred was victorious. This put him in a stronger position to negotiate terms. As a result, this time the agreement, known as the Treaty of Wedmore, involved Guthrum agreeing to be baptized "with Alfred standing as his godfather."[198] The pious Alfred was undoubtedly seeking to save Guthrum's soul. Nevertheless, he was also moving the situation with the Vikings in England in the right direction. By seeking to convert the Vikings to Christianity, Alfred was effectively working to establish a *shared* system of values and beliefs. And, in the case of Guthrum (and scores of others), it seems to have (finally) worked. This time he honored his agreement. Guthrum even adopted a baptismal name, Athelstan, which he subsequently used as the ruler of East Anglia. He even issued coins under his new Christian name.[199] The *Anglo-Saxon Chronicle* also took a kinder view to the former heathen, showing a certain level of respect upon his death that had been entirely absent earlier: "And the northern king, Guthrum, whose baptismal name was Athelstan, died. He was King Alfred's godson, and he lived in East Anglia and was the first to settle that land."[200] Guthrum's transformation was what one historian describes as "an encouraging sign of the willingness of some Vikings to accept that the religion which they rejected with such ferocious contempt represented a higher form of culture than Heathendom, if only in its aspirations towards a better way of living."[201]

Aspire and Adapt. It is also possible to create this sort of surprise when you deliberately adjust one or more of your own norms, values or beliefs. In the case of the Viking leader Canute (or Cnut) the Great, for example, who became the king of England, the surprise came not from his willingness to impose Viking norms, values and beliefs on the Anglo-Saxons of England, but from how skillfully he often adopted and adapted to the best of English norms, customs, values, and beliefs. In one instance, for example, "at a Parliament at Oxford, Cnut adopted the laws of the late King Edgar, seen as one of the greatest of all English monarchs. Edgar's reign was perceived as a Golden Age, a time of peace and prosperity. This was a canny move by Cnut."[202] It was, writes one historian, "the first sign that there was something to this young man other than the attributes of a rip-roaring Viking raider..."[203]

[TECHNOLOGICAL SURPRISE]

Reap Unsurpassed Advantages with an Unexpected Innovation, Process, or Tech: Oleg the Viking River King Overcomes Constantinople by Sailing His Ships Overland

"Any sufficiently advanced technology is indistinguishable from magic."
—Arthur C. Clarke, Inventor, Futurist, Science Writer, TV Host

In 907 A.D., when he suddenly learned that a Viking fleet was descending upon his city, Constantinople, the Byzantine Emperor Leo VI was shocked and distraught. According to the report, Oleg the Seer was in command of a fleet of 2,000 Viking longships, with some 80,000 warriors, and he was sailing across the Black Sea to attack the great double-walled city. The alarming news triggered a sudden frenzy of orders and last minute preparations.

It had been nearly a half a century since the Vikings or anyone else had attempted to sack Constantinople. And, yet, the last time these ruthless Viking raiders attacked, in 860 A.D., it had left an indelible imprint on the memory of the city. Photios, the Archbishop of Constantinople at the time, wrote about how the Vikings had descended "like a thunderbolt from heaven," assaulting the city "as a swarm of wasps."[204]

Fortunately, for the people living in Constantinople, the capital of the Byzantine (Eastern Roman) Empire,[205] the Vikings previous naval assault on their city had failed. This was due largely to Constantinople's elaborate system of Roman fortified walls, first built by the Roman emperor Constantine the Great and later reinforced by Theodosius II, but also the use of their mysteriously unquenchable "Greek fire." For hundreds of years, these two technological advantages led to one military victory after another.

However, unlike the immediate threat, the 860 A.D. siege of Constantinople by the legendary Viking leader Rurik of Novgorod was launched with just 200 ships. Even then, before Rurik had determined that the walls of Constantinople were impenetrable and, therefore, decided to sail away, his Viking raiders had spent nearly six *weeks* devastating the surrounding suburbs and hinterland, setting homes and churches on fire, slaughtering innocent people, and drowning others in the sea. In

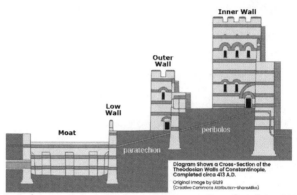

Diagram Shows a Cross-Section of the Theodosian Walls of Constantinople, Completed circa 413 A.D.
Original Image by Gigia
(Creative Commons Attribution-ShareAlike)

short, the looming 2,000-ship-strong, 10X threat Emperor Leo faced in 907 A.D. was of a different order of magnitude.[206]

Recovering from his initial shock, Leo ordered his men to fortify the Bosporus Strait (the narrow waterway running from the Black Sea down to Constantinople and on into the Mediterranean). He also ordered the giant Byzantine iron chain to be raised, preventing access to the Golden Horn (the estuary on the northeast side of the city, which is also where the city's defenses were most vulnerable, due to a single track of sea walls). Unlike the rapid currents of the Bosporus Strait, gaining access to the Golden Horn, with its calm and comparatively still waters, would also allow the safe anchorage of enemy ships. Furthermore, shielding nearly a third of the city's perimeter, occupying the Golden Horn would also force the city's defenders to be further dispersed.[207] In short, the giant chain that blocked access to the Golden Horn was vital to the defense of the city.

<u>Win the Battle in Your Mind First</u>. The Vikings, known by the Byzantines as Varangians or Rus ("men who row"), were being led by Prince Oleg of Novgorod (a city in Russia). Also known as "Oleg the Seer" or "Oleg the Prophet," Prince Oleg wanted access to and better trade terms with Miklagard (i.e. "Great City"), the Norse name for Constantinople. Constantinople was "the world's greatest city, the heir to Rome, the very center of civilization,"[208] and Oleg understood how favorable trade terms would lead to great wealth and transform the lives of his people. Given Viking culture and his hunger for glory and fame, Oleg also viewed the great and famously impregnable walled city as a challenge too tempting to pass up.[209]

"By sailing upriver from the Baltic sea, portaging [i.e. carrying the ships] for a relatively short distance and sailing downriver to the Black Sea, the Vikings had reasonably easy access to Constantinople."[210] Given that portage was common in this region of river routes—not just to travel from one river to another, but also to get around rocky rapids and treacherous falls[211]—the Viking vessels used were probably smaller than the typical longship.[212]

By the time Oleg's fleet arrived at Constantinople in 907, the *Primary Russian Chronicle* reports, the Byzantines had already "fortified the strait and closed up the city."[213] Oleg, however, was undeterred. "He disembarked and ordered the ships to be beached, after which the attackers went on to inflict dreadful atrocities on the natives. Palaces were destroyed, churches were burned, and prisoners were taken, tortured and thrown into the sea."[214] Despite the devastation around the city, however, the people inside the walls of Constantinople had so far remained safe.

Convert the Known into the Unknown. But then Oleg turned his attention to the great walled city itself. Determined to get his ships inside the Golden Horn, Oleg devised a scheme to circumvent the massive iron chain that blocked the entrance. Oleg instructed his men to build wheeled carts for the ships. The Vikings next mounted each ship on its own cart and then, the colorful *Russian Chronicle* reports, "when the wind was favorable they spread the sails and bore down upon the city from the open country."[215]

The surreal site of 2,000 Viking ships sailing across *land* to attack their city must have seemed otherworldly to the Byzantines because, we are told, despite hundreds of years of successfully defending the city from foreign invaders, "they were afraid."[216] "It was now that the defenders realized they were in trouble."[217] "Sending messengers to Oleg, they implored him not to destroy the city and offered to submit to such tribute as he should desire."[218]

Why this subterfuge subdued the emperor is unclear. Did the ships, viewed from the distant walls of the city, appear to be floating across the land? Or perhaps Emperor Leo was simply surprised by the technological ingenuity and recognized the determination of this Viking river king and, along with the size of the Viking army, was persuaded that trading with these people might prove a more prosperous route?[219]

Regardless of "whatever terrified them," historian Susan Wise Bauer writes in *The History of the Medieval World*, "the people of Constantinople agreed to pay a huge tribute so that the Rus would retreat."[220] And, as a result, Oleg halted the assault, achieving what master strategist Sun Tzu referred to as "the supreme art of war."[221] "To win 100 victories in 100 battles is not," Sun Tzu wrote, "the acme of skill. To subdue the enemy without fighting is the supreme excellence."[222]

After a failed attempt to kill the Viking conqueror with a peace offering of wine and food, which "Oleg the Prophet" correctly suspected was poisoned, the "terrified"[223] Byzantines accepted his demand for a substantial tribute—12 grivna for each and every one of the 80,000 Viking warriors under his command.[224] The terms of the subsequent peace and trade treaty established the Rus Vikings as "favored residents and merchants in Constantinople."[225]

Technological Surprise (How): Leverage the Advantage of Unforeseen Advances, Innovations, or Tech. Technological advances and breakthrough innovations have been used to gain a strategic advantage since the beginning of time. But they are particularly effective when their deployment comes as a surprise—regardless of whether others are unaware of the new technology or innovation entirely or because they did not foresee that an existing tool, asset, or resource could be used, converted, or combined in such a way. In the case of the Byzantines, for example, there was nothing surprising about ships with sails or carts with wheels, it was the never-before-seen combination of the two that reportedly triggered the Byzantine Emperor's surprise.

Furthermore, the greater or more advanced the innovation, or the more difficult to deconstruct, the better able you are to both intensify and extend the surprise, along with all of the strategic advantages that go with it. This is why secrecy is so often critical. The English inventor and futurist Arthur C. Clarke once said, "any sufficiently advanced technology is indistinguishable from magic." So long as it remains a mystery or is at least poorly understood by your target audience, competitor, or foe, you can easily maintain your "magical" strategic advantage, even after the element of surprise has played out.

As much power and influence as you can gain as the magician, however, the point is not to be the one who invented the magic trick—though that *can* lead to a considerable competitive advantage. The key is to stay attuned to new developments and think carefully about how to use them to your advantage or, at least, avoid being at a disadvantage without them.

In the case of the Vikings at Miklagard (i.e. Constantinople), we can certainly credit Oleg the Seer for his "improvisational talent that led him to transform a fleet of ships into wheeled wagons,"[226] and which, as a result, opened up for the Vikings "the great marketplace of Constantinople."[227] But this was just one illustration of the great many strategic advantages the Vikings gained from the versatile and technologically advanced Viking ship—not just Oleg and the Rus Vikings, but all Vikings across the Viking Age.

Harness Innovation to Achieve Strategic Surprise: 5 Viking Ship Advances and their Secrets for Strategists Today. The Viking ship was one of the most important technological advances of the age, giving the Vikings tactical and strategic advantages which played an indispensable role in their surprising success. The following are the five most critical innovations of the Viking ship and how you can put the underlying principles into play:

(A.) *Flexible Modes of Power*. First, the Viking ships were built so they could be both rowed and sailed. This gave them their first strategic advantage. Even if they were unable to sail for a lack of wind, they could still row faster (up to 50 miles per day) than any medieval army could march (up to 15 miles per day).[228] This was also part of what enabled them to travel such long distances and, therefore, surprise targets in the most faraway places.

Technological innovations that increase *flexibility* or help facilitate resilience can play a crucial role in achieving strategic surprise. This is true both in terms of better enabling you to capitalize on unexpected opportunities, but also in terms of better enabling you to respond effectively to unexpected threats, changes in the environment, or the actions of adversaries.

(B.) *Secure Source of Mobile Supplies*. Rather than having long, land-locked, slow-moving, and vulnerable baggage trains with food and supplies like most armies, the Vikings carried everything on their ships, which were equipped with sea chests and cargo holds below the removable planks of the deck. Even when large parts of their forces were on land, there was often a fleet shadowing their movements along the coast, carrying whatever food, provisions, and supplies they might require. What's more, the often substantial "carrying capacity of their ships meant that they could be used as mobile supply dumps for provisions or loot."[229] Particularly in England in the early decades of the Viking age—that is, before any significant Anglo-Saxon naval activities—the Vikings ready source of provisions and supplies made it possible to "campaign in hostile territory for years at a time."[230] The Viking Great Army and the Viking's Great Summer Army both exploited this advantage to "devastating effect" when they conquered three of the four kingdoms of England, and very nearly the fourth, between 865 and 889.[231]

As the Vikings clearly demonstrated, by extending your operational reach and ability to project power over greater distances or in unexpected forums, *mobility* can also play a decisive role in strategic surprise. The greater your ability to move quickly and efficiently, maneuver around obstacles, outflank opponents, and rapidly deploy people and resources to different locations or platforms, the greater your strategic advantage, but also the more unpredictable you become and, therefore, the greater your ability to achieve strategic surprise.

As the Vikings made clear in their surprisingly persistent assault on England, mobility also plays a role in *sustaining* operational reach which can contribute to strategic surprise by enabling your quickly reinforced and resupplied forces to maintain their momentum and pressure on adversaries or engagement with customers, constituents, followers, or fans.

(C.) *Easy Access with Shallow Drafts*. A third important innovation of the Viking ship was the shallow draft (the distance from the waterline down to the bottom of the hull). Unlike most other warships of the age, this is what allowed the Vikings to travel in the rivers and up narrow fjords. These shallow drafts, usually less than two or three feet, along with retractable rudders and symmetrical ends, also allowed the Vikings to race right up to the shore and jump out onto the beach. "This meant that the Vikings' ships could get very close to the coast when they had to load and unload heavy goods or surprise an enemy."[232] Because there was no need to anchor offshore and transfer to a smaller boat and then row to shore, they were able save considerable time as well as the space required to stow however many smaller boats. Their symmetrical, double-ended design also allowed them to back out of certain dangers (e.g. ground, reefs, icebergs, or an enemy ship) and immediately begin rowing in reverse.

Their shallow drafts and easy maneuvering also gave them a crucial agility when dealing with an enemy fleet. In 896, for example, when the Vikings were raiding a village at an estuary in Dorset, they were suddenly surprised by the appearance of Alfred the Great's nascent fleet of English ships, which were at the mouth of the estuary, blocking the Vikings' exit to the sea. As the tide was going out, however, the inexperienced English fleet made the mistake of moving in on the Viking fleet, half of which was beached. The remainder of both fleets, including all 9 of the English ships, quickly ran aground bringing the naval battle to a sudden halt. When the tide finally started to come back in, it was the lighter, shallower Viking fleet that was first able to rise up out of the mud and sail past the stranded English ships and out into the freedom of the sea.

As it better enables a less predictable and more proactive approach to seizing opportunities and responding to threats, technology or innovations that increase *agility* can also play a powerful role in achieving strategic surprise. Whether in business, politics, sports, or war, to be agile is to better anticipate and respond to sudden developments, new information, or changing situations. This can be useful both in achieving surprise and in avoiding being surprised.

Like Viking warships, agile organizations make quick decisions, capitalize on unexpected developments, and rapidly adapt in ways that may not be possible for those less agile organizations who, like cumbersome cargo ships, are often dangerously inflexible and slow to respond. Viking warships were able to instantly change direction, elude enemy vessels, and raid new lands before defenders even realized an attack was underway. Agile organizations, likewise, gain the power to achieve strategic surprise through their swift decision making and rapid response times, tactical and logistical flexibility, and readiness to quickly pivot, change course, or respond—enabling them to seize unexpected opportunities, evade or subdue sudden threats, employ unconventional strategies and tactics for which competitors are unprepared, and blindside rivals before they have time to react.

Imagine the fear in the villagers as they see a fleet of Viking warships suddenly materialize from the mist to plunder their unsuspecting coastal town. In a similar way, organizations with the nimbleness, speed, and agility to change course at a moment's notice gain the power to surprise, blindsiding sluggish competitors, giving them a vital strategic edge. Through their speed, decisiveness and readiness to change tactics in an instant, agile organizations mimic the ability of the Viking longships to achieve strategic and tactical surprise, raiding and outstripping opponents who react too slowly.

(D.) *The Supremacy of Speed.* One of the most common blunders in attempting to achieve strategic surprise is neglecting to take sufficient measures to ensure the speed necessary for the effective *execution* of surprise. In contrast to land-based raiders like Genghis Khan's Mongolian horde or Attila's Huns, "the crucial difference with the Viking raid was speed; they appeared as if from nowhere, although, in fact, they came from the sea on their fast ships."[233]

The Viking warship was *designed* for speed. "With its large sail and slim hull, it was able to travel surprisingly fast,"[234] *averaging* "over 40 miles per day."[235] "The particular combination of sail and keel allowed for a reach and a speed that were unprecedented."[236] "They could average up to four knots and reach eight to ten if the winds or currents were with them."[237] This gave the Vikings what was undoubtedly their greatest strategic advantage, and "ensured that the element of surprise would nearly always be with the Vikings."[238]

But this was not only when sailing. "Under oar they were nearly as fast. One Viking fleet rowed up the hundred and fifty miles of the Seine—against the current and fending off two Frankish attacks—to reach Paris in three days."[239] In stark contrast, Brownworth reports, "the medieval armies they faced, assuming they had access to a good Roman roads, could only average between twelve and fifteen miles per day."[240] Maxing out at maybe 25 to 30 miles a day if conditions were *ideal*, not even an elite *cavalry* force could keep pace with Vikings under oar.

Combined with its maneuverability and shallow draft, this unprecedented speed ensured "the ship was perfectly built for the surprise attacks that the Vikings' victims feared."[241] As historian Elise Christensen writes, "their speed and ability to sail tight into the beach and discharge wave after wave of warriors, then disappear before the English had a chance to mount a defense, made the Vikings' ships seem invincible."[242] As a result, as Brownworth puts it in *The Sea Wolves*, "the most frightening thing about them was their speed."[243]

The speed of their ships also served the Vikings when it came to war. In fact, their warships "were the Vikings' strongest weapon."[244] Again and again, "using their fast, maneuverable vessels, warring Vikings employed the same tactics as when raiding: lightning attacks that paralyzed the enemy."[245] "It was this speed—the ability to move up to five times as fast as their enemies—that made Viking attacks so lethal."[246]

(E.) *Sufficiently Light to Carry (Portage).* Your capacity to adapt and adjust your tactics, technology, or techniques in response to unforeseen circumstances, a changing environment, or new information can also play a powerful role in achieving strategic surprise. The ability to adapt and evolve can make teams, entrepreneurs, and organizations more difficult for competitors to predict. Like a river carving its path through a landscape, adaptability can also make it easier for you to find alternative routes to your goal, circumventing obstacles and exploiting weaknesses. Adaptability can help you outmaneuver unprepared competitors and exploit the flaws and limits of opponents. Adaptability can make it easier to discover and implement new processes, innovations or technical advances that can heighten your probability of success. By staying ahead of the technological curve, learning from experience, and being an early adopter of new or emerging technologies and innovations, you can also achieve surprise by employing new tools and advanced developments for which your competitors or opponents may not be prepared or even aware. Adapt, adjust, advance; these are the keys to technological surprise.

In the case of the Vikings, a fifth key strategic advantage was that they designed their ships so they would be light enough to carry, which also made them faster and more flexible in the water. Carrying ships over land was a fairly common practice for Vikings, especially the Rus Vikings, or Varangians, who spent far more time in the rivers than the seas. In navigating the 1,200 mile river route from Sweden's coast on the Baltic Sea in the north to the Black Sea in the south, carrying ships between waterways or around rapids was standard fare. As Viking age archaeologist Cat Jarman writes in *River Kings: A New History of the Vikings from Scandinavia to the Silk Road*, "the dragging or carrying of ships overland in between waterborne routes...became a critical element of their success in eastern Europe."[247] This was also part of what was so terrifying about the Vikings. The fact that their ships were capable of being carried meant that they could show up in the most unexpected place.

As opposed to sailing or even rowing, carrying the ships was "no doubt strenuous work, but," as Bartlett adds, "the relatively streamlined design of Viking ships made it at least possible."[248] This "relatively streamlined design" was not by luck or accident, however; it was more a point of cultural pride.

In *The Saga of Olaf Tryggvason*, for instance, the 13th century Icelandic historian Snorri Sturluson relates a story that demonstrates the lengths to which the Vikings would go to excel at their craft. King Olaf's saga tells of the time, circa 1000 A.D., when the shipbuilder Thorberg the Woodcarver was part of a large team building King Olaf's great Viking longship known as *Long Serpent*. Olaf's team of shipbuilders were all happy with how the ship was coming along, but not Thorberg.

One night someone snuck into the shipyard and hacked deep wedges into the planks down one whole side. The next morning, King Olaf came to admire the ship only to discover that it had been sabotaged in the night. Everyone said that the ship was ruined.

Olaf was furious. He swore that whoever did this would be killed and he promised a reward to anyone who revealed the culprit.

At this point, Thorberg came forward and said that he would reveal the culprit. He then admitted that *he* was the one who had hacked the planks of the ship. He explained that although he knew it would anger the king, he sabotaged the ship because he was so disappointed with the work of Olaf's team of shipbuilders. Olaf then said that Thorberg was to repair the ship to his satisfaction or he would be killed. When Thorberg was finished everyone declared that the ship was far superior to the original and more handsome as well. "In fact, what Thorberg had done to significantly raise the quality of the ship was to make the planks not just smoother but thinner and lighter as well, and therefore more flexible in the water."[249] King Olaf was so pleased with the result that he made Thorberg his master-builder, gave him the name Thorberg Skafhogg ("Smoothing Stroke"), and put him in charge of completing *Long*

Serpent. When the great ship was finished, Thorberg Skafhogg had become the most famous shipbuilder in Norway.

Long before it was recorded by Snorri in *The Saga of Olaf Tryggvason*, the Vikings had been telling and retelling the story of Thorberg Skafhogg for more than 200 years. It was a part of their culture. And it demonstrates the importance the Vikings placed on advancing technology and the lengths to which they were willing to go to excel at their craft, particularly building ships, which were central to their exploits as explorers, merchants, raiders, and conquerors. Indeed, the Viking ship was so important that many of the most powerful Viking leaders "took their ship with them to the grave."[250]

Fuel the Drive for Technological Surprise. Viking ships were one of the great technological advancements of the age. They helped to make Scandinavians perhaps not "invincible,"[251] as some historians have argued, but certainly the dominant force in Europe for nearly 300 years.[252] "Their sea voyages and foreign encounters led to new ideas and customs that changed the north forever. And behind their success, were some of the most advanced ships of the age."[253]

With their technologically advanced ships, the Vikings ruled the "northern waters of Europe," which "not only includes the seas and oceans...but also the river systems of Western Europe and of Russia..."[254] In his course, entitled "The Vikings," Tulane professor Kenneth Harl refers to the development of Viking ships as "a revolution in shipbuilding,"[255] which included certain innovations and breakthroughs without which "the Viking Age would be impossible."[256]

As essential and impressive as their ships were, and remain to this day, it was the Vikings themselves that seemed to possess a drive for innovation and technological advancement. Perhaps not surprisingly, given their skill as sailors, they were also pioneers in the use of navigational tools, such as sun boards, sun stones, and bearing dials.[257] The Vikings also invented a practical magnetic compass,[258] made from magnetite, an abundant resource in Scandinavia. They were also known for their superior swords, which were fashioned from bog iron and the bones (carbon) of their ancestors, leading to a rudimentary form of steel that was significantly stronger than the typical iron sword of the age.[259]

Beyond ships, weapons, and navigational tools (as well as decorative combs and hair dyes—yes, appearance was an important part of Viking identity), the Vikings themselves were some of the most advanced warriors of the age. To be sure, the favorable treaty that Oleg the Prophet was able to secure following his surprise assault on Constantinople included an opportunity for the Vikings to partner with the Byzantine Emperor himself. In effect, Leo VI had been so impressed with the Vikings that he immediately started recruiting them into his army. Written into the treaty were also terms "established to encourage the Rus to convert to Orthodox Christianity and to join the emperor's military service."[260] With a reputation as fierce warriors, the Vikings soon earned a place of honor as a special unit within the Byzantine army. This elite guard of fearless Viking warriors eventually became known as the *Varangian Guard*, and they were the best-paid troops in the Byzantine empire, serving for some 300 years.[261]

Exploit the Enduring Surprise Power of the Ability to Swiftly Adapt: The Transformation of Rollo from a Viking Warrior to the Duke of Normandy.

In 911 A.D., late in the dark of night, a large crew of Viking warriors would leave their fortified settlement, row up the River Seine, beach their ships, and walk toward the walls of Rouen to continue digging. Rouen was one of the largest and richest cities of medieval Europe, and the Viking leader Rollo (c. 860—932 A.D.), in command of a fleet of 15 Viking ships, was determined to sack the city.

Rollo's crew of veteran Viking warriors worked hard for several nights digging deep, well-positioned ditches between the walls of the city and the river. Each ditch was filled with sharp spikes and, more than likely, several poisonous snakes. Finally, after carefully covering and concealing each pit with disguised turf, the Vikings were ready to begin their assault.

On the day of the attack, the Vikings amassed outside the city walls and lured the city's defenders into a fight. Expecting to easily defeat the Vikings, who were all on foot, Rouen's cavalry soon came racing out of the gates, followed close behind by foot soldiers. Suddenly, the Vikings all turn and run at full speed, retreating back to their ships along the safe, narrow, carefully disguised paths they had marked out in advance.

Assuming the Vikings are desperately rushing to escape, Rouen's soldiers hasten ahead hoping to cut the heathens down before they sail away. Suddenly, soldiers and cavalry alike begin to vanish from view.

As they approach the ships, the Vikings start to turn around. To their utter delight, they see that nearly all of the city's defenders are now gone. Their carefully concealed traps worked even better than they expected. Almost to a man, Rouen's defenders dropped down to their deaths in the deadly pits. Indeed, as Robert Ferguson reports in *The Hammer and the Cross*, "the trick was so successful that they were able to enter Rouen unopposed."[262]

This was not the first time that Rollo and his Viking warriors had successfully raided one of the northern coastal cities or towns in West Francia. In fact, Rollo (also known as Rolf or, in Old Norse, Hrólfr), is believed to have been in West Francia as early as the siege of Paris in 885 A.D., when he was probably around age 25, and already a junior commander.[263] Furthermore, writes Bauer, Rollo had returned to West Francia "on a regular basis ever since: raiding, fighting, accepting payment, withdrawing, and then raiding again."[264]

The King of West Francia, Charles the Simple, had grown uncomfortably accustomed to Rollo's presence in this region of his kingdom, but he could no longer afford to pay the *danegeld* Rollo demanded. A danegeld, as Rudyard Kipling wrote in his poem "Dane-Geld," is when you "call upon a neighbor and...say: 'We invaded you last night—we are quite prepared to fight, Unless you pay us cash to go away.'"[265] The problem was that Charles was unable to pay. What's more, Charles had also long ago realized that, again as Kipling put it, "once you have paid him the Dane-geld, you never get rid of the Dane."[266] Alas, "as an armed and agile nation," the danegeld would be for the Vikings "always a temptation"—that is until Charles finally hit upon what he thought was his own clever manipulation.[267]

The Vikings aspired for much more than riches and a reputation as ruthless raiders. After 20 or more years of fighting, many of Rollo's veteran warriors were "keenly interested in acquiring land."[268] They wanted to settle down, cultivate the land, support themselves and their growing families, and live a prosperous life. Rollo wanted that too, but, "following the traditions of the great legends of Scandinavia," Rollo also wanted to continue to reign as the leader of the Vikings in West Francia.[269] He wanted to retire as a great sea king, just as did his namesake, the legendary Danish king Hrólfr Kraki. "Hrólfr Kraki raided widely, built a great hall in Denmark, and retired as a great king."[270]

Not long after Rollo had firmly established himself in Rouen, Charles sent Rollo a royal invitation.[271] He wanted to negotiate a truce, but rather than paying yet another danegeld that he could not afford, he had a very different proposal in mind.

At last, sitting across the table from one other, Charles explained to Rollo that he wanted the Vikings to stop raiding his towns and cities. Furthermore, he said, he wanted Rollo to help make them stop.

At this point, the fierce Viking warrior undoubtedly looked at this soft, fragile king, dripping in opulence, and thought to himself, 'Why would I do that? And who's going to make me?' But then Charles said something that would forever alter Rollo's life and change the course of history in Europe. He told Rollo that if he would be baptized as a Christian and agree to defend West Francia from Viking raiders, Charles would, in exchange, give to Rollo all of the lands around Rouen and the lower Seine. What's more, to seal the deal, Rollo would marry Charles' daughter, Gisela.[272]

The offer was exceptionally generous. The lands were some of the most beautiful and abundant lands in the kingdom. The idea of marrying the daughter of a king also appealed to Rollo's pride and ambition. As far as the baptism, Rollo was "more than willing to do that."[273] He understood that Jesus was a powerful God over these lands and, moreover, given all of the gods in the Norse religion, he saw no reason why Jesus could not be a part of his pagan pantheon, taking a place alongside Odin, Thor, Frigg, Freya, and Frey.[274] In short, Rollo eagerly accepted the king's proposal which led to the signing of the

Treaty of Saint-Clair-sur-Epte and the creation of the Duchy of Normandy in 911 A.D.

Charles was elated. He had effectively transformed the deadliest of foreign foxes into the game warden of his kingdom.[275] The Vikings were equally pleased. Rollo had delivered on their desire to acquire land, and the land was as rich and bountiful as they had ever seen. Rollo got what he wanted as well, including transforming himself into a respectable duke in one of the four great kingdoms of Western Europe.

As much as this transformation of Rollo was a surprise turning point, the really big surprise was how successfully he adapted to and succeeded in his new position.

Rollo and the Vikings understood that they had attained "one of the premier areas of northern France," and they soon "transformed themselves from warriors into landlords and began to learn how to fight as mounted cavalry."[276]

Rollo also understood how to exploit the military strength of the Vikings and his growing dukedom of vassals (i.e. men who, in exchange for land and protection, agreed to fight for their lord when needed), who were "extremely good and aggressive at patrolling the Norman coast."[277] In fact, the Vikings turned out to be "very, very good at stopping Viking attacks."[278]

Initially, this was the most significant result of the treaty with Charles: The Vikings helped end the era of Viking attacks on the Carolingian Empire.[279] But the other key reason for the success of Rollo, as well as his successors, is that "as descendants of Vikings themselves, they were more than willing to bring in colonists."[280] In other words, in many cases, there was no need to fend off the Vikings because they were welcomed to stay and farm the land. "They had no objections to taking in Scandinavians," Kenneth Harl explains, "but they weren't going to tolerate any raids anymore than they were going to tolerate any kind of indiscipline on the part of their vassals. And, so, Normandy really turns out to be a successful model of how to create a kingdom."[281]

As pleased as King Charles was about the end of the era of ruthless raiders, Rollo was turning out to be "far more energetic and far more successful than the King probably really wanted."[282] Rollo's remarkable ability to adapt to his new role was leading to a level of power and influence in West Francia well beyond what Charles had expected.

No question, it would be a mistake to underestimate the role of his military power,[283] but what is perhaps most interesting is that Rollo's success was far more a matter of strategy than strength.[284] To begin with, Rollo's first and most vital step was to learn and adopt the French language.[285] Then, not only did he also immediately adapt to "French and Frankish style institutions, he also learned to forge an alliance with the clergy within Normandy, particularly the bishops of Rouen, and the great monasteries."[286] Unlike earlier, when monasteries were considered prime targets, Rollo now established a "very close alliance with both the prelates, as well as the monastic institutions."[287] He also aligned himself with the counts of Paris and other members of powerful families in the kingdom. Finally, he was unusually generous with his patronage to the church and support for "the monastic reforms emanating from Cluny,"[288] which included encouraging art, and caring for the poor.

Beyond giving generously to the church, Rollo also learned from the example of the Carolingian kings by appointing his own people to positions of power within the church and, thus, another important part of his success came down to his ability to adapt to and co-opt existing institutions.[289]

Furthermore, following Rollo's lead, the Vikings themselves were also embracing the people and culture of West Francia and thriving as a result. Within a generation of Rollo's treaty with Charles, the "Vikings had intermarried with local women, given up their Norse tongue, and become Christians."[290]

Surprise Agility (How): Develop the Enduring Power of the Capacity to Quickly Adapt. Agility is another potentially powerful approach to surprise. Strategic agility is about being *flexible* and *quick* to respond and *adapt* effectively to a new situation, sudden development, or unexpected change. There are a number of vital strategic advantages of agility itself (as discussed in an upcoming chapter), but agility can also help create surprise, leading to additional advantages, which often include an important psychological edge.

We all tend to operate according to countless assumptions about the range of possibilities in a given situation, what someone or some group or organization is or is not capable of, what something is made for, or how something works. When people's assumptions are overturned by your surprise agility or your ability to quickly adapt to new circumstances or an unanticipated development or sudden change it can disrupt their equilibrium, and, in a competitor or opponent, create confusion, uncertainty, doubt, or fear. For potential allies and supporters, in contrast, your surprise agility can attract interest, build loyalty, and strengthen commitment to you and your cause.

In Rollo's case, his unexpected agility led to virtually every one of these benefits. As he adapted to his new role as the Duke of Normandy, it increased his hold on power not just with his veteran warriors, or even the scores of Scandinavians who learned of Rollo's dukedom in Normandy and moved down to settle. His ability to adapt to this new role also led to considerable influence with the powerful elites, noble families, and religious leaders of West Francia, many of whom were dissatisfied with the Carolingian rulers and were impressed with Rollo's successful integration with the church and governing institutions of the kingdom, as well as his remarkable transformation into a respectable, civilized European ruler.

Rollo's agility, his ability to effectively adapt and grow in power and influence, also forced King Charles onto his back foot and, in one instance, literally onto his back. In fact, it was likely at their first public ceremony together that Charles started having misgivings about their treaty. Rollo was expected to kiss the king's foot as an act of submission to Charles' authority as king. But such a demonstration of extreme subservience was not the kind of display a powerful Viking warrior was keen to perform. It would make him look weak to his men, perhaps even undermine their respect for his authority. On the other hand, he understood that refusing to do this would create a conflict with the king or might even derail the agreement. Demonstrating his flexibility and capacity to swiftly adjust course without losing the initiative, Rollo orders one of his warriors to kiss the king's foot. Instead of showing submissive deference, however, this big hulking warrior grabs a hold of the king's ankle and pulls his foot up to his mouth. This causes the king to fall back on his rear. But then the Viking warrior does actually kiss the king's foot. So, it's a bit of a humbling compromise. Rollo does symbolically kiss the king's foot, but not at all in the way the king wished.[291]

In some ways, this incident foreshadowed their relationship.[292] Rollo would continue to push the boundaries and build his power in the process. By ruling his dukedom with "excellent rights and judicious laws," according to one contemporary account, "in a short time he won over people of different origin and of various skills and so made one people out of a mixture of different ones. In this way he quickly grew so strong, that his [people] became more numerous and stronger than the neighboring realms and kingdoms."[293]

Charles was so stunned by Rollo's growing power and prosperity that he eventually came to see Rollo as a threat to his own power. Several efforts were made to try and repossess the Duchy of Normandy from Rollo and the Normans who settled there.[294] But those efforts failed. "In all instances," Harl writes, "the Normans proved themselves the equals to any invading French army. They quickly learned to make use of heavy cavalry and to build motte-and-bailey castles. These stockades, erected at strong points and manned by cavalry, enabled the Normans to dominate the countryside."[295]

Convert to Survive, Transform to Thrive: The Vikings' Quick Switch from Merchants to Marauders and More. The transformation of Rollo from a fierce Viking warrior into a powerful Christian nobleman is a compelling example of the Vikings remarkable ability to quickly adapt to a new environment. But he was an exemplar, not an exception. To be sure, there are a number of examples of Viking leaders who were able to change and adapt. The Viking jarl Guthrum, for example, also converted to Christianity, changed his name to an Anglo-Saxon name, Athelstan, became an ally of his former enemy, and settled down to rule the English kingdom of East Anglia.

The transformation of the Viking warrior Canute (or Cnut) the Great (discussed further below), is an even more powerful illustration of Viking agility and how it could help create strategic surprise. No question, part of this can be attributed to the complexity and flexibility of the man himself. As Bartlett explains, "Cnut is a man with a foot in so many camps, which makes him a complex, intriguing subject. He is a Viking but at the same time a staunch defender of Christianity. He is a lover of Norse sagas but also a generous donor to the Church. He stands at a crossroads in history and was an outstanding political leader at a time when the world was experiencing huge change. He managed to live and thrive in more than one world at the same time."[296]

But it wasn't just Viking leaders like Rollo, Guthrum and Canute; it was really the Vikings themselves who were so surprisingly agile. The Vikings were much more than mere ruthless raiders. "They appeared in many guises: as pirates, traders, extortioners of tribute, mercenaries, conquerors, rulers, warlords, emigrating farmers, explorers and colonizers of uninhabited regions."[297]

Contrary to the way they are often portrayed today, the Vikings spent at least as much time engaged in trading as they did in raiding, and there were "many individuals who combined both activities."[298] Some Vikings even switched from merchant to marauder in the midst of the same journey; "sometimes they might raid and other times they might trade depending on circumstance."[299]

The Vikings were also capable of bending and blending with circumstances when things did not work out in their favor. In 873, for example, "after ravaging various towns, raising fortresses to the ground, burning churches and monasteries and turning cultivated land into a desert,"[300] the Vikings were besieged at Angers and forced to terms by Charles the Bald. Rather than leaving Francia, however, many opted to stay. They agreed to be baptized as Christians and asked Charles for permission to setup trading operations in a busy market area nearby. Charles agreed and the Vikings were soon stacking considerable coin. Rather than being unusual, the agility they demonstrated after Angers is "a direct reference to the chameleon-like flexibility of the Vikings, equally adept as raiders and traders, just as much at home when acting as merchants or as warriors. There was also clearly a suppleness of conscience that allowed such men to undergo baptism as an acceptable cost to be incurred in return for useful trading concessions."[301]

Use Speed and Mobility to Maneuver and Surprise: Viking Agility in War. Viking agility was perhaps most apparent in raiding and war. This is also where any surprise achieved as a result of their agility would likely prove most disruptive to their enemies. When the Viking Great Army invaded East Anglia, for example, they forced King Edmund to supply their army with horses from the well-stocked royal studs. "By procuring horses, they became a mounted body, giving them maneuverability and flexibility,"[302] including "much the same mobility on land as they had previously enjoyed on water, with all the tactical advantages that went with it."[303] According to Haywood, "the real secret to the Vikings' success was their mobility, which meant that they, rather than the defenders, usually held the initiative."[304]

The Vikings had already possessed a strategic advantage with their ships, but now "with their horses they would be able to move swiftly around England, enabling them to launch surprise attacks inland just as surely as their ships allowed them to do on the coast."[305] As Hjardar and Vike write in *Vikings at*

War, "speed and mobility had always been their trademark at sea, and they now applied this talent on land."[306] The armies of England were subsequently surprised and discouraged to learn that the Vikings "were fine horsemen as well as seafarers."[307]

The Vikings also learned to make good use of their enemies own defenses. After spending time on the ground in England, traversing the Roman roads, Price writes, "the Vikings had shown themselves to be completely in tune with the English systems of defense. They knew all about the networks of strategic communications in the form of *herepaths*, or 'army-roads', and used them to their advantage. They understood the signal beacons on high ground, which they sometimes lit themselves to confuse the local militias."[308]

Another aspect of Viking agility was born out of their skill at building forts and strongholds. "The Vikings," Harl explains, "were...extremely good at building fortifications,"[309] and they used these fortifications in a variety of different ways. They could be used as a means of defense or as the base for an attack or counterattack. They could also be used to trick an enemy into "making an unwise tactical choice," or to bait him into a trap.[310]

As experts in building fortifications, the Vikings also had flexibility in terms of where they set up camp. They could establish a fortified base just about anywhere. This was key because "it enabled the Vikings to control a territory or remain in an area for any length of time. With a fortress as a base, they could explore the surrounding country and invade further, or they could establish themselves in an area."[311]

<u>Discover Resources, Assets and Tools to Cultivate Agility and Trigger Surprise: The Versatility of the Viking Ship</u>. There is one final factor that was an indispensable aspect of the Vikings' versatility, flexibility, and ability to quickly adapt: The Viking longship. The Vikings' *technologically* advanced ships (see section above) were by far the greatest factor in Viking *agility*, and it was also often critical to their ability to create strategic surprise. "The longships could accommodate up to a hundred men, but could be handled on the open sea by as few as fifteen. They were agile enough to slip past coastal defenses, roomy enough to store weeks of loot, sturdy enough to cross the stormy Atlantic, and light enough to be dragged between rivers."[312] But the greatest advantage was their speed, which helped to ensure that surprise would nearly always be on the Vikings' side.[313]

No doubt, the Viking longship was an incredible ship, capable of enabling a number of tactical or strategic surprises. Naturally, this was by design. In fact, the *flexibility* and *versatility* of the Viking ship was also part of Viking culture, a culture which was heavily influenced by Norse or Scandinavian mythology.

In Norse mythology, there is a famous magical ship named *Skidbladnir*, which belongs to Freya's brother, the god Frey. *Skidbladnir* was forged by the same dwarves who made Mjölnir, the mighty hammer of the god Thor. *Skidbladnir* was large enough to fit all of the gods with all of their weapons, and its sails were filled with the perfect wind the moment they were unfurled.

Skidbladnir's wood was so thin and it was so well-crafted that once the gods had sailed to their destination, Freyr could simply fold *Skidbladnir* up like a cloth napkin and keep it in his pocket.[314]

Given the powerful influence of Norse mythology on the Vikings' values, ambitions, and beliefs, it is no surprise that the Vikings were driven to create such flexible and versatile ships. In time, through continuous refinements and trial and error, the Vikings learned to create different parts of their ships with particular parts of the tree. The trunk, for example, would become the keel. Large branches would become the ribs and so on. Carefully selecting their timber, they even used the grain and natural curve of the lumber to align with certain sections of the ship.[315]

"In this way optimal use was made of the natural strength and flexibility of the wood, and the joints between the hull and the frame were made flexible by the use of ties or treenails."[316] "They were very, very cleverly adapting the materials to the construction of the ship. They also built the ships from rather green and unseasoned timber and that was again to retain the flexibility so that Viking vessels almost bent with the waves."[317] Much like fiberglass surfboards today (as opposed to epoxy), rather than potentially snapping under the force of a large wave, according to recent reports sailing replicas, Viking ships did actually *bend* slightly and spring back with bigger waves.

Along with the advantages of having a vessel that could either be sailed or rowed,[318] there were also advantages to having one large sail, which could be quickly lowered in a storm or to hide, or raised to speed an attack or escape. Beyond the sail, on some ships the mast itself could be easily lowered or raised. This allowed them to travel under low bridges and adapt to other circumstances, "including military cover maneuvers and surprise attacks."[319] As opposed to multiple masts and multiple sails, this also made the ships lighter, faster, and easier to carry.

Of course, despite the considerable flexibility and versatility, none of these various innovations magically transformed their ships into foldable napkins. But they did make them "faster, lighter, more flexible and more easily maneuverable than other ships of the time."[320] And all of this, together with their prowess as navigators, helped to increase their agility, extend their ability, and ensure that the Vikings were a surprisingly powerful and effective force throughout Europe, Russia, and beyond.

The ability to quickly and strategically adapt to rapid changes in your environment can mean the difference between failure and success. It can prove especially useful in those times and circumstances when it is least expected. Indeed, as it was with Rollo in West Francia, perhaps the greatest opportunity is when no one expects you or your team or organization to be able to successfully change, evolve, and adapt—when *even you* have your doubts. Treat these pivotal moments as rare opportunities and dig in. Do whatever it takes to discover the inner resources and external support you need to succeed, and perhaps, like Rollo and his Viking warriors, you and your team or organization will surprise everyone with your ability to become the new rulers of an emerging empire.

Optimize, Revolutionize, or Revitalize with Sudden, Unforeseen Allies: Canute the Great, from Viking Conqueror to Premier European Monarch of the North Sea Empire

After falling from his horse on February 3, 1014, just 5 weeks after claiming the English crown by right of conquest, Sweyn Forkbeard, the first Viking to claim to be king of England, was dead.[321] Forkbeard's son, Canute (also spelled Cnut), assumed the English crown would pass to him.[322] But the roughly 19-year-old (born c. 995) was in for a harsh surprise and a valuable lesson in English politics.

Forkbeard was feared by the ealdormen and nobles of Anglo-Saxon England, his teenage son was not. Rather than paying homage to this foreign-born son of a Viking, the Anglo-Saxons immediately moved to recall their unpopular but native king, Æthelred the Unready, who was in exile in Normandy at the court of his brother-in-law, Duke Richard II.[323]

Suddenly, caught off guard by the surprise attack of Æthelred's army on his camp at Gainsborough, Canute barely escaped with his life. Though he was recognized as king by Danelaw (i.e. the citizens, mostly Danes and other Norsemen, living in northern and eastern England), the young Viking and would-be English king fled back to his fleet at Sandwich and returned to Denmark.[324]

In the summer of 1015, just over a year later, Canute was back in England with a fleet of 200 Viking longships and some 10,000 Vikings from across Scandinavia, along with a fierce determination to secure the English throne. Old and ailing, Æthelred was forced to rely on his rebellious 25-year-old son, Edmund Ironside, to lead the defense of England against the Viking invaders.[325]

The first surprise alliance happened soon after Canute's invasion. Seeing the scale of Canute's Scandinavian army, Æthelred's own son-in-law, Eadric Streona, with his 40 ships, defected to the Vikings.[326] The public desertion was the final disgrace for the dying King, one that would win undying infamy for Streona as "the most notorious traitor in English history."[327]

For the next year, despite the defection of a powerful ally, Edmund Ironside proved a formidable adversary. It even started to look as if Edmund might gain the upper hand. This led Eadric Streona to betray Canute and seek to rejoin the English. It was at this point that Edmund Ironside made the devastating decision that led to his downfall. Rather than imprisoning Streona for treason and adding Streona's men to his own army, which he desperately needed, Edmund welcomed his backstabbing brother-in-law back into the fold. According to the *Anglo-Saxon Chronicle*, "No greater error of judgment was ever made than this."[328]

Soon afterwards, as Edmund's army marched through Essex, Canute caught them by surprise in open country. The two armies fought hard in what became known as the Battle of Ashingdon, but "at the climactic moment" Edmund's traitorous brother-in-law yet *again* deserted his own countrymen, effectively handing victory to the Vikings.[329]

Worse still for the Anglo-Saxons was that Edmund—who had been crowned king in April following the death of his father—was wounded in the battle. Recognizing that Edmund's days were numbered, Canute agreed to generous terms, allowing him to retain the southern portion of England. Upon his death, however, per the terms of their agreement, all of England went to Canute. Six weeks later, Edmund Ironside was dead—allegedly on the orders of Streona, his brother-in-law[330]—and the Anglo-Saxons now accepted Canute as king of the entire realm. On January 6, 1017, Canute became the first Viking to be officially crowned as the King of England.[331] "Little more than a century after Alfred had defeated the Vikings, his descendants had ceded it all to the Danes."[332]

Canute was now the "undisputed king over all England."[333] Whereas Ivar the Boneless had given the Vikings "their first firm foothold in England,"[334] Canute "had finished the job," fulfilling the Vikings' shared ambition of ruling all of England, bringing "to a successful conclusion a long-term military campaign pursued, with exemplary and unwavering patience, towards just this end."[335] To the Icelandic poet Sigvat Thordarson, known as "the greatest skald of them all," Canute's ascension to the English throne in 1016 was "the heroic realization of a plan that had been fashioned by his Viking ancestors over 150 years earlier."[336]

Make Allies of Enemies, But Put Trust Above All. What surprised the English was not that Canute quickly crushed the handful of English nobles that he suspected of treachery. That much was expected. As Lars Brownworth explains, "If history had taught Cnut anything, it was that English crowns did not sit easily on Viking heads. He had already lived through one coronation that had failed because the English preferred even the most unpopular native monarch to a foreign one."[337]

But what about Eadric "the Grasper"[338] Streona who had actually helped Canute at the decisive moment in the final battle, the battle that led to Canute becoming the king of England? Streona was at the top of Canute's list. Unlike Edmund Ironside, Canute was smart enough to realize that Streona could *never* be trusted. Indeed, at three major, public betrayals, Streona had an astonishingly long history of treachery.

Canute ordered Streona's head to be chopped off and "placed upon a pole on the highest battlement of the tower of London."[339] In this way, he fulfilled his promise to Streona to, as Canute put it, "exalt you, as it merits, higher than all the nobles of England."[340] But this was not the greatest surprise either.

What surprised the English was the steps Canute took to further strengthen and secure his throne, surprise alliances which, in time, transformed him in the minds of the English from an illegitimate Viking conqueror to one of Europe's preeminent monarchs.[341]

Canute's first and perhaps most famously surprising alliance was with Emma of Normandy, the widow of King Æthelred the Unready. Of Scandinavian decent, Emma was the great-granddaughter of Rollo, one of the most famous Viking leaders in history and the founder of Normandy (i.e. the "Land of the Northmen"). Emma was also reported to be the richest woman and a major landowner in England. As queen consort of England since she was 18—nearly 14 years—she had also become a major power broker in England with a clear grasp of English politics (she would later become the great-aunt of William the Conqueror). But Emma also had a daughter and two sons from her marriage with Æthelred, which many Anglo-Saxons still saw as rightful heirs to the English throne. In fact, Emma's own brother, Richard II, Duke of Normandy, wanted to take up their cause and overthrow Canute.[342]

Instead of killing Emma's sons or facing Richard in battle, however, the shrewd and practical circa 23-year-old Canute sought the circa 33-year-old Emma's hand in marriage. Emma agreed to his proposal and they were married in the summer of 1017.[343] Emma became a key figure in Canute's government, advising him on important matters of state and helping him to build key alliances with important English leaders and institutions all of which helped to strengthen his hold on power, but which also made it easier to defend the realm against external threats.

Choose Very Carefully, Then Stick With Your Choice. Canute's other surprising alliance was with an obscure English noble, Godwin of Wessex, who had proven implacably loyal to King Æthelred. When both Æthelred and Edmund were dead, Godwin sought to serve Canute. At first, however, aware of Godwin's loyalty to Æthelred, Canute balked. When so many other English nobles had pledged their loyalty to Canute early on, why should he trust someone who had proven so loyal to his *enemy*? Godwin responded by saying that he had sworn an oath to Æthelred and that he was honor-bound to uphold that oath even in the darkest hour, which is exactly what he did. Now that Æthelred was dead, he was free to swear a new oath to a new king. Furthermore, Godwin argued, it was all those English nobles who *failed* to uphold their oaths to Æthelred of which Canute should be suspicious.

Canute was impressed with Godwin and so convinced by his argument that he made Godwin the first Earl of Wessex and kept him on as a key advisor.[344] Canute later arranged for Godwin to marry his sister-in-law, Gytha Thorkelsdóttir. "The formerly obscure noble became the most powerful native earl in England."[345] By the time of Canute's death in 1035, Godwin had become one of the most powerful men in the entire realm and an advisor to both of Canute's sons, King Harold Harefoot and King Harthacnut (or Hardicanute), as they ruled over England in succession.[346] Godwin and Gytha had a number of children, including Harold Godwinson who himself became king of England before dying from an arrow shot through his eye at the famed Battle of Hastings in 1066, the end of the Viking Age.

Canute also sought to build alliances with other leading figures across Europe, arranging marriages, and becoming an enthusiastic supporter of the church.[347] "He also appointed allies into key positions of influence in the Church, such as when Æthelnoth was made archbishop of Canterbury in 1020. This helped to build his influence and reputation, and further strengthen his position."[348]

His nearly two-decade-long prosperous and generally peaceful reign, along with his effective relationships with other powerful European leaders, helped to build his reputation as an esteemed monarch and, in the words of English historian Sir Frank Stenton, "the first Viking leader to be admitted into the civilized fraternity of Christian kings.'"[349]

Rise Above Differences to Expand Your Rule. When Canute's older brother, King Harald II of Denmark died in 1018, Canute sailed with his English and Viking army to press his claim, becoming King of Denmark and the most powerful leader in Scandinavia. In 1026, Canute conquered the Norwegians and Swedes at the Battle of Helgeå, becoming the King of Norway and parts of Sweden. By 1027, Canute had become "one of the premier monarchs of Europe," a status "confirmed," writes Brownworth, "when the Pope personally invited him to watch the coronation of the new Roman Emperor Conrad II."[350]

"To be in attendance at this ceremony was a great mark of recognition for a man who was effectively a Viking king. It made a great impression on many at home and in Europe."[351] In fact, as Bartlett explains, it was "a remarkable achievement" for a former Viking, a "heathen," to even be permitted an audience with the Pope, never mind being in the Pope's entourage at "the coronation of the Holy Roman Emperor, then the most powerful man in Europe."[352]

As the King of England, Denmark, and Norway, as well as parts of Sweden and Ireland, Canute was himself one of the most powerful monarchs in Europe. Ruling over "a vast northern Empire," Canute had attained heights of power, wealth, and fame beyond the most wild fantasies of those early Vikings who first stormed the coasts of Europe in the late eighth century.[353] "He had become the greatest of the sea-kings, ruler of the only North Sea Empire in history."[354]

Once a consummate outsider, when the great Viking leader died of illness in 1035, "genuinely mourned" by both his Viking and Anglo-Saxon subjects, he was entombed in the Anglo-Saxon royal crypt in the great cathedral at Winchester.[355]

Confederate Surprise (Who): Profit from the Power of Unexpected Allies. In his 2,500 year-old strategy book, *The Art of War*, the ancient Chinese military strategist Sun Tzu wrote, "If you know the enemy and know yourself, you need not fear the result of a hundred battles. If you know yourself but not the enemy, for every victory gained you will also suffer a defeat." No doubt, the ancient admonition to "know your enemy" remains sound advice. The mistake, however, is to think of people only as they currently are, while ignoring what they might quickly and easily become.

Avoid Being Surprised: Play a Rigorous Defensive Game. To be clear, the idea is not to run through every conceivable alliance or potential scenario, which would be impossible anyway. On the other hand, in terms of playing defense, it is a mistake to avoid considering some of the most obvious or most threatening potential alliances, or loss of powerful allies, and how you might thwart or alleviate any negative effects.

In Canute's case, the natural allies of Æthelred were his former subjects, the Anglo-Saxons that Canute initially assumed he would rule, but who instead recalled Æthelred and aided the march of English forces on Canute's camp at Gainsborough. "Badly caught out by a surprise attack on his camp," Canute just barely escaped with his life.[356]

In the case of Edmund Ironside, he failed to think of Eadric Streona, his ally and brother-in-law, as a potential enemy not just once, which might be forgiven, but *twice*. And he lost his life as a result.

In the case of the 843 A.D. attack on Nantes, the game-changing threat to the city came when the Vikings partnered with a traitorous ally from within the city. "The people of Nantes had felt secure from Viking attack, believing that no strangers could navigate their way through the maze of shoals in the Loire's estuary."[357] They felt particularly safe in the summer when, writes Jones, "the sandbanks, shallows, and uncertain watercourses...were judged an absolute protection from naval assault."[358] "However, these Vikings had been supplied with a pilot by Lambert, a local count, who was in rebellion against King Charles and hoped the Vikings would help him get his hands on Nantes."[359]

The lesson in each of these instances is clear: If it takes only one simple pilot to navigate the maze or betray your secrets, then your city is not as safe as you think.

Play a Game-Changing Offense: Convert Enemies into Friends. In terms of playing the offense, teaming up with the right partner can open up a whole new world of possibilities. In Canute's case, while everyone else assumed Emma of Normandy was his opponent, Canute had the foresight to imagine how she might become a powerful ally.

Another surprise alliance from the Viking age occurred in 911 A.D. when Charles the Simple, the King of West Francia, transformed the great Viking warrior Rollo from a fierce enemy into a loyal ally through a prized marriage as well as gifts, titles, and extensive lands.

Led by the Viking leader Rognvald, a similar situation unfolded around the mouth of the Loire near Nantes circa 916—917 A.D., but which ultimately failed in large part because of a failure to build alliances—which was not surprising, given the hostilities between the two sides, but was nevertheless a lost opportunity that closed the door on a world of possibilities.[360]

Rather than simply accepting things as they are now, make it a habit to think beyond the *current* status of relationships. Get your head outside of the status quo. Look for potential, mutually beneficial alliances, even amongst your *current* competitors or opponents, and you may find those who can help you achieve a surprise objective that you could not otherwise achieve.

It may seem obvious to choose allies who are strong where you are weak, or, often even more important, who can boost or accelerate your strengths. But the hard part for most people is in gaining a clear and candid understanding of their strengths and weaknesses and knowing which ones matter most. In Canute's case, for example, perhaps his greatest liability was his status as a foreigner and, worse still, a Viking "heathen." His greatest alliance, therefore, arguably, was his surprise marriage to Emma of Normandy, which immediately foiled the plans of all those rebellious nobles who hoped to overthrow Canute with the supporters of one of Æthelred's heirs.

Regardless of the need or extent of surprise, the key to building effective alliances is trust. No doubt, each new alliance of Eadric Streona came as a sudden surprise (to Edmund, anyway), but he was betraying trust and he lost his life as a result. In Canute's case, in stark contrast, he was building new, surprisingly effective alliances, not betraying old friends. And, furthermore, forging alliances firmly grounded in trust helped him to build one of the greatest empires in history.

Perpetuate Power: Maintain Mystery to Sustain Strategic Surprise.

Regardless of your field of practice, surprise can be a tremendously powerful tool. Surprise can help to capture attention, engage an audience, spark curiosity, boost learning and recall, or deepen interest. Surprise can make a game-changing difference to the successful execution of your strategic plan. In competitive situations, surprise is indispensable. It can enable you to triumph over the greatest strategic advantage of a competitor, or it can bring your opponents to their knees. Ultimately, surprise is power.

Surprise was an instrumental part of the Vikings' success and the primary reason why they continued to succeed for so long. The extent to which they made use of surprise helped forge the Vikings into a force unlike any Europe had seen since the legions of ancient Rome. But it was the broad array of different types of surprise that compounded and multiplied to make the Vikings such a powerful, menacing threat.

From the very beginning, the Vikings appeared in unexpected places (positional surprise), at unexpected times or seasons (temporal surprise), and, over time, in unanticipated numbers (mass surprise). They also used unexpected methods and maneuvers (tactical surprise), and acted in unanticipated ways (doctrinal surprise). They could be shockingly versatile and quick to adapt (surprise agility) and, on occasion, they joined forces with unsuspected agents or allies (confederate surprise). Finally, throughout the three-century-long Viking age, they benefited immensely from the technological advances and innovations that were unknown or unfamiliar to their targets (technological surprise), primarily in the form of the legendary Viking longship.

"Know thy enemy and know yourself;
in a hundred battles, you will never be defeated."

—Sun Tzu

In time, as the Vikings slowly lost much of their ability to surprise, they lost one of their most important strategic advantages. As their enemies came to better understand the Vikings—their capabilities, their methods, their beliefs, their ships—writes Gwyn, "their initial advantages of surprise and mobility were whittled away."[361]

Further, the more the Anglo-Saxons and Franks understood their own weaknesses and limitations, the better prepared they were to prevent, neutralize, or respond to the Vikings and their surprise attacks. Once described by chroniclers as "warriors distinguished by superhuman strength and subhuman destructiveness," as time and experience accumulated, the much more mundane reality of England's own need for manpower, organization, and logistics began to take hold.[362]

In one of the earliest cases, for example, Alfred the Great began to place greater emphasis on the Fyrd system—a form of conscripted, self-armed army—and certain reforms, including more systematic deployment. "It was a system that made the most of England's manpower and other resources to face the Viking challenge full on. [...] By the close of Alfred's reign, he had at least 27,000 men available for garrison duty and probably more. This completely changed the dynamics of warfare in England from a Viking perspective."[363] "It meant that some of their military advantages were negated. There was now less chance of catching their Anglo-Saxon opponents by surprise; raids could now expect to achieve only limited penetration before a defense was organized. The character of war therefore changed and the rate of attrition that the Vikings could expect to suffer increased."[364]

Given their extensive and effective use of surprise, perhaps the overriding lesson we learn from the Vikings is not so much that surprise is powerful, everywhere possible, and often relatively easy to achieve, but that it is today so remarkably underutilized.

Indeed, the possibilities for game-changing surprise are all around us. The key is to recognize its potential power and explore the possibilities for putting this tremendous power into play.

10

EXPLOIT THE UNEXPECTED GENIUS OF SIMPLICITY: ALEXANDER THE GREAT FULFILLS THE PROPHECY OF THE GORDIAN KNOT

"The strength of any strategy lies in its simplicity."[1]
—Willie Pietersen, Columbia Business School

"Simplicity in planning fosters energy in execution. Strong determination in carrying through a simple idea is the surest route to success. The winning simplicity we seek, the simplicity of genius, is the result of intense mental engagement."[2]

—Carl von Clausewitz

According to legend, when the chief priests of Gordion finally gathered to select a leader they eventually decided that the next citizen of the town to travel with a cart up one of the main roads to the temple would be their new king. That man turned out to be a poor farmer from Macedonia named Gordias. When Gordias arrived at the temple, an eagle landed on the pole of his ox-cart. Gordias was widely considered an honorable citizen and a pillar of the community, and with all three of their conditions met, the leading priests and elders took the landing eagle to be a clear sign. Gordias was soon crowned as King of Gordion.

As a sign of respect to their gods, when Gordias began his reign as King of Gordion he left his cart on the acropolis, within the temple of Zeus. Here his cart would be preserved. In fastening his cart to a pillar inside the shrine, Gordias tied an exceptionally large, elaborate knot, hiding the ends of the hefty rope inside the knot itself. When he finished, no one was able to loosen its ends, but all who visited the temple "admired its design and strength."[3] The rope was then covered with the bark of the cornel tree, in effect making it impossible to untie.

Gordias' cart and the puzzle of the great Gordian Knot soon became an attraction for travelers. When rulers and leaders visited from other cities, custom was for them to try and loose the ends of the intricate knot. More than 100 years passed and no one was able to unfasten the knot. The legend was that whoever could "loose the ends" of the Gordian Knot would become the king of Gordion and would come to conquer all of Asia.

In the midst of his Asiatic campaign in 333 B.C., Alexander the Great stopped in Gordion to refuel his army. On his way out of town, preparing to resume his conquest, Alexander was told of the legend and tradition of the Gordian Knot. He immediately went to have a look.

Like the others, Alexander struggled to loosen or even find the ends of the knot. Suddenly, in a stroke of insight, he turned to the large crowd that had gathered around and said, "What does it matter how I 'loose the ends'?"

With that, he quickly unsheathed his sword and sliced the huge knot in two, immediately exposing both of its previously hidden ends.

The crowd let out a collective gasp; momentarily paused, and then erupted in cheers. No one had ever challenged the assumption of how to loosen the ends of the great Gordian Knot. The problem of the intricately complex knot seemed to seduce all prior participants into a search for a correspondingly complex solution. But the actual solution turned out to be piercingly simple.

Alexander's bold, direct approach to the Gordian Knot gives us just a glimpse of his preference for the power of simplicity, particularly with respect to strategy. But it also gives us a glimpse of the ways he profited from this approach. "…In the chaos and complexity of strategy, Alexander benefited from the fact that he maintained a straightforward approach (simplicity);"[4] explains strategy professor David Lonsdale, "meeting complexity with complexity will most likely only increase levels of friction."[5]

And *friction*, wrote Carl von Clausewitz, the renowned Prussian strategist who coined the term, "is the…concept that…distinguish[es] real war from war on paper,"[6] and it includes all those surprising things that occur in wartime that make even "the simplest thing…difficult."[7] Indeed, as Alexander well understood and clearly demonstrated at Gordion and again and again throughout his military career, "the temptation to pursue nuanced and sophisticated answers to strategic problems needs to be tempered,"[8] restricted, and restrained.[9]

Spurn Complexity, Simplify to Excel

"No problem can be solved until it is reduced to some simple form. The changing of a vague difficulty into a specific, concrete form is a very essential element in thinking."[10]

—J. P. Morgan (1837-1913), American Financier

Scores of the greatest leaders and thinkers throughout history, in virtually every field of endeavor—from business, politics and war to science, education and the arts—have emphasized the power and central importance of simplicity. Alexander the Great, Sun Tzu, Joan of Arc, Napoleon Bonaparte, Leonardo da Vinci, Abraham Lincoln, Mahatma Gandhi, Albert Einstein, Jack Welch, Steve Jobs—this is but a tiny fraction of some of the most influential people in history who have championed the power and importance of simplicity to success.

"Great leaders are almost always great simplifiers," wrote General Colin Powell, "who can cut through argument, debate and doubt to offer a solution everybody can understand."[11] In modern U.S. military doctrine, *simplicity* is considered one of the nine primary principles of war.[12]

"The concept of simplicity is just as valid in planning business strategy as it is in conducting military campaigns," writes Major General William Cohen.[13] "An analysis conducted by the prestigious Booz Allen Hamilton consulting firm showed that in one industry after another, large traditional companies faced the identical problem: overcomplicating their business. The strategies they developed to run their businesses had become so complex that profit margins had almost disappeared."[14]

The problem with complexity is that it causes confusion, conflict, and friction, and it increases unpredictability, heightens risks, and multiplies costs. "Complexity" is also, writes Robbins, "the enemy of execution."[15]

In contrast, in a study of the world's largest 500 companies, simplicity proved to be a critical component of the success of the top performing firms, as measured by "compound annual growth rate for organic revenue."[16] According to the lead researchers of a recent report by Heidrick & Struggles, these companies, referred to as "super accelerators," along with "deliberately designing simplicity into their strategy, operating model and culture, they embed simplicity as a way of behaving, thinking and working."[17] In short, these companies seemed to be contemporary reflections of Ralph Waldo Emerson's maxim, written over a century and a half ago, "Nothing is more simple than greatness; indeed, to be simple is to be great."[18]

Simplicity was a driving factor in the success of pioneering automobile manufacturer and business tycoon Henry Ford, who is often credited with creating the middle class. "When he was 45, and a moderately successful industrialist, Henry Ford took a brave stand that shook the world. The decision not only created his fortune but made him a leading architect of the twentieth century and one of the most celebrated and influential people on the planet. He decided to simplify and democratize the automobile."[19] Ford himself said of his ground-breaking new car, the Model T, that "… its most important feature was its simplicity."[20] In his autobiography, recalling the great watershed of his life and the key distinguishing factor that set his automobile apart, Ford wrote, "Our automobile was less complex than any other."[21] "There were but four constructional units in the car—the power plant, the frame, the front axle, and the rear axle…" Ford explained, "I thought it was up to me as the designer to make the car so completely simple that no one could fail to understand it. That works both ways and applies to everything. The less complex an article, the easier it is to make, the cheaper it may be sold, and therefore the greater number may be sold."[22] In the beginning, he even went as far as simplifying the color options. "you can get the Model T in any color you like," Ford said, "as long as its black."[23]

It would be easy to argue that simplicity simply does not apply to large, multinational conglomerates. But not according to legendary business titan Jack Welch, who is said to have "rivaled" the great Leonardo da Vinci "in the range of his achievements."[24] "Welch ran General Electric, the world's largest conglomerate, for 20 years of stunning success, from 1981 to 2001. At a time when other companies sought greater focus on one or two major businesses, Welch succeeded in a dozen different sectors, from aircraft engines to mortgage insurance to a major television network."[25] When *Harvard Business Review (HBR)* asked him, "How can it be 'simple' to run a $50 billion enterprise?" Welch replied: "People always overestimate how complex business is. This isn't rocket science…there aren't that many things you can do with a business. It's not as if you're choosing among 2,000 options."[26]

Foster an Affinity for Simplicity

"The art of war does not require complicated maneuvers; the simplest are the best, and common sense is fundamental. From which one might wonder how it is generals make blunders; it is because they try to be clever."[27]

—Napoleon Bonaparte, January 29, 1818, while imprisoned on St. Helena

The problem is that the tendency to complicate things is exceedingly common. "Men rush toward complexity," wrote the English philosopher G.K. Chesterton, despite the fact that we "yearn for simplicity."[28] Over 2,500 years ago, the ancient Chinese philosopher Confucius wrote, "Life is really simple, but we insist on making it complicated."[29]

Recent research has even revealed what social scientists refer to as a *complexity bias*. In essence, when faced with two competing theories, people often have an *irrational* tendency to favor the more complex explanation. Similarly, when faced with a problem, people frequently tend to ignore the simple solution. Unlike Alexander the Great, most people mindlessly opt for the more complex solution instead. The simple solution just seems too obvious or incomplete.

People do this for a variety of different reasons, including a lack of initiative, apathy, or sloth. If the solution is complex, they can put it off, dismiss it, or have someone else deal with it. They avoid responsibility by making the challenge seem more complex.

Another common reason is a lack of confidence. People avoid what they perceive to be simple because they are afraid of how it will appear. They try to hide mediocre ideas in a fog of fancy words, sophisticated sounding explanations, convoluted arguments and pointless complexity. In a chapter titled "Simplicity," William Zinsser writes in his celebrated book, *On Writing Well*, "Clutter is the disease of American writing. We are a society strangling in unnecessary words, circular constructions, pompous frills and meaningless jargon…Our national tendency is to inflate and thereby sound important."[30]

People fear being found inferior or inadequate so they try to compensate or cover over every conceivable crack. As Jack Welch told *HBR*, "You can't believe how much people fear being simple."[31] "Insecure managers create complexity," he said.[32] "Frightened, nervous managers use thick, convoluted planning books and busy slides filled with everything they've known since childhood."[33] "You can't believe how hard it is for people to be simple, how much they fear being simple. They worry that if they're simple," Welch said, "people will think they're simpleminded. In reality, of course, it's just the reverse. Clear, tough-minded people are the most simple," Welch said.[34]

Of course, it's not just insecurity. Former rocket scientist turned McKinsey consultant Peter Eckart, in his book, *Simplicity for Success in Business*, wrote that, "simplicity is probably the most neglected managerial art, on the one hand, because of people's fear of being considered simple-minded, on the other hand, because it's so hard to achieve."[35] Steve Jobs put it this way, "Simple can be harder than complex: You have to work hard to get your thinking clean to make it simple. But," Jobs added, "it's worth it in the end because once you get there, you can move mountains."[36]

"Everything in strategy is very simple," wrote Clausewitz, the celebrated Prussian military strategist, "but that does not mean that everything is very easy."[37] "Simple doesn't mean easy," Jack Welch similarly said, "especially as you try to move this approach down through the organization."[38]

Complexity often *begins* with a complex strategic vision, but this leads to a cascade effect, "...giving rise to complexity problems elsewhere..."[39] "Whatever actions strategists decide upon must ultimately be implemented, or nothing happens. But the more elements that make up each action, the greater the likelihood that one or more will fail."[40] As General Cohen writes, "If the actions you must take to implement a strategy are overly complex, you may have difficulty keeping them straight. Others may have difficulty following their part of the plan. The more complex the plan, the more problems can crop up."[41] "If your strategy is too complex then inevitably your organization will be too complex, your processes will become too complex and you will probably have too many markets, customers, products and services to look after."[42] All of this can easily lead to disconnected efforts and diluted effectiveness, and, in all likelihood, confusion and conflict. To be sure, "complexity has caused many brilliantly designed plans to fail when executed," and, therefore, Cohen concludes, "simplicity itself is powerful and compelling."[43]

Naturally, this goes well beyond the world of business. "Failure to incorporate the principle of keeping plans simple has caused failures in all fields of human endeavor,"[44] writes Cohen in *The Art of the Strategist*.

Regardless of your domain, simplicity remains a critical part of how you succeed. If you are lost in complexity, slowed by complexity, or you are creating complexity for yourself or your organization, you are needlessly jeopardizing your own success. It's that simple. Unnecessary complexity is the enemy of success. And, to be sure, most complexity is indeed unnecessary. The bottom line is complexity and confusion are a couple of "the worst enemies of successful business or military operations."[45] As Clausewitz said, "...Every effort should be made to keep operations as simple as possible..."[46] Regardless of whether there may be a "natural tendency" toward complexity "in all human activities" it "must constantly be resisted," because "if you don't focus on simplicity, you get complexity by default."[47]

5 Key Tactics and Tools to Best Exploit the Power of Simplicity

"Truth is ever to be found in the simplicity,
and not in the multiplicity and confusion of things."[48]

—Isaac Newton (1643—1727), Father of Modern Science

"Nearly all of the great success stories of the twentieth century—right up to the present day—are stories of simplifying..." write the authors of *Simplify: How the Best Businesses in the World Succeed*; "clever and creative simplifying has and continues to ...lead to extraordinary success."[49] Detailing case studies of business titans such as Henry Ford, Walt Disney, Herb Kelleher, Akio Morita, Steve Jobs, and others, management consultants Koch and Lockwood conclude, "If you make a list of the people who have been most successful in the last hundred years...a large majority of them have been great simplifiers."[50]

To be clear, simplicity is not the end goal or final point. The point is effectiveness. The point is truth. The point is excellence and success. But as a strategist, a strategic leader, or even an individual with ambitious goals, simplicity is a key part of *how* to get there. "The greater the simplicity with which you can execute your plans, the greater the power and force you can bring to bear on achieving your objectives."[51] Toward that end, the following are five (5) key tactics and tools to employ in order to best exploit the power of simplicity.

(1.) *Expect Resistance, Have the Courage to Persevere.*

"Courage is rightly esteemed the first of human qualities,
because...it is the quality which guarantees all others."[52]

—Winston Churchill

On November 19, 1863, the day that Abraham Lincoln delivered his historic Gettysburg Address, there was another speaker, former U.S. Secretary of State Edward Everett, who was the former president of Harvard (where he had taught Ralph Waldo Emerson) and one of the most popular orators of his day. Everett spent weeks researching and preparing his speech, even visiting the battlefield and speaking with eye-witnesses before the day of his stirring two hour talk.[53]

In contrast, Lincoln's speech lasted less than a few minutes. As is often the case with charismatic leaders, President Lincoln understood "the importance of reducing complexity and ruthlessly simplifying" his speech so that his message would land easily and be long remembered.[54]

Afterwards, numerous newspapers, particularly partisan rags, heaped praise on Everett's speech, but belittled or dismissed the words of Lincoln. Harrisburg's *Patriot & Union*, for instance, said, "We pass over the silly remarks of the President."[55] A correspondent for *The London Times* was equally dismissive, writing that, "the ceremony was rendered ludicrous by some of the sallies of that poor President Lincoln. ...Anything more dull and commonplace it would not be easy to produce."[56] *The Chicago Times* wrote, "The cheeks of every American must tingle with shame as he reads the silly, flat, and dishwatery utterances."[57]

Everett, in contrast, recognized right away the powerful impact of Lincoln's clear and concise address. He wrote to Lincoln the following day; praising what he called the "eloquent simplicity & appropriateness" of Lincoln's remarks, Everett said, "I should be glad, if I could flatter myself that I came as near to the central idea of the occasion, in two hours, as you did in two minutes."[58]

Today, scarcely anyone remembers Edward Everett's name, never mind his own beautiful, meticulously researched two-hour address at Gettysburg. Lincoln's Gettysburg Address, in contrast, is considered one of the greatest speeches in American history and one of the most influential and iconic proclamations of our shared national purpose.

The first key to tapping the power of simplicity is having the self-confidence and courage to persevere. There is often considerable resistance to simplicity, particularly among those who are anxious to appear intelligent or informed. As Lincoln often experienced, these self-styled intellectuals or "disciples of complexity" prefer to criticize and condemn what is simple and clear, dismissing it as simplistic rather than actually doing the deeds that need to be done.[59] As Jack Welch explains, "One of the hardest things for a manager is to reach that ["all-important"[60]] threshold of self-confidence where being simple is comfortable..."[61] And, yet, Welch adds, "For a large organization to be effective, it must be simple. For a large organization to be simple, its people must have self-confidence and intellectual self-assurance."[62] In the words of German economist E. F. Schumacher, author of *Small Is Beautiful: Economics as if People Mattered*, "Any intelligent fool can make things bigger, more complex, and more violent. It takes a touch of genius—*and a lot of courage*—to move in the opposite direction."[63]

(2.) *Avoid Oversimplifying. Preserve the Essence.*

The second key step is to preserve the essence of what you are simplifying. In other words, avoid *over*simplifying. To be simple is *not* to be simplistic. When you make the complex simple, you preserve what is essential. You preserve its essence, the key elements, or what makes it powerful, meaningful, or distinct. If you make something simplistic, on the other hand, you lose much of what made it meaningful, useful, important, or distinct. As Albert Einstein famously said: "Make things as simple as possible, but not simpler."[64]

To be clear, the point is not to deny the reality of complexity. The point is to tame it. The point is to face it and ruthlessly deflate it, not completely eliminate it. If you eliminate too much, you risk oversimplifying or making it simplistic. "Identifying the fine line between simple and simplistic is undoubtedly not easy," writes Eckart; "the distinction between the two lies in the ability to understand what is essential and meaningful as opposed to what is not..."[65]

It is worth noting that, in *certain* contexts, preserving some *small* amount of complexity is often desirable. If something is too simple it may bore or be ignored.[66] If you maintain a bit of complexity, in contrast, it can help to keep things interesting and alluring. A dash of complexity can also be perceived as a "mark of mastery," a sign of affiliation within a group, or like "a touch of spice that can elevate and enrich..."[67] The key is in being clear and concise, purposeful and precise.

(3.) *Prioritize Around Your Purpose.*

Beginning in 1958, American aeronautical engineer Kelly Johnson was head of Lockheed Martin's Skunk Works program, which developed a number of advanced aircraft for the U.S. military, including the P-38 Lightning (the first fighter jet to exceed 400 mph), the F-117A Nighthawk (the first stealth aircraft), and the U-2 (a high altitude reconnaissance plane). Johnson also helped develop the Model 10 Electra, flown by Amelia Earhart, as well as the Constellation (the first pressurized airliner) for billionaire businessman Howard Hughes. And all of this is just a partial list. So, what accounted for such a remarkable string of accomplishments?

Despite a steady stream of the most sophisticated aircrafts in aviation history, keeping things simple was a cornerstone of Johnson's leadership philosophy. In his biography, Kelly Johnson's successor, Ben Rich, described Johnson's "highly successful Skunk Works operation" as "a concentration of a few good people...applying the simplest, most straightforward methods possible to develop and produce new products."[68] Johnson himself wrote, "Keep it simple, stupid—KISS—is our constant reminder."[69]

Indeed, Johnson reportedly coined the KISS acronym when, in 1960, he was giving instructions to a team of design engineers for an advanced military jet. Johnson understood that the purpose of the aircraft was to help win wars and save lives. He also understood the reality of the necessary repairs often required in the field, the combat conditions under which those repairs might need to take place, the limited tools that would be available, and the level of training and experience of the average mechanic in the armed forces. As a result, Johnson wanted to make sure his engineers designed an engine that was as simple as possible to fix. When Johnson addressed his team of engineers at the beginning of the project, he gave them a clear, visual reminder of their purpose. He handed them a *small set of tools* with instructions to make sure that the aircraft could be repaired by the average military mechanic with *these tools alone*. He then added his final instruction, which became their "constant reminder": "Keep it simple, stupid."[70]

As a strategic leader or strategist, your job may never match the risks and intensity of combat conditions. You may have the luxury of access to other experts and tools. Nonetheless, in a rapidly changing world where attention is at an absolute premium, you cannot afford to lose sight of your primary purpose. Any time you deviate from your purpose by adding superfluous parts, processes, policies, or people, or otherwise adding anything that is not absolutely necessary, not only do you risk losing focus and wasting time and energy, but you may also put your ultimate purpose at risk.

Thus, the third key to effectively exploiting the power of simplicity is staying focused on and prioritizing around your primary purpose. This was one of the key themes in the writings of Prussian general and military theorist Carl von Clausewitz. "The lesson here is simple," writes Lonsdale, "and is the very essence of Clausewitz's advice in *On War*: Ensure that every military action is guided by the policy objective, not in some general, ethereal way, but in a detailed, concrete manner."[71]

In short, to maximize the power of simplicity is to begin with clear goals and objectives.[72] To fail to establish a clear direction and destination, in contrast, is to dilute focus, foster confusion, and invite complexity. "Amongst the complexities of strategy, the...objective represents a lens that enables the strategist to focus on what is important and necessary."[73] The strategist's definite, chief purpose is "the ultimate yardstick by which actions must be judged. Maintaining this focus," Lonsdale argues, "should allow the strategist to filter out much of the noise and chaos of strategy."[74]

(4.) *Organize, Categorize, Collapse.*

Effective organization is another essential factor in fostering simplicity. In fact, regardless of what it is you are dealing with—information, tasks, skills, systems, policies, politics, problems, processes, products, projects, people, clients, customers, constituents, stakeholders, followers, et cetera—one of the biggest contributing factors to complexity is a failure to adequately organize, categorize, combine, and collapse.

In most cases, a failure to effectively organize is more or less a failure to stop and think. Lazy thinkers make things messy and complex, or even incomprehensible. In fact, whenever you are confronted with complexity, rather than accepting it as the nature of the beast, one of the first things to do is ask yourself how it can be better organized so that it does not seem so complex.

Of course, a failure to organize is not always a lack of effort. There is a certain aptitude involved in effective organization. Ineffective, inefficient, or insufficient organization may stem from a flawed or inadequate understanding of the history, purpose, or context, or perhaps some critical component, category, or part. Oftentimes, recognizing how best to group and order something may seem like common sense. In other cases, however, the most effective way to organize and systematize something may require identifying recurring themes or patterns; taking a systems perspective; recognizing key requirements, priorities, or frequencies; or getting clear about the connections, interdependencies, and relationships between particular parts or with the whole. In essence, then, complexity can also be caused by a flawed or inadequate understanding. The less clear you are about what matters and what doesn't, the more likely you are to keep adding more.[75]

The celebrated American football coach, Vince Lombardi, was a big believer in simplicity and the power of a well-organized game plan. Rather than forcing his players to remember dozens of complicated plays, for example, Lombardi asked his players to focus on learning just a small number of plays, but to learn them so well that they were practically instinctual.[76] As a result, Vince Lombardi's "playbook was simpler and smaller" than other NFL coaches.[77] "Once these few basic plays became second nature, he asked his players to become equally familiar with a dozen or more options that might be run off each of those core plays. Suddenly, the playbook included "hundreds" of plays," writes his son, Vince Lombardi Jr., "but they were organized logically and simply in each player's mind as collections of related options, simple, but full of possibilities."[78]

In essence, rather than giving his players the impossible task of committing hundreds of complex plays to memory, Lombardi used a well-organized system to reduce the options down to a handful of fundamental plays— perhaps five to seven—with an additional twelve options.

Lest you imagine that this small set of core plays limited their potential for success, consider this: There was just *one* play—the "Power Sweep" or the "Lombardi Sweep"—that Vince Lombardi drilled into his team again and again and again.

"This is the lead play in our offense," Lombardi would explain to his team. "We must make it go. We will make it go. We will run it again and again and again, and we will make it go."[79]

What's more, Lombardi's "relentless"[80] focus on this one play was not just when he was the head coach of the Green Bay Packers. It started when he was with the New York Giants, and it continued to grow from there. He once led a football clinic for coaches, dedicating two of the four days to this one play.[81] Even more to the point, with Lombardi as head coach, "the Green Bay Packers won five league championships, including the first two Super Bowls because of that one play."[82]

(5.) *Ruthlessly Reduce—Filter, Subtract, and Eliminate.*

> *"Perfection is reached not when there is nothing left to add,*
> *but when there is nothing left to take away."*[83]

—Antoine de Saint-Exupéry (1900—1944), French Writer and Pioneering Aviator

Success is never about having infinite options. In fact, infinitely more often, the opposite is true, as Lombardi demonstrated with his relentless focus on mastering that single move. This leads to the final strategy for exploiting the power of simplicity: Take away everything that you can. "In a world that says you have to provide more choices, create more products, run hundreds of plays and be everything to everyone if you want to be successful, there is something very powerful about simplicity, clarity and leading with your strengths."[84] Rather that letting an unclear purpose, perfectionism, doubt, or fear drive you to continue adding until everything ends up crowded, chaotic, and complex; simplify and focus on being your absolute best with a well-chosen, well-defined set. "Success is about doing the right thing, not about doing everything right."[85]

Knowing what to ignore is not always as easy as it seems, but it is essential to your success.[86] "Half of your mastery of power comes from what you do not do, what you do not allow yourself to get dragged into."[87] Harvard Business School professor Michael Porter, known as the founder of the modern strategy field, says that "the essence of strategy is choosing what not to do."[88]

This was one of the areas where Albert Einstein excelled; he was a master at filtering the few essential factors out from the great mass of nonessentials.[89] When everyone else was lost in the complexity, derailed by the disorder, or carried away by the clutter, Einstein was able to home in on the essence. As he said himself, "I soon learned to scent out what was able to lead to fundamentals and to turn aside from everything else, from the multitude of things that clutter up the mind."[90]

It wasn't Einstein's ability to grasp complex concepts that was so remarkable, argues American theoretical physicist John Wheeler. It was his ability to ruthlessly reduce, subtract, and eliminate complexity. It was his ability to simplify. "Many a man in the street thinks of Einstein as a man who could only make headway in his work by dint of pages of complicated mathematics; the truth is the direct opposite. As Hilbert put it, 'Every boy in the streets of our mathematical Gottingen understands more about four-dimensional geometry than Einstein. Yet, despite that, Einstein did the work and not the mathematicians.' Time and again, in the photoelectric effect, in relativity, in gravitation, the amateur grasped the simple point that had eluded the expert."[91] Einstein himself said that "genius is making complex ideas simple, not making simple ideas complex."[92]

But this was not a skill he was born with so much as one he acquired. In fact, for several years early in his career, this was a central aspect of his job. When he worked as a clerk in the Swiss patent office, he was required to sift through all of the unnecessary, nonessential information and ideas to get the core concept of each patent application. What's more, he had to learn to do this quickly in order to excel at his job. As Wheeler explains in his biographical memoir of Albert Einstein, "Over and above the applications and the models was the boss, a kind man, a strict man, and a wise man. He gave strict instructions: explain very briefly, if possible in a single sentence, why the device will work or why it won't; why the application should be granted or why it should be denied. Day after day Einstein had to distill the central lesson out of objects of the greatest variety that man has power to invent."[93]

The management consulting firm Booz Allen Hamilton has said that what work young people do and who they work with in their first job has more of an effect on their "future than anything else one can easily analyze."[94] In Einstein's case, his first job was in the Swiss patent office in Bern and, over a period of seven years, he developed a deep appreciation for the value of simplicity, along with a swift, unparalleled skill at filtering out complexity, at stripping everything down to focus in on what matters most. This explains better than anything, according to Wheeler, the great "miracle" of Einstein's mind. Who else "but a patent office clerk," Wheeler argues, "who else knew out of the welter of facts to fasten on that which is absolutely central?"[95] "Who else could have distilled this simple central point from all the clutter of electromagnetism than someone whose job it was over and over to extract simplicity out of complexity."[96]

When you are thinking about how much to reduce and subtract, a good rule of thumb is the Pareto principle, otherwise known as the 80:20 rule. First posited by Italian economist Vilfredo Pareto, this rule is based on the rather surprisingly widespread observation in a variety of different domains that "the lion's share of the effect comes from a relatively small number of causes."[97] In other words, generally speaking, 80% of the outputs you are seeing are coming from 20% of the inputs. For example, 80% of your revenue is likely to come from only 20% of your customers. Similarly, 80% of your results are likely coming from only 20% of your activities. On the flip side, 20% of all defects are creating 80% of all problems. Thus, when thinking about ruthlessly reducing complexity, the Pareto principle would suggest that only about 20% of what you are dealing with is vital and, therefore, must be preserved. Keep in mind that this is just a guideline or rule of thumb to get you started, and that there are almost certainly some important exceptions. Nevertheless, there is considerable evidence for the notion that there is substantial waste and unnecessary excess in virtually every realm. Even in nature, as Pareto himself found, 80% of the peas in his garden were reaped from just 20% of the peapods.[98] "This extraordinarily stark pattern," writes billionaire venture capitalist Peter Thiel in Zero to One, "in which a small few radically outstrip all rivals, surrounds us everywhere in the natural and social world."[99]

Most of the intelligence strategists collect is immaterial. Much of the time spent planning, formulating, implementing, and executing strategy is wasted. To avoid this wasted time and effort, you must get good, really good, at discerning what matters most. Key conceptual tools for filtering out the excess 80% include the following:

(A.) **Strategic Purpose:** Eliminate activities and behaviors that are not aligned with your chief purpose or strategic intent.

(B.) **Keystone Goals:** A limited number of goals and the activities and behaviors involved in pursuing those goals have a disproportionate impact on your success or the achievement of your purpose; all other goals should be filtered out.

(C.) **Timeless Principles:** Seek to eliminate all activities, actions and behaviors that are in conflict with timeless, universal principles (e.g. honesty, integrity, responsibility, industry, self-discipline, service, respect, etc.).[100]

(D.) **Conceptual Frameworks:** Models, mental maps, and frameworks—such as the strategist code framework—can be used to make meaning, organize information and input, and filter out excess or superfluous data, redundant or irrelevant information, and noise.[101]

(E.) **Urgency vs. Importance:** Prioritize work that is important, while carefully eliminating that which appears urgent, but which is actually unimportant.[102]

(F.) **Circle of Influence:** Rather than getting distracted by issues in the larger circle of concern (issues that concern you, but over which you have no control), limit yourself to focusing on the smaller circle of influence (the subset of issues which also concern you, but over which you do have some influence or control).[103]

The story of Alexander the Great's simple, bold approach to the Gordian knot turns out to be a telling illustration of his general approach to strategy and his affinity for simplicity. "Although Alexander sometimes appeared to take the route less travelled, his plans and operations were rarely complicated," strategy professor David Lonsdale writes in his book, *Alexander the Great: Lessons in Strategy*.[104] "Indeed, his great battles are testament to this."[105] In fact, according to one of Canada's most renowned military strategists and historians, Lieutenant-Colonel Dr. Angelo Caravaggio, Alexander the Great was, much like Vince Lombardi, victorious in his three greatest battles because of one simple maneuver: The right flank.[106] Perhaps it is no surprise then, as foretold, that Alexander the Great did indeed go on to conquer Asia, fulfilling the prophecy of the Gordian knot.

This is undoubtedly one of the simplest yet most important lessons we learn from master strategists in virtually every field: There is great power in simplicity. "In war," wrote Clausewitz, "it is often less important what one does than how one does it. Strong *determination* and *perseverance* in carrying through a *simple idea* are the surest routes to one's objective."[107]

11

FOCUS YOUR FORCES, AMASS YOUR RESOURCES, CONCENTRATE ON JUST ONE THING: CLEOPATRA REGAINS AND SUSTAINS HER EGYPTIAN REIGN

"Concentration is the secret of strength in politics, in war, in trade,
in short in all management of human affairs."[1]
—Ralph Waldo Emerson, *The Conduct of Life*

"Not many things indifferently, but one thing supremely, is the demand of the hour.
He who scatters his efforts...cannot hope to succeed."[2]
—Orison Swett Marden, *Pushing to the Front*

On the Ides of March in 44 B.C., more than 40 senators of the Roman Republic encircled Julius Caesar inside the Theatre of Pompey in Rome with daggers hidden in their cloaks. Within minutes, the murderous conspirators descended upon their defenseless Roman dictator, wildly attacking and stabbing him until, after his flesh was pierced 23 times, he lie alone on the cold, hard floor bleeding to death.

The assassination of Julius Caesar meant that Cleopatra's hold on power in Egypt was once again in jeopardy. Julius Caesar had been Cleopatra's lover and he was the father of her son, Caesarion ("Little Caesar"). It was also Julius Caesar who had commanded the Roman legions on her behalf to take the Egyptian throne back from her little brother's murderous, scheming advisors. Now, with Caesar dead, Cleopatra feared that Egypt would once again fall prey to the will of the domineering and rapacious Roman senate.

The intelligent, highly educated, and politically savvy Cleopatra, as a concession to Egyptian tradition, had agreed to marry her brother, Ptolemy XIII, in 51 B.C., but she refused to surrender to the patriarchal ideas of her brother's power-hungry advisors. In fact, Cleopatra had every intention of ruling Egypt herself—just as she had been prepared and equipped to do from early childhood, and just as she had been doing since her father, Ptolemy XII, had made her his co-regent when she was still just 17. But this was no mere vague aspiration or fanciful dream. Despite the long line of almost exclusively male rulers across some 3,000 years of Egyptian history and tradition, Cleopatra was resolved to rule Egypt and she was prepared to summon all of her strength and power and whatever resources were required.

The assassination of Julius Caesar, however, presented a number of new problems for Cleopatra. With the poisoning of her second brother in July 44 B.C., the greatest threat to her power now was not from inside her own family, but from within the same body that had just murdered one of their own and Cleopatra's most important ally. The fact that Cleopatra had been Caesar's lover meant that she automatically had a number of powerful enemies. However, that she bore him a son, a potential heir, made her an even greater threat to Rome, particularly to those vying to replace Caesar as Rome's new dictator. What made her position even more tenuous was that most Romans looked down on Cleopatra as an immoral seductress leading a nation of barbarians. Worse still, writes historian Bridget McDermott, "the Romans regarded a female ruler with abhorrence..."[3]

Given that Rome was the most powerful empire in the world at the time, Cleopatra knew that she had little choice if she hoped to remain on the Egyptian throne. Just as her father had done throughout his reign, and in contrast to the will of her other siblings, Cleopatra understood that Egypt's best interests were in building dependable alliances with powerful leaders in Rome. What she "desperately needed," in other words, was a powerful ally in Rome's Senate.[4]

Visiting Rome at the time of Caesar's assassination, Cleopatra was understandably alarmed. She soon bolted back to Egypt while Rome descended into civil war.

In 42 B.C., the forces of the Second Triumvirate—Mark Antony, Lepidus, and Octavian (Caesar's adopted son and chosen heir)—defeated the forces of Caesar's assassins, Cassius and Brutus, at the Battle of Philippi. Antony and Octavian then divided the government between themselves, with Antony taking the lion's share of Rome's provinces in the North and East, including the client kingdom of Egypt.

Antony soon began writing letters to Cleopatra, summoning her to his government's headquarters in Tarsus (later, the birthplace of St. Paul). As one of the three leaders of Rome, there were important matters of state to discuss. There was also a grave misunderstanding that had to be addressed—Cleopatra was mistakenly believed to have supported Cassius, one of Caesar's assassins, during the civil war.

Antony was under no obligation to back Cleopatra's claim to the Egyptian throne. To be sure, he had backed the claim of Cleopatra's sister, Arsinoe, in 44 B.C. "and there was no assurance that he would not now decide that replacing Cleopatra with her younger sister might allow him to exploit Egypt's and Cyprus' resources more effectively."[5]

Master the Art of Timing.

According to the ancient Greek historian Plutarch, Cleopatra "received a number of letters from both Antony and his friends demanding her presence." As much as she needed Antony as an ally, "Cleopatra...was no fool."[6] Rather than appearing desperate and needy, eagerly rushing to obey his summons, Cleopatra began her campaign to win Antony over by rebuffing his requests to meet.[7] Her refusals were intended to demonstrate her high value, but also inflame Antony's curiosity and arouse his interest.[8] Her initial refusals would also help to heighten Antony's expectations once Cleopatra finally agreed to meet.[9]

Once Cleopatra made up her mind to make the trip, she began making the most extravagant preparations and plans. "With her gift for spotting a good opportunity," writes historian Diana Preston, "she planned her campaign with as much care and calculation as her former lover Caesar had planned his military ventures, assessing her target's vulnerabilities, one of which, she knew, was a predilection for beautiful, flamboyant women."[10]

"Already playing a brilliant political game," Cleopatra wanted to ensure that the "preparations were in place to make the Roman's first encounter with Egypt's queen one to remember."[11]

In fact, another part of Cleopatra's delay in responding to one of Rome's most powerful leaders was that her full-scale campaign to win Antony over required considerable time to prepare.[12] "In an age when the great majority of the population in Alexandria or Rome was illiterate," writes Preston, "spectacle was the medium for communicating with the masses. Just as Caesar's magnificent Triumphs celebrating Rome's mastery of the world had wrung roars of approval from near-hysterical crowds, so Cleopatra intended to create a pageant of royal wealth and divine beauty that would not be easily forgotten."[13]

She would fully exploit the considerable means at her disposal, milking her strengths to maximum effect—her deep charisma, her wealth and power, her cunning and wit. "Drawing on her family's long tradition of building luxurious pleasure craft,"[14] Cleopatra would make the most dazzling entrance that the world had ever seen. "Her father would no doubt have been proud of such a performance."[15]

She also made sure she "equipped herself with plenty of gifts and money."[16] "Above all, however," Plutarch explains, "she went there relying on herself and on the magical arts and charms of her person."[17]

By the time she was finally prepared to embark, "in the most spectacular style,"[18] Cleopatra had done virtually everything in her power, including gathering intelligence on Antony, to ensure that her efforts were a resounding success. "Cleopatra dramatically played on Mark Antony's fascination for Greek culture and his love of luxury. She approached Tarsus by sailing up the Cydnus River in a magnificent boat..."[19] Plutarch describes the extravagant arrival of Egypt's Queen, sailing in a barge gilded in gold, "its purple sails billowing in the wind, while her rowers caressed the water with oars of silver which dipped in time to the music of the flute, accompanied by pipes and lutes."[20] "Instead of a crew the barge was lined with the most beautiful of her waiting-women...some at the rudders, others at the tackle of the sails, and all the while an indescribably rich perfume...was wafted from the vessel to the riverbanks. Great multitudes accompanied this royal progress, some of them following the queen on both sides of the river from its very mouth, while others hurried down from the city of Tarsus to gaze at the sight."[21]

It was a sensational entrance. Cleopatra was pulling out all the stops, the most critical of which was her own appearance. "As musicians played, Cleopatra reclined under a gold-embroidered canopy dressed as Aphrodite, Greek goddess of love. She was fanned by youths dressed as Eros and waited upon by girls dressed as sea nymphs..."[22]

Maintain the Initiative, Use Spectacle to Capture and Control.

Antony was overwhelmed by the spectacle, which was unlike anything anyone in Rome would ever conceive. "While she drifted towards Mark Antony like a creature from myth, she refused to disembark. As queen of Egypt, she expected Antony to wait on her. Mark Antony's temper was inflamed, but so were his passions."[23] Antony was helpless in the face of Cleopatra's charisma and her seductive, self-reliant powers.

Attempting to regain the initiative, a slightly perplexed Antony sent Cleopatra a dinner invitation. Still in full command, however, and "unwilling either to surrender the initiative or to break the spell she had cast," she countered with an invitation to a banquet on her royal barge.[24] In effect, though she had traveled across the Mediterranean Sea, by ensuring that Antony came to her, she was subtly reversing the power dynamic and neutralizing his summons.[25] Antony was coming to her domain for a taste of Egypt in an atmosphere she controlled, where she "wined and dined"[26] him on the delicacies of Egypt. "The banquet that followed was brightly illuminated by carefully arranged clusters of lamps. The luxury, opulence and spectacle of the Ptolemaic court were displayed to full effect."[27] "Cleopatra's looks and her subtlety and tricky wit in conversation," writes Plutarch, led her to "have the greatest influence over him.'"[28]

"Antony loved pleasure and spectacle... Everything was geared to suggest to him the superiority of the Egyptian way of life over the Roman, at least when it came to pleasure. The Romans were boring and unsophisticated by comparison. And once Antony was made to feel how much he was missing in spending his time with his dull soldiers and his matronly Roman wife, he could be made to see Cleopatra as the incarnation of all that was exciting. He became her slave."[29] "Cleopatra had also displayed the abundance of her realm...this opulence...was a clear promise that the queen could mobilize this wealth to Antony's service."[30]

Cleopatra's entrance to Tarsus has since been the subject of a number of famous paintings, including André Bauchant's "Cleopatra's Barge," George Frederick Bensell "Cleopatra Entering Her Barge," Agostino Tassi's "The Arrival of Cleopatra at Tarsus," Sir Lawrence Alma-Tadema's "The Meeting of Antony and Cleopatra" and William Etty's "The Triumph of Cleopatra."

Cleopatra's efforts were indeed a triumph. With Antony as an ally, she further secured her hold over Egypt and continued to rule for another 11 years. "Keen to please his Egyptian Queen, Antony agreed to orchestrate the death of Arsinoe and, in 41 B.C., Cleopatra's last remaining sibling was dragged out of sanctuary and murdered on the steps of the Temple of Artemis."[31] Cleopatra also initiated one of the greatest love affairs in history. In 37 B.C., the two lovers became husband and wife and, furthermore, "Cleopatra would go on to bear Antony three children."[32]

To be clear, Cleopatra was no simple seductress. In contrast to the Hollywood version of Cleopatra as an infamous femme fatale, the reality is that she was "a commanding woman versed in politics, diplomacy and governance, fluent in nine languages, silver-tongued and charismatic."[33] Cleopatra understood the nature of power and influence and, as a result, she persuaded both Mark Antony and Julius Caesar, two of the most powerful men in the world at the time, "to do her bidding."[34]

"For his grand finale, Antony finally let any guise of Roman loyalty fall away. He distributed lands held by Rome and Parthia to his new wife and their children, then in his most shocking move yet, proclaimed Caesarion, not Octavian, Caesar's legitimate son and true heir. Rome was outraged."[35]

For the proud and pompous Romans, Antony "going native" was an unforgivable crime. But Antony too was proud and, backed by Cleopatra, the wealthiest and most powerful woman in the world, he no longer saw fit to maintain his alliance with Octavian. His mistake, however, was in underestimating his enemy and, by playing his hand openly, surrendering the initiative.[36]

No doubt, more than Antony, it was Cleopatra who wanted Caesarion in control of Rome. It was Cleopatra's "years of pragmatic power plays and investment" that had won over Antony's allegiance, despite a lifetime of loyalty to Rome.[37] "Ever the showman, she wrapped him in purple robes, draped him in jewels and thrust a golden scepter into his hand. The queen of the Nile would need a king as splendid as her, and upsetting Octavian was exactly what she wanted to do."[38]

In the end, Antony's proclamation, his infidelity to his wife, Octavia, the sister of Octavian, and the rivalry for ultimate power created a split between these two co-rulers of Rome. This split led to yet another civil war in which Octavian emerged victorious over Antony and Cleopatra at the Battle of Actium. The two lovers were at last doomed to a tragic fate: Suicide—Antony because he mistakenly thought Cleopatra was dead and Cleopatra because Antony was dead and she refused to be dragged through the streets of Rome caged like an Egyptian lioness.

Master the Power of Concentration—
The Superseding Principle of Strategic Success

*"There are many good generals in Europe, but they see too many things at once;
I see only one thing; namely, the enemy's main body. I strive to destroy it,
confident that secondary matters will work themselves out."* [39]

—Napoleon Bonaparte, Emperor of the French

The importance of concentrating your resources gets to the heart of strategy. The whole point of strategy is born out of the reality of limited resources. You only have so much time, money, staff, soldiers, hardware, supplies, et cetera and, therefore, you develop a strategy to use the resources you have to achieve the end you desire. "No individual, no business, even no country has unlimited resources." [40] "If resources were not limited, there would be no need to select one objective over another." [41]

Concentrating your forces is about maximizing the limited resources you have to focus on the point where those resources can have the greatest impact. Referring to the concept of "massing, concentration, or focus," which he explains as "three names for essentially the same thing," General Cohen argues that "every strategy must incorporate this concept as part of its basic makeup. In fact," he adds, "many experts consider this principle to be the basis of all strategy." [42] The influential British military historian and strategist Sir Liddell Hart went even further, writing that "the principles of war, not merely one principle, can be condensed into a single word—'concentration.'" [43]

Napoleon Bonaparte was fiercely devoted to the principle of concentration for this same reason. [44] To effectively execute strategy is to concentrate your forces. In the words of the great 19th century Prussian strategist Carl von Clausewitz, "there is no higher and simpler law of strategy than that of *keeping one's forces concentrated*." [45]

Despite the fact that, "at the core, strategy is about focus," the reality is that "most complex organizations don't focus their resources. Instead, they pursue multiple goals at once, not concentrating enough resources to achieve a breakthrough in any of them." [46] In business, the most common mistake is thinking that *everyone* is a part of your potential audience or customer base. But this approach, virtually by definition, is the exact opposite of effective strategy.

"The opposite of concentration is *diffusion of effort*—a tendency to offer too many products and services to too many types of customers, in too many ways, with too many different price points. This inevitably leads to loss of energy, overextension, excessive costs, and the diversion of key talents away from the areas where great success is possible." [47]

Explaining the power of this principle by using water as a metaphor, the 19th century Scottish historian Thomas Carlyle writes, "The weakest living creature, by concentrating his powers on a single object, can accomplish something; whereas the strongest, by dispersing his [powers] over many, may fail to accomplish anything. The drop, by continually falling, bores its passage through the hardest rock. The hasty [dispersed] torrent rushes over it with hideous uproar and leaves no trace behind."[48]

Most business failures are the result of people rushing across the rocks like Carlyle's violent flood. They are loud and full of energy. Their efforts cover a broad path. But they lack a clear focus and, therefore, they fail to succeed in penetrating the market.

To succeed as a strategist you must master this principle of concentration—amassing your resources and focusing your forces on *just one thing*. As with Cleopatra's success in gaining and maintaining her hold over Egypt, "successful people all seem to have this special ability to *concentrate their forces* and mass their energies on *the critical task* where great success and victory is possible."[49] After decades of extraordinary success as a business consultant and executive coach, Brian Tracy concluded that "your ability to decide exactly what you want and then to concentrate all your energies on achieving your most important goals probably determines your success and happiness more than any other decision you make."[50]

To maximize the power of this principle, focus on the following five (5) subfactors of concentration:

#1. Win by Concentrating On One Wildly Important Aim: Russia's Running Start Over the States in the Race to Outer Space

"The giants of the race have been men of concentration, who have struck sledgehammer blows in one place until they have accomplished their purpose. The successful men of today are men of one overmastering idea, one unwavering aim, men of single and intense purpose."[51]

—Orison Swett Marden, *Pushing to the Front*

The end of World War II put the United States and the Soviet Union on a collision course with history. On March 5, 1946, Winston Churchill traveled with President Harry Truman to Westminster College in Missouri to deliver what would become Churchill's most famous post-World War II address.

Despite expressing his "strong admiration" for Joseph Stalin as a key ally in the defeat of Adolf Hitler's Nazi war machine, Churchill was nevertheless alarmed by the increasing influence and communist control of formerly independent nations by Stalin's Soviet Russia.[52] "A shadow has fallen upon the scenes so lately lighted by the Allied victory," Churchill said. "From Stettin in the Baltic to Trieste in the Adriatic, an iron curtain has descended across the Continent. Behind that line lie all the capitals of the ancient states of Central and Eastern Europe. Warsaw, Berlin, Prague, Vienna, Budapest, Belgrade, Bucharest and Sofia, all these famous cities and the populations around them lie in what I," Churchill continued, "must call the Soviet sphere, and all are subject in one form or another, not only to Soviet influence but to a very high and, in many cases, increasing measure of control from Moscow."[53]

Churchill's famous "Iron Curtain" speech both predicted and, in retrospect, marked the beginning of the Cold War between the United States and the Soviet Union,[54] a period noted for its heightened geopolitical tensions, proxy wars in foreign lands, and attempts to best and bury one another without triggering the *mutually assured destruction* (MAD) of nuclear war.[55]

As the years advanced and technology progressed, the two former allies were both intent on achieving superiority in the ballistic missile-based nuclear arms race which, for purposes of national security, quickly expanded into a general competition for superiority in space.

Under the leadership of premier Nikita Khrushchev, the Soviet Union took the lead in the Space Race in October 1957 with the successful launch of Sputnik 1, the first Earth-orbiting satellite in history. When the Soviets successfully launched Sputnik 2 the following month, this time carrying a dog, Laika, another historic first, public fear in the West of a perceived technological gap became known as the Sputnik crisis.

When the Soviets succeeded yet again, this time launching the first human, Yuri Gagarin, into space on April 12, 1961, and returning him safely to Earth, the newly elected President John F. Kennedy was determined to eliminate the perceived gap and secure the lead in exploring the final frontier.

Casting his epic vision in a historic speech, Kennedy called on America to concentrate its forces, focus its energies and resources and, he said, "commit itself to achieving the goal, before this decade is out, of landing a man on the Moon..."[56] This was the key moment that the race for space began to change. While America was zeroing in on one heroic ambition, the Soviets inexplicably began to disperse their efforts.

In the U.S., NASA had one project, Project Apollo, led by one chief, James Webb, who "ensured absolute focus" on one thing, landing a man on the moon.[57] In the U.S.S.R., in contrast, efforts were scattered. In the words of one historian, the Soviet Union's "greatest problem was a lack of focus."[58] Rather than concentrating and uniting around one wildly important aim, the Soviets were divided and at odds. They even had two different lunar schemes which further divided their limited resources.[59] One was led by Soviet rocket engineer and spacecraft designer Sergei Korolev, who insisted that, as opposed to multiple stages, his design, the N1 rocket, could fly to the moon with one single launch.[60] The other scheme, led by "rival engineer Vladimir Chelomei proposed that his smaller rocket, the Proton, should send separate modules into orbit, where they would dock before heading for the Moon."[61]

Unfortunately, rather than sharing information and working collaboratively together toward one shared, preeminent purpose, their efforts were divided and dispersed. As recently explained by Sergei Khrushchev, the son of former premier Nikita Khrushchev, there were also "different designers who competed with one another."[62]

Rather than serving as a friendly competition that worked to spur on the two teams to "beat the Americans," they criticized and attacked each other's ideas instead. Russian cosmonaut and Air Force Major General Alexey Leonov claimed that the rivalry undermined them both. In fact, Leonov, who worked with Korolev at the time, admitted to a Russian newspaper in 2010 that "very complicated relations between Korolev and Chelomei and their rivalry harmed our common cause."[63]

The two programs were further undermined by the leadership of the "emotional" and "unpredictable" Nikita Khrushchev, who led the Soviet Union from 1953 to 1964.[64] Khrushchev sometimes took resources away, telling Korolev that they were running out of money for the space program. But then he would later switch priorities, telling Korolev, "We won't give up the Moon to the Americans! Take all the resources you need!"[65]

Well within the ten-year timeline Kennedy set in his moon speech, America eventually triumphed over the Soviets in the Space Race when, on July 20, 1969, with NASA's focus on one wildly important aim, the Apollo 11 crew landed safely on the moon.

Paint One Canvas at a Time.

"It is those who concentrate on but one thing
at a time who advance in this world."[66]

—Og Mandino, *The Greatest Salesman in the World*

"The one prudence in life is concentration," wrote Emerson; "the one evil is dissipation: And it makes no difference whether our dissipations are coarse or fine."[67] To succeed, Emerson said, you must put a decisive end to all miscellaneous activity and concentrate your power "on one or a few points." Learn from the example of the gardener, he said, who "by severe pruning, forces the sap of the tree into one or two vigorous limbs, instead of suffering it to spindle into a sheaf of twigs."[68]

Despite his success as a writer, playwright, and social philosopher, as well as a spy, conman, politician and diplomat, today the world remembers Giacomo Casanova (1725—1798) as history's greatest lover—and for good reason: Casanova was a legendarily notorious seducer and rake.

The Italian adventurer, entrepreneur and author was born at the dawn of the Age of Enlightenment, into a family of lowly, but popular Venetian actors. Casanova's ability to completely immerse himself in a craft to the point of mastery helped him to find success in a wealth of diverse pursuits—*one pursuit at a time.*

Accepted to the University of Padua, a premier Italian university, at age *twelve*, graduating with a law degree at age seventeen, Casanova, a masterful storyteller, went on to become a brilliant and prolific writer. He soon came to be celebrated as the "prince of Italian adventurers," earning the esteem of the most elevated in European society.[69]

The same intense focus and attention to detail that Casanova applied to his other pursuits, he applied to his prodigious pursuit of women. And it was this, more than his physical appearance, that Casanova himself attributed to his success with the fairer sex. It was his ability to focus his attention so completely on winning over the woman of his desire that helped to ensure that Casanova rarely ever failed.[70]

Casanova's strategy was simple. First, he never pursued more than one woman at once. When he met a woman he desired he would immediately begin to study her, becoming a veritable student of the woman, finding out everything he could about her: What made her happy? What were her dreams, her desires, her fears? What was she missing? Did she want to feel like a lady? Was it friendship? Lofty conversation? Romance?[71]

As his study of the woman he was pursuing continued, and he began to understand her, he would seek to meet her needs anyway he could. However long the affair would last, Casanova would think of no one but her. His focus was so intense and absolute that it was as if he totally surrendered himself to her. "He would do anything for her, even risk his life, which in fact he sometimes did."[72] Casanova understood that concentrated, sweeping focus was key. If his attention wandered, even for a moment, the usual doubts would seep back in and his charm would be broken.[73] Finding his complete concentration extremely seductive, women would swiftly fall under his spell.[74] In the end, this total focus often took considerable effort—which is precisely why it is so rare, and enthralling—but it was, Casanova believed, well worth the work.

"Not surprisingly, the principle of massing your resources applies to everything you do in life," writes William Cohen in his book, *The Art of the Strategist*.[75] "It is important to emphasize," he argues, "that Casanova massed his resources and did not pursue more than one woman at a time. While he pursued one, he concentrated on that woman *alone*, and *thought of nothing and no one else* until his conquest was complete, whether this took days or months. Casanova carried the strategy concept of massing his resources into everything he did in life."[76][e.a.] Well beyond his pursuit of women, Robert Greene writes in *The 48 Laws of Power*, "Casanova attributed his *success in life* to his ability to concentrate on a single goal and push at it until it yielded. It was his ability to give himself over completely to the women he desired that made him so intensely seductive. For the weeks or months that one of these women lived in his orbit, he thought of no one else."[77][e.a.]

In the end, Casanova lived a richly varied and colorful life. And, yet, regardless of the particular pursuit, he painted but one canvas at a time, and he gave his undivided attention to each stroke of the brush. In the words of the Spanish Proverb, "If you would be pope, you must think of nothing else."[78] Summing up his success in words worth repeating, Casanova himself later wrote, "I have always believed that when a man gets it into his head to do something, and when he exclusively occupies himself in that design, he must succeed, whatever the difficulties. That man will become Grand Vizier or Pope."[79]

Concentrate Your Power, Fly Like an Arrow to Your Singular Mark.

"This is my one aim."[80]
—Saint Paul, Letter to the Philippians

Far too many people fail due to a lack of disciplined concentration and sustained focus. They fear they will never succeed with one rocket to the moon, one line of business, or one new product line, so they attempt to take two, three, four or more lines all at the same time, never giving everything they have to any single one. But "here is the prime condition of success," wrote the Scottish American steel baron Andrew Carnegie, one of the richest men in history, "concentrate your energy, thought and capital exclusively upon the business in which you are engaged. Having begun on one line, resolve to fight it out on that line, to lead in it, adopt every improvement, have the best machinery, and know the most about it."[81]

As marketing legend Al Ries writes, "the biggest single barrier to the development of an effective corporate strategy is the strongly held belief that a company has to appeal to the entire market. More money has been wasted reaching out to a company's 'noncustomers' than any other single endeavor."[82] Ries, co-author with Jack Trout of *The 22 Immutable Laws of Marketing*, further adds, "The attempt to appeal to everybody is *the biggest single mistake a business can make*. Better to stake out your own ground and write off everyone else."[83] Better, in other words, to focus on one supreme rocket, and make it the best that you possibly can.

Fearful that it will be difficult to get work playing other types of characters at some unknown point in the future, many Hollywood actors work hard to avoid being "typecast." In many cases, however, playing to type is the most lucrative line of work an actor can expect. As Jonathan Frakes, who played Commander William Riker in the Star Trek television series, told the BBC, "it's better to be type-cast than not to be cast at all."[84] "An actor or an actress who plays the same role over and over again often becomes a big star. If BMW is the ultimate driving machine, John Wayne was the ultimate macho cowboy. Marilyn Monroe was the ultimate sex symbol. And Clint Eastwood is the ultimate strong, silent type."[85]

Playing the same type of character may not always be the most intellectually stimulating or personally rewarding for the actor, but in terms of succeeding in a fiercely competitive industry, focus works for actors much the same way it does in business, politics, and war. "In essence, big Hollywood stars are focused. They play themselves, which simplifies their jobs and makes them a lot of money."[86]

Once told by her mother that "actresses go hungry while movie stars have everything,"[87] Elizabeth Taylor, went on to become the highest paid movie star in the world. Many of today's highest paid stars are also known for regularly playing to type. Adam Sandler owns the likable goofball. Jennifer Aniston owns the romcom gal pal. Samuel Jackson owns the no nonsense tough guy. Arnold Schwarzenegger owns the ultimate action hero. Cameron Diaz is the funny hottie; Jim Carey, the eccentric goof; Morgan Freeman, the wise, older guide; Dwayne Johnson, the charming, rugged hero. In a sense, these superstars all have their own brand identity and this is a big part of why they are so successful. As with "virtually every other superstar of the past...focus got them to the top. Focus kept them there."[88]

"Focusing will do more to propel a company into the stratosphere than any other single activity. But it's not easy. [...] What management needs to do is search for the *one thing* that is working and then focus the entire company behind that single effort."[89] In his book, *Focus: The Future of Your Company Depends On It*, Ries brings the key point home:

> *"Focus is the art of carefully selecting your category and then working diligently in order to get yourself categorized. It's not a trap to avoid; it's a goal to achieve. Don't let mindless criticism detract you from this goal. If you're a Hollywood star, a Wall Street luminary, or a corporate executive, it's hard enough to burn your way into the mind with a single character. Why would you want to weigh yourself down with multiple personalities? Nothing succeeds in life...or in business...like a carefully selected, carefully chiseled focus."*[90]

The great 19th century Prussian military theorist Carl von Clausewitz similarly advised strategists to, "pursue *one* great decisive aim with force and determination."[91]

In Cleopatra's case, her one great aim was to rule over all of Egypt and to rule it well. Even as a young woman, she was determined to be the queen no matter what the cost. In terms of how to achieve her ambition, Cleopatra understood that Rome was a rapidly expanding superpower with both military and economic superiority throughout the Mediterranean and Middle East. She was also well aware of the large debts Egypt racked up with Rome, and the lack of sufficient flooding of the Nile, which withered crops and led to the ongoing famine. As a result, Cleopatra believed that the pivotal factor in holding power in Egypt was in maintaining strong alliances with powerful leaders in Rome. And she focused everything she had on securing this one vital relationship above all, first with Julius Caesar and, years later, with Mark Antony.

As hard as this is for ambitious leaders to accept, the brutal truth is that "the more you try to do, the less you actually accomplish. This is a stark, inescapable principle that we all live with," writes Sean Covey.[92] Like an arrow flying straight to its singular mark, Cleopatra was not simultaneously targeting multiple additional rulers or executing multiple additional plans.[93] She focused on one thing, "one great decisive aim" where she knew she was strong, and she employed all of the necessary resources at her disposal to achieve it.

#2. Focus Your Forces on a Precise Strategic Position: British Vice Admiral Horatio Nelson Faces Napoleon's Fleet at the Battle of Trafalgar

"Every great man has become great, every successful man has succeeded, in proportion as he has confined his powers to one particular channel." [94]

—Orison Swett Marden, *Pushing to the Front*

On October 21, 1805, in the midst of the Napoleonic Wars, British Vice Admiral Horatio Nelson was about to do the unthinkable. With a dangerous storm approaching off the Cape of Trafalgar in the southwest of Spain, Nelson was intentionally sailing the Royale Navy straight into a massive broadside cannon bombardment by Napoleon Bonaparte's combined French and Spanish fleet. Worse still, the light North-West wind ensured that the British fleet was crawling directly into the enemy's cannon fire at a mere 1.5 miles per hour, about half the average adult's walking speed. Still confident in his ultimate success, Nelson had previously written to Admiral Collingwood, who was now leading the other, parallel column of British ships of the line, "We have only one great object in view, that of annihilating our enemies." [95]

Britain's heroic Vice Admiral Lord Nelson desperately wanted to destroy Napoleon's fleet, solidify British dominance of the seas, and rid the continent of France's new "upstart" emperor once and for all. But sailing directly perpendicular into 33 enemy ships of the line—a few of which were equipped with 3 levels of gun decks—was filled with potentially catastrophic risks. In fact, *leading* the charge, Nelson's ship—the 104-gun, 3-deck HMS *Victory*— was headed directly in the vicinity of the 4-deck Spanish flagship, *Santísima Trinidad*, a floating military fortress equipped with 140 guns. But Lord Nelson was also sailing the HMS *Victory* directly into his carefully selected *strategic position*, the 86-gun flagship, *Bucentaure*, of the allied fleet's commanding officer, the cautious, indecisive French Admiral Pierre Villeneuve. [96]

Previously, Napoleon had sent orders to halt the action and remove Admiral Villeneuve from command, writing that "Villeneuve does not possess the strength of character to command a frigate. He lacks determination and has no moral courage." But Villeneuve refused to surrender his post. "Aware that his career was already in serious jeopardy, he ordered preparations to sail despite the poor condition of most of his vessels which lacked adequate armament and trained crews." [97] Hoping to "redeem himself by battle," [98] Villeneuve disobeyed Napoleon's orders to *avoid* engaging with the English and instead sailed the allied fleet directly into disaster.

Given the lack of cannons at the bow and stern, naval tactics of this period, going back 150 years, [99] dictated that ships would form up end-to-end in a single line of battle, parallel with the enemy. This prevailing tactical orthodoxy, a widely practiced convention, ensured that they could train the greatest number of their cannons on the enemy's line. While it maximized the exposure of their own ships, it also helped to protect the more vulnerable bow and stern.[100] In this way, victory usually came down to some combination of the skill, speed, discipline, and courage of the sailors as well as the size, quality, and number of the cannons and ships. "This strategy was such an integral part of naval warfare at the time that it had inspired the name 'ship of the line' for the vessels that took part in it. But Nelson had other plans."[101]

As it happened, given that the French and Spanish combined had 33 ships of the line with a total of 2,568 guns, Nelson's fleet of 27* ships and 2,088 guns was both outnumbered and outgunned.[102] Nelson, nonetheless, a clever strategist and inspiring leader who "sought glory above all else," was resolved to do whatever was necessary to win.[103] Arranging for one final message to his men, the HMS *Victory*'s signal flag system read: "England expects that every man will do his duty."[104]

To be sure, compared with Villeneuve's allied French and Spanish fleet, Nelson's men had a number of advantages, including greater experience, a superior communication system, a cunning and courageous strategic leader, and higher morale. As Nelson and Collingwood's two columns headed, at full sail and with the wind at their back, directly into enemy fire, they also had one other temporary advantage: A significant sized swell in the Atlantic made it difficult for the allies to hit their distant targets. Still, as a result of the light wind, the two approaching British columns were in range of the enemy's cannons for nearly an hour and, therefore, were forced to weather considerable damage as they crawled closer and closer to the allied line.

Exploit the Advantages of the Unorthodox Approach.

Despite what appeared to be an unorthodox suicide mission and a violation of standard naval doctrine, Lord Nelson was actually in the midst of unleashing a risky, but carefully calculated and devastatingly clever strategic plan. Nelson had divided his ships into two parallel columns with the goal of splitting the Franco-Spanish line of 33 ships into 3 parts—a head, a body, and a tail. Once Nelson's two columns began to break through the enemy's line, the brilliance of Nelson's attack quickly became alarmingly clear.

First, after Nelson's two columns successfully endured the broadside bombardments of their initial approach, once they broke through the line they then had the advantage of unleashing their own broadside attacks, only now at a much closer and more concentrated range, while the relatively defenseless allied ships had to struggle to reposition to return fire.

Second, leading the northern, windward British column, Nelson effectively cut the head or vanguard of the Franco-Spanish line off from the battle. Headed north, the ships in the vanguard (approximately 10 or 11) were given the signal to loop back around, but the calm wind ensured that it would be too late by the time they made it back. This cut the allies down to a size (23 or 22 ships) where Nelson's 27 ships had a more concentrated advantage.

Third, by specifically breaking the line right in front of *Bucentaure*, the French flagship (i.e. the vessel used by the commanding officer—in this case, Villeneuve), the concentrated attack of Nelson's column disrupted the flagship's signals, making it nearly impossible for Villeneuve to communicate with the other ships to coordinate a response. Nelson, in contrast, also had the advantage of a superior communication system (signal flags) to better coordinate and concentrate his forces,[105] and the devastating blows from both the front and rear ensured that Villeneuve's *Bucentaure* was the first ship to surrender.

Fourth, the concentrated attack on the body or center of the Franco-Spanish line from *both* the windward and leeward British columns simultaneously ensured that a number of ships were quickly destroyed. In short, following the lead of Admiral Villeneuve, one by one the French and Spanish ships of the line started to surrender.

Nelson had effectively concentrated his forces on breaking the enemy's line into three much more manageable parts "before destroying two of them piecemeal"[106] at close range—which, given the superior gunnery and discipline of the British, was yet another example of Nelson concentrating his advantages.[107] Once the vanguard of the enemy line had made its way back around to the battle, the devastation of the Combined Fleet's rear caused them to turn back north to escape.

In the end, Napoleon's rogue admiral lost 22 allied ships, while Britain's Admiral Nelson lost not a single one.[108] "The victory at Trafalgar allowed Britain to step up its economic war against France."[109] It also helped ensure that there would be no other major naval battle during the Napoleonic wars, and it effectively foiled Napoleon's long-held hopes of invading England.

Identify Your Strategic Focus Point.

"If you chase two rabbits, you will not catch either one."[110]
—Russian Proverb

Clausewitz wrote that "the talent of the strategist is to identify the *decisive point* and to concentrate everything on it, removing forces from secondary fronts and ignoring lesser objectives."[111] The celebrated Swiss military strategist, Antoine Henri de Jomini—who served in Napoleon Bonaparte's army and whose writings, like Clausewitz, are still studied at the world's top military academies, such as West Point—also argued for the central importance of concentration. In fact, Jomini believed that concentration was *the* fundamental principle of the whole discipline of strategy—but, "specifically, concentration of forces at the decisive point on the battlefield."[112] Napoleon Bonaparte himself was implacably committed to concentration, but, again, *not just anywhere*.[113] The key is not *only* to amass or concentrate your forces. The key is also to amass your resources at the *most strategic, decisive point*—the point where you can have an overwhelming advantage, or at least a superior and decisive one.

In essence, the principle of concentration has two key parts. First, amassing your resources, as Nelson did by coordinating the Royale Navy into two parallel columns. Second, focusing those amassed resources on a key strategic position, as Nelson did in three ways: (1.) First, by concentrating his columns on splitting the enemy fleet into three smaller, more manageable parts, which also temporarily removed the vanguard from the battle; (2.) Second, by focusing foremost on the enemy's flagship, which hindered their ability to communicate; and (3.) Third, by concentrating his initial attack on the body (middle third) of the enemy line, hitting it with broadsides from both the windward and leeward columns; in effect, concentrating his power on one segment of the enemy fleet at a time.

In his business book, *Good Strategy, Bad Strategy*, adopting the word "focus," Richard Rumelt explains the same concept from a business perspective, "This particular pattern—attacking a segment of the market with a business system supplying more value to that segment than the other players can—is called focus. Here, the word "focus" has two meanings. First, it denotes the coordination of policies that produces extra power through their interacting and overlapping effects. Second, it denotes the application of that power to the right target."[114]

Focusing your resources on a precise target is the opposite of a broad offensive, which disperses and weakens your power. As Napoleon said, "war is a business of positions."[115] Thus, "the essence of strategy," he said, "...is always to have more force at a crucial point than the enemy."[116]

Clausewitz referred to this key strategic point as your opponent's "center of gravity," and in order "to score a decisive victory,"[117] Clausewitz said, "we must mass our forces at *the hub of all power and movement*, the enemy's 'Center of Gravity.'"[118][e.a.] This is the point "on which everything depends,"[119] and, he added, "the point against which all our energies should be directed."[120]

"Clausewitz recognized that the critical point might be a capital city or the coherence of an alliance,"[121] but also that "there might be no obvious single focal point, if the enemy did not present itself in that way."[122]

That the "single focal point" may not be "obvious," however, does not mean that it is any less critical. Regardless of how difficult it may be to determine, "there is no more powerful concept in strategic thinking than centre of gravity," writes Stephens and Baker in *Making Sense of War: Strategy of the 21st Century*.[123] "History is replete with examples of campaigns that failed because the wrong centers of gravity were attacked and protected, and with those that succeeded because one set of competing strategists got its center-of-gravity analysis more or less right."[124]

"Because resources are always limited, you must make constant tradeoffs as to where they will be used."[125] To attempt to be strong everywhere is a fool's errand. "If you try to do this, you will fail because," almost inevitably, at it least *one* of those points, *"you will be weak..."*[126] and, therefore, you will create a vulnerability, a point at which your opponents can effectively amass and focus their forces against *you*. The key, instead, is to accept the inevitability of a tradeoff and concentrate your strength at the decisive point.

Amass Your Resources at the Strategic Focus Point.

The great advantage of concentrating your forces at the crucial point is that it gives you a decisive advantage *at that point*, even in the face of a competitor or opponent who is much more powerful or numerically superior *overall*.[127]

Napoleon Bonaparte applied the principle of concentration to masterful effect again and again throughout his career—perhaps most notably in his most famous battle. On December 2, 1805, less than two months after Nelson's decisive victory at Trafalgar, Napoleon faced the joint forces of Russia and Austria at the Battle of Austerlitz. With the allies of the Third Coalition rapidly closing in, Napoleon concentrated his corps of some 67,000 men and 157 guns just outside the town of Austerlitz in the south of the Austrian Empire. Allied against him, in what is also known as the Battle of Three Emperors, was Alexander I, Emperor of Russia, and Francis I, Emperor of Austria (the last Holy Roman Emperor) whose combined forces totaled 85,000 men and, at 318, more than twice the number of Bonaparte's guns.[128]

When Napoleon arrived on the battle scene he immediately recognized the key strategic point—Pratzen Heights, which was the high point of a hill in the center of the battlefield, which was then occupied by the Russians.[129] Napoleon knew that if he could take this key strategic position he could bring in his reserve forces and dominate the battle.[130] Keeping his main reserves in the center, hidden behind a brew of fog and wood smoke, Napoleon intentionally had his right flank thinly guarded in an attempt to lure the enemy into a trap.

As the Russians began to take the bait of his deceptively weakened right flank, Napoleon turned to one of his marshals and said, "One sharp blow and the war is over."[131] He then ordered an attack, concentrating the bulk of his forces, about 45,000 men, on seizing the commanding heights of the battlefield.[132]

Suddenly aware of the threat to his center on the heights, Russian general Mikhail Kutuzov—the commander-in-chief of the combined Russo-Austrian force—attempted a desperate counter-attack in support of the center, but it was too late. Bonaparte succeeded in taking Pratzen Heights and the now disoriented enemy began to falter. Within two hours the battle was over.

With French losses totaling some 8,300 killed or wounded and Russo-Austrian losses totaling some 16,000 killed or wounded, plus another 20,000 captured, it was a resounding victory for Napoleon.

The principle of concentration had once again played a decisive role in Napoleon's success. Indeed, in the words of one historian, "Napoleon's genius was in continually shifting his forces so that he had superior numbers at each point of attack."[133] Just as he had demonstrated in one decisive battle after another, his success at Austerlitz was likewise, "a classic application of the principle of mass."[134]

The proper application of this principle is equally effective in business, sports (e.g. Lombardi power sweep), politics (e.g. swing states), foreign policy (e.g. Cuban Missile Crisis), dating (e.g. Casanova), and more. In the marketplace, for example, "a strategic position can be a target market, a business, an industry, a product, or a geographical location."[135]

In Cleopatra's case, she identified the "decisive point" as the leading rulers in Rome, specifically Julius Caesar in 48 B.C., but even more pointedly Mark Antony in 41 B.C. Given that Antony was the most experienced member of the Second Triumvirate, the ruling body of the greatest empire in the world, it made perfect sense for Cleopatra to focus all of her efforts on winning Antony as a political ally for Egypt—just as she had done years earlier with Julius Caesar, right after he defeated Pompey in the final battle of Rome's Civil War.

Concentrating your forces at a strategic position can also help you to stand out in a crowded market. You can exploit this principle, for example, by focusing your advertising dollars in a particular geographic area, or with an advertising blitz over a narrow period of time, or simply by focusing your limited resources on your greatest opportunity.[136]

No matter what strategic position you choose, writes General Cohen, "unless you mass your resources against a clearly defined objective, so you are stronger than your competition at that point, you will have little chance of success."[137]

Concentrate Your Power, Alter Your Trajectory.

"Beware of dissipating your powers; strive constantly to concentrate them."[138]
—Johann Wolfgang Von Goethe

British Admiral Lord Nelson concentrated his ships at a decisive point in the enemy's line at the Battle of Trafalgar and, though significantly outnumbered, won a stinging victory over the French, a triumph which altered Napoleon's trajectory and changed the course of history as a result. In fact, more than a few historians argue that it was Britain's victory at Trafalgar and, therefore, her continued mastery of the seas ("the whale"), that served as a crucial counterweight to Napoleon's dominance on land ("the elephant"). By controlling the coasts of Europe, Britain continued to threaten Napoleon's hold on power while keeping him from further expanding his empire. As Napoleon himself later admitted in 1815, "If it had not been for you English, I should have been Emperor of the East. But wherever there is water to float a ship, we are sure to find you in our way."[139]

Britain's control of the coasts of Europe enabled the shielded and secure supply of General Arthur Wellesley, Duke of Wellington who eventually, defeated Napoleon at the Battle of Waterloo. In short, Lord Nelson's successful concentration of forces at Trafalgar was the beginning of the end for Napoleon. As French historian Jean Tulard put it, "after Trafalgar the emperor was beaten, though he did not yet know it."[140]

The Battle of Trafalgar is also remembered for the death of one of its greatest heroes. Long before this decisive naval victory, Lord Nelson had gained a heroic reputation for his triumph over the French at the Battle of the Nile in 1798 and his defeat of the Royal Danish Navy at Copenhagen in 1801. By the time of Trafalgar, Nelson was considered "a tactical genius" who was "adored by his men," and "unflinching in his pursuit of the enemy."[141] Alas, at Trafalgar, commanding the battle at close range dressed in full military regalia, standing boldly defiant on the quarterdeck of HMS *Victory*, Nelson was shot through the spine by a sniper from the crow's nest of the French ship *Redoutable*. He felt the blood seeping into his lungs as he fell to his hand and knees. Nelson knew immediately that he would soon be dead. One of the most feared and respected naval commanders of the day, Nelson had already lost both an arm and an eye in service to his country. As he approached his final hour on Earth, his mind was still focused on victory. He instructed his face to be covered to avoid demoralizing his men as he was carried below to the cockpit.

Nelson's decisive victory over Napoleon's fleet at Trafalgar combined with his own heroic end left an indelible imprint "on the psyche of the British people."[142] "With their god of war buried in the crypt of St. Paul's in London, the bittersweet victory at Trafalgar morphed into optimism and a renewed energy and commitment to British strength and the imperial project."[143] In the end, Lord Nelson's decisive victory at Trafalgar ensured that Britain retained its "mastery of the seas"[144] "for over a century,"[145] making Admiral Horatio Nelson an eternal hero of the British Empire.

#3. Identify and Amass Your Resources:
Giacomo Casanova's Great Prison Escape

"When you have resolved to fight a battle, collect your forces.
Dispense with nothing. A single battalion sometimes decides the day."[146]

—Napoleon Bonaparte

On July 26, 1755, at age 30, the Italian adventurer and libertine Giacomo Casanova was arrested and thrown into prison. Casanova's licentious lifestyle and reputation for an endless stream of sexual conquests and scandalous escapades had finally caught the attention and subsequent scrutiny of the Venetian Inquisition. Their investigation further revealed that Casanova owned several forbidden books and was allegedly practicing black magic and fake alchemy. The Inquisition convicted Casanova of witchcraft and imprisoned him in "The Leads" under the roof of the Doge's Palace in Venice, the most notorious prison in Europe, the dungeon in the attic from which no man had ever escaped.

Casanova, however, was not about to resign himself to a destiny behind bars, rotting in prison by the corrupt power and reason of the Venetian Inquisition. Letting others, no matter how powerful, determine his fate was inconsistent with his philosophy of life. "Man is a free agent," he wrote, "but he is not free if he does not believe it, for the more power he attributes to Destiny, the more he deprives himself of the power which God granted him when he gave him reason."[147]

In short, the power of reason that God had gifted to Casanova told him that a life behind bars would be more intolerable than death and, therefore, come what may, Casanova was determined to escape. "I have loved women even to madness," wrote the infamous rake, "but I have always loved liberty better."[148]

Fortunately, for Casanova, his ability to concentrate all of his mental and physical resources on a single point of focus was more than merely his strategy of seduction. It was his philosophy of success. Whatever he did, he gave himself to it fully. Now, imprisoned in The Leads, he would give himself fully to his escape.

For the next year, Casanova worked out his plan to leave his wretched residence under the roof—boiling hot in the summer, in the winter bone-chilling cold. After his first escape plan was foiled when he was abruptly moved to a new cell, he soon began to conspire with another prisoner, Father Balbi, a renegade priest in an adjacent cell. Using an iron rod, Casanova discovered in the prison attic while exercising, they carved holes in the ceiling and then pried their way through the heavy lead plates on the roof. From the rooftop they spied an empty room in another part of the castle. They then precariously lowered themselves down with bed sheets and broke in through the window. They chanced upon new clothes in one of the rooms and quickly changed out of their prison attire.

They then rested until morning.

As they drifted to sleep hidden away in a spare bedroom in the back of the palace, they contemplated how they would complete their escape the next day.

Concentrate Everything You Have.

In his definition of strategy, Carl von Clausewitz advised the strategist not just to identify the "*decisive point*," but "to concentrate *everything* on it." The strategist's goal is never to merely scrape by, eke out a victory, or needlessly leave certain critical factors to chance. The goal is to avoid dispersing your forces and, instead, amass every resource necessary to guarantee your success. Clausewitz was not advocating the use of wasteful, overwhelming force. He was emphasizing the vital importance of victory, the need to be prepared and equipped for the unexpected, particularly given "the fog of war" (e.g. volatility, ambiguity, uncertainty), and, therefore, the need to amass sufficient resources to ensure your *decisive* success.

Unfortunately, this is not how most businesses are run. Even the greatest, most resource rich organizations often fail to bring sufficient resources to bear, usually because they are trying to tackle too many different fronts at once. As Rumelt writes, "At the core, strategy is about focus, and most complex organizations don't focus their resources. Instead, they pursue multiple goals at once, not concentrating enough resources to achieve a breakthrough in any of them."[149]

In Cleopatra's case, she had many strengths and resources that she could bring to "concentrate" on her "decisive point," including her intelligence, education, courage, and cunning as well as her personal charisma, powers of persuasion, and an obvious talent for compelling presentations. As the ruler of Egypt, one of the richest nations in the world at the time, she also had the wealth and power of the state at her beck and call.

The strengths and resources Cleopatra had at her disposal did not simply enable her to effectively execute her strategy, they also helped determine it. When she sailed up the river to meet with Antony, virtually every one of her assets were on full display, effectively overwhelming Marcus Antonius, the great Roman general and politician.

But Cleopatra did not always find herself in control of such vast resources. Fortunately, vast resources are not always required. In fact, what's required depends on what you are up against. As Liddell Hart explains in his book, *Strategy*, the principle of concentration must be understood as the "concentration of strength against weakness."[150]

When her first brother-husband banished her from Egypt in 48 B.C., Cleopatra suddenly found herself powerless and virtually alone with very few resources at her disposal. Brimming with confidence, charisma, and deep self-belief, however, she "concentrated everything" she had on winning over Julius Caesar who was then "arguably the most powerful man in the known world."[151] In stark contrast to her dazzling entrance sailing up the river to meet Antony in Tarsus, however, when she met Caesar, Cleopatra found herself in a much less resourceful situation.

Nevertheless, she made the most of everything she had. Both clever and charming, Cleopatra knew how to stroke a man's ego and, ever the diligent student, she well understood her target audience, her "decisive point"—in this case, Julius Caesar. "Cleopatra studied this complex and sophisticated man as meticulously as Hannibal researched his Roman opponents. She knew all about his stunning military success in Gaul, his womanizing, his tastes, and his vanity."[152] She knew about his love of spectacle and how he staged the gladiatorial games in Rome.

She soon had herself smuggled into the city at night, rolled up in a fine Egyptian rug.[153] Caesar and his generals were "dazzled at the sight" of this royal seductress "appearing before them suddenly as if in a dream."[154] "They were astounded at her daring and theatricality."[155]

Her sudden, mysterious and captivating entrance itself appealed to Caesar's love of spectacle, as she suspected it would.[156] Furthermore, she was aware of his interest in Egyptian history,[157] and the great leaders and heroes of history—

particularly, she learned, how "Caesar was obsessed with comparisons to Alexander the Great. Once, when Caesar had seen a statue of Alexander, he wailed that he had done so little at an age when this great Macedonian had already conquered half the world."[158]

And, so, Cleopatra shrewdly, subtly highlighted her distinguished, royal ancestry and connection to Alexander the Great—Cleopatra descended from a long line of Macedonian-Greek pharaohs, known as the Ptolemaic Dynasty, which began after Alexander seized Egypt from the Persians.[159]

But Cleopatra also understood the value of powerful allies, and how a special bond with Egypt would benefit Caesar as well. In short, as historian Frances White put it, "Caesar needed Egypt as much as Egypt needed Rome and she would use that fact to her advantage."[160] Despite the stark lack of resources at her immediate disposal, Cleopatra "concentrated everything" she could bring to bear on her "decisive point" and it worked.[161] Julius Caesar was enthralled with the bright, colorful, and charismatic Egyptian Queen and she was soon back on the Egyptian throne.

Resources are All Around, Rethink What's Possible, Make Use of Whatever You Can.

In the case of Casanova's escape, given that he was in prison, it would be natural to assume that he had no useful resources at all, particularly with respect to *mounting a prison escape*. After all, "a dungeon in Venice from which no one had previously escaped,"[162] is not the sort of place you'd expect to spy Harry Houdini's tools and tricks of the trade, particularly given that Casanova "had no prior experience either with prisons, or the means of escaping from them."[163]

But when combined with his own cunning, courage, and determination, and when brought to bear 'against the weaknesses' of an old building and poorly trained prison guards, the exceedingly limited resources he had at his disposal, along with those he was able to access through craftiness and chance, proved to be sufficient to attempt an escape. Naturally, the material and human resources Casanova would have relied on would have been very different if he had been "out of prison...but," as he said himself, "up there I had to make use of everything."[164]

"Everything" started out with the various uncommon components he needed to work on his plan in the dark. With Lucca oil from his salad, cotton wicks from his quilt, a piece of steel from his belt, punk from his coat, and some flint and matches, which he gained from the jailer by pretending to have a toothache and a rash, he fashioned his own lamp. This lamp allowed him to read at night, which he says helped him to keep his sanity, but which also helped to avoid raising the suspicions of the guard. The real purpose of the lamp was to be able to carve his way out of his cell at *night* and, therefore, without the danger of being discovered by the guard. Upon successfully fashioning the lamp, Casanova recorded his glee, "For me, there were no more nights. Farewell salad! I was very fond of it, but I did not regret it; I thought that oil was created only to give us light."[165]

With the exception of his own intelligence and the efforts of the people who aided him (either knowingly or through Casanova's clever manipulation[166]), his most important resource was undoubtedly the tool he happened upon by chance. Casanova was constantly on the lookout for even the most seemingly insignificant resource he might discover to aid in his single-minded plan to escape. As he explains in *History of My Life*, he was allowed "the privilege of walking in the garret for half an hour every day"[167] for exercise and which, he adds, "I found...very good for my health and for my plan of escaping."[168] Once there, he continues, "I examined everything in it. One of the big chests was filled with fine paper, pieces of cardboard, untrimmed goose quills, and balls of string; the other was nailed shut. A piece of black polished marble an inch thick, six inches long, and three wide caught my eye; I took it with no particular purpose and put it under my shirts in my cell."[169] It was also in the loft that he discovered a "perfectly straight bolt as thick as my thumb and a foot and a half long,"[170] which proved to be the key instrument of his escape. Casanova soon discovered that he could use the marble stone as a means of sharpening the bolt.

As he explains, "as soon as I was alone I found that the latter made a perfect whetstone, for, after rubbing the end of the bolt against the marble for a long time I saw that it showed a flat edge."[171] Despite the fact that he had nothing "with which to wet and soften the iron on which I wanted to put a point...but my saliva," he writes, "inspired by the hope of possessing a tool which must be strictly forbidden up there," he nevertheless, "toiled for two weeks" until at last, after suffering what he called "torture of a kind...even the Sicilian tyrants did not invent," he had a long iron rod with an end forged into a sharp "perfect point."[172] As he put it, "the result was an octagonal stiletto as well proportioned as one could have expected from a good cutler."[173] "Thus," by making maximum use of his exceedingly limited resources, he writes, "did God provide me with what I needed for an escape which was to be a wonder if not a miracle."[174]

Nonetheless, it was not all smooth sailing from here. In fact, at one point, after using his iron stiletto to carve through three layers of wood flooring, Casanova found his efforts blocked by a layer of marble, against which his iron rod had no effect. Then, suddenly, Casanova writes, "I remembered Hannibal, who, according to Livy, had opened a passage through the Alps by chopping away the rock which he had softened through the action of vinegar—a thing I had considered incredible, not so much because of the power of the acid but because of the prodigious quantity of vinegar he must have had."[175] Fortunately, Casanova too had plenty of vinegar and, he writes, "I poured into my excavation a bottle of strong vinegar...and the next morning, whether as the result of the vinegar or of greater patience, I saw that I should succeed."[176]

It might seem strange that Casanova would call to mind an ancient Carthaginian military general while trapped in an 18th century Venetian prison, but, as one of history's greatest strategists, Hannibal's example undoubtedly had more than a few insights to offer a wide range of difficult challenges Casanova might of faced. When Hannibal found that his army was trapped in the river valley of Campania, for example, he obviously lacked the vast resources military leaders often rely on today. Rather than wasting time worrying about what he didn't have, he made the best possible use of what was available. Fortunately, it was dry so there was plenty of brush and dry sticks. He had also procured an abundance of cattle from nearby lands. And with just these two simple, common resources, Hannibal created an escape plan that echoes throughout history to this day.

Ultimately, after being moved to another cell, Casanova was forced to use his sharp iron rod to carve his way through the roof instead. Finally, on November 1, 1756, the morning after he and Father Balbi broke out of their cell and spent the night sleeping in a spare bedroom, the two renegades made their spectacular daybreak escape. The confident and charismatic Casanova convinced the outer guard that they had been inadvertently locked inside following an official function in the Doge's Palace the night before. The pair of prisoners then descended the grand staircase and simply walked out of the front door of the harshest, most difficult-to-escape prison in all of Europe.

Now a fugitive, certain to be hunted by the Venetian Inquisition, Casanova immediately left Venice and headed for Paris where news of his escape made him an instant celebrity. Overnight, he became the delight of the city of lights, the toast of Paris, the high society man who had escaped the inescapable prison. Casanova's getaway quickly became known as "the most famous escape in history," everywhere he was suddenly regarded as a hero.

Casanova had "concentrated on the single goal of escape to an incredible degree. He massed every limited resource he had at his disposal toward that single objective,"[177] and, although he had never before been imprisoned, never mind escaping from one, he had, against incredible odds, succeeded in setting himself free. Recall how Casanova later explained his success, "when a man gets into his head to do something, and when he exclusively occupies himself in that design, he must succeed, whatever the difficulties."[178]

Casanova relished his newfound fame and took such pleasure in sharing the story of his magnificent escape that he soon wrote a full account of the daring escapade which became an 18th century bestseller. "There is no such thing as destiny," Casanova wrote. "We ourselves shape our lives."[179]

#4. Move Rapidly When the Timing is Right or the Situation is Ripe: The Whites Versus the Reds in the Russian Civil War.

"Now" or "as soon as possible" is often the answer to the question of when to make your move.[180] Most targets in life are in constant motion. The most critical point of attack or target of action in one moment is unlikely to be the most critical point in the next.

As much as leaders often feel rightly compelled to rush into action, however, a general sense of urgency must yield to the fact that, in strategy, as in life, timing can be everything. Success, therefore, is often about learning and preparing and staying vigilant, but *waiting* until the timing is right or circumstances are ripe.

When Hannibal Barca sought to escape from the river valley of Campania, in which the Roman general Fabius Maximus had the Carthaginians effectively pinned, he did not wait for his food or supplies to run low before attempting an escape. But he did wait long enough for Fabius and his men to begin to relax. He did not wait merely until it was dark to sneak past the soldiers guarding the pass. He waited until it was a moonless night. He did not wait merely until the Romans had likely fallen asleep. He waited until three in the morning, the time when he knew the Roman soldiers would likely be in their deepest sleep.

In Cleopatra's case, she had good reasons for waiting to respond to Antony's summons. It can take time to amass your forces and coordinate your resources. She also calculated that a certain level of resistance (i.e. delay) was key to building anticipation, triggering (and, later, releasing) frustration, and, therefore, ultimately, heightening the impact of her theatrical presentation. After all, as she well understood, a critical part of concentrating your forces is overwhelming your target.

Nevertheless, there were also risks in delay. The emotional Antony might easily have lost patience and acted rashly against Cleopatra. There was also the possibility that her sister Arsinoe would beat her to the punch. In fact, according to historian Adrian Goldsworthy, Antony undoubtedly met with Arsinoe while he was nearby in Ephesus.[181] Fortunately, for Cleopatra, Arsinoe was no strategist and she failed to emerge as a significant threat.

In the case of Napoleon, he was known for attacking in unusual locations, places that were off the beaten path. But he was also known for the lightning speed of his attacks. In essence, Bonaparte used speed to ensure that his enemy would not have time to amass their own defenses at his point of attack.

Russia remains a communist dictatorship today, in part, because of a failure of the Whites, during the Russian Civil War, to coordinate and concentrate their forces in their march on Moscow to defeat the Reds (the Bolsheviks, led by Marxist revolutionary Leon Trotsky). "There were times when the Bolsheviks themselves thought that they'd lost the civil war, and were almost preparing to abandon Moscow. In early 1919, for example," British military historian Antony Beevor explains, "there was a sudden advance by the White General Kolchak's troops all the way to the Volga. The trouble was that the great advance of General Denikin from the south did not coincide with that—and by the time Denikin's march on Moscow started, Kolchak's advance was in full retreat."[182]

By October, the Russian Civil War had so completely turned around that the European allies were in shock. Winston Churchill, who was then Secretary of State for War and Air, was in a state of disbelief. In a message to a British intelligence officer, Churchill asked incredulously, "I can't believe this. The Reds were in full retreat, and now suddenly they seem to be beating the Whites on every front. What's happened?"[183]

In effect, rather than facing a concentrated enemy force, the Reds, under unified command, were able to amass their own forces, first in the south to defeat Denikin, and then in the east to defeat Kolchak. The Reds won, in other words, Beevor explains, "purely because the Bolsheviks had reinforced that eastern front at a crucial moment, [and] then—with the advantage of their internal lines—[had] been able to bring troops back very rapidly to transform the whole situation."[184] If the White generals, Kolchak and Denikin, had better coordinated their efforts to attack the Red Army, *at the same time*, Russia might very well have a far more open and democratic government today.[185]

The most effective concentration of your forces will almost invariably change over time depending on various internal and external factors, including the readiness of your opponent. President Abraham Lincoln faced a similar dilemma during the Civil War. The Union army had the advantage in numbers, but the Confederate army had the advantage of occupying a central position. In other words, the Confederate army could easily shift their mass of forces anywhere within their central position (known as "interior lines") in order to meet an external threat. The Union army, in contrast, would have to cover a much greater distance to go around the enemy's central position (known as "exterior lines") in order to meet an attack. As a result, Lincoln's two main generals operating in the western theaters, Henry W. Halleck and Don C. Buell, who were separated by the Cumberland River, continued to hesitate to attack. Lincoln pressed them to join together in a coordinated attack, but they both complained that they were not ready. Halleck wrote to Lincoln, "To operate on exterior lines against an enemy occupying a central position will fail. It is condemned by every military authority I have ever read."[186]

Lincoln could see that the solution was a matter of timing and he did his utmost to persuade his generals of this fact. The strategy he explained in a letter to both Halleck and Buell was thus, "we have the greater numbers, and the enemy has the greater facility of concentrating forces upon points of collision; that we must fail, unless we can find some way to making our advantage an over-match for his; and that this can be only done by menacing him with superior forces at different points, at the *same time*..."[187(e.a.)] In this way, Lincoln further explained, "we can safely attack, one, or both, if he makes no change; and if he weakens one to strengthen the other, forbear to attack the strengthened one, but seize and hold the weakened one, gaining so much."[188] In essence, as Lincoln clearly understood, timing could overcome the advantage of central position. Princeton historian James McPherson explains, "Lincoln clearly expressed here what military theorists define as 'concentration in time' to counter the Confederacy's advantage of interior lines that enabled Southern forces to concentrate in space. The geography of the war required the North to operate generally on exterior lines while the Confederacy could use interior lines to shift troops to the point of danger. By advancing on two or more fronts *simultaneously*, Union forces could neutralize this advantage, as Lincoln understood but Halleck and Buell seemed unable to grasp."[189(e.a.)] Fortunately, when General Ulysses S. Grant was given the reins, President Lincoln at last had a commander in place who both immediately grasped the wisdom of this strategy and who was far less hesitant to attack.[190]

In summary, it is not enough to amass and focus your resources, the speed and timing of your action can make the decisive difference between victory and defeat. When Henri Becquerel discovered radioactivity in Paris on March 1, 1896, he presented his discovery to the French Academy of Sciences the very next day. Unknown to Becquerel, Silvanus P. Thompson was working independently in London at the same time as Becquerel, on the same thing. Thompson observed the same "strange action of uranium rays and named the phenomenon 'hyper-phosphorescence.'"[191] If Becquerel had not acted so swiftly, Silvanus Thompson, "a dangerous competitor in the race that led to the discovery of radioactivity," would have received the credit and the Nobel Prize that went with it.[192]

In Casanova's case, timing was a critical part of his escape. From the moment he had first been thrown into the Doge's prison, just as he had been gathering resources, he had begun to gather intelligence. Nearly a year before he escaped, he had gathered a bit of intelligence about Lorenzo, the main prison guard. "The State Inquisitors and even the Secretary went every year to spend the first three days of November in some village on the mainland. During these three days when his masters were on vacation Lorenzo got drunk in the evening, slept until the Terza, and did not appear under the Leads until very late."[193] "Prudence," therefore, Casanova concluded in his book, "demanded that, if l was to escape, I must choose one of these three nights, in order to be certain that my flight would not be discovered until fairly late in the morning."[194] As Casanova's plans came together that fall, he became increasingly aware of the calendar and the clock. "It was the 25th of October," he wrote, "and the days were nearing when I must either carry out my project or abandon it forever."[195] Make your necessary preparations and plans,

Napoleon Bonaparte once said, "take time to deliberate, but when the time for action comes, stop thinking and go in."[196]

In his book on strategy, the influential 20th century strategist Captain Liddell Hart advised his readers, "do not throw your weight into a stroke whilst your opponent is on guard—whilst he is well placed to parry or evade It. The experience of history shows that, save against a much inferior opponent, no effective stroke is possible until his power of resistance or evasion is paralyzed."[197] In regard to Casanova's escape, it seems ludicrous to point out that he should not attempt to escape while the prison guards were in the midst of their rounds (i.e. "whilst your opponent is on guard"). And, yet, do we not see people and organization's carrying out some version of this approach time after time, often with appalling results? In war, business, politics, sports, whether driven by pride or ignorance, we go head to head with our rivals, putting our best against their best with significant risks and costs to both sides.

Best remembered for the strategy of the indirect approach, Liddell Hart was formulating his key ideas shortly after World War I, a "war of trenches" and one of the deadliest wars in history. Hart argued that strategists should never waste resources engaging directly with an entrenched enemy, concentrating their forces at the same time and place.[198] "His theory was, of course, influenced by the ghastly trench warfare of World War I and its direct assaults across open ground. Hart insisted that instead of grinding our strength against enemy strength we should seek interesting alternative routes to achieve our objectives. We should shroud our moves and attentions in mystery and we should keep our competitors off balance and ignorant of our aims."[199]

To be an effective strategist, you too must think carefully about the role timing plays—including the clock and the calendar, but also seasons, stages, and speed—in amassing your resources, and factor timing into your execution plans. "In strategy," Hart wrote, "the longest way around is often the shortest way home."

#5. Persist to Surpass the Threshold Effect:
Marie Curie's Breakthrough Concentration of Power

"Life is not easy for any of us. But what of that?
We must have perseverance and above all confidence in ourselves.
We must believe that we are gifted for something, and that this thing,
at whatever cost, must be attained."[200]

—Marie Curie

On June 6, 1898, Marie Curie made a surprising discovery. Always a meticulous recorder of even the most banal observations, on this day her and her husband Pierre Curie's "laboratory notebook shows a sudden outburst of excitement that even Marie's self-control could not contain."[201] After measuring a sample of what she suspected contained a new, undiscovered element, she recorded the result at the bottom of the page, both underlined and in bold letters for emphasis: "**150 times more active than uranium!**"[202]

Further efforts to isolate the element produced even more radioactive results.[203] It was an astonishing discovery, one with revolutionary implications.

"By June 27th Marie was precipitating substances about 300 times more active, and recording the triumph in her notebook in even bolder strokes. There was now no doubt. They had discovered a new element."[204] In July 1898, Marie and Pierre Curie quickly prepared a paper for publication, in which they wrote, "If the existence of this new metal is confirmed, we propose to call it *polonium...*"[205] This was also the paper in which they coined the term *radioactive*.

By December, they had discovered yet another element. Five days later, on December 26, 1898, they published their latest discovery with the French Academy of Sciences. If this new element could also be confirmed, they proposed to name it *radium*. It was a heady time for the Curies to be sure.

The problem was that the existence of these new metals was *not* confirmed and, especially given the potentially profound implications of what their reported discoveries suggested, this was not something scientists would simply accept at face value. After all, the special properties that they were attributing to these two new elements "upset fundamental theories in which scientists had believed for centuries."[206]

"How was one to explain the spontaneous radiation of the radioactive bodies? The discovery upset a world of acquired knowledge and contradicted the most firmly established ideas on the composition of matter."[207] For one to fundamentally alter the scientific understanding of the very nature of reality and the assumption about the indivisibility of the atom (from the Greek *atomos*, meaning "indivisible"), irrefutable proof would be required.

"The attitude of the chemist was even more downright," explains Ève Curie, the younger daughter of Marie and Pierre.[208] "By definition, a chemist only believes in the existence of a new substance when he has seen the substance, touched it, weighed and examined it, confronted it with acids, bottled it, and when he has determined its 'atomic weight.'"[209]

But at this point, no one had ever seen either one of these purported "new metals," never mind knowing their atomic weights. Not surprisingly, therefore, true to the principles of their field, the chemists were unwavering, 'No atomic weights, no new elements. Let us see some of this so-called polonium or radium and then we will believe you.[210]

Of course, Marie and Pierre were already completely concentrated on doing just that. In fact, it was not long before, in light of the astonishing development of Marie's results, that Pierre had abandoned "his study of crystals...in order to join his efforts to hers in the search for the new substance."[211] "The available force was now doubled. Two brains, four hands, now sought the unknown element in the damp little workroom in the Rue Lhomond."[212]

What the Curies did not know, however, was the magnitude of the task before them. The startlingly high radioactive measurements they had thus far obtained were actually being emitted from "imperceptible traces" of polonium and radium hidden in the ore and minerals with which they were working (i.e. pitchblende—an expensive uranium-rich mineral and ore discovered in the mines of Bohemia).[213] While they initially began working in *grams* of pitchblende and thinking in terms of weeks, they would eventually be working in *tons* of pitchblende, carrying out hard physical labor in an increasingly radioactive environment for more than four *years*.[214]

The goal was to isolate these new metals, obtaining the purest form of radium and polonium,[215] but to do that would require a hillside of pitchblende. According to Ève Curie, as she writes in her biography, *Madame Curie*, the Curies would have been shocked and distressed "if they had known that the radioactive element they were hunting down did not count for more than a millionth part of pitchblende ore."[216]

What's more, to methodically, meticulously sift through that hillside of pitchblende "no matter how or where they could find it, would cost money, and it would require space...."[217] In the words of Albert Einstein, "science is a wonderful thing if one does not have to earn one's living at it."[218] Unfortunately, in her case, "money, or the lack of it, provided major conflicts throughout Marie's life."[219]

Do the Work.

Nevertheless, largely unaware of the towering task ahead, energized by the thrill of their discoveries, and buoyed by the collaborative efforts of other scientists and the contributions of colleagues, the Curies located an old shed with a leaky roof, procured a "a mountain of black rubble strewn with pine needles—from the Bohemian mines," and "began trying to extract measurable amounts of their new elements."[220] This was the beginning of the heroic period of their lives "that has become legendary."[221]

Marie Curie began her journey into the unknown with "intense powers of concentration."[222] To be sure, it was her sustained power of concentration that got her to this point in the first place. She was only able to realize that she might be on the trail of discovering a new element because "in her preceding experiments, Marie had already examined *all known chemical elements*."[223] In other words, it was only because of the unique experience she had endured that she knew immediately that the radioactivity she was detecting in the pitchblende, which led to her discovery of polonium, was at a level never before seen.

Now, in their effort to isolate these two new elements, she would reveal her ability to maintain her "intense powers of concentration" over an extended period of time. What's more, writes biographer Robert Reid in his book, *Marie*

Curie, "the way in which she approached this next stage of her career, with absolute refusal to tolerate any thought of deflection, is all the more remarkable when it is remembered that she launched into it physically debilitated after a wretched year of pregnancy and its after effects."[224] Marie herself later wrote, "I was taught that the way of progress was neither swift nor easy."[225]

The work in "this miserable old shed" was hard labor indeed, Marie wrote.[226] It was here where the painstaking and protracted work of separation, measurement, and analysis was conducted. "Marie carried out the chemical separations, Pierre undertook the measurements after each successive step. Physically it was heavy work for Marie. She processed 20 kilos [44 pounds] of raw material at a time. First of all she had to clear away pine needles and any perceptible debris, then she had to undertake the work of separation."[227]

"Sometimes," Marie wrote, "I had to spend a whole day stirring a boiling mass with a heavy iron rod nearly as large as myself. I would be broken with fatigue at day's end."[228] But the pioneering couple was nevertheless committed, Marie writes, explaining how she and Pierre "passed the best and happiest years of our life, devoting our entire days to our work."[229]

The Curies were united in what was, Marie later wrote, "our desire to concentrate our entire effort on the work in which we were engaged."[230] To be sure, despite struggling financially, they refused some of the most lucrative offers for work including, in Pierre's case, the Chair of Physics at the University of Geneva, because, she wrote, "he feared the interruption of our investigations which such a change must involve."[231]

Nail the Process, Then Persist.

Interest from other scientists followed the initial reports of their discoveries, but the real game changer came only after they had irrefutable proof. And this proof came only after nearly four years[232] of hard labor working with four hundred tons of rinsing waters and forty tons of chemicals.[233] Along the way they learned that radium glowed in the dark and, miraculously, emitted its own heat and light, apparently forever.[234]

Finally, on March 28, 1902, they managed to isolate one-tenth of a gram of radium into a chemical body sufficiently pure to determine its atomic weight.[235]

With this, Marie wrote, "the existence and character of radium were definitely established."[236] "The demonstration that cost so much effort" was also, she said, "the basis of the new science of radioactivity."[237]

The following year, 1903, in light of the discovery of new radioactive elements, Marie and Pierre Curie, together with Henri Becquerel, were awarded the Nobel prize. This was the transforming event in their quest. After crossing this threshold, everything began to change. This was also the "event," Marie said, which "greatly increased the publicity of our work."[238]

"The award of the Nobel prize was a great honor. It is also known that the material means provided by this prize was much greater than is usual in prizes for science. This," Marie wrote, "was a great help in the continuation of our researches."[239]

Chemists came to see the Curie's discovery and isolation of radium as "the greatest event in chemistry since the discovery of oxygen."[240] "For the first time in history," the recognition that "an element could be transmuted into another element, revolutionized chemistry and signified a new epoch."[241] Radium, thereby, became, as Reid put it, "the jewel in Marie Curie's crown."[242]

Surpass the Threshold, Catapult Your Success.

The principle of concentration requires persevering until you obtain your objective. While you may never have to persist through years of hardship as Marie and Pierre Curie did, there is virtually nothing to be gained from a mere flash of concentration. In fact, it is often the case that you will fail to see any of the fruits of your efforts until and unless you can surpass a certain critical threshold or tipping point,[243] usually within a certain period of time.

In the sciences this is known as a *threshold effect*. "A 'threshold effect' exists when there is a critical level of effort necessary to affect the system. Levels of effort below this threshold have little payoff," if any at all.[244] In the case of the Curies, for example, when they published their findings with the French Academy of Sciences on December 26, 1898, they certainly had compelling evidence that they had discovered two new elements, but they did not yet have satisfactory proof. Until they had a sufficiently pure form of a substance that could be touched, weighed, examined, bottled, and so on, until they surpassed that all-important threshold of an atomic weight, the payoff would be equally unsatisfactory.

"When there are threshold effects," Rumelt writes in *Good Strategy, Bad Strategy*, "it is prudent to limit objectives to those that can be affected by the resources at the strategist's disposal."[245] In essence, in the face of a demanding threshold, concentrating your forces becomes more important than ever. This is undoubtedly part of why the Curies turned down lucrative offers for work despite struggling financially. Given their understanding and assumptions at the time (e.g. that they needed several weeks, not 4 years), they were understandably concerned that they would spread themselves too thin; the limited resources they had might have proved insufficient to reach that threshold, the threshold that changed everything, including their financial situation, but also our understanding of reality itself.

The concept of threshold effects helps to explain why just a small amount of effort for a limited time may lead to no rewards at all. This holds true in many different areas—from advertising and networking, to dieting, dating, and diplomacy. After some sufficient amount of effort, however, or after a certain period of time, then the rewards start to roll in, often to a surprising degree. In business, for example, the "Marketing Rule of 7" suggests that consumers typically have to see an advertisement seven times before it will start to have an effect on sales.[246] Once that magic number or threshold is reached, a product can quickly go from low or no sales to a sellout success.

"Due to similar forces, business strategists will often prefer to dominate a small market segment over having an equal number of customers who represent only a sliver of a larger market. Politicians will often prefer a plan that delivers a clear benefit to a recognizable group over one that provides larger benefits spread more thinly across the population."[247]

Part of the power of threshold effects is rooted in human psychology and the limits of human awareness and attention. People tend to ignore or overlook weak signals or one-offs.

In contrast, people instinctively give their attention to stronger signals, and signals that repeat. People tend to notice *recurring* themes and patterns. They tend to believe past success will lead to future success. They place more faith in *frequency*, and more trust in *consistency*.[248] People are also more likely to *believe* what is repeated—even, unfortunately, if what is repeated is an outright lie. Nevertheless, this helps to explain why concentration and persistence are key factors in your success.

Momentum, another factor that frequently helps facilitate success, further highlights the importance of concentration. Whether you are operating within a market niche, a limited geographic area, or a narrow customer base, the more you amass your resources on that precise strategic point, the faster you are likely to build and benefit from momentum. But even with sufficient concentration, momentum often takes time and effort to build and, therefore, also requires perseverance to reach that all-important threshold or tipping point.[249] This also helps to explain why *small wins* are so important. They help generate momentum and, if continued over time, the perception that you are a rock star and your team or organization is a winner.

Absorb the Blows, Continue the Work.

Alas, life's struggles were not over. Given the incessant interruptions and urgent requests, celebrity proved to be a significant, time-consuming challenge, particularly for Marie, who loved her freedom, and peace and quiet.

Then, on April 19, 1906, tragedy struck when Pierre Curie fell in front of a horse-drawn wagon while crossing a busy street in the rain in Paris. He died instantly.

Shocked by the sudden death of her husband and best friend, Marie was completely broken. In time, still only 38 and with two young daughters to care for, Marie turned to "the toughness and perseverance that were fundamental aspects of her character."[250]

Still feeling "crushed by the blow" of losing the man she said was "my closest companion and best friend," she nevertheless said that she, "could not forget what my husband used sometimes to say, that, even deprived of him, I ought to continue my work."[251]

The University of Paris (the Sorbonne) offered Pierre's position as the chair of the physics department to Marie, which she accepted, thus becoming the first woman appointed as a professor at the Sorbonne.

She went on to win the Nobel Prize in chemistry in 1911. After becoming, in 1903, the first *woman* to win a Nobel prize, she was now the first *person* to win a Noble prize in two different scientific fields.

"Marie Curie's relentless resolve and insatiable curiosity made her an icon in the world of modern science. Indefatigable, despite a career of physically demanding and ultimately fatal work, she discovered polonium and radium, championed the use of radiation in medicine and fundamentally changed our understanding of radioactivity."[252] "A few of her books and papers are still so radioactive that they are stored in lead boxes."[253] In the words of the Nobel Foundation, "It seems fitting that Curie left a scientific legacy that is literally untouchable."[254]

Follow All the Way Through

When Cleopatra set out to win over the new Roman Triumvir, she concentrated so much effort into her luxurious and enchanting spectacle sailing up the river in Tarsus, "adorned like a painting of Aphrodite,"[255] and "display[ing] the abundance of her realm,"[256] that she completely overwhelmed Mark Antony in that first encounter. But she didn't stop there. She generated the momentum she needed with her concentrated blitz, but she still needed to close the sale.

The brilliantly illuminated banquet that followed in the evening of her arrival was also carefully crafted to captivate Cleopatra's target and her wealth, charisma, and power were on full display.[257] But she didn't stop there either. Cleopatra continued to focus all of her energy, attention, and resources on the Roman Triumvir, drawing him back to Alexandria where she had complete control over whatever resources she might need. In no time, following all the way through, Cleopatra had Mark Antony completely under her spell. If there was threshold to winning him over, she had clearly surpassed it. "Within a year she would bear him twins, a son and a daughter."[258]

Amass Your Resources, Focus Your Forces

The Queen of Egypt, Cleopatra Philopator, understood intuitively the power of concentration. She knew her strengths and weaknesses. She knew what she needed to maintain her hold on power. She zeroed in on the target and task at hand. And she succeeded on an epic scale as a result. Indeed, living in an age dominated by men, Cleopatra emerged as a shrewd strategist and a cunning leader who, for 21 years, in the face of plague, famine, and the ever-present possibility of foreign intervention or domestic revolt, ruled one of the greatest kingdoms in the world and, at the peak of her power, nearly the whole of the eastern Mediterranean coast.[259] "For a fleeting moment she held the fate of the Western world in her hands."[260] And she did all this despite nearly 3,000 years of entrenched cultural norms and traditions opposed to female rule. "Her tenure alone speaks to her guile," Stacy Schiff writes in *Smithsonian*. "She knew she could be removed at any time by Rome, deposed by her subjects, undermined by her advisers—or stabbed, poisoned and dismembered by her own family."[261] In a reign remembered for its relative peace and prosperity, Cleopatra "...sustained a vast, rich, densely populated empire in its troubled twilight"[262] and stands today as one the most famous Egyptian rulers of all.

As with Cleopatra, the great men and women of history, in virtually every realm of human affairs, are those who learned to concentrate their powers on the most critical points.[263] "In warfare, the ability to mass your forces at the right time and place is a force multiplier that enables smaller forces to conquer a larger enemy."[264] In an unmistakably similar way, an average person with standard capability and typical opportunities can achieve exceptional results by "concentrating on doing one thing, the most important thing," and doing it exceptionally well.[265]

"Success demands singleness of purpose," wrote Vince Lombardi, widely considered the greatest coach in football history.[266] "It is those who concentrate on but one thing at a time who advance in this world."[267] "There are many qualities that are helpful in achieving success," Brian Tracy writes in *Victory: Applying the Proven Principles of Military Strategy*, "but the qualities of focus and concentration are indispensable. With the ability to mass your powers, all things are possible. You become unstoppable and your ultimate victory is virtually guaranteed."[268]

CATAPULT AND SHIELD YOUR POWER THROUGH MUTUALLY ASSURED SUCCESS: THE ROTHSCHILDS VERSUS THE REPUBLIC OF PIRATES

"No matter how brilliant your mind or strategy,
if you're playing a solo game, you'll always lose out to a team."[1]
—Reid Hoffman, Founder of LinkedIn

Unearth Unparalleled Power in Unified, Unbreakable Bonds: The Rothschilds and the Greatest Banking Empire on Earth

When Mayer Amschel Rothschild, the founder of the Rothschild banking dynasty, was on his deathbed in 1812, he gathered his five sons around him one last time. Rothschild wanted not just to bid them farewell, but to impart his one last, ultimate piece of wisdom.

Rothschild desperately wanted his sons to succeed in carrying on his legacy and he used his final moments to dramatize the importance of his last words, this final, definitive lesson. Less than an hour before he died, he shared a story with them, a story attributed to the ancient Greek historian Plutarch, in a book titled *Sayings of Kings and Commanders.*[2]

In the 2nd century B.C., Rothschild began, Scilurus was the king of Scythia. Scilurus was also both the son of a king, and the father of a king. According to legend, when Skilurus was on his own deathbed, he gathered his 80 sons around him. To each son, Skilurus offered a bundle of arrows which were bound tightly together. He then instructed his sons to try and break their bundle of arrows. Many of his sons tried in earnest to break their bundle, imagining they would gain favor with their father if they proved stronger than the other brothers. But no one could do it. Securely bound together, the bundle was simply unbreakable. An old, weak, and dying man, Scilurus then pulled an arrow out of each bundle and easily broke each single arrow with his own hands.[3]

Stretching as far back as the ancient Greek storyteller Aesop, with his fable "The Father and His Quarreling Sons," various versions of this story have been told throughout history. According to the 16th century German poet Hieronymus Osius, the lesson is that in unity there is great power, but "a quarrelsome life deprives people of their strength."[4] In his own telling, Aesop put it this way, "My sons, if you are of one mind, and unite to assist each other, you will be as this bundle of sticks, uninjured by all the attempts of your enemies; but if you are divided among yourselves, you will be broken as easily as these sticks."[5]

Mayer Rothschild, now mere minutes away from his own death, commanded his five sons to do likewise, urgently advising them that their greatest power was in being *unified*. Rothschild then turned to his oldest son. "Amschel," he said, "keep your brothers together and you will become the richest people in Germany."[6]

Start Where You Are, Concentrate on Your One Thing.

Already well on their way to remarkable wealth, the Rothschilds (from German "Roth Schild," literally "Red Shield") had not always been rich. In fact, the story of Mayer Rothschild is a rags to riches story, from a Jewish ghetto in Frankfurt to financing the defeat of Napoleon Bonaparte.

It wasn't just poverty, however, or the dark, grossly crowded ghetto that Goethe once described as a 'hellish slum' that the Rothschilds had to overcome. Medieval Europe was also rabidly anti-Semitic. As Jews growing up in late 18th century Frankfurt, the Rothschilds were part of a culture and community which had been facing fierce persecution in Germany since the Early Medieval Period. Lacking freedom of movement, special permission was required just to travel beyond their cities bounds. What's more, most rulers forbid Jews from owning property.[7]

So, how on Earth could Rothschild possibly break out to become "the world's banker?"[8]

First, the prohibition on property led generations of Jewish men to do business in the financial sector, where assets were liquid. And here was the silver lining. Christians, in Medieval Europe, were forbidden from lending money with interest. This left the highly profitable business of money lending almost entirely in the hands of the Jews. As they gained experience as money lenders, and expanded to the world of finance more generally, many Jews became increasingly recognized for their valuable expertise in all manner of financial matters. Before long, it became common practice for the nobility to outsource their finances to Jews in order to circumvent the laws against Christians charging interest.

As with many Jewish families at the time, the Rothschild's were deeply involved in finance. Even Rothschild's father specialized in exchanging currencies.

Mayer Rothschild developed a specialty in collectible coins. Beginning in the early 1760s, Rothschild's increasingly extensive collection of coins began attracting attention. In time, some of the wealthiest aristocrats in Europe began to have dealings with Rothschild, including William I, the crown prince (i.e. heir apparent) of Hesse, a central state in Germany. William actually began to rely on Rothschild for his finances. When William's father died in 1785, William became the Landgrave of Hesse-Kassel (which is akin to a duke, essentially a territorial ruler), *and* he inherited what then was one of the largest fortunes in Europe.

"A man who seeks power needs friends with power."[9]
—Genghis Khan

Given their ongoing, decade-long relationship, William then turned to the trusty Rothschild to manage his massive estate, making Rothschild his *Hofjude* (i.e. German for "Court Jew"). The income provided Rothschild with a comfortable living, though it was far from enough to build a fortune.

Create Your Five Cities Strategy.

But Rothschild was clever and ambitious and boldly resourceful. To begin with, he was providing banking services to a number of other nobles in Germany. Rothschild's stroke of genius, however, the move for which he is most famous, was spreading his banking and finance business beyond the borders of Germany, building five different financial houses in leading cities across Europe, one for each of his five sons. With branches of the Rothschild banking empire established in Frankfurt, London, Naples, Vienna, and Paris, the Rothschilds had one of the first truly international banking systems in the history of the world.

The advantages of an international system were considerable. First, the bank as a whole was largely impervious to political and economic threats faced by any of the *individual* branches. With eyes and ears spread across Europe, the Rothschilds also had a more complete view of important social, political, military, and economic developments. This enabled them to share valuable information that could prove highly profitable, and, indeed, they developed complex systems of communication, including the use of the swiftest couriers in Europe as well as carrier pigeons to increase the speed of their communications.

Whereas the wealth of nobles had always been threatened by the possibility of violence, civil unrest, or seizure by the ruling powers, the Rothschilds further shielded their wealth from local attacks through the use of financial instruments such as debts, stocks and bonds traded in markets and exchanges in Venice, Belgium, and London, and, later, Philadelphia and New York. In essence, writes historian Paul Johnson, "their real wealth was beyond the reach of the mob, almost beyond the reach of greedy monarchs."[10]

Most importantly, the five sons of Mayer Amschel Rothschild stayed true to their father's final wish. They stayed true to one another and the Rothschild family business. In fact, as one Rothschild biographer wrote, "few have honored the commandments of a parent more faithfully than the five sons of Mayer Amschel Rothschild."[11] But they also went beyond themselves and "made a determined effort to pass on the founder's dream of unbreakable unity to the next generation [of Rothschilds]."[12]

Vital to their family's remarkable success, they repeated this message of shared commitment, unity, and trust again and again, "emphatically—in their wills, during partnership negotiations, on their deathbeds."[13] And, in time, in no small part because of their unbreakable unity and shared commitment to the family's business, the Rothschilds came to possess the largest private fortune in the history of the modern world, and they came to have a lasting influence on the economic and political history of Europe as a result.

Rise Above the Limits of Flying Solo.

"Surely you need guidance to wage war, and victory is won through many advisers."[14]
—Proverbs 24:6

In the West, particularly in the United States, we naturally admire the self-made, self-reliant individual. Many even imagine that independence—financial, intellectual, emotional—is a sort of ideal end goal. No doubt, self-reliance is a critical component of success, and, moreover, you must maintain a basic level of psychological independence before you can effectively work interdependently with others. Independence always precedes true interdependence.

But independence has its limits. There is only so much that individuals operating on their own can do to succeed. As billionaire internet entrepreneur and LinkedIn co-founder Reid Hoffman writes, "No matter how brilliant your mind or strategy, if you're playing a solo game, you'll always lose out to a team."[15]

Unfortunately, too often leaders fail to achieve their greatest ambitions and goals because they are unable or unwilling to get the help they need. They keep trying to do it all on their own. They refuse to ask for help or collaborate with others. Of course, they often have all sorts of sensible sounding or even compelling explanations for why they don't delegate or seek out the help they need to succeed (e.g. the challenge of finding good people to collaborate with, or the challenge of trusting the people they find), but these explanations are still just excuses, self-deceptive attempts to absolve themselves of responsibility, rationalizations masking weaknesses that can and must be overcome.

Foster Friendships and Forge Alliances
to Build Power, Influence, and Strength.

The hard truth is that there are many things that you simply cannot do for yourself or on your own. As long as you continue to work predominantly as a solo-operator, you will continue to place decisive limits on your success. When you develop a tight circle of family and friends, or close colleagues and staff, however, people you can count on and trust, your probability of success increases exponentially.

This same principle holds true for reliable allies and even temporary coalitions in international relations. As the evil Nazi dictator Adolf Hitler learned the hard way and Vladimir Putin is learning today, "even the strongest individual state [can] be defeated by an organized coalition ranged against it and determined to restore equilibrium to the international system."[16] This was also one of the key lessons learned from the eventual defeat of Napoleon Bonaparte, one of the most brilliant strategists in the history of the world. As Lawrence Freedman writes in *Strategy: A History*, "the basic lesson from the Napoleonic

Wars [is] that there was only so much one country's army, whatever the brilliance of its operations, could do against a much stronger alliance..."[17]

Forging trusting alliances was one of the secrets of the early success of ancient Rome as well. Amidst numerous *small* ancient republics, the vast territory of Rome was the exception to the rule. But how did Rome get so large? Not so much through conquest, at least not at first. "Rome...grew large...through the alliances it formed, in which neighboring peoples gradually united with Rome to form a larger whole. It was only *after* Rome had spread throughout southern Italy in this way that it truly began to advance by conquest."[18]

Regardless of the realm or scale, there are a number of advantages to working closely together with trusted allies, including greater access to resources, people, and intelligence; greater productivity; increased perspective and potential for useful feedback; and, ultimately, greater power and strength. To be sure, this strength is the key. *There is extraordinary, synergistic power in banding together and forging unbreakable bonds with other like-minded people. This is how you build the kind of power which is exponentially greater than any single leader could ever realistically imagine.*

Military historians and strategists have recognized the importance of strategic coalitions and alliances "as a source of strength"[19] at least as far back as Thucydides, the Athenian general and "father of scientific history" who wrote the *History of the Peloponnesian War* in the 4th century B.C. This is also the essence of what Mayer Rothschild emphasized to his sons. No doubt, your mutual success might never be guaranteed. However, by carefully building strategic, unbreakable bonds with others, your success is increasingly assured by your increasing power, resources, and collective strength.

Champion Cooperative Communication, a Cognitive Superpower.

"Two people are better off than one, for they can help each other succeed. If one person falls, the other can reach out and help. But someone who falls alone is in real trouble. Likewise, two people lying close together can keep each other warm. But how can one be warm alone? A person standing alone can be attacked and defeated, but two can stand back-to-back and conquer. Three are even better, for a triple-braided cord is not easily broken."[20]

—Ecclesiastes 4:9-12, NLT

To succeed at the highest levels, building collaborative, trusting relationships with others is key. "It is the long history of humankind (and animal kind, too)," wrote Charles Darwin, "those who learned to collaborate and improvise most effectively have prevailed."[21]

This is one of the leading factors that differentiates us from every other species on Earth, including other species of humans (e.g. Neanderthals, homo erectus, homo ergaster, etc.), some of which were bigger, and had bigger brains, explains Duke University professor of neuroscience Brian Hare and Vanessa Woods in their groundbreaking book, *Survival of the Friendliest.*[22]

"What allowed us to thrive while other humans went extinct was a kind of cognitive superpower: a particular type of friendliness called cooperative communication. We are experts at working together with other people, even strangers. We can communicate with someone we've never met about a shared goal and work together to accomplish it."[23]

Unlike other species, including the cognitively sophisticated chimpanzees, humans develop the ability to synchronize our behavior, coordinate different roles, pass on our innovations, and communicate complex requests all before we can walk or talk.[24]

Provided we actually put these advanced skills into effective practice, they enable us to survive and thrive in a highly developed social, cultural, and political world.[25] "They allow us to plug our minds into the minds of others and inherit the knowledge of generations. They are the foundation for all forms of culture and learning," writes Hare and Woods.[26] In essence, humans have the proven ability "to flourish where other smart human species didn't because we excel at a particular kind of collaboration."[27]

The ability to foster effective collaboration, the ability to cultivate fruitful relationships and build trust, the ability to work cooperatively together toward a shared vision, to build a business, a movement, or an empire; this is the nucleus of what makes us the most superior species on Earth. Naturally, this cognitive superpower varies, often greatly, from individual to individual. And, yet, each and every one of us can do so much more when we're united, working collaboratively with others, than we can on our own. Truly, wrote the English priest and politician John Donne, "no man is an island."[28]

To be sure, even those legends and heroes of history who we imagine as virtual archetypes of independence, self-reliance, and personal achievement were virtually never operating entirely on their own. Daniel Boone, for example, frequently traveled with his family or a small group of explorers, including his wife Rebecca Boone and his brother Squire Boone. The great American women's rights activist Susan B. Anthony had Elizabeth Cady Stanton and Lucy Stone, known together as the 19th-century "triumvirate" of women's suffrage. The fearless frontier lawman Sherriff Wyatt Earp had Doc Holliday, but also his brothers, lawmen Morgan and Virgil Earp. Henry David Thoreau had Ralph Waldo Emerson. Socrates, the "Father of Western Philosophy," mentored Plato, the "Father of Political Philosophy;" Plato mentored Aristotle, the "father of political science, logic, rhetoric, and psychology;" and Aristotle mentored Alexander the Great, who became Plato's first "philosopher king." Though it was a solo flight that made Charles Lindbergh famous, he too was supported by a small team of people who helped him with everything from financing to building and maintaining the plane. Amelia Earhart, likewise, benefitted immensely from her own inner circle, including other renowned pilots, the famous publicist and promoter, George

P. Putnam (whom Earhart married), and her indispensible mechanic, Ruckins McKneely Jr. Even the fictional character the Lone Ranger, whose very *name* evokes independence, fought injustice alongside of his Native American friend Tonto, and their horses, of course, Silver and Scout.

But there is also something beyond *interdependence.*

Crack the Code of Consummate Collaboration: 5 Strategies to Ensure Mutual Commitment and Shared Success

"A grand dream doesn't become a significant reality through the actions of a single person. It requires a team effort. It requires solid trust and strong relationships.

It requires deep competence and cool confidence. It requires group collaboration and individual accountability."[29]

—James Kouzes & Barry Posner, *The Leadership Challenge*

It's one thing to work together cooperatively, relying on one another to make things happen and get things done. It is something else entirely to be mutually committed to ensuring one another's success because you are all working together as one.

Mutually assured success means looking out for one another's interests, supporting one another beyond what might normally be expected, and having one another's backs or being in each other's corner even, perhaps especially, in the midst of the most trying circumstances. Mutually assured success is also about working for the success of others just as much as your own, and going beyond expectations for the whole group, organization, family, or team. It's about enduring commitment and, at times, it means making significant sacrifices, but it also means much greater rewards for all.

Mutually assured success is both a mindset and a set of behaviors, but it is also a proven philosophy of success. To catapult your power and probability of strategic success, cracking the code of effective, collaborative bonds and mutually assured success is indispensable. What follows are the five (5) most critical factors for creating the kind of collaborative relationships strategists need to succeed in building the sort of unparalleled power that we see in history's most successful organizations, alliances, families, and teams.

(1.) *Synthesize Power from Shared Interests Forged into Common, Collaborative Bonds: The Republic of Pirates and the Flying Gang.*

"We must all hang together or most assuredly we shall all hang separately."[30]
—Benjamin Franklin, to the Continental Congress after signing
the Declaration of Independence from Great Britain

In the wee hours of the morning on April 2, 1803, a small landing force of sailors from the HMS *Aigle* disembarked at Easton, a village on the Isle of

Portland in Dorset, England. Known as a "press gang," the sailors were ordered by Captain George Wolfe to abduct as many able-bodied men as they could.

They were hoping to catch their fellow English citizens while they slept, but this was their second attempt and the town was on high alert. When the sailors tried to drag one Robert Bennett away, a large group of citizens suddenly rounded the corner and began wrestling to set the man free. Within minutes, the captain and his crew opened fire. Seconds later, three townsfolk were left dead. A fourth, the 21 year-old Mary Way, died from her wounds within days. Standing trial for murder in what became known as the Easton Massacre, Captain Wolfe and his crew were easily acquitted and immediately resumed their deadly coastal recruitment campaign.

Life on a ship in Britain's Royal Navy during this period, the Age of Sail (mid-16th to mid-19th centuries), was so dreadful and dangerous that Parliament sanctioned the use of these notorious press-gangs to round up recruits. If any able-bodied man refused to volunteer, he was knocked unconscious with a club and carried onto the ship. Along with ordinary citizens, naval ships were also manned with criminals, men who were forced to serve in the navy as punishment for their crimes.[31] Described as a floating concentration camp, more than half of a ship's crew could be composed of such conscripts, particularly in wartime, and, to curtail desertion, these men had to be shackled whenever in port.

"Punishments were harsh and capricious: whippings, imprisonment below deck, and even hangings were standard fare in the Royal Navy."[32] Those who were not killed by cannon or did not die of disease—usually from rotten food or dirty water—could count themselves lucky if they did not die in a fire or drown in the sea. Those sailors who managed to survive all such harrowing hazards still found the daily regimen and discipline onboard could be incredibly brutal and unfair, even for those who had volunteered.

Later known as "the King of Pirates," Henry Avery's experience was typical. After spending most of his life at sea, including a period as a junior officer in the Royal Navy, "...he and his fellow sailors had experienced beatings and humiliations from officers, eaten rotten or substandard food courtesy of corrupt pursers, and their salaries had gone unpaid for years on end. It was a beggar's life for shipmates who lost arms, legs, hands, feet, or eyes in accidents or battle. Sailors said that prisoners led a better life, and after more than two decades at sea, Avery had to agree."[33]

Unfortunately, living in an age of widespread injustice and extreme inequality, life on land was barely much better. "About half of the population of England at this time was living in abject poverty, and it caused people, in their desperation for lack of means to feed themselves, to do something as dangerous as going to sea, which was often a death sentence..."[34]

Given the conditions of the Royal Navy, many sailors sought to do similar work on merchant vessels instead, but life there was no less cruel and, depending on the captain or the businessmen behind the endeavor, it might be more severe. As University of Pittsburgh historian Marcus Rediker writes, "merchant seamen got a hard, close look at death: disease and accidents were commonplace in their occupation, rations were often meager, and discipline was brutal. Each ship was 'a little kingdom' whose captain held a near-absolute power which he often abused."[35]

Fight for the Freedom to Write Your Own Team's Rules. "Low pay and poor working conditions incited many ship crews to mutiny."[36] In fact, it was a merchant ship mutiny that helped spawn the dawn of the Golden Age of Piracy. When the crew of the *Charles II*—a fast, 46-gun warship owned by a London financier—was left without pay, laying at anchor in a northern Spanish harbor while their families back home struggled to survive, Henry Avery, the first mate, led a mutiny. They stole the ship, elected Avery captain, renamed the ship *Fancy* (for their shared vision of a "fancy life"), combined forces with five other pirate captains,[37] which elected Avery as admiral, and proceeded to win the biggest pirate prize in all of Asia, if not the world—the Grand Mughal's fleet, worth the equivalent of tens of millions of dollars today.[38] When word got out that he escaped and retired to a life of luxury, Avery's successful "exploits inspired songs, books and plays, including one called "The Successful Pyrate" that was performed on London stages for several years."[39]

"To abused young sailors and cabin boys, Avery had become a hero. He was one of their own, a man who stuck up for his fellow sailors and led them to a promised land, a sailor's heaven on earth. A champion of the ordinary man," writes American journalist and historian Colin Woodard, "the Avery of legend was a symbol of hope for a new generation of oppressed mariners, as well as a role model for the men who would one day become the most famous and fearsome pirates in history."[40]

After being ripped from their homes and forced to serve under the cruel conditions, brutal discipline, and petty tyranny of smug naval officers and greedy merchant captains, is it any wonder that great multitudes of mariners opted instead to join the "merry,"[41] rum-loving life of pirates in order to survive? And, possibly, get filthy, stinkin' rich?

No doubt, the life of pirates was filled with danger and violence, but it was still healthier and less hostile, and in some ways safer and more secure than serving in the navy or on a merchant ship.[42] But this didn't occur by chance. It happened because life on the high seas, far from state sanctioned authority of any sort, afforded pirates the *freedom* to work together however they saw fit. And what they saw as fit was a very different code or set of rules than what they had experienced in the Royale Navy, on merchant ships, or even among the landlubbers back in so called "civilized society."

Create Your Pirate Code. In essence, to cope, the pirates collaborated. In response to the tyranny they experienced on board naval and merchant vessels, the pirates, virtually without exception, opted for a more democratic and egalitarian system—that is, one based on a belief in equality, one in which everyone, regardless of race,[43] had a voice—a remarkably advanced system for its day. They even created their own written code, known as "the pirate code," which outlined the rules of engagement and terms of agreement between the captain and his or her crew. Despite covering a number of relevant topics and being shared across an even greater number of pirate captains—each with their own unique personalities and styles of leadership—the pirate code was strikingly consistent from one ship to the next (which undoubtedly speaks to the general agreement with the core principles).[44]

For starters, pirates elected their own captains, often from among their own ranks, and likewise deposed them by popular vote. Pirate captains essentially served with the consent and by the authority of the crew and could be removed from command for poor leadership, an act of cruelty or cowardice, or a failure to act on behalf of the crew.[45]

Akin to James Madison's idea in *Federalist No. 51* that "ambition must be made to counteract ambition," the pirates even provided for a certain separation of powers. To prevent the captain from abusing his authority, a quartermaster was elected to protect the "Interest of the Crew" and, as such, created a sort of "dual executive" as a check or balance to the captain's power.[46] The quartermaster's role included serving as judge over minor disputes, distributing grub, rum, and treasure, and, in some cases, leading an attack on a prize or captaining a captured ship in a growing fleet.[47] As Rediker put it, "He served as a 'civil Magistrate' and dispensed necessaries 'with an Equality to them all.'"[48]

Pirates were also known for reserving their most important decisions, those "decisions that had the greatest bearing on the welfare of the crew,"[49] to "an open council,"[50] "a body usually including every man on the ship."[51] "The council determined such matters as where the best prizes could be taken and how disruptive dissension was to be resolved. Some crews continually used the council, 'carrying every thing by a majority of votes;' others set up the council as a court. The decisions made by this body constituted the highest authority on a pirate ship: even the boldest captain dared not challenge a council's mandate."[52] All of this was "in sharp contrast to the dictatorial regimes" found in the Royal Navy or on merchant ships.[53] Not unlike the dictators of the ancient Roman republic, the only time a pirate captain exercised absolute power was in the midst of battle or chase.[54]

Furthermore, unlike the excessive inequality found in large corporations today (where CEOs, according to a recent *Fast Company* report, make up to *1,000 times* the *median* employee's annual income![55]), pirates shared their rewards equally among crew members, allowing their captain to take no more than 1.5 to 2 times the booty of the rest of the crew. Pirates also shared in the hardships and consequences of their endeavors. In fact, by contributing a portion of their booty to a "common fund," pirates created an early form of worker's compensation or social security which was paid out to anyone who lost a limb or an eye or who sustained a lasting injury in battle or in an accident at sea.[56] Requiring everyone to contribute to the common fund, upon which any unlucky pirate might come to rely, also helped to strengthen their commitment to protecting one another in the midst of a battle or fierce storm. In his book, *Culture Code: The Secrets of Highly Successful Groups*, this is what Daniel Coyle refers to as "shared vulnerability" and, according to Coyle's research, it is one of the keys to exceptionally high performing teams.

Forge a Common Culture and Community. The willing readiness of pirates to collaborate went beyond the ship. "Pirates showed recurrent willingness to join forces at sea and in port."[57] When an opportunity or threat emerged, they would "combine...their powers," and they "frequently invoked an unwritten code of hospitality to forge spontaneous alliances."[58]

The bonds between pirates went beyond traditional borders as well. "Though conflict between pirate bands was not unheard of, the groups were largely cooperative, even across national boundaries."[59] As Woodard explains in *The Republic of Pirates*, "despite differences in nation, race, religion, and even language, they forged a common culture. When meeting at sea, pirate vessels frequently joined forces and came to one another's aid, even when one crew was largely French and the other dominated by their traditional enemies, the English."[60]

The pirate system they created worked so well that it continued to attract new mariners to their ranks. "Dissatisfaction was so great aboard merchant vessels that typically when the pirates captured one, a portion of its crew enthusiastically joined their ranks."[61] "Even the Royal Navy was vulnerable; when HMS *Phoenix* confronted the pirates at their Bahamian lair in 1718, a number of the frigate's sailors defected, sneaking off in the night to serve under the black flag. Indeed, the pirates' expansion was fueled in large part by the defections of sailors, in direct proportion to the brutal treatment in both the navy and merchant marine."[62]

There are also known instances where blacks joined the crews of pirate ships when slave ships were captured at sea. Unlike the nations from which pirates were typically spawned, blacks could be treated as equal members of pirate crews and several became pirate captains. Black Caesar of Blackbeard's crew is one famous example. Black Caesar later became a pirate captain in his own right and there are other cases in which, Kenneth Kinkor reports, "blacks are accordingly found as leaders of predominantly white crews."[63] According to Rediker, "black pirates also made up part of the pirates' vanguard, the most trusted and fearsome members of the crew who boarded a prospective prize."[64]

Living in a time of extreme religious persecution and mass hysteria (e.g. the Salem witch trials occurred in 1692-93), pirate ships were also open to religious minorities who could join the crew "without the fear of persecution"—which is perhaps no surprise, history professor Rebecca Simon writes, "seeing as pirate ships were not generally bastions of Christian purity."[65]

While it is true that "there were very few women on pirate ships," and they were actually forbidden in many cases, as per the pirate code, there were certainly some women, most famously, Anne Bonny and Mary Read who "developed a significant role within the crew."[66] There were also more than a handful of women who became pirate captains, including Grace O'Malley, who led an entire 20-ship fleet, Charlotte de Berry, and Jacquotte "Back from the Dead Red" Delahaye who, according to legend, after taking over a small Caribbean island, established the first "freebooter republic."[67] "It was here, so the legend goes, that she died, defending her pirate utopia from attackers."[68]

Build a Base of Operations. Taken together these factors helped ensure, for a time at least, the continued growth of piracy. By the early 1700s, there were several dozen pirate ships and as many as 5,000 pirates haunting maritime trading routes across the world. With this growth and continued collaboration came increasing strength and control. Pirate strongholds started cropping up in places like Madagascar, Tortuga, Port Royal, and Sierra Leone, but perhaps most famously in Nassau on New Providence island. These safe havens allowed pirates to repair and resupply their ships and sell their plunder to unscrupulous merchants. These were also places where pirate captains could recruit new crew members, build alliances for joint operations, and gather and share intelligence on their mutual enemies.

No doubt, given that their very lives were at stake, these collaborative opportunities were no trifling advantages. As anthropologist Krystal D'Costa writes in *Scientific American*, "They literally needed to hang together, or could find themselves hanging separately, which bred a sense of fraternity that spread among pirates and manifested in cooperative tendencies at sea and in port."[69]

Given the need to hide or escape capture by pirate hunters or avoid battle with navy warships, pirate havens tended to be located in areas with adequate places to hide, such as secret coves, veiled inlets, or uncharted isles. As 19th century British admiral Sir Henry Keppel once explained, "As surely as spiders abound where there are nooks and crannies, so have pirates sprung up wherever there is a nest of islands offering creeks and shallows, headlands, rocks and reefs—facilities in short for lurking, for surprise, for attack, for escape."[70]

While the story of captain Jacquotte "Back from the Dead Red" Delahaye's "freebooter republic" is reportedly a legend, she was not the only pirate leader who dreamed of a pirate republic. In fact, in 1706, this dream was nearly realized when the British-controlled island of New Providence in the Bahamas was effectively abandoned following attacks by a combined French and Spanish fleet. With no government to contend with, pirate Captain Benjamin Hornigold took over the failed British colony and founded the first so-called pirate republic.[71]

Undoubtedly, the greatest pirate collaboration in the history of the Golden Age of Piracy, the pirate republic was basically ruled by a group of pirates which called themselves the Flying Gang. This bold band of outlaws included Hornigold and his bitter rival, Henry Jennings, as well as a number of the most famous and cunning pirates of the day, men and women such as Edward "Blackbeard" Teach, John "Calico Jack" Rackham, Mary Read, Anne Bonny, Stede "the Gentleman Pirate" Bonnet, Edward England, John Martel, Paulsgrave Williams, Olivier "the Buzzard" Levasseur, Samuel "Black Sam" Bellamy, and Charles Vane. Most all of these famous seafaring freebooters already knew each other—in many cases, they had served with one or another on a navy or merchant ship. (Some historians have suggested that they were joining forces to set up this pirate republic not so much as a means of better facilitating their common thievery, but as a "conscious social revolt" in response to their shared experience of tyranny.[72])

Either way, as a base of operations for pirates, the bountiful New Providence island, with plenty of fresh water and fresh fruit and meat, worked exceptionally well. Because of the frequent need to hide or escape, pirates favored ships with shallow drafts which increased their ability to sail close to land, over reefs, into coves, or even up rivers. In the case of New Providence, along with the protection offered by the harbor and the many reefs, channels, coves, cays, and bays, the surrounding waters were shallow enough to keep the navy's warships at a distance, but deep enough for pirate ships as well as other small boats which were built to attack any large, slow-to-maneuver warship that approached the island. There was also a harbor and a military fort at Nassau, which was ideal for defense.

With cannons from captured ships, the Flying Gang worked together to rearm the fort and keep it manned. They also wrecked ships at the entrance of the harbor to further fortify Nassau from foreign attacks. As word got out, pirates from all around flocked to the island. At its height, there were said to be some 1,000 pirates along with a 100 or so inhabitants, scores of escaped slaves, and a number of unscrupulous merchants and wild women.

Grounded in their shared interests in freedom and prosperity, guided by the pirate code, and built on common, collaborative, mutually beneficial bonds, these pirates overcame their internal rivalries and factional divisions to create—if not a full-fledged republic, then, at the very least—a unified, cooperative community so powerful and successful that "soon governors, slave merchants, plantation owners, and shipping magnates—the entire power structure of British America—was clamoring for something to be done."[73]

Identify Shared Interests, Find Common Ground. Contrary to the popular myth that "opposites attract," scientific evidence repeatedly reveals that we like people who are like us. We are drawn to those who are similar to us in obvious ways, such as appearance, age, and ethnicity, but also less obvious ways, such as personal interests and values, sense of humor, background, education, income level, and political and religious beliefs. Of course there are exceptions and a few big or obvious differences can easily be neutralized by a greater number of similarities. Nevertheless, the scientific evidence is clear: "We like people who are similar to us."[74]

The primary reasons for this come down to trust, comfort, and success. If people are *too* different it almost invariably creates challenges and leads to conflict and confusion, undermines happiness, disrupts comfort, and threatens the ability to cooperate and achieve one's goals. As the author of one study reported in the esteemed *Journal of Personality and Social Psychology*, "you try to create a social world where you're comfortable, where you succeed, where you have people you can trust and with whom you can cooperate to meet your goals. To create this, similarity is very useful..."[75]

Contrary to the visual differences that people often mistakenly imagine as most important, research also reveals that one of the most important factors is being like-minded, particularly with regard to those "things that matter most to the individuals personally."[76] In other words, the people we are most comfortable with are the people who think like us about the issues that matter to us most. Interestingly, in terms of forming relationships or even building alliances, what matters most is *perceived similarity*—in other words, what matters most is *not* that you *actually have* a lot in common, but that you *believe* you have a lot in common.[77]

In the case of the Rothschilds, a mere handful of brothers working together to build a family business seems perfectly natural, indeed, almost expected given their wealth of shared interests. But what about the pirates?

Given that there were thousands of them coming from all over the world, it could easily have been one of the most diverse gatherings of the day. And yet, despite their differences, they also had much in common. Whether one had a background serving time in the navy or on a merchant ship, or whether one was a former slave, we know that most all of them experienced one form of tyranny or another. What's more, given that they ultimately turned to piracy, we can also make certain general assumptions about their backgrounds (with rare exceptions for someone like Stede Bonnet, the "Gentleman Pirate"), their limited options back on land, their values (e.g. the pirate code), and their appetite for risk. In other words, pirates had much in common, and perhaps most particularly in regards to the all-important factor of being *like-minded* on those things that mattered to them most (i.e. survival, treasure, freedom, and, perhaps, rum). Furthermore, given what we know about pirate culture, language, and lifestyle, whatever their *actual* differences, they undoubtedly *perceived* themselves to be quite similar to one another, at least in comparison to those who were not pirates, and even more so to those who they were fighting against. Finally, and most importantly, they shared the same interests and desires, the same potential opportunities and threats. Building powerful alliances begins on common ground, and the pirates' shared interests created a firm foundation for effective collaboration and, therefore, *power*.

Within several years of establishing themselves at Nassau on New Providence island, what Woodard calls "a zone of freedom in the midst of an authoritarian age,"[78] this collaborative community of pirates became so powerful that they threatened not just passing ships and supplies, but entire colonies and networks of trade.[79] "They occupied British outposts in the Leeward Islands, threatened to invade Bermuda, and repeatedly blockaded South Carolina. In the process, some accumulated staggering fortunes, with which they bought the loyalty of merchants, plantation owners, even the colonial governors themselves."[80]

What made matters more dangerous for the authorities was the fact that many ordinary colonists saw these so-called "monsters"[81] as "folk heroes"[82] boldly fighting the good fight against corrupt authorities and the excessively wealthy and powerful elites. "At their zenith they succeeded in severing Britain, France, and Spain from their New World empires, cutting off trade routes, stifling the supply of slaves to the sugar plantations of America and the West Indies, and disrupting the flow of information between the continents. The Royal Navy went from being unable to catch the pirates to being afraid to encounter them at all."[83]

<u>Beware of Betrayal, Self-Interest, and Fragile Bonds: Pardons, Pirates, and Pirate Hunters</u>. By 1717, the British had finally devised a clever two-part divide-and-conquer strategy to rid the seas of pirates. To implement their new strategy, they appointed a tough, savvy former privateer, Captain Woodes Rogers, to be the new Governor of the Bahamas.

In September of 1717, Rogers distributed a royal proclamation issued by King George I of Great Britain that promised to pardon all those pirates who surrendered, so long as they forever swore off piracy within a year. They were even allowed to keep whatever treasures they had collected up to that point. For the considerable number of pirates who were actually looking to get out or who feared the "agony of slowly being strangled to death" in a gruesome public spectacle, the royal pardon was a godsend.[84]

This one maneuver alone effectively split the pirate community at Nassau in two. Some 400 pirates reportedly accepted the royal pardon.[85]

Still, at less than half of the pirates at Nassau alone, this was not enough to rid the seas of pirates.[86]

The second part of the strategy was to offer substantial rewards to any pirate crew member who aided in the capture of their captains. The Bahamas' newly minted Governor Woodes Rogers also hired some of the best pirate captains who accepted the pardon to join him in his mission to end piracy by becoming paid pirate hunters "who would spend their time scouring the seas looking for the swashbuckling thieves."[87]

Rather than conveying the idea that "we share risk here,"[88] which is so critical to effective collaborations, the pirates were no longer safe. In fact, their very lives were at risk, even from former long-time members of their own crews.

The most surprising turn was the man most responsible for the pirate republic, Benjamin Hornigold. Now the Benedict Arnold of pirates, Hornigold became a pirate hunter and helped Rogers track down and slaughter his former pirate friends and allies. In essence, the English used the pirates themselves to intensify their campaign against piracy to "great and gruesome effect."[89]

Unlike the Royale Navy with their "press gangs," the pirates lacked a reliable source of recruits to replace those who turned or were killed in action.[90] In July 1718, less than a year after the royal pardon, Rogers recaptured New Providence island after Captain Charles Vane, the leader of the resistance to British rule, abandoned the island, but made a spectacular escape by punching through Rogers squadron with a fire ship.[91] The captains and crews of the pirate resistance quickly dispersed, making it even more difficult to "mobilize their collective strength"[92] to mount a defense.

Alas, the bonds that united the pirates had always been fragile and fundamentally flawed. Pirates were individuals who were willing to flout the law to serve their own ends and, in most cases, commit vicious acts of savagery and murder along the way—not exactly the sort of characters who make reliable allies. Nevertheless, it was not until the English effectively exploited their self-interest that their divided and scattered forces became easy prey.[93] In the end, circa 1730, it was their own lack of shared commitment and mutual trust, the betrayal by so many of their own, that helped bring an end to the Golden Age of Piracy.

The lesson is clear: There can be no mutually assured success without unified, unbreakable bonds. As Benjamin Franklin said to the Continental Congress after signing the Declaration of Independence from Great Britain, which was seen as an act of treason by the English Parliament, "We must all hang together or most assuredly we shall all hang separately."[94] Abraham Lincoln, quoting Christ from the Synoptic Gospels, put it this way, "a house divided against itself cannot stand."[95]

The mutually beneficial collaboration of the Flying Gang's so-called pirate republic was a clear turning point in the Golden Age of Piracy. With a home base, an armed fortress, and an island ideal for defense, some 1,000 pirates, including many of the most notorious and cunning pirates of the age, fended off the best efforts of the English and Spanish navies for more than a decade (1706—1718). It was a remarkably long run given that they were riding almost exclusively on shared interests and common ground. As with the majority of failed alliances, collaborations, and teams, however, they lacked the shared vision, shared commitment, and mutual trust necessary to strengthen and expand their alliances and bolster the bonds they had built.

(2.) *Create and Consistently Communicate a Clear,*
** *Compelling, and Shared Strategic Intent.***

The second key to fostering and profiting from collaborative relationships is establishing an inspiring, clearly defined, obtainable objective or strategic intent. As discussed in the first chapter, effective strategists, leaders, and teams are all decidedly future-oriented. Guided by a clear set of values, they all have a future in mind, a clear and compelling vision that they eagerly want to achieve. "Without a powerful vision," Ridgley writes, "effective strategy is non-existent."[96]

It cannot be *your vision and values alone*, however. Whether you are collaborating with one other person, a team, an organization, or a nation, your purpose and principles must be shared. Your vision must be informed, shaped, and held in common with the people involved. *Nothing* will sustain commitment like a vision that is grounded in the common needs, hopes and dreams of the people involved. *Fortune* magazine even went as far as declaring the idea of a "shared vision"[97] to be one of the most important leadership ideas in the twentieth century.[98] MIT's Peter Senge similarly said, "Few, if any, forces in human affairs are as powerful as a shared vision."[99] In contrast, visions that trickle down from the top, rather than being rooted in the shared dreams of the people, never inspire the kind of courage, commitment, and collaboration *necessary* to achieve the extraordinary.

To Achieve the Vision, Live Its Values. The Rothschild family certainly achieved extraordinary wealth, but was wealth the *summum bonum* (the supreme good) of their shared vision and values? Mayer Amschel Rothschild's last words to his eldest son were, "Amschel, keep your brothers together and you will become the richest people in Germany."[100] No doubt, building wealth was an intrinsic part of their calculus. And to be sure, as Zig Ziglar often said, "anybody that says they're not interested in money will lie about other things too."[101]

But what's interesting is how frequently and consistently they emphasized not so much being the richest people in Germany, Europe, or the world, but the fraternal accord part of the equation—that is, the "keep your brothers *together*" part of their father's last words. The core of the vision, in other words, was *prosperity through unity*.

As Niall Ferguson writes in The House of Rothschild, "of all their father's advice, his last commandment—to maintain fraternal unity—had the greatest and most enduring impact."[102] This was the lodestar they looked to again and again. "That advice was often invoked when the brothers quarreled—as they frequently did in the turbulent years immediately after Mayer Amschel's death."[103] "Our blessed father ordered us to live in peace," Salomon Rothschild, the second son, said to Nathan Rothschild, the third, after a bitter attack on Carl, the fourth.[104] Only a week later, Salomon again turns to this familial guidepost. "My good brother, dear Nathan, our blessed father ordered us to live in peace, otherwise we shall lose our courage. Let us have peace."[105]

When Nathan died over two decades later, the Rothschilds North Star was burning as bright as ever. In fact, as Ferguson put it, they "elaborately enshrined"[106] this guiding star in their new partnership agreement:

> "We wish to offer a proof of our reverence for the holiest memory of our father...[who] laid the foundation of our good fortune...when, almost forty years ago, he took his sons into partnership with him in his business, [and] told them that acting in **unison** would be a sure means of achieving success in their work, and always recommended **fraternal concord** to them as a source of divine blessing. In accordance with his venerable wishes, and following the promptings of our own hearts, we therefore wish today, through this renewed agreement, to reinforce our **mutual dependence** and hope, in this new league of **brotherly love**, to guarantee the success of the future activities of our House. May our children and descendants in the future be guided by the same aim, so that with the constant maintenance of **unity** the House of Rothschild may blossom and grow into full ripeness... ; and may they remain as mindful as we of the hallowed precept of our noble ancestor and present to posterity the godly image of **united** love and work."[107]

Not surprisingly, this would not be the last time the Rothschilds would communicate this vision of *prosperity through unity*. Nor would it be the last time they would link this vision with the story of their father. When their agreement was modified again years later, there too was their polestar of "paternally ordained brotherly unity."[108] The blessings of the House of Rothschild would continue to be fulfilled in the future, including "the protection of the Almighty; the success of our undertakings; the prosperity of our family and the continuing honor and respect of our reputation and name," but only, they wrote, if they "always preserved concord, love and faith" with each other.[109] So long as they continued to live by these values, they wrote, "'in the future [as in the past] the blessing of our blessed father and grandfather upon our House and our family'" would be continue to be fulfilled.[110]

Employ Story and Repetition and Watch the Vision and Values Do the Heavy Lifting. A clear and compelling shared vision has a number of advantages—it provides direction, helps to clarify priorities, and, ideally, it helps to motivate, inspire and foster resilience. And it generally increases the probability of success. If it's a really inspiring vision, people will want to work to make it happen. As research in the field of leadership demonstrates again and again, people work harder for a vision that inspires.[111]

In the case of the Rothschilds, theirs was not the most specific or clearly defined vision, but it was inspiring and beneficial because it was ingrained with values, rich with meaning, and wrapped in story. Their vision of *prosperity through unity* was also shared in common and communicated consistently again and again.

They understood how to put their shared purpose into play. They used it as a compass and they referred to it repeatedly. They put their vision to work similar to the way that Coyle describes vision in relation to high performing groups and teams. "Purpose," he writes, "isn't about tapping into some mystical internal drive but rather about creating simple beacons that focus attention and engagement on the shared goal. Successful cultures do this by relentlessly seeking ways to tell and retell their story."[112]

The other vital part of their vision was how it prioritized their relationships with one another and, therefore, helped to further define their identity, including their principles, priorities, and purpose. "In order to move toward a target," Coyle writes, "you must first have a target. Listing your priorities, which means wrestling with the choices that define your identity, is the first step. Most successful groups end up with a small handful of priorities (five or fewer), and many, not coincidentally, end up placing their in-group relationships—how they treat one another—at the top of the list."[113] This is exactly what Salomon Rothschild was doing in the example above and, as Coyle concludes, "This reflects the truth that many successful groups realize: Their greatest project is building and sustaining the group itself. If they get their own relationships right, everything else will follow."[114]

The pirates, in contrast, had no shared vision. Of course, they all dreamed of treasures, and their ships were operated according to certain surprisingly democratic values, but there was no storytelling and retelling or even a connection between the two. They began with shared interests, but they were not bound together by a shared vision of the future. In fact, very few pirates imagined they would be pirating for very long. They collaborated out of convenience, so long as it suited their purposes, but most all of them hoped to retire rich as soon as they captured their next big treasure ship.

(3.) *Be Selective. Build Bonds Based on Shared Commitment, Requisite Variety, and Mutual Trust.*

"No man will make a great leader who wants to do it all himself, or to get all the credit for doing it. That spirit is fatal, and the sure proof of a small mind."[115]
—Andrew Carnegie (1835-1919), Scottish-American Steel Baron

The third factor critical to building and benefiting from effective collaboration is getting the right people on board.

<u>Profit from Requisite Variety</u>. The smaller the group or enterprise, the more selective you can afford to be. To be exclusive, however, is not to be exclusionary. To be clear, ethical arguments aside, variety or diversity can be a considerable competitive advantage. Diverse teams simply perform better. As Karl Weick explains with his law of requisite variety, "No[team] is ever free to do what [it] can't think of. That's why requisite variety produces adaptation."[116] "In recent years," according to *Harvard Business Review (HBR)*, "a body of research has revealed another, more nuanced benefit of workplace

diversity: non-homogenous teams are simply smarter. Working with people who are different from you may challenge your brain to overcome its stale ways of thinking and sharpen its performance."[117]

No doubt, diversity can be taken to unproductive extremes (particularly when there is no longer a shared set of values), but so too can a lack of diversity. A total lack of diversity can even threaten an organism's ability to survive. In contrast, as Charles Darwin argued, 'diversity in the gene pool creates strength and survivability in any species.'[118] This is part of the problem with inbreeding, which was a common practice amongst royalty and aristocrats in Mayer Amschel Rothschild's day, and which he too pressed onto his descendants in his will.[119]

Seek Shared Commitment and Mutual Trust. Nevertheless, the point is to build alliances with those who share your *commitment*—which is reliant on a shared vision, shared values and common interests—and upon whom you can *trust*—which is reliant on both *character* and *competence*.[120]

By insisting on keeping ownership of the bank strictly in the hands of his family, Mayer Amschel Rothschild both increased the likelihood of mutual *trust* and helped ensure a shared *commitment* to the success of the family's business.

This is not to suggest that families are paragons of virtue, communication, and trust—never mind siblings or brothers. The Rothschilds certainly had their quarrels. One historian even speculated that "perhaps one reason the brothers stuck together was that they were so far apart geographically. They carried on their business, for the most part, through correspondence, sparing them too many face-to-face confrontations and shouting matches."[121] Nevertheless, as with *most* successful families, however much they might quarrel, quibble, and debate, the brothers knew they could trust one another more than any associate, colleague, or mate.[122]

Encourage Candid Dialogue Behind the Scenes. Clearly, trust is not about agreement. Trust is about being honest with one another, including when you disagree. You cannot trust people who *always* agree with you anymore than you can trust those who *always disagree*. To be an effective strategist or leader, you must have people around you that you can trust, people who will, respectfully, tell you the truth as they see it regardless of what you think or how you feel.

In 1945, soon after Harry Truman was sworn in as President of the United States, following the sudden death of F.D.R., his good friend and ally, Speaker of the House Sam Rayburn, gave Truman a priceless piece of advice.

> *"Harry," he said, "this will be the last time I will address you in such an informal manner, calling you by your first name. From here on out, I will address you as 'Mr. President,' because that's the way I think our relationship ought to be. But I just have one other thing I want to say to you. While you are President of the United States, you are going to have a staff around you that is going to tell you day in and day out that*

you are the smartest man in the world, and that's going to have a real effect on you. But the truth is, Mr. President, you and I both know it's a damn lie."[123]

Of course, it also matters *how* your circle disagrees—and *when* and *where*. Presenting a unified front in public is very often vitally important. Behind the scenes, however, the best leaders work to ensure vigorous, candid dialogue and healthy, informed debate.

Select According to Commitment, Remove for a Lack of Trust. Naturally, selection and recruitment are very different matters for a much larger and far more informal enterprise such as the pirate republic. Nevertheless, there was still significant selection happening in terms of the pirate crews electing their captains and removing those who lacked commitment—which usually amounted to a failure of courage to attack (e.g. Charles Vane was deposed for calling off an attack on a French navy warship) or the unwillingness of a captain to attack a vessel of his home country (e.g. Benjamin Hornigold was deposed for refusing to take English prizes).

Pirates also removed captains who they felt they could no longer *trust*—whether from a lack of *character* or *competence*. In regards to trust in character, for example, the crew of Captain Charles Martel "deposed him on account of his cruelty in the treatment of crew and captives and chose a 'more righteous' man in his place."[124] In regards to trust in competence, Captain Stede Bonnet, known as the "Gentleman Pirate," was removed from command by Blackbeard and crew because of his ignorance of nautical matters and incompetent leadership.[125]

On the other hand, as Woodard writes in *The Republic of Pirates*, "If the men trusted their leader and were satisfied with his performance, they would follow him to the bitter end."[126]

The opportunities these seafaring freebooters had to influence their leaders, shape their futures, and ensure shared commitment and trust extended beyond electing the captain; it included the "quartermaster and lesser officers as well, particularly if a crew had more than the minimum number of skilled workers such as carpenters. One crew carried the logic so far as to elect a boatswain's mate!"[127] "Freebooters also knew of the naval tradition—the council of war—in which the top officers in a ship or fleet met to plan strategy, and," Marcus Rediker writes in *Villains of All Nations*, "they democratized the naval custom. The floating town meeting acknowledged the truth of the old proverb 'We are all in this boat together.'"[128]

In many instances, these pirate councils even decided such matters as where to search for prizes and how to deal with troublemakers on board.[129] "They loved to vote, claimed a captured captain, 'all the Pyrates['] Affairs being carried by that.' Indeed, there was 'so little Government and Subordination' among pirates that 'they are, on Occasion, all Captains, all Leaders.'"[130]

The pirates also used *the pirate code* to ensure shared commitment and trust. Any pirate who deserted in the midst of battle, for example, "was punished with death or marooning."[131] There were also articles against "Drunkenness in time of Engagement,"[132] or "Cowardice in the Time of Engagement,"[133] and another that required the crew to always "keep their piece, pistols, and cutlass clean and fit for service."[134] Captain Bartholomew Roberts even had an article that forbid the pirates from "talk of breaking up their way of living."[135]

Regardless of the exact degree of influence you have over the particular people you collaborate with, the key is to do whatever possible to ensure shared commitment and mutual trust. Without these fundamental essentials all will eventually be lost. Rivalry and betrayal will bring an end to even the most securely established nation, corporation, or group. In the case of the once emerging pirate republic, it was obliterated by betrayal.

The Rothschilds likewise endured a substantial decline in wealth and power with the fading of their shared commitment and trust. In fact, once the richest family on Earth, the Rothschilds' family fortune declined dramatically with the end of their system of five brothers and their successor sons, which resulted in the five branches operating as independent banks.[136] What's more, following the *lack of commitment* to "managing the business" by subsequent generations of Rothschilds, "the family saw its fortunes decline substantially thereafter."[137]

(4.) *Share Information Rapidly, Transparently, and Often.*

The fourth factor fundamental to effective collaborations is the swift and frequent sharing of valuable information and insight. Intelligence alone can create a significant strategic advantage and it is often one of the main reasons why people, organizations, and nations collaborate. It may not be possible or even desirable to share everything (particularly when trust is in doubt, or surprise is in play), but the greater the degree of timely intelligence sharing, the greater the potential strategic advantage.

Intelligence sharing can also greatly increase the collective power of those involved and improve the probability of success. In the case of World War II, for example, General Dwight Eisenhower said that intelligence sharing played a "decisive" role in the Allied victory.[138] The secret intelligence sharing between the Allies "shortened the war by several years," saved countless lives, and brought an end to Adolf Hitler and his Third Reich.[139]

The powerful role that intelligence sharing played in the Allied victory in World War II spurred a number of the allied nations to seek more permanent collaborations. In Winston Churchill's famous Iron Curtain speech, delivered on March 5, 1946, he made compelling case for such an alliance, arguing that, "Neither the sure prevention of war, nor the continuous rise of world organization will be gained without what I have called the fraternal association of the English-speaking peoples. This means a *special relationship* between the British Commonwealth and Empire and the United States... the continuance of the intimate relationship between our military advisers, leading to common study of potential dangers..."[140(e.a.)]

Not coincidentally, March 5, 1946 was also the birth of UKUSA, which later became Five Eyes—an intelligence alliance between Australia, Canada, New Zealand, the United Kingdom, and the United States.[141] Five Eyes is "the most exclusive intelligence pooling club in the world," writes Canadian professor of international affairs Srdjan Vucetic, and the most secret (until the Edward Snowden disclosures).[142]

Intelligence sharing was also one of the key ingredients in the Rothschilds' success. The ability to be transparent came largely from the trust they had in one another, but they also had to communicate quickly, clearly, concisely, and frequently in order to maximize the often highly profitable advantages to one another and the bank as a whole. In order to achieve this, they created the most superior intelligence gathering operation and communication system of the age. The rapid, frequent sharing of intelligence from each of the five European cities where their branches were established (Frankfurt, London, Naples, Vienna, and Paris) gave them a tremendous competitive advantage, even above major European governments[143]—not because the ruling monarchs didn't have the means to construct the fastest and most reliable intelligence sharing network in the world, but because, in many cases, they didn't grasp its importance to the extent that the Rothschilds did. Instead, they were content to rely on others, and, in a few instances, these governments received their intelligence from the Rothschilds, such as the time when Nathan Mayer Rothschild learned of Napoleon's defeat at Waterloo two days before anyone else in London could verify his report.

The pirates were also reasonably good about sharing intelligence with one another, at least in regard to their shared enemies (i.e. foreign navies and pirate hunters), but it was not at all systematic or equally shared. Instead, it was more-or-less haphazard and circumstantial, spreading like gossip from one outlaw to the next.

The pirate code of John Phillips, captain of *Revenge*, went as far as leaving a pirate for dead if he was found to be hiding intelligence. According to Article II of his code, "If any Man shall...keep any Secret from the Company, he shall be marooned with one Bottle of Powder, one Bottle of Water, one small Arm, and Shot."[144]

Nevertheless, following the appointment of Woodes Rogers and the royal pardon that divided the pirate republic, a time when the frequent, rapid sharing of intelligence was more important than ever, communications between pirates were fraught with disloyalty, deception, and doubt—all of which further undermined their ability to effectively collaborate.

(5.) *To Maximize the Power of the Many,*
Surrender to the Power of the One.

Calls for unity are so common today that they are virtually invisible and practically meaningless. No one doubts that unity gives families, teams, organizations, and even nations great strength. Everyone agrees that unity is crucial to effective collaboration. But what does the term *unity* really mean, particularly in regards to strategy and success? What is it that's lost when most leaders preach about this concept today? And what transpires when this apparently commonplace principle is revered as a sacred pledge?

Unity is more than just working well together. It's more than harmonizing or being a team player. Unity, from the Latin *unitas* or *unus*, literally translates as *oneness* or *one*. To have team unity, therefore, is to function as *one*.

Prior to adopting "In God We Trust" in 1956, the de facto motto of the United States was *e pluribus unum*, which is Latin for "out of many, *one*," or "from many, *one*." What is too often lost with the use of the concept of *unity* or the phrase *e pluribus unum* is the *sacrifice* made by the "many" or the willingness to surrender to the "one." There is tremendous potential power in unity, but only when the "many" put the "one"—the indivisible *whole—first*.

This can be challenging, of course, particularly in highly individualistic cultures such as the United States (according to Hofstede's research, the U.S. is ranked number one on individualism, followed by Australia, the U.K., the Netherlands, and New Zealand). Without a shared vision and values and a shared commitment and trust, it can be nearly impossible.

On the other hand, it is also difficult to overstate the potential power gained in forging unified, unbreakable bonds. In the words of Sir Edward Coke, the most celebrated English jurist of the Elizabethan age, "*Eritis insuperabiles, si fueritis inseparabiles*" ("You will be insurmountable if you are inseparable.").

This was the essence of Mayer Amschel Rothschild's "last commandment to his sons;" maintain "unbreakable unity," he said.[145] And, according to one historian, "never has a father's last testament been carried out more conscientiously and more profitably."[146]

Many great families and winning teams can boast of sharing a genuine commitment to unity. The thing that stands out about the Rothschilds, however, "the impressive thing about the Rothschilds," writes Ferguson, is how "*zealously*" they heeded their father's call to "*unbreakable unity*," even decades after his death.[147]

As one early 19th century historian explained, "Since his death, any proposal, no matter where it comes from, is the object of collective discussion; each operation, even if it is of minor importance, is carried out according to an agreed plan and with their combined efforts; and each of them has an equal share in its results."[148]

As sound and simple as this advice may be, maintaining and sustaining unity and accord requires continuous vigilance and effort. Perhaps this best explains why, *decades* later, Rothschild's sons continued to repeatedly and vigorously emphasize this "same, all-important nexus between unity and success."[149] In the words of the eldest son, Amschel Rothschild,

*"**Unity** was what our blessed father, with his last words, enjoined me to uphold as [our] first and holiest of duties...It is my conviction," he wrote to the other bank partners (i.e. his brothers and their sons), "and I am sure it is yours too, that, along with God's blessing, we owe not only our wealth but also our honorable position in society primarily to the [spirit of] **unity** and **co-operation** [that binds together] all our partners, bank houses and establishments. I therefore request most urgently that you, beloved brothers and nephews, will always take care to implant in your heirs the same consciousness of **concord** and **togetherness**, so that the same [spirit of] **unity** and **co-operation** continues to exist for as long as is at all possible. To do so will be of benefit both to you and to your descendants."[150]*

The Rothschilds even went as far as creating a symbol to represent their father's final lesson—a hand grasping five arrows, one for each of the five sons, all bound together in unity. In 1818, Nathan Mayer Rothschild adopted the bundle of five arrows for the family's coat of arms. Two hundred years later, that same bundle of arrows appears on everything from the Rothschilds corporate logo and letterhead to bookplates, porcelain and even jewelry.[151]

In the case of the pirates, they too often acted in unity and accord. In fact, they could never have brought about such an unprecedented cooperative community of outlaws if they had not sought, "to minimize conflict not only on each ship but also among separate bands of pirates. Indeed, one of the strongest indicators of consciousness of kind lies in the manifest *absence of discord* between different pirate crews."[152][e.a.] What's more, Rediker adds, "in no way was the pirate sense of fraternity...more forcefully expressed than in the threats and acts of revenge taken by pirates. Theirs was truly a case of hanging together or being hanged separately."[153]

Like the Rothschilds, the Golden Age pirates also found ways to signal their shared identity and fraternity both to each other, as a means of cooperation, and to outsiders. "Pirates also affirmed their unity symbolically,"[154] which included the Jolly Roger, but also "extended into the domain of language."[155] "Certainly the best known symbol of piracy is the flag, the Jolly Roger. Less known and appreciated is the fact that the flag was very widely used: no fewer, and probably a great many more, than two thousand five hundred men sailed under it."[156] As Rediker explains, "so general an adoption indicates an advanced state of group identification."[157]

In the end, however, unlike the Rothschilds who, for generations, profited greatly from their unyielding unity, the pirates of Nassau were far less unified and committed and, therefore, much more exposed and susceptible to internal weaknesses and external threats. Ultimately, they were divided by the royal pardon and, thus, in essence, conquered by themselves.

Despite the innumerable differences between a family of wealthy Jewish bankers and a gang of notorious pirate captains, there is one exceptionally important similarity. It is a principle we can see at play in every one of the most powerful groups throughout history. From secret societies like the

Bavarian Illuminati and the Order of the Assassins to Yale's Skull & Bones; from religious, fraternal and political organizations such as the Knights Templar, the Freemasons, and the Sons of Liberty; from powerful families such as the Medicis, the Kennedys, and the Khans to cult-like corporations, Viking raiders, and even criminal gangs; humans have been organizing into restricted clans, selective groups, elite forces, and tight-knit families and tribes since the beginning of time, and for all manner of mixed aims, but always with one critically important purpose in mind: To increase their power and assure their success. Every one of these groups serves as a testament to the fact that *there is extraordinary, synergistic power in banding together with other like-minded people and forging unified, unbreakable bonds.*

13

BELIEVE ABSOLUTELY TO INSPIRE ABSOLUTE BELIEF: JOAN OF ARC TURNS THE TIDE OF THE HUNDRED YEARS' WAR

"The one thing that will guarantee the successful conclusion of a doubtful undertaking is faith in the beginning that you can do it...
Belief creates the actual fact."[1]
—William James (1842—1910)

Joan of Arc was born into a peasant family in northeastern France during the Late Medieval Era, at a time when France and England were still in the midst of the Lancastrian phase (i.e. the third and final phase) of the Hundred Years' War. Raised on a farm, spending most of her time, as she put it, "work[ing] at common tasks about the house," including "sewing and spinning," Joan of Arc was still in her early teens when, in 1425, she was first inspired to lead a divine military mission.[2]

Professing to see visions and hear the voices of St. Catherine, St. Margaret, and St. Michael the Archangel, Joan made a 300-mile journey, traveling at night through enemy territory when she was still only 16, in order to request an audience with Charles VII, the Dauphin of France (i.e. the heir to the French throne). Joan wanted the future king to give her command of his army so that she might drive the English from France.[3]

After the death of his father, Charles VI, the Dauphin had been idly languishing in a castle while the English continued to strengthen their hold over France. Joan was now promising to lead France's military forces to victory over the English, restore Charles to his proper place of power, and ensure his coronation as the rightful King of France.

Of course, the idea that an unknown, illiterate peasant girl from a tiny village out in the boondocks would be given command of French troops was utterly preposterous. Add the fact that Joan was a 16-year-old girl with no experience fighting anyone for anything, never mind any training in leadership, logistics, strategy, tactics, or weapons, and the notion of her leading an army becomes even more absurd. Indeed, when she first met with Sir Robert de Baudricourt at the castle of Vaucouleurs, her request was met by the governor and the chief officers of the garrison with "a great and general burst of *laughter.*"[4] The governor then instructed Joan's Uncle Laxart, who was standing by her side, "Harkye!—take this mad child home and whip her soundly. That is the best cure for her ailment."[5]

But the French were desperate, and Joan of Arc was an exceptional girl with an extraordinary story. What's more, she seemed to know things that were impossible for her to know. She was also extraordinarily confident, and she held her beliefs, including belief in herself and her destiny, with such articulate, irresistible conviction that it was difficult not to believe everything she said.

Besides all of that, everything that the twenty-six year old Charles VII heard made him increasingly curious about this young maiden and her prophecy, and he was cautiously open to the possibility of divine intervention or supernatural power.

When Joan easily picked him out in a crowded room of nobles and courtiers, despite his disguise, he allowed the poor, young, uneducated farm girl to speak. "Most illustrious Lord Dauphin, I come and am sent from God to give assistance to you and the kingdom."[6] She then told him about the visions of angels and saints and her divine mission. It was a stunningly bold claim, but Charles admired her courage, conviction, and grit, and he was intrigued by her story.

After having her undergo a theological examination and having her claims and background fully investigated by an official commission, Charles decided to allow her to lead the French troops in a relief expedition to Orléans. Escaping what was almost certain death, including being wounded by an arrow in the shoulder, Joan of Arc inspired the French troops with her daring presence on the battlefield, and, after less than a week, under her aggressive and decisive leadership, the French troops ended the siege and rescued the strategic and symbolically significant city of Orléans—and with immaculate timing too given that the French leader of Orléans was on the brink of surrendering to the English. If the English *had* succeeded in taking Orléans, the general consensus at the time was that it would be the end of France as an independent nation. Instead, it was a key French victory, and it proved to be a watershed in the Hundred Years' War.

With her mass of supporters growing by the day, Joan of Arc's next critical mission was to clear enemy-held territory all the way to Reims where, according to her prophecy, the Dauphin would be crowned, and, given the traditions of the time, where he *had* to be crowned in order to be recognized as the legitimate king of France.

True to her promise, Joan of Arc led the French army to clear territory held by the English, liberating along the way the towns of Auxerre, Troyes, and Chalons. Finally, she led the army to a decisive victory over the English on June 18, 1429 at the Battle of Patay where English losses totaled some 2,500, mostly English longbowmen, to France's 100.

At last, Charles VII, the Dauphin of France, was free to leave Chinon, and, accompanied by the young French heroine, he traveled to Reims. Arriving on July 16, the gates of the city of kings had finally opened, and the following day, July 17, 1429, the Dauphin was crowned King Charles VII of France, *fulfilling Joan of Arc's prophecy.*

Conceive and Believe to Achieve

"Whatever the mind can conceive and believe, it can achieve."[7]
—Napoleon Hill, *Think and Grow Rich*

The story of Joan of Arc's success as a military commander is one of the most astonishing stories in the entire history of war. But just how was it that an illiterate teenage peasant girl with no military training or experience whatsoever was able to lead the French army to victory again and again and, ultimately, help turn the tide in the Hundred Years War? A close examination of the extraordinary story of Joan of Arc reveals five (5) key factors that helped forge her remarkable success.

Start with What is Worth Believing.

"I would give all the wealth of the world,
and all the deeds of all the heroes, for one true vision." [8]

—Henry David Thoreau

Most people are hungry for belief. They are starving for a bright vision, for hope in a compelling future. They are desperate to believe in something special, something extraordinary, something mystical, romantic, or supernatural.[9] They want to be lifted out of their dull lives or dire circumstances.

As a result, when someone comes along with something worth believing in, most everyone will stop, look and listen, and some will follow and obey. Still others will make great sacrifices, marching without question to whatever the orders of the day.

The problem for most leaders is they fail to understand the importance of believing in something or, even more commonly, they don't believe in anything worthwhile themselves. This is the place to begin.

Focus First on the Need to Believe. Belief begins with desire. If your audience *wants* to believe you, your job of persuading them to believe and convincing them to follow will be far easier. When someone wants to believe something, any lingering reservations, questions, or doubts will automatically lean in your favor. If they don't *want* to believe you, however, all those lingering reservations will lean decidedly against belief.

As anyone in sales will tell you, what your audience *wants* to believe determines *everything*—from what you say, to how and when you say it, to whether you say it at all. The place to begin, therefore, is with understanding your audience—*who* they are, what they *want*, and *why* they want it. As marketing maven Dan Kennedy writes, "The important 'secret' here to grasp is that providing *reasons* to believe is a rather ordinary, commonly understood exercise in persuasion, but it is "low power" unless and until it is paired with an inspired *desire* to believe."[10]

Stop Working So Hard to Win the World Over. The reality is you cannot always create a desire in someone where no desire exists. In fact, you may very well be wasting your time because if someone does not *want* to believe, *they are unlikely to even listen.*

Former Louisiana Governor Huey Long was one of the most charismatic and persuasive figures of his era. In the words of Long biographer Richard White, "Always mesmerizing, he cast a spell upon his listeners."[11] As compelling and persuasive as he could be, however, even Huey could not always reach those who were opposed to his message. In one instance, for example, when Huey spoke at a county fair one summer, "a man who hated him stood to the side of the crowd, then disappeared. Later, one of Huey's supporters saw the man and asked why he left. "I left because I was afraid. That guy was convincing me. I had to get out."[12]

Rather than trying to reach those who refuse to even listen, far better to identify your ideal audience, the people who *want* or *need* to believe, or at least those who are receptive to how it may be in their own interest to believe.

Understand: The far too common but costly *mistake* is to try to win *everyone* over. It is far more effective and efficient to turn away from those who are unlikely to be persuaded anyway. It is far wiser to focus your efforts and center your message around your *ideal* target or niche.

In the case of Joan of Arc, one of the secrets to her success in persuading the Dauphin to allow her to lead the French troops was that he already *wanted* to take his rightful place as the King of France. In other words, he desperately *wanted* to believe her; the *desire* to believe she could help him was already there. He wanted to believe that God was looking out for him, that his legacy could be saved. Of course he had doubts about this young, illiterate peasant girl, and he did his due diligence in investigating her claims, but he was also desperate to find out that she was indeed the real thing. Thus, that *crucial* step in the process was already done.

The lesson is clear: Don't start by giving people reasons to believe. Instead, start with a worthwhile belief. In other words, *first* make sure that it is in your audience's own best interest to believe, that there is a clear and compelling benefit your audience will gain. Once they have the desire to believe you, then you can lay out the case for why they should.

Act Only from Deep Self-Belief.

"There is but one cause of human failure.
And that is man's lack of faith in his true Self." [13]

—William James (1842—1910), Harvard Psychologist

Nothing explains Joan of Arc's remarkable rise and ultimate impact better than her unflinching, unshakeable sense of self-belief. Virtually everything of consequence that she said and did can be traced back to her belief. From the very beginning, Joan of Arc boldly, confidently, without pride or malice, asserted that *she* was the one who would lead the French forces to victory over the English. *She* was the one who would restore Charles VII to power. *She* was the one who, she said, "must be at the King's side." "There will be no help (for the kingdom)," she said, "if not from me."[14]

"For no one in all the world," she said, "neither kings nor dukes nor the daughter of the King of Scotland, nor any other person, can recover the kingdom of France, and there is no other help than mine."[15] "And why had all this happened to her, instead of someone else? Because it pleased God, she said, to drive back the king's enemies by means of a simple maid."[16]

Activate the Virtuous Circle of Self-Belief. Regardless of how you interpret Joan's visions, in her mind, they were real. She was set apart. She was chosen for a divine purpose. She was destined to be a vessel for God. And her unblinking, unshrinking belief in her destiny made the most improbable difference. In fact, her whole story is a testament to a simple truth: The greater your self-belief, the greater your power to transform your world.[17] "Having supreme confidence makes you fearless and persistent, allowing you to overcome obstacles that stop most people in their tracks. It makes others believe in you as well. And the most intense form of self-belief is to feel a sense of destiny impelling you forward."[18]

In Joan's case, while it all began with her own unshakeable sense of self-belief (i.e. the belief that God chose to work through *her*), it by no means ended there. In fact, it was the extent to which her belief transformed the beliefs of so many others that made the real, lasting difference.

When her parents attempted to marry her off at age 16—beginning with her own unshakeable self-belief—it was the local court's belief in her divine mission and her vow of chastity that enabled her to prevail over her parents, setting the stage for her legend as The Virgin Warrior.

After his initial resistance to the unknown teen's request—again, beginning with her own unshakeable self-belief—it was the garrison commander's belief in her gift of prophecy that enabled her to secure an armed escort through hostile territory to speak to the Dauphin of France.

When Charles waffled about whether to let Joan lead the army to Orléans, it was belief in the growing legend of Joan that led to thousands of new recruits swelling the French army and which, in turn, helped Charles, who was already forced to rely on volunteers, to make up his mind in her favor.

And, finally, on the field of battle—again, beginning with her own unshakeable self-belief—it was the French soldiers' belief in her that inspired them to fight like lions.

Reap the Rewards of Supreme Belief. No doubt, as with Constantine, Charlemagne, Martin Luther, Harriet Tubman, Abraham Lincoln, Theodore Roosevelt,[19] Martin Luther King, and countless others; those who, like Joan of Arc, believe that they are called to a divine mission by a loving, *all-powerful* God are at an even greater advantage. People like this often appear utterly fearless in the face of grave risks, including the threat of assassination or execution. Indeed, in many cases, this sort of belief in Providence is everything. As Joan of Arc herself said, "…to live without belief, that is a fate more terrible than *dying*."[20]

To succeed, the ancient Chinese military strategist Sun Tzu once said, "you *must* believe in yourself."[21] Sadly, the great majority of people slog through life without ever truly recognizing just how vital it is to believe. Rather than believing that they have what it takes to succeed, that they too can be chosen by Providence, that they have the capacity to rise up and conquer whatever challenges they face, and achieve whatever seemingly impossible goals they set; most people saddle themselves with self-doubt and fear. And, as a result, they place false limits and artificial constraints on their success. "What we can or cannot do, what we consider possible or impossible, is rarely a function of our true capability. It is more likely a function of our beliefs about who we are."[22] "Our beliefs are like unquestioned commands," writes Anthony Robbins, "telling us how things are, what's possible and impossible and what we can and cannot do. They shape every action, every thought, and every feeling that we experience. As a result, changing our belief systems is central to making any real and lasting change in our lives."[23]

Make Big, Bold Promises with Unflinching Belief.

"All battles are first won or lost, in the mind." [24]
—Joan of Arc

Make an Irresistible Promise. Grounded in her unshakable belief, the third factor critical to Joan of Arc's surprising influence was the bold, irresistible promises she made, and how she made them—without a hint of hesitation, reservation, or doubt.

The promise is a vital part of all forms of leadership and influence. The only reason leaders exist is because followers believe (or at least *hope*) that the leader will deliver on the promise. If there is no promise, there is no leader, no follower, no relationship, and no influence. Even fans of rock stars or influencers are banking on the promise—regardless of whether the promise is explicit, hidden, or assumed. And the moment fans no longer feel that special feeling or connection or sense of belonging or status from following the star, the moment they will cease to be fans.

The bigger and bolder the promise the greater and more powerful the effect (so long as your audience believes you). What Joan of Arc was promising was something no one in France had been able to do in nearly a hundred years: She was promising to drive the English out of France. She was promising to restore French pride and honor and a sense of self-determination. She was promising something irresistible, and she was making that promise with unflinching faith.

Communicate with Conviction. Joan of Arc's unwavering, unmistakable *conviction* was another vital element of her extraordinary influence. "Self-belief must be communicated to potential followers."[25] The acceptance of the leader, "the *acceptance* of the leader's ideas and program, has much to do with 'the *intensity* of the leader's convictions' and…*the strength of their expression.*"[26][e.a.] "Rhetoric, as always, is a powerful tool."[27]

This was, in fact, a critical part of why she stood out amongst so many others, explains historian Juliet Barker; "Joan had absolute faith in the divine origins of her mission and was utterly convinced that her voices were real, which made her a convincing, fearless and charismatic leadership figure, especially in a divided country which, until she arrived, had believed that God was on the side of the English."[28]

Mark Twain explained it this way, "she was a rock of convictions in a time when men believed in nothing and scoffed at all things; she was unfailingly true to an age that was false to the core..."[29] In fact, when she was first questioned by the Dauphin's best theologians, an examination that lasted for three weeks, it was her unwavering conviction that stood out most. As one historian put it, "These men believed that God hadn't made women to be soldiers, let alone lead armies, but she was so utterly convinced of what the voices had apparently told her, that they couldn't decide whether she was indeed a messenger from God, or an envoy of the devil."[30]

The beauty of Joan of Arc's promises, and the *reason her unwavering conviction was key*, is that the more the French people believed in what she was saying, the more likely they were to publicly support her, spread the word, take actions, make sacrifices, and *fight* to make her words come true. The promises she made, in other words, were promises that her followers wanted to believe *and* over which they had some control.

Broadcast Your Belief. As with Joan of Arc, the intensity of *your* belief is critical to *your* success. Your beliefs work as limits on your ability to influence others. The more you believe in what you're saying or doing, the more others will believe in it too. Your belief operates like a radio signal. If it is strong, others will pick up on it and get the message. The stronger it is the better and more clearly they will receive it and the more likely they are to believe it. The depth of your belief in what you're doing manifests as confidence, conviction and congruence—all of which you can learn to develop and which, in turn, will strengthen your signal and help broadcast your message.

Illustrate the Intensity of Your Belief. When Joan first attempted to approach the French court when she was sixteen, she was rebuffed. The following year, she demonstrated even greater conviction. Indeed, the very fact that she was returning was a sign of conviction. But she also returned with a retinue of supporters, including two French nobleman, Bertrand de Poulengy and Jean de Metz.[31] Thus, it was more than just the desperation of the French that helped her to rise to take command. It was the confidence and conviction of Joan of Arc. "...Confidence is a critical component of persuasion. If people don't think you say what you mean or mean what you say, they have no reason whatsoever to listen to a word you say."[32]

As with Joan of Arc, who was overcome with belief in her divine mission, Napoleon Bonaparte, another heroic French leader, "inspired in the population profound belief and faith in him simply because he had been overcome by belief in himself."[33] We see this same principle of persuasion at work throughout history—from the great military and political leaders to the titans of business and industry. "Because they believed so strongly in what they were telling us," writes political consultant Frank Luntz, "we were inclined to trust and believe in them as well. That's no small point."[34]

"Trust is an integral part of communication and persuasion, and you can't really build trust if people don't think you actually believe in what you're saying."[35] Real estate tycoon and media proprietor Mort Zuckerman adds, "For me, the *most important element of persuasion* is that you really need to believe what you're trying to persuade people to share."[36][e.a.]

Promise and Promise Again. When the French people heard about Joan of Arc and her prophecy, they hoped it was true. But not everyone believed. So, they asked for a sign. But because she, initially, could not make them believe by offering proof, *she fed their hope with one bold promise after another*. "In the name of God," she said, "I have not come to...give signs; but take me to Orléans, and I will show you the signs for which I am sent."[37]

"Give me an army," she said on another occasion, "and I'll break the siege myself."[38]

Indeed, there were a number of instances in which Joan made bold promises—always with utter confidence and conviction—as a means of overcoming resistance or boosting motivation and morale. The moment Joan first arrived at Orléans, for example, she told their leader, Jean de Dunois, "I bring you better succor than has ever come to any general or town whatsoever—the succor of the King of Heaven."[39]

In another instance, on May 6, after a long day of fighting, the French had been victorious, but they had not yet succeeded in taking the primary English stronghold in Orléans, the Tourelles. However, with the road east cleared, the city could now "be supplied indefinitely."[40]

At this point, Joan of Arc's fearfully cautious generals were determined to call for a halt until they could be reinforced. At a council of war meeting, to which she was deliberately excluded, the self-congratulatory generals talked themselves out of further fighting. "The town is full of supplies; we could keep it well while we await fresh succor, which the King could send us; it does not seem expedient to the Council that the army should go forth tomorrow," one knight reported to Joan afterwards.[41]

Joan was having none of it.

"Go back to that council," she said, "and tell them this!"[42]

"You have been to your council and I have been to mine. Now, believe me when I say that the Counsel of God will be accomplished and succeed; yours, on the contrary, will fail!"[43]

It was just another promise. But, once again, it was a bold promise, backed by unflinching belief.

Lean on Belief to Prevail and Persevere.

"Remember, conviction has the power to drive you to action, to push you through all kinds of obstacles."[44]

—Anthony Robbins, Awaken the Giant Within

Beliefs are the bedrock of perseverance, resilience and grit. What you believe about whether or not you ought to persist in a quest will determine whether or not you do. As Anthony Robbins writes, "Beliefs can either give us the resolve to take action, or weaken and destroy our drive."[45] Your beliefs and the words and actions that flow out of your beliefs will also have a powerful influence on the beliefs of those around you and the words and actions that flow out of their beliefs.

Naturally, the idea that an unknown, illiterate, peasant girl might be given command of the French army was ludicrous—particularly given the warped ways of the Medieval world, which included severe restrictions against women. It is no surprise, therefore, despite her message of hope, that the first time Joan of Arc petitioned for an armed escort to travel to Chinon to speak to the Dauphin of France, she was immediately, unceremoniously rebuffed; brushed away by the Dauphin's garrison commander like some pesky, stray dog. Gaining access to the heir apparent to the throne of France in a time of war would take more than a little effort and a fantastic claim.

Most people would have given up right there. In his bestselling business book, *Think and Grow Rich*, Napoleon Hill argues that "the majority of people are ready to throw their aims and purposes overboard, and give up at the *first sign* of opposition or misfortune."[46] Furthermore, a "lack of persistence," Hill argues, "is one of the major causes of failure."[47]

But Joan of Arc would *not* give up. She would not back down or surrender. She refused to be denied. And it was all *because of what she believed.*

Joan of Arc believed she was being sent by God. She believed it was her destiny to "drive the English out of France"[48] and no man, no matter how powerful and deep their doubt, was going to stop her.

Following the governor's rejection of her request for a military escort through hostile territory, Joan of Arc revealed her resolve to fulfill her mission. As she was walking away, she turned and said, " You refuse me the soldiers, I know not why, for it is my Lord that has commanded you. Yes, it is He that has made the command; therefore I must come again, and yet again; then I shall have the men-at-arms."[49] Reflecting on his harsh rejection later, she said to a friend, "Nevertheless, before mid-Lent, I must be with the Dauphin, even if I have to wear my legs down to my knees!"[50]

Meanwhile, as she contemplated her next move, Joan continued to speak openly about her visions, particularly in court when she defended herself against a devious marriage suitor who, sadly, was supported by her own parents.[51] As news of her successful and "ingenious"[52] self-defense, which impressed even the judge, spread to surrounding villages, word of her visions caused stirrings that she might be the virgin prophesied to lead France to victory over the English.

Unfortunately, these excited whisperings soon led to Joan of Arc's village getting sacked by Burgundian forces which were allied with the English. Rather than silencing her, however, this only reinforced her will to defeat the English and their supporters. But it also helped to spread the word of her visions, which led to increasing support for her cause. In fact, Joan of Arc soon became a minor celebrity. By the time she returned in the spring of 1429 to speak with the garrison commander, Robert de Baudricourt, news of the famous girl prophet and her divine military mission had spread across France, greatly increasing her authority and social proof.

Sir Robert de Baudricourt was no longer laughing.

When he discovered that she somehow knew of the outcome of the Battle of the Herrings days before word could possibly have reached her, he was at last convinced. He immediately arranged to have her outfitted in men's clothing (a disguise for protection) and provided her with a horse and an armed military escort so she could travel the 300 miles through hostile enemy territory to the Dauphin's castle at Chinon.[53] At long last, Joan's confidence and conviction was so thoroughly compelling that she was granted an audience with Charles, the Dauphin of France, the man who would be king.

Identify and Adopt the Beliefs You Need. As with Joan of Arc, we all face difficult obstacles and challenges. Most everyone gets frustrated or discouraged, or finds it difficult to bounce back from a big setback. What separates those who, like Joan of Arc, prevail and persevere is what they believe. If you find yourself giving up too often or too soon, stop and examine your beliefs. If your beliefs are no longer supporting you, then resolve to replace those old, limiting beliefs with new more resourceful and empowering beliefs.

Ask yourself what you would need to believe (e.g. about yourself, the world, your relationship with God, or your purpose) in order to bounce back and persevere in the face of difficult obstacles, setbacks and defeat? Then, look for the supporting evidence or references or personal experiences you need to reinforce the beliefs you desire with the feeling of certainty they require.[54]

To be clear, you *can* change your beliefs. In fact, within reason, you can find evidence for almost anything you want to believe. As critical theorist Erich Heller wrote in *The Disinherited Mind*, "Be careful how you interpret the world; it *is* like that."[55]

But understand this: The point is not to be *realistic*. Joan of Arc was not being realistic. "Great leaders are rarely 'realistic.'"[56] They are smart, and they are strategic, "but they are not realistic," at least not according to the beliefs and standards of others.[57] What is realistic for you may sound like madness to someone else, depending on *their* experience, evidence, knowledge, and beliefs.[58] Joan of Arc believed a 17-year-old illiterate peasant girl could lead a great army, and drive the English out of France. "Gandhi believed he could gain autonomy for India without violently opposing Great Britain—something that had never been done before."[59] President Kennedy believed we could put a man on the moon. Not one of these leaders was being "realistic," but they all proved to be right.[60]

What matters, therefore, is not what society says is realistic or possible for you. What matters is identifying and adopting the most resourceful beliefs for which you can identify some compelling point of reference or evidence or support until you feel *certain* about that belief. What matters is having beliefs that serve, strengthen, and empower you. "What matters is which one is most empowering," writes Robbins.[61] "We all can find someone to back up our belief, and make us feel more solid about it. This is how human beings are able to rationalize. The key question...is whether this belief is strengthening or weakening...empowering or disempowering..."[62]

Deliver on the Promise.

"I shall last a year, and but little longer; we must think to do good work in that year. Four things are laid upon me: to drive out the English; to bring you to be crowned and anointed at Reims; to rescue the Duke of Orléans from the hands of the English; and to raise the siege of Orléans."[63]

—Joan of Arc to Charles VII of France

Finally, the fifth factor critical to Joan of Arc's surprising success was the extent to which she fulfilled her word and, driven by belief in her divine destiny, delivered on the promises she made. It's easy enough to *talk* a good game. But the real *lasting* power and influence comes from actually delivering on the promises you make. Indeed, perhaps nothing inspired the French people to believe more than when Joan of Arc began to fulfill the promises she made.

Few things have the power to strengthen belief—both your own sense of self-belief and the belief of others—better than the twin pillars of integrity and success. If you promise to do or achieve something extraordinary, or even noteworthy, and then you do what you said you would do by successfully achieving what you said you would achieve, you will both strengthen your own sense of self-efficacy, self-respect, and self-belief, and you will increase your influence with others.

When you honor your word, when you follow through on the promises you make to others, when people learn that they can count on what you say, you gain their trust, strengthen their connection, increase their hope, and further expand your influence and power. All of this, in turn, will increase the likelihood of your future success—particularly if, as was the case with Joan of Arc, your future success depends on the engagement and morale of others. The greater the promises you keep, the faster and further your influence and power will grow.[64]

At Orléans, immediately after she sent the knight to rebuke the war council for making plans opposed to her own, she turned to her confessor, Father Jean

Pasquerel, and said, "Rise tomorrow morning even earlier than you did today; do your best; keep always near me; for tomorrow I shall have yet more to do, and much greater things; tomorrow blood shall flow from my body, above the breast."[65]

The following day, Joan had all the lords and captains brought "before the captured fort, to consult as to what more should be done. French knights could hardly show timidity in front of a teenage girl," so they fought after all, just as Joan had promised.[66]

Interestingly, exactly as she prophesied to Father Pasquerel, she was also wounded the following day and blood did indeed flow from her "body, above the breast."[67] As Joan explains, "I was the first to set a ladder against the fortress on the bridge, and, as I raised it, I was wounded in the throat by a crossbow bolt."[68] According to one eyewitness, Jean de Dunois, the "Bastard of Orléans," the bolt "penetrated half-a-foot between the neck and the shoulder."[69] Joan was immediately removed from the battlefield, and both the English and the French thought she was mortally wounded.

Without Joan to lead them onward, French morale and resolve began to slip. Toward the end of the day the assault on the Tourelles looked like it would fail. It was 8 o'clock at night, and the exhausted French called a retreat.

But then, in what seemed to many like a miracle, the still seriously wounded Joan of Arc suddenly appeared at the front.

"At sight of her the English trembled, and were seized with sudden fear," Dunois reported.[70] "Our people, on the contrary, took courage and began to mount and assail the Boulevard, not meeting any resistance."[71]

"Be not afraid!" Joan yelled to the French troops.[72] "The English will have no more power over you."[73]

"In, in," she said when her standard touched the fortress wall, "the place is yours!"[74]

After hours of one of the bloodiest battles in the long war, with painfully little progress to show for it, the French troops—based solely on the promise of Joan—now believed that victory was theirs. They immediately went in.

And they won.

"After seven months of siege Joan had freed Orléans in a matter of four days. This was proof, her supporters now claimed, that God had indeed sent her, and news of her miraculous victory began to spread far and wide. Joan's conviction was now stronger than ever. Orléans had been her test and victory was her sign. Now came her true purpose—to crown the Dauphin and drive the English out of France forever."[75]

Fulfill One Promise After Another. Every time Joan of Arc honored her word or fulfilled a promise, her influence increased. When she successfully defended herself against a false marriage suitor, protecting her reputation and belief in her divine mission as the "Virgin Warrior," her influence grew. When De Baudricourt received official news of the French army's defeat at the Battle of Herrings, just as Joan had said days before anyone could possibly have traveled to Vaucouleurs with the news, her influence grew. When De Baudricourt finally relented, just as Joan said he would, and sent her with an armed guard to Chinon to request an audience with the Dauphin, her influence grew. When she successfully identified Charles in a crowded room of courtiers, despite his deliberate disguise, her influence grew. When she sent for a sword that her voices told her was buried behind the altar in the church of St. Catherine de Fierbois, a sword that no one else knew about, not even the clergy of the church, and the astonished priests found the sword, her influence grew.[76] When she successfully lifted the Siege of Orléans as she had boldly promised, her influence grew. And on and on it went; with each fulfilled promise, with each successful step in the fulfillment of her divine military mission, her influence grew. Regardless of what you believe about *how* she knew some of the things she knew, the result was the same: She made a certain claim or promise, the promise was fulfilled, and her influence grew.

Mark Twain once described the times in which Joan of Arc lived as "the brutalest, the wickedest, the rottenest in history since the darkest ages."[77] Rather than infecting Joan or corrupting her leadership, however, the brutal realities of the age helped her to stand out as a bright shining example. "The contrast between her and her century," writes Twain, "is the contrast between day and night. She was truthful when lying was the common speech of men; she was honest when honesty [had] become a lost virtue; she was a keeper of promises when the keeping of a promise was expected of no one;…"[78] Consequently, not only did she stand out in a striking and virtuous way, but this also helped to make her all the more heroic and, for all those believers who shared her faith—which included most of the French at the time—all the more convinced that she was on a divine mission from God.

Joan of Arc's promise to drive the English from France was not entirely fulfilled within her lifetime. Yet, under Joan of Arc's command, in 13 different engagements, French troops triumphed over the English 9 different times. What's more, another 30 or more cities, towns and villages simply surrendered to Joan of Arc and her army as soon as they saw her banner, returning their allegiance to France.[79]

Most important by far was Joan of Arc's vital initial victory at Orléans, along with her subsequent historic "Bloodless March" to Reims (a miraculous military procession through enemy territory in which, relying solely on "the mere force of her name," Joan of Arc captured every English-occupied city or fort along the way, all without spilling a single drop of blood).[80] This led directly to the fulfillment of her first and foremost promise: The coronation of King Charles VII of France in Reims Cathedral, which linked him to the kings of Israel, including the legendary King David of the Old Testament.[81] It was the fulfillment of this most pivotal, long-awaited promise, a "masterpiece of diplomacy," writes Twain, which gave France "an advantage of incalculable importance."[82] It reinvigorated the hope and will of the French people and reignited the courage and fighting spirit of France, paving the way for the recovery of Paris and Normandy, and France's final, decisive victory over England at the Battle of Castillon in 1453, which marked the end of the Hundred Years' War.

Believe to Achieve Miraculous Results.

> *"You can have anything you want—if you want it badly enough.*
> *You can be anything you want to be, have anything you desire, accomplish anything you set out to accomplish—if you will hold to that desire with singleness of purpose; if you will understand and BELIEVE in your own powers to accomplish."*[83]
>
> —Robert Collier, *The Secret of the Ages*

Joan of Arc's story remains one of the most remarkable stories in the long history of military leadership. Consider this singular, striking distinction: "Since the writing of human history began, Joan of Arc is the only person, of either sex, who has ever held supreme command of the military forces of a nation *at the age of seventeen.*"[84] In the words of Winston Churchill, "Joan of Arc was a being so uplifted from the ordinary run of mankind that she finds no equal in a thousand years."[85]

What set Joan of Arc apart more than anything else was her unshakable belief, both in herself and in the divine destiny that defined her life. It was belief that drove Joan of Arc to make fantastic claims and take fearless actions. It was belief that drove her to brook great risks, defy standing conventions, challenge powerful monarchs, and stir slumbering armies.[86] It was belief that gave Joan of Arc unrivaled spiritual, psychological and symbolic power. And it was Joan of Arc's belief that inspired the people to believe in a new, inspiring future for France. Indeed, Joan of Arc's great source of power came almost entirely from her belief, which was so powerful, so faultless and absolute, that it inspired belief in the minds of millions of others.[87] What other power on the planet could possibly match the power of belief?[88]

"Teachers like Jesus and Buddha have been telling us the same story for millennia. Now science is pointing in the same direction. It is not our genes but our beliefs that control our lives."[89] And your beliefs are under your control. As William Shakespeare wrote in *Julius Caesar*, "Men at some time are masters of their fates: The fault, dear Brutus, is not in our stars, But in ourselves, that we are underlings."[90]

And the stronger your belief in yourself and your vision, the more you will inspire others to believe, the more likely your vision will come true. Your belief becomes a self-fulfilling prophecy. The power is in the strength of belief—both yours and those you inspire to believe.

In the case of Joan of Arc, unfortunately, the English were well aware of her symbolic power, and they assumed, mistakenly, that to capture her would be to destroy the symbolic power of France. Alas, in 1430, in the midst of battle at the Siege of Compiègne, Joan was thrown off her horse, captured by English allies, and sold to the English for an enormous sum.

She was soon charged with the capital offenses of heresy and witchcraft and sentenced to be burned at the stake. Other than proclaiming her innocent of the charges, the ungrateful Charles, now "the Well-Served" King of France, did nothing to help her. She was offered life imprisonment if she would simply confess to being a witch, but she refused.[91] "My Voices *did* come from God," she said, "and everything that I have done was by God's order."[92] And, so, on May 30, 1431, refusing to lie or beg for her life, Joan of Arc, the savior of France, was burned alive at the stake.

Twenty years later, following an investigation that included analyzing the testimony of 115 witnesses, the retrial of Joan of Arc "overturned the guilty verdict that condemned her to death."[93]

In 1803, France's revered and beloved Joan of Arc was officially recognized as a national symbol of France by none other than Napoleon Bonaparte.

In 1920, following the discovery of the transcripts of the previous trials, Joan of Arc was canonized as a saint by the Catholic Church.[94]

In 1895, Samuel Langhorne Clemens, known popularly as Mark Twain, "the father of American literature," after spending 12 years researching her story and another 2 years writing it, published a biography of Joan of Arc, a book about which he said, "I like *Joan of Arc* best of all my books; and it is the best."[95] In this book, Twain captures the essence of Joan of Arc's story with the following passage:

> "The work wrought by Joan of Arc may fairly be regarded as ranking any recorded in history, when one considers the conditions under which it was undertaken, the obstacles in the way, and the means at her disposal. Caesar carried conquests far, but he did it with the trained and confident veterans of Rome, and was a trained soldier himself; and Napoleon swept away the disciplined armies of Europe, but he also was a trained soldier, and he began his work with patriot battalions inflamed and inspired by the miracle-working new breath of Liberty breathed upon them by the Revolution—eager young apprentices to the splendid trade of war, not old and broken men-at-arms, despairing survivors of an age-long accumulation of monotonous defeats; but Joan of Arc, a mere child in years, ignorant, unlettered, a poor village girl unknown and without influence, found a great nation lying in chains, helpless and hopeless under an alien domination, its treasury bankrupt, its soldiers disheartened and dispersed, all spirit torpid, all courage dead in the hearts of the people through long years of foreign and domestic outrage and oppression, their King cowed, resigned to its fate, and preparing to fly the country; and she laid her hand upon this nation, this corpse, and it rose and followed her. She led it from victory to victory, she turned back the tide of the Hundred Years' War, she fatally crippled the English power, and died with the earned title of Deliverer of France, which she bears to this day."[96]

14

MODEL THE MASTERS OF STRATEGIC AGILITY; ENGINEER THE FLEXIBILITY AND MOBILITY TO QUICKLY AND CLEVERLY ADAPT: GENGHIS KHAN AND HIS SAVAGE SLAYERS CONQUER THE ISLAMIC WORLD

*"The fact was that I was not a master of my actions because I was not so insane
as to attempt to bend events to conform to my policies. On the contrary,
I bent my policies to accord with the unforeseen shape of the events."*[1]
—Napoleon Bonaparte

In 1218, while still at war with the Jin dynasty in China, Genghis Khan sent a trade delegation, including a large caravan of commercial traders, to Otrar, the frontier post of the great Khwarazmian empire.

The Khwarezmians had a reputation for producing high quality steel and armor, and Genghis Khan was eager to explore the possibility of becoming partners in trade.[2] He was also curious to learn more about what, as a result of his recent conquests, was now his new neighbor to the west.[3] Anticipating a lucrative trade relationship that would benefit both nations, Genghis Khan wrote to his neighbor, "I am the sovereign of the rising sun, and you are the sovereign of the setting sun. Let us conclude a firm agreement of friendship and peace."[4]

But the ruler of the Khwarezmian empire, Ala ad-Din Muhammad II, known as the sultan or shah, distrusted Genghis Khan and let his fear and suspicion get the best of him. Shah Muhammad, "who controlled most of the eastern Muslim world,"[5] instructed his uncle, Inalchuq, the Governor of Otrar, to accuse the delegation of being spies and have them all arrested. The Shah then had Genghis Khan's entire trade caravan slaughtered, killing some 450 merchants, 100 cavalrymen escorts, and the personal envoy of Genghis Khan.[6]

When a camel driver escaped and returned with the news, Genghis Khan was furious. "The shah," according to one historian, "had offered him a gross personal insult, had offended against all the canons of the then rudimentary international law and was, even by medieval standards, guilty of a war crime."[7]

Nevertheless, hopeful it might be an egregious error on the part of the Shah's renegade uncle, Genghis sought to give the Shah the benefit of the doubt. His next move was to send a single Muslim ambassador, accompanied by two Mongol diplomats, directly to the Shah with a demand for swift justice. The Shah responded by beheading Genghis Khan's ambassador and shaving the heads and beards of his two Mongol diplomats—a show of disrespect intended to emasculate the men. The Shah, in effect, "rebuked the Khan in the most publicly dramatic and offensive manner he knew."[8]

When Genghis learned of this latest affront, writes the 13th century Persian historian Juvaini, "the whirlwind of anger cast dust into the eyes of patience and clemency while the fire of wrath flared up with such a flame that it drove the water from his eyes and could be quenched only by the shedding of blood."[9]

With his own reputation now on the line, Genghis Khan was left with few options. Rather than being completely consumed by his anger and launching abruptly into a new war, however, Genghis Khan took time to stop and think. While he commanded some 70,000 to 80,000[10] Mongol troops, the Shah "had some 400,000 men under arms across his empire."[11] Further, the Mongols were still engaged in the war in China and, moreover, if they attacked, the Khwarezmians would be "fighting with the home advantage on their own territory."[12]

Seeking wisdom, Genghis Khan went up to the mountaintop of Burkhan Khaldun and, for three nights and days, he reflected and prayed.

"I was not the author of this trouble;" he said, finally, "grant me strength to exact vengeance."[13]

Now resolved to destroy his enemy, Genghis still did not rush into battle, but he did send a final message to the Shah: "You kill my men and my merchants and you take from them my property. Prepare for war, for I am coming against you with a host you cannot withstand."[14]

The Khwarezmian ruler knew that he commanded far more men than the Mongols. What he did not know was that Genghis Khan was unlike any commander he had ever confronted before. It wasn't just the battlefield skills of the Mongols, born out of a lifetime of incessant military training, or the courage, cruelty and ferocity of the Mongolian Horde. What made the real difference was the strategic genius and agility of Genghis Khan—which played out in a number of important ways.

Learn from the Legends of Strategic Agility

Continue to Collect Timely Intelligence.

"It is a military axiom that time spent on reconnaissance is never wasted."[15]
—Alan Stephens & Nicola Baker, Making Sense of War: Strategy of the 21st Century

To begin with, in stark contrast to the Shah, Genghis Khan understood the necessity of good intelligence. After a few days of deep reflection, the Khan's first step in dealing with the Shah was to ramp up his intelligence gathering. "Genghis always made a point of studying potential rivals to an obsessive degree,"[16] and, in this particular case, there was still much he had to learn about Shah Muhammad II, the Khwarezmian people, and the internal politics of the empire. As eager as he was to swiftly respond to this unprovoked act of war, he knew better than to rush into a conquest of such magnitude without careful observation and a clear understanding of his enemy first.[17]

Unlike Muhammad, Genghis Khan already had what at the time was one of the most sophisticated espionage and intelligence systems in history, including agents who "had penetrated the Shah's inner councils" and loyal moles who made regular, timely reports.[18] But now a flood of Genghis Khan's intelligence agents would swamp the Shah's empire, "picking up gossip at markets and merchant caravans."[19]

"As information trickled back, it soon became apparent that despite the steely façade, all was not well in Khwarezmia."[20] "Genghis even knew that the Iranian soothsayers had warned the shah that the omens for the coming war were not favorable"[21]

In the interim, Genghis and his generals pored over the various maps of the Shah's difficult terrain, which included many deserts and semi-deserts, mountains, rivers, jungles, and steppes.[22] British historian Frank McLynn observes, "the geography of Khwarezmia alone was a tough nut for an invader to crack…Each separate area would throw up different problems relating to the horses, food supplies and logistics, and all would have to be carefully 'war-gamed' beforehand."[23]

"Meanwhile," focused primarily on his own protection in the capital, "the Shah devoted his energies to surrounding Samarkand with immense fortifications, which were never finished."[24] For his own part, the Shah completely failed to gather adequate intelligence. Instead, he relied on old accounts of the Mongols, dated information that was no longer accurate. For example, "sadly for his own ambitions," writes McLynn, "Muhammad had imbibed the myth that the Mongols were hopeless at siegecraft, which his agents based on the lackluster performance in the campaign against Hsi-Hsia in 1209–11."[25]

To be sure, earlier in his reign, Genghis Khan had been unprepared for siege warfare. "The Mongols initially lacked the weapons [and] knowledge to break down the massive city walls," and, thus, "they wreaked havoc in the surrounding countryside and then disappeared, only to reappear again just when it seemed that the city was safe."[26]

Look and Listen, Learn and Adapt.

"Strategic thinking is a proposition that says we can affect the future through a strategic learning process that positions strategists as adaptive influencers in this ominously unpredictable environment, rather than as victims or as controllers."[27]

—Julia Sloan, Professor of Strategy, Columbia University

Genghis Khan, however, was an agile strategist; he was constantly watching and listening, learning and adapting to the situation at hand. And, therefore, relying on dated accounts of the Mongols' military capabilities proved to be the Shah's first critical mistake. "He had no idea that, as a result of their war with the Jin, the Mongols' expertise had proceeded almost exponentially, and the well-defended fortress of Otrar held no terrors for [the Mongols]."[28]

The Shah's intelligence failure amounted to more than merely being surprised by the Khan's emerging expertise in siege warfare, however. It also meant that the Shah had foolishly squandered his greatest advantage, his numerical superiority. Rather than concentrating his forces to face the Mongol Horde in battle, the Shah opted "to shelter inside heavily fortified cities,"[29] essentially surrendering his advantage in numbers by dispersing his army across multiple garrisons, giving Genghis *local* superiority in numbers.[30]

It would not have taken much effort for the Shah to gather the intelligence he so desperately needed. Indeed, nearly four years had passed since, in 1215, Genghis Khan and his Horde had used siege weapons and tactics to conquer Beijing, an event so catastrophic that it alone left its mark on history. What's more, beyond Beijing, through his ongoing conquest of China, "the sieges of Chinese cities" had enabled the Mongols to gain "the best in siege technology and expertise: battering rams, scaling ladders, four-wheeled mobile shields, trebuchets with fire- and smoke-bombs, flame-throwing tubes, and the huge double- and triple-bowed siege bows, which could fire arrows like small telegraph poles."[31]

Through his own intelligence, Genghis was also able to exploit the Shah's lack of intelligence and "internal weaknesses even before the fighting started."[32] He was now determined to crush Khwarezmia just as he had already crushed so many walled cities in China. Traveling with his own livestock and heavy siege equipment, Genghis sent his second son, Chagatai Khan, "ahead with the vanguard to build bridges to take them across the...rivers, making sure they could bear the weight of heavy transport wagons. Chagatai had many faults but he completed this task with supreme efficiency, building forty-eight timber bridges wide enough for two heavy carts to drive across side by side."[33]

Once they finally arrived at Otrar, the Mongol Horde immediately began to assemble and position their weapons and prepare for battle. "Inalchuq, the governor responsible for the original atrocity, and general Qaracha, sent by the shah with 50,000 men to bolster the governor's original 10,000 garrison, are said to have been caught completely off guard by the Mongol host appearing outside the walls, with the neighing of armored horses and the braying of chain-armored mules."[34]

"Gradually they pounded the walls and cut off all supplies of food and water."[35] Otrar resisted the Mongolian onslaught for "five bitter months,"[36] but ultimately, "by their fierce discipline," and now considerable expertise at siege warfare, "the numerically inferior nomad army triumphed over an enemy who should have been able to resist."[37] According to one account,[38] when Genghis Khan's sons, Chagatai and Ogedei, finally seized Inalchuq, the murderous governor whose actions first put the two nations on the path to war, they "killed him by pouring molten gold down his throat."[39]

Conquering Otrar and killing Inalchuq was only the first round, however. After all, the real culprit was the Shah, and Otrar was only an outpost of his vast empire.

Prepare to Scale to Adapt.

The significant size of the Khwarezmian empire had in fact been an important concern for the Khan from the outset. To adapt to this challenge, "the Mongols used all kinds of tricks to exaggerate their numbers."[40] Beyond the *perception* of strength, however, Genghis knew that he also needed to scale up the *actual* size of his army and, therefore, from the moment he had first began to ramp up his intelligence gathering, he simultaneously began recruiting allies from across the region. To be sure, Genghis was taking the steps necessary to build "an enormous army…"[41] Along with the Mongol Horde and Chinese recruits, 10,000 Uighurs, 6,000 Qarluq Turks[42] and "a contingent from Almaliq made a hefty reinforcement; Ongud, Khitans, Solons, Kirghiz and Kem Kemjiut are also mentioned among the recruits."[43]

This much larger army of some 150,000 troops[44] provided Genghis with the flexibility he needed to expand his strategic options and, thereby, better surprise and overwhelm his enemy. The increased numbers also enabled him to temporarily split his forces and flank his enemy. As a matter of fact, taking a multi-pronged approach, Genghis split his army into four divisions.[See Endnote No. 45 on *force concentration*.]

Surmount Resistance Through Speed and Surprise.

While Chagatai and Ogedei, the second and third sons of Genghis, were dealing a death blow to Otrar and, thereby, drawing the Shah's panicked attention to the east, Genghis Khan's eldest son, Jochi, was in the north leading, at lightning speed, a second Mongol army of some 30,000 troops[46] across the treacherous Tian Shan mountains.[47] A remarkable feat accomplished in record time, Jochi's dangerous crossing, entirely unexpected by the Shah, was itself a premier example of the Mongols ability to swiftly adapt to new and difficult challenges and terrain. Jochi then immediately proceeded to capture all the cities and towns along the Syr Darya River. When he finally reached Jend on April 20, 1220, "the citizens had the good sense to surrender."[48] With this, the Mongols had effectively won the second round of the war.

Employ Experts, Exploit Assumptions.

Meanwhile, with his fourth son, Tolui, and a division of some 40,000 riders, Genghis embarked on yet another incursion into the Khwarezmian empire. In a strategic masterstroke, Genghis pulled off what one historian described as a "seemingly impossible…march of nearly 300 miles through one of the most fearsome deserts in the world."[49] What's more, he pulled off this "dramatic venture" with some "40,000 to 50,000 men, and even more horses," and he did it with "complete secrecy."[50]

Traveling to Transoxiana by crossing over the endless, red, pyramidal sand dunes of the reportedly "impassable"[51] Kyzylkum Desert was considered by many to be a "miraculous" achievement,[52] but Genghis Khan was virtually never formulating strategy or devising tactics out of courage or creativity alone. Rather, he was exploring his options and doing his due diligence and, in this case, "using local guides to navigate the oases"[53] and "trusting that the intelligence from his agents and local spies was good and that sufficient wells and waterholes could be located to water a large army."[54] Of course, Genghis also understood, as renowned military strategist and historian Captain Liddell Hart famously said, "in strategy, the longest way round is often the shortest way there."[55]

When the Shah received word that Genghis Khan had "suddenly appeared outside the gates of Bukhara," in other words, behind the Shah's defensive lines, he was "stupefied."[56] Beside himself with disbelief, he repeatedly asked "whether Genghis Khan was really to the west of him, and how this could have happened."[57] With Mongol divisions already occupying the north, east, and south, the Shah was now basically surrounded.[58] "At one blow the Shah's whole line was turned, and his communications severed with his more distant westerly States, whose forces had still to arrive."[59]

It was a coup of epic proportions. According to Captain Hart, "Rarely, if ever, in the history of war has the principle of surprise been so dramatically or completely fulfilled."[60] McLynn put it this way, "without question Genghis's march through the Kizil Kum [Kyzylkum] to outflank the shah is one of the greatest exploits in all military history, revealing him once again as a strategist of genius. He was at the height of his powers in this war against Khwarezmia, brilliant, original, innovative, creative, richly endowed with improvisatory genius and an unparalleled instinct for reading maps and understanding spaces."[61]

Probe for Openings, Profit from Your Opponent's Weaknesses, Limitations, and Fears.

The Shah's hopes now turned to Bukhara, the religious capital[62] of his empire and "the richest and busiest city of Transoxiana."[63] "Bukhara was one of the largest cities in the Islamic world,"[64] and the Shah was desperately hoping that the garrison of some 20,000 Turks, along with a relief column that he was sending in, would be sufficient to deter the Mongol threat.[65]

"Theoretically, Bukhara should have been impenetrable," but the city had its flaws.[66] To begin with, the Shah continued to operate under the assumption that "the Mongol army was still in its infancy as regards siegecraft."[67]

Genghis, moreover, was always looking beyond military strategy and tactics to consider the broader social, political, and economic context. In so doing, he would often find ways "to further undermine his enemies by exploiting any internal…turmoil or rift he could identify."[68] In the case of Bukhara, "Genghis thought the acute class conflict within the city might be his entering wedge."[69] According to McLynn, "Genghis hoped to use the slum dwellers as a fifth column; in any case they would be useful when it came to getting the elite to disgorge their wealth."[70]

What's more, the Shah had a serious loyalty problem. This made him unwilling to unify his army under a single commander, "lest a victor become a future rival."[71] The Shah's lack of *unity of command* (widely considered a core principle of effective military action), was in stark contrast to Genghis Khan's command over the four Mongol divisions which, with a highly developed messenger system, remained in near continuous communication as they concentrated and closed in on their enemies.

The Shah's lack of loyalty also meant that he was in constant fear of desertion or defection to the Mongol ranks. "Moreover, although he had a huge force of defenders at his command, Muhammad must have known that the overwhelming majority of influential oligarchs and merchants had no appetite for a fight to the death with Genghis Khan."[72] "All these were weaknesses that Genghis Khan was determined to exploit."[73]

Given their surprising advances in siege warfare, the Mongols quickly began to "batter…down Bukhara as if it had been a sandcastle."[74] Almost as expected, this led the Shah's disloyal garrison of 20,000 Turks to try to escape in the night. But they were quickly discovered and completely slaughtered by the Horde. The people of Bukhara were now utterly defenseless. The Shah's lack of loyalty was not limited to the army, however. "There were profound divisions among the Shah's subjects and also among his high officials," writes Turnbull.[75] Thus, not surprisingly, when they learned the Shah's troops had abandoned Bukhara, "the townspeople, unwilling to be killed for the sake of a sultan they despised, opened the gates."[76]

The Mongols proceeded to level the city. As Bukhara burned and thick smoke hovered overhead, Genghis Khan had the leading citizens summoned to the main mosque. As the city crumbled all around, Genghis stormed the pulpit to deliver one of his most famous sermons. Declaring himself the "Punisher of God," he proceeded to chastise the leaders for their sins. "Know that you have committed great sins, and that the great ones among you have committed these sins. If you ask me what proof I have for these words, I say it is because I am the punishment of God. If you had not committed great sins, God would not have sent a punishment like me upon you."[77]

Because the townspeople willingly surrendered, rather than destroying them, Genghis drafted all those with skills or knowledge into his army or sent them back to Mongolia. Those townspeople who lacked skills, however, were forced into manual labor, digging moats and hauling weapons.[78] "The fall of Bukhara had made manifest" the many different divisions and "various latent…weaknesses in the Khwarezmian empire,"[79] which Genghis would continue to exploit as he turned his attention to Samarkand, the Shah's political capital, "where the people were severely demoralized by the fall of their sister city."[80]

Win the Psychological Game: Employ Propaganda to Persuade, Confuse and Misinform.

All eyes at last turned to Samarkand, the home of the Shah himself, and the place where he "had taken refuge…with a force which Juvaini puts at 110,000 men, including 60,000 elite Qangli Turks and twenty war elephants imported from India."[81] Surrounding his enemy on all sides, "Genghis now closed in on the Shah's headquarters from the west, at the same time sending orders for his detached armies to rendezvous outside the city."[82]

The only question that remained was just *how* the Khwarezmian empire's final stronghold would fall. With each new encounter, Genghis Khan seemed to demonstrate his tactical and strategic superiority over his enemy in a new way. In Samarkand, his long game would again bear fruit, revealing his mastery of the psychological dimension of warfare.

Throughout their war against Khwarezmia, beginning with the brutal murder of the Governor of Otrar, who had a cauldron of molten gold poured down his throat, the Mongols had been simultaneously conducting a terror campaign in an effort to win the psychological game. To be clear, few question whether Genghis Khan was a viciously cruel conqueror who was willing to engage in all manner of atrocities to defeat his opponents. Rather than simply the sadistic work of a twisted mind, however, he used such brutal tactics and terror as a psychological weapon of war. Genghis Khan loathed to lose the lives of his men. In fact, his warriors were prohibited from even talking about death or injury in battle.[83] As a result, like Blackbeard and the pirates of the Golden Age of Piracy, Genghis Khan used terror in an effort to induce his enemies to surrender and *submit without a fight*. If the stories of his vicious cruelty could persuade a city to surrender before the battle even began, then Genghis would not only avoid the inevitable loss of a certain number of Mongols, but he might also gain a wealth of new recruits.

This psychological dimension of war went well beyond brutal rape, pillage, and murder. The swift, surprise attack through the treacherous Tian Shan mountains, the impossible crossing of the impassable Kyzylkum Desert, surrounding the enemy on all sides, attacking on multiple fronts, hitting him when or where he thought he was safe; all of these efforts served, in part, to shock, frighten and overwhelm the enemy and, thus, further induce him to surrender or make a costly emotional mistake.

One of Genghis Khan's most vicious and despicable tactics was the use of prisoners and slaves as human shields, which the Mongols used on the front lines both as protection from archers, but also as a deterrent—which worked particularly well when these poor souls, often captured in a neighboring village or town, could be seen and, in some cases, recognized by the facing army.

Following their decisive victory at neighboring Bukhara, "Genghis now had a plentiful supply of human shields and, more importantly, the psychological upper hand."[84] As the Mongol juggernaut rolled up on Samarkand, "driving crowds of prisoners," and setting up camp all around the city walls, a dark cloud of doom hovered overhead.[85] By this time, now more panicked than ever, the Shah "abandoned his people and fled west with 30,000 soldiers."[86] Promising to return with troops from Persian Iraq, he left a garrison of some 60,000 behind. While he fled, however, he urged "everyone along his route to get out, because resistance was useless."[87]

Genghis Khan's greatest weapon in the psychological war was not the Mongols' grotesque acts of violence, however. His greatest weapon was the pen. With an impressive understanding of the power of propaganda, and, writes historian Jack Weatherford, "with his penchant for finding a use for everything he encountered, he devised a powerful way to exploit the high literacy rate of the Muslim people, and turned his unsuspecting enemies into a potent weapon for shaping public opinion."[88] Rather than relying on the brutal actions of his Mongol warriors to spread terror, Genghis Khan believed that the words of his enemy's own scholars and scribes would be far more effective. "In an era before newspapers, the letters of the intelligentsia played a primary role in shaping public opinion, and in the conquest of central Asia," Weatherford writes, "they played their role quite well on Genghis Khan's behalf."[89]

Genghis also used Muslim scribes to spread misinformation, sow further division, and exploit the Shah's "strains with his Muslim neighbors"[90] and the "numerous divisions within his own lands and family,"[91] including with his quarrelsome mother, Terken Qatun, who created "almost unbelievable problems" for him.[92]

Given the various divisions and conflicting loyalties, writes McLynn, "Khwarezmia was a gift for masters of disinformation. It was the easiest thing in the world to issue bogus decrees, purporting to come from the shah or from Terken Qatun, snarling the military and bureaucracy up into a tangle of confusion."[93] "On this occasion Genghis surpassed himself by circulating rumors that Terken Qatun intended to join the Mongols, that she would rather be their prisoner than submit to Muhammad and [his son] Jalal al-Din."[94]

His efforts soon paid off, convincing scores of disloyal men to jump ship. "Advisors defected to the Mongol ranks, and Genghis began sending messengers out with false orders, forging letters claiming that scores of soldiers were abandoning the shah due to his ill treatment of his mother. He even wrote to the shah's mother, offering her the throne if she betrayed her son. The resultant chaos drove many to simply lay down their arms and flee."[95]

Finally, just three days into the siege of Samarkand, "the people opened the gates" to the Mongols while the remaining garrison withdrew to the citadel.[96] Witnessing the cowardly escape of Muhammad, "the merchant princes and clerics of Samarkand, unprepared to risk death for such a man, sued for peace and received similar treatment to the inhabitants of Bukhara, with Mongol commanders and their families taking their pick of possessions, women and artisans."[97]

"The citadel of Samarkand was then surrounded and subjected to the usual barrage of arrows and flaming naphtha [a flammable liquid], after which the Mongols stormed the [fortress]. There were now only 1,000 defenders left and the fighting was over in a few hours, or as Juvaini puts it, 'the space between two prayers.'"[98] "Samarkand's leading religious figure negotiated a surrender—securing safe passage for 50,000 scholars and nobles..."[99] "The Qangli garrison suffered the usual massacre, but the population was allowed to return home after paying a fine."[100]

Meanwhile, desperate to save his own life, the Shah became a fugitive. Hunted down by the sons of Genghis, the Shah continued to flee further and further away until he finally died of pneumonia on an island in the Caspian Sea in 1221.

From the outpost of Otrar to the capital of Samarkand, Genghis Khan—a brilliant and agile strategist, moving with speed and fluidity, adapting to the maneuvers and weaknesses of his enemy and the challenges and constraints of the terrain—had now conquered virtually every major town and city in Shah Muhammad's once-mighty empire, bringing the Khwarazmian war to its decisive end. Not only did this campaign "mark the transition of Genghis' empire from an essentially East Asian to a global power," writes historian Chris Peers, but it had also, in just four years, "utterly destroyed what had been the greatest Muslim power in Central Asia and took the Mongol armies to the western perimeter of the continent, opening up an entire new world of which they had previously been unaware."[101]

Reigning for more than two decades, the two-year-long war against Shah Muhammad gives us just a glimpse of the strategic genius and agility of Genghis Khan. But the war against the Khwarezmian empire is also a revealing illustration of how a man, Temujin ("blacksmith"), from such humble origins, once an outcast, a fatherless nomad, would first survive, and then learn, adapt, and grow to become the great Genghis Khan ("Universal Leader"), one of the most fearsome and formidable conquerors in human history.

Be Mindful of How You Perceive the World

"To change ourselves effectively, we first [have] to change our perceptions."[102]
—Stephen Covey, *The Seven Habits of Highly Effective People*

Keep Your Perceptions in Perspective.

It is easy to perceive ways in which the world is becoming increasingly complex, plagued by uncertainty, turbulence, and relentless change. Traditionally limited to a military context, the VUCA acronym (volatile, uncertain, complex, ambiguous) is now regularly applied to everything from politics and international relations to business, entertainment, education, and healthcare. But is this really, *objectively* true? And if we are living in a more VUCA world, is that really what matters? Or is the crux of the issue really about perspective, perception, and preparation, including appropriate training and tools?

After losing control of the capital of his empire and fleeing for his life, the Shah of Khwarezmia undoubtedly felt overwhelmed as his world came crumbling down. Given his persistent struggles with leadership, perhaps he always perceived the world to be chaotic, uncertain, and complex. But was the world really the way he perceived it, or was it more a matter of lacking the leadership, wisdom, discipline, training, and tools for dealing with the unstable, uncertain, and complex world in which he found himself?

Chaos and complexity can be stressful and confusing, and, under extreme, protracted conditions, it can make even the best of leaders feel frustrated, powerless, and incompetent, or perhaps even angry, fearful and overwhelmed. But the real failure comes when they compound the problem by neglecting to better understand their reality and manage their perceptions.

When most leaders are confronted with what they perceive as a chaotic, uncertain, and complex world, they will do either one of two things. The first typical reaction is to downplay and disregard it. These leaders will hunker down and focus on doing what they have always done, often becoming increasingly rigid and unresponsive to their rapidly changing world. These leaders often struggle to adapt and they "may cling to old habits and practices until those practices become counterproductive, distracting them from the more important new work that needs to be done."[103]

The second typical reaction is to surrender and capitulate to it. These leaders will throw up their hands and give up trying to plan or strategize at all, letting the chaos of uncontrolled, unmanaged internal and external forces reign supreme. Both of these reactive responses fail, but in different ways. Rigidity leads to extinction; chaos to disaster.

What about Genghis Khan? Perhaps he would have agreed that theirs was a world of uncertainty, complexity, and instability. After all, what was life like in 13th century Eurasia? Unprovoked, surprise raids from strange people; inexplicable weather patterns, floods and droughts; painfully slow and unreliable communication by horse and ship; crop failures that devastated entire villages; mysterious plagues that wiped out big chunks of the population—would people today not describe such a life as volatile, uncertain, ambiguous, and complex?

To be sure, there is nothing new about VUCA. To be a soldier in Alexander's army at the Battle of the Hydaspes in India in 326 B.C. was to experience a situation every bit as volatile, uncertain, complex, and ambiguous as the situation faced by the soldier in General Dwight Eisenhower's Easy Company regiment in the midst of the Battle of the Bulge during World War II.

In short, it is your perspective, expectations, and beliefs that shape your reality, far more than the other way around. According to a popular paraphrase of a passage by the ancient Roman emperor Marcus Aurelius in *Meditations*, "Everything we hear is an opinion, not a fact. Everything we see is a perspective, not the truth."[104] "The question is not what you look at," wrote Thoreau, "but what you see."[105] Perception is reality. It is, therefore, not about what challenges you face so much as your confidence, expectations, and readiness to face them.

Knowledge and training can change everything. Learning and development programs that include sufficient focus on mindsets and mental models, and equipping participants to think critically and strategically, can be particularly beneficial. Recent research in neuroscience and psychology is revealing how this may be even more true than we previously realized.

Scientists have long known about the astonishing power of positive and negative self-fulfilling prophecies, what is new is the research showing how mental frameworks can actually change the brain, including determining "memory capacity, concentration and fatigue during hard mental tasks, and creativity in problem solving. Even someone's intelligence—long considered to be an immutable trait—may climb or fall according to their expectations," reports award-winning science writer David Robson; "these findings are causing some scientists to question the fundamental limits of the brain, suggesting that we may all have untapped mental reserves that we can free if we develop the right mindset."[106]

As Stanford psychologist Alia Crum put it, "our minds aren't passive observers simply perceiving reality as it is; our minds actually change reality. In other words the reality that we will experience tomorrow is in part a product of the mindsets we hold today."[107]

The best part is that you can decide which mindset you are going to adopt. Recall the words of Heller, "be careful how you interpret the world; it is like that."[108] You can choose to see the world as volatile, uncertain, and complex, or you can adopt the much more empowering mindset of Pistol in Shakespeare's *The Merry Wives of Windsor*, who said, "The world is my oyster,"[109] or William Ernest Henley who wrote in "Invictus,"

"It matters not how strait the gate,
How charged with punishments the scroll,
I am the master of my fate,
I am the captain of my soul."[110]

You can adopt either one of these mindsets. You can make any mindset your own. But make no mistake, Crum said, "the mindsets we choose to hold influence the outcomes that will result. Mindsets change what we pay attention to. Mindsets change what we're motivated to do. Mindsets change how we feel and expect to feel. And mindsets change what our bodies are prepared to do."[111] What's more, she continues, "through cascading effects on these psychological, behavioral, and physiological mechanisms; *mindsets can create the reality that's implied*. In other words, having the mindset that *stress is enhancing*, ironically, is what makes those enhancing effects more likely. So, as influential leaders and decision makers it's essential to recognize that mindsets are not *peripheral* but *central* to health and behavior."[112]

In essence, the choice is yours. You can choose to see volatility, uncertainty, and complexity as an overwhelming threat or as a situation teeming with opportunities, so long as you maintain the mindset and employ the tools you need to exploit them.[113]

Model the Masters of Strategic Agility, Resolve to Thrive in a Volatile, Uncertain, Complex, and Ambiguous World

Regardless of how he might have described the complexity and volatility of war or the world over which he ruled, rather than being overwhelmed or paralyzed by it, Genghis Khan was able to thrive. In fact, it was precisely because he had the strategies, tactics, tools, and resources he needed to capitalize on the chaos and uncertainty of war that he was able to surpass his rivals and triumph over his enemies.

What makes the 13th century world so different from ours is not just the incredible problems that we have to confront, but also the vast knowledge and extraordinary tools we have to confront them. As has been the case throughout history, when the world becomes more complex, uncertain, and ambiguous, we improve our understanding, we invent tools and develop methods for managing it, conquering it, or turning it to our advantage. Indeed, this is the fundamental business of civilization. And those who, like Genghis Khan, are best able to deal with the world as it is, thriving in the midst of chaotic change and, thus, teaching us how to thrive, are those we remember best.

Rather than making strategy irrelevant, the madness of the modern world makes our capacity to create effective, sustainable strategy more important than ever.[114] And, moreover, the case for developing strategic thinking skills, writes Columbia's Julia Sloan, "becomes all the more compelling."[115]

The key to creating effective, sustainable strategy in today's world is agility. Formulating strategy cannot be seen as a final solution or ultimate destination to reach, writes *Harvard Business Review (HBR)*. "Strategy is not...a problem to be solved and settled. It's a journey. It needs continuous, not intermittent, leadership. It needs a strategist."[116]

This was the secret to the strategic genius of Genghis Khan: Agility. The "brilliance" of history's greatest strategic minds, explains Stanley Ridgley in his course, *Strategic Thinking Skills*, "lies not in offering an explicit set of maxims for the conduct of war but in his recognition of the fluid nature of reality and how any practitioner of strategy must constantly and swiftly adapt to that reality."[117]

Humans are creatures of habit. We easily fall into certain ways of thinking and acting. We even take pride in staying true to our convictions, opinions, and beliefs. But the problem is that the world is rapidly, continuously changing and evolving. It is impossible to thrive in a world of rapid growth and change without learning or *relearning*, without reexamining your habitual behaviors, or rethinking your habits of mind. To thrive, you must be willing to continuously learn, grow, and adapt. In other words, to be a master strategist, *agility is key*.

Strategic agility is about being flexible and swift to respond and adapt optimally to a dynamic, changing environment. The key words are *flexibility* and *adaptation*, but agility is also about *speed* and *mobility*, and using good *intelligence* and swift, accurate *communication* in order to rapidly respond and successfully adapt to and exploit the benefits of change.

Rather than thinking of agility as the opposite of rigidity, think of agility as being on a continuum between rigidity and anarchy.[118] On the rigidity end stands the inflexible, authoritarian leader who refuses to listen, learn, or change. On the other end you have chaos and confusion swirling around the erratic and impulsive leader who constantly changes course and achieves very little as a result. The agile leader is in the middle, representing the balance between the two—flexible, but with a solid inner core; ready and willing to adapt when necessary, but, when it suits the leader's strategic purpose, equally capable of standing firm and forcing circumstances or others to change instead.

To strike the right balance requires having a stable, consistent core which gives leaders and organizations strength and direction and helps to hold the endeavor together. This stable backbone or core consists of the more-or-less "non-negotiables" of the endeavor, organization or team, such as the chief purpose and key principles, which evolve only very slowly and only after thoughtful, thorough consideration. It might also include your or your organization's basic operational code or the underlying operating system itself.

But how does the strategist cultivate, encourage, and exercise agility? In the research investigating history's masters of strategic agility, the following are the five (5) most salient factors to surface:

Always Be Gathering and Analyzing Good, Timely Intelligence.

"If you know the enemy and know yourself, your victory will not stand in doubt;
if you know Heaven and know Earth, you may make your victory complete."[119]

—Sun Tzu, Art of War

"The Lord said to Moses, 'Send some men to explore the land of Canaan'...
When Moses sent them to explore Canaan, he said, 'Go up through the Negev and on
into the hill country. See what the land is like and whether the people who live there
are strong or weak, few or many. What kind of land do they live in? Is it good or bad?
What kind of towns do they live in? Are they unwalled or fortified? How is the soil? Is
it fertile or poor? Are there trees in it or not? Do your best to bring back some of the
fruit of the land.'"[120]

—Book of Numbers 13:1-2, 17-20

Agility requires intelligence. It is impossible to effectively respond to change if you are unaware of exactly how and what changes are taking place. The better you understand what's happening, the more likely you can use it to your advantage. Sometimes just one good piece of intel is enough to gain a considerable strategic advantage. Perhaps the biggest intelligence coup in history occurred when Alan Turing cracked the code on Germany's Enigma machine, allowing the Allies to read German communications in real time, which completely changed the war. While most intelligence coups are far more modest, they can nevertheless be a decisive component of success.

When Genghis Khan first thought of a surprise attack on the Shah through the fearsome, impassable Kyzylkum Desert, he knew he would need expert intelligence to pull it off. To obtain this intelligence, he captured the city of Zarnuk, "for the sole purpose of acquiring a man who had lived in the Kyzylkum Desert all his life and knew where the oases were located."[121] While Genghis Khan understood the need to crosscheck his intelligence, and he did rely on other guides, it was the local knowledge of this sole guide that "enabled the Mongol army to cross the desert from one water hole to another and fall upon the largely unguarded capital city of Bukhara from the rear."[122] "With Bukhara captured, the Khwarezmian Empire was cut in half,"[123] leading one historian to describe the capture of the guide of Zarnuk as "one of the great intelligence maneuvers of history."[124]

Without question, it is often critical to use multiple sources. "Like all the Mongol campaigns," Captain Liddell Hart writes in *Great Captains Unveiled*, "the invasion of [the Khwarezmian empire] was prepared for by the employment of an extensive spy system, combining propaganda among the enemy peoples with a wonderful service of information to the Mongol command."[125] Throughout the war, Genghis Khan used secret agents that had penetrated the Shah's inner council, but he also used spies who masqueraded as merchants throughout the marketplace. As with many other great military commanders, Genghis could also frequently be found on the front lines, collecting *unfiltered* intelligence with his own eyes and ears. "Those people in the field are closest to the problem, closest to the situation; therefore," Colin Powell once said, "that is where the real wisdom is."[126] What's more, Genghis also had a reputation for being curious, engaged, and open to explore—all of which, mixed with his mastery as a strategist, amounted to a potent cocktail of characteristics for an agent of intelligence.

Along with continuously scanning the external environment, effective strategists also understand the value of receiving feedback from a variety of different internal functions. You are not looking for agreement or support. You are looking for relevant facts and information. You want to explore and analyze alternative perspectives and conflicting sources in order to gain understanding and, ultimately, wisdom. In this regard, feedback and even constructive criticism can be immensely useful.

One of the leading causes of Mao Zedong's catastrophic failure in his attempt to modernize China's economy, the so-called "Great Leap Forward," was that his lieutenants were afraid to tell him the truth about how poorly his plans and policies were playing out. The fear of being purged caused the subordinates of Mao's lieutenants to exaggerate their numbers as well. In fact, there were multiple layers of deceptive reporting. By the time Mao received the totals they were so inflated that he believed China had a *surplus* of food—so much so that he was *exporting* food around the world while millions of Chinese peasants starved to death. As a result, Mao's short-sighted overreliance on fear ultimately led to a dramatic decrease in his own power and influence as tens of millions of Chinese died.

Fear has led to similar intelligence failures in Russia under the dictatorial leadership of President Vladimir Putin. Particularly in the early stages of Russia's invasion of Ukraine, surrounded by military advisors afraid to tell him anything he does not want to hear, Putin consistently overestimated the capabilities of his armed forces and underestimated the resistance he would face from Ukraine and the Western world.

In stark contrast, Dwight Eisenhower, a masterful political and military strategist, often made an explicit point of openly, sometimes publicly, seeking feedback. On the eve of D-Day, as the Supreme Commander for the Allied Powers, General Eisenhower exemplified this mindset in his address to the troops: "Here we are on the eve of a great battle. The Force Commanders will brief you on their plans. I would emphasize one thing: I consider it to be the duty of anyone who sees a flaw in the plan not to hesitate to say so. I have no sympathy with anyone, whatever his station, who will not brook criticism. We are here to get the best possible results..."[127] "Criticism may not be agreeable," Winston Churchill later added, "but it is necessary. It fulfills the same function as pain in the human body; it calls attention to the development of an unhealthy state of things. If it is heeded in time, danger may be averted; if it is suppressed, a fatal distemper may develop."[128]

In short, the best strategists are humble enough to realize that no individual is better than a team. We all have biases, blind spots, imperfect and incomplete mental maps, and habits of mind that can undermine even the most intelligent, well-intentioned efforts. Effective strategists, therefore, adopt the attitude of President Woodrow Wilson who said, "I not only use all the brains I have, but all I can borrow, and I have borrowed a lot..."[129]

Engineer Flexibility into Your Frameworks.

"One does not plan and then try to make circumstances fit those plans.
One tries to make plans fit the circumstances. I think the difference between success
and failure in high command depends upon the ability, or lack of it, to do just that."[130]

—General George S. Patton, *War as I Knew It*

The agile strategist is flexible virtually by definition. The most effective strategists, however, take flexibility beyond the need to bend or adjust to changing circumstances. Indeed, with the exception of a backbone of support or a stable core, the best strategists integrate flexibility into virtually every aspect of their operation. Take, for example, the case of Genghis Khan:

(1.) <u>Foster a Flexible Mindset</u>. To begin with, flexibility was a part of his operational code, and central to what enabled him to rise in the first place. Temujin did not become Genghis Khan, the lord of the nomadic tribes of Northeast Asia, because he was the strongest or greatest warrior, or the chief of the largest or oldest tribe. "He managed to weld all of these tribes together under his leadership," ultimately having himself proclaimed "universal emperor" by an assembly of Mongol chieftains in 1206, through a broad set of skills adapted to the situation at hand, including "a combination of military prowess, diplomacy, ruthlessness, and organizational ability."[131] Genghis Khan was not merely a hammer, seeing every challenge as a nail. He was a strategist, open and flexible, applying a suite of different tools to whatever best suited the situation at the time.

Nor did Genghis Khan hesitate to do things differently if he saw a superior way—even if that meant going against longstanding tradition, custom or culture. For example, in the face of considerable resistance from all those noble families who were benefiting from the status quo, he abolished the system of inherited aristocratic titles, replacing it with a system based solely on merit. Despite their deeply entrenched way of life, this decision helped bring an end to the constant tribal warring. Rather than surrendering to sentimentality for the past, Genghis allowed himself a range of options, choosing the most able advisors and generals, even those from the most humble backgrounds or recently conquered lands. "The picture we gain is not of a man weighed down by dogma or preconceived ideas, but of a man apparently open and flexible to whatever ideas work best."[132]

(2.) <u>Favor Flexible Tactics with a Strategy Able to Bend</u>. As the supreme chief, it was this same flexibility that continued to govern his strategic and tactical approach to war. Whether he sought to build alliances or obliterate an enemy, employ propaganda and psychological warfare, or unleash his strategic genius to force a surrender, Genghis Khan adjusted his plan to the people, situation, and context at hand.

At the start of the war with Khwarezmia, for example, when his initial plan for a surprise attack with his main army on the Shah's rear was foiled, "for the simple reason that Muhammad was afraid to take the bait,"[133] Genghis immediately regrouped to maintain the initiative and readied his army for a siege. As historian Chris Peers writes, "If Genghis' original plan had been thwarted as suggested, he showed his versatility as soon as this became clear by adopting a new one..."[134]

Flexibility also played a critical role in the execution of the Mongols' tactics in battle. In some cases, Genghis adopted certain measures in advance so that his warriors would have greater flexibility once on the field of battle. Historians believe, for example, that the Mongols were the first to develop the *metal* stirrup, which provided Khan's warriors with unparalleled stability and flexibility and, therefore, a major advantage in a fight.[135]

Along with giving horse-mounted archers the ability to better stand and twist around to the side, the design and sturdiness of their metal stirrups also allowed them to ride backwards in the saddle so that they could continue to devastate a pursuing army even in the midst of retreat.[136] This tactic worked so well that the Mongols practiced retreating as an offensive maneuver, allowing them even greater flexibility. According to one historian, "riding with stirrups gave the forces of Genghis Khan and his descendants a previously unimaginable tactical advantage."[137]

The Mongols also wore silk shirts under their overlapping layers of clothes, leather, and iron breastplates. This silk undershirt better enabled them to move their arms and twist their torsos and, essentially, "maintain...flexibility, allowing the Mongol warrior to perform the 'Parthian shot,' in which he would gallop full tilt away from an enemy while turning back in his saddle to fire an arrow."[138]

(3.) <u>Devise a Pliable Organizational Structure</u>. Flexibility was also built into the Mongol army itself, including how it was structured. Known as the "Horde," Genghis Khan organized his army into multiples of 10. The largest unit, known as a *touman*, comprised 10,000 men.[139] The smallest unit, known as an *arban*, comprised 10 men. Each *arban* had to be entirely self-sufficient, able to break off at a moment's notice without concern for food, clothing, weapons, or supplies. The leaders of each *arban* were also empowered with significant autonomy and latitude in terms of *how* they executed their orders. This command structure gave the Horde considerable flexibility. They could come together *en masse* to attack a large army, or they could swiftly divide into groups of 1,000 each (a *mingghan*), 100 (a *zuun*), or 10, depending on the situation.

(4.) Ensure Flexible Resource Allocation. The Mongols also had a mind for flexibility in the deployment and allocation of resources. Each man was responsible for up to 5 or 6 mounts, for example, lessening the burden on each horse. When required by extreme situations, they were also able to live off of their animals. The Mongols frequently drank their mare's milk, for example, but there were also times when they had to open a vein and then drink some of their horse's blood before sealing the vein again. While the Mongols cherished their mounts, and wrapped them in yak hides as protection from snowstorms, there were also rare occasions when a horse collapsed in the snow or from exhaustion or bloodletting, and the Mongols quickly killed and consumed the horse to survive.[140]

Unlike traditional armies, which required a massive supply caravan spread out in a long, often vulnerable, column, the warriors of the Mongol armies were self-sufficient; carrying their own food supplies or hunting in small groups or on their own. They were also more spread out, ensuring their horses had sufficient grasses, bushes, and shrubs to eat.

Beyond his own army, Genghis Khan also sought to make good use of the people he conquered. Naturally, as a military leader, he was particularly interested in making the most of any resources that might give him a competitive advantage in war. Rather than merely borrowing and building on ideas for weapons of war, for instance, "Genghis Khan acquired the engineering intelligence needed to create them. The Mongols eagerly rewarded engineers who defected to them and, after each battle, carefully selected engineers from among the captives and impressed them into Mongol service. Genghis," in fact, Weatherford explains, "made engineering units a permanent part of the Mongol army, and with each new battle and each conquest, his war machinery grew in complexity and efficiency."[141]

Unfortunately, Genghis Khan was also devilishly flexible with his morals, which worked to his advantage at times. Siege warfare, for example, was unusually labor intensive. In order to build siege towers and catapults, dig tunnels and construct earthworks, Genghis relied on the slave labor of the thousands of civilians the Mongols had captured in surrounding villages and towns. Even worse was the fact that many of these slaves were women and children. But the most terrible part was that, once the assault on the city began, the Mongols used these innocent men, women, and children as human shields.[142] As cruel and callous as it was, it "had the advantage of both lowering Mongol casualties and giving the defenders the horrible dilemma of having to kill their fellow countrymen, sometimes relatives or friends, or allowing the Mongols to reach the walls and take the city."[143]

(5.) <u>Counterpunch: Seek Support in a Solid Core</u>. Genghis Khan's affinity for flexibility was part of who he was as a leader, and his leadership provides a powerful example of the importance of being fluid and adaptable, open to exploring different options, and willing to try alternative routes. The point, however, is not to be flexible about *everything*. Thus, Genghis Khan also provides a compelling example of what *not* to do. While he is often remembered as a great conqueror, his reputation is severely undermined by the fact that he was also a brutal, bloodthirsty mass murderer who slaughtered some 40 million people.[144] Genghis Khan, in other words, took moral flexibility to the ultimate immoral extreme, committing crimes against humanity for which he would be convicted by a war crimes tribunal today.

The point of flexibility is to keep your options open, *not* swap out your principles to suit your current circumstances (though Genghis Khan would undoubtedly argue that his core principle was to save Mongol lives). Nevertheless, the *limits* of flexibility go beyond the value of having a solid, principle-centered core. Being flexible about *everything* is a recipe for chaos, not agility and success. In fact, it is with a relatively stable vision and values in place that you are best able to adapt to new challenges, opportunities and threats in an effective and advantageous, but still respectable way. A clear purpose and principles helps to guide your actions the way that sailors once navigated by the North Star.[145]

Nor is the point of agility to underestimate the power of consistency and conviction. In fact, as we learned from Joan of Arc's story (see chapter 13), there is tremendous potential power in consistency and conviction. The point is to avoid becoming so attached to your position that you are no longer willing to *think*—revisiting existing beliefs, understandings, and opinions to see if they still make sense. If something about you, your situation, or your world has fundamentally changed, it serves to reason that your understanding will need to change too. "A foolish consistency," Emerson wrote in *Self-Reliance*, "is the hobgoblin of little minds, adored by little statesmen and philosophers and divines."[146]

As Adam Grant explains in his book, *Think Again*, "Most of us take pride in our knowledge and expertise, and in staying true to our beliefs and opinions."[147] The problem is that that pride can be become a major obstacle to our own success, particularly given that "we live in a rapidly changing world, where we need to spend as much time rethinking as we do thinking."[148]

The key, then, paradoxically, to being truly agile, writes McKinsey, is to "learn to be both stable (resilient, reliable, and efficient) and dynamic (fast, nimble, and adaptive)."[149] The way to master this paradox is to build your strategy around a stable backbone, a core set of relatively unchanging elements, including your purpose and principles, but perhaps also certain basic processes and a core leadership or organizational structure, while simultaneously creating "looser, more dynamic elements that can be adapted quickly to new challenges and opportunities."[150]

The other key to mastering this paradox is cultivating the willingness to think and *think again*. Once accused of changing his position on an important issue, the celebrated British economist John Maynard Keynes responded with his usual wit, "When I get new information, I adjust my conclusions. What, sir, do you do with new information?"[151]

"Rethinking is a skill set, but it's also a mindset," Grant writes in *Think Again*.[152] "We already have many of the mental tools we need. We just have to remember to get them out of the shed and remove the rust."[153] Adjusting your rusty conclusions may require a bit of effort at times, but, for the master strategist or, as Emerson put it, "the great soul," it certainly beats the alternative. "With consistency," he said, "a great soul has simply nothing to do. He may as well concern himself with his shadow on the wall."[154]

Make a Core Competency of Quick, Clear Communication.

From small businesses and team sports to presidential campaigns and multinational conglomerates, communication is vital to virtually every field of human interaction. In high stakes competitive situations, effective communication is paramount. When it comes to strategic agility, communication must also be swift.

Operating in a time of war, Genghis Khan's generals obviously had to know the precise plan in order to execute it effectively. But it's virtually never enough to get the game plan only in advance of the game. An unfolding battle or conflict will almost invariably require some modifications if not major change. To paraphrase the preeminent 19th century Prussian military strategist Helmuth von Moltke the Elder, 'No plan can survive with any certainty beyond first contact with the enemy.'[155]

For Genghis Khan and his Mongolian horde, being able to rapidly respond to a dynamic situation presented a serious challenge, particularly given that, leading up to the final assault on the sultan, the different Mongol divisions were spread out across vast distances.

Adding to the challenge was the fact that the officers were illiterate. This meant that all communication had to be both oral and, to ensure accuracy and precision, *memorized*. To overcome these hurdles, the Mongols used a system of rhymes that every soldier was required to learn. This system included "a set of fixed melodies and poetic styles into which various words could be improvised according to the meaning of the message. For a soldier," Weatherford explains, "hearing the message was like learning a new verse to a song that he already knew. The soldiers, like bands of riders on the steppe still do today, frequently sang as they rode in their small groups. In addition to singing about what soldiers always sing about—home, women, and fighting— the Mongol soldiers sang their laws and rules of conduct," he continues, "which had also been set to music so that every man might know them. By memorizing the laws and constantly practicing the format of their message songs, every man was ready, at any moment's notice, to learn a new message, in the form of a new verse to these well-rehearsed songs, and take it where ordered."[156]

Dealing with the often vast distances was a different matter. To be successful, Genghis also had to remain in regular, close contact with the different divisions. This was accomplished through his remarkable messenger system. In fact, among his many accomplishments, Genghis Khan is also remembered for the empire-wide postal system he established. Known as the *Yam*, this messenger system included an extensive network of relay stations, placed about 20 to 40 miles apart, that provided food, shelter and spare horses (from among the 50,000 horses in service[157]) for the Mongol messengers, who rode the horses as hard and fast as possible, traveling, in some cases, up to 190 miles per day.[158]

Designed to speed up the process of sharing information and intelligence, the *Yam* was regulated by the *Yassa*, the code of laws of the Mongol empire, which ensured that messengers were given special privileges and that their swift and secure travel was given precedence over any of the other duties of Mongol citizens.

Along with a means of swift communication for other matters of state, this messenger system was critical to his successful military leadership. With regular riders "travelling at great speed using relays of horses," the Mongols were able to "concentrate quickly" to adapt to changing circumstances or the unexpected actions of a vigilant enemy.[159]

Along with the use of other riders as needed, Genghis used this system in order to coordinate his attack across great distances. For shorter distances, the Mongols used a "a sophisticated and well-drilled system of flags, torches and messengers" to ensure more continuous channels of communication between the different divisions and units.[160]

In essence, the Mongols' multiple methods of swift and sophisticated communication helped to make the Mongol Horde "far more agile" and responsive to the dangerously dynamic realities of war.[161]

Hierarchy is often one of the biggest hurdles to quick and clear communication. Hierarchical systems tend to be rigid with strict levels of authority, which discourages flexibility, transparency, and speed.

A recent example of this is the 2022 Russian invasion of Ukraine. In contrast to the trust and initiative-taking encouraged by Ukraine's military leadership, Russia's reliance on a rigid command structure has compounded Vladimir Putin's problems. Rather than getting accurate information swiftly, he has often been oblivious to how poorly particular aspects of the invasion were unfolding until it was too late to effectively respond or adapt.

"Putin's mistakes were not unique; they were typical of those made by autocratic leaders who come to believe their own propaganda. [...] But he also relied on a rigid and hierarchical command structure that was unable to absorb and adapt to information from the ground and, crucially, did not enable Russian units to respond rapidly to changing circumstances."[162] As British historian Sir Lawrence Freedman concludes in *Foreign Affairs*, "Inflexible command systems can lead to excessive caution, a fixation on certain tactics even when they are inappropriate, and a lack of "ground truth," as subordinates dare not report problems and instead insist that all is well."[163]

Respond with Rapidity. Design for Mobility and Speed.

"The world is changing very fast. We are moving from an old model economy to a new one, and every business has to find a way of transforming itself for this new economy which is coming upon us with lightning speed. Big will not beat small any more. It will be the fast beating the slow."[164]
—Rupert Murdoch (1931—), Newspaper Baron, Interview in *The Guardian* in 1999

In war, business, politics—speed is a force multiplier. The ancient Chinese military strategist Sun Tzu said, "mastering speed is the essence of war."[165] Harvard Business School professor John Kotter put it this way, "Speed is one of the most important strategic issues in a leap into the future."[166]

Being able to think, act, and *move* quickly is also a definitive part of what it means to be agile. In essence, strategic agility necessitates speed and mobility.

In the case of the Mongols, who grew up hunting on the Asian Steppe, being able to think and act quickly was a matter of life and death, often determining what and when their families were able to eat. Born into a culture of migrating and roaming to find food, a mobility mindset was a natural artifact of their nomadic lifestyle.

Not surprisingly, the nomadic way of life of the Mongol people was embodied in Genghis Khan and reflected in his army. They were experts with horses and "incredibly nimble hunters," and "Genghis Khan adapted these agile, extremely effective hunting techniques to warfare, building a highly mobile army that was fast, efficient, and could execute and iterate on a dime."[167] Indeed, according to many historians, a significant part of the success of Genghis Khan can be attributed to the speed and mobility of his army which, made up of "horse archers with no more baggage than a reserve of spare horses," was able to "move fast and strike hard before the enemy had any chance to do anything about it."[168] As the influential British strategist Liddell Hart writes in *Great Captains Unveiled*, "The Mongol force was a machine which worked like clockwork, and this very mobility made it irresistible to troops far more strongly armed and numerous."[169]

The ability to rapidly respond to a change in circumstances was built into the Mongol army by design. Consider the following four factors in terms of the mobility (which coincides with flexibility, discussed above) and, more specifically, the speed which enabled Genghis Khan to succeed:

(1.) Enable Self-Sufficient, Self-Managing, Accountable Action. One of the greatest contributors to the speed and mobility of the Mongol horde was derived from their organizational structure and the self-sufficiency of the individual units, which prevented them from requiring a long and slow baggage train. "Every trooper carried a complete set of tools, individual camp-kettle, and iron ration, for his own maintenance and subsistence in the field. He had also a water-tight bag in which he carried a change of clothes, and which could be inflated for crossing rivers."[170] Each *arban* (squad of 10) also had its own doctor and commander, but they all shared in the necessary work. "As his warriors moved without a cumbersome supply train, they swept across the land at a blistering pace, raiding and plundering as they went."[171]

(2.) Create a Network or System Comprised of Empowered Teams.[172] Their organizational structure also facilitated greater speed and mobility in terms of formations. By structuring the Mongol army into stable, self-sufficient units of 10—which could be quickly and easily adapted and scaled to meet a changing need or focus on a shared mission—Genghis Khan ensured that the Mongol Horde possessed a lethal, unprecedented level of flexibility, mobility, and speed.

(3.) Produce and Distribute Resources to Maximize Mobility and Speed. They also gained an advantage in speed with their extraordinary supply of horses. Each rider had as many as 5 spare horses galloping alongside, enabling the Horde to travel long distances much more quickly than any army relying on one horse per soldier.

(4.) Train, Develop and Deploy Winning, Standardized Methods of Moving and Working.[173] Finally, the Mongols relied on *skill* to increase their speed and mobility. They were, for example, trained to swap mounts while still galloping. With such resources and training, Genghis Khan's army could "travel vast distances…at unprecedented speeds—conventional armies had little hope of defeating them."[174] They were so fast, in fact—many sources reporting upwards of 60 miles a day—that their opponents frequently assumed they were facing a Mongol Horde five or six times the strength of its actual number.[175]

Napoleon Bonaparte would later use a similarly flexible approach, though on a grander scale, to reorganize his *Grande Armée*. In a system that became known as the *corps system*, Napoleon created what amounted to between 5 and 7 mini, self-contained armies. Each army, typically consisting of between 20,000 and 30,000 troops, was commanded by its own Marshal and had its own infantry, cavalry, and artillery, as well as all of the other necessary support services.

This allowed each army to operate independently whenever necessary or advantageous, including when foraging, following separate routes, or maneuvering to surprise an opponent. Given that smaller units made it easier to live off the land and scattered villages, rather than being constrained by the long, slow and vulnerable supply train, the corps system also gave Napoleon an advantage in *speed* and, therefore, *surprise*.

Rather than commanding one massive, slow-moving, ponderous and predictable beast, Napoleon designed the corps system to increase *speed* and *mobility*. And, as Chandler writes, Napoleon's "...insistence on speed and mobility was a basic feature of the Emperor's campaigns from beginning to end," and, furthermore, it was "the feature of his warfare that most confused and unsettled the majority of his opponents."[176]

Rather than contradicting the principle of concentration, however, Napoleon ensured that these self-contained *corps d'armée* were never more than about 20 miles apart, usually less, and, moreover, that they were all working in close, carefully orchestrated concert with one another. Thus, while being slightly dispersed when moving along separate routes, Napoleon ensured they were concentrated at the *decisive point* prior to contact with the enemy.[177]

This highly flexible system was far superior to the organization of any other army of the day. It helped to ensure that Napoleon's campaigns were "quicker and more fluid," writes Major James Wasson, and it gave Napoleon a "decisive advantage over his opponents."[178] As a result, Napoleon's *corps d'armée* system was eventually imitated by armies around the world.

Napoleon used these same principles—flexibility, mobility, and speed—in regards to the battles he chose to fight. According to Clausewitz, this was an important part of Napoleon's success.[179] He kept his army moving until he saw an opportunity to win. Of course, the goal was always the same: Defeat the enemy or force a surrender. But when and where he would engage the enemy depended entirely on the situation and circumstances. "When he saw a battle he could win, he chose to fight. If he saw no battle that he could win, he just kept moving, out of reach of the enemy but always looking for a better time and place to attack."[180]

This is what Napoleon meant when he said, "Instead of obstinately seeking to control circumstances, I obeyed them."[181] It's not that he abandoned his purpose or surrendered his goals to fate. It's that, rather than fooling himself, he acknowledged the realities of whatever circumstances he faced and adjusted his plans or rerouted his course to adapt. Interestingly, as a result of this strategy, Columbia Business School professor William Duggan writes, "Napoleon passed up more battles than he fought. But in so doing, he won more battles than any other general in history."[182]

Naturally, these same core strategic principles went beyond Napoleon Bonaparte and Genghis Khan. To be sure, the recognition of the vital importance of speed and mobility in the implementation of strategy can be traced back over thousands of years of warfare, most notably to master strategists such as Alexander the Great, Hannibal Barca and Julius Caesar. "Alexander's thundering heavy cavalry, Hannibal's agile light horsemen, and Caesar's lightning infantry thrusts—these were the agents of success. In their hands, even elephants could be made to move with grace," writes Cornell historian Barry Strauss, "as when Hannibal's elephants were cajoled onto rafts across the Rhône. They traveled light, with little in the way of a supply train. Their men lived off the land..."[183] "Speed was their watchword, mobility their hallmark."[184]

Learn. Experiment. Test. Take Risks and Dare to Adapt.

"It is not the strongest of the species that survives, nor even the most intelligent. The species that survives is the one most responsive to change."[185]

—Charles Darwin

Strategic agility is ultimately about effectively adapting to change. To effectively adapt in a turbulent, rapidly changing environment, or to respond optimally and advantageously to the unexpected development or course change, this is the essence of strategic agility. It makes little strategic sense to gather intelligence, or build in flexibility, mobility, clear communication, and speed if you are only going to fail to effectively adapt when it suits your own strategic purpose.

For our purposes here, it is important to draw a distinction between being *flexible,* which is more *tactical* and *short-term,* and being *adaptable* which is more *strategic* and *long-term.* Both are essential; but they are different. Rather than quickly adjusting to more or less predictable events, which requires *flexibility,* being *adaptive* is about making more significant or lasting changes to a new, often unanticipated, developments.

When the branches or trunk of a tree bends and sways in a storm, rather than breaking apart, it is flexible. When a tree regenerates from its root system following a wildfire it is adaptive. When a tree endures a dry spell or loses and regenerates its leaves with the seasons, it is flexible. When a tree is transplanted to warmer climate and it survives by changing the amount of water the leaves retain, it is adaptive. To be flexible, then, is to bend or adjust. To be adaptive is to change, evolve, or transform.

<u>Take Bold Risks, Borrow the Expertise of Others</u>. As a strategic military leader, Genghis Khan demonstrated considerable flexibility, but he also demonstrated a remarkable readiness to learn, experiment, and adapt. This goes a long way toward explaining how he was able to rise from such humble beginnings (e.g. living in poverty as a nomad, being abandoned, along with his mother and brothers, by their tribe) to become one of history's greatest conquerors.

In 1209, when the Mongols attacked Ningxia, the capital of Xi Xia, Genghis Khan knew virtually nothing of siege warfare. To lay siege to a city was what historian Borja Pelegero described as "the Achilles' heel of nomadic armies, which were skilled at swift maneuvers on the open field but ineffective at forcing walled cities to surrender."[186] It was, therefore, no surprise that, without proper siege engines or knowledge of siege warfare, Genghis Khan's "first siege of a large fortified city did not go as planned."[187] As a matter of fact, the siege of Ningxia was a *disaster*.

The Mongols worked hard digging for days in a Herculean effort to divert the flow of the Yellow River toward the walls of the city. Instead of washing away the foundations or toppling the walls of the city, however, the Mongols flooded their own camp.

Fortunately, as humiliating as this was for Genghis Khan—and probably hilarious for the defenders of Ningxia—the king of the city was so impressed by the scale of the effort and the will and grit of Genghis and the horde that he decided that they would make far better allies than enemies. He even agreed to swear allegiance to the great Khan and marry off one of his own daughters to him to seal the deal.[188]

Without siege weapons, however, the Mongols were still only able to capture towns and cities that were poorly defended or vulnerable to surprise attacks.[189] But Genghis Khan was a shrewd and tenacious strategist who was "also unusually innovative and adaptable, proving more than willing to try out new strategies when faced with unfamiliar situations."[190] In time, the Mongols "were able to steadily augment their army with powerful siege engines, which they acquired by recruiting Chinese engineers, deserters who had the technical knowledge the Mongols needed."[191]

Not surprisingly, Genghis Khan and the Mongols eventually "mastered siege warfare,"[192] because, as one historian put it, "where Khan was truly a military genius was in his ability to adapt to new strategies..."[193] In fact, in 1214, five years after his torrential failure to lay siege to Ningxia, by incorporating this new expertise into his arsenal, including the use of catapults and battering rams, Genghis Khan successfully besieged the city of Zhongdu and its nearly one million inhabitants, one of the largest city's of the day (known today as Beijing).[194]

<u>Learn What Works, Build on the Best Ideas of Others</u>. While the Mongols were best known for their mastery of the composite bow, they continued to adopt new technology, expanding their arsenal of weaponry as they swept

across Eurasia, borrowing and building on the best ideas of others. "The Mongols were lethal warriors," but what made them such a powerful, unparalleled threat was that they were also "brilliant learners: Any weapon used successfully against them would quickly become part of their own arsenal."[195] Furthermore, historian Keith Blanchard writes, "the Mongols were masters at quickly learning and adapting. Not only were they able to overcome whatever enemies threw at them—they were able to understand the value of those weapons and tactics, and quickly adapt them for their own use."[196] By combining the design components of catapults from both the Chinese and Persians, for example, the Mongols created a superior catapult that could launch projectiles well over 1,000 feet.[197]

To be sure, a vital contributing factor to the Mongol's success was "the adoption of their enemies' tactics and technology that allowed them to defeat established military powers in China, Persia, and Eastern Europe."[198] But it wasn't just "tactics and technology"[199] or even "foreign knowledge and expertise"[200] that made them such victorious conquerors.

The Mongols also adapted to new cultures. "When Genghis Khan occupied a sovereign nation, his appointed representatives bonded with the local cultures; and in fact, many were assimilated by those cultures."[201] Genghis Khan himself "embraced the cultures of his conquered nations and allowed [significant] religious freedom within his empire, embracing Confucianism, Buddhism, Nestorian Christianity, Islam, and his own religion: Tengrism."[202]

But he was also prepared to reject those practices, even those from his own cultural norms and traditions, which did not serve his strategic purpose. Unlike the long history of special status and privilege afforded to those with "proper" hereditary affiliations, for example, Genghis Khan would promote talent wherever he found it, which was itself an adaptive measure. As a result, rather than resting on the laurels of their lineage, tribal heritage, or political connections, Khan's generals brought ability, ambition and a fresh, dynamic perspective. By building an army based on talent and choosing leaders based on ability, "Genghis Khan established a large cadre of very able officers to which he could delegate with complete confidence."[203]

He was so committed to this principle that one of his generals, Jebe, had once been a former enemy. Jebe had even once shot at Genghis Khan in the midst of battle. "But the conqueror appreciated talent wherever he found it, and he pardoned Jebe, who became a trusted Mongol general."[204]

Given his upbringing, perhaps it's no surprise that agility was such a central part of Genghis Khan's mastery as a strategist. In the words of one historian, "as nomads of the steppe, the Mongolians had to be agile in order to survive."[205]

Do What Works. Adapt to Win. If there is one key to Genghis Khan's ready willingness to adapt it was his pragmatism. He adapted a meritocratic system because it led to better leaders. He delegated power and authority to women[206] because they were just as effective as men. He adopted the weapons of his enemies because he experienced their indisputable power in battle.

Genghis Khan was an open-minded pragmatist who refused to let antiquated ideas or flawed thinking stand in his way. To be clear, it wasn't about popular ideas or public opinion. It was about letting the best ideas and the best people rise to the top.

What mattered to him was what worked. What mattered was winning. His focus, therefore, was quickly learning what worked and swiftly adapting to it to win.

The lesson is clear. "People weighed down by a system and inflexible ways of doing things cannot move fast, cannot sense or adapt to change. They lumber around more and more slowly until they go the way of the brontosaurus. Learn to move fast and adapt or you will be eaten."[207]

This ability to rapidly learn and adapt was the real secret of Genghis Khan's success, and it was a vital part of what made him such an effective strategist. In the words of one historian, Genghis Khan and the Mongols "were nothing if not adaptable."[208] Perhaps this is not a surprise given that learning and adapting was a natural part of life for Genghis Khan and his horde of Mongolian warriors. It enabled them to survive the difficulties of life as nomads on the plains. And it enabled them to thrive as savage slayers across the Eurasian Steppe. "Their ability to absorb and adapt [also] enabled the Mongol Empire to grow amazingly quickly. By the time of Genghis Khan's death, it was already twice the size of the Roman Empire at its peak and the empire only kept growing under his successors, until it roughly doubled in size again, stretching from the Black Sea in the West all the way to the Pacific Ocean in the East."[209]

Unlike ancient Rome, America, and most every other culture throughout the history of the world, for the Mongols, there was no honor in fighting or even dying in battle. "On and off the battlefield," explains historian and anthropologist Jack Weatherford, "the Mongol warrior was forbidden to speak of death, injury, or defeat. Just to think of it might make it happen. Even mentioning the name of a fallen comrade or other dead warrior constituted a serious taboo. Every Mongol soldier had to live his life as a warrior with the assumption that he was immortal, that no one could defeat him or harm him, that nothing could kill him."[210]

What's perhaps even more interesting is that, because the Mongols did not find honor in fighting, but only in winning, it opened their minds to all of the possible ways of winning. Agility, in other words, was born out of their focus on winning. Winning was the only thing that mattered. "They had a single goal in every campaign—total victory. Toward this end," Weatherford writes in *Genghis Khan and the Making of the Modern World*, "it did not matter what tactics were used against the enemy or how the battles were fought or avoided being fought. Winning by clever deception or cruel trickery was still winning and carried no stain on the bravery of the warriors, since there would be plenty of other occasions for showing prowess on the field."[211]

Regardless of the source of his agility, whatever it was that drove him to win no matter what, Genghis Khan was not alone. The greatest strategists throughout history were all remarkably agile; they were flexible, responsive, and willing and able to quickly adapt. "They were soldiers for all seasons," Strauss writes in *Masters of Command*.[212] "When the conditions of combat changed, they retooled."[213]

Alexander, having mastered conventional warfare across western Asia, swiftly shifted to guerrilla tactics against stubborn Sogdian tribes and Persian rebels in Central Asia. Hannibal switched smoothly from open battles to covert ambushes. Caesar conquered capably in conventional combat but charged heroically into chaotic urban warfare in Alexandria, somehow snatching victory from defeat.[214]

In Napoleon's case, he showed himself capable of quickly adapting to a remarkable range of different circumstances and conditions. Over and again he proved himself adept at surmounting "every species of difficulty," writes Chandler.[215] In Egypt, he traversed deserts and trounced the Mamelukes, renowned for their courage and skill. In Italy, he twice crossed the Alps at the most perilous passes, during the most difficult seasons. In Spain, he passed through the Pyrenees to crush four Spanish armies. In essence, from Germany's river valleys to Russia's eastern steppes, crossing bleak alpine heights, frozen tundra, craggy mountains, dense forests, and trackless plains, no army, no weapon, no natural obstacle could be found to arrest the rapid advance of Napoleon's relentless sweep.[216] In every case, from the great military commanders to the titans of industry, winning was what mattered and, in order to win, agility was, and remains, indispensable.

15

Wield Power with Wisdom, Get Both in and Out of the Game: Martin Luther King Jr. Assumes Leadership, Becomes the Symbol of the Civil Rights Movement

"Follow effective action with quiet reflection.
From the quiet reflection will come even more effective action."[1]
—Peter Drucker

On January 30, 1956, a dark and cold night in Montgomery, Alabama, Reverend Dr. Martin Luther King Jr. was leading a mass meeting at his local church when his house was bombed. By the time he arrived home, a large and angry crowd of his friends and supporters had already gathered in his front yard. They wanted revenge. And with guns, knives, clubs and broken bottles in hand, they were prepared to take it.[2] Some in the crowd angrily taunted the local police on the scene. King pushed through the crowd and raced passed the people inside to see if his wife and daughter were okay. Meanwhile, the crowd outside was spiraling out of control, and a confrontation with the local police appeared imminent.[3]

This was a defining moment in the life of Martin Luther King, and a pivotal moment in the fight for civil rights. As a minister, King was an ambassador of Christ on Earth. He was also a fierce advocate of the non-violent teachings of Mahatma Gandhi (who was assassinated eight years earlier on that same day, January 30) and Henry David Thoreau, and this was undoubtedly King's greatest trial thus far. His wife, Coretta Scott King, later recalled: "In some ways it was the most important hour of his life. His own home had just been bombed, his wife and baby could have been killed; this was the first deep test of his Christian principles and his theories of nonviolence."[4]

The "precipitating factor," King later wrote in his 1958 book, *Stride Toward Freedom*, was the arrest of Rosa Parks on December 1, 1955, just two months before King's house was bombed.[5] Parks had refused to give up her seat to a white passenger on a Montgomery city bus. At the time, Dr. King was only twenty-six, just one year on the job as a minister at the Dexter Avenue Baptist Church in Montgomery, and still planning to one day become a professor.[6] When King first reflected "seriously on the nature of the boycott method,"[7] and the call to boycott Montgomery's bus system, "he did not immediately endorse [the plan]."[8]

Increase Your Influence Through Strategic
Action Informed by Critical Reflection

Begin with Reflection-Before-Action.

Martin Luther King understood that a boycott of the Montgomery bus system was a serious step that could have far-reaching consequences and, therefore, he was determined to further think it through *before* taking action.

Along with sharpening his awareness, this process of pre-action reflection—known in the research literature as "reflection-before-action," also better enabled King to gauge and navigate his experience in the midst of having it.

King was no coward.[9] He was certainly willing to take bold, daring action to fight injustice. In fact, as he once told a black reporter in Montgomery, "Once you become dedicated to a cause, personal security is not the goal. What will happen to you personally does not matter. My cause, my race is worth dying for."[10]

But King was no emotional reactionary either. He was a moral leader and a visionary strategist and, therefore, he had to believe that the action was the morally right, and strategically wise thing to do. Rather than rushing into action with unchecked emotional zeal, King was inclined to explore the options, and how they would be received, carefully considering both the immediate and long-term effects.

Building a case for a more effective and enduring alternative strategy, for example, King was firmly opposed to *riots*. "The limitation of riots, moral questions aside," he said, "is that they cannot win and their participants know it. Hence, rioting is not revolutionary," King continues, "but reactionary because it invites defeat. It involves an emotional catharsis, but it must be followed by a sense of futility."[11]

In regards to bus segregation, "what had given King pause about endorsing the boycott was a concern that it might be unethical and unchristian," writes Harvard historian Louis Menand.[12] "The boycott might be unethical because, if it shut down Montgomery buses, it would deprive other riders of a service that they depended on, and deprive bus drivers of the way that they made a living. It might be unchristian," he continues, "because it was a response to an injury by inflicting an injury. It was revenge. King felt that he had to work through these worries about the movement before he could lead it."[13]

"As I thought further," King himself explains in his autobiography, "I came to see that what we were really doing was withdrawing our cooperation from an evil system, rather than merely withdrawing our support from the bus company. The bus company, being an external expression of the system, would naturally suffer, but the basic aim was to refuse to cooperate with evil."[14]

King wasn't just rationalizing. Thinking through this both shaped how the boycott would be conducted (i.e. non-violently, and with openness and transparency, and with support from whites,[15] indeed from a great many Americans), but also how he would think about change in America, *and* how he would communicate the need for change to Americans.

"At this point," King recalls, "I began to think about Thoreau's 'Essay on Civil Disobedience.' I became convinced that what we were preparing to do in Montgomery was related to what Thoreau had expressed. We were simply saying to the white community, 'We can no longer lend our cooperation to an evil system.'"[16]

Now, after further reflection and prayer, Dr. King was ready not just to support the boycott (or "an act of massive noncooperation,"[17] as he was determined to frame it), but to take an active leadership role, including, at the very least, offering "a room in the basement of his church for the organizers to meet."[18]

Practice Reflection-in-Action.

The plan to boycott the Montgomery bus system took shape within hours of Rosa Parks' arrest. On Monday, December 5, 1955—just four days after Parks' Thursday arrest, and now with Dr. King's full support—the Montgomery Bus Boycott was in full effect. And it was a resounding success. When the first bus passed his house that morning, King could hardly believe it. Usually packed with passengers by this time, the bus was empty. Scarcely able to contain his excitement, King recalled, "I jumped in my car and for almost an hour I cruised down every major street and examined every passing bus. [...] Instead of the 60 percent cooperation we had hoped for," he wrote, "it was becoming apparent that we had reached almost 100 percent. A miracle had taken place."[19]

While some folks carpooled, thousands more walked many miles to their destinations. "Men were seen riding mules to work, and more than one horse-drawn buggy drove the streets of Montgomery."[20] "They knew why they walked," King said, "and the knowledge was evident in the way they carried themselves. And as I watched them I knew that there is nothing more majestic than the determined courage of individuals willing to suffer and sacrifice for their freedom and dignity."[21] One elderly grandmother said at the time, "It used to be my soul was tired and my feet rested; now my feet's tired, but my soul is rested."[22]

Later that Monday afternoon, Dr. King and a few dozen other local ministers, civic leaders and working professionals gathered to establish the Montgomery Improvement Association (MIA) to oversee the boycott.

The 26-year old King was quickly, though unexpectedly, nominated and unanimously elected President. "The action had caught me unawares," King recalled. "It had happened so quickly I did not even have time to think it through. It is probable that if I had, I would have declined the nomination."[23]

A mass meeting for the boycott was scheduled to begin just a short while later that evening, and King, now that he was president, was expected to deliver an address.

Martin Luther King had always had a strong preference for thoughtful preparation. He knew he needed time to get outside of the arena, to go up to the mountaintop. For his Sunday sermons, he said that he "needed at least fifteen hours to prepare."[24] Now, in what he described as "the most decisive speech of my life," he had "only twenty minutes to prepare."[25] "He says in his autobiography that he wasted five of those twenty minutes having a panic attack. Fifteen minutes later, he was picked up and driven to the Holt Street Church"[26] to deliver the opening address of the Montgomery Improvement Association.

Hoping for a strong turnout, King was stunned when he was caught in a traffic jam as they approached the church. Once inside, King found close to a thousand people crammed into the church, "spilling into the aisles, standing on the sides and in the back. An estimated four thousand more people were crowded together outside on the lawn and in the streets listening to what was being said from a loud-speaker that had been mounted on the church's roof."[27] Despite his lack of preparation, the mass turnout, and the row of television cameras recording the meeting for a national audience, King was moved to deliver a riveting speech, and the Montgomery Bus Boycott was off to a spectacular start.[28]

Less than a year later, in November 1956, as a result of the bus boycott, the United States Supreme Court ruled that Alabama's laws on bus segregation were unconstitutional. It was a major victory for the Civil Rights Movement, and for the leadership of Martin Luther King. As the bus "boycott's chief architect," King "became nationally recognized as one of the Civil Rights Movement's most high-profile leaders."[29] A savvy strategist and inclusive moral leader, "King hailed the decision as a victory for *all* Americans…"[30]

Get in the Game. 'Get Action.'

"Get action. Seize the moment. Man was never intended to become an oyster."[31]
—Theodore Roosevelt, 26th U.S. President

"The path to success is to take massive, determined action."[32]
—Anthony Robbins

As history repeatedly demonstrates and common sense makes clear, taking massive action in pursuit of your vision is critical to your ultimate success. As Joel Barker put it, "Vision without action is merely a dream."[33] To be sure, action is *key,* but action *alone* is never enough.

Leaders who are driven by action *alone* can be grouped into two different types of failure. The first group consists of those who are committed to action, but who have undisciplined minds. When they are in the arena or on the battlefield, their attention is easily pulled from one new shiny object or apparently urgent matter to another. They struggle to stay focused on the task at hand. They are constantly reacting to the words and actions of others.[34] They are easily "infected by all of the drama that others churn up."[35] Whatever the stimulus, rather than being guided by wisdom and reason, they *react* according to how they feel.

As a result, they unwittingly surrender their power. Their moods and emotions drive the decisions they make, the goals they set, and how they see and make sense of the world. The consequence, not surprisingly, is an endless stream of bad decisions and unfulfilled dreams.[36] Without a clear strategic vision and framework to filter and guide their decisions, without a disciplined commitment to their definite chief purpose and principles, they struggle to reach their goals or achieve anything worthwhile.[37] Ruled by circumstances, other people, and their own turbulent emotions, these leaders are the least effective as strategists.

The second group includes those leaders who have developed a certain level of self-discipline and self-restraint. These leaders are better able to shut out the outside world as they narrow their focus on the immediate tasks and objectives.[38] Now, in the arena, they are consumed only with the direct, pressing concerns of the game.

The danger for this group is getting disconnected or stuck in a mental rut. If you stay in this mode of operating for too long, you begin to stagnate and lose perspective. Your ideas begin to fester and your self-awareness recedes. Engrossed in the heat of the moment or the urgency of pressing concerns, your thinking becomes increasingly tactical, your focus almost completely short-term. In time, your sense of perspective and proportion diminish as the broader picture, context, and overarching purpose begins to fade. Your discernment about direction and priorities becomes increasingly dull, constricted, and ill-informed. Your bearings begin to loosen and your judgment often suffers as a result. Think, for example, of Winston Churchill at the end of World War II. No longer in synch with the British people and their desire to rebuild, the hero of the half century, still consumed with the threat of war, was suddenly thrown out of office.

Unfortunately, driven by our emotions, subject to our own limited experience, these scenarios are far more common than most people think. As Harvard Kennedy School professor Ronald Heifetz explains, "Rather than maintain perspective on the events that surround and involve us, we often get swept up by them."[39]

Fortunately, there is a simple and practical solution.

Get Out of the Game. Get Reflection.

"Rarely do we find men who willingly engage in hard, solid thinking.
There is an almost universal quest for easy answers and half-baked solutions.
Nothing pains some people more than having to think."[40]

—Martin Luther King Jr.

Only when you get sufficient distance from the arena—the dramatic action, the psychological drama, the adrenaline rush, the spectacle, the dirt and sweat and tears—are you really free to make meaning of your experience in fresh and novel ways. When you get outside of the game, when you "elevate yourself above the battlefield,"[41] or get "on the balcony," as Heifetz puts it in his book, *Leadership Without Easy Answers,*[42] your brain—both consciously and unconsciously—will begin to process the experience in fresh, resourceful ways. This gives you a better chance to consider the big picture and place circumstances and events in their broader context. It also creates the space to rethink goals, reexamine priorities, make fresh comparisons, update historical analogies, recognize new patterns and themes, and reassess key factors and prevailing forces.

"Events in life mean nothing if you do not reflect on them in a deep way."[43] This practice of getting "on the balcony" enables you to peer under the surface, penetrate pretenses, better detect self-deception, and look beyond the symptoms and surface-level distractions to identify the root cause, or discover what's really going on. All of this better enables you to generate new ideas and insights and see things through new frames, leading to improved decisions and more effective action.[44] In short, getting some distance, "observing the patterns of action from afar," writes Harvard Kennedy School professor David Gergen, helps to foster more effective action.[45] As the celebrated management consultant Peter Drucker put it, "Follow effective action with quiet reflection. From the quiet reflection will come even more effective action."[46] Your essential task, as Walt Whitman described it, is to be "both in and out of the game."[47]

This practice of getting "out of the game" can look very different depending on your situation, purpose, and preferences. In the case of Genghis Khan, seeking wisdom prior to his declaration of war on the Sultan of the Khwarezmian empire, he went up to the mountaintop of Burkhan Khaldun and reflected and prayed on the situation for three nights and three days.

In one of America's most famous sojourns outside the arena or trips to the mountaintop—and, by far, the longest—Henry David Thoreau spent two *years* living in the woods at Walden Pond. "I went to the woods because I wished to live deliberately," Thoreau later wrote, "to front only the essential facts of life, and see if I could not learn what it had to teach, and not, when I came to die, discover that I had not lived."[48] The experience of living alone in the woods had a profound effect on Thoreau and his thinking. Indeed, it was here where he first began writing his influential essay, "Civil Disobedience," which went on to have a significant influence on Leo Tolstoy, Mahatma Gandhi, and Martin Luther King.

In King's case, arrested nearly 30 times,[49] he often used his time in jail as an opportunity to get "on the balcony," to think, write, and reflect. And it was here where he wrote one of his most influential essays, the "Letter From a Birmingham Jail."[50]

Write, Journal, Reflect.

Whatever your individual circumstances or preferences, whether you can afford a week, or just several minutes a day, one of the best ways to use your time out of the game is by writing or journaling.

Writing is actually an exceptional tool for leaders. Writing helps to clarify your thoughts, and expand your thinking. Writing can also help you to gain perspective, particularly if you're writing with multiple different audiences in mind, as Martin Luther King often was. What's more, when you go back and read what you've written, you can often gain even greater perspective and, often, surprising insight and clarity. After reading what you've written, you may find that you see it differently, which may lead to further insight, or a more resourceful point of view—this is especially true if you are also reading what others have written about the topic (as King was doing, perhaps most famously, with Jesus, Gandhi, and Thoreau, but also several of his professors and contemporary influences, including Howard Thurman, Reinhold Niebuhr, Bayard Rustin, and Billy Graham).

This helps to explain why so many effective leaders are also writers—not just Thoreau, Gandhi, and King. Julius Caesar, Marcus Aurelius, Napoleon Bonaparte, Theodore Roosevelt, Susan B. Anthony, Elizabeth Cady Stanton, Winston Churchill, Eleanor Roosevelt, John F. Kennedy, and Nelson Mandela; these leaders were all powerfully effective writers. They were masters of language and communication, which is vital to leadership. As Mark Twain once quipped, "The difference between the right word and the almost right word is the difference between lightning and the lightning bug."[51]

Whether you choose to write, consult with a coach or mentor, or engage in dialogue with your mastermind or team, this practice of getting outside of the arena is crucial to maximizing your effectiveness as a leader and as a strategist.

If you find yourself struggling with what to write, start by writing out a few basic questions, and then answer those questions. One of the most practical reflection methods consists of simply answering the following three questions: What? So what? And now what?[52]

(1.) *What?* Start by asking yourself: What is the action, incident, or event that I'm reflecting on? What is basically happening or not happening? Why is it happening or not? Who are the key players involved? What are their various roles? Who benefits?

(2.) *So what?* With this question, you're basically asking yourself: Why is this *important*? What does it ultimately mean, or how does it matter? What does this mean for the big picture? Does it matter differently to different people? Does it matter in the short-term or the long-term or both?

(3.) *Now what?* This question is focused on application. The point here is to use critical reflection to generate more strategic action. Questions here include: How can I use or apply this going forward? What are the key takeaways, or lessons learned? What goals, objectives, or tasks do I now want to set?

See endnotes for a collection of other useful reflection tools. [53]

In the case of Martin Luther King and the Civil Rights Movement, taking time to get outside of the arena gave him a chance to better contemplate, assess and understand his various audiences, which helped him to better adapt his message to them, "depending on whether he was speaking to his home congregation, an unfamiliar congregation, a sympathetic interviewer, a hostile reporter, the viewers of a television talk show, or the readers of an elite magazine." [54] Taking time to stop and step back also enabled King to develop a better "sense of when to listen, when to compromise, and when to hold his ground," writes Harvard psychologist Howard Gardner in *Leading Minds*. [55] What's more, given the intensity of the situation, and the flagrant brutality of racists like Police Commissioner Eugene "Bull" Connor of Birmingham—the man who unleashed dogs and high pressure fire hoses on peaceful protestors— as well as the blatant immorality of racists like Governor George Wallace of Alabama, "King repeatedly had to decide where to go, whom to confront, how hard to push, when to turn on the heat, and when to allow things to cool off" [56]—all things which benefited from increased perspective, careful reflection, and strategic thinking.

Rather than reacting out of emotion, King's well-established habit of taking time to get out of the game—to think, to read, to write and reflect—became a powerful tool, better enabling him to respond to even the most vicious attacks, with a calm and collected mind. This is why thoughtful, critical reflection is such a central practice for your ultimate success.

Rather than "reacting to what others give you," or being constricted and controlled by the grip of your emotions, you will find, "with a calm spirit," that you are able to "entertain a wide range of options and solutions." [57] As Robert Green writes in *The Laws of Human Nature*, "like an athlete continually getting stronger through training, your mind will become more flexible and resilient. Clear and calm, you will see answers and creative solutions that no one else can envision." [58]

The night of the bombing, several minutes after Martin Luther King disappeared into his house to check on his wife and daughter, he emerged on his front porch. Shards of glass from the shattered living room windows cracked under his weight as he carefully stepped up to the railing. He could still smell the dynamite as he looked out on the angry crowd which now extended into the street.[59] He raised his hand and, within seconds, a silence fell over group. Everyone was now suddenly still. King spoke calmly: "My wife and baby are all right;" he paused, "I want you to go home and put down your weapons."[60] He continued, "We cannot solve this problem through retaliatory violence. We must meet violence with nonviolence. Remember the words of Jesus: 'He who lives by the sword will perish by the sword.' We must love our white brothers, no matter what they do to us. We must make them know that we love them. Jesus still cries out across the centuries, "Love your enemies." This is what we must live by. We must meet hate with love."[61]

Miraculously, the angry and hostile spirit of the crowd was subdued. Someone shouted out "Amen;" and another cried "God bless you."[62] Others followed and the crowd slowly dispersed. White police officers would later report that Dr. King saved their lives. "A night that had been on the verge of chaos came to a quiet, if uneasy, close. Pictures of King urging calm from his shattered porch made the newspapers across the country, and support for the civil rights movement swelled."[63]

Martin Luther King Jr., a preacher by profession, proved to be a powerful moral leader by his exceptional example, and his influence and stature grew significantly as a result. Several years later, in 1963, he was featured on the cover of *TIME* magazine, and, after living true to his words again and again, always leading by example, with great courage and determination and extraordinary empathy, compassion and love, Reverend Dr. Martin Luther King Jr. was awarded the Noble Peace Prize the following year.

16

EXECUTE FROM THE VITAL CENTER OF THE ACTION. MASTER THE SECRETS OF STRATEGY EXECUTION AT THE FRONT: CAPTAIN HENRY MORGAN OUTWITS A SPANISH ARMADA

"There are two principal things a leader can influence when it comes to producing results: Your strategy...and your ability to execute that strategy."[1]
—Sean Covey et al, *The 4 Disciplines of Execution*

"Knowledge is not power—it's potential power. Knowledge is not mastery. Execution is mastery. Execution will trump knowledge every day of the week."[2]
—Anthony Robbins (1960—), Author, Speaker, Life & Business Strategist

On April 17, 1669, the Spanish Navy finally had their most fearsome enemy trapped. "The most famous and successful of all the buccaneers,"[3] Captain Henry Morgan had been wreaking havoc on Spanish villages and vessels throughout the Caribbean for years. And, yet, as eager as the Spaniards were to see his body hanging from the gallows or his head on a pike, Captain Morgan—the Welshman who, according to some reports, was once abducted and sold as a white slave[4]—had thus far proved impossible to capture.

After several months of fruitless pirate patrols across the Caribbean,[5] when Spain's Admiral Don Alonso del Campo y Espinosa first learned that Captain Morgan was raiding Spanish villages along the coast of Maracaibo, he was ecstatic. Given the geography, this "was incredible news," Stephan Talty explains in *Empire of Blue Water: Captain Morgan's Great Pirate Army*.[6] "His enemy was now within his reach, trapped like a dog, without the possibility of escape. How the words must have sung in [his] ears!"[7] To be sure, this was Admiral Don Alonso's great chance and he was not going to miss it; "his career, not to mention the fortunes of his king and nation, now depended on stopping Morgan."[8]

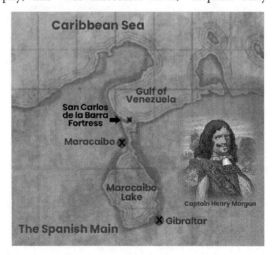

Leading a squadron of three warships from the Spanish Armada, Don Alonso quickly sailed into the Gulf of Venezuela in time to block Captain Morgan's escape from Maracaibo Lake, which had only a narrow channel leading out to the Gulf and into the Caribbean Sea.

In stark contrast to Captain Morgan's small ships, "mere water taxis meant to shuttle the rogues from one sacking to the next,"[9] Don Alonso was in command of "heavy warships bristling with cannon, manned by competent soldiers, and far superior in firepower to any pirate ship in the world. They were even commanded by an admiral," Don Alonso, "who had been given one and only one mission: 'To clean the coasts of the [Spanish West] Indies of the pirates which infest them.'"[10] Now on the cusp of fulfilling the heart of his mission; the Spanish Admiral "would be the instrument of royal, indeed of divine, retribution. Henry Morgan was going to surrender or die."[11]

To the Spanish, Captain Morgan was nothing more than a common criminal, a bloodthirsty buccaneer. But Morgan never saw himself as a pirate; "he was a military man" with a "letter of marque," and that made him a privateer.[12] Besides, unlike most pirates, Morgan did not attack just any vessel or village, he attacked the enemies of England. He attacked the Spanish Empire in the Caribbean, which included the Spanish West Indies and the Spanish Main.

Furthermore, whenever Morgan and his men attacked, it was immediately clear that this was no typical band of pirates *or* privateers. Bearing down on their enemies "with drums beating and colors flying,"[13] Henry Morgan's buccaneers were more akin to a military regiment; complete with expert marksmen, ferocious fighters, tacticians, and spies. As Scottish historian Angus Konstam writes, "These men were trained to fight in ranks in a military fashion, and although they lacked harsh military discipline, they were united in a common goal: the capture and plundering of enemy towns."[14]

Living in a social order of sea dogs and maritime marauders, Morgan styled himself the "Admiral of the Coast,"[15] and, no doubt, he was something of a "top dog in what was otherwise a society of equals."[16] More importantly, unlike the typical Caribbean Sea devil, Captain Henry Morgan was a clever strategist, a bold risk-taker, and a charismatic[17] leader of men.

Lead from the Front or Develop Those Who Can

"Follow after me, for the Lord has delivered
your enemies, the Moabites, into your hands."[18]

—Ehud ben-Gera, Military Leader of the Tribe of Benjamin

On March 9, 1669, acting on the intelligence of one of his lieutenants,[19] Captain Morgan and his fleet of 7 small ships first entered the narrow passage into Lake Maracaibo, a huge tidal bay, in order to raid and plunder the Spanish towns of Maracaibo and Gibraltar.

As they approached the narrow channel from the Gulf of Venezuela into Lake Maracaibo, they were surprised to find that the entrance was now guarded by a well-positioned Spanish military fort known as San Carlos de la Barra Fortress. Morgan took a chance and boldly charged ahead.

Suddenly, the Spanish soldiers manning the fort began firing on Morgan's fleet. Morgan leapt into action, ordering the crews to anchor the ships at a safe distance and prepare to attack the fort by land.

Rather than directing the operation from the safety of his ship, Morgan personally led the attack. This proved to be a life-saving move,[20] but it was also generally expected—a leadership lesson Morgan first learned under fire. As American historian Benerson Little explains, "Buccaneers all considered themselves leaders, and buccaneer leaders were expected to lead from the front in battle."[21]

The fort turned out to be manned with fewer than a dozen Spanish soldiers who, by sunset, simply stopped firing, enabling Morgan and his men to approach. Strangely, when they entered the fort there was no one there. While his men were relieved and suspected cowardice, Morgan suspected a trap.

As they walked around searching the fort room by room, Morgan soon got a whiff of a distinct acrid smell. Suddenly, he began racing forward to find the source. Minutes later, inside the arsenal of the fort he found a lit fuse that was burning straight toward a stockpile of barrels filled with gunpowder. With barely an inch left to burn, Morgan stomped on the fuse with just seconds to spare, saving the lives of at least half of his roughly 200 men.[22]

After spiking the cannons and burying them in the sand so they could not be used against them on the way back out of the lake, they loaded up the welcome stash of military hardware they found—which, along with enough gun powder to blow up the fort, included a number of muskets, flints, ramrods, and other "military provisions."[23] Now, "armed to the teeth," the English privateers advanced on the wealthy Spanish town of Maracaibo.[24]

After sacking and plundering Maracaibo, Gibraltar, and the surrounding coast and hinterlands for a few weeks, and exerting tortuous effort extracting every last *piece of eight* (the name for the Spanish dollar, the first international currency), Captain Morgan knew it was time to go. Surely, by now, the soldiers that had guarded the fort would have "galloped off to the centers of power" to raise the alarm.[25] Morgan ordered the buccaneers to board the ships to return to Port Royal.[26]

Alas, it was too late. Just as Morgan was ready to depart, he received word that a Spanish squadron was anchored at the fort, guarding their only way of escape. "There was no chance of escape overland."[27] Worse still, Spain's Admiral Don Alonso had already re-drilled and remounted the cannons and refortified and rearmed the fort "with guns, and men, and all sorts of ammunition."[28]

Captain Morgan immediately sent a ship to do some reconnaissance, after which he learned that there were three ships—Don Alonso's flagship, the *Magdalen*, which had 48 guns and 250 men, the *Santa Louisa*, with 38 guns and 200 men, and the *La Marquesa*, with 24 guns and 150 men.[29] In effect, Don Alonso had three times as many men, a flagship with more cannons than Morgan's entire 7-ship fleet *combined*, and a fully-manned military fort. "The admiral's vessels were arrayed across the channel so that no other vessel could pass without coming under direct fire from at least one of them. They acted as the cork in a bottle, and Morgan was caught inside."[30]

"That was it. It was over. How could Morgan possibly get out of this situation? His fleet was outgunned in every respect."[31] The idea that his little fleet, weighed down with booty and provisions, might safely pass so closely by those great ships seemed impossible.[32] "They could see no way of escaping by sea or by land. Morgan and his men were trapped."[33]

After being overjoyed by their newfound riches, the buccaneers were now suddenly dismayed and filled with dread. In his book, *The Buccaneers of America* (1678), Captain Morgan's French surgeon, Alexander Exquemelin, wrote that the Captain himself was judged by all to be despondent and "hopeless."[34]

Take Every Step to Ensure Your Success

Quickly recovering his brash boldness, Morgan soon insisted that it was Don Alonso who *must* surrender. Exquemelin explains, "under these necessities, Captain Morgan resumed new courage…resolving to show himself still undaunted, he boldly sent a Spaniard to the admiral of those three ships, demanding of him a considerable ransom for not putting the city of Maracaibo to the flames."[35]

Recognizing his considerable advantage, Don Alonso was not about to budge. "I have with me very good soldiers," he wrote back to Captain Morgan, "who desire nothing more ardently than to revenge on you, and your people, all the cruelties, and base infamous actions, you have committed upon the Spanish nation in America."[36]

Hoping to keep their ill-gotten gains, Morgan and his men voted to fight on, but not in the way that Don Alonso and his Spanish soldiers expected or hoped. "Captain Morgan…knew he had to quickly devise a ruse that would gain him surprise, and thus advantage."[37]

He directed his buccaneers to scour the town for as much "'pitch, tar and brimstone [as] they could find.'"[38] They were going to build the most explosive fire ship that the Spanish had ever seen. Unlike a typical fire ship, however, Captain Morgan ensured that his fire ship would be exceptionally well disguised. On the decks of the ship, they set up logs and branches handsomely dressed up like men in colorful clothes, wearing hats and montera caps, "and armed with swords, muskets, and bandoleers."[39] They then cut additional portholes in the hull with hollow logs sticking out—covered in pitch, tar, and brimstone—to look like the ship was heavily armed with cannons.[40] "Under each of the logs disguised as cannon they laid large amounts of powder and cut [additional] holes in the ship to ensure that once ignited the powder would have a maximum blast range."[41]

With barrels of gunpowder placed strategically around the ship, Morgan then had grappling irons strung into the rigging to ensure it would become entangled with the rigging of the target ship, Don Alonso's flagship, the *Magdalen*.[42]

Further adding to the deception, the chosen vessel was disguised to look like the best ship in the fleet, Morgan's own flagship.[43] A lesser ship might have raised more suspicions, but surely, the Spaniards must have reasoned, Morgan would not sacrifice his own flagship in such a risky manner when an inferior ship would work just as well. To complete the disguise, Morgan flew an English flag[44] at the stern in order, writes Exquemelin, "to persuade the enemy she is one of our best men-of-war going to fight them.'"[45]

To further "mislead the enemy" and ensure their success, Morgan had another ship that was made to look like a *real* fire ship, complete with "kindled rope smoking on deck."[46] While this fake fire ship added to the anxiety of the Spanish soldiers, it was sailed at a distance so that it was not perceived to be an immediate threat. This, of course, helped to fool the Spanish into thinking that their immediate threat was not a fire ship—which they could probably sink or sail away from before it reached them—but the rapidly approaching, heavily armed English man-of-war.

At dawn, on May 1, 1669, while still fairly dark, Captain Morgan's fleet sailed toward the Spanish squadron. Sailing some distance ahead, the fire ship set her sights directly on Don Alonso's *Magdalen*, the largest of the three Spanish warships.[47]

"The rest of the buccaneer fleet would split up and attack the other two Spanish ships, with Morgan leading the attack on the second largest ship, the thirty-eight-gun *Santa Louisa*."[48]

As another tactical precaution, Morgan had his men wait as long as possible before lighting the ship on fire. To do this, a handful of men remained on the fire ship, steering her directly toward the *Magdalen* until the last possible minute. After lighting various fires throughout the ship, the men dove off the stern into water and climbed into the canoes that had been hidden in tow behind.

By this time, the Spaniards began to assume that the buccaneers planned to board. "And for this the Spaniards were ready. Did not the Spanish sailor and sea soldier fight his fiercest in boarding actions?"[49] By the time the Spanish recognized the fire ship for what it really was, however, it was too late. With perfect execution, the fire ship collided directly with Don Alonso's flagship as smoke began pouring out from the hatches.[50] As pockets of gunpowder exploded, the fiery inferno seized the "timber and tackling" of the *Magdalen*.[51]

Terror and pandemonium struck the crew when the Spanish flagship's magazine exploded, engulfing the ship in flames as she suddenly began to sink into the sea.[52]

Working feverishly to get away from the fire ship, a second Spanish ship, *Santa Louisa*, sailed toward the safety of the fort, only to run aground. In a desperate attempt to ensure the buccaneers would not get it and add it to their fleet, the Spanish torched and sunk their own ship before escaping to the fort.[53] Swamped by Morgan's fleet, the third Spanish crew had little choice but to surrender their ship, *La Marquesa*, which Captain Morgan took for himself.

Against incredible odds, Captain Morgan and his buccaneers had triumphed, obliterating, in short order, the "cream of Spain's New World maritime defenses."[54] They were overjoyed. In the words of Exquemelin, "The pirates being extremely glad at this signal victory so soon obtained, and with so great an inequality of forces, conceived greater pride than they had before…"[55]

Alas, far from free, Captain Morgan and his men were in for a sudden, unfortunate surprise.

Be Ready to Rapidly Respond

"Victory in the next war will depend on execution, not plans."[56]
—General George S. Patton

Suddenly, as Captain Morgan's buccaneers made their way to the lake's bottleneck, expecting to sail easily past the fort and into the freedom of the open sea, their brief victory spree came to an abrupt end when they came within range of the fort's cannons. Facing a crushing curtain of cannon fire, Morgan had little choice but to abandon the final part of his plan and order a hasty retreat.[57] After a short-lived attack on the fort "had proved to be fruitless as the Spanish resistance had been too strong,"[58] the buccaneers sailed back to town to reformulate their strategy to escape, and to divide their spoils in case a ship was lost.

"To make matters worse, Don Alonso had escaped the inferno of the *Magdalen* and managed to get to the castle, which was now under his direct command. This meant that the garrison there, reinforced days earlier by Don Alonso, would not easily give in."[59] Indeed, with his reputation now in tatters, Don Alonso was determined to make maximum use of the fort for its intended purpose. He would destroy Morgan's fleet as they attempted to escape through the narrow channel into the Gulf of Venezuela. Even with the addition of *La Marquesa*, "a much larger and faster ship than the fourteen-gun vessel he'd been using,"[60] the heavily reinforced Spanish fort still "had the higher ground and more firepower than Morgan's combined fleet."[61] What's more, unlike when they first entered the lake, the fort was now swarming with soldiers and sailors alike, with reinforcements soon on the way. Besides, how could they possibly sail a fleet so closely past a fort that was designed for the very purpose of preventing the passage of unwanted ships?

Maintain the Initiative.

Captain Henry Morgan remained undaunted. This was but another chance to make use of his mastery as a strategist. In the words of former U.S. Navy SEAL Benerson Little, "Here was an opportunity for tactics in their purest form: victory via deception!"[62]

To begin with, Captain Morgan sent a message to Don Alonso, once again threatening to burn Maracaibo to the ground if they were not permitted safe passage. It is unlikely that Morgan expected Don Alonso to relent. The point was to boost Don Alonso's confidence by making him believe he still had the upper hand and that Morgan had no real viable options. As Morgan well understood, overconfidence leads to poor judgment and mistakes.

Earlier, when the buccaneers took the fort on the way in, Captain Morgan had taken measure of the strengths and weaknesses of the fort. Assuming that Don Alonso would also be aware of any weak points in his fortification, Morgan sought to turn the Spaniard's attention to his weakness, and, thereby, exploit any natural anxiety or defensiveness he might have about it. The weakness, in this case, was a landward attack on the western wall.

Morgan then directed his men to build a number of scaling ladders. Next, he anchored his fleet at a safe distance from the reach of the guns of the fort, but still well within view. He then had his men make dozens of trips by canoe from the ships to an area of land within walking distance of the fort. Though still some distance away, the Spaniards could easily see what was happening, except the shoreline where they landed, which was hidden under mangrove trees. "The foliage was thick and a perfect place for men to hide while they prepared a land assault against the fort."[63] As each canoe arrived, the ladders were unloaded along with all of the men, who were "armed to the teeth with muskets, swords, pikes and so on," with the exception of the few who rowed back to the ships to pick up more men, weapons, and ladders.[64]

As the hours of the day wore on and the unloading of fully-armed men and ladders continued, all of which the Spaniards watched with great interest from the ramparts, Don Alonso assumed the obvious: The buccaneers were landing in preparation "for a full-scale land attack."[65] The idea that Morgan was preparing for a land attack was undoubtedly reinforced in Don Alonso's mind by the fact that Morgan had done the same thing when he entered the lake five weeks earlier. Imagining that he was learning what his enemy was like, Don Alonso was preparing to "fight the last war."[66]

This time, however, rather than fleeing the fort, as the badly outnumbered Spanish soldiers did last time, Don Alonso would fight to the bitter end.

The Spanish admiral knew exactly what to do to prepare for the impending attack too. Of course, to Don Alonso's way of thinking, it made perfect sense that Morgan would seek to attack the fort where it was weak. What other option did he have? In order to compensate for this weakness, Don Alonso immediately swung into action and ordered his men to move the cannons from the seaward to the landward wall in order to rebuff the attack.

Given the size and weight of the cannons, and the not insignificant distance to the landward wall, it took the Spaniards, laboring under the scorching sun and intense tropical humidity, some time to dismount the cannons, haul them across the fortress and remount them along the wall where their defenses were weakest.[67] When they had finally finished, it was after dark and, with the exception of a few guards, Don Alonso directed his soldiers to get some rest before the battle the following morning.

Remember: Timing is Everything.

Suddenly, in the middle of the night, Don Alonso was awoken by the sound of 7 cannons firing from out in the Gulf. Timed with the outgoing tide, the buccaneers had "slipped anchor and let the ships drift with the tide" from Maracaibo Lake into the Gulf of Venezuela so as not to raise the alarm of the guards.[68] Just as they were passing the fort, they quickly unfurled their sails, and passed swiftly through the channel, with each one of Morgan's seven-ship fleet firing a victory salvo as they made it through.

Don Alonso knew instantly that he had been fooled. Captain Morgan's men had never actually gotten off the canoes. On the return trip to the ships, the men had merely laid down in the canoes so that they could no longer be seen. The ladders that had been dropped off at the landing site were merely part of an elaborate ploy. Captain Morgan never intended to attack the fort, he only wanted to make Don Alonso think that he did so that the Spaniards would move the cannons away from the seaward wall.

With "characteristic cunning and audacity,"[69] Captain Morgan had once again proven his salt, unleashing his strategic genius, "expert timing,"[70] and mastery of surprise "on the battered, tortured, and now fully humiliated Spaniards."[71] The following morning Captain Morgan graciously released some of the prisoners, "whom the Spaniards had given up for dead," allowing them to take canoes back to the fort.[72] "He also gave a barque to the rest of the prisoners and let them sail off in it."[73]

The buccaneers were free to sail safely out into the sea. Captain Henry Morgan and his men returned to Port Royal, sailing into the harbor on May 17, 1669, as exceedingly rich and soon-to-be famous buccaneers.[74] "That single raid brought more than thirty thousand pounds back to Jamaica, a vast sum for the times."[75] "When the buccaneers swarmed ashore with their newly won wealth the merchants, innkeepers and prostitutes did their best to relieve them of it while the city celebrated."[76]

"In port, Morgan's men taunted the captains who had not sailed with him and flaunted their sudden riches."[77] Returning as a hero, hundreds of pirates were soon in an uproar, "clamoring to cruise with Morgan."[78] On October 24, 1670, when he finally put out a call for some 500 new recruits for a raid on

Panama, a stunning 2,000 men and 36 ships answered his call at Tortuga.[79] It was the largest army of privateers that had ever gathered in the Caribbean to that date, a mark of "Morgan's leadership ability"[80] and renown.[81]

Master the Seven Secrets to Successful Strategy Execution

"Execution is not just tactics—it is a discipline and a system.
It has to be built into a company's strategy, its goals, and its culture.
And the leader of the organization must be deeply engaged in it."[82]

—Larry Bossidy and Ram Charan, *Execution: The Discipline of Getting Things Done*

A clear and inspiring vision, a brilliant strategy, the most clever tactics— these factors can all help to ensure your success. But they are worth precious little if you are unable to carry them out. Effective execution reigns supreme. In fact, we create strategy in large part so that we know what actions to take. Without action, without execution, there is no point to strategy.

General Colin Powell argued that strategy *is* execution. "Strategy equals execution...all the great ideas and visions in the world are worthless," Powell wrote, "if they can't be implemented rapidly and efficiently."[83]

The most common way that leaders screw this up is by failing to stay closely engaged with the execution of their strategy. They may formulate and even implement a brilliant strategy, but then they hand it off to their lieutenants, expecting others to carry it through. The biggest problem with this mindset is that, in order to succeed, the strategy may very well need to be adapted or adjusted as the execution of strategy unfolds.

Recall the words the Prussian military strategist Helmuth von Moltke wrote in an 1871 essay on military strategy, 'No plan can survive with any certainty beyond first contact with the enemy.'[84] The point is not that the strategy *will* fall apart, or that strategic planning is worthless—*not at all*. The point is that the strategy will meet with certain resistance, or perhaps a major obstacle, setback, or surprise which will almost certainly require some adjustments, or patches, or at least a few tweaks and repairs.

This is why so many of history's greatest leaders were so often found leading from the front, including, despite the risks, some of the most indispensable, irreplaceable leaders such as Napoleon Bonaparte,[85] George Washington, Julius Caesar, Joan of Arc, Shaka Zulu, Genghis Khan, Hannibal Barca, Horatio Nelson, and Alexander the Great. In the case of Napoleon, for example, he "led from the front, as at Lodi bridge," Columbia Business School's William Duggan explains, in order to "better...see in a glance the battle unfolding and make adjustments along the way."[86]

In the case of Alexander the Great, his "active role in combat was a consistent element in his campaigns. He [repeatedly] exercised heroic command. Not only was he present on the battlefield," writes history professor Justin Lyons, "he fought in the front lines at great personal hazard. Again and again, Alexander led the charge of the Companion Cavalry and was among the first to scale the walls of a besieged fortress."[87]

In ancient Greece, Columbia's Julia Sloan similarly explains in her book, *Learning to Think Strategically*, "the front lines were the best place to get a feel for the 'becoming' of events, to implement plans, or to adapt plans as circumstances changed. Strategists understood that strategy making also happened here."[88] As Captain Henry Morgan repeatedly demonstrated, "strategists…were expected to be at or connected to the points where action took place in order to reinterpret things."[89]

Despite her age and total lack of military experience and training, Joan of Arc understood intuitively the power of leading from the front—not just as a drum major leading the way to the action, but also as a tactician discerning where her soldiers needed to be in order to gain an advantage. In an interview with a 15th century chronicler, she explained, "Personally, I don't know how to fight. But I have a large banner which all of my soldiers recognize. What I do is to look at the battlefield and see where the important action is and where it is crucial that we be in order to win. I ride to that position. My soldiers see my banner and where I have ridden. They follow me, and we win."[90]

March Toward the Sound of the Guns.

This also helps explain why failing to lead from the front or failing to at least be closely engaged with what's happening at the front, can easily lead to disaster. On July 1, 1898, when Theodore Roosevelt was leading the Rough Rider regiment in Cuba during the Spanish American War, he found himself and his men stuck in a holding pattern on the front line. General Shafter had given them orders to maintain their position until they received orders to advance. "In characteristic Roosevelt fashion, he had already sent someone back to hurry those orders along."[91]

The problem was that Roosevelt's regiment was enduring heavy fire from the Spaniards on the top of the hill. "The Mauser bullets drove in sheets through the trees and the tall jungle grass," remembered Roosevelt, "making a peculiar whirring or rustling sound."[92]

Meanwhile, as they sat in a position at the bottom of the hill, where it was difficult to return fire, the Rough Riders were sustaining heavy casualties. Given that the narrow trail was packed with infantrymen itching to advance, it was equally impossible to retreat.

Worse still was the fact that the portly General Shafter, suffering with gout and swollen ankles, was attempting to manage the battle from nearly a mile back. Given the deep mud puddles from the previous night's rain and the narrow, mountainous trail, sending and receiving messages with Shafter was a difficult, time-consuming affair. If Shafter had been on the front line, or at least close enough to fully appreciate the dire circumstances and the pointlessness of remaining put, he almost certainly would have given Roosevelt the order to advance.

As the minutes raced on and his men continued to drop, Roosevelt, desperate to advance, sent another runner back to press the request. Watching his men being picked off, Roosevelt became increasingly frantic to advance in spite of the obvious dangers. He sent at least three messengers back down the line, he wrote, "to the rear to try to get authority to attack the hills in front," but not one of his messengers returned.[93] "I wish they'd let us start, I wish they'd let us start," Roosevelt was repeatedly heard saying.[94]

However hazardous, in Roosevelt's mind there was only one clear solution to this deadly impasse: Bold, enthusiastic action. He would lead a charge up San Juan Hill, and force the enemy to fight or flee. Fixed in his mind was the old military maxim, "go to the sound of the guns."[95]

Suddenly, when Roosevelt "was just about making up my mind," he said, "that in the absence of orders I had better 'march toward the guns,'" an officer, Lieutenant Colonel Dorst, "came riding up through the storm of bullets with the welcome command" from General Sumner "to move forward and support the regulars in the assault on the hills in front."[96]

TR was elated. "The instant I received the order I sprang on my horse and then my 'crowded hour' began."[97] Following the plan to take Kettle Hill, Roosevelt began at the rear of the regiment, where it was custom for a colonel to stay. But the troops were advancing slowly under a torrent of bullets.[98] Earnestly hoping to reassure and arouse the troops,[99] despite the dangers of making himself a conspicuous target, Roosevelt insisted on charging on Little Texas, his horse. "Are you afraid to stand up when I am on horseback?" he shouted at his regiment.[100] Still, the Spanish sharpshooters continued to pick them off. At last, he'd seen enough. There was nothing left to do but charge the hill and crush the enemy. "The Spaniards had a hard position to attack, it is true," he later said, "but we could see them, and I knew exactly how to proceed."[101]

Be Close By or Tightly Tuned In.

"If you want to accomplish impossible missions—high-velocity, first-to-market new product introductions with extreme turnarounds, or wildly effective, unexpected competitive strategies against larger and more powerful competitors—you've got to be right on the firing line, regardless of hardship or risk. You cannot lead from an air-conditioned office," Major General William Cohen argues in Secrets of Special Ops Leadership, "you must be out there where things are happening."[102]

Considered a master tactician even by his enemies, German General Erwin Rommel was known for leading his troops from the front. But it wasn't merely a matter of inspiring leadership. "The German general stayed with his troops at the front so he could quickly take advantage of developing opportunities."[103] Rommel seemed to have an intuitive grasp of the decisive power of initiative, momentum, and speed, all of which were easier to maximize and exploit at the front, where the action was unfolding. As a result of his bold daring, as well as his cunning, strategic mind, "legends about the Desert Fox began to circulate, and Rommel started to gain an almost mythical status among his followers."[104] While in Africa in command of a unit of German tanks, even while he was outranked by his Italian ally, General Italo Gariboldi, Rommel's mastery as a strategist was so self-evident that he was given control of most of Italy's mobile units as well. "The German and Italian soldiers noticed how their general was always in the thick of the action on the front line. He lived, sweated, slept and ate like his men. Several times, while driving close to the front in his command car, he met British patrols and only escaped by luck. Such courage won the respect of his troops."[105]

A *failure* to be at or near the front is also believed to have contributed to General Douglas MacArthur's downfall during the war in Korea. MacArthur was nowhere near the front line. In fact, he wasn't even in Korea. MacArthur was leading the allied effort against North Korea while he himself was safely tucked away in Tokyo, more than 700 miles away. Clearly, there was very little he would be seeing with his own eyes. "He was a classic absentee general," writes historian Hampton Sides, author of *On Desperate Ground, The Epic Story of Chosin Reservoir, the Greatest Battle of the Korean War*, "he never slept a single night on Korean soil during the whole conflict, and would only occasionally fly over from Japan for a quick photo-op or aerial reconnaissance."[106]

During World War II, MacArthur soldiers named him "Dugout Doug" because he was never even near the field of battle. As a matter of fact, CNN reports, "MacArthur only visited his troops in Bataan once on January 10, 1942. Some viewed this as cowardice and lack of leadership, at a time when his men needed a morale boost."[107]

Of course, distance itself does not *automatically* translate to a failure of execution. But it does increase the probability of error. Distance also heightens the urgency of speed and the need for trust in the people who *are* leading from the front, but also everyone in between.

Unfortunately, rather than surrounding himself with a highly competent staff, MacArthur, like King Louis XIV, surrounded himself with a "simpering and reverential" court.[108] Five-star general George Marshall reportedly once said as much to MacArthur's face. "You don't have a staff, General. You have a court."[109] After visiting MacArthur in Tokyo, American journalist Joseph Alsop (a descendant of both presidents Theodore Roosevelt and James Monroe) wrote that MacArthur's relationship with his staff "was proof of the basic rule of armies at war: the farther one gets from the front, the more laggards, toadies and fools one encounters."[110]

The problem with being surrounded by sycophants was that MacArthur "isolated himself from criticism and unwelcome advice."[111] "This sycophancy," Alsop concluded, "was what tripped him up in the end."[112]

Interestingly, in executing his bold amphibious landing at Inchon, described in Colonel Robert Brunson's book as "an example of brilliant generalship and military genius," MacArthur was far more closely engaged, personally overseeing the 1st Marine Regiment on the road to take back Seoul.[113]

Regardless of whether you are leading from the front, you are closely engaged with the front, or you have effectively delegated leadership—including sufficient autonomy and decision making authority—to one or more trusted lieutenants at the front, in order to profit from the power of effective strategy, the successful execution of that strategy is key. Toward that end, the following are the seven (7) cardinal pillars of successful strategy execution:

(1.) *Ownership: Foster Ownership of the Purpose, Strategy, and Actionable Goals.*

The first key to effective strategy execution is assuming extreme ownership of and dedication to the objective or strategic intent. Without this single-minded commitment and culture of ownership, even the perfect strategy can easily fail. Sadly, a lack of commitment is surprisingly common. In one large international study, researchers found that nearly *half* of the people surveyed lacked commitment to achieving their organization's goal. As Covey et al write in *The 4 Disciplines of Execution*, "Only 51 percent could say that they were passionate about the team's goal, leaving almost half the team simply going through the motions."[114]

Along with consistent communication, part of commitment comes down to ensuring the goals are clear, actionable, measurable, and concrete. But the real secret to commitment is giving people a voice. Remember: People support what they help create. In their book, *Execution: The Discipline of Getting Things Done*, Larry Bossidy and Ram Charan write, "To be effective, a strategy has to be *constructed* and owned by those who will execute it."[115]

When they learned they were trapped in Maracaibo Lake, the buccaneers were discouraged, anxious, and doubtful about their odds. Captain Morgan refrained from telling his men what they had to do, however. Instead, he laid out the situation before them and let them all vote on how to respond. It would be easy to imagine, given that they were fighting for their lives, that their vote made little difference. Perhaps they would fight just as hard even if Captain Morgan had forced them to fight their way out. But these were free men fighting not just for their lives, or the considerable treasure they had acquired, but for a life of freedom and independence, and against tyranny. And when Captain Morgan put the matter to a vote, he was reinforcing that freedom and sense of ownership over their choices and, ultimately, their destiny. They were not merely fighting to keep a job or to avoid execution, they were fighting for a life worth living.

While the long-standing military maxim that 'one volunteer soldier is worth ten who have been drafted'[116] may exaggerate the case, there is *no question* that forced compliance impedes commitment or that motivation and morale very often make a decisive difference. Recall the words of Napoleon

Bonaparte, "An army's effectiveness depends on its size, training, experience, and morale, and morale is worth more than any of the other factors combined."[117]

The sense of ownership and commitment found in those who join of their own volition often stands in stark contrast to those who are forced to fight or who fight only for pay, particularly when their lives are on the line. In *The Prince*, Niccolò Machiavelli writes, "mercenaries and auxiliaries are useless and dangerous, and if anyone keeps his state based on the arms of mercenaries, he will never stand firm or sure, as they are disunited, ambitious, without discipline, faithless, bold amongst friends, cowardly amongst enemies, they have no fear of God, and keep no faith with men."[118]

Furthermore, because the buccaneers were free to share their thoughts and ideas with Captain Morgan and, ultimately, vote together on the plan, there was far less second-guessing, backseat driving, and disharmony among the crew when it came to executing their plan. They made the decision together and they would work together to see it through. Naturally, the application of this principle is not limited to freedom loving pirates.

Challenging and questioning the strategy, tactics, and goals of any organization not only reveals a lack of commitment, but it also actively undermines execution. According to research reported in *Harvard Business Review (HBR)*, "71% of respondents in weak-execution companies thought that decisions were being second-guessed, whereas only 45% of those from strong-execution organizations felt that way."[119] But what other causes could be at work?

(2.) *Synchronization: Coordinate and Orchestrate People and Resources with Clear Roles and Goals.*

> *"Synchronization is essential for excellence in execution."*[120]
> —Larry Bossidy and Ram Charan, *Execution: The Discipline of Getting Things Done*

Another key part of effective execution is synchronization, including coordination, calibration, orchestration, and alignment. Coordination and calibration are about ensuring everyone fits the culture ("the right people on the bus"[121]), is in the right position ("the key seats on the bus"[122]), and that they are confidently equipped with the knowledge and skills, and effectively supplied with the resources and provisions they need to succeed. In *Execution*, Bossidy and Charan argue that "having the right people in the right place" is "the job no leader should delegate."[123] It may not be the most glamorous responsibility, they admit, "but over time, choosing the right people," "people who understand how to execute" your strategy, "is what creates that elusive sustainable competitive advantage."[124]

Synchronization is also about orchestration and alignment—ensuring that everyone is working together in harmony, carefully arranged with clear roles and responsibilities, *all* geared toward supporting the team or organization's shared purpose and corresponding goals. In short, everything must be effectively positioned, provisioned, and aligned to support the strategic intent.

The most inspired strategy is worthless if you can't "make sure your organization has or can get what's required to execute it, including the right resources and the right people"[125] in the right places and positions of power. This begins first and foremost with the leaders.

As is often the case with leaders, including 17th century pirates, how well the captain is aligned with the vision, values, and culture of the crew can make or break the organization. Pirates and privateers like Captain Morgan "had to display both courage and intelligence, and above all, they had to be successful or the crew would turn them out. Men who aspired to lead their buccaneer brethren had to prove themselves in the same way, and it was here in the ugly, violent world of the close fight that Morgan doubtless first made his name."[126]

(3.) *Intelligence: Ensure that Quality, Timely, Trustworthy Intelligence Flows Quickly and Easily to All Decision Makers.*

The third critical factor of effective strategy execution is intelligence. With rare exceptions, as discussed above, history's greatest strategists have all been intimately involved in the execution of their plans, often operating on the front lines or in the center of the action. "The vital center" President John F. Kennedy called it—"the center of the center of the action."[127] Kennedy wanted to be "in the very thick of the fight." Indeed, he said, this was the duty of the president. President Theodore Roosevelt likewise spoke of the need for leaders to be "actually in the arena," where your "face is marred by dust and sweat and blood."[128]

Learn What's Happening as It's Happening. For leaders, being on the front lines or at the center of the action has a number of advantages—including an opportunity to lead by example, build connections with followers on the front lines (which can help to maintain morale, boost engagement and improve performance), but also to get information that might not surface in formal reports or which followers might be reluctant to share.

For strategists, the critical factor is strategic intelligence. The big advantage of being on the front lines or in the center of the action is knowing what's happening *as* its happening, so you can more quickly and easily adapt. In fact, a large part of what effective execution entails is having quality, timely intelligence (i.e. information that has been processed, contextualized, analyzed, and interpreted) so you are better able to *anticipate* and, thereby, *influence* what is going to happen rather than merely *react* to what already happened.

Of course, getting the best most reliable information as quickly as possible does not always necessitate being on the front lines, particularly given the technology available today. What is essential, however, is getting quality, pertinent, unfiltered information that you can trust *as quickly as possible*. In war, business, politics and sports, speed is a force multiplier. Speed can take limited time, money, people, or other resources and multiply their influence or overall effects. Moreover, writes Mark McNeilly in *Sun Tzu and the Art of Business*, "Speed in execution is essential for a number of reasons; speed is a substitute for resources, it shocks and surprises your competitors, it is critical to exploiting weaknesses and opportunities, and it allows you to build momentum."[129]

Reap Speed Through Trust. The two greatest challenges strategists face with not being on the front lines are speed and trust. Receiving good intelligence but not trusting it, or after it is too late, is scarcely much better than not receiving it at all (although, if it's the best available, questionable intelligence may at least provide leads or hypotheses or something that can be further investigated or disproven). As Stephen Covey put it, "Nothing is as fast as the speed of trust."[130]

In June 1941, Germany and Russia were at peace—at least that's what Joseph Stalin believed, as per the Molotov-Ribbentrop Pact signed in 1939. Both U.S. and British intelligence sources, however, tried to warn Stalin that a German invasion of Russia was imminent. Stalin's own intelligence sources likewise warned him that a German attack was looming. But he ignored them all, including direct contact from Winston Churchill.[131]

When Stalin received reports from Soviet military sources that the Germans were amassing along Russia's Western border, including 19 Panzer divisions (i.e. 3,000 tanks, 2,500 aircraft, and 7,000 artillery pieces[132]), Stalin *still* refused to believe that an invasion was imminent. Later, he received a warning of a German invasion from Chairman Mao Zedong, but, again, he refused to believe it.[133]

At the same time, Stalin was being bombarded with misinformation from the Germans. "Hitler had a very good eye for the weaknesses of his opponents," explains British historian Richard Evans in *Rise of the Nazis;* "Stalin was a very suspicious kind of man. He was prone to conspiracy theories, and that of course means that you can supply Stalin with many kinds of information and misinformation that he will believe."[134]

In essence, rather than trusting his own sources or taking steps to gather intelligence that he *would* actually trust, Stalin believed the German propaganda instead. "It was an epic failure on his part."[135]

After receiving another warning from one of his own spies, Richard Sorge, "Stalin remained implacable, insisting that Hitler was not 'such an idiot' as to risk a war on two fronts."[136] When Stalin's own Soviet military units began to report that they were *actually under attack*, Stalin *still refused to believe it*. He even sent orders to "avoid provocative actions of any kind."[137]

At this point, Stalin's belief in the non-aggression pact with Hitler was pure delusion.[138]

The only thing that might convince him otherwise, it seemed, would be a visit to the 1,800-mile front[139] to see with his own eyes what remains today the largest invasion in human history.

Instead, however, Cambridge University's David Reynolds explains, "He made the predicament of the Soviet Union much worse...by his overconfidence, complacency and failure to really understand what was going on at the front."[140]

Instead of coming to terms with what was unfolding, Stalin, for two full weeks, went silent, retreating to his country house outside of Moscow. During this period, according to Soviet Premier Nikita Khrushchev, Stalin suffered a nervous breakdown.[141]

A few weeks after he received his spymaster's report, Stalin was shown to be "spectacularly wrong."[142] Some 1,200 Soviet planes were wiped off the airfields on the first morning alone.[143] By the time the Germans made it hundreds of miles into Russia on their march to Moscow, 420,000 Soviet soldiers had lost their lives.[144] In response, Stalin said, "Lenin founded our state and we've f@c#ed it up."[145]

(4.) *Communication: Cultivate Crisp, Clear, and Consistent Communication.*

Clear and consistent communication is another essential factor in the effective execution of strategy. Quality, timely intelligence is worthless if it is miscommunicated or misunderstood. Likewise, communicating abstract, complex, fuzzy, or poorly defined goals and objectives does not inspire commitment.

The lack of a clear objective, clearly communicated, is one of the major reasons why strategy execution fails. In their extensive surveys, Covey et al's researchers found that a mere 15 percent of employees were able to name at least one of their organization's most important goals. "The other 85 percent named what they thought was the goal, but it often didn't remotely resemble what their leaders had said."[146] Not surprisingly, the researchers also found that "the further from the top of the organization, the lower the clarity."[147] In the end, the reason strategy so often failed is because, according to Covey, "people simply didn't understand the goal they were supposed to execute."[148]

Beyond the organization's wildly important goals, according to *HBR*, "a staggering 95 percent of employees don't understand or are unaware of their company's strategy."[149] Thus, as HBR's Catherine Cote concludes, "when it comes to strategy execution, the power of clear communication can't be overlooked."[150]

(5.) *Observation: Watch and Weigh Progress and Performance.*
   Prepare to Rapidly Respond.

Rather than a one-off event, strategy execution is a process. The longer the process the more apt it is to go off track or require adjustment to adapt. In order to effectively execute a strategy, therefore, it is important to closely observe its progress. This often includes collecting data, or gathering information and feedback about what is actually happening on the ground or at the points where the strategy is unfolding. The idea is to continuously appraise your progress in context so that, if necessary, you can rapidly recalibrate and respond.[151]

It takes leadership and initiative and a certain level of humility in order to quickly respond to an unexpected development or disruption to one's strategy, tactics, or plan. As General George S. Patton once said, "Unsuccessful commanders issue orders and then return to their card games at headquarters. They believe the simple act of issuing an order will immediately cause everything to fall into place, and the battle will go their way just because they said so. They expect everything to go exactly according to their plans. That is as unrealistic as it is stupid. A successful commander," on the other hand, Patton continued, "issues an order and then makes damn sure it's not only carried out but working as planned. If things go wrong, or a situation changes, the commander will be aware of it immediately and be able to change the orders in response..." in short, Patton concluded, "don't jump to conclusions and don't make assumptions. Follow up on everything."[152]

In the case of Captain Morgan, the original plan was to use the fire ship to sail past the fort and on to the safety of the sea. Instead, despite their initial success, once his fleet came under fire from the fort, Captain Morgan was forced to order a hasty retreat. This was not part of the initial plan and though the buccaneers had eliminated part of the threat (the Spanish squadron), they were nevertheless still trapped in the lake. Fortunately, for Morgan, given that he was leading the battle and, therefore, monitoring its progress firsthand, he was able to quickly adjust, retreat and regroup, and reformulate a new, surprise plan to escape.

In contrast to Captain Morgan, Admiral Alonso's lack of humility proved to be major liability, leading him to underestimate his enemy more than once. Rather than adequately adapting to the unanticipated change to his plan (e.g. the destruction of his ships), or closely monitoring the unfolding of his plan (e.g. observing the tides, watching Morgan's fleet closely, even, perhaps especially, at night), Don Alonso's arrogance led him to make one faulty assumption after another. As historian Graham Thomas writes in *The Pirate King: The Incredible Story of the Real Captain Morgan*, "While Morgan was capable of adapting quickly, Don Alonso was rigid, traditional, bound by duty to his king and, more importantly, bound by his arrogance and belief in his superior birthright."[153]

(6.) *Accountability: Collect and Share Feedback and Hold Yourself and Others Accountable to the Results.*

Another factor essential to the long-term effectiveness of strategy execution is accountability. Top performing teams are made up of members who are clear about their role and responsibilities, how their specific actions contribute to the strategy and goals, and the rewards they can expect as a result of success. High performing teams also receive timely, objective feedback so they are clear about how they are performing, or what they might need to adjust.

The biggest problem here is the general lack of accountability. According to Covey's research, "a staggering 81 percent of the people surveyed said they were not held accountable for regular progress on the organization's goals."[154]

The next most common problem is a lack of clarity around goals and the specific actions needed to achieve those goals. In other words, the authors conclude, "the goals were not translated into specific actions;" in fact, a whopping "87 percent had no clear idea what they should be doing to achieve the goal."[155]

In the case of the buccaneers, both as individuals and as a crew, to a considerable extent, accountability was built into the hard realities of the lives they led and the consequences of their performance as privateers. Poor performance meant that they would soon be captured, imprisoned, or hung. The next lowest level meant that some number of the crew might be missing an arm, an eye, or a leg. Or it might mean that they were alive and able-bodied, but starving or suffering from scurvy. If they were performing reasonably well, then their bellies were full and they were probably drunk on rum. But if they performed really well then they were rich or even, in rare cases, retired.

There were also rules relating to accountability written into the pirate code, which outlined the conditions of service, codes of conduct and discipline, and defined the punishments, which varied widely from flogging and marooning to having one's ears and nose slit.[156] The pirate codes on many ships outlined "minor offenses such as quarreling, mistreatment of equipment, or neglect of duties,"[157] as well as more serious derelictions of duty, such as being drunk in a time of engagement, "desert[ing] the ship or their quarters in battle"[158] or "cowardice in the time of engagement."[159] The punishment for these more severe infractions usually amounted to a gruesome death sentence. In one form of punishment, for example, known as keelhauling, the offender was tied up and dragged across the barnacles on the bottom of the ship, resulting in severe lacerations.

There were also often rewards for stellar service. In the pirate code of Captain Edward Low and George Lowther, for example, the crew member who was first to spot the sail of a ship was rewarded with "the best Pistol or Small Arm"[160] that was later stolen from that ship.

The captains of pirate ships had ultimate accountability and if they were not performing they could be voted out. Basically serving "at the mercy of the crew," a pirate captain could also be "removed from his position for acts of cowardice, cruelty, or failure to act in the best interest of the crew."[161] Pirate captains were also rewarded for their success with a double portion of any booty or prize captured.

The key point to remember here is that accountability can be a powerful, constructive force. When the only person you have to answer to is yourself, success usually proves more elusive. On the other hand, there is power in working together with a team and holding each other accountable for the shared dream. This is especially true when you partner with the right people,

"people who believe in you and want to see you grow."[162] We are social animals by nature and accountability can sharpen the focus and deepen the drive of even the most ambitious.

Even if you are working more or less on your own, your likelihood of success increases dramatically when you have adequate accountability.[163] "The support and accountability afforded by a group committed to seeing you succeed is one of the most important soft assets for any business-builder."[164]

Lacking an accountability partner or group, the inventor Thomas Edison relied on the public and the press. Edison was well aware of "how much better he worked under pressure," and so he would "deliberately talk to the press about an idea before it was ready. This would create some publicity and excitement in the public as to the possibilities of the proposed invention. If he dropped the ball or let too much time pass, his reputation would suffer, and so his mind would spark into high gear and he would make it happen."[165] The place to start is with specific, measurable, actionable goals which are aligned with your strategy. Then, set deadlines and create an accountability plan.

(7.) *Resolve: Persist Until You Succeed.*

The Battle of the Bulge was Nazi dictator Adolf Hitler's last major offensive in World War II. If he could split the Allied forces on the Western Front, he could encircle and destroy the Allied forces one piece at a time. He could then return to the Eastern Front to concentrate his forces against Russia and win the war. Everything depended on splitting the Allied line.

The Nazis' initial surprise attack on the four American divisions ensured the Nazis had the upper hand. But the Americans put up unexpectedly fierce resistance.

In one key battle, the Siege of Bastogne in Belgium, paratroopers from the 101st Airborne Division, together with the all African American 969th Artillery Battalion, combined into some 22,000 U.S. troops. They were tasked with holding the perimeter around Bastogne, an important crossroads town during the Battle of the Bulge, against a massive force of Germans which, with 54,000 troops, was two and a half times their size. Despite operating on a limited supply of ammunition and scarce food, the Americans, commanded by Brigadier General Anthony McAuliffe, desperately sought to hold out against the well-supplied division of panzers (armored corps), commanded by German General Heinrich Freiherr von Lüttwitz.[166]

The odds were so heavily stacked against the Americans that Lüttwitz sent a delegation to the Americans with an ultimatum, which read, "To the U.S.A. Commander of the encircled town of Bastogne. The fortune of war is changing. This time the U.S.A. forces in and near Bastogne have been encircled by strong German armored units. [...]There is only one possibility to save the encircled U.S.A. troops from total annihilation: that is the honorable surrender of the encircled town."[167]

Allowing 2 hours "to think it over," Lüttwitz concluded, "If this proposal should be rejected one German Artillery Corps and six heavy A. A. Battalions are ready to annihilate the U.S.A. troops in and near Bastogne. The order for firing will be given immediately after this two hours term."[168]

Given that they were completely surrounded and badly outnumbered, the situation indeed seemed hopeless. Nevertheless, U.S. Brigadier General Anthony McAuliffe was so dumbfounded by the request that all he could say in response to the delegation was "NUTS!"[169]

Minutes later, it was decided that that would be the official American response. When Lüttwitz received the document, all it said was, "To the German commander, NUTS! –The American commander."[170]

When the Germans asked for an interpretation, the translator explained, "It means 'Go to Hell!'"[171]

Despite the dire circumstances—suffering enormous casualties in bitter cold weather with a lack of ammunition and supplies, all while being surrounded by a ruthless enemy—the U.S. troops valiantly continued to hold the perimeter for days afterwards. Word of their stubborn resistance spread across the entire Western Front, boosting Allied morale.

At last, on December 26, General George Patton's Third Army reached the besieged town and rescued the regiments, who later became known as the "Battered Bastards of Bastogne," for their heroic hold of the critical crossroads. Immediately, the Americans began retaking positions and gaining new ground. Less than a month later, the Allied Forces would emerge victorious in the Battle of the Bulge. It was the beginning of the end of Nazi Germany.

Follow All the Way Through. This is the final key factor in effective strategy execution. You must resolve to follow all the way through *until* you succeed. Perseverance is everything. "There is no value in anything until it is finished,"[172] said Genghis Khan; "the merit of an action lies in finishing it to the end."[173]

People very often succeed for the simple fact that they refuse to quit. In the words of Napoleon Bonaparte, "victory belongs to the most persevering."[174] "If courage is the first characteristic of the soldier," Napoleon said, "perseverance is the second."[175]

The opposite is equally true. People often fail for no other reason than the simple fact that they fail to follow through—too often, unfortunately, when success is around the very next corner or on the other side of the very next hill. "Throughout history, great battles have been won and then lost because of the failure of a commanding general to follow through and complete the victory."[176] On March 27, 1943, in the Battle of the Komandorski Islands, U.S. Rear Admiral Charles McMorris was sent with a fleet 6 ships (1 heavy cruiser, *Salt Lake City*; 1 light cruiser, *Richmond*; and 4 destroyers) to stop Imperial Japan from supplying their forces on the Aleutian Islands off Alaska. McMorris expected the fleets to be equally matched, but when they finally encountered the Japanese fleet about 100 miles south of the Komandorski islands it had been reinforced to 8 ships (2 heavy cruisers, 2 light cruisers, and 4 destroyers).

After nearly 4 hours of exchanging fire, the Japanese fleet was on the cusp of victory. The *Salt Lake City* had been severely damaged. Two of the four U.S. destroyers had also been slightly damaged. One of Japan's heavy cruisers, *Nachi*, had sustained moderate damage and the other heavy cruiser, *Maya*, only slight damage. Japan's Admiral Hosogaya did not realize, however, the significant damage he had inflicted on the *Salt Lake City*, the Americans only heavy cruiser, which had temporarily stopped, had taken on some water, and was listing (tilting due to flooding).

What's more, because they had run out of armor piercing ammunition, the Americans started firing high-explosive incendiary (HEI) ammunition, which resulted in large splashes of water shooting up on impact with the ocean's surface. Given the heavy cloud cover and the clever use of smoke screens—to hide the damage sustained by the *Salt Lake City*, and to make it a more elusive target—Hosogaya thought these splashes were from bombs being dropped by U.S. war planes above. As a result, rather than pressing his considerable advantage, he turned and sailed his fleet away. What was very nearly a great victory for Imperial Japan was tantamount to a strategic victory for the U.S. Navy instead.

Thomas Edison once wrote that "many of life's failures are people who did not realize how close they were to success when they gave up."[177] Most people give up far too often and quit far too soon. They may begin with great enthusiasm or a short burst of boldness, but the moment the inevitable challenges and obstacles arise, or when they simply fail to succeed right away, they start searching for excuses to quit.

Perhaps the biggest problem with this pattern is not just that it is a complete waste of energy, resources, and time. The real danger is that the cycle of failed attempts can become crippling. Every time you waste valuable resources and time you'll never get back, something inside you shifts. With each surrender, your determination dwindles, your fortitude falls, until giving up becomes second nature, until resignation is more comfortable than struggle. Call it a weakness or lack of resolve, but the truth is darker—quitting begets quitting, until quitting becomes a habit.

The solution is to first *choose your goal very carefully* and then resolve to stick it out. "Never launch an initiative unless you're personally committed to it and prepared to see it through until it's embedded in the DNA of [your] organization."[178] Do whatever is necessary to make sure that everyone understands this: "You are simply going to keep going until you get there."[179] "Press your advantage and push through to complete victory. Never relax until your objective has been attained."[180] "Follow-through is the cornerstone of execution," writes Bossidy and Charan, "and every leader who's good at executing follows through religiously."[181]

"The good news," Fortune 500 consultant Brian Tracy maintains, "is that your chances of great success are extremely high if you know what you want, put your whole heart into it, and then persist until you succeed."[182] This is why history's greatest strategists have so often emphasized the need for and power of resolve. In *The Outlook*, a magazine for which he was associate editor following his presidency, Theodore Roosevelt once wrote, "perhaps there is no more important component of character than steadfast resolution. The boy who is going to make a great man," Roosevelt wrote, "or is going to count in any way in after life, must make up his mind not merely to overcome a thousand obstacles, but to win in spite of a thousand repulses or defeats."[183]

In October 1941, Winston Churchill was invited to speak at Harrow, a boarding school for boys in London and Churchill's alma mater. Despite the fact that the country was in the midst of World War II and, moreover, that Churchill was the absurdly busy Prime Minister of the United Kingdom at the time, he accepted the invitation. He apparently had something important to say.

When the day and moment arrived, Churchill flew in, took to the stage, looked out into the eyes of his young, eager audience and said these unforgettable words: "Never give in, never give in, never, never, never, never—in nothing, great or small, large or petty—never give in except to convictions of honor and good sense. Never yield to force; never yield to the apparently overwhelming might of the enemy."[184] Churchill then abruptly exited the stage and returned to 10 Downing Street.

Implement and Execute Like Hell

"In real life, strategy is actually very straightforward. You pick a general direction and implement like hell."[185]

—Jack Welch (1935—2020), American Business Titan

When reading over the historical record of master strategists and tacticians like Henry Morgan, it's easy to get caught up in thinking about *what* the strategy is rather than *how* it was implemented. If the strategy fails or comes up short, rather than examining the execution of the plan, the tendency is to want to find fault with the plan itself. But even the most brilliant strategic plan is at best only half of the battle. Magazine publishing magnate Felix Dennis put it even more emphatically, "Ideas don't make you rich. The correct execution of ideas does."[186] Tech titan Steve Jobs similarly said, "Ideas are worth nothing *unless executed*. They are just a multiplier. Execution is worth millions."[187]

Do not misunderstand: Strategy is vital. Tactics are indispensable. And, yet no matter how inspired your strategy or clever your tactics, execution is still key. Execution is where the dream becomes reality. It is here where you "mesh strategy with reality, align people with goals, and achieve the promised results."[188]

This is where Captain Morgan excelled. No doubt, he was a master strategist. In fact, he is typically described today as "a brilliant strategist and tactician" who was "able to adapt to his environment and willing to take risks in order to achieve his objectives."[189] But Captain Morgan was also an effective leader of men. He was able to devise a winning strategy and tactics, but he was also able to ensure the superb execution of his strategy and tactics to achieve the promised result.

Following his dramatic escape from Maracaibo Lake, Captain Morgan's continuing success as a privateer in the Caribbean created such a stir that it increased tensions between England and Spain. In 1672, in an effort to keep the fragile peace, King Charles II of England had Captain Morgan arrested and brought back to England for trial. Once in England, however, Captain Morgan was celebrated as a hero. Far too successful and valuable to rot in prison, he was instead knighted by the King.

Known from that day forward as Sir Henry Morgan, with his days as a privateer at an end, he retired to a life of luxury in Jamaica as a wealthy plantation owner, where he was appointed Lt. Governor and, later, Acting Governor. "In his final years he was rich, owned several plantations, drank heavily with former buccaneers and "privateers," made enemies of a few simpering politicians, cursed much, and was accused of consorting with pirates."[190]

In 1688, at age 53, Captain Morgan died from alcoholism. "The quintessential English buccaneer" was, reportedly, when he passed away, "so bloated from drink that he could not move from his hammock."[191] A state funeral was held for him back in England, a rare and exceptional tribute. Today, Captain Morgan is best known for having a popular brand of rum named in his honor.

THE END

REFERENCES & NOTES

For a free large print version of the REFERENCES & NOTES visit: http://classicinfluence.com/strategist/

|PART 1: INTRO|

Think Like a Strategist, Exploit the Proven Power of a Superior Strategic Plan: Napoleon Bonaparte Assumes First Command

1. McLynn, Frank (2015). *Genghis Khan: His Conquests, His Empire, His Legacy*. Boston: Da Capo. Pg. 274.
2. Schom, Alan (1997). Napoleon Bonaparte. NYC: HarperCollins. Pg. 49.
3. Gilbert, Adrian (2022, April 17 [Last Accessed]). "Siege of Toulon." Encyclopedia Britannica. https://www.britannica.com/event/Siege-of-Toulon
4. Wilde, Robert (2019, March 4). "Napoleon and the Siege of Toulon 1793." ThoughtCo. https://www.thoughtco.com/napoleon-and-the-siege-of-toulon-1221693
5. Dwyer, Philip (2007). Napoleon: The Path to Power, 1769—1799. New Haven: Yale University Press. Pg. 115.
6. Chandler, David G. (1966). The Campaigns of Napoleon: The Mind and Method of History's Greatest Soldier. NYC: Scribner. Pg. 104.
7. Haskew, Michael {Editor)(2021). "The Star of Napoleon Ascendant." All About History Napoleon, 4th Edition. Bournemouth: Future Publishing Limited. Pg. 16.
8. Zamoyski, Adam (2018). *Napoleon: The Man Behind the Myth*. London: William Collins. Pg. 128.
9. Roberts, Andrew (2014). Napoleon: A Life. NYC: Viking. Pg. 58.
10. Cronin, Vincent (1988). Napoleon. NY: Penguin. Pg. 86.
11. Grehan, John (Editor)(2018). *Napoleon Bonaparte: Master of War*. Lincolnshire: Key Publishing Ltd. Pg. 15.
12. Chandler (1966), Pg. 106.
13. Roberts (2014), Pg. 57.
14. Englund, Steven (2004). *Napoleon: A Political Life*. NYC: Scribner. Pg. 62.
15. Chandler (1966), Pg. 106.
16. Zamoyski (2018), Pg. 127.
17. Zamoyski (2018), Pg. 127.
18. Chandler (1966), Pg. 109.
19. Nester, William (2021). Napoleon and the Art of Leadership: How a Flawed Genius Changed the History of Europe and the World. NYC: Frontline Books. Pg. 77.
20. Chandler (1966), Pg. 110.
21. Chandler (1966), Pg. 110.
22. Chandler (1966), Pg. 107.
23. Nester (2021), Pg. 77.
24. Chandler (1966), Pgs. 107-108.
25. Cronin (1988), Pg. 87.
26. Chandler (1966), Pg. 108.
27. Cronin (1988), Pg. 87.
28. Chandler (1966), Pg. 108.
29. Chandler (1966), Pg. 108.
30. Cronin (1988), Pg. 87.
31. Dwyer (2007), Pg. 115.
32. Dwyer (2007), Pg. 115.
33. Asprey, Robert (2000). The Rise of Napoleon Bonaparte. NYC: Basic Books. Pg. 81.
34. Nester (2021), Pg. 78.
35. Roberts (2014), Pg. 58.
36. Chandler (1966), Pg. 109.
37. Asprey (2000), Pg. 82.
38. Asprey (2000), Pg. 82.
39. Asprey (2000), Pg. 82.
40. Haskew, Michael (Editor)(2021). "The Star of Napoleon Ascendant." All About History Napoleon, 4th Edition. Bournemouth: Future Publishing Limited. Pg. 16.
41. Haskew (2021), Pg. 16.
42. Asprey, Robert (2000), Pg. 82.
43. Zamoyski (2018), Pg. 130.
44. Palumbo, Paolo (2020, August 21). "Was the Siege of Toulon the Military Birth of Napoleon?" SOFREP. https://sofrep.com/news/was-the-siege-of-toulon-the-military-birth-of-napoleon-bonaparte/
45. Roberts (2014), Pg. 58.
46. Asprey (2000), Pg. 82.
47. Asprey (2000), Pg. 82.
48. Asprey (2000), Pg. 82.
49. Chandler (1966), Pg. 106.
50. Chandler (1966), Pg. 24.
51. Asprey (2000), Pg. 84.
52. Nester (2021), Pg. 78.
53. Westlake, Hannah (Editor)(2018). "The Star of Napoleon Ascendant." *History of War Book of the Napoleonic Wars*, Second Edition. Bournemouth: Future Publishing Limited. Pg. 20.
54. Zamoyski (2018), Pg. 131.
55. Dwyer (2007), Pg. 117.
56. Nester (2021), Pg. 78.
57. Asprey (2000), Pg. 85.
58. Asprey (2000), Pg. 85.
59. Zamoyski (2018), Pg. 131.
60. Asprey (2000), Pg. 85.
61. Asprey (2000), Pg. 85.
62. Zamoyski (2018), Pg. 131.
63. Chandler (1966), Pg. 25.
64. Zamoyski (2018), Pg. 133.
65. Chandler (1966), Pg. 111.
66. Dwyer (2007), Pg. 118.
67. Zamoyski (2018), Pgs. 133-134.
68. Chandler (1966), Pg. 111.
69. Zamoyski (2018), Pgs. 133-134.
70. Cronin (1988), Pg. 88.
71. Chandler (1966), Pg. 111.
72. Hoefer, Richard (2019). Advocacy Practice for Social Justice, 4th Edition. Oxford: Oxford University Press. Pg. 87.
73. Roberts (2014), Pg. 59.
74. Roberts (2014), Pg. 59.
75. Roberts (2014), Pg. 59.
76. Roberts (2014), Pg. 59.
77. Cronin (1988), Pg. 90.
78. Roberts (2014), Pg. 60.
79. Roberts (2014), Pg. 60.
80. Roberts (2014), Pg. 60.
81. Cronin (1988), Pg. 90.
82. Dwyer (2007), Pg. 119.
83. McLynn, Frank (2011). Napoleon: A Biography. NYC: Arcade Publishing. Pg. 75.
84. Asprey (2000), Pg. 88.
85. Durant, Will & Ariel (1975). The Age of Napoleon: The Story of Civilization, Volume 11. NYC: Simon & Schuster. Pg. 309.
86. Sloan, Julia (2006). Learning to Think Strategically. San Diego: Butterworth-Heinemann. Pg. 42.

87. Covey, Stephen (2004). The 8th Habit: From Effectiveness to Greatness. NYC: Free Press. Pg. 131.

88. Malnight, Thomas W. & Buche, Ivy (2022, January-February). "The Strategic Advantage of Incumbency." Harvard Business Review, Volume 100, Number 1. Boston: Harvard Business School Publishing. Pg. 45.

89. Lafley, A.G. and Martin, Roger (2013). Playing to Win: How Strategy Really Works. Boston: Harvard Business Review Press. Pg.13.

90. Lafley (2013), Pg.13.

91. Sloan (2006), Pg. 42.

92. Sloan (2006), Pg. 42.

93. Sloan (2006), Pg. 42.

94. Chandler (1966), Pg. 109.

95. Levine, Michael (1996). Take it from Me: Practical and Inspiring Career Advice from the Celebrated and the Successful. NYC: Berkley Publishing Group. Pg. 76.

96. Gold, Eugene (2019, September 12). "The Curse Of Indecisiveness." Forbes. https://www.forbes.com/sites/theyec/2019/09/12/the-curse-of-indecisiveness/

97. Hoefer, Richard (2019). Advocacy Practice for Social Justice, 4th Edition. Oxford: Oxford University Press. Pg. 87.

98. Chandler, Steve (1998). Reinventing Yourself: How to Become the Person You've Always Wanted to Be. Franklin Lakes: Career Press. Pg. 191.

99. Wiercinski, Andrzej (2020). Existentia Hermeneutica: Understanding as the Mode of Being in the World, International Studies in Hermeneutics and Phenomenology, Vol. 11. Zurich: Lit Verlag. Pg. 30.

100. Paine, Thomas (1925). The Life and Works of Thomas Paine. William M. Van der Weyde (Editor). New Rochelle: Patriots' Edition. Pg. 66.

101. Tracy, Brian (2022). Speak to Win: How to Present with Power in Any Situation. New York: AMACOM. Pg. 111.

102. Tracy, Brian (2022). Speak to Win: How to Present with Power in Any Situation. New York: AMACOM. Pgs. 110-111.

103. Mortensen, Kurt W. (2004). Maximum Influence: The 12 Universal Laws of Power Persuasion. NYC: Amacom. Pg. 18.

104. King Jr., Martin Luther (1963). Strength to Love. Boston: Beacon Press. Pg. 2.

105. Duggan, William (2002). Napoleon's Glance: The Secret of Strategy. NYC: Thunder's Mouth Press. Pg. 3.

106. Greene, Robert (2021). The Daily Laws: 366 Meditations on Power, Seduction, Mastery, Strategy, and Human Nature. NYC: Viking. Pg. 308.

107. In thinking about how to achieve their vision and goals, strategists are guided by the following seven questions, often returning to them again and again throughout the process of formulating, implementing, and executing their strategy: (a.) Where are we now? (b.) Where do we want to go? (c.) How do we get there? (d.) What do we need to do to get there? (e.) What strengths and resources do we have or can we get? (f.) Who or what obstacles and resistance will we face? (g.) Who is with us?

108. Napolitan, Joseph (2003). "Napolitan's Rules: 112 Lessons Learned from a Career in Politics." In Faucheux, Ronald A. (Editor) Winning Elections: Political Campaign Management, Strategy, & Tactics. Lanham: Rowman & Littlefield.

109. HBR Guides to Building Your Strategic Skills Collection. Cambridge: Harvard Business School Publishing.

110. Echevarria II, Antulio J. (2017). Military Strategy: A Very Short Introduction. Oxford: Oxford University Press. Pg. 146.

111. McKeown, Max (2020). The Strategy Book: How to Think and Act Strategically to Deliver Outstanding Results, 3rd Edition. London: Pearson. Pg. 2.

112. Stephens, Alan and Baker, Nicola (2006). Making Sense of War: Strategy of the 21st Century. NYC. Pg. 5.

113. Duggan, William (2007). Strategic Intuition: The Creative Spark in Human Achievement. NYC: Columbia Business School Publishing. Pg. 55.

114. Ridgley, Stanley K. (2012). Strategic Thinking Skills: The Great Courses. Chantilly, Virginia: The Teaching Company, LLC. Lecture 1.

115. Ridgley, Stanley K. (2012). Strategic Thinking Skills: The Great Courses. Chantilly, Virginia: The Teaching Company, LLC. Lecture 1.

116. Duggan, William (2015). The Seventh Sense: How Flashes of Insight Change Your Life. NYC: Columbia University Press. Pg. 71.

117. Duggan (2007), Pg. 55.

118. Duggan (2007), Pg. 55.

119. Duggan (2007), Pg. 55.

120. Duggan (2007), Pg. 55.

121. Duggan (2015), Pg. 71.

122. Duggan, William (2003). The Art of What Works. NYC: McGraw-Hill. Pg. 4.

123. Duggan (2007), Pg. 55.

124. Wilson, Andrew R. (2012). Masters of War: History's Greatest Strategic Thinkers. The Great Courses. Chantilly, Virginia: The Teaching Company, LLC. Lecture10. See Also: Clausewitz, Carl von (2008). On War. Translated by Michael Eliot Howard and Peter Paret. Princeton: Princeton University Press. Pg. 198.

125. Duggan (2015), Pg. 71.

126. Duggan (2003), Pg. 4.

127. Baillergeon, Rick (2011, November-December). "Book Review: Sun Tzu at Gettysburg: Ancient Military Wisdom in the Modern World." Military Review. Pg. 86.

128. Chandler, Steve (1998). Reinventing Yourself: How to Become the Person You've Always Wanted to Be. Franklin Lakes: Career Press. Pg. 191.

129. Colson, Bruno (2015). Napoleon: On War. Translated by Gregory Elliott. NYC: Oxford University Press. Pg. 106

130. Duggan (2007), Pg. 59.

131. Colson, Bruno (2015). Napoleon: On War. Translated by Gregory Elliott. NYC: Oxford University Press. Pg. 107

132. Colson, Bruno (2015). Napoleon: On War. Translated by Gregory Elliott. NYC: Oxford University Press. Pg. 107

133. Nester, William (2021). Napoleon and the Art of Leadership: How a Flawed Genius Changed the History of Europe and the World. NYC: Frontline Books. Pg. 24.

134. Hart, Captain B.H. Liddell (1971). Why Don't We Learn from History? Sophron. Pg. 8.

135. Duggan (2007), Pgs. 58-59, 78.

136. Meadows, Donella (2008). Thinking in Systems: A Primer. London: Earthscan. Pg. 145.

137. Greene, Robert (2001). The Art of Seduction. NYC: Penguin. Pg. 241.

138. Chandler, David G. (Editor)(2015). Napoleon's Military Maxims. Cheltenham, England: The History Press. Pg. 74.

139. Ross, Steven T. (1988). "Napoleon and Maneuver Warfare." In Borowski, Harry (Editor) The Harmon Memorial Lectures in Military History, 1959—1987: A Collection of the First Thirty Harmon Lectures Given at the United States Air Force Academy. Washington, D.C.: Office of Air Force History. Pg. 310. **See also:** Bonaparte, Napoleon (1845). *Military Maxims of Napoleon*. Translated by J. Akerly. NYC: Wiley and Putnam. Pg. 95.

140. Jobs, Steve (1998, May 25). "Steve Jobs: There's Sanity Returning." Interview in BusinessWeek. Full Quote: "Everything just got simpler. That's been one of my mantras -- focus and simplicity. Simple can be harder than complex: You have to work hard to get your thinking clean to make it simple. But it's worth it in the end because once you get there, you can move mountains." (Google Cache) https://www.bloomberg.com/news/articles/1998-05-25/steve-jobs-theres-sanity-returning

141. Zamoyski (2018), Pg. 21.

142. Grehan, John (Editor)(2018). *Napoleon Bonaparte: Master of War*. Lincolnshire: Key Publishing Ltd. Pg. 15.

143. Colson, Bruno (2015). Napoleon: On War. Translated by Gregory Elliott. NYC: Oxford University Press. Pg. 121

144. Colson, Bruno (2015). Napoleon: On War. Translated by Gregory Elliott. NYC: Oxford University Press. Pg. 123

145. Colson, Bruno (2015). Napoleon: On War. Translated by Gregory Elliott. NYC: Oxford University Press. Pg. 123

146. Keller, Gary (2013). The ONE Thing: The Surprisingly Simple Truth Behind Extraordinary Results. Austin: Bard Press. Pg. 24.

147. Pietersen, Willie (2016, February 12). "Von Clausewitz on War: Six Lessons for the Modern Strategist." Strategy: Ideas at Work. Columbia Business School. https://www8.gsb.columbia.edu/articles/ideas-work/von-clausewitz-war-six-lessons-modern-strategist

148. Atkinson, Charles Francis (1910). "French Revolutionary Wars." Encyclopedia Britannica, Eleventh Edition, Volume XI, Franciscans to Gibson. NYC: The Encyclopedia Britannica Company. Pg. 188. Full Quote: "The essence of strategy," said Napoleon in 1797, "is, with a weaker army, always to have more force at a crucial point than the enemy."

149. Hart, B.H. Liddell (1991). Strategy, Second Revised Edition. NYC: Meridian. Pg. 334

150. Jean-Andoche Junot first gained Napoleon's attention at Toulon for displaying the sort of coolness under fire with which Napoleon loved to surround himself. Junot was writing a dispatch which Napoleon was dictating when a bursting shell exploded right near Junot, scattering dirt across the paper on which he was writing. Rather than yelling or running for cover, he coolly remarked "Good! I need no sand!" (i.e. to dry the ink). Source: Bent, Samuel Arthur (1887). *Familiar Short Sayings of Great Men*, 6th Edition. Boston: Ticknor and Co. https://www.bartleby.com/br/344.html

151. Sun Tzu (1996 [circa 5th century B.C.]) The Complete Art of War. Ralph D. Sawyer (Translator). NYC: Westview Press. Pg. 108.

152. Michaelson, Gerald (2003). Sun Tzu for Success: How to Use The Art of War to Master Challenges and Accomplish the Important Goals in Your Life. Avon, MA: Adams Media Corporation. Pg. 160.

153. Zamoyski (2018), Pg. 131.

154. Heifetz, Ronald A. (1994). Leadership Without Easy Answers. Cambridge, MA: Harvard University Press. Pg. 252. See Also: Greene Pg. 184. See Also: Sobel, Andrew and Panas, Jerold (2012). Power Questions: Build Relationships, Win New Business, and Influence Others. NYC: John Wiley & Sons. Pg. 81.

155. Roosevelt, Theodore (1910, April 23). "Citizenship in a Republic." Public Address at the Sorbonne. Paris, France.

156. Hinterhuber, Hans H. and Popp, Wolfgang (1992, January-February). "Are you a Strategist or Just a Manager?" Harvard Business Review. https://hbr.org/1992/01/are-you-a-strategist-or-just-a-manager

157. Richard, Rumelt (2022). The Crux: How Leaders Become Strategists. Pg. 136.

158. Cronin (1988), Pg. 91.

159. Cronin (1988), Pg. 91.

160. Cronin (1988), Pg. 91.

161. Cronin (1988), Pg. 91.

162. McLynn (2011), Pg. 76.

163. Nester (2021), Pg. 77.

164. Chandler (1966), Pg. 114.

165. Cronin (1988), Pg. 92.

166. Westlake (2018), Pg. 20.

167. Roberts (2014), Pg. 60.

168. Roberts (2014), Pg. 60.

169. McLynn (2011), Pg. 76.

170. Duggan (2007), Pg. 60.

171. Anonymous (1846). Anecdotes of Napoleon Bonaparte, His Ministers, His Generals, His Soldiers and His Times. Manchester: S. Johnson & Son. Pg. 122-123.

172. Roberts (2014), Pg. 60.

173. Anonymous (1846). Anecdotes of Napoleon Bonaparte, His Ministers, His Generals, His Soldiers and His Times. Manchester: S. Johnson & Son. Pg. 28.

|PART 2: OVERVIEW|

Reap the Rewards, Rule Your World

1. Groysberg, Boris (2014, March 18). "The Seven Skills You Need to Thrive in the C-Suite." Harvard Business Review. https://hbr.org/2014/03/the-seven-skills-you-need-to-thrive-in-the-c-suite See also: "Top Executive Management Skills Needed to Succeed in the C-Suite." Wharton Business School, University of Pennsylvania. https://executivemba.wharton.upenn.edu/top-executive-management-skills-needed-in-the-c-suite/

2. Kabacoff, Robert (2014, February 7). "Develop Strategic Thinkers Throughout Your Organization." Harvard Business Review. https://hbr.org/2014/02/develop-strategic-thinkers-throughout-your-organization

3. Kabacoff, Robert (2014, February 7). "Develop Strategic Thinkers Throughout Your Organization." Harvard Business Review. https://hbr.org/2014/02/develop-strategic-thinkers-throughout-your-organization

4. Kabacoff, Robert (2014, February 7). "Develop Strategic Thinkers Throughout Your Organization." Harvard Business Review.

https://hbr.org/2014/02/develop-strategic-thinkers-throughout-your-organization

5. Carnegie, Dale (1981 [1936]). How to Win Friends and Influence People. NYC: Pocket Books.

6. Kouzes, James and Posner, Barry (2002). The Leadership Challenge: The Most Trusted Source on Becoming a Better Leader, 3rd Edition. San Francisco: Wiley and Sons, Inc. Pg. 363.

7. McKee, Robert (2023). McKee Story. https://mckeestory.com/is-it-possible-to-bring-storytelling-into-marketing/ See also: Dykes, B. (2019). Effective Data Storytelling: How to Drive Change with Data, Narrative and Visuals. Hoboken: Wiley. Pg. 27.

8. Head, Tom (2017). World History 101: From Ancient Mesopotamia and the Viking Conquests to Nato and Wikileaks, an Essential Primer on World History. Avon, MA: Adams Media. Pg. 7.

9. Kouzes, James and Posner, Barry (2012). The Leadership Challenge: How to Make Extraordinary Things Happen in Organizations, 5th Edition. San Francisco: Wiley. Pg. 321.

10. Roosevelt, Theodore. (1926). The Works of Theodore Roosevelt. Hermann Hagedorn (Editor). NYC: Charles Scribner's Sons. Pg. 7.

11. Robbins, Anthony (1986). Unlimited Power: The New Science of Personal Achievement. NYC: Simon and Schuster. Pg. 43.

12. Farrell, C. (2011). The New Frugality: How to Consume Less, Save More, and Live Better. United States: Bloomsbury USA. Pg. 68. Note: This quote is often attributed to Albert Einstein, but the claims seem dubious.

13. Peterson, Jordan B. (2018). 12 Rules for Life: An Antidote to Chaos. NYC: Random House . Pg. 169.

14. Weatherford, Jack (2005). Genghis Khan and the Making of the Modern World. NYC: Three Rivers Press. Pg. 92. Weatherford paraphrases Genghis Khan as saying "There is no good in anything until it is finished."

15. Lamb, Harold (1927). Genghis Khan: The Emperor of All Men. Garden City, NY: Garden City Publishing. Pg. 66. Lamb translates Genghis Khan as saying; "the merit of an action lies in finishing it to the end," others translate the quote as "the merit in action..."

16. Kettering, Charles Franklin (1959). In Memoriam, Charles F. Kettering. Birmingham: Southern Research Institute. Pg. 17.

17. Hill, Napoleon (2019). The Lost Prosperity Secrets of Napoleon Hill. Landover: Gildan Media, LLC. Pg. 51.

18. Schocker, Larua (2015, August 5). "6 Science-Backed Reasons To Go Read A Book Right Now." Huffington Post. http://www.huffingtonpost.com/2015/08/05/health-benefits-reading_n_4081258.html See Also: Ward, Marguerite (2016, November 16). "Warren Buffett's reading routine could make you smarter, science suggests." CNBC. https://www.cnbc.com/2016/11/16/warren-buffetts-reading-routine-could-make-you-smarter-suggests-science.html

19. Cuban, Mark (2004, May 25). "Success and Motivation P4." Blog Maverick: The Mark Cuban Weblog. http://blogmaverick.com/2004/05/25/success-and-motivation-p4/

20. Baer, Drake (2014, September 2). "9 Books Billionaire Warren Buffett Thinks Everyone Should Read." Business Insider. http://www.businessinsider.com/warren-buffett-favorite-business-books-2014-8/#e-intelligent-investor-by-benjamin-graham-1

21. Kane, Libby (2014, June 17). "What Rich People Have Next to Their Beds." Business Insider. http://www.businessinsider.com/rich-people-read-self-improvement-books-2014-6

|PART 3: THE STRATEGIST CODE|
|1|

Appropriate the Extraordinary Secret Psychology of Strategic Mastery: The Strategist Mindset as the Cornerstone of Alexander the Great's Empire Building Success

1. Marquis De Noailles (Editor)(1923). The Life and Memoirs of Count Molé (1781-1855), Volume 1 (1804-1815). London: Hutchinson & Co. Pg. 90.

2. Green, Peter (2007). Alexander the Great and the Hellenistic Age: A Short History. London: Weidenfeld and Nicolson. Pg. 5.

3. Green (2007), Pg. 5.

4. Everitt, Anthony (2019). Alexander the Great: His Life and His Mysterious Death. NYC: Random House. Pg. 108.

5. Everitt (2019), Pg. 110.

6. Roos, Dave (2019, September 9). "How Alexander the Great Conquered the Persian Empire." The History Channel. United States: A&E Television Networks, LLC. https://www.history.com/news/alexander-the-great-defeat-persian-empire

7. Everitt (2019), Pg. 111.

8. Ledwidge, Frank (2017). Losing Small Wars: British Military Failure in the 9/11 Wars, 2nd Ed. New Haven: Yale University Press. Pg. 205.

9. Pound, Jeremy (2015, January). "Alexander the Great: The Empire Builder." History Revealed, Issue 12. Bristol: Immediate Media Co. Pg 73

10. Lonsdale, David J. (2007). Alexander the Great: Lessons in Strategy. London: Routledge. Pg. 146.

11. Schuhly, Thomas (Producer), Stone, Oliver (Director). (2004). Alexander [Film]. United States: Warner Bros. Pictures.

12. Bose, Partha (2004). Alexander the Great's Art of Strategy: The Timeless Lessons of History's Greatest Empire Builder. NYC: Gotham. Pgs. 1-2.

13. Bolman, Lee and Deal, Terrence (2017). Reframing Organizations: Artistry, Choice and Leadership, 6th Edition. San Francisco: Jossey-Bass. Pg. 205.

14. Shaw, George Bernard (1933, May), "Quotable Quotes." Reader's Digest, Volume 23. The Reader's Digest Association. Pg. 16. Hat Tip to Quote Investigator: https://quoteinvestigator.com/2014/02/20/shaw-think/

15. Ridgley, Stanley K. (2012). Strategic Thinking Skills: The Great Courses Course Guidebook. The Great Courses. Chantilly, Virginia: The Teaching Company, LLC. Pg. 3.

16. Twelve of the most widely cited strategy frameworks used in today's business world include: (1.) **SWOT Analysis**—widely applicable beyond business, this tool consists of identifying the strengths, weaknesses, opportunities and threats that are most applicable to the organization's success. (2.) **Gap Analysis**—also

known as Needs Assessment or Need-Gap Analysis, this model focuses on determining where you are now and where you want to be and then how best to bridge the gap between the two. (3.) **PESTEL Analysis**—a tool for analyzing the political, economic, social, technological, environmental, and legal factors that may impact an organization's strategy. (4.) **Porter's Five Forces**—this framework focuses on identifying the key factors that effect the success of a company from among the five fundamental forces: threat of entry, threat of substitutes, bargaining power of customers, bargaining power of suppliers, competitive rivalry among existing organizations. (5.) **Fishbone Diagram**—a visual tool for identifying and analyzing the potential causes of a problem or issue by brainstorming and organizing potential causes into categories based on different factors or areas of the process. See Chapter 4. (6.) **The McKinsey 7-S Framework**—this model emphasizes the alignment of the organization's seven key elements: structure, strategy, system, skill, style (leadership), staff, shared values (norms, values, beliefs) (7.) **Benchmarking**—this amounts to measuring the organization against external benchmarks or industry standards. (8.) **Balanced Scorecard**—a framework for measuring and managing organizational performance across multiple dimensions, such as financial, customer, internal processes, and learning and growth. (9.) **Ansoff Matrix**—identifies different growth strategies by analyzing the relationship between products and markets. (10.) **BCG Matrix** (Boston Box)—a strategic management tool used to analyze a company's product portfolio, based on two dimensions (market share and market growth rate, to make decisions about resource allocation and product development. (11.) **Lewin's Three Stage Model of Change**—unfreeze, change, refreeze. (12.) **Scenario Planning**—this model proposes assessing the likelihood and implications of multiple potential outcomes as a means of evaluating options to prepare for uncertainty and change.

17. Fitzgerald, F. Scott (1936, February). "The Crack-Up: A desolately frank document from one for whom the salt of life has lost its savor." Esquire. Page 41, Column 1, Esquire Inc., Chicago, Illinois. (Esquire archive at classic.esquire.com).

18. Thompson, Derek (2017). Hit Makers: The Science of Popularity in an Age of Distraction. Pg. 55.

19. Arrian (1884). The Anabasis of Alexander; or, The history of the Wars and Conquests of Alexander the Great. E.J. Chinnock (Translator). London: Hodder and Stoughton. Chapter X.

20. Schuhly, Thomas (Producer), Stone, Oliver (Director). (2004). Alexander [Film]. United States: Warner Bros. Pictures.

21. Senge, Peter (1994). The Fifth Discipline Fieldbook: Strategies and Tools for Building a Learning Organization. New York: Doubleday. Pg. 17.

22. Lonsdale, David J. (2007). Alexander the Great: Lessons in Strategy. London: Routledge. Pg. 6.

23. Lonsdale, David J. (2007). Alexander the Great: Lessons in Strategy. London: Routledge. Pg. 6.

24. Everitt (2019), Pg. 110.

25. Jian, Kuodi (Editor)(2017). Operations Research: The Art of Making Good Decisions. Rijeka, Croatia: InTech. Pg. 3.

26. Connolly, Fergus (2017). Game Changer: The Art of Sports Science. Las Vegas: Victory Belt Publishing, Inc. Pg. 133.

27. Wooden, John (2023, March 3: LA). Wooden on Leadership: Pyramid of Success. CoachWooden.com https://coachwooden.com/files/PyramidThinkingSuccess.jpg

28. Bronson, Po and Merryman, Ashley (2013). *Top Dog: The Science of Winning and Losing.* Pg. 17.

29. Bronson, Po and Merryman, Ashley (2013). Top Dog: The Science of Winning and Losing. Pg. 17.

30. Bronson, Po and Merryman, Ashley (2013). Top Dog: The Science of Winning and Losing. Pg. 17.

31. Bronson, Po and Merryman, Ashley (2013). Top Dog: The Science of Winning and Losing. Pg. 17.

32. Bronson, Po and Merryman, Ashley (2013). Top Dog: The Science of Winning and Losing. Pg. 17.

33. Bronson, Po and Merryman, Ashley (2013). Top Dog: The Science of Winning and Losing. Pg. 17.

34. Bronson, Po and Merryman, Ashley (2013). Top Dog: The Science of Winning and Losing. Pg. 18.

35. Bronson, Po and Merryman, Ashley (2013). Top Dog: The Science of Winning and Losing. Pg. 17.

36. Kurke, Lance (2004). *The Wisdom of Alexander the Great: Enduring Leadership Lessons From the Man Who Created an Empire.* NYC: Amacom. Pg. 55.

37. Senge, Peter (1994). The Fifth Discipline Fieldbook: Strategies and Tools for Building a Learning Organization. New York: Doubleday. Pg. 17.

38. Reeves, Richard (1993). *President Kennedy: Profile of Power.* NYC: Simon & Schuster. Pg. 45.

39. Heifetz, Ronald A. (1994). *Leadership Without Easy Answers.* Cambridge, MA: Harvard University Press.

40. De Gaulle, Charles [1932] Hopkins, G. (translator). *The Edge of the Sword.* NYC: Criterion Books. Pg. 23.

41. Sobel, Andrew and Panas, Jerold (2012). Power Questions: Build Relationships, Win New Business, and Influence Others. NYC: John Wiley & Sons. Pg. 81.

42. Horwath, Rich (2023, LA). "The Strategic Thinking Manifesto." Strategic Thinking Institute. Pg. 7. https://www.strategyskills.com/pdf/The-Strategic-Thinking-Manifesto.pdf?gclid=ClaV2fGOv88CFcVIfgodSBUM8A

43. Greene, Robert (2006). The 33 Strategies of War. NYC: Penguin Books. Pg. 18.

44. This battle is also the inspiration for the marathon race owing to the heroic day-long dash from Athens to Sparta by the Athenian messenger Pheidippides, who was sent to seek Sparta's help, but also the Athenian army's rapid 26-mile march to head off the Persian armada back in Athens.

45. Roos, Dave (2019, September 9). "How Alexander the Great Conquered the Persian Empire." The History Channel. United States: A&E Television Networks, LLC. https://www.history.com/news/alexander-the-great-defeat-persian-empire

46. Roos, Dave (2019, September 9). "How Alexander the Great Conquered the Persian Empire." The History Channel. United States: A&E Television Networks, LLC. https://www.history.com/news/alexander-the-great-defeat-persian-empire

47. Pound, Jeremy (2015, January). "Alexander the Great: The Empire Builder." History Revealed, Issue 12. Bristol: Immediate Media Co. Pg. 73.

48. Lyons, Justin D. (2023, Spring). "Challenging Poseidon: Alexander the Great's 332 BC Siege of Tyre was won by his daring strategy." Military History Quarterly. P. 72.

49. White, Jon (Editor)(2016). All About History Book Of Myths and Legends. Bournemouth: Imagine Publishing Ltd. Pg. 26.

50. White, Jon (Editor)(2016). All About History Book Of Myths and Legends. Bournemouth: Imagine Publishing Ltd. Pg. 26.

51. Miller, Tim (2016, May). "Alexander's Triumph at Granicus." Military Heritage, Volume 17, Number 6. McLean VA: Sovereign Media. Pg. 67.

52. Desmond, William (2011). Philosopher-Kings of Antiquity. Continuum. Pgs. 49–51.

53. Bose, Partha (2004). Alexander the Great's Art of Strategy: The Timeless Lessons of History's Greatest Empire Builder. NYC: Gotham. Pg. 1.

|2|

Be Future focused and Mission Driven, Tap the Power and Promise of Your Purpose to Perform: Charlemagne Becomes the Father of Europe

1. Brown, Paul B. (2005). Fast Company: The Rules of Business: 55 Essential Ideas to Help Smart People (and Organizations) Perform at Their Best. NYC: Doubleday. Pg. 149.

2. Fried, Johannes. Lewis, Peter (Translator)(2016). Charlemagne. Cambridge: Harvard University Press. Pg. 414.

3. Editors of Encyclopedia Britannica (2020, June 8). "Saint Leo III." Encyclopedia Britannica. https://www.britannica.com/biography/Saint-Leo-III

4. Nelson, Janet L. (2019). King and Emperor: A New Life of Charlemagne. Oakland: University of California. Pg. 391.

5. Mann, Horace Kinder (1913). "Pope St. Leo III." Catholic Encyclopedia, Volume 9. https://en.wikisource.org/wiki/Catholic_Encyclopedia_(1913)/Pope_St._Leo_III

6. Fried, Johannes. Lewis, Peter (Translator)(2016). Charlemagne. Cambridge: Harvard University Press. Pg. 412.

7. Fried, Johannes. Lewis, Peter (Translator)(2016). Charlemagne. Cambridge: Harvard University Press. Pg. 412.

8. Fried, Johannes. Lewis, Peter (Translator)(2016). Charlemagne. Cambridge: Harvard University Press. Pg. 409.

9. Fried, Johannes. Lewis, Peter (Translator)(2016). Charlemagne. Cambridge: Harvard University Press. Pg. 409.

10. Skoda, Hannah (2020, May 27). "How Bloody Was Medieval Life?" History Extra. BBC History Magazine. Bristol: Immediate Media Co. https://www.historyextra.com/period/medieval/life-violence-middle-ages-murder-crime/

11. Skoda, Hannah (2020, May 27). "How Bloody Was Medieval Life?" History Extra. BBC History Magazine. Bristol: Immediate Media Co. https://www.historyextra.com/period/medieval/life-violence-middle-ages-murder-crime/ Note: Given the lack of reliable statistics and the changing definition of legal terms, assessing the relative degree of violence in the Middle Ages is a rather complicated and controversial topic among historians. And while this period may not have been quite as violent as most people think, or as Hollywood would like us to believe, historians widely agree that interpersonal violence (which does not include war, genocide, or other forms of institutional violence, or violence on a mass scale) was generally much greater during the Medieval Era than it is today.

12. Wilkes, Jonny (2016, January). "Charlemagne: Bringing Light to the Dark Ages." History Revealed, Issue 25. Bristol: Immediate Media Company. Pg. 67.

13. Wilkes, Jonny (2016, January). "Charlemagne: Bringing Light to the Dark Ages." History Revealed, Issue 25. Bristol: Immediate Media Company. Pg. 67.

14. Hobbes, Thomas (2016). The Essential Leviathan: A Modernized Edition. Stanlick, Nancy (Editor). Cambridge: Hackett Publishing. Pg. 69.

15. Wilkes, Jonny (2016, January). "Charlemagne: Bringing Light to the Dark Ages." History Revealed, Issue 25. Bristol: Immediate Media Company. Pg. 67.

16. Hart, Michael H. (1992). The 100: A Ranking of the Most Influential Persons in History. NYC: Citadel Press. Pg. 492.

17. Ziglar, Zig (2019). Goals: How to Get the Most Out of Your Life. Shippensburg, PA: Nightingale Conant. Pg. 92.

18. Fried, Johannes. Lewis, Peter (Translator)(2016). Charlemagne. Cambridge: Harvard University Press. Pg. 106.

19. Davis, Jennifer R. (2015). Charlemagne's Practice of Empire. Cambridge: Cambridge University Press. Pg. 10.

20. Wilkes, Jonny (2016, January). "Charlemagne: Bringing Light to the Dark Ages." History Revealed, Issue 25. Bristol: Immediate Media Company. Pg. 69.

21. Nelson, Janet (2019, August). "Janet Nelson on How Charlemagne Built an Empire." [Interview.] BBC History Magazine, Volume 20, Number 8. Bristol: Immediate Media Company. Pg. 72.

22. Nelson, Janet (2019, August). "Janet Nelson on How Charlemagne Built an Empire." [Interview.] BBC History Magazine, Volume 20, Number 8. Bristol: Immediate Media Company. Pg. 72.

23. Kulikowski , Michael (2016, November 18). "The Father of Europe." The Wall Street Journal. https://www.wsj.com/articles/the-father-of-europe-1479506153

24. This quote is typically attributed to Mark Twain, but the source is likely unknown. It was popularized by E.Campbell, see: Campbell, Ernest T. (1970, January 25). "Give Ye Them to Eat": Luke 9:10-17. [Sermon]. NYC: The Publications Office, Riverside Church. Pg. 8. See also: https://quoteinvestigator.com/2016/06/22/why

25. Kaufmann, Scott Barry (2019, May/June). "When Does Intelligence Peak? Maybe that's not even the right question." Scientific American Mind, Volume 30, Number 3. Pg. 28.

26. Kaufmann, Scott Barry (2019, May/June). "When Does Intelligence Peak? Maybe that's not even the right question." Scientific American Mind, Volume 30, Number 3. Pg. 28.

27. Kaufmann, Scott Barry (2019, May/June). "When Does Intelligence Peak? Maybe that's not even the right question." Scientific American Mind, Volume 30, Number 3. Pg. 28.

28. Straus, Ernst (1980). Einstein: A Centenary Volume. A.P. French. Pg. 32.

29. Einstein, Albert (1982). Albert Einstein: Historical and Cultural Perspectives. (Edited by Gerald James Holton and Yehuda Elkana) Courier Corporation. Pg. 420.

30. Ziglar, Zig (2019). Goals: How to Get the Most Out of Your Life. Shippensburg, PA: Nightingale Conant. Pg. 92.

31. Maltz, Maxwell (1960). Psycho-Cybernetics. NYC: Simon and Schuster. Pg. 128.

32. Warren, Rick (2002). The Purpose-Driven Life: What on Earth Am I Here For? Grand Rapids: Zondervan. Pg 30.

33. Brown, Paul B. (2005). Fast Company: The Rules of Business: 55 Essential Ideas to Help Smart People (and Organizations) Perform at Their Best. NYC: Doubleday. Pg. 149.

34. Whaley, Barton (2007). Stratagem: Deception and Surprise in War. Norwood, MA: Artech House. Pg. 65.

35. Michaelson, Gerald A. & Michaelson, Steven W. (2004). Sun Tzu Strategies for Marketing: 12 Essential Principles for Winning the War for Customers. NYC: McGraw-Hill. Pg. 40.

36. Kluth, Andreas (2011). Hannibal and Me: What History's Greatest Military Strategist Can Teach Us About Success and Failure. NYC: Riverhead Books. Pg. 154.

37. Kluth, Andreas (2011). Hannibal and Me: What History's Greatest Military Strategist Can Teach Us About Success and Failure. NYC: Riverhead Books. Pg. 154.

38. Zufelt, Jack M. (2005). "The DNA of Success." in E, Steven & Beard, Lee's Seizing Success. Laguna Beach: Little Seed Publishing, LLC. Pg. 37.

39. Seneca. L. Annaeus Seneca On Benefits. Stewart, Aubrey (Editor). Note: Quote is paraphrased from Chapter XXVIII by an unknown author. https://www.gutenberg.org/files/3794/3794-h/3794-h.htm

40. Ridgley, Stanley K. (2012). Strategic Thinking Skills: The Great Courses Course Guidebook. The Great Courses. Chantilly, Virginia: The Teaching Company, LLC. Pg. 2.

41. Fried, Johannes. Lewis, Peter (Translator)(2016). Charlemagne. Cambridge: Harvard U. Press. Pg. 42.

42. Murrow, Edward R. "Winston Churchill's Way With Words." NPR. https://www.npr.org/transcripts/156720829 Note: This sentence borrows from a quote from Edward Murrow and, later, President John F. Kennedy who said of Winston Churchill, "In the dark days and darker nights when England stood alone—and most men save Englishmen despaired of England's life—he mobilized the English language and sent it into battle."

43. Johnsen, William T. et al (1995, August 1). "The Principles of War in the 21st Century: Strategic Considerations." Strategic Studies Institute, U.S. Army War College, Carlisle Barracks, PA. Pg. 4.

44. Johnsen, William T. et al (1995, August 1). "The Principles of War in the 21st Century: Strategic Considerations." Strategic Studies Institute, U.S. Army War College, Carlisle Barracks, PA. Pg. 4.

45. Rarick, Charles A., Vitton, J. (1995). "Mission Statements Make Cents." Journal of Business Strategy, 16, Pgs. 11-12.

46. Malnight, Thomas; Buche, Ivy; and Dhanaraj, Charles (2020). "Put Purpose at the Core of Your Strategy." Chapter 13 in HBR Guide to Setting Strategy. Boston: Harvard Business Review Press. Pg. 106.

47. Malnight, Thomas; Buche, Ivy; and Dhanaraj, Charles (2020). "Put Purpose at the Core of Your Strategy." Chapter 13 in HBR Guide to Setting Strategy. Boston: Harvard Business Review Press. Pg. 105.

48. Davis, Jennifer R. (2015). Charlemagne's Practice of Empire. Cambridge: Cambridge U. Press. Pg. 10.

49. Nixon, Richard (1982). Leaders: Profiles and Reminiscences of Men Who Have Shaped the Modern World. NYC: Simon and Schuster. Pg. 5.

50. Senge, Peter M. (1990). The Fifth Discipline: The Art and Practice of the Learning Organization. NYC: Doubleday. Pg. 209.

51. Nanus, Burt (1992). Visionary Leadership. San Francisco: Jossey-Bass. Pg. 27.

52. Maxwell, John (2003). Leadership Promises for Everyday: A Daily Devotional. Nashville, TN: Thomas Nelson, Inc. Pg. 219.

53. Nelson, Janet (2019, August). "Janet Nelson on How Charlemagne Built an Empire." [Interview.] BBC History Magazine, Volume 20, Number 8. Bristol: Immediate Media Company. Pg. 72.

54. Palos, Joan-Lluis (2018, March-April). "Isabella's Play for Power: The Queen of Castile." National Geographic History. Washington, D.C.: National Geographic Partners, LLC. Pg. 65.

55. Palos, Joan-Lluis (2018, March-April). "Isabella's Play for Power: The Queen of Castile." National Geographic History. Washington, D.C.: National Geographic Partners, LLC. Pg. 64.

56. Palos, Joan-Lluis (2018, March-April). "Isabella's Play for Power: The Queen of Castile." National Geographic History. Washington, D.C.: National Geographic Partners, LLC. Pg. 68.

57. Palos, Joan-Lluis (2018, March-April). "Isabella's Play for Power: The Queen of Castile." National Geographic History. Washington, D.C.: National Geographic Partners, LLC. Pg. 65.

58. History: The Definitive Visual Guide. Pg. 226

59. Johnsen, William T. et al (1995, August 1). "The Principles of War in the 21st Century: Strategic Considerations." Strategic Studies Institute, U.S. Army War College, Carlisle Barracks, PA. Pg. 4.

60. Sloan, Julia (2006). Learning to Think Strategically. San Diego: Butterworth-Heinemann. Pg. 6.

61. Phillips, Derek (1986). Toward a Just Social Order. Princeton: Princeton University Press. Pg. 410.

62. Tracy, Brian (2000). The 100 Absolutely Unbreakable Laws of Business Success. San Francisco: Berrett-Koehler Publishers, Inc. Pg. 164.

63. Freedman, Lawrence (2013). Strategy: A History. Oxford: Oxford University Press. Pg. 238.

64. Hill, Napoleon (1965). The Master Key to Riches. NYC: Ballatine Books. Pg. 63.

65. Thoreau, Henry David (1910). Walden. NYC: Thomas Y. Crowell & Co. Pg. 315.

66. Maxwell, John (2003). Thinking for a Change: 11 Ways Highly Successful People Approach Life and Work. NYC: Warner Business Books. Pg. 66.

67. Stephens, Alan and Baker, Nicola (2006). Making Sense of War: Strategy of the 21st Century. NYC. Pg. 13.

68. "Charlemagne." (2019, June 6) History.com NYC: A&E Television Networks. https://www.history.com/topics/middle-ages/charlemagne

69. Fried, Johannes. Lewis, Peter (Translator)(2016). Charlemagne. Cambridge: Harvard University Press. Pg. 218.

70. Nelson, Janet (2019, August). "Janet Nelson on How Charlemagne Built an Empire." [Interview.] BBC History Magazine, Volume 20, Number 8. Bristol: Immediate Media Company. Pg. 72.

71. Dunford, Chauney (Editor)(2019). Leaders Who Changed History. NYC: DK Publishing. Pg. 45.

72. Fried, Johannes. Lewis, Peter (Translator)(2016). Charlemagne. Cambridge: Harvard University Press. Pg. 218.

73. Senge, Peter M. (1990). The Fifth Discipline: The Art and Practice of the Learning Organization. NYC: Doubleday. Pg. 206.

74. Murphy, Charles J.V. and Davenport, John (1945). "The Lives of Winston Churchill." LIFE. Volume 18, Number 21. May 21, 1945. Pg. 93.

75. Merriam-Webster.com Dictionary, s.v. (2023, February 20 Last Accessed). "Finis coronat opus." ("The end crowns the work.") https://www.merriam-webster.com/dictionary/finis%20coronat%20opus.

76. Nelson, Janet L. (2019). King and Emperor: A New Life of Charlemagne. Oakland: University of California. Pg. 392.

77. Nelson, Janet L. (2019). King and Emperor: A New Life of Charlemagne. Oakland: University of California. Pg. 396.

78. Fried, Johannes. Lewis, Peter (Translator)(2016). Charlemagne. Cambridge: Harvard University Press. Pg. 415.

79. Fried, Johannes. Lewis, Peter (Translator)(2016). Charlemagne. Cambridge: Harvard University Press. Pgs. 415-416.

80. Nelson, Janet L. (2019). King and Emperor: A New Life of Charlemagne. Oakland: University of California. Pgs. 396-397.

81. Hudson, Fiona (Editor)(2016) "Charlemagne." All About History Book of Kings & Queens, Fifth Edition. San Francisco: Future Publishing Limited. Pg. 59.

82. Hudson, Fiona (Editor)(2016) "Charlemagne." All About History Book of Kings & Queens, Fifth Edition. San Francisco: Future Publishing Limited. Pg. 59.

83. Hart, Michael H. (1992). The 100: A Ranking of the Most Influential Persons in History. NYC: Citadel Press. Pg. 493.

84. Dunford, Chauney (Editor)(2019). Leaders Who Changed History. NYC: DK Publishing. Pg. 45.

85. Wilkes, Jonny (2016, January). "Charlemagne: Bringing Light to the Dark Ages." History Revealed, Issue 25. Bristol: Immediate Media Company. Pg. 66.

86. Wilkes, Jonny (2016, January). "Charlemagne: Bringing Light to the Dark Ages." History Revealed, Issue 25. Bristol: Immediate Media Company. Pg. 69.

87. Weir, William (2001). 50 Battles that Changed the World: The Conflicts that Most Influenced the Course of History. Franklin Lakes: New Page Books. Pg. 173.

88. Hart, Michael H. (1992). The 100: A Ranking of the Most Influential Persons in History. NYC: Citadel Press. Pg. 491.

89. Wilkes, Jonny (2016, January). "Charlemagne: Bringing Light to the Dark Ages." History Revealed, Issue 25. Bristol: Immediate Media Company. Pg. 66.

90. Dunford, Chauney (Editor)(2019). Leaders Who Changed History. NYC: DK Publishing. Pg. 45.

91. Ferrell, Robert H. (1994). Harry S. Truman: A Life (Missouri Biography Series). University of Missouri Press. Pg. 120.

92. Hill, Napoleon (1987). Success Through a Positive Mental Attitude. NYC: Simon and Schuster. Pg. vii.

93. Marden, Orison Swett (1920). You Can, But Will You? NYC: Thomas Y. Crowell Company. Pg. 265.

94. Thoreau, Henry David (1910). Walden. NYC: Thomas Y. Crowell & Co. Pg. 427.

95. Lickerman, Alex (2012). The Undefeated Mind: On the Science of Constructing an Indestructible Self. Deerfield Beach: Health Communications, Inc. Pg. 25.

96. Khan, Vilayat Inayat (1999). Awakening: A Sufi Experience. NYC: Penguin. Pg. 198. Actual Quote: "The power that you gain by pursuing your interest will give you the ability to take upon yourself a greater challenge than you have taken on so far. We gain in power by pursuing our purpose in life." (Vilayat Inayat Khan is quoting here his father, Hazrat Inayat Khan, the founder of Sufism)

97. Spears, Larry (1998). Insights on Leadership. The University of Michigan Press. Pg. 42.

|3|

Think Proactively, Seize, Sustain, and Exploit the Initiative. Win by Playing an Offensive Game: Mary Tudor's Bloody Fight for the Throne:

1. Montgomery, Cynthia (2012). The Strategist: Be the Leader Your Business Needs. Cambridge: Harvard Business Review. Pg. 157.

2. Herman, Eleanor (2018). The Royal Art of Poison. NYC; St. Martin's Press. Pg. 105.

3. Herman (2018), Pg. 105.

4. Porter, Linda (2010). Mary Tudor: The First Queen. London: Hachette. Pg. 107.

5. Marsh, Katharine (Editor)(2018). Everything You Need to Know About the Tudors, 1st Edition. Bournemouth: Future Publishing Limited. Pg. 66.

6. Marsh (2018), Pg. 66.

7. Porter, Linda (2010). Mary Tudor: The First Queen. London: Hachette. Pg. 125.

8. Marsh, Katharine (Editor)(2018). Everything You Need to Know About the Tudors, 1st Edition. Bournemouth: Future Publishing Limited. Pg. 66.

9. Marsh, Katharine (Editor)(2018). Everything You Need to Know About the Tudors, 1st Edition. Bournemouth: Future Publishing Limited. Pg. 66.

10. Porter, Linda (2010). Mary Tudor: The First Queen. London: Hachette. Pg. 123.

11. Porter, Linda (2010). Mary Tudor: The First Queen. London: Hachette. Pg. 125.

12. Porter, Linda (2010). Mary Tudor: The First Queen. London: Hachette. Pg. 125.

13. Porter, Linda (2010). Mary Tudor: The First Queen. London: Hachette. Pg. 127.

14. Whitelock, Anna (2009). Mary Tudor: Princess, Bastard, Queen. NYC: Random House. Pg. 137.

15. Porter, Linda (2010). Mary Tudor: The First Queen. London: Hachette. Pg. 129.

16. Porter, Linda (2010). Mary Tudor: The First Queen. London: Hachette. Pgs. 126-127.

17. Porter, Linda (2010). Mary Tudor: The First Queen. London: Hachette. Pg. 128.

18. Ackroyd, Peter (2012). Tudors: The History of England from Henry VIII to Elizabeth I, Volume II. London: Macmillan. Pg. 143.
19. Whitelock, Anna (2009). Mary Tudor: Princess, Bastard, Queen. NYC: Random House. Pg. 139.
20. Porter, Linda (2010). Mary Tudor: The First Queen. London: Hachette. Pg. 129.
21. Porter, Linda (2010). Mary Tudor: The First Queen. London: Hachette. Pg. 129.
22. Beer, Barrett L. (1979, Spring). "Northumberland: The Myth of the Wicked Duke and the Historical John Dudley." Albion: A Quarterly Journal Concerned with British Studies, Volume 11, Number 1. Pgs. 2-3. Note: Consistent with the rumors of the day, a handful of historians have argued that Northumberland *did* have the young king poisoned in order to gain personal control of the crown.
23. Porter, Linda (2010). Mary Tudor: The First Queen. London: Hachette. Pg. 129.
24. Porter, Linda (2010). Mary Tudor: The First Queen. London: Hachette. Pg. 129.
25. Porter, Linda (2010). Mary Tudor: The First Queen. London: Hachette. Pg. 130.
26. Samson, Alexander (2020, April). "Mary: Brutal But Brilliant." BBC History Magazine. Bristol: Immediate Media Co. Pg. 32.
27. Whitelock, Anna (2009). Mary Tudor: Princess, Bastard, Queen. NYC: Random House. Pg. 139.
28. Ackroyd, Peter (2012). Tudors: The History of England from Henry VIII to Elizabeth I, Volume II. London: Macmillan. Pg. 143.
29. Porter, Linda (2010). Mary Tudor: The First Queen. London: Hachette. Pg. 129.
30. Porter, Linda (2010). Mary Tudor: The First Queen. London: Hachette. Pg. 129.
31. Whitelock, Anna (2009). Mary Tudor: Princess, Bastard, Queen. NYC: Random House. Pg. 139.
32. Frost, Robert (1952, December 13). "Television: Men of Faith by Philip Hamburger." The NYCer. NYC: The New Yorker Magazine Inc. Page 169.
33. Porter, Linda (2010). Mary Tudor: The First Queen. London: Hachette. Pg. 129.
34. Gristwood, Sarah (2016). Game of Queens: The Women Who Made Sixteenth-Century Europe. NYC: Basic Books. Pg. 241.
35. Porter, Linda (2010). Mary Tudor: The First Queen. London: Hachette. Pg. 129.
36. Tallis, Nicola (2017). "Bloody Mary on Trial: Henry VIII's Deadliest Daughter or Victim of Protestant Propaganda?" All About History, Issue 48. Bournemouth: Imagine Publishing, Ltd. Pg. 35.
37. Balch, Thomas Willing (1909). "French Colonization in North Africa." in The American Political Science Review, Volume III. Baltimore: The Waverly Press. Pg. 551.
38. Downey, Kirstin (2014). Isabella: The Warrior Queen. NYC: Anchor Books. Pg. 2.
39. Gristwood, Sarah (2016). Game of Queens: The Women Who Made Sixteenth-Century Europe. NYC: Basic Books. Pg. 243.
40. Porter, Linda (2010). Mary Tudor: The First Queen. London: Hachette. Pg. 129.
41. Gristwood, Sarah (2016). Game of Queens: The Women Who Made Sixteenth-Century Europe. NYC: Basic Books. Pg. 241.
42. Gristwood, Sarah (2016). Game of Queens: The Women Who Made Sixteenth-Century Europe. NYC: Basic Books. Pg. 241.
43. Gristwood, Sarah (2016). Game of Queens: The Women Who Made Sixteenth-Century Europe. NYC: Basic Books. Pg. 241.
44. Porter, Linda (2010). Mary Tudor: The First Queen. London: Hachette. Pg. 129.
45. Gristwood, Sarah (2016). Game of Queens: The Women Who Made Sixteenth-Century Europe. NYC: Basic Books. Pg. 241.
46. Ackroyd, Peter (2012). Tudors: The History of England from Henry VIII to Elizabeth I, Volume II. London: Macmillan. Pg. 143.
47. Ackroyd, Peter (2012). Tudors: The History of England from Henry VIII to Elizabeth I, Volume II. London: Macmillan. Pg. 143.
48. Gristwood, Sarah (2016). Game of Queens: The Women Who Made Sixteenth-Century Europe. NYC: Basic Books. Pg. 241.
49. Ackroyd, Peter (2012). Tudors: The History of England from Henry VIII to Elizabeth I, Volume II. London: Macmillan. Pg. 143.
50. Porter, Linda (2010). Mary Tudor: The First Queen. London: Hachette. Pg. 130.
51. Porter, Linda (2010). Mary Tudor: The First Queen. London: Hachette. Pg. 130.
52. Porter, Linda (2010). Mary Tudor: The First Queen. London: Hachette. Pg. 130.
53. Ackroyd, Peter (2012). Tudors: The History of England from Henry VIII to Elizabeth I, Volume II. London: Macmillan. Pg. 143.
54. Samson, Alexander (2020, April). "Mary: Brutal But Brilliant." BBC History Magazine. Bristol: Immediate Media Co. Pg. 32.
55. Ackroyd, Peter (2012). Tudors: The History of England from Henry VIII to Elizabeth I, Volume II. London: Macmillan. Pg. 143.
56. Whitelock, Anna (2009). Mary Tudor: Princess, Bastard, Queen. NYC: Random House. Pg. 140.
57. Ackroyd, Peter (2012). Tudors: The History of England from Henry VIII to Elizabeth I, Volume II. London: Macmillan. Pg. 143.
58. Tallis, Nicola (2017). "Bloody Mary on Trial: Henry VIII's Deadliest Daughter or Victim of Protestant Propaganda?" All About History, Issue 48. Bournemouth: Imagine Publishing, Ltd. Pg. 35.
59. Ackroyd, Peter (2012). Tudors: The History of England from Henry VIII to Elizabeth I, Volume II. London: Macmillan. Pg. 143.
60. Tallis, Nicola (2017). "Bloody Mary on Trial: Henry VIII's Deadliest Daughter or Victim of Protestant Propaganda?" All About History, Issue 48. Bournemouth: Imagine Publishing, Ltd. Pg. 35.
61. Richards, Judith (2007, December) "Edward VI and Mary Tudor: Protestant King and Catholic Sister." History Review. Pg. 22.
62. Tallis, Nicola (2017). "Bloody Mary on Trial: Henry VIII's Deadliest Daughter or Victim of Protestant Propaganda?" All About History, Issue 48. Bournemouth: Imagine Publishing, Ltd. Pg. 35.
63. Porter, Linda (2010). Mary Tudor: The First Queen. London: Hachette. Pg. 129.
64. Ackroyd, Peter (2012). Tudors: The History of England from Henry VIII to Elizabeth I, Volume II. London: Macmillan. Pg. 143.

65. Ackroyd, Peter (2012). Tudors: The History of England from Henry VIII to Elizabeth I, Volume II. London: Macmillan. Pg. 143.
66. Gristwood, Sarah (2016). Game of Queens: The Women Who Made Sixteenth-Century Europe. NYC: Basic Books. Pgs. 241.
67. Ackroyd, Peter (2012). Tudors: The History of England from Henry VIII to Elizabeth I, Volume II. London: Macmillan. Pg. 143.
68. Ackroyd, Peter (2012). Tudors: The History of England from Henry VIII to Elizabeth I, Volume II. London: Macmillan. Pg. 143.
69. Tallis, Nicola (2017). "Bloody Mary on Trial: Henry VIII's Deadliest Daughter or Victim of Protestant Propaganda?" All About History, Issue 48. Bournemouth: Imagine Publishing, Ltd. Pg. 34.
70. Braddock, Robert C. (1974, Winter). "The Character and Composition of the Duke of Northumberland's Army." Albion: A Quarterly Journal Concerned with British Studies, Volume 6, Number 4. Pg. 342.
71. Tallis, Nicola (2017). "Bloody Mary on Trial: Henry VIII's Deadliest Daughter or Victim of Protestant Propaganda?" All About History, Issue 48. Bournemouth: Imagine Publishing, Ltd. Pg. 35.
72. Tallis, Nicola (2017). "Bloody Mary on Trial: Henry VIII's Deadliest Daughter or Victim of Protestant Propaganda?" All About History, Issue 48. Bournemouth: Imagine Publishing, Ltd. Pg. 35.
73. Solly, Meilan (2020, March 12). "The Myth of 'BloodyMary.': History remembers the English queen as a murderous monster, but the real story of Mary I is far more nuanced." Smithsonian Magazine. https://www.smithsonianmag.com/history/myth-bloody-mary-180974221/
74. Collier, Robert (2008). The Secret of the Ages. Radford: Wilder Publications, Pg. 122.
75. Chandler, David G. (Editor)(2015). Napoleon's Military Maxims. Cheltenham, England: The History Press. Pg. 82.
76. Cohen, William A. (2004). The Art of the Strategist: 10 Essential Principles for Leading Your Company to Victory. NYC: AMACOM. Pg. 44.
77. Montgomery, Cynthia (2012). The Strategist: Be the Leader Your Business Needs. Harvard Business Review. Pg. 157.
78. Cohen, William A. (2004). The Art of the Strategist: 10 Essential Principles for Leading Your Company to Victory. NYC: AMACOM. Pg. 49.
79. Johnsen, William T. et al (1995, August 1). "The Principles of War in the 21st Century: Strategic Considerations." Strategic Studies Institute, U.S. Army War College, Carlisle Barracks, PA. Pgs. 6-7. https://www.files.ethz.ch/isn/47517/Principles_War_21st.pdf
80. Johnsen, William T. et al (1995, August 1). "The Principles of War in the 21st Century: Strategic Considerations." Strategic Studies Institute, U.S. Army War College, Carlisle Barracks, PA. Pg. 6. https://www.files.ethz.ch/isn/47517/Principles_War_21st.pdf
81. Johnsen, William T. et al (1995, August 1). "The Principles of War in the 21st Century: Strategic Considerations." Strategic Studies Institute, U.S. Army War College, Carlisle Barracks, PA. Pg. 7. https://www.files.ethz.ch/isn/47517/Principles_War_21st.pdf
82. Stephens, Alan and Baker, Nicola (2006). Making Sense of War: Strategy of the 21st Century. NYC. Pg. 20.
83. Whitelock, Anna (2009). Mary Tudor: Princess, Bastard, Queen. NYC: Random House. Pg. 137-138.
84. Greene, Robert (2006). The 33 Strategies of War. NYC: Penguin Books. Pg. 152.
85. Greene, Robert (2006). The 33 Strategies of War. NYC: Penguin Books. Pg. 152.
86. Greene, Robert (2006). The 33 Strategies of War. NYC: Penguin Books. Pg. 152.
87. Ackroyd, Peter (2012). Tudors: The History of England from Henry VIII to Elizabeth I, Volume II. London: Macmillan. Pg. 145.
88. Ridgley, Stanley K. (2012). Strategic Thinking Skills: The Great Courses Course Guidebook. The Great Courses. Chantilly, Virginia: The Teaching Company, LLC. Pg. 31.
89. Cohen, William A. (2004). The Art of the Strategist: 10 Essential Principles for Leading Your Company to Victory. NYC: AMACOM. Pg. 44.
90. Greene, Robert (2006). The 33 Strategies of War. NYC: Penguin Books. Pg. 152.
91. Cancian, Mark F. (2021, January). Inflicting Surprise: Gaining Competitive Advantage in Great Power Conflicts. Center for Strategic & International Studies. Lanham: Rowman & Littlefield. Pg. 57.
92. Cancian, Mark F. (2021, January). Inflicting Surprise: Gaining Competitive Advantage in Great Power Conflicts. Center for Strategic & International Studies. Lanham: Rowman & Littlefield. Pg. 57.
93. Cancian, Mark F. (2021, January). Inflicting Surprise: Gaining Competitive Advantage in Great Power Conflicts. Center for Strategic & International Studies. Lanham: Rowman & Littlefield. Pg. 57.
94. Cohen, William A. (2004). The Art of the Strategist: 10 Essential Principles for Leading Your Company to Victory. NYC: AMACOM. Pg. 44.
95. Canfield, Jack (2005). The Success Principles: How to Get from Where You Are to Where You Want to Be. NYC: HarperCollins. Pg. 98.
96. Canfield, Jack (2005). The Success Principles: How to Get from Where You Are to Where You Want to Be. NYC: HarperCollins. Pg. 98.
97. Canfield, Jack (2005). The Success Principles: How to Get from Where You Are to Where You Want to Be. NYC: HarperCollins. Pg. 98.
98. Canfield, Jack (2005). The Success Principles: How to Get from Where You Are to Where You Want to Be. NYC: HarperCollins. Pg. 98.
99. Canfield, Jack (2005). The Success Principles: How to Get from Where You Are to Where You Want to Be. NYC: HarperCollins. Pg. 98.
100. Canfield, Jack (2005). The Success Principles: How to Get from Where You Are to Where You Want to Be. NYC: HarperCollins. Pg. 98.
101. McCaulay, Philip Martin (2009). Sun Tzu's the Art of War. Raleigh: Lulu. Pg. 25.
102. McCullough, David (2001). Mornings on Horseback: The Story of an Extraordinary Family, a Vanished Way of Life, and the Unique Child Who Became Theodore Roosevelt. NYC: Simon and Schuster. Pg. 30.
103. Tracy, Brian (2004). The Psychology of Selling. San Francisco: Nashville: Thomas Nelson. Pg. 17.
104. Greene, Robert (2006). The 33 Strategies of War. NYC: Penguin Books. Pg. 200.
105. Greene, Robert (2006). The 33 Strategies of War. NYC: Penguin Books. Pg. 200.

106. Greene, Robert (2006). The 33 Strategies of War. NYC: Penguin Books. Pg. 200.
107. Greene, Robert (2006). The 33 Strategies of War. NYC: Penguin Books. Pg. 193.
108. Greene, Robert (2006). The 33 Strategies of War. NYC: Penguin Books. Pg. 200.
109. Ridgley, Stanley K. (2012). Strategic Thinking Skills: The Great Courses Course Guidebook. The Great Courses. Chantilly, Virginia: The Teaching Company, LLC. Pgs. 31-32.
110. Cohen, William A. (2004). The Art of the Strategist: 10 Essential Principles for Leading Your Company to Victory. NYC: AMACOM. Pg. 58.
111. Musashi, Miyamoto (2005 [c. 1645]). The Book of Five Rings: A Classic Text on the Japanese Way of the Sword. Thomas Cleary (Translator). Boston: Shambhala Publications.
112. Porter, Linda (2010). Mary Tudor: The First Queen. London: Hachette. Pg. 130.
113. Whitelock, Anna (2009). Mary Tudor: Princess, Bastard, Queen. NYC: Random House. Pg. 142.
114. Whitelock, Anna (2009). Mary Tudor: Princess, Bastard, Queen. NYC: Random House. Pgs. 142-143.
115. Whitelock, Anna (2009). Mary Tudor: Princess, Bastard, Queen. NYC: Random House. Pg. 143.
116. Whitelock, Anna (2009). Mary Tudor: Princess, Bastard, Queen. NYC: Random House. Pg. 140.
117. Greene, Robert (2006). The 33 Strategies of War. NYC: Penguin Books. Pg. 191.
118. Greene, Robert (2006). The 33 Strategies of War. NYC: Penguin Books. Pg. 167.
119. Tallis, Nicola (2017). "Bloody Mary on Trial: Henry VIII's Deadliest Daughter or Victim of Protestant Propaganda?" All About History, Issue 48. Bournemouth: Imagine Publishing, Ltd. Pg. 35.
120. Gristwood, Sarah (2016). Game of Queens: The Women Who Made Sixteenth-Century Europe. NYC: Basic Books. Pg. 242.
121. Marsh, Katharine (Editor)(2018). Everything You Need to Know About the Tudors, 1st Edition. Bournemouth: Future Publishing Limited. Pgs. 66-69.
122. Samson, Alexander (2020, April). "Mary: Brutal But Brilliant." BBC History Magazine. Bristol: Immediate Media Co. Pg. 32.
123. Tallis, Nicola (2017). "Bloody Mary on Trial: Henry VIII's Deadliest Daughter or Victim of Protestant Propaganda?" All About History, Issue 48. Bournemouth: Imagine Publishing, Ltd. Pg. 38.
124. Samson, Alexander (2020, April). "Mary: Brutal But Brilliant." BBC History Magazine. Bristol: Immediate Media Co. Pg. 35.
125. Solly, Meilan (2020, March 12). "The Myth of 'Bloody Mary': History remembers the English queen as a murderous monster, but the real story of Mary I is far more nuanced." Smithsonian Magazine. https://www.smithsonianmag.com/history/myth-bloody-mary-180974221/

|4|

Champion Critical Thinking to Craft Cunning Solutions and Achieve Superior Success: President John F. Kennedy Transforms His Decision-Making System from the Bay of Pigs Fiasco to the Missile Crisis in Cuba

1. Collins, Mrs. Philip L. (1964, January 11). "Strength in Difference, Letter from: Mrs. Philip L. Collins." The Dallas Morning News, Section: Letters From Readers, Section 4, Page 2, Column 4, Dallas, Texas. Online: https://archives.dallasnews.com/uncategorized/IO_726218f8-841a-48dd-a8c4-eaf7d7097950/ Pg. 28.
2. Frankel, Max (2002, October). "Learning from the Missile Crisis: What Really Happened on Those Thirteen Fateful Days in October." Smithsonian Magazine. https://www.smithsonianmag.com/history/learning-from-the-missile-crisis-68901679
3. Frankel (2002).
4. Frankel (2002).
5. Bohn, Michael (2015). Presidents in Crisis: Tough Decisions inside the White House from Truman to Obama. NYC: Arcade Publishing. Michael Beschloss similarly called it "probably the most alarming address ever delivered by an American president."
6. Kennedy, John F. (1962, October 22). "Radio and television address to the American people on the Soviet arms build-up in Cuba, 22 October 1962." John F. Kennedy Presidential Library and Museum, Boston, MA. Digital Identifier: JFKWHA-142-001 https://www.jfklibrary.org/learn/about-jfk/historic-speeches/address-during-the-cuban-missile-crisis
7. Janis, Irving (1983). Groupthink: Psychological Studies of Policy Decisions and Fiascoes, 2nd Edition. Boston: Houghton Mifflin Company. Pg. 138.
8. Kennedy, John F. (1962, October 22). "Radio and television address to the American people on the Soviet arms build-up in Cuba, 22 October 1962." John F. Kennedy Presidential Library and Museum, Boston, MA. Digital Identifier: JFKWHA-142-001 https://www.jfklibrary.org/learn/about-jfk/historic-speeches/address-during-the-cuban-missile-crisis
9. Kennedy, John F. (1962, October 22). "Radio and television address to the American people on the Soviet arms build-up in Cuba, 22 October 1962." John F. Kennedy Presidential Library and Museum, Boston, MA. Digital Identifier: JFKWHA-142-001 https://www.jfklibrary.org/learn/about-jfk/historic-speeches/address-during-the-cuban-missile-crisis
10. Kennedy, John F. (1962, October 22). "Radio and television address to the American people on the Soviet arms build-up in Cuba, 22 October 1962." John F. Kennedy Presidential Library and Museum, Boston, MA. Digital Identifier: JFKWHA-142-001 https://www.jfklibrary.org/learn/about-jfk/historic-speeches/address-during-the-cuban-missile-crisis
11. Chapman, Lionel (Producer) Wiley, Foster (Director)(1992). The Missiles of October: What the

World Didn't Know. [Documentary Film]. United States: Washington Media Associates.

12. Burns, James MacGregor (2007). Running Alone: Presidential Leadership from JFK to Bush II. NYC: Basic Books. Pg. 49.

13. Janis, Irving (1983). Groupthink: Psychological Studies of Policy Decisions and Fiascoes, 2nd Edition. Boston: Houghton Mifflin Company. Pg. 14.

14. Janis, Irving (1983). Groupthink: Psychological Studies of Policy Decisions and Fiascoes, 2nd Edition. Boston: Houghton Mifflin Company. Pg. 16.

15. Wicker, Tom; Finney, John W.; Frankel, Max; and Kenworthy, E.W. (1966, April 25). "C.I.A.: Maker of Policy, or Tool?" NYC Times. Pg. 20.

16. Neustadt, Richard & May, Ernest (1986). Thinking in Time: The Uses of History for Decision Makers. NYC: The Free Press. Pg. 210.

17. Thomas, Evan (1995). The Very Best Men: Four Who Dared: The Early Years of the CIA. NYC: Simon & Schuster. Pg. 266.

18. Thomas, Evan (1995). The Very Best Men: Four Who Dared: The Early Years of the CIA. NYC: Simon & Schuster. Pg. 266.

19. Thomas, Evan (1995). The Very Best Men: Four Who Dared: The Early Years of the CIA. NYC: Simon & Schuster. Pg. 266.

20. Kennedy, President John F. (1961, April 21). "The President's News Conference." Online by Gerhard Peters and John T. Woolley, The American Presidency Project. https://www.presidency.ucsb.edu/node/234701

21. Savranskaya, Svetlana (2022, October 3). "The Underwater Cuban Missile Crisis at 60." National Security Archive, George Washington University. https://nsarchive.gwu.edu/briefing-book/russia-programs/2022-10-03/soviet-submarines-nuclear-torpedoes-cuban-missile-crisis

22. Kennedy, Robert F. (1969). Thirteen Days: A Memoir of the Cuban Missile Crisis. NYC: Penguin Books. Pg. 49.

23. Nye, Joseph S. (1989, March 13). "Where Were You in 62?: Cuban Graffiti" The New Republic. Pg. 16.

24. Chomsky, Noam (2012, October 15). "Cuban missile crisis: how the US played Russian roulette with nuclear war." The Guardian. http://www.theguardian.com/commentisfree/2012/oct/15/cuban-missile-crisis-russian-roulette

25. Plummer, Matt (2019, October 11). "A Short Guide to Building Your Team's Critical Thinking Skills." Harvard Business Review. https://hbr.org/2019/10/a-short-guide-to-building-your-teams-critical-thinking-skills

26. Tolle, Eckhart (2004). The Power of Now. Vancouver: Namaste Publishing. Pg. 7.

27. Drucker, Peter F. (2017). The Peter F. Drucker Reader: Selected Articles from the Father of Modern Management Thinking. Boston, MA: Harvard Business Review. Pg. viii.

28. Coleman, John (2022, April 22). "Critical Thinking is About Asking Better Questions." Harvard Business Review. https://hbr.org/2022/04/critical-thinking-is-about-asking-better-questions

29. Bregman, Peter (2015, December 7). "Are You Trying to Solve the Wrong Problem?" Harvard Business Review. https://hbr.org/2015/12/are-you-solving-the-wrong-problem

30. Bregman, Peter (2015, December 7). "Are You Trying to Solve the Wrong Problem?" Harvard Business Review. https://hbr.org/2015/12/are-you-solving-the-wrong-problem

31. Spradlin, Dwayne (2012, September) "Are You Solving the Right Problem?" Harvard Business Review. Cambridge: Harvard Business Publishing. https://hbr.org/2012/09/are-you-solving-the-right-problem

32. Spradlin, Dwayne (2012, September) "Are You Solving the Right Problem?" Harvard Business Review. Cambridge: Harvard Business Publishing. https://hbr.org/2012/09/are-you-solving-the-right-problem

33. Spradlin, Dwayne (2012, September) "Are You Solving the Right Problem?" Harvard Business Review. Cambridge: Harvard Business Publishing. https://hbr.org/2012/09/are-you-solving-the-right-problem

34. Spradlin, Dwayne (2012, September) "Are You Solving the Right Problem?" Harvard Business Review. Cambridge: Harvard Business Publishing. https://hbr.org/2012/09/are-you-solving-the-right-problem

35. Spradlin, Dwayne (2012, September) "Are You Solving the Right Problem?" Harvard Business Review. Cambridge: Harvard Business Publishing. https://hbr.org/2012/09/are-you-solving-the-right-problem

36. *The Holy Bible*, English Standard Version (2016). Proverbs 16:32 Biblegateway.com. Biblica, Inc. https://www.biblegateway.com/passage/?search=Proverbs+16%3A32+&version=ESV

37. Kennedy, Robert F. (1969). Thirteen Days: A Memoir of the Cuban Missile Crisis. NYC: Penguin Books. Pg. 33.

38. Kennedy, Robert F. (1969). Thirteen Days: A Memoir of the Cuban Missile Crisis. NYC: Penguin Books. Pg. 33.

39. Janis, Irving (1983). Groupthink: Psychological Studies of Policy Decisions and Fiascoes, 2nd Edition. Boston: Houghton Mifflin Company. Pgs. 132-158.

40. Janis, Irving (1983). Groupthink: Psychological Studies of Policy Decisions and Fiascoes, 2nd Edition. Boston: Houghton Mifflin Company. Pgs. 132-158.

41. Gracián, Baltasar (1892). Jacobs, Joseph (Translator). The Art of Worldly Wisdom. London: MacMillan and Co. Pg. 295 (#287).

42. Kennedy, Robert F. (1969). Thirteen Days: A Memoir of the Cuban Missile Crisis. NYC: Penguin Books. Pg. 54.

43. Kennedy, Robert F. (1969). Thirteen Days: A Memoir of the Cuban Missile Crisis. NYC: Penguin Books. Pg. 55.

44. Kennedy, Robert F. (1969). Thirteen Days: A Memoir of the Cuban Missile Crisis. NYC: Penguin Books. Pg. 55.

45. Kennedy, Robert F. (1969). Thirteen Days: A Memoir of the Cuban Missile Crisis. NYC: Penguin Books. Pg. 86.

46. Kennedy, Robert F. (1969). Thirteen Days: A Memoir of the Cuban Missile Crisis. NYC: Penguin Books. Pg. 86.

47. Kets de Vries, Manfred (2010). Reflections on Leadership and Career Development. San Francisco: Jossey Bass. Pg. 33.

48. Pieta, Ewa (2006). "The Red Button & the Man Who Saved the World". logtv.com. https://logtv.com/redbutton/

49. Pieta, Ewa (2006). "The Red Button & the Man Who Saved the World". logtv.com. https://logtv.com/redbutton/

50. Pieta, Ewa (2006). "The Red Button & the Man Who Saved the World". logtv.com. https://logtv.com/redbutton/

51. Lebedev, Anastasiya (2004, May 21). "The Man Who Saved the World Finally Recognized." MosNews. https://web.archive.org/web/20110721000030/http://www.worldcitizens.org/petrov2.html

52. Staff Writer (2017, September 21). "Stanislav Petrov, 'the man who saved the world' from nuclear war, dies at 77." Los Angeles Times. https://www.latimes.com/local/obituaries/la-me-stanislavsky-petrov-20170921-story.html

53. Falcon, Andrea (2022, Spring). "Aristotle on Causality." The Stanford Encyclopedia of Philosophy , Edward N. Zalta (Editor) https://plato.stanford.edu/archives/spr2022/entries/aristotle-causality/ See Also: http://classics.mit.edu/Aristotle/physics.mb.txt

54. Einstein, Albert (1946, June 23). "The Real Problem Is in the Hearts of Men." The NYC Times. https://www.nytimes.com/1946/06/23/archives/the-real-problem-is-in-the-hearts-of-men-professor-einstein-says-a.html

55. Ruiz, Don Miguel (1997). The Four Agreements: A Practical Guide to Personal Freedom. San Rafael, CA: Amber-Allen Publishing. Pg. 64.

56. Gore, Al (2007). Earth in the Balance: Forging a New Common Purpose. NYC: Earthscan. Pg. 41.

57. Engel, Jeffrey; Lawrence, Mark; and Preston, Andrew (Editors)(2014). America in the World: A History in Documents from the War with Spain to the War on Terror. Princeton: Princeton University Press. Washington, D.C. Pg. 204.

58. Engel, Jeffrey; Lawrence, Mark; and Preston, Andrew (Editors)(2014). America in the World: A History in Documents from the War with Spain to the War on Terror. Princeton: Princeton University Press. Washington, D.C. Pg. 204.

59. Kennedy, Robert F. (1969). Thirteen Days: A Memoir of the Cuban Missile Crisis. NYC: Penguin Books. Pgs. 117-118.

60. Kennedy, Robert F. (1969). Thirteen Days: A Memoir of the Cuban Missile Crisis. NYC: Penguin Books. Pgs. 117-118.

61. Kennedy, Robert F. (1969). Thirteen Days: A Memoir of the Cuban Missile Crisis. NYC: Penguin Books. Pg. 117.

62. Kennedy, Robert F. (1969). Thirteen Days: A Memoir of the Cuban Missile Crisis. NYC: Penguin Books. Pg. 124.

63. Kennedy, Robert F. (1969). Thirteen Days: A Memoir of the Cuban Missile Crisis. NYC: Penguin Books. Pg. 119.

64. Kennedy, Robert F. (1969). Thirteen Days: A Memoir of the Cuban Missile Crisis. NYC: Penguin Books. Pg. 119.

65. Kennedy, Robert F. (1969). Thirteen Days: A Memoir of the Cuban Missile Crisis. NYC: Penguin Books. Pg. 119.

66. Kennedy, Robert F. (1969). Thirteen Days: A Memoir of the Cuban Missile Crisis. NYC: Penguin Books. Pg. 119.

67. Kennedy, Robert F. (1969). Thirteen Days: A Memoir of the Cuban Missile Crisis. NYC: Penguin Books. Pg. 117.

68. Kennedy, Robert F. (1969). Thirteen Days: A Memoir of the Cuban Missile Crisis. NYC: Penguin Books. Pg. 117.

69. Kennedy, Robert F. (1969). Thirteen Days: A Memoir of the Cuban Missile Crisis. NYC: Penguin Books. Pg. 46.

70. Frankel, Max (2002, October). "Learning from the Missile Crisis: What Really Happened on Those Thirteen Fateful Days in October." Smithsonian Magazine. https://www.smithsonianmag.com/history/learning-from-the-missile-crisis-68901679

71. Hargrove, Erwin C. (2014). The Effective Presidency: Lessons on Leadership from John F. Kennedy to Barack Obama, Second Edition. NYC: Routledge. Pg. 24. Full Quote: "Kennedy failed at the Bay of Pigs and succeeded in the missile crisis. His virtues in the latter case were intelligence, detachment, and judgment. He did not so much manage the process as guide it. He asked hard questions and gradually felt his way to a decision."

72. Janis, Irving (1983). Groupthink: Psychological Studies of Policy Decisions and Fiascoes, 2nd Edition. Boston: Houghton Mifflin Company. Pgs. 132-158.

73. Kennedy, John F. (1961, April 27). "The President and the Press." Presidential Address Before the American Newspaper Publishers Association, Waldorf-Astoria Hotel, NYC City. https://www.jfklibrary.org/archives/other-resources/john-f-kennedy-speeches/american-newspaper-publishers-association-19610427

74. McManus, John C. (2004). The Americans at D-Day: The American Experience at the Normandy Invasion. NYC: Forge Books. Pg. 87.

75. Manchester, William (1978). American Caesar: Douglas MacArthur 1880—1964. NYC: Back Bay Books. Pg. 348.

76. Kennedy, Robert F. (1969). Thirteen Days: A Memoir of the Cuban Missile Crisis. NYC: Penguin Books. Pg. 118.

77. Kennedy, Robert F. (1969). Thirteen Days: A Memoir of the Cuban Missile Crisis. NYC: Penguin Books. Pgs. 115-116.

78. Welch, Johnny (2016). Mastering the Power of Grit. San Diego: By the People Books.

79. Welch, Johnny (2016). Mastering the Power of Grit. San Diego: By the People Books.

|5|

Cultivate the Hidden Power of Concentrated Curiosity: The Secret Success Factor of Marco Polo and Kublai Khan

1. Disney, Walt; Smith, Dave (2001). The Quotable Walt Disney. Los Angeles: Disney Editions. Pg. 137.

2. Brown, Robin (2011). Marco Polo: Journey to the End of the Earth. Gloucestershire: History Press. Pg. 8.

3. Tarcher, Jeremy P. (Ed.)(2007). The Prosperity Bible: The Greatest Writings of All Time on the Secrets to Wealth and Prosperity. NYC: Penguin. Pg. 43.

4. Strathern, Paul (2013). The Venetians: A New History: From Marco Polo to Casanova. NYC: Pegasus Books. Pg. 19.

5. Strathern, Paul (2013). The Venetians: A New History: From Marco Polo to Casanova. NYC: Pegasus Books. Pg. 19.

6. Bergreen, Laurence (2007). Marco Polo: From Venice to Xanadu. NYC: Alfred A. Knopf. Pg. 6.

7. Bergreen, Laurence (2007). Marco Polo: From Venice to Xanadu. NYC: Alfred A. Knopf. Pgs. 6-7.

8. Bergreen, Laurence (2007). Marco Polo: From Venice to Xanadu. NYC: Alfred A. Knopf. Pgs. 6-7.

9. Bergreen, Laurence (2007). Marco Polo: From Venice to Xanadu. NYC: Alfred A. Knopf. Pg. 308.

10. Maxwell, John (2012). The 15 Invaluable Laws of Growth: Live Them and Reach Your Potential. NYC: Center Street. Pg. 196.

11. McNeese, Tim (2005). Marco Polo and the Realm of Kublai Khan (Explorers of New Lands). NYC: Chelsea House Publishers. Pg. vi.

12. Leslie, Ian (2014). Curious: The Desire to Know and Why Your Future Depends On It. NYC: Basic Books. Pg. xv

13. Bergreen, Laurence (2007). Marco Polo: From Venice to Xanadu. NYC: Alfred A. Knopf. Pg. 27.

14. Meagher, Thomas (2007). The Gigantic Book of Horse Wisdom. NYC: Skyhorse Publishing. Note: This quote is widely attributed to Genghis Khan, but other sources contend that it was said to Genghis Khan by his top military advisor, Yelü Chucai, a Confucian scholar. Pg. 408.

15. Bergreen, Laurence (2007). Marco Polo: From Venice to Xanadu. NYC: Alfred A. Knopf. Pg. 32, 33.

16. Ratti, Antonio (2019, September-October). "There and Back Again: The Travels of Marco Polo." National Geographic History, Volume 5, Number 4. Washington, D.C.: National Geographic Partners, LLC. Pg. 68.

17. Bergreen, Laurence (2007). Marco Polo: From Venice to Xanadu. NYC: Alfred A. Knopf. Pgs. 32-33.

18. Bergreen, Laurence (2007). Marco Polo: From Venice to Xanadu. NYC: Alfred A. Knopf. Pgs. 32-33.

19. Bergreen, Laurence (2007). Marco Polo: From Venice to Xanadu. NYC: Alfred A. Knopf. Pg. 33.

20. Bergreen, Laurence (2007). Marco Polo: From Venice to Xanadu. NYC: Alfred A. Knopf. Pg. 27.

21. Bergreen, Laurence (2007). Marco Polo: From Venice to Xanadu. NYC: Alfred A. Knopf. Pg. 27.

22. Ratti, Antonio (2019, September-October). "There and Back Again: The Travels of Marco Polo." National Geographic History, Volume 5, Number 4. Washington, D.C.: National Geographic Partners, LLC. Pg. 68.

23. Ratti, Antonio (2019, September-October). "There and Back Again: The Travels of Marco Polo." National Geographic History, Volume 5, Number 4. Washington, D.C.: National Geographic Partners, LLC. Pg. 68.

24. Strathern, Paul (2013). The Venetians: A New History: From Marco Polo to Casanova. NYC: Pegasus Books. Pg. 19.

25. Brown, Robin (2011). Marco Polo: Journey to the End of the Earth. Gloucestershire: History Press. Pg. 29.

26. Strathern, Paul (2013). The Venetians: A New History: From Marco Polo to Casanova. NYC: Pegasus Books. Pg. 19.

27. Bergreen, Laurence (2007). Marco Polo: From Venice to Xanadu. NYC: Alfred A. Knopf. Pg. 27.

28. Ratti, Antonio (2019, September-October). "There and Back Again: The Travels of Marco Polo." National Geographic History, Volume 5, Number 4. Washington, D.C.: National Geographic Partners, LLC. Pg. 64.

29. Ratti, Antonio (2019, September-October). "There and Back Again: The Travels of Marco Polo." National Geographic History, Volume 5, Number 4. Washington, D.C.: National Geographic Partners, LLC. Pg. 72.

30. Ratti, Antonio (2019, September-October). "There and Back Again: The Travels of Marco Polo." National Geographic History, Volume 5, Number 4. Washington, D.C.: National Geographic Partners, LLC. Pg. 64.

31. Mead, Margaret (1979). Some Personal Views. Sydney: Angus & Robertson. Pg. 89.

32. Holman, Katherine (2003). Historical Dictionary of the Vikings. Oxford: The Scarecrow Press, Inc. Pg. 203.

33. Meslow, Scott (2013, March 2). "Vikings creator Michael Hirst on violent warriors, historical drama, and pagan religions." The Week. https://theweek.com/articles/467102/vikings-creator-michael-hirst-violent-warriors-historical-drama-pagan-religions

34. Holman, Katherine (2003). Historical Dictionary of the Vikings. Oxford: The Scarecrow Press, Inc. Pg. 203.

35. Leslie, Ian (2014). Curious: The Desire to Know and Why Your Future Depends On It. NYC: Basic Books. Pg. 12.

36. Meslow, Scott (2013, March 2). "Vikings creator Michael Hirst on violent warriors, historical drama, and pagan religions." The Week. https://theweek.com/articles/467102/vikings-creator-michael-hirst-violent-warriors-historical-drama-pagan-religions

37. Meslow, Scott (2013, March 2). "Vikings creator Michael Hirst on violent warriors, historical drama, and pagan religions." The Week. https://theweek.com/articles/467102/vikings-creator-michael-hirst-violent-warriors-historical-drama-pagan-religions

38. Holman, Katherine (2003). Historical Dictionary of the Vikings. Oxford: The Scarecrow Press, Inc. Pg. 16.

39. Holman, Katherine (2003). Historical Dictionary of the Vikings. Oxford: The Scarecrow Press, Inc. NOTE: Some sources cite Bjarni Herjólfsson as the first Scandinavian to sight land in North America, though he did not make landfall.

40. Cordell, Linda S.; Lightfoot, Kent; McManamon, Francis; Milner, George (2009). "L'Anse aux Meadows National Historic Site," Archaeology in America: An Encyclopedia. ABC-CLIO. Pg. 82. Carbon dating estimates the Norse settlement at L'Anse aux Meadows was sometime between 990 and 1050 B.C. Pg. 82.

41. Friis, Erik J. (Editor)(1917). The King's Mirror. (Translated by Laurence Marcellus Larson). NYC: Twayne Publishers, Inc. Pg. 142.

42. Gruber, Matthias; Gelman, Bernard; Ranganath, Charan (2014). "States of Curiosity Modulate Hippocampus-Dependent Learning via the Dopaminergic Circuit." Neuron, Volume 84, Issue 2, Pgs. 486-496. See also: Cell Press. (2014, October 2). How curiosity changes the brain to enhance learning. Science Daily. www.sciencedaily.com/releases/2014/10/141002123631.htm See also: Livio, Mario (2017, August 23). "The 'Why' Behind Asking Why: The Science of Curiosity." Knowledge@Wharton. https://knowledge.wharton.upenn.edu/article/makes-us-curious/

43. Leslie, Ian (2014). Curious: The Desire to Know and Why Your Future Depends On It. NYC: Basic Books. Pg. 132.

44. Leslie, Ian (2014). Curious: The Desire to Know and Why Your Future Depends On It. NYC: Basic Books. Pg. 111.

45. Leslie, Ian (2014). Curious: The Desire to Know and Why Your Future Depends On It. NYC: Basic Books. Pg. 111.

46. Isaacson, Walter (2008). Einstein: His Life and Universe. NYC: Simon & Schuster. Pg. 548.

47. Isaacson, Walter (2008). Einstein: His Life and Universe. NYC: Simon & Schuster. Pg. 548.

48. Isaacson, Walter (2008). Einstein: His Life and Universe. NYC: Simon & Schuster. Pg. 853.

49. Isaacson, Walter (2008). Einstein: His Life and Universe. NYC: Simon & Schuster. Pg. 548.

50. Csikszentmihalyi, Mihaly (2013). Creativity: Flow and the Psychology of Discovery and Invention. NYC: HarperCollins. Pg. 459.

51. Williams, Pat (2004). How to Be Like Walt: Capturing the Disney Magic Every Day of Your Life. Deerfield Beach, Florida: Health Communications, Inc. Pgs. 353-354.

52. Williams, Pat (2004). How to Be Like Walt: Capturing the Disney Magic Every Day of Your Life. Deerfield Beach, Florida: Health Communications, Inc. Pg. 350.

53. Williams, Pat (2004). How to Be Like Walt: Capturing the Disney Magic Every Day of Your Life. Deerfield Beach, Florida: Health Communications, Inc. Pg. 350.

54. Williams, Pat (2004). How to Be Like Walt: Capturing the Disney Magic Every Day of Your Life. Deerfield Beach, Florida: Health Communications, Inc. Pg. 351.

55. Anderson, Stephen J. [Director]. (2007). "Meet the Robinsons." [Film.] Walt Disney Pictures, Walt Disney Animation Studios. See Also: Williams, Pat (2004). How to Be Like Walt: Capturing the Disney Magic Every Day of Your Life. Deerfield Beach, Florida: Health Communications, Inc. Pg. 350.

56. Leslie, Ian (2014). Curious: The Desire to Know and Why Your Future Depends On It. NYC: Basic Books. Pg. 12.

57. Leslie, Ian (2014). Curious: The Desire to Know and Why Your Future Depends On It. NYC: Basic Books. Pg. xv.

58. Livio, Mario (2017). Why: What Makes Us Curious. NYC: Simon & Schuster. Pg. 102.

59. Berger, Warren (2015, September 11). "Why Curious People are Destined for the C-Suite." Harvard Business Review. https://hbr.org/2015/09/why-curious-people-are-destined-for-the-c-suite

60. Orben, Robert (1974 July 28). "Quips and Quotes." The Gallup Independent, Section: Family Weekly (Newspaper Supplement), Pg. 15, Column 2, Gallup, New Mexico. Hat tip to Quote Investigator for tracking this down: https://quoteinvestigator.com/2016/05/03/expense/

61. Leslie, Ian (2014). Curious: The Desire to Know and Why Your Future Depends On It. NYC: Basic Books. Pg. 12.

62. Berger, Warren (2015, September 11). "Why Curious People are Destined for the C-Suite." Harvard Business Review. https://hbr.org/2015/09/why-curious-people-are-destined-for-the-c-suite

63. Hoare, James (2022). "Wrath of the Khans." All About History: Genghis Khan and the Mongol Empire. Bournemouth: Imagine Publishing, Ltd. Pg. 86.

64. McNeese, Tim (2005). Marco Polo and the Realm of Kublai Khan (Explorers of New Lands). NYC: Chelsea House Publishers. Pg. 113.

65. McNeese, Tim (2005). Marco Polo and the Realm of Kublai Khan (Explorers of New Lands). NYC: Chelsea House Publishers. Pg. 113.

66. **Firestein, Stuart (2012). *Ignorance: How It Drives Science*. NYC: Oxford University Press. Pg. 7.**

67. Leslie, Ian (2014). Curious: The Desire to Know and Why Your Future Depends On It. NYC: Basic Books. Pgs. 129-130.

68. Livio, Mario (2017). Why: What Makes Us Curious. NYC: Simon & Schuster. Pgs. 112-113.

69. Wilkes, Jonny (2021, March). "Michelangelo: Renaissance Man." History Revealed, Issue 92. Bristol: Immediate Media Company. Pg. 63.

70. Wilkes, Jonny (2021, March). "Michelangelo: Renaissance Man." History Revealed, Issue 92. Bristol: Immediate Media Company. Pg. 63.

71. Isaacson, Walter (2018). Leonardo Da Vinci. NYC: Simon & Schuster. Pg. 22.

72. Isaacson, Walter (2018). Leonardo Da Vinci. NYC: Simon & Schuster. Pg. 21.

73. "Leonardo da Vinci" (2020). *All About History Book of the Renaissance*, Fifth Edition. Bournemouth: Future Publishing Limited. Pg. 50.

74. Man, John (2014). Marco Polo: The Journey that Changed the World. NYC: William Morrow. Pg. 184.

75. McNeese, Tim (2005). Marco Polo and the Realm of Kublai Khan (Explorers of New Lands). NYC: Chelsea House Publishers. Pg. 67.

76. McNeese, Tim (2005). Marco Polo and the Realm of Kublai Khan (Explorers of New Lands). NYC: Chelsea House Publishers. Pg. 114.

77. Brown, Robin (2011). Marco Polo: Journey to the End of the Earth. Gloucestershire: The History Press. Pg. 46.

78. Ratti, Antonio (2019, September-October). "There and Back Again: The Travels of Marco Polo." National Geographic History, Volume 5, Number 4. Washington, D.C.: National Geographic Partners, LLC. Pg. 64.

79. Man, John (2014). Marco Polo: The Journey that Changed the World. NYC: William Morrow. Pg. 184.

80. Livio, Mario (2017). Why: What Makes Us Curious. NYC: Simon & Schuster. Pg. 112.

81. Livio, Mario (2017). Why: What Makes Us Curious. NYC: Simon & Schuster. Pg. 112.

82. Isaacson, Walter (2018). *Leonardo Da Vinci*. NYC: Simon & Schuster. Pg. 22.

83. Isaacson, Walter (2018). *Leonardo Da Vinci*. NYC: Simon & Schuster. Pg. 22.

84. Isaacson, Walter (2018). *Leonardo Da Vinci*. NYC: Simon & Schuster. Pg. 21.

85. Keller, Gary (2013). The ONE Thing: The Surprisingly Simple Truth Behind Extraordinary Results. Austin: Bard Press. Pg. 111.

86. Leonardo da Vinci, 1452-1519. (1888). The Notebooks of Leonardo da Vinci, Volume I. Translated by Jean Paul Richter. Oxford: Oxford's World Classics. Pg. 435.

87. Kemp, Martin (2006). Leonardo da Vinci: The Marvelous Works of Nature and Man. Oxford: Oxford University Press. Pg. 85.

88. Kemp, Martin (2006). Leonardo da Vinci: The Marvelous Works of Nature and Man. Oxford: Oxford University Press. Pg. 85.

89. Isaacson, Walter (2008). Einstein: His Life and Universe. NYC: Simon & Schuster. Pg. 548.

90. Firestein, Stuart (2012). Ignorance: How It Drives Science. NYC: Oxford University Press. Pg. 7.

91. Keller, Gary (2013). The ONE Thing: The Surprisingly Simple Truth Behind Extraordinary Results. Austin: Bard Press. Pg. 111.

92. Maxwell, John C. (2012). *The 15 Invaluable Laws of Growth: Live Them and Reach Your Potential*. NYC: Hachette. Pg. 189.

93. Goldsmith, Barbara (2005). *Obsessive Genius: The Inner World of Marie Curie*. NYC: Atlas Books. Pg. 78.

94. Goldsmith, Barbara (2005). *Obsessive Genius: The Inner World of Marie Curie*. NYC: Atlas Books. Pg. 78.

95. Curie, Eve (1937). Madame Curie: A Biography by Eve Curie. NYC: Doubleday. Pg. 184.

96. Goldsmith, Barbara (2005). Obsessive Genius: The Inner World of Marie Curie. NYC: Atlas Books. Pg. 78.

97. Curie, Eve (1937). Madame Curie: A Biography by Eve Curie. NYC: Doubleday. Pg. 184.

98. Curie, Eve (1937). Madame Curie: A Biography by Eve Curie. NYC: Doubleday. Pg. 184.

99. Curie, Eve (1937). Madame Curie: A Biography by Eve Curie. NYC: Doubleday. Pgs. 184-185.

100. Goldsmith, Barbara (2005). Obsessive Genius: The Inner World of Marie Curie. NYC: Atlas Books. Pg. 78.

101. Goldsmith, Barbara (2005). Obsessive Genius: The Inner World of Marie Curie. NYC: Atlas Books. Pg. 91.

102. McKelvey, Tara (2015, July 21). "When the U.S. President Travels, the World Stands Still." BBC News. https://www.bbc.com/news/magazine-33561051

103. McKelvey, Tara (2015, July 21). "When the U.S. President Travels, the World Stands Still." BBC News. https://www.bbc.com/news/magazine-33561051

104. Baime, A.J. (2017). The Accidental President: Harry S. Truman and the Four Months that Changed the World. Boston: Houghton Mifflin Harcourt. Pg. 334.

105. Tackett, Michael (2019, March 27). "Some Presidents Felt Trapped in the White House Bubble. Trump Thrives in It." The NYC Times. https://www.nytimes.com/2019/03/27/us/politics/trump-white-house-travel.html

106. Tackett, Michael (2019, March 27). "Some Presidents Felt Trapped in the White House Bubble. Trump Thrives in It." The NYC Times. https://www.nytimes.com/2019/03/27/us/politics/trump-white-house-travel.html

107. Murray, Frank J. (1993, January 15). "Clinton chafes at security." The Washington Times, Pg. A3.

108. Carpenter, Francis B. (1872). Six Months at the White House: The Inner Life of Abraham Lincoln. Cambridge: Riverside Press. Pg. 281.

109. Carpenter, Francis B. (1872). Six Months at the White House: The Inner Life of Abraham Lincoln. Cambridge: Riverside Press. Pg. 279.

110. Carpenter, Francis B. (1872). Six Months at the White House: The Inner Life of Abraham Lincoln. Cambridge: Riverside Press. Pg. 281.

111. Carpenter, Francis B. (1872). Six Months at the White House: The Inner Life of Abraham Lincoln. Cambridge: Riverside Press. Pg. 282.

112. Brown, Robin (2011). Marco Polo: Journey to the End of the Earth. Gloucestershire: The History Press. Pg. 25.

113. Walker, Veronica (2020, March-April). "Kublai Khan's Realm." National Geographic. Washington, D.C.: National Geographic Partners, LLC. Pg. 70.

114. Walker, Veronica (2020, March-April). "Kublai Khan's Realm." National Geographic. Washington, D.C.: National Geographic Partners, LLC. Pg. 70.

115. Walker, Veronica (2020, March-April). "Kublai Khan's Realm." National Geographic. Washington, D.C.: National Geographic Partners, LLC. Pg. 71.

116. Walker, Veronica (2020, March-April). "Kublai Khan's Realm." National Geographic. Washington, D.C.: National Geographic Partners, LLC. Pg. 71.

117. Brown, Robin (2011). Marco Polo: Journey to the End of the Earth. Gloucestershire: The History Press. Pg. 25.

118. Brown, Robin (2011). Marco Polo: Journey to the End of the Earth. Gloucestershire: The History Press. Pg. 23.

119. Brown, Robin (2011). Marco Polo: Journey to the End of the Earth. Gloucestershire: The History Press. Pg. 23.

120. Maxwell, John C. (2012). The 15 Invaluable Laws of Growth: Live Them and Reach Your Potential. NYC: Hachette. Pg. 224.

121. Isaacson, Walter (2008). Einstein: His Life and Universe. NYC: Simon & Schuster. Pg. 688 (eBook).

122. Isaacson, Walter (2008). Einstein: His Life and Universe. NYC: Simon & Schuster. Pg. 548.

123. Isaacson, Walter (2008). Einstein: His Life and Universe. NYC: Simon & Schuster. Pg. 548.

124. Bradenburger, Adam (2022, Spring). "To Change the Way You Think, Change the Way You See." Harvard Business Review, On Point. Pg. 34.

125. Bradenburger, Adam (2022, Spring). "To Change the Way You Think, Change the Way You See." Harvard Business Review, On Point. Pg. 34.

126. Senior, Jennifer (2017, November 1). "Walter Isaacson's 'Leonardo da Vinci' Is the Portrait of a Real Renaissance Man." The NYC Times. https://www.nytimes.com/2017/11/01/books/review-leonardo-da-vinci-biography-walter-isaacson.html

127. Isaacson, Walter (2018). Leonardo Da Vinci. NYC: Simon & Schuster. Pg. 6.

128. Isaacson, Walter (2018). Leonardo Da Vinci. NYC: Simon & Schuster. Pg. 6.

129. Isaacson, Walter (2018). Leonardo Da Vinci. NYC: Simon & Schuster. Pg. 6.

130. Bouguet, Cyril; Barsoux, Jean-Louis; Wade, Michael (2022, Spring). "Stop Sabotaging Your Ability to Innovate." Harvard Business Review, On Point. Pg. 14.

131. Wykes, Alan (1969). Doctor Cardano, Physician Extraordinary. Muller. Pg. 26.

132. "Leonardo da Vinci" (2020). All About History Book of the Renaissance, Fifth Edition. Bournemouth: Future Publishing Limited. Pg. 53.

133. Kalb, Claudia (2019, May). "Leonardo's Enduring Brilliance." National Geographic. Washington, D.C.: National Geographic Partners, LLC. Pg. Pg. 82.

134. Senior, Jennifer (2017, November 1). "Walter Isaacson's 'Leonardo da Vinci' Is the Portrait of a Real Renaissance Man. The NYC Times. https://www.nytimes.com/2017/11/01/books/review-leonardo-da-vinci-biography-walter-isaacson.html

135. Leslie, Ian (2014). Curious: The Desire to Know and Why Your Future Depends On It. NY: Basic Books. Pg. 12.

136. Ovid (2004 [circa 8 B.C.]). Metamorphoses. R. J. Tarrant (Editor). Oxford University Press.

137. Leslie, Ian (2014). Curious: The Desire to Know and Why Your Future Depends On It. NY: Basic Books. Pg. 12.

138. Leslie, Ian (2014). Curious: The Desire to Know and Why Your Future Depends On It. NY: Basic Books. Pg. 12.

139. Isaacson, Walter (2018). Leonardo Da Vinci. NYC: Simon & Schuster. Pg. 25.

140. Ratti, Antonio (2019, September-October). "There and Back Again: The Travels of Marco Polo." National Geographic History, Volume 5, Number 4. Washington, D.C.: National Geographic Partners, LLC. Pg. 68.

141. Ratti, Antonio (2019, September-October). "There and Back Again: The Travels of Marco Polo." National Geographic History, Volume 5, Number 4. Washington, D.C.: National Geographic Partners, LLC. Pg. 73.

142. Hart, Henry (1967). Marco Polo: Venetian Adventurer. Norman, OK: University of Oklahoma Press. Pg. 258.

|6|
Reap the Wisdom of History: Profit from the Power of the Past to Influence the Future

1. Wilson, Andrew R. (2012). Masters of War: History's Greatest Strategic Thinkers. The Great Courses. Chantilly, Virginia: The Teaching Company, LLC.

|6.1|
Tap the Power of History to Illuminate, Illustrate, and Inspire: Alexander the Great Emulates the Greek Legends, Heroes & Myths

2. McKeown, Max (2020). The Strategy Book: How to Think and Act Strategically to Deliver Outstanding Results, 3rd Edition. London: Pearson. Pg. xix.
3. Plutarch (1832 [75 A.D.]). Plutarch's Lives of the Most Select and Illustrious Characters of Antiquity. Langhorne, John and Langhorne, William (Translators) NYC: W.C. Borradaile.
4. Everitt, Anthony (2019). Alexander the Great: His Life and His Mysterious Death. NYC: Random House. Pg. 100.
5. Note: To be clear, writes historian Paul Johnson, "no one in [Alexander's] day (or for long after) had any doubt that what Homer described had actually happened."HeroesJohnson30
6. Everitt, Anthony (2019). Alexander the Great: His Life and His Mysterious Death. NYC: Random House. Pg. 100.
7. Doleac, Miles (2014). In the Footsteps of Alexander: The King Who Conquered the Ancient World. NYC: Metro Books. Pgs. 49-53. See Also: Everitt, Anthony (2019). Alexander the Great: His Life and His Mysterious Death. NYC: Random House. Pg. 99.
8. Doleac, Miles (2014). In the Footsteps of Alexander: The King Who Conquered the Ancient World. NYC: Metro Books. Pg. 46.
9. Bose, Partha (2004). Alexander the Great's Art of Strategy: The Timeless Lessons of History's Greatest Empire Builder. NYC: Gotham Books. Pg. 111.
10. Clausewitz, Carl von (2007). On War. Translated by Michael Eliot Howard and Peter Paret. Oxford: Oxford University Press. Pgs. 146-147.
11. Dietrich, William (2015). Napoleon's Rules: Life and Career Lessons from Bonaparte. Burrows Publishing. Pg. 85.
12. Everitt, Anthony (2019). Alexander the Great: His Life and His Mysterious Death. NYC: Random House. Pg. 99.
13. Fox, Robin Lane (2004). Alexander the Great. London: Penguin Group. Pg. 113.
14. Doleac, Miles (2014). In the Footsteps of Alexander: The King Who Conquered the Ancient World. NYC: Metro Books. Pg. 53.
15. Fox, Robin Lane (2004). Alexander the Great. London: Penguin Group. Pg. 60.
16. Bose, Partha (2004). Alexander the Great's Art of Strategy: The Timeless Lessons of History's Greatest Empire Builder. NYC: Gotham Books. Pg. 39.
17. Bose, Partha (2004). Alexander the Great's Art of Strategy: The Timeless Lessons of History's Greatest Empire Builder. NYC: Gotham Books. Pg. 39.
18. Fox, Robin Lane (2004). Alexander the Great. London: Penguin Group. Pg. 60.
19. Bose, Partha (2004). Alexander the Great's Art of Strategy: The Timeless Lessons of History's Greatest Empire Builder. NYC: Gotham Books. Pg. 39.
20. Fox, Robin Lane (2004). Alexander the Great. London: Penguin Group. Pgs. 60-61.
21. Bose, Partha (2004). Alexander the Great's Art of Strategy: The Timeless Lessons of History's Greatest Empire Builder. NYC: Gotham Books. Pg. 113.
22. Fox, Robin Lane (2004). Alexander the Great. London: Penguin Group. Pg. 115
23. Bose, Partha (2004). Alexander the Great's Art of Strategy: The Timeless Lessons of History's Greatest Empire Builder. NYC: Gotham Books. Pg. 113.
24. Kurke, Lance (2004). The Wisdom of Alexander the Great: Enduring Leadership Lessons From the Man Who Created an Empire. NYC: Amacom. Pg. 87.
25. Fox, Robin Lane (2004). Alexander the Great. London: Penguin Group. Pg. 115.
26. Fox, Robin Lane (2004). Alexander the Great. London: Penguin Group. Pg. 115.
27. Fox, Robin Lane (2004). Alexander the Great. London: Penguin Group. Pg. 115.
28. Fox, Robin Lane (2004). Alexander the Great. London: Penguin Group. Pg. 116.
29. Worthington, Ian (2014). By the Spear : Philip II, Alexander the Great, and the Rise and Fall of the Macedonian Empire. Oxford: Oxford University Press. Pg. 141
30. Bose, Partha (2004). Alexander the Great's Art of Strategy: The Timeless Lessons of History's Greatest Empire Builder. NYC: Gotham Books. Pg. 111.
31. Fox, Robin Lane (2004). Alexander the Great. London: Penguin Group. Pg. 60.
32. Fox, Robin Lane (2004). Alexander the Great. London: Penguin Group. Pg. 58.
33. Fox, Robin Lane (2004). Alexander the Great. London: Penguin Group. Pg. 58.
34. Fox, Robin Lane (2004). Alexander the Great. London: Penguin Group. Pg. 60.
35. Bose, Partha (2004). Alexander the Great's Art of Strategy: The Timeless Lessons of History's Greatest Empire Builder. NYC: Gotham Books. Pg. 112.
36. Bose, Partha (2004). Alexander the Great's Art of Strategy: The Timeless Lessons of History's Greatest Empire Builder. NYC: Gotham Books. Pg. 113.
37. Bose, Partha (2004). Alexander the Great's Art of Strategy: The Timeless Lessons of History's Greatest Empire Builder. NYC: Gotham Books. Pg. 113.
38. Fox, Robin Lane (2004). Alexander the Great. London: Penguin Group. Pg. 115.
39. Bowden, Hugh (2014). Alexander the Great: A Very Short Introduction. Oxford: Oxford U. Press. Pg. 61.
40. The Battle of the Granicus is generally recognized by historians as one of the most difficult to reconstruct. The descriptive accounts are said to be too vague. Interestingly, assuming that we are relying on the account recorded by Alexander's official historian, Callisthenes, this may be because Callisthenes, undoubtedly under Alexander's direction, was attempting to paint Alexander as the new Achilles. Rather than an overview, the Battle of Granicus, historian Hugh Bowden explains, is written as a "series of single combats fought by Alexander" which "resembles passages from Homer's Iliad more than anything else." Bowden, Hugh (2014). Alexander the Great: A Very Short Introduction. Oxford: Oxford

University Press. Pg. 61. "The resemblance to Homer may in fact have been deliberate...Early in the description of Achilles' one day of fighting in the Iliad, Homer describes how the hero leaps into the river Scamander in pursuit of the Trojans, and battles with the river itself. Alexander claimed descent from Achilles," writes Bowden, "and Callisthenes' description of the battle—first the leap into the river, and then the sequence of single-combats—will have been as much influenced by a wish to bring out the relationship between the two heroes as by any concern for accurate reportage." Bowden, Hugh (2014). Alexander the Great: A Very Short Introduction. Oxford: Oxford University Press. Pg. 61.

41. Hart, Captain B.H. Liddell (1971). Why Don't We Learn from History? Sophron. Pg. 7.

42. Polybius (1922—1927 [c. 2nd century B.C.]). Paton, William Roger (Translator). The Histories. Cambridge: Harvard University Press. Book 1, Pg. 5.

43. Neustadt, Richard & May, Ernest (1986). Thinking in Time: The Uses of History for Decision Makers. NYC: The Free Press. Pg. 232.

44. Hare, Brian and Woods, Vanessa (2020). Survival of the Friendliest: Understanding Our Origins and Rediscovering Our Common Humanity. NYC: Random House. Pg. xxv.

45. Hare, Brian and Woods, Vanessa (2020). Survival of the Friendliest: Understanding Our Origins and Rediscovering Our Common Humanity. NYC: Random House. Pg. xxv.

46. Hare, Brian and Woods, Vanessa (2020). Survival of the Friendliest: Understanding Our Origins and Rediscovering Our Common Humanity. NYC: Random House. Pg. xxv.

47. Hare, Brian and Woods, Vanessa (2020). Survival of the Friendliest: Understanding Our Origins and Rediscovering Our Common Humanity. NYC: Random House. Pg. xxv.

48. Santayana, George. (2011). The Life of Reason Or The Phases of Human Progress: Reason in Society, Volume VII, Book II. Cambridge: MIT Press. "Those who cannot remember the past are condemned to repeat it."

49. Aesop (1909—1914 [6th century B.C.]), "The Lion, the Fox, and the Beasts." Aesop's Fables, The Harvard Classics, Volume 17, Part 1. As retold by Joseph Jacobs. NYC: P.F. Collier & Son. https://www.bartleby.com/17/1/73.html

50. Machiavelli, Niccolò (1908 [1532]). The Prince. Marriott, W.K. (Translator). J. M. Dent & Company. Pg. 83.

51. Machiavelli, Niccolò (1908 [1532]). The Prince. Marriott, W.K. (Translator). J. M. Dent & Company. Pgs. 83-84.

52. Fox, Robin Lane (2004). Alexander the Great. London: Penguin Group. Pg. 115.

53. Fox, Robin Lane (2004). Alexander the Great. London: Penguin Group. Pg. 115.

54. Grabsky, Phil (Producer). Grabsky, Phil (Director). (1993). The Great Commanders. Alexander the Great—The Battle of Issus (Episode 1) [Documentary Film]. United Kingdom: Ambrose Video Publishing. 6:46.

55. Kemal, Salim et al (Editors)(1998). Nietzsche, Philosophy and the Arts. Cambridge: Cambridge University Press. Pg. 149.

56. Kurke, Lance (2004). The Wisdom of Alexander the Great: Enduring Leadership Lessons From the Man Who Created an Empire. NYC: Amacom. Pg. 87

57. Kurke, Lance (2004). The Wisdom of Alexander the Great: Enduring Leadership Lessons From the Man Who Created an Empire. NYC: Amacom. Pg. 88

58. Kurke, Lance (2004). The Wisdom of Alexander the Great: Enduring Leadership Lessons From the Man Who Created an Empire. NYC: Amacom. Pg. 88

59. Robbins, Anthony (1986). Unlimited Power: The New Science of Personal Achievement. NYC: Simon and Schuster. Pg. 29

60. Irvin, William and Johnson, David K. (2009). Heroes and Philosophy: Buy the Book, Save the World. NYC: Wiley. Pg. 2

61. Emerson, Ralph Waldo (1856). Representative Men: Seven Lectures. Boston: Phillips, Sampson and Company. Pgs. 9-10.

62. Emerson, Ralph Waldo (1856). Representative Men: Seven Lectures. Boston: Phillips, Sampson and Company. Pgs. 9-10.

63. Cartledge, Paul (2004). Alexander the Great. NYC: Vintage Books. Pg. 227.

64. Cartledge, Paul (2004). Alexander the Great. NYC: Vintage Books. Pg. 112.

65. Bose, Partha (2004). Alexander the Great's Art of Strategy: The Timeless Lessons of History's Greatest Empire Builder. NYC: Gotham Books. Pg. 40.

66. Cartledge, Paul (2004). Alexander the Great. NYC: Vintage Books. Pg. 227.

67. Cartledge, Paul (2004). Alexander the Great. NYC: Vintage Books. Pg. 227.

68. Kurke, Lance (2004). The Wisdom of Alexander the Great: Enduring Leadership Lessons From the Man Who Created an Empire. NYC: Amacom. Pg. 87

69. Fox, Robin Lane (2004). Alexander the Great. London: Penguin Group. Pg. 59.

70. Johnson, Paul (2009). Heroes: From Alexander the Great and Julius Caesar to Churchill and De Gaulle. NYC: HarperCollins. Pg. 30.

71. Emerson, Ralph Waldo (2007). The Collected Works of Ralph Waldo Emerson: Society and Solitude, Volume VII. Cambridge: Harvard University Press. Pg. 96.

72. Fox, Robin Lane (2004). Alexander the Great. London: Penguin Group. Pg. 115.

73. Garvey, Patrick (2016, May 2). "Alexander the Great's 3 Heroes." Ancient Heroes. http://ancientheroes.net/blog/alexander-the-greats-3-heroes

74. Garvey, Patrick (2016, May 2). "Alexander the Great's 3 Heroes." Ancient Heroes. http://ancientheroes.net/blog/alexander-the-greats-3-heroes

75 . Bowden, Hugh (2014). Alexander the Great: A Very Short Introduction. Oxford: Oxford University Press. Pg. 115.

76 . Bowden, Hugh (2014). Alexander the Great: A Very Short Introduction. Oxford: Oxford University Press. Pg. 115.

77. Arrian, Flavius (1884). The Anabasis of Alexander; or, The history of the Wars and Conquests of Alexander the Great. E.J. Chinnock (Translator). London: Hodder and Stoughton.

78 . Bowden, Hugh (2014). Alexander the Great: A Very Short Introduction. Oxford: Oxford University Press. Pg. 115.

79. Marden, Orison Swett (1911). Pushing to the Front. Petersburg, NY: The Success Company's. Pg. 810.

80. Marden, Orison Swett (1911). Pushing to the Front. Petersburg, NY: The Success Company's. Pg. 810.

81. Marden, Orison Swett (1911). Pushing to the Front. Petersburg, NY: The Success Company's. Pg. 809.

82. Marden, Orison Swett (1911). Pushing to the Front. Petersburg, NY: The Success Company's. Pg. 809.

83. Marden, Orison Swett (1911). Pushing to the Front. Petersburg, NY: The Success Company's. Pg. 809.

84. Marden, Orison Swett (1911). Pushing to the Front. Petersburg, NY: The Success Company's. Pg. 804.

85. Marden, Orison Swett (1911). Pushing to the Front. Petersburg, NY: The Success Company's. Pg. 804.

86. Marden, Orison Swett (1911). Pushing to the Front. Petersburg, NY: The Success Company's. Pg. 807.

87. Hellmann, John (1999). The Kennedy Obsession: The American Myth of JFK. NYC: Columbia University Press. Pg. 29.

88. Gergen, David (2001). Eyewitness to Power: The Essence of Leadership Nixon to Clinton. NYC: Simon & Schuster. Pg. 44.

89. Cronin, Thomas E. (2008). "'All the World's a Stage...' Acting and the Art of Political Leadership." Leadership Quarterly, Volume 19, Number 4. Pg. 460.

90. Maney, Patrick J. (1992). The Roosevelt Presence: The Life and Legacy of FDR. Los Angeles: University of California Press. Pg. 202.

91. Dalton, Kathleen (2002). Theodore Roosevelt: A Strenuous Life. NYC: Random House. Pg. 521.

92. Strauss, Leo (2018). On Political Philosophy: Responding to the Challenge of Positivism and Historicism. London: The University of Chicago Press. Pg. 123.

93. Axelrod, Alan (2013). Catherine the Great CEO: 7 Principles to Guide and Inspire Modern Leaders. NYC: Sterling. Pgs. 59-60.

94. Axelrod, Alan (2013). Catherine the Great CEO: 7 Principles to Guide and Inspire Modern Leaders. NYC: Sterling. Pg. 183

95. Axelrod, Alan (2013). Catherine the Great CEO: 7 Principles to Guide and Inspire Modern Leaders. NYC: Sterling. Pg. 182

96. Axelrod, Alan (2013). Catherine the Great CEO: 7 Principles to Guide and Inspire Modern Leaders. NYC: Sterling. Pg. 183.

97. Greene, Robert (1998). The 48 Laws of Power. NYC: Penguin Books. Pg. 60.

98. Greene, Robert (1998). The 48 Laws of Power. NYC: Penguin Books. Pg. 60.

99. Franklin, Benjamin ([1750], 1914). Poor Richard's Almanack. Waterloo, Iowa: The U.S.C. Publishing Co. Pg. 61 (#651).

100. Fujii, Satoshi (Editor)(2015). Beyond Global Capitalism. Tokyo: Springer. Pg. 73.

101. Hart, Captain B.H. Liddell (1971). Why Don't We Learn from History? Sophron. Pg. 5.

102. Polybius (1922—1927 [c. 2nd century B.C.]). Paton, William Roger (Translator). The Histories. Cambridge: Harvard University Press. Book 1, Pg. 5.

103. Polybius (1922—1927 [c. 2nd century B.C.]). Paton, William Roger (Translator). The Histories. Cambridge: Harvard University Press. Book 1, Pg. 99.

104. Unger, Miles J. (2011). Machiavelli: A Biography. NYC: Simon & Schuster. Pg. 270.

105. Hart, Captain B.H. Liddell (1971). Why Don't We Learn from History? Sophron. Pg. 5.

106. Hart, Captain B.H. Liddell (1971). Why Don't We Learn from History? Sophron. Pg. 5.

107. Burns, James MacGregor (Senior Editor)(2004). Encyclopedia of Leadership, Volume 1. Thousand Oaks: Sage. Pg. 664.

108. Burns, James MacGregor (Senior Editor)(2004). Encyclopedia of Leadership, Volume 1. Thousand Oaks: Sage. Pg. 664.

109. Burns, James MacGregor (Senior Editor)(2004). Encyclopedia of Leadership, Volume 1. Thousand Oaks: Sage. Pg. 664.

110. Aesop (1909—1914 [6th century B.C.]), "The Lion, the Fox, and the Beasts." Aesop's Fables, The Harvard Classics, Volume 17, Part 1. As retold by Joseph Jacobs. NYC: P.F. Collier & Son. https://www.bartleby.com/17/1/73.html

111. Stewart, Andrew (1993). Faces of Power: Alexander's Image and Hellenistic Politics. Berkeley: University of California Press. Pg. 85.

112. Stewart, Andrew (1993). Faces of Power: Alexander's Image and Hellenistic Politics. Berkeley: University of California Press. Pg. 85.

|6.2|

Make History Work:
Napoleon Bonaparte Taps the Power
of the Past to Shape the Future

1. Foch, General Ferdinand (1918). The Principles of War. J.Morinni (Translator). NYC: The H.K. Fly Co. Pg. 19.

2. Bonaparte, Napoleon (1845). Military Maxims of Napoleon. Translated by J. Akerly. NYC: Wiley and Putnam. Pgs. 67-70.

3. The Holy Bible, English Standard Version (ESV)(2016). Proverbs 16:16. Biblegateway.com. Biblica, Inc. https://www.biblegateway.com/passage/?search=Proverbs+16%3A16&version=ESV

4. Roberts, Andrew (2014). Napoleon: A Life. NYC: Viking. Pg. 207.

5. Anonymous (1846). Anecdotes of Napoleon Bonaparte, His Ministers, His Generals, His Soldiers and His Times. Manchester: S. Johnson & Son. Pg. 193.

6. Schom, Alan (1997). Napoleon Bonaparte. NYC: HarperCollins. Pg. 273.

7. Schom, Alan (1997). Napoleon Bonaparte. NYC: HarperCollins. Pg. 274.

8. Roberts, Andrew (2014). Napoleon: A Life. NYC: Viking. Pg. 207.

9. Schom, Alan (1997). Napoleon Bonaparte. NYC: HarperCollins. Pg. 274.

10. Anonymous (1846). Anecdotes of Napoleon Bonaparte, His Ministers, His Generals, His Soldiers and His Times. Manchester: S. Johnson & Son. Pg. 191.

11. Anonymous (1846). Anecdotes of Napoleon Bonaparte, His Ministers, His Generals, His Soldiers and His Times. Manchester: S. Johnson & Son. Pg. 193.

12. Roberts, Andrew (2014). Napoleon: A Life. NYC: Viking. Pg. 208.

13. Roberts, Andrew (2014). Napoleon: A Life. NYC: Viking. Pg. 208.

14. Alberge, Dalya (2014, September 27). "Plot to kill Napoleon linked to British cabinet minister." The Guardian. https://www.theguardian.com/world/2014/sep/2

7/plot-kill-napoleon-linked-to-cabinet-minister-castlereagh

15. Markham, Felix (1966). Napoleon. NYC: Mentor. Pg. 101

16. Cronin, Vincent (1988). Napoleon. NYC: Penguin. Pg. 302.

17. Westlake, Hannah (Editor)(2018). "The Star of Napoleon Ascendant." History of War Book of the Napoleonic Wars, Second Edition. Bournemouth: Future Publishing Limited. Pg. 23.

18. Westlake, Hannah (Editor)(2018). "The Star of Napoleon Ascendant." History of War Book of the Napoleonic Wars, Second Edition. Bournemouth: Future Publishing Limited. Pg. 23.

19. Cronin, Vincent (1988). Napoleon. NYC: Penguin. Pg. 302.

20. Roberts, Andrew (2014). Napoleon: A Life. NYC: Viking. Pg. 208.

21. Cronin, Vincent (1988). Napoleon. NYC: Penguin. Pg. 301.

22. Markham, Felix (1966). Napoleon. NYC: Mentor. Pg. 100.

23. Cronin, Vincent (1988). Napoleon. NYC: Penguin. Pg. 301.

24. Cronin, Vincent (1988). Napoleon. NYC: Penguin. Pg. 301.

25. Cronin, Vincent (1988). Napoleon. NYC: Penguin. Pg. 313 (ebook).

26. Markham, Felix (1966). Napoleon. NYC: Mentor. Pg. 100

27. McLynn, Frank (2011). Napoleon: A Biography. NYC: Arcade Publishing. Pg. 296.

28. Markham, Felix (1966). Napoleon. NYC: Mentor. Pg. 100

29. Cronin, Vincent (1988). Napoleon. NYC: Penguin. Pg. 304.

30. Cronin, Vincent (1988). Napoleon. NYC: Penguin. Pg. 300.

31. Roberts, Andrew (2015, June). "Why We'd Be Better Off if Napoleon Never Lost at Waterloo." Smithsonian Magazine. Washington, D.C.: Smithsonian Institution. https://www.smithsonianmag.com/history/we-better-off-napoleon-never-lost-waterloo-180955298/

32. Bonaparte, Napoleon (1845). Military Maxims of Napoleon. Translated by J. Akerly. NYC: Wiley and Putnam. Pgs. 67-70.

33. Anonymous (1846). Anecdotes of Napoleon Bonaparte, His Ministers, His Generals, His Soldiers and His Times. Manchester: S. Johnson & Son. Pg. 311.

34. Anonymous (1846). Anecdotes of Napoleon Bonaparte, His Ministers, His Generals, His Soldiers and His Times. Manchester: S. Johnson & Son. Pg. 311.

35. Roberts, Andrew (2014). Napoleon: A Life. NYC: Viking. Pg. 208.

36. McLynn, Frank (2011). Napoleon: A Biography. NYC: Arcade Publishing. Pg. 297.

37. Cronin, Vincent (1988). Napoleon. NYC: Penguin. Pg. 303.

38. Anonymous (1846). Anecdotes of Napoleon Bonaparte, His Ministers, His Generals, His Soldiers and His Times. Manchester: S. Johnson & Son. Pg. 310.

39. Cronin, Vincent (1988). Napoleon. NYC: Penguin. Pg. 306.

40. Cronin, Vincent (1988). Napoleon. NYC: Penguin. Pg. 306.

41. Westlake, Hannah (Editor)(2018). "The Star of Napoleon Ascendant." History of War Book of the Napoleonic Wars, Second Edition. Bournemouth: Future Publishing Limited. Pg. 23.

42. The cover of this book, as well as the symbol we use for our podcast, Classic Influence, is from a coin of Napoleon Bonaparte portrayed as Julius Caesar, crowned with a laurel wreath. The olive tree is also a frequent symbol in the Old Testament. In Genesis, for example, after spending a year on the Ark, a dove returns with an olive leaf, which let Noah know that it was now safe to open the Ark and return to land.

43. Cronin, Vincent (1988). Napoleon. NYC: Penguin. Pg. 306.

44. Westlake, Hannah (Editor)(2018). "The Star of Napoleon Ascendant." History of War Book of the Napoleonic Wars, Second Edition. Bournemouth: Future Publishing Limited. Pg. 23.

45. Knighton, Andrew (2016, March 14). "5 Ways Napoleon Made Himself into the New Charlemagne." War History Online. Irving, TX: Timera.

46. Duggan, William (2003). The Art of What Works. NYC: McGraw-Hill. Pg. xi.

47. Emmanuel, comte de Las Cases (1890). Memoirs of the Life, Exile, and Conversations of the Emperor Napoleon. NYC: Worthington, Co. Pg. 140.

48. Humes, James C. (1997). Confessions of a White House Ghostwriter: Five Presidents and Other Political Adventures. Washington, D.C.: Regenery Publishing, Pgs. 28-29.

49. Mansfield, Stephen (1995). Never Give In: The Extraordinary Character of Winston Churchill. Nashville: Cumberland House. Pg. 200.

50. Gilbert, Martin (1966). Winston S. Churchill: Never Despair, 1945—1965. Hillsdale: Hillsdale College Press. Pg. 459.

51. Gergen, David (2001). Eyewitness to Power: The Essence of Leadership Nixon to Clinton. NYC: Simon & Schuster. Pg. 42.

52. Gabriel, Richard A. (2001). Great Captains of Antiquity. Westport, CT: Greenwood Publishing Group. Pg. xvi.

53. Hart, Captain B.H. Liddell (1971). Why Don't We Learn from History? Sophron. Pg. 8.

54. Hart, Captain B.H. Liddell (1971). Why Don't We Learn from History? Sophron. Pg. 7.

55. Hart, Captain B.H. Liddell (1971). Why Don't We Learn from History? Sophron. Pg. 7.

56. Mansfield, Stephen (1995). Never Give In: The Extraordinary Character of Winston Churchill. Nashville: Cumberland House. Pg. 200.

57. Roberts, Andrew (2014). Napoleon: A Life. NYC: Viking. Pg. 305.

58. Roberts, Andrew (2014). Napoleon: A Life. NYC: Viking. Pg. 305.

59. Roberts, Andrew (2014). Napoleon: A Life. NYC: Viking. Pg. 305.

60. Emmanuel, comte de Las Cases (1890). Memoirs of the Life, Exile, and Conversations of the Emperor Napoleon. NYC: Worthington, Co. Pg. 140.

61. Emmanuel, comte de Las Cases (1890). Memoirs of the Life, Exile, and Conversations of the Emperor Napoleon. NYC: Worthington, Co. Pg. 141.

62. Emmanuel, comte de Las Cases (1890). Memoirs of the Life, Exile, and Conversations of the Emperor Napoleon. NYC: Worthington, Co. Pg. 141.

63. Williams, Robert C. (2007). The Historian's Toolbox: A Student's Guide to the Theory and Craft of History, 2nd Edition. London: M.E. Sharpe. Pg. 156.

64. Murrow, Edward R. "Winston Churchill's Way With Words." NPR. https://www.npr.org/transcripts/156720829

65. Thompson, Derek (2017). Hit Makers: The Science of Popularity in an Age of Distraction. Pg. 28.

66. Thompson, Derek (2017). Hit Makers: The Science of Popularity in an Age of Distraction. Pg. 29.

67. Thompson, Derek (2017). Hit Makers: The Science of Popularity in an Age of Distraction. Pg. 11.

68. Knighton, Andrew (2016, March 14). "5 Ways Napoleon Made Himself into the New Charlemagne." War History Online. Irving, TX: Timera.

69. Cialdini, Robert (2001). Influence: Science and Practice, 4th Edition. Boston: Allyn and Bacon. Pg. 154.

70. Cialdini, Robert (2001). Influence: Science and Practice, 4th Edition. Boston: Allyn and Bacon. Pg. 154.

71. Thompson, Derek (2017). Hit Makers: The Science of Popularity in an Age of Distraction. Pg. 11.

72. Zarzeczny, Matthew (2005). "Napoleon and the Unification of Europe." The Napoleon Series. https://www.napoleon-series.org/research/napoleon/c_unification.html

73. Roberts, Andrew (2001). Napoleon & Wellington: The Battle of Waterloo and the Great Commanders Who Fought It. NYC: Simon & Schuster. Pg. 298.

74. Zarzeczny, Matthew (2005). "Napoleon and the Unification of Europe." The Napoleon Series. https://www.napoleon-series.org/research/napoleon/c_unification.html

75. Knighton, Andrew (2016, March 14). "5 Ways Napoleon Made Himself into the New Charlemagne." War History Online. Irving, TX: Timera.

76. Knighton, Andrew (2016, March 14). "5 Ways Napoleon Made Himself into the New Charlemagne." War History Online. Irving, TX: Timera.

77. Knighton, Andrew (2016, March 14). "5 Ways Napoleon Made Himself into the New Charlemagne." War History Online. Irving, TX: Timera.

78. Roberts, Andrew (2014). Napoleon: A Life. NYC: Viking. Pg. 246.

79. Roberts, Andrew (2014). Napoleon: A Life. NYC: Viking. Pg. 246.

80. Roberts, Andrew (2014). Napoleon: A Life. NYC: Viking. Pg. 246.

81. Roberts, Andrew (2014). Napoleon: A Life. NYC: Viking. Pg. 246.

82. Roberts, Andrew (2014). Napoleon: A Life. NYC: Viking. Pg. 246.

83. Roberts, Andrew (2014). Napoleon: A Life. NYC: Viking. Pg. 246.

84. Knighton, Andrew (2016, March 14). "5 Ways Napoleon Made Himself into the New Charlemagne." War History Online. Irving, TX: Timera.

85. Knighton, Andrew (2016, March 14). "5 Ways Napoleon Made Himself into the New Charlemagne." War History Online. Irving, TX: Timera.

86. Hood, Jeff (2017, January 5). "The Power of Symbols." St. Luke's Innovative Resources. https://innovativeresources.org/the-power-of-symbols/

87. Hood, Jeff (2017, January 5). "The Power of Symbols." St. Luke's Innovative Resources.

88. Hood, Jeff (2017, January 5). "The Power of Symbols." St. Luke's Innovative Resources. https://innovativeresources.org/the-power-of-symbols/

89. Jung, Carl G. (1998). Jung on Mythology. Segal, Robert A. (Editor). Princeton: Princeton University Press. Pg. 96.

90. Westlake, Hannah (Editor)(2018). "The Star of Napoleon Ascendant." History of War Book of the Napoleonic Wars, Second Edition. Bournemouth: Future Publishing Limited. Pg. 16.

91. Newton, Isaac (1675, February 5). "Letter from Sir Isaac Newton to Robert Hooke." Historical Society of Pennsylvania. https://digitallibrary.hsp.org/index.php/Detail/objects/9792

|6.3|

Build an Arsenal of Analogies, a Foundation of Relevant History, Recurring Patterns and Themes: President Harry Truman Taps History to Navigate the U.S. Ship of State

1. Miller, Merle (1974). *Plain Speaking: An Oral Biography of Harry S. Truman.* NYC: Berkley Publishing. Pg. 46.

2. *The Holy Bible, New International Version* (2011). Book of Ecclesiastes. Biblegateway.com. Biblica, Inc. https://www.biblegateway.com/passage/?search=Ecclesiastes+1%3A9&version=NIV

|6.3.1|

Construct a Foundation to Accelerate Learning, Wisdom,and Growth: Harry Truman Takes the Reigns of the Presidency Following the Death of FDR

3. Boller Jr., Paul F. (2007). Presidential Diversions: Presidents at Play from George Washington to George W. Bush. Orlando: Harcourt, Inc. Pg. 244.

4. Wikipedia contributors. (2022). "Historical rankings of presidents of the United States." Wikipedia, The Free Encyclopedia. Note: Polls used cover a broad political spectrum, including Schlesinger, C-SPAN, Wall Street Journal, Times, Siena, USPC, APSA, and PSN. https://en.wikipedia.org/wiki/Historical_rankings_of_presidents_of_the_United_States

5. Truman, Harry S. (1955). The Memoirs of Harry S. Truman, Volume 1: Year of Decisions: 1945. NYC: Doubleday. Pg. 5.

6. McCullough, David (1992). Truman. NYC: Simon and Schuster. Pg. 260. (ebook)

7. McCullough, David (1992). Truman. NYC: Simon and Schuster. Pg. 260. (ebook)

8. McCullough, David (1992). Truman. NYC: Simon and Schuster. Pg. 260. (ebook)

9. McCullough, David (1992). Truman. NYC: Simon and Schuster. Pg. 262. (ebook)

10 . Truman, Harry S. (1955). The Memoirs of Harry S. Truman, Volume 1: Year of Decisions: 1945. NYC: Doubleday. Pgs. 19-20.

11. McCullough, David (1992). Truman. NYC: Simon and Schuster. Pg. 262. (ebook)

12. McCullough, David (1992). Truman. NYC: Simon and Schuster. Pg. 262. (ebook)

13. McCullough, David (1992). Truman. NYC: Simon and Schuster. Pg. 433.

14. McCullough, David (1992). Truman. NYC: Simon and Schuster. Pg. 433.

15. McCullough, David (1992). Truman. NYC: Simon and Schuster. Pg. 433. (ebook261)

16. Grubin, David (Producer). (1997). Truman. American Experience. PBS. [Documentary Film]. United States: David Grubin Productions, Inc. Transcript: http://www.shoppbs.pbs.org/wgbh/amex/truman/filmmore/pt.html

17. McCullough, David (1992). Truman. NYC: Simon and Schuster. Pg. 267. (ebook)

18. Plato (1875). The Dialogues of Plato. B. Jowett (Translator). Oxford: Oxford University Press. Pg. 85.

19. Truman, Harry S. (1955). The Memoirs of Harry S. Truman, Volume 1: Year of Decisions: 1945. NYC: Doubleday. Pgs.11-12

20. Truman, Margaret (1990). Where the Buck Stops: The Personal and Private Writings of Harry S. Truman. NYC: Grand Central Publishing. Pg. 15.

21. Truman, Margaret (1990). Where the Buck Stops: The Personal and Private Writings of Harry S. Truman. NYC: Grand Central Publishing. Pg. 15.

22. Staff Writer (2015, June 18). "Recommended Reading from Harry Truman." Truman Library Institute. https://www.trumanlibraryinstitute.org/tru-history/

23. Levine, Timothy R. (Editor)(2014). Encyclopedia of Deception, Volume 1. Los Angeles: Sage. Pg. 454.

24. Levine, Timothy R. (Editor)(2014). Encyclopedia of Deception, Volume 1. Los Angeles: Sage. Pg. 454.

25. Machiavelli, Niccolò (1883 [1531]). Discourses on the First Decade of Titus Livius. Ninian Hill Thomson (Translator). London: Kegan Paul, Trench & Co. Book III, Pg. 43.

26. Allgood, Jay R. (2004). Embracing History's Lessons: What Every College Graduate Should Know. Agreka Books. 23

27. Allgood, Jay R. (2004). Embracing History's Lessons: What Every College Graduate Should Know. Agreka Books. 24

28. Allgood, Jay R. (2004). Embracing History's Lessons: What Every College Graduate Should Know. Agreka Books. 24

29. Kagan, Donald (2001). "While America Sleeps." American Diplomacy, Volume VI, Number 1. https://ciaotest.cc.columbia.edu/olj/ad/ad_v6_1/kad01.html See also: https://www.fpri.org/article/2000/11/while-america-sleeps/

30. Aurelius, Marcus (2002 [Circa 170-180 A.D.). The Meditations. NYC: Random House, Inc. Pg. 113.

31. Hooker, Roderick et al (2017). Physician Assistants: Policy and Practice, 4th Edition. Philadelphia: F.A. Davis Company. Pg. 15.

32. Lincoln, Abraham (1862, December 1). "Annual Message to Congress—Concluding Remarks." In Collected Works of Abraham Lincoln, Basler, Roy P. (Editor) Washington, D.C. https://www.abrahamlincolnonline.org/lincoln/speeches/congress.htm Note: Lincoln was talking to the legislature about how they would be judged by history. Nevertheless, his remark captures the essence of the idea that history is a record of the past that will influence our perceptions in the future and, thereby, the future itself.

33. Jung, Carl (1968). The Collected Works of C.G. Jung: Civilization in Transition, Volume 10. Princeton: Princeton University Press. Pg. 130.

34. Lee, Walter (2022). Principles and Laws in World Politics. Singapore: World Scientific Publishing Co. Pg. 147.

35. Humes, James C. (1997). Confessions of a White House Ghostwriter: Five Presidents and Other Political Adventures. Washington, D.C.: Regenery Publishing, Pgs. 28-29.

36. Bailey, Mark (2017, August 11). "History Teaches You How to Run the Country." The Times. https://www.thetimes.co.uk/article/history-teaches-you-how-to-run-the-country-7nsz3xrns

37. Wikipedia contributors. (2022). "Historical rankings of presidents of the United States." Wikipedia, The Free Encyclopedia. https://en.wikipedia.org/wiki/Historical_rankings_of_presidents_of_the_United_States

38. Beschloss, Michael R. (2003). The Presidents: Every Leader from Washington to Bush. NY: Crown Books. Pg. 327.

39. Staff Writer (2015, June 18). "Recommended Reading from Harry Truman." Truman Library Institute. https://www.trumanlibraryinstitute.org/tru-history/

40. McCullough, David (1992). Truman. NYC: Simon and Schuster. Pg. 43.

41. McCullough, David (1992). Truman. NYC: Simon and Schuster. Pg. 43.

42. Truman, Harry S. (1955). The Memoirs of Harry S. Truman, Volume 1: Year of Decisions: 1945. NYC: Doubleday. Pg.209

43. McCullough, David (1992). Truman. NYC: Simon and Schuster. Pg. 43.

44. McCullough, David (1992). Truman. NYC: Simon and Schuster. Pg. 58.

45. Truman, Harry S. (1955). The Memoirs of Harry S. Truman, Volume 1: Year of Decisions: 1945. NYC: Doubleday. Pg.209

46. Truman, Harry S. (1955). The Memoirs of Harry S. Truman, Volume 1: Year of Decisions: 1945. NYC: Doubleday. Pg.208-209

47. McCullough, David (1992). Truman. NYC: Simon and Schuster. Pg. 58.

48. Truman, Harry S. (1955). The Memoirs of Harry S. Truman, Volume 1: Year of Decisions: 1945. NYC: Doubleday. Pg.208

49. Truman, Harry S. (1955). The Memoirs of Harry S. Truman, Volume 1: Year of Decisions: 1945. NYC: Doubleday. Pg.210

50. Truman, Harry S. (1955). The Memoirs of Harry S. Truman, Volume 1: Year of Decisions: 1945. NYC: Doubleday. Pg.208

51. Humes, James C. (1997). Confessions of a White House Ghostwriter: Five Presidents and Other Political Adventures. Washington, D.C.: Regenery Publishing, Pgs. 28-29.

52. Truman, Harry S. (1955). The Memoirs of Harry S. Truman, Volume 1: Year of Decisions: 1945. NYC: Doubleday. Pg. 46

53. Franklin, Benjamin (1818). Memoirs of the Life and Writings of Benjamin Franklin. London: A.J. Valpy. Pg. 60.

54. Cairnes, William E. (Editor)(2016). The Military Maxims of Napoleon. NYC: Skyhorse Publishing. Pg. 205 (Maxim LXXVIII).

55. Neustadt, Richard E. (1990). Presidential Power and the Modern Presidents: The Politics of Leadership from Roosevelt to Reagan. NYC: The Free Press. Pgs. 304-305.

56. Williams, Ryan (2016). The Influencer Economy: How to Launch Your Idea, Share It With the World, and Thrive in the Digital Age. San Bernardino, CA: Ryan Williams. Pg. 14.

57. Gabriel, Richard A. (2001). Great Captains of Antiquity. Westport, CT: Greenwood Publishing Group. Pg. xvi.

58. Grubin, David (Producer). (1997). Truman. American Experience. PBS. [Documentary Film]. United States: David Grubin Productions, Inc. Transcript: http://www.shoppbs.pbs.org/wgbh/amex/truman/filmmore/pt.html

59. Emerson, Ralph Waldo (2000). "Power," and "Wealth," essays in The Conduct of Life [1860]. The Essential Writings of Ralph Waldo Emerson. NYC: The Modern Library. London: William Clowes and Sons. Pg. 696.

60. The Holy Bible, New International Version (2011). Book of Matthew 25:29. Biblegateway.com. Biblica, Inc. https://www.biblegateway.com/passage/?search=Matthew+25%3A29&version=NIV

61. The Holy Bible, New International Version (2011). Book of Matthew 25:24-30. Biblegateway.com. Biblica, Inc. https://www.biblegateway.com/passage/?search=Matthew+25%3A24-30&version=NIV

62. Rigney, Daniel (2010). The Matthew Effect: How Advantage Begets Further Advantage. NYC: Columbia University Press. Pg. vii.

63. Leslie, Ian (2014). Curious: The Desire to Know and Why Your Future Depends On It. NYC: Basic Books. Pg. 115.

64. Leslie (2014), Pg. 121.

65. Leslie (2014), Pg. 121.

66. Leslie (2014), Pg. 121.

67. Leslie (2014), Pg. 114.

68. Leslie (2014), Pg. 114.

69. Leslie (2014), Pg. 114.

70. Connors, Michael; Burns, Bruce; and Campitelli, Guillermo (2011, October 7). "Expertise in Complex Decision Making: The Role of Search in Chess 70 Years After de Groot." Cognitive Science, Volume 35, Issue 8. Pg. 1567. https://onlinelibrary.wiley.com/doi/full/10.1111/j.1551-6709.2011.01196.x#b22

71. Connors, Michael; Burns, Bruce; and Campitelli, Guillermo (2011, October 7). "Expertise in Complex Decision Making: The Role of Search in Chess 70 Years After de Groot." Cognitive Science, Volume 35, Issue 8. Pg. 1567. https://onlinelibrary.wiley.com/doi/full/10.1111/j.1551-6709.2011.01196.x#b22

72. Recht, D. R., & Leslie, L. (1988). Effect of prior knowledge on good and poor readers' memory of text. Journal of Educational Psychology, 80(1), Pgs. 16-20. https://doi.org/10.1037/0022-0663.80.1.16

73. Wexler, Natalie (2019, April 29). "Why Memorizing Stuff Can Be Good for You." Forbes. https://www.forbes.com/sites/nataliewexler/2019/04/29/why-memorizing-stuff-can-be-good-for-you/?sh=34d927193c4f

74. Wexler, Natalie (2019, April 29). "Why Memorizing Stuff Can Be Good for You." Forbes. https://www.forbes.com/sites/nataliewexler/2019/04/29/why-memorizing-stuff-can-be-good-for-you/?sh=34d927193c4f

75. Leslie (2014), Pg. 114.

76. Diaz de Chumaceiro, Cora (1999). "Serendipity." In Encyclopedia of Creativity, Volume 2. San Diego: Academic Press. Pg. 547.

77. Leslie (2014), Pg. 131.

78. Young, James Webb (2007). A Technique for Producing Ideas. NYC: McGraw-Hill. Pg. 9. See also: Leslie, Ian (2014). Curious: The Desire to Know and Why Your Future Depends On It. NYC: Basic Books. Pg. 131.

79. Leslie (2014), Pg. 131.

80. Seaman, John T. and Smith, George David (2012, December). "Your Company's History as a Leadership Tool." Harvard Business Review. https://hbr.org/2012/12/your-companys-history-as-a-leadership-tool

81. Seaman, John T. and Smith, George David (2012, December). "Your Company's History as a Leadership Tool." Harvard Business Review. https://hbr.org/2012/12/your-companys-history-as-a-leadership-tool

82. Seaman, John T. and Smith, George David (2012, December). "Your Company's History as a Leadership Tool." Harvard Business Review. https://hbr.org/2012/12/your-companys-history-as-a-leadership-tool

83. Seaman, John T. and Smith, George David (2012, December). "Your Company's History as a Leadership Tool." Harvard Business Review. https://hbr.org/2012/12/your-companys-history-as-a-leadership-tool

84. Note: Interestingly, meteorologists are far more accurate forecasters than most people imagine. Shepherd, Marshall (2019, April 2). "How Meteorologists Compare to Other Professions That Predict the Future." Forbes. https://www.forbes.com/sites/marshallshepherd/2019/04/02/how-meteorologists-compare-to-other-professions-that-predict-the-future/?sh=2704cfd85698

85. Abshire, David M. (2008). A Call to Greatness: Challenging our Next President. NYC: Roman and Littlefield Publishers, Inc. Pg. 7

86. Plato (c. 380 B.C. [1992]). Republic. Cambridge, MA: Hackett Publishing Co. Pg. 216.

87. Durant, Will (1955). "The Greatest Ten Thinkers: A Scholar Places Our Times in the Context of Ideas, Ranking These Minds High." The Rotarian, February 1955. Pg. 39.

88. Aristotle (1883). The Politics of Aristotle. Translated by J.E.C. Welldon, M.A. London: Macmillan and Co.

89. Paraphrasing the great philosopher, President Woodrow Wilson said that Aristotle, "outlined a cycle of degeneracies and revolutions through which, as he conceived, every State of long life was apt to pass," and "the cycle is completed," Wilson continues, when "democracy...loses its early respect for law, its first amiability of mutual concession. It breaks out into license and Anarchy, and none but a Caesar can bring it back to reason and order. The throne is set up again, and a new series of deteriorations and revolutions begins." Source: Wilson, Woodrow (1889). The State:

Elements of Historical and Practical Politics (Classic Reprint) Boston: D.C. Heath & Co. Pgs. 577-578.

The record of leaders and historians and political philosophers pointing to the importance of recurring patterns, cycles and themes continues on to this day. Perhaps most familiar is Karl Marx, who wrote in the beginning of the Communist Manifesto: "The history of all hitherto existing society is the history of class struggles. Freeman and slave, patrician and plebeian, lord and serf, guild-master and journeyman, in a word, oppressor and oppressed, stood in constant opposition to one another, carried on an uninterrupted, now hidden, now open fight, a fight that each time ended, either in a revolutionary reconstitution of society at large, or in the common ruin of the contending classes." **Source**: Marx, Karl & Engels, Friedrich (2008). The Communist Manifesto (Oxford World's Classics). NYC: Oxford University Press. Pg. 3.

Many historians have written persuasively about the cycle from conqueror to conquered or the rise and fall and rebirth of civilizations.WhyHistoryRepeats8 Other historians and leading thinkers tend toward the investigation of recurring themes or the back-and-forth of the pendulum. Still others prefer the spiral or the upward circular movement of the single helix. The presidential historian, Arthur M. Schlesinger Jr. writes: "Wise men have remarked on patterns of alternation, of ebb and of flow, in human history. 'The two parties which divide the state, the party of Conservatism and that of Innovation,' wrote [Ralph Waldo] Emerson in 1841, 'are very old, and have disputed the possession of the world ever since it was made... Now one, now the other gets the day, and still the fight renews itself as if for the first time, under new names and hot personalities.' Innovation presses ever forward; Conservativism holds ever back. We are reformers spring and summer, in autumn and winter we stand by the old; reformers in the morning, conservers at night." **Source**: Schlesinger Jr., Arthur M. (1999). The Cycles of American History. NYC: First Mariner Books. Pg. 23.

90. Soros, George (1997, February). "The Capitalist Threat." *Atlantic Monthly*, Volume 279, No. 2, February 1997. Pgs. 45-58. Last Accessed: August 8, 2011. https://www.theatlantic.com/magazine/archive/1997/02/the-capitalist-threat/376773/

91 . Machiavelli, Niccolò (1883 [1531]). Discourses on the First Decade of Titus Livius. Ninian Hill Thomson (Translator). London: Kegan Paul, Trench & Co. Pgs. 332-333.

92. Hobbes, Thomas; Thucydides, Homer (1840). The English Works of Thomas Hobbes of Malmesbury, Volume VI. London: John Bohn. Pg. 418.

93. Locke, John (1821). Two Treatises of Government. London: Whitmore and Fenn, Charing Cross; and C. Brown. Pgs. 370-371.

94. Truman, Harry S. (1955). The Memoirs of Harry S. Truman, Volume 1: Year of Decisions: 1945. NYC: Doubleday. Pg. 210.

95. Rushay Jr., Samuel W. (2009). "Harry Truman's History Lessons." Prologue Magazine, Volume 41, Number 1. http://www.archives.gov/publications/prologue/2009/spring/truman-history.html

96. Rushay Jr., Samuel W. (2009). "Harry Truman's History Lessons." Prologue Magazine, Volume 41, Number 1.

http://www.archives.gov/publications/prologue/2009/spring/truman-history.html

97. Rushay Jr., Samuel W. (2009). "Harry Truman's History Lessons." Prologue Magazine, Volume 41, Number 1. http://www.archives.gov/publications/prologue/2009/spring/truman-history.html

98. Consider, for example, the following six potential benefits.

(1.) Enhances Understanding. Isaiah Berlin once said, "to understand is to perceive patterns" (pg. 129). In fact, the British historian and political theorist wrote, "to offer historical explanations is not merely to describe a succession of events, but to make it intelligible; to make it intelligible is to reveal the basic pattern..." (pg. 129). In today's world we are flooded with facts and information. As you become adept at identifying and investigating patterns—both from the broad sweep of history as well as the more immediate past—you can learn to screen out the mass of data and noise and focus on the facts and relationships that matter most. You can improve your comprehension of the road traveled and, thereby, enhance your understanding and insight for the road ahead. **Source**: Berlin, Isaiah (1949 [2000]). *The Proper Study of Mankind: An Anthology of Essays.* NYC: Farrar, Straus and Giroux. Pg. 129. Full quote: "To understand is to perceive patterns. To offer historical explanations is not merely to describe a succession of events, but to make it intelligible; to make it intelligible is to reveal the basic pattern—not one of several possible patterns, but the one unique plan which, by being as it is fulfills only one particular purpose, and consequently is revealed as fitting in a specifiable fashion within the single 'cosmic' overall schema which is the goal of the universe, the goal in virtue of which alone it is a universe at all, and not a chaos of unrelated bits and pieces. The more thoroughly the nature of this purpose is understood, and with it the pattern it entails in the various forms of human activity, the more explanatory or illuminating—the 'deeper'—the activity of the historian will be."

(2.) Helps to Identify Direction and Improve Vision. Recognizing the patterns of history can help in detecting the broader movement and direction of society, industries within society, and other key environmental forces. One of the key attributes of visionary leaders is their grasp of history. As Harvard Kennedy School professor David Gergen, advisor to five U.S. Presidents, writes in his book, Eyewitness to Power, "Nixon was accustomed to measuring time in decades and centuries, so he liked to think about what forces would be at work a decade or century hence. [...] His capacity as a visionary exceeds that of other presidents in modern times and was squarely based upon his understanding of history." **Source**: Gergen, David (2001). Eyewitness to Power: The Essence of Leadership Nixon to Clinton. NYC: Simon & Schuster. Pgs. 42-43.

(3.) Improves Planning and Preparation, and Proactive Thinking. By offering glimpses of the future, we can more easily plan and prepare. Of course, as George Lucas reminds us through Jedi Master Yoda in Star Wars, "impossible to see the future is." **Source**: Lucas, George and Hales, Jonathan (2001). "Star Wars: Episode II Attack of the Clones." Screenplay. Last

Accessed: August 8, 2011.
http://www.scenebyscene.net/ii/aotcscript.txt

Yet, having a more reliable sense of potential or even probable outcomes or possible future scenarios can help to encourage a productive move toward anticipation and planning, rather than simply worrying while waiting to see. And, as Churchill said, it is far more effective to "let our advance worrying become advance thinking and planning." **Source:** Giuliani, Rudolph W. (2002). Leadership. NYC: Hyperion. Pg. 295.

(4.) <u>Facilitates Intervention</u>. Even if you are unable to predict the future precisely, by recognizing the patterns and contemplating possible future scenarios, you better equip yourself to deal with and navigate the road ahead; potentially disrupting dangerous or destructive developments early on; perhaps lessening the length or width or depth of a future crisis or, in some cases, avoiding catastrophe altogether (e.g. averting a second Great Depression). This is often how these cycles are broken. Only when we understand the pattern at play, with an eye to the future, are we able to make the necessary adjustments to interrupt the pattern and prevent the cycle from endlessly repeating in the future.Source: Greene, Robert (2006). The 33 Strategies of War. NYC: Penguin Books. Pg. 157. In fact, as George Washington argued, this is the whole point. "We should not look back," he said, "unless it is to derive useful lessons from past errors, and for the purpose of profiting by dearly bought experience." Source: Pine, Joslyn T. (2012)(Editor). Wit and Wisdom of the American Presidents: A Book of Quotations. Mineola, NY: Dover Publications. Pg. 2.

(5.) <u>Broadens Perspective and Strengthens Strategic Thinking</u>. Grasping the repeating or expanding patterns of history can also serve to broaden your frame of reference. It can help to reduce complexity, bring order to chaos, and simplify problem solving by helping you to focus on the big picture, screen out irrelevant or superfluous data and, thereby, focus on critical points and defining trends. This, in turn, can serve as a valuable input to decision making, allowing strategists to extrapolate and, thus, more effectively engage in scenario development and systems thinking. Indeed, pattern recognition can be a key input to thinking strategically.

(6.) <u>Cultivate Intuition and Foster Confidence</u>. All of these factors can work together to boost courage and confidence and enhance your sense of having greater control over your destiny and the future of those you lead. With the broader scope in perspective and a better-grounded and more informed sense of the direction of society, strategists are almost invariably more rightly trusting of their institution and, therefore, more apt to operate in a calm and collected manner when dealing with chaos and disorder.

99. Truman, Harry S. (1955). The Memoirs of Harry S. Truman, Volume 1: Year of Decisions: 1945. NYC: Doubleday. Pg. 211.
100. Aristotle; Gillies, John (1893). Aristotle's Ethics: Comprising His Practical Philosophy. London: George Routledge and Sons, Ltd. Pgs. 63-79.
101. Plato. (1894). The Works of Plato. Volume II. Translated by Henry Davis, M.A. London: George Bell & Sons.
102. Covey, Stephen R. (1991). *Principle-Centered Leadership*. NYC: Simon & Schuster. Pg. 19.
103. Truman, Harry S. (1955). The Memoirs of Harry S. Truman, Volume 1: Year of Decisions: 1945. NYC: Doubleday. Pg. 210.
104. Emmanuel, comte de Las Cases (1890). Memoirs of the Life, Exile, and Conversations of the Emperor Napoleon. NYC: Worthington, Co. Pg. 140-142.
105. Axelrod, Robert and Forster, Larissa (2017, March). "How historical analogies in newspapers of five countries make sense of major events: 9/11, Mumbai and Tahrir Square." Research in Economics, Volume 71, Issue 1. Pg. 10. https://www.sciencedirect.com/science/article/pii/S1090944316301636
106. McCullough, David (1992). Truman. NYC: Simon and Schuster. Pg. 58.
107. Truman, Harry S. (1956). The Memoirs of Harry S. Truman, Volume 2: Years of Trial and Hope. NYC: Doubleday. Pg. 204.
108. Truman, Harry S. (1956). The Memoirs of Harry S. Truman, Volume 2: Years of Trial and Hope. NYC: Doubleday. Pg. 204.
109. Axelrod, Robert and Forster, Larissa (2017, March). "How historical analogies in newspapers of five countries make sense of major events: 9/11, Mumbai and Tahrir Square." Research in Economics, Volume 71, Issue 1. Pg. 10. https://www.sciencedirect.com/science/article/pii/S1090944316301636
110. Ross, Steven T. (1988). "Napoleon and Maneuver Warfare." In Borowski, Harry (Editor) The Harmon Memorial Lectures in Military History, 1959—1987: A Collection of the First Thirty Harmon Lectures Given at the United States Air Force Academy. Washington, D.C.: Office of Air Force History. Pg. 309.
111. Ross, Steven T. (1988). "Napoleon and Maneuver Warfare." In Borowski, Harry (Editor) The Harmon Memorial Lectures in Military History, 1959—1987: A Collection of the First Thirty Harmon Lectures Given at the United States Air Force Academy. Washington, D.C.: Office of Air Force History. Pg. 309.
112. Shaw, Colonel Donald P. (1980, January 7). "The Other Sides of George S. Patton, Jr." Vignettes of Military History, Volume III, No. 140. Carlisle Barracks, PA: U.S. Army Military History Institute.
113. Lowe, Maj. John (2013, January-February). "Professional Development Bookshelf: Reviews of Books that Teach Us About Our Craft." The Georgia Guardsman. Marietta, GA: Georgia Department of Defense Public Affairs Office. Pg. 14.
114. Ross, Steven T. (1988). "Napoleon and Maneuver Warfare." In Borowski, Harry (Editor) *The Harmon Memorial Lectures in Military History, 1959—1987: A Collection of the First Thirty Harmon Lectures Given at the United States Air Force Academy*. Washington, D.C.: Office of Air Force History. Pg. 309.
115. Santayana, George (1905). The Life of Reason, Volume 1: Reason in Common Sense. Pg. 284. "Those who cannot remember the past are condemned to repeat it."
116. Rushay Jr., Samuel W. (2009). "Harry Truman's History Lessons." Prologue Magazine, Volume 41, Number 1. http://www.archives.gov/publications/prologue/2009/spring/truman-history.html

117. Hess, Jerry N. & Feeney, Joseph G. (1966, September 20). "Oral History Interview with Joseph G. Feeney," Washington, D.C. The Harry S. Truman Library and Museum. National Archives and Records Administration.
https://www.trumanlibrary.gov/library/oral-histories/feeney

118. Rushay Jr., Samuel W. (2009). "Harry Truman's History Lessons." Prologue Magazine, Volume 41, Number 1.
http://www.archives.gov/publications/prologue/2009/spring/truman-history.html

119. Hess, Jerry N. & Feeney, Joseph G. (1966, September 20). "Oral History Interview with Joseph G. Feeney," Washington, D.C. The Harry S. Truman Library and Museum. National Archives and Records Administration.
https://www.trumanlibrary.gov/library/oral-histories/feeney

120. Truman, Margaret (1990). Where the Buck Stops: The Personal and Private Writings of Harry S. Truman. NYC: Grand Central Publishing. Pg. 90.

121. Rushay Jr., Samuel W. (2009). "Harry Truman's History Lessons." Prologue Magazine, Volume 41, Number 1.
http://www.archives.gov/publications/prologue/2009/spring/truman-history.html

122. Truman, Margaret (1990). Where the Buck Stops: The Personal and Private Writings of Harry S. Truman. NYC: Grand Central Publishing. Pgs. 90-91.

|6.3.2|

Exploit the Power of Analogy to SharpenDecisions, Expand Options, and Increase Your Probability of Success

1. Machiavelli, Niccolò (2009 [c. 1517]). Discourses on Livy I. Harvey C. Mansfield (Translator). Chicago: University of Chicago Press. Pg. 39.

2. Truman, Harry S. (1956). The Memoirs of Harry S. Truman, Volume 2: Years of Trial and Hope. NYC: Doubleday. Pg. 332.

3. Grubin, David (Producer). (1997). Truman. American Experience. PBS. [Documentary Film]. United States: David Grubin Productions, Inc. Transcript:
http://www.shoppbs.pbs.org/wgbh/amex/truman/filmmore/pt.html [1:08:20]

4. Truman, Harry S. (1956). The Memoirs of Harry S. Truman, Volume 2: Years of Trial and Hope. NYC: Doubleday. Pg. 332.

5. Truman, Harry S. (1956). The Memoirs of Harry S. Truman, Volume 2: Years of Trial and Hope. NYC: Doubleday. Pgs. 332-333.

6. Truman, Harry S. (1956). The Memoirs of Harry S. Truman, Volume 2: Years of Trial and Hope. NYC: Doubleday. Pg. 333.

7. Truman, Harry (1947, March 12). "Truman Doctrine." Presidential Address to a Joint Session of Congress. Document 171; 80th Congress, 1st Session; Records of the United States House of Representatives; Record Group 233; National Archives.
https://www.archives.gov/milestone-documents/truman-doctrine

8. Truman, Harry S. (1956). The Memoirs of Harry S. Truman, Volume 2: Years of Trial and Hope. NYC: Doubleday. Pg. 333.

9. Note: The Blair House, also known as The President's Guest House, was located directly across from the White House on Pennsylvania Avenue. Truman lived at the Blair House during the White House Reconstruction, 1949-1952.

10. Truman, Harry S. (1956). The Memoirs of Harry S. Truman, Volume 2: Years of Trial and Hope. NYC: Doubleday. Pg. 334.

11. Truman, Harry S. (1956). The Memoirs of Harry S. Truman, Volume 2: Years of Trial and Hope. NYC: Doubleday. Pg. 335.

12. Truman, Harry S. (1956). The Memoirs of Harry S. Truman, Volume 2: Years of Trial and Hope. NYC: Doubleday. Pg. 334.

13. Grubin, David (Producer). (1997). Truman. American Experience. PBS. [Documentary Film]. United States: David Grubin Productions, Inc. Transcript:
http://www.shoppbs.pbs.org/wgbh/amex/truman/filmmore/pt.html

14. Grubin, David (Producer). (1997). Truman. American Experience. PBS. [Documentary Film]. United States: David Grubin Productions, Inc. Transcript:
http://www.shoppbs.pbs.org/wgbh/amex/truman/filmmore/pt.html

15. McCullough, David (1992). Truman. NYC: Simon and Schuster. Pg. 930.

16. Truman, Harry S. (1956). The Memoirs of Harry S. Truman, Volume 2: Years of Trial and Hope. NYC: Doubleday. Pg. 341.

17. Seaman, John T. and Smith, George David (2012, December). "Your Company's History as a Leadership Tool." Harvard Business Review.
https://hbr.org/2012/12/your-companys-history-as-a-leadership-tool See Also: Abshire, David M. (2008). A Call to Greatness: Challenging our Next President. NYC: Roman and Littlefield Publishers, Inc. Pg. 7.

18. Neustadt, Richard & May, Ernest (1986). Thinking in Time: The Uses of History for Decision Makers. NYC: The Free Press. Pg. 232.

19. Neustadt, Richard & May, Ernest (1986). Thinking in Time: The Uses of History for Decision Makers. NYC: The Free Press. Pg. 232. See also: Bose, Partha (2004). Alexander the Great's Art of Strategy: The Timeless Lessons of History's Greatest Empire Builder. NYC: Gotham Books. Pg. 6.

20. Stockdale, James Bond (1983, March 30). "Educating Leaders." The Washington Quarterly, Volume 6, Issue 1. Pgs. 49-52.

21. Truman, Harry S. (1956). The Memoirs of Harry S. Truman, Volume 2: Years of Trial and Hope. NYC: Doubleday. Pg. 273.

22. Seaman, John T. and Smith, George David (2012, December). "Your Company's History as a Leadership Tool." Harvard Business Review.
https://hbr.org/2012/12/your-companys-history-as-a-leadership-tool

23. Seaman, John T. and Smith, George David (2012, December). "Your Company's History as a Leadership Tool." Harvard Business Review.
https://hbr.org/2012/12/your-companys-history-as-a-leadership-tool See Also: Abshire, David M. (2008). A Call to Greatness: Challenging our Next President. NYC: Roman and Littlefield Publishers, Inc. Pg. 7.

24. Seaman, John T. and Smith, George David (2012, December). "Your Company's History as a Leadership Tool." Harvard Business Review.
https://hbr.org/2012/12/your-companys-history-as-a-leadership-tool

25. Neustadt, Richard & May, Ernest (1986). Thinking in Time: The Uses of History for Decision Makers. NYC: The Free Press. Pg. 36.

26. Neustadt, Richard & May, Ernest (1986). Thinking in Time: The Uses of History for Decision Makers. NYC: The Free Press. Pg. 36.

27. Bartha, Paul (2019, Spring). "Analogy and Analogical Reasoning." The Stanford Encyclopedia of Philosophy. Edward N. Zalta (ed.). https://plato.stanford.edu/archives/spr2019/entries/reasoning-analogy/

28. Bartha, Paul (2019, Spring). "Analogy and Analogical Reasoning." The Stanford Encyclopedia of Philosophy. Edward N. Zalta (ed.). https://plato.stanford.edu/archives/spr2019/entries/reasoning-analogy/

29. Bartha, Paul (2019, Spring). "Analogy and Analogical Reasoning." The Stanford Encyclopedia of Philosophy. Edward N. Zalta (ed.). https://plato.stanford.edu/archives/spr2019/entries/reasoning-analogy/

30. Holyoak, Keith & Thagard, Paul (1994). Mental Leaps: Analogy in Creative Thought. Cambridge: MIT Press. Pg. 6.

31. Holyoak, Keith & Thagard, Paul (1994). Mental Leaps: Analogy in Creative Thought. Cambridge: MIT Press. Pg. 186

32. Holyoak, Keith & Thagard, Paul (1994). Mental Leaps: Analogy in Creative Thought. Cambridge: MIT Press. Pg. 187

33. Holyoak, Keith & Thagard, Paul (1994). Mental Leaps: Analogy in Creative Thought. Cambridge: MIT Press. Pg. 187

34. Gavetti, Giovanni and Rivkin, Jan W. (2005, April). "How Strategists Really Think: Tapping the Power of Analogy." Harvard Business Review. https://hbr.org/2005/04/how-strategists-really-think-tapping-the-power-of-analogy Full Quote: "Reasoning by analogy is prevalent among strategy makers because of a series of close matches: between the amount of information available in many strategic situations and the amount required to draw analogies; between the wealth of managerial experience and the need for that experience in analogical reasoning; and between the need for creative strategies and analogy's ability to spark creativity. Reflecting these matches, business schools typically teach strategy by means of case studies, which provide an abundance of analogies from which the students can draw. [...] Similarly, some of the foremost strategy consultants are famed for their ability to draw lessons from one industry and apply them to another. Thus we have ample reason to believe that analogical reasoning is a key implement in the toolbox of the typical real-world strategist."

35. Gavetti (2005).

36. Gavetti (2005).

37. Truman, Harry S. (1955). The Memoirs of Harry S. Truman, Volume 1: Year of Decisions: 1945. NYC: Doubleday. Pgs. 211-212

38. Truman, Harry S. (1955). The Memoirs of Harry S. Truman, Volume 1: Year of Decisions: 1945. NYC: Doubleday. 211.

39. Neustadt, Richard & May, Ernest (1986). Thinking in Time: The Uses of History for Decision Makers. NYC: The Free Press. Pg. 42.

40. Neustadt, Richard & May, Ernest (1986). Thinking in Time: The Uses of History for Decision Makers. NYC: The Free Press. Pg. 4, 35.

41. Axelrod, Alan (2013). Catherine the Great CEO: 7 Principles to Guide and Inspire Modern Leaders. NYC: Sterling. Pgs. 182-183.

42. Truman, Harry S. (1955). The Memoirs of Harry S. Truman, Volume 1: Year of Decisions: 1945. NYC: Doubleday. Pg. 46

43. Truman, Harry S. (1955). The Memoirs of Harry S. Truman, Volume 1: Year of Decisions: 1945. NYC: Doubleday. Pg. 46

44. Truman, Harry S. (1955). The Memoirs of Harry S. Truman, Volume 1: Year of Decisions: 1945. NYC: Doubleday. Pg. 212.

45. Truman, Harry S. (1955). The Memoirs of Harry S. Truman, Volume 1: Year of Decisions: 1945. NYC: Doubleday. Pgs. 210-211.

46. Truman, Harry S. (1955). The Memoirs of Harry S. Truman, Volume 1: Year of Decisions: 1945. NYC: Doubleday. Pgs. 210-211.

47. Truman, Harry S. (1956). The Memoirs of Harry S. Truman, Volume 2: Years of Trial and Hope. NYC: Doubleday. Pg. 1.

48. Nazaretyan, Akop (2020). "The Twenty-First Century's 'Mysterious Singularity' in the Light of the Big History." In The 21st Century Singularity and Global Futures: A Big History Perspective. Andrey Korotayev & David LePoire (Editors). Cham, Switzerland: Springer. Pg. 345.

49. Smoler, Fredric (2001, November/December). "Fighting The Last War—and The Next." American Heritage, Volume 52, Issue 8. https://www.americanheritage.com/fighting-last-war-and-next

50. Smoler, Fredric (2001, November/December). "Fighting The Last War—and The Next." American Heritage, Volume 52, Issue 8. https://www.americanheritage.com/fighting-last-war-and-next

51. Smoler, Fredric (2001, November/December). "Fighting The Last War—and The Next." American Heritage, Volume 52, Issue 8. https://www.americanheritage.com/fighting-last-war-and-next

52. Holyoak, Keith & Thagard, Paul (1994). Mental Leaps: Analogy in Creative Thought. Cambridge: MIT Press. Pg. 157

53. Holyoak, Keith & Thagard, Paul (1994). Mental Leaps: Analogy in Creative Thought. Cambridge: MIT Press. Pg. 157

54. "Godwin's Law, n." Oxford English Dictionary Online, Oxford University Press. www.oed.com/view/Entry/340583

55. Plato (2010 [360 B.C.]). Cratylus. Benjamin Jowett (Translator). Rockville, MD: Wildside Press. Section 402a. http://classics.mit.edu/Plato/cratylus.html

56. Plato (2010 [360 B.C.]). Cratylus. Benjamin Jowett (Translator). Rockville, MD: Wildside Press. Section 402a. http://classics.mit.edu/Plato/cratylus.html

57. Lewis, C. S. (1980). The Chronicles of Narnia : The Voyage of the Dawn Treader. United States of America: Harper Collins Publisher.

58. Smoler, Fredric (2001, November/December). "Fighting The Last War—and The Next." American Heritage, Volume 52, Issue 8.

https://www.americanheritage.com/fighting-last-war-and-next

59. Richards, Michael (2001, February). "Historical Analogies: Handle With Care." Origins: Current Events in Historical Perspective. Ohio State University.

60. Sheets, Dutch and Ford III, William L. (2004). History Makers: Your Prayers Have the Power to Heal the Past and Shape the Future. Ventura: Regal. Pg. 173.

61 Hill, Howard C. (1920, January-December). "History for History's Sake." In The Historical Outlook, Volume XI. Philadelphia: McKinley Publishing Company. Pg. 311.

62. Allgood, Jay R. (2004). Embracing History's Lessons: What Every College Graduate Should Know. Agreka Books. 21.

63. Holyoak, Keith & Thagard, Paul (1994). Mental Leaps: Analogy in Creative Thought. Cambridge: MIT Press. Pg. 163

64. Allgood, Jay R. (2004). Embracing History's Lessons: What Every College Graduate Should Know. Agreka Books. 24

65. Kagan, Donald (2001). "While America Sleeps." American Diplomacy, Volume VI, Number 1. https://ciaotest.cc.columbia.edu/olj/ad/ad_v6_1/kad01.html

66. Neustadt, Richard & May, Ernest (1986). Thinking in Time: The Uses of History for Decision Makers. NYC: The Free Press. Pg. 42.

67. Neustadt, Richard & May, Ernest (1986). Thinking in Time: The Uses of History for Decision Makers. NYC: The Free Press. Pg. 42.

68. Neustadt, Richard & May, Ernest (1986). Thinking in Time: The Uses of History for Decision Makers. NYC: The Free Press. Pg. 42.

69. Dallek, Robert (1986). "Thinking in Time: The Uses of History for Decision Makers." [Book Review.] The New Republic, Volume 195, Issue, 1. Pgs 46.

70. Dallek, Robert (1986). "Thinking in Time: The Uses of History for Decision Makers." [Book Review.] The New Republic, Volume 195, Issue, 1. Pgs 46.

71. Dallek, Robert (1986). "Thinking in Time: The Uses of History for Decision Makers." [Book Review.] The New Republic, Volume 195, Issue, 1. Pgs 46.

72. Mattson, Mark P. (2014, August 22). "Superior pattern processing is the essence of the evolved human brain." Frontiers in Neuroscience, Volume 8, Article 265. Pg. 1.

73. Neustadt, Richard & May, Ernest (1986). Thinking in Time: The Uses of History for Decision Makers. NYC: The Free Press. Pg. 41.

74. Schnaars, Steven P. (1987). "Thinking in Time: The Uses of History for Decision Makers." [Book Review.] International Journal of Forecasting, Volume 3. Pg. 330.

75. Neustadt, Richard & May, Ernest (1986). Thinking in Time: The Uses of History for Decision Makers. NYC: The Free Press. Pg. 39.

76. Neustadt, Richard & May, Ernest (1986). Thinking in Time: The Uses of History for Decision Makers. NYC: The Free Press. Pg. 41.

77. Holyoak, Keith & Thagard, Paul (1994). Mental Leaps: Analogy in Creative Thought. Cambridge: MIT Press. Pg. 163.

78. Rich, Frank (2009, September 26). "Obama at the Precipice." The NYC Times. https://www.nytimes.com/2009/09/27/opinion/27rich.html

79. Staff Writer (1986, August 24). "Advisers, Then and Now." The NYC Times. https://www.nytimes.com/1986/08/24/opinion/advisers-then-and-now.html

80. Holyoak, Keith & Thagard, Paul (1994). Mental Leaps: Analogy in Creative Thought. Cambridge: MIT Press. Pgs. 163-164.

81. Neustadt, Richard & May, Ernest (1986). Thinking in Time: The Uses of History for Decision Makers. NYC: The Free Press. Pg. 37.

|6.3.3|

Think in Time to Influence the Future, Make the Most of the Power of the Past with a Systematic Plan

1. Cousins, Norman (1978, April 15). "Editorial." *Saturday Review.*

2. McCullough, David (1992). *Truman.* NYC: Simon and Schuster. Pg. 930.

3. Grubin, David (Producer). (1997). *Truman. American Experience.* PBS. [Documentary Film]. United States: David Grubin Productions, Inc. Transcript: http://www.shoppbs.pbs.org/wgbh/amex/truman/filmmore/pt.html

4. Ibid.

5. Ibid.

6. Ibid.

7. Ibid.

8. Ibid.

9. Malkasian, Carter (2001), *The Korean War 1950-1953.* NYC: Osprey Publishing Ltd. Pg. 8.

10. Grubin, David (Producer). (1997). Truman. American Experience. PBS. [Documentary Film]. United States: David Grubin Productions, Inc. Transcript: http://www.shoppbs.pbs.org/wgbh/amex/truman/filmmore/pt.html

11. Gonzalez, Ariel (2010, June 28). "McClellan, MacArthur, McChrystal: Militarizing the presidency obviously undermines the principle of civilian control, which the McChrystal kerfuffle brought to the forefront." Huffington Post. https://www.huffpost.com/entry/mcclellan-macarthur-mcchr_b_626651

12. Grubin, David (Producer). (1997). Truman. American Experience. PBS. [Documentary Film]. United States: David Grubin Productions, Inc. Transcript: http://www.shoppbs.pbs.org/wgbh/amex/truman/filmmore/pt.html

13. Grubin, David (Producer). (1997). Truman. American Experience. PBS. [Documentary Film]. United States: David Grubin Productions, Inc. Transcript: http://www.shoppbs.pbs.org/wgbh/amex/truman/filmmore/pt.html

14. Rothkopf, David J. (2005). Running the World: The Inside Story of the National Security Council and the Architects of American Power. NYC: Public Affairs. Pg. 260.

15. Fatmi, H. A. and Young, R.W. (1970, October 3). "A Definition of Intelligence." Nature, Volume 288. Pg. 97.

16. Likierman, Andrew (2020, January-February). "The Elements of Good Judgment." Harvard Business Review. https://hbr.org/2020/01/the-elements-of-good-judgment

17. Likierman, Andrew (2020, January-February). "The Elements of Good Judgment." Harvard Business

Review. https://hbr.org/2020/01/the-elements-of-good-judgment

18. Likierman, Andrew (2020, January-February). "The Elements of Good Judgment." Harvard Business Review. https://hbr.org/2020/01/the-elements-of-good-judgment

19. Likierman, Andrew (2020, January-February). "The Elements of Good Judgment." Harvard Business Review. https://hbr.org/2020/01/the-elements-of-good-judgment

20. Greene, Robert (2021). The Daily Laws: 366 Meditations on Power, Seduction, Mastery, Strategy, and Human Nature. New York: Viking. Pg. 164.

21. Wikipedia contributors. (2022). "Historical rankings of presidents of the United States." Wikipedia, The Free Encyclopedia. https://en.wikipedia.org/wiki/Historical_rankings_of_p residents_of_the_United_States

22. Wyszomirski, Margaret Jane (1987, May). "Thinking in Time: The Uses of History for Decision Makers. by Richard E. Neustadt and Ernest R. May." The Journal of Politics, Volume 49, Number 2. Pg. 605.

23. Dallek, Robert (1986). "Thinking in Time: The Uses of History for Decision Makers." [Book Review.] The New Republic, Volume 195, Issue, 1. Pgs. 45-46.

24. Neustadt, Richard & May, Ernest (1986). Thinking in Time: The Uses of History for Decision Makers. NYC: The Free Press. Pgs. 32-33.

25. Weiss, E.L. (1987, February 1). "Thinking in Time: The Uses of History for Decision Makers." [Book Review.] Management Review, Volume 76, Issue 2. Pg. 70.

26. Neirotti R. A. (2021). "The importance of asking questions and doing things for a reason." Brazilian Journal of Cardiovascular Surgery, Volume 36, Number 1. https://doi.org/10.21470/1678-9741-2021-0950

27. Neustadt, Richard & May, Ernest (1986). Thinking in Time: The Uses of History for Decision Makers. NYC: The Free Press. Pg. 39.

28. Neustadt, Richard & May, Ernest (1986). Thinking in Time: The Uses of History for Decision Makers. NYC: The Free Press. Pg. 37.

29. Dallek, Robert (1986). "Thinking in Time: The Uses of History for Decision Makers." [Book Review.] The New Republic, Volume 195, Issue, 1. Pg. 46.

30. McCullough, David (1992). Truman. NYC: Simon and Schuster. Pg. 930.

31. Wyszomirski, Margaret Jane (1987, May). "Thinking in Time: The Uses of History for Decision Makers. by Richard E. Neustadt and Ernest R. May." The Journal of Politics, Volume 49, Number 2. Pg. 606.

32. Neustadt, Richard & May, Ernest (1986). Thinking in Time: The Uses of History for Decision Makers. NYC: The Free Press. Pg. 38.

33. Wyszomirski, Margaret Jane (1987, May). "Thinking in Time: The Uses of History for Decision Makers. by Richard E. Neustadt and Ernest R. May." The Journal of Politics, Volume 49, Number 2. Pg. 606.

34. Neustadt, Richard & May, Ernest (1986). Thinking in Time: The Uses of History for Decision Makers. NYC: The Free Press. Pgs. 269-270.

35. Neustadt, Richard & May, Ernest (1986). Thinking in Time: The Uses of History for Decision Makers. NYC: The Free Press. Pgs. 32-33.

36. Neustadt, Richard & May, Ernest (1986). Thinking in Time: The Uses of History for Decision Makers. NYC: The Free Press. Pg. 41.

37. Neustadt, Richard & May, Ernest (1986). Thinking in Time: The Uses of History for Decision Makers. NYC: The Free Press. Pg. 41.

38. Wyszomirski, Margaret Jane (1987, May). "Thinking in Time: The Uses of History for Decision Makers. by Richard E. Neustadt and Ernest R. May." The Journal of Politics, Volume 49, Number 2. Pg. 605.

39. Neustadt, Richard & May, Ernest (1986). Thinking in Time: The Uses of History for Decision Makers. NYC: The Free Press. Pg. 8.

40. Neustadt, Richard & May, Ernest (1986). Thinking in Time: The Uses of History for Decision Makers. NYC: The Free Press. Pg. 8.

41. Neustadt, Richard & May, Ernest (1986). Thinking in Time: The Uses of History for Decision Makers. NYC: The Free Press. Pg. 8.

42. Neustadt, Richard & May, Ernest (1986). Thinking in Time: The Uses of History for Decision Makers. NYC: The Free Press. Pg. 9.

43. Neustadt, Richard & May, Ernest (1986). Thinking in Time: The Uses of History for Decision Makers. NYC: The Free Press. Pg. 9.

44. Neustadt, Richard & May, Ernest (1986). Thinking in Time: The Uses of History for Decision Makers. NYC: The Free Press. Pg. 9.

45. Staff Writer (2021, November 23). "Cuban Missile Crisis." John F. Kennedy Presidential Library and Museum. Boston, MA. https://www.jfklibrary.org/learn/about-jfk/jfk-in-history/cuban-missile-crisis

46. Staff Writer (2021, November 23). "The Cuban Missile Crisis, October 1962." Office of the Historian, United States Department of State. https://history.state.gov/milestones/1961-1968/cuban-missile-crisis

47. Neustadt, Richard & May, Ernest (1986). Thinking in Time: The Uses of History for Decision Makers. NYC: The Free Press. Pg. 41.

48. Neustadt, Richard & May, Ernest (1986). Thinking in Time: The Uses of History for Decision Makers. NYC: The Free Press. Pg. 206.

49. Weiss, E.L. (1987, February 1). "Thinking in Time: The Uses of History for Decision Makers." [Book Review.] Management Review, Volume 76, Issue 2. Pg. 70.

50. Neustadt, Richard & May, Ernest (1986). Thinking in Time: The Uses of History for Decision Makers. NYC: The Free Press. Pg. 133.

51. Wyszomirski, Margaret Jane (1987, May). "Thinking in Time: The Uses of History for Decision Makers. by Richard E. Neustadt and Ernest R. May." The Journal of Politics, Volume 49, Number 2. Pg. 606.

52. Wyszomirski, Margaret Jane (1987, May). "Thinking in Time: The Uses of History for Decision Makers. by Richard E. Neustadt and Ernest R. May." The Journal of Politics, Volume 49, Number 2. Pg. 606.

53. Truman, Harry S. (1956). The Memoirs of Harry S. Truman, Volume 2: Years of Trial and Hope. NYC: Doubleday. Pg. 101.

54. Truman, Harry S. (1956). The Memoirs of Harry S. Truman, Volume 2: Years of Trial and Hope. NYC: Doubleday. Pgs. 101-102.

55. Truman, Harry S. (1956). The Memoirs of Harry S. Truman, Volume 2: Years of Trial and Hope. NYC: Doubleday. Pgs. 101-102.

56. Ferrell, Robert H. (1994). Harry S. Truman: A Life (Missouri Biography Series). University of Missouri Press. Pg. 182.
57. Ferrell, Robert H. (1994). Harry S. Truman: A Life (Missouri Biography Series). University of Missouri Press. Pg. 182.
58. Lincoln, Abraham (1902). Political Debates Between Abraham Lincoln and Stephen A. Douglas. Cleveland: The Arthur H. Clark Company. Pg. 293.
59. Dallek, Robert (1986). "Thinking in Time: The Uses of History for Decision Makers." [Book Review.] The New Republic, Volume 195, Issue, 1. Pg. 46.
60. Dallek, Robert (1986). "Thinking in Time: The Uses of History for Decision Makers." [Book Review.] The New Republic, Volume 195, Issue, 1. Pg. 46.
61. Dallek, Robert (1986). "Thinking in Time: The Uses of History for Decision Makers." [Book Review.] The New Republic, Volume 195, Issue, 1. Pg. 46.
62. Dallek, Robert (1986). "Thinking in Time: The Uses of History for Decision Makers." [Book Review.] The New Republic, Volume 195, Issue, 1. Pg. 46.
63. Dallek, Robert (1986). "Thinking in Time: The Uses of History for Decision Makers." [Book Review.] The New Republic, Volume 195, Issue, 1. Pg. 46.
64. MacArthur, Douglas (1964, April 9). "Texts of Accounts by Lucas and Considine on Interviews with MacArthur in 1954." *The NYC Times.* https://www.nytimes.com/1964/04/09/archives/texts-of-accounts-by-lucas-and-considine-on-interviews-with.html

|6.3.4|

Lean on History as a Guide, Mine the Wisdom of History to Decide

1. Emerson, Ralph Waldo (2000). "Power," and "Wealth," essays in The Conduct of Life [1860]. The Essential Writings of Ralph Waldo Emerson. NY: The Modern Library. London: William Clowes & Sons. Pg. 696.
2. Moran, Tom (2016, October 5). "The Tale of President Harry S. Truman and Gen. Douglas MacArthur." Chicago Tribune. https://www.chicagotribune.com/entertainment/books/ct-books-general-vs-the-president-hw-brand-20161005-story.html
3. Moran, Tom (2016, October 5). "The Tale of President Harry S. Truman and Gen. Douglas MacArthur." Chicago Tribune. https://www.chicagotribune.com/entertainment/books/ct-books-general-vs-the-president-hw-brand-20161005-story.html
4. Sides, Hampton (2019, November 11). "Douglas MacArthur Is One of America's Most Famous Generals. He's Also the Most Overrated." *Time.* https://time.com/5724009/douglas-macarthur-is-one-of-americas-most-famous-generals-hes-also-the-most-overrated/
5. Sides, Hampton (2018). On Desperate Ground: The Marines at the Reservoir, the Korean War's Greatest Battle. NYC: Doubleday. Pg. 172.
6. Sides, Hampton (2019, November 11). "Douglas MacArthur Is One of America's Most Famous Generals. He's Also the Most Overrated." Time. https://time.com/5724009/douglas-macarthur-is-one-of-americas-most-famous-generals-hes-also-the-most-overrated/
7. Sides, Hampton (2019, November 11). "Douglas MacArthur Is One of America's Most Famous Generals. He's Also the Most Overrated." Time. https://time.com/5724009/douglas-macarthur-is-one-of-americas-most-famous-generals-hes-also-the-most-overrated/
8. Sides, Hampton (2019, November 11). "Douglas MacArthur Is One of America's Most Famous Generals. He's Also the Most Overrated." Time. https://time.com/5724009/douglas-macarthur-is-one-of-americas-most-famous-generals-hes-also-the-most-overrated/
9. Sides, Hampton (2018). On Desperate Ground: The Marines at the Reservoir, the Korean War's Greatest Battle. NYC: Doubleday. Pg. 244.
10. Halberstam, David (2007). The Coldest Winter: America and the Korean War. NYC: Hyperion. Pg. 687.
11. Sides, Hampton (2019, November 11). "Douglas MacArthur Is One of America's Most Famous Generals. He's Also the Most Overrated." Time. https://time.com/5724009/douglas-macarthur-is-one-of-americas-most-famous-generals-hes-also-the-most-overrated/
12. Sides, Hampton (2019, November 11). "Douglas MacArthur Is One of America's Most Famous Generals. He's Also the Most Overrated." Time. https://time.com/5724009/douglas-macarthur-is-one-of-americas-most-famous-generals-hes-also-the-most-overrated/
13. McCullough, David (1992). "Truman Fires MacArthur." Military History Quarterly, Volume 5, Number 3. —The Quarterly Journal of Military History. History Net. Arlington, VA: World History Group, LLC. https://www.historynet.com/truman-fires-macarthur.htm
14. Manchester, William (1978). American Caesar: Douglas MacArthur 1880—1964. NYC: Back Bay Books. Pg. 613.
15. Manchester, William (1978). American Caesar: Douglas MacArthur 1880—1964. NYC: Back Bay Books. Pg. 613.
16. Halberstam, David (2007). The Coldest Winter: America and the Korean War. NYC: Hyperion. Pg. 687.
17. Dotinga, Randy (2014, April 30). "The Most Dangerous Man in America." The Christian Science Monitor. https://www.csmonitor.com/Books/Book-Reviews/2014/0430/The-Most-Dangerous-Man-in-America
18. McCullough, David (1992). "Truman Fires MacArthur." Military History Quarterly, Volume 5, Number 3. —The Quarterly Journal of Military History. History Net. Arlington, VA: World History Group, LLC. https://www.historynet.com/truman-fires-macarthur.htm
19. Halberstam, David (2007). The Coldest Winter: America and the Korean War. NYC: Hyperion. Pg. 687.
20. Manchester, William (1978). American Caesar: Douglas MacArthur 1880—1964. NYC: Back Bay Books. Pg. 612.
21. Moran, Tom (2016, October 5). "The Tale of President Harry S. Truman and Gen. Douglas MacArthur." Chicago Tribune. https://www.chicagotribune.com/entertainment/books/ct-books-general-vs-the-president-hw-brand-20161005-story.html
22. McCullough, David (1992). Truman. NYC: Simon and Schuster. Pg. 836.
23. McCullough, David (1992). Truman. NYC: Simon and Schuster. Pg. 836.

24. Moran, Tom (2016, October 5). "The Tale of President Harry S. Truman and Gen. Douglas MacArthur." Chicago Tribune. https://www.chicagotribune.com/entertainment/books/ct-books-general-vs-the-president-hw-brand-20161005-story.html

25. McCullough, David (1992). Truman. NYC: Simon and Schuster. Pg. 836.

26. McCullough, David (1992). Truman. NYC: Simon and Schuster. Pg. 837.

27. McCullough, David (1992). "Truman Fires MacArthur." Military History Quarterly, Volume 5, Number 3. —The Quarterly Journal of Military History. History Net. Arlington, VA: World History Group, LLC. https://www.historynet.com/truman-fires-macarthur.htm

28. McCullough, David (1992). "Truman Fires MacArthur." Military History Quarterly, Volume 5, Number 3. —The Quarterly Journal of Military History. History Net. Arlington, VA: World History Group, LLC. https://www.historynet.com/truman-fires-macarthur.htm

29. McCullough, David (1992). "Truman Fires MacArthur." Military History Quarterly, Volume 5, Number 3. —The Quarterly Journal of Military History. History Net. Arlington, VA: World History Group, LLC. https://www.historynet.com/truman-fires-macarthur.htm

30. McCullough, David (1992). Truman. NYC: Simon and Schuster. Pg. 838.

31. Pearlman, Michael D. (2008). Truman and MacArthur: Policy, Politics and the Hunger for Honor and Renown. Bloomington: Indiana University Press. Pg. 183.

32. McCullough, David (1992). "Truman Fires MacArthur." Military History Quarterly, Volume 5, Number 3. —The Quarterly Journal of Military History. History Net. Arlington, VA: World History Group, LLC. https://www.historynet.com/truman-fires-macarthur.htm

33. Gonzalez, Ariel (2010, June 28). "McClellan, MacArthur, McChrystal." The Huffington Post. https://www.huffpost.com/entry/mcclellan-macarthur-mcchr_b_626651

34. Manchester, William (1978). American Caesar: Douglas MacArthur 1880—1964. NYC: Back Bay Books. Pg. 16.

35. Gonzalez, Ariel (2010, June 28). "McClellan, MacArthur, McChrystal." The Huffington Post. https://www.huffpost.com/entry/mcclellan-macarthur-mcchr_b_626651

36. Dunford, Chauney (Editor)(2019). Leaders Who Changed History. NYC: DK Publishing. Pg. 202.

37. Truman, Harry (1951, April 6). "Diary Entry of President Harry S. Truman, April 6, 1951." Harry S. Truman Papers: President's Secretary's Files. https://www.trumanlibrary.gov/library/truman-papers/diaries-file-1947-1953/1951?documentid=2&pagenumber=1

38. Truman, Harry (1951, April 6). "Diary Entry of President Harry S. Truman, April 6, 1951." Harry S. Truman Papers: President's Secretary's Files. https://www.trumanlibrary.gov/library/truman-papers/diaries-file-1947-1953/1951?documentid=2&pagenumber=1

39. Donovan, Robert J. (1996). Tumultuous Years: The Presidency of Harry S. Truman, 1949—1953. Columbia: University of Missouri Press. Pg. 355.

40. Brands, H.W. (2016). The General vs. the President: MacArthur and Truman at the Brink of Nuclear War. Pg. 379.

41. Brands, H.W. (2016, September 28). "The Redacted Testimony That Fully Explains Why General MacArthur Was Fired." Smithsonian Magazine. https://www.smithsonianmag.com/history/redacted-testimony-fully-explains-why-general-macarthur-was-fired-180960622/

42. Brands, H.W. (2016, September 28). "The Redacted Testimony That Fully Explains Why General MacArthur Was Fired." Smithsonian Magazine. https://www.smithsonianmag.com/history/redacted-testimony-fully-explains-why-general-macarthur-was-fired-180960622/

43. Grubin, David (Producer). (1997). Truman. American Experience. PBS. [Documentary Film]. United States: David Grubin Productions, Inc. Transcript: http://www.shoppbs.pbs.org/wgbh/amex/truman/filmmore/pt.html

44. McCullough, David (1992). "Truman Fires MacArthur." Military History Quarterly, Volume 5, Number 3. —The Quarterly Journal of Military History. History Net. Arlington, VA: World History Group, LLC. https://www.historynet.com/truman-fires-macarthur.htm

45. Gonzalez, Ariel (2010, June 28). "McClellan, MacArthur, McChrystal." The Huffington Post. https://www.huffpost.com/entry/mcclellan-macarthur-mcchr_b_626651

46. Gonzalez, Ariel (2010, June 28). "McClellan, MacArthur, McChrystal." The Huffington Post. https://www.huffpost.com/entry/mcclellan-macarthur-mcchr_b_626651

47. Gonzalez, Ariel (2010, June 28). "McClellan, MacArthur, McChrystal." The Huffington Post. https://www.huffpost.com/entry/mcclellan-macarthur-mcchr_b_626651

48. Gonzalez, Ariel (2010, June 28). "McClellan, MacArthur, McChrystal." The Huffington Post. https://www.huffpost.com/entry/mcclellan-macarthur-mcchr_b_626651

49. Gonzalez, Ariel (2010, June 28). "McClellan, MacArthur, McChrystal." The Huffington Post. https://www.huffpost.com/entry/mcclellan-macarthur-mcchr_b_626651

50. Greenstein, Fred I. (2000). The Presidential Difference: Leadership Style from Roosevelt to Clinton. NYC: The Free Press. Pg. 31.

51. McCullough, David (1992). "Truman Fires MacArthur." Military History Quarterly, Volume 5, Number 3. —The Quarterly Journal of Military History. History Net. Arlington, VA: World History Group, LLC. https://www.historynet.com/truman-fires-macarthur.htm

52. Manchester, William (1978). American Caesar: Douglas MacArthur 1880—1964. NYC: Back Bay Books. Pgs. 618-619.

53. Brands, H.W. (2016). The General vs. the President: MacArthur and Truman at the Brink of Nuclear War. Pg. 78.

54. Bohn, Michael (2015). Presidents in Crisis: Tough Decisions inside the White House from Truman to Obama. NYC: Arcade Publishing. Pg. 15.

55. Manchester, William (1978). American Caesar: Douglas MacArthur 1880—1964. NYC: Back Bay Books. Pg. 619.
56. Manchester, William (1978). American Caesar: Douglas MacArthur 1880—1964. NYC: Back Bay Books. Pg. 619.
57. Manchester, William (1978). American Caesar: Douglas MacArthur 1880—1964. NYC: Back Bay Books. Pg. 619.
58. Hart, Captain B.H. Liddell (1971). Why Don't We Learn from History? Sophron. Pg. 5.
59. McCullough, David (1992). Truman. NYC: Simon and Schuster. Pg. 837.
60. McCullough, David (1992). Truman. NYC: Simon and Schuster. Pg. 837.
61. McCullough, David (1992). Truman. NYC: Simon and Schuster. Pg. 839.
62. McCullough, David (1992). Truman. NYC: Simon and Schuster. Pg. 839.
63. McCullough, David (1992). Truman. NYC: Simon and Schuster. Pg. 839.
64. McCullough, David (1992). Truman. NYC: Simon and Schuster. Pg. 839.
65. McCullough, David (1992). Truman. NYC: Simon and Schuster. Pg. 838.
66. McCullough, David (1992). Truman. NYC: Simon and Schuster. Pg. 839.
67. Manchester, William (1978). American Caesar: Douglas MacArthur 1880—1964. NYC: Back Bay Books. Pg. 614.
68. Manchester, William (1978). American Caesar: Douglas MacArthur 1880—1964. NYC: Back Bay Books. Pg. 614.
69. McCullough, David (1992). Truman. NYC: Simon and Schuster. Pg. 840.
70. McCullough, David (1992). Truman. NYC: Simon and Schuster. Pg. 837.
71. "Wall and Pool of Remembrance." Korean War Veterans Memorial, National Park Service. United States of America. Washington, D.C. https://www.nps.gov/kowa/learn/historyculture/wall-and-pool-of-remembrance.htm
72. McCullough, David (1992). "Truman Fires MacArthur." Military History Quarterly, Volume 5, Number 3. —The Quarterly Journal of Military History. History Net. Arlington, VA: World History Group, LLC. https://www.historynet.com/truman-fires-macarthur.htm
73. Moran, Tom (2016, October 5). "The Tale of President Harry S. Truman and Gen. Douglas MacArthur." Chicago Tribune. https://www.chicagotribune.com/entertainment/books/ct-books-general-vs-the-president-hw-brand-20161005-story.html
74. Sides, Hampton (2019, November 11). "Douglas MacArthur Is One of America's Most Famous Generals. He's Also the Most Overrated." Time. https://time.com/5724009/douglas-macarthur-is-one-of-americas-most-famous-generals-hes-also-the-most-overrated/
75. Manchester, William (1978). American Caesar: Douglas MacArthur 1880—1964. NYC: Back Bay Books. Pg. 615.
76. Moran, Tom (2016, October 5). "The Tale of President Harry S. Truman and Gen. Douglas MacArthur." Chicago Tribune. https://www.chicagotribune.com/entertainment/books/ct-books-general-vs-the-president-hw-brand-20161005-story.html
77. Manchester, William (1978). American Caesar: Douglas MacArthur 1880—1964. NYC: Back Bay Books. Pg. 617.
78. Sides, Hampton (2019, November 11). "Douglas MacArthur Is One of America's Most Famous Generals. He's Also the Most Overrated." Time. https://time.com/5724009/douglas-macarthur-is-one-of-americas-most-famous-generals-hes-also-the-most-overrated/
79. Dagle, Robbin M. (2020, September 8). "Liberator or 'Dugout Doug'?: MacArthur's legacy in the Philippines revisited." CNN. https://www.cnnphilippines.com/life/culture/2020/9/8/douglas-macarthur-history-controversy.html Note: General Douglas MacArthur was named "Dugout Doug" by his men in Bataan for "hiding inside a tunnel while his troops faced death."
80. Manchester, William (1978). American Caesar: Douglas MacArthur 1880—1964. NYC: Back Bay Books. Pg. 615.
81. Manchester, William (1978). American Caesar: Douglas MacArthur 1880—1964. NYC: Back Bay Books. Pg. 614.
82. Manchester, William (1978). American Caesar: Douglas MacArthur 1880—1964. NYC: Back Bay Books. Pg. 615.
83. Truman, Harry S. (1956). The Memoirs of Harry S. Truman, Volume 2: Years of Trial and Hope. NYC: Doubleday. Pg. 172.
84. Hart, Captain B.H. Liddell (1971). Why Don't We Learn from History? Sophron. Pg. 7.
85. Seaman, John T. and Smith, George David (2012, December). "Your Company's History as a Leadership Tool." Harvard Business Review. https://hbr.org/2012/12/your-companys-history-as-a-leadership-tool
86. Mansfield, Stephen (1995). Never Give In: The Extraordinary Character of Winston Churchill. Nashville: Cumberland House. Pg. 200.
87. Gonzalez, Ariel (2010, June 28). "McClellan, MacArthur, McChrystal." The Huffington Post. https://www.huffpost.com/entry/mcclellan-macarthur-mcchr_b_626651
88. Brands, H.W. (2016, September 28). "The Redacted Testimony That Fully Explains Why General MacArthur Was Fired." Smithsonian.com. http://www.smithsonianmag.com/history/redacted-testimony-fully-explains-why-general-macarthur-was-fired-180960622
89. Brands, H.W. (2016). The General vs teh President: MacArthur and Truman at the Brink of Nuclear War. NYC: Doubleday. Pg. 463.
90. Brands, H.W. (2016, September 28). "The Redacted Testimony That Fully Explains Why General MacArthur Was Fired." Smithsonian.com. http://www.smithsonianmag.com/history/redacted-testimony-fully-explains-why-general-macarthur-was-fired-180960622
91. Brands, H.W. (2016, September 28). "The Redacted Testimony That Fully Explains Why General MacArthur Was Fired." Smithsonian Magazine. https://www.smithsonianmag.com/history/redacted-testimony-fully-explains-why-general-macarthur-was-fired-180960622/
92. Brands, H.W. (2016, September 28). "The Redacted Testimony That Fully Explains Why General MacArthur Was Fired." Smithsonian Magazine. https://www.smithsonianmag.com/history/redacted-testimony-fully-explains-why-general-macarthur-was-fired-180960622/

93. Gonzalez, Ariel (2010, June 28). "McClellan, MacArthur, McChrystal." The Huffington Post. https://www.huffpost.com/entry/mcclellan-macarthur-mcchr_b_626651
94. Tootle, Stephen (2022). "Truman Fires MacArthur." Bill of Rights Institute. https://billofrightsinstitute.org/essays/truman-fires-general-douglas-macarthur
95. Brands, H.W. (2016). The General vs. the President: MacArthur and Truman at the Brink of Nuclear War. Pgs. 363-364.
96. McCullough, David (1992). "Truman Fires MacArthur." Military History Quarterly, Volume 5, Number 3. —The Quarterly Journal of Military History. History Net. Arlington, VA: World History Group, LLC. https://www.historynet.com/truman-fires-macarthur.htm
97. "Historical Notes: Giving Them More Hell" (December 3, 1973). Time. https://web.archive.org/web/20071012203926/ht tp://www.time.com/time/magazine/article/0,917 1,908217,00.html
98. "Historical Notes: Giving Them More Hell" (December 3, 1973). Time. https://web.archive.org/web/20071012203926/ht tp://www.time.com/time/magazine/article/0,917 1,908217,00.html
99. Nietzsche, Friedrich; Breazeale, Daniel (Editor); Hollingdale, R.J. (Translator)(1997). Untimely Meditations. Cambridge Texts in the History of Philosophy. Cambridge: Cambridge U. Press. Pg. 68.
100. Wikipedia contributors. (2022). "Historical rankings of presidents of the United States." Wikipedia, The Free Encyclopedia. Note: Polls used cover a broad political spectrum, including Schlesinger, C-SPAN, Wall Street Journal, Times, Siena, USPC, APSA, and PSN. https://en.wikipedia.org/wiki/Historical_rankings_of_presidents_of_the_United_States
101. Nietzsche, Friedrich; Breazeale, Daniel (Editor); Hollingdale, R.J. (Translator)(1997). Untimely Meditations. Cambridge Texts in the History of Philosophy. Cambridge: Cambridge University Press. Pg. 68.
102. Nietzsche, Friedrich (1997). Twilight of the Idols, Or How to Philosophize with the Hammer. Translated by Richard Polt. Cambridge: Hackett Publishing. Pg. 66.

|6.4|

Exploit to Exceed the Example of the Exemplars: Alexander the Great and the Siege of Aornos Rock

1. Covey, Stephen (2004). The 8th Habit: From Effectiveness to Greatness. NYC: Free Press. Pg. 43.
2. Dahlquist, Allan (1977). Megasthenes and Indian Religion: A Study in Motives and Types. Delhi: Motilal Banarsidass. Pg. 59.
3. Siculus, Diodorus (Diodorus of Sicily)(1963[1st Century B.C.]). Bibliotheca Historica [Historical Library], XVII. LXXXV. [17.85.2]Loeb Classical Library, University of Chicago. https://penelope.uchicago.edu/Thayer/e/roman/t exts/diodorus_siculus/home.html
4. Stein, Aurel (1927, December). "Alexander's Campaign on the Indian North-West Frontier: Notes from Explorations between Upper Swat and the Indus (Continued)." The Geographical Journal, Volume 70, Number 6. Pg. 515.
5. Dahlquist (1977), Pg. 122.
6. Best, Amy (Editor)(2021). "Greek Legend." All About History Book of Greek Mythology. Bath: Future Publishing Limited. Pg. 79.
7. Best (2021), Pg. 80.
8. Stein, Aurel (1927, November). "Alexander's Campaign on the Indian North-West Frontier: Notes from Explorations between Upper Swat and the Indus." The Geographical Journal, Vol. 70, No. 5. Pg. 437.
9. Doleac, Miles (2014). In the Footsteps of Alexander: The King Who Conquered the Ancient World. NYC: Metro Books. Pg. 149.
10. Yenne, Bill (2010). Alexander the Great: Lessons from History's Undefeated General. NYC: St. Martin's Press. Pg. 139.
11. Ashley, James R. (1998). The Macedonian Empire: The Era of Warfare Under Philip II and Alexander the Great, 359-323 B.C. Jefferson, North Carolina: McFarland & Company, Inc. Pg. 313.
12. Doleac (2014), Pg. 149.
13. Worthington, Ian (2014). By the Spear : Philip II, Alexander the Great, and the Rise and Fall of the Macedonian Empire. Oxford: Oxford University Press. Pg. 241.
14. Moritani, Kimotoshi and Zahir, Muhammad (2018). "Alexander the Great at Aornos (Mount Pir-Sar), District Shangla, Khyber Pakhtunkhwa Province, Pakistan: Report on Historical and Archaeological Field Investigations (2017 – 2018)." Pakistan Heritage, Volume 10. Pg. 163. https://www.researchgate.net/publication/34253 4421_Alexander_the_Great_at_Aornos_Mount_Pi r-Sar_District_Shangla_Khyber_Pakhtunkhwa_Provi nce_Pakistan_Report_on_Historical_and_Archaeol ogical_Field_Investigations_2017_-2018
15. Bose, Partha (2004). Alexander the Great's Art of Strategy: The Timeless Lessons of History's Greatest Empire Builder. NYC: Gotham Books. Pg. 215.
16. Moritani, Kimotoshi and Zahir, Muhammad (2018). "Alexander the Great at Aornos (Mount Pir-Sar), District Shangla, Khyber Pakhtunkhwa Province, Pakistan: Report on Historical and Archaeological Field Investigations (2017 – 2018)." Pakistan Heritage, Volume 10. Pg. 163. https://www.researchgate.net/publication/342534421 _Alexander_the_Great_at_Aornos_Mount_Pir-Sar_District_Shangla_Khyber_Pakhtunkhwa_Province_ Pakistan_Report_on_Historical_and_Archaeological_Fi eld_Investigations_2017_-2018
17. Bose (2004), Pg. 215.
18. Doleac (2014), Pg. 149.
19. Bose (2004), Pg. 216.
20. Bose (2004), Pg. 215.
21. Stein, Aurel (1927, December). "Alexander's Campaign on the Indian North-West Frontier: Notes from Explorations between Upper Swat and the Indus (Continued)." The Geographical Journal, Volume 70, Number 6. Pg. 526
22. Moritani, Kimotoshi and Zahir, Muhammad (2018). "Alexander the Great at Aornos (Mount Pir-Sar), District Shangla, Khyber Pakhtunkhwa Province, Pakistan: Report on Historical and Archaeological Field

Investigations (2017 – 2018)." Pakistan Heritage, Volume 10. Pg. 163.
https://www.researchgate.net/publication/34253 4421_Alexander_the_Great_at_Aornos_Mount_Pir-Sar_District_Shangla_Khyber_Pakhtunkhwa_Province_Pakistan_Report_on_Historical_and_Archaeological_Field_Investigations_2017_-2018

23. Stein, Aurel (1927, December). "Alexander's Campaign on the Indian North-West Frontier: Notes from Explorations between Upper Swat and the Indus (Continued)." The Geographical Journal, Volume 70, Number 6. Pg. 516

24. Kurke, Lance (2004). The Wisdom of Alexander the Great: Enduring Leadership Lessons From the Man Who Created an Empire. NYC: Amacom. Pgs. 37-38.

25. Worthington, Ian (2014). By the Spear : Philip II, Alexander the Great, and the Rise and Fall of the Macedonian Empire. Oxford: Oxford University Press. Pg. 242.

26. Bose, Partha (2004). Alexander the Great's Art of Strategy: The Timeless Lessons of History's Greatest Empire Builder. NYC: Gotham Books. Pg. 217.

27. Moritani, Kimotoshi and Zahir, Muhammad (2018). "Alexander the Great at Aornos (Mount Pir-Sar), District Shangla, Khyber Pakhtunkhwa Province, Pakistan: Report on Historical and Archaeological Field Investigations (2017 – 2018)." Pakistan Heritage, Volume 10. Pg. 168.
https://www.researchgate.net/publication/34253 4421_Alexander_the_Great_at_Aornos_Mount_Pir-Sar_District_Shangla_Khyber_Pakhtunkhwa_Province_Pakistan_Report_on_Historical_and_Archaeological_Field_Investigations_2017_-2018

28. Moritani, Kimotoshi and Zahir, Muhammad (2018). "Alexander the Great at Aornos (Mount Pir-Sar), District Shangla, Khyber Pakhtunkhwa Province, Pakistan: Report on Historical and Archaeological Field Investigations (2017 – 2018)." Pakistan Heritage, Volume 10. Pg. 167.
https://www.researchgate.net/publication/34253 4421_Alexander_the_Great_at_Aornos_Mount_Pir-Sar_District_Shangla_Khyber_Pakhtunkhwa_Province_Pakistan_Report_on_Historical_and_Archaeological_Field_Investigations_2017_-2018

29. Worthington, Ian (2014). By the Spear : Philip II, Alexander the Great, and the Rise and Fall of the Macedonian Empire. Oxford: Oxford U. Press. Pg. 242.

30. Worthington, Ian (2014). By the Spear : Philip II, Alexander the Great, and the Rise and Fall of the Macedonian Empire. Oxford: Oxford U. Press. Pg. 242.

31. Bose, Partha (2004). Alexander the Great's Art of Strategy: The Timeless Lessons of History's Greatest Empire Builder. NYC: Gotham Books. Pg. 217.

32. Bose, Partha (2004). Alexander the Great's Art of Strategy: The Timeless Lessons of History's Greatest Empire Builder. NYC: Gotham Books. Pg. 217.

33. Covey, Stephen (2004). The 8th Habit: From Effectiveness to Greatness. NYC: Free Press. Pg. 54.

34. Siculus, Diodorus (Diodorus of Sicily)(1963[1st Century B.C.]). Bibliotheca Historica [Historical Library], XVII. LXXXV. Pg. 401. Loeb Classical Library, University of Chicago.

https://penelope.uchicago.edu/Thayer/e/roman/texts/diodorus_siculus/home.html

35. Garvey, Patrick (2016, May 2). "Alexander the Great's 3 Heroes." Ancient Heroes.
http://ancientheroes.net/blog/alexander-the-greats-3-heroes

36. Covey, Stephen (2004). The 8th Habit: From Effectiveness to Greatness. NYC: Free Press. Pg. 43.

37. "Beginnings" (2021). All About History Book of Alexander the Great, Third Edition. San Francisco: Future Publishing Limited. Pg. 12.

38. "Beginnings" (2021). All About History Book of Alexander the Great, Third Edition. San Francisco: Future Publishing Limited. Pg. 12.

39. Cartledge, Paul (2004). Alexander the Great. NYC: Vintage Books. Pg. 221.

40. Stewart, Andrew (1993). Faces of Power: Alexander's Image and Hellenistic Politics. Berkeley: University of California Press. Pg. 86.

41. Stewart, Andrew (1993). Faces of Power: Alexander's Image and Hellenistic Politics. Berkeley: University of California Press. Pg. 120.

42. Harl, Kenneth W. (2010). Alexander the Great and the Macedonian Empire. The Great Courses. The Teaching Company, LLC. Lecture 9, 25:38—25:54.

43. Everitt, Anthony (2019). Alexander the Great: His Life and His Mysterious Death. NYC: Random House. Pgs. 97-98.

44. Bose, Partha (2004). Alexander the Great's Art of Strategy: The Timeless Lessons of History's Greatest Empire Builder. NYC: Gotham Books. Pg. 214.

45. Bose, Partha (2004). Alexander the Great's Art of Strategy: The Timeless Lessons of History's Greatest Empire Builder. NYC: Gotham Books. Pg. 214.

46. Bose, Partha (2004). Alexander the Great's Art of Strategy: The Timeless Lessons of History's Greatest Empire Builder. NYC: Gotham Books. Pg. 214.

47. Bose, Partha (2004). Alexander the Great's Art of Strategy: The Timeless Lessons of History's Greatest Empire Builder. NYC: Gotham Books. Pgs. 214-215.

48. Bose, Partha (2004). Alexander the Great's Art of Strategy: The Timeless Lessons of History's Greatest Empire Builder. NYC: Gotham Books. Pg. 215.

49. Bose, Partha (2004). Alexander the Great's Art of Strategy: The Timeless Lessons of History's Greatest Empire Builder. NYC: Gotham Books. Pg. 215.

50. Harl, Kenneth W. (2010). Alexander the Great and the Macedonian Empire. The Great Courses. The Teaching Company, LLC. Lecture 9, 25:38—25:45.

51. Harl, Kenneth W. (2010). Alexander the Great and the Macedonian Empire. The Great Courses. The Teaching Company, LLC. Lecture 9, 25:38—25:54.

52. Siculus, Diodorus (Diodorus of Sicily)(1963[1st Century B.C.]). Bibliotheca Historica [Historical Library], XVII.LXXXV. Loeb Classical Library, University of Chicago. Pg. 367.
https://penelope.uchicago.edu/Thayer/e/roman/texts/diodorus_siculus/home.html

53. Siculus, Diodorus (Diodorus of Sicily)(1963[1st Century B.C.]). Bibliotheca Historica [Historical Library], XVII.LXXXV. Loeb Classical Library, University of Chicago. Pg. 367.
https://penelope.uchicago.edu/Thayer/e/roman/texts/diodorus_siculus/home.html

54. Siculus, Diodorus (Diodorus of Sicily)(1963[1st Century B.C.]). Bibliotheca Historica [Historical Library],

XVII.LXXXV. Loeb Classical Library, University of Chicago. Pg. 367-369. https://penelope.uchicago.edu/Thayer/e/roman/texts/diodorus_siculus/home.html

55. Colvin, Geoffrey (2006, October 30). "What It Takes to Be Great." Fortune Magazine, Volume 154, Number 9. Pg. 102.

56. Langer, Ellen J. (1989). Mindfulness. Menlo Park: Addison-Wesley. Pg. 76.

57. Coyle, Daniel (2009). The Talent Code: Greatness isn't Born. It's Grown. Here's How. NYC: Bantam. Pg. 65. **See also:** Owen, Frederick A. (1929). "Letters to the Editor." Normal Instructor and Primary Plans, Volume 39. Dansville: F.A. Owen Publishing Company. Pg. 19. **Note:** The quote in context is even more interesting: "Who said, 'If people knew how hard I had to work to gain my mastery, it would not seem so wonderful at all.'? Michelangelo is said to have made this remark to a friend who found him in his studio destroying numerous sketches which had been used in developing his masterpieces."

58. Colvin, Geoffrey (2006, October 30). "What It Takes to Be Great." Fortune Magazine, Volume 154, Number 9. Pg. 88.

59. Colvin, Geoffrey (2006, October 30). "What It Takes to Be Great." Fortune Magazine, Volume 154, Number 9. Pg. 72.

60. Johnson, Paul (2009). Heroes: From Alexander the Great and Julius Caesar to Churchill and De Gaulle. NYC: HarperCollins. Pg. 33.

61. Doleac, Miles (2014). In the Footsteps of Alexander: The King Who Conquered the Ancient World. NYC: Metro Books. Pg. 17.

62. Best, Amy (Editor)(2021). "Greek Legend." All About History Book of Greek Mythology. Bath: Future Publishing Limited. Pg. 89.

63. Best, Amy (Editor)(2021). "Greek Legend." All About History Book of Greek Mythology. Bath: Future Publishing Limited. Pg. 89.

64. Everitt, Anthony (2019). Alexander the Great: His Life and His Mysterious Death. NYC: Random House. Pg. 317.

65. Johnson, Paul (2009). Heroes: From Alexander the Great and Julius Caesar to Churchill and De Gaulle. NYC: HarperCollins. Pg. 33.

66. Lyons, Lynn (2022). The Anxiety Audit: Seven Sneaky Ways Anxiety Takes Hold and How to Escape Them. NYC: Simon & Schuster. Pg. 126.

67. "Beginnings" (2021). All About History Book of Alexander the Great, Third Edition. San Francisco: Future Publishing Limited. Pg. 11.

68. Cartledge, Paul (2004). Alexander the Great. NYC: Vintage Books. Pg. 222.

69. Cartledge, Paul (2004). Alexander the Great. NYC: Vintage Books. Pg. 222.

70. Cartledge, Paul (2004). Alexander the Great. NYC: Vintage Books. Pg. 222.

71. Nietzsche, Friedrich (1997). Twilight of the Idols, Or How to Philosophize with the Hammer. Translated by Richard Polt. Cambridge: Hackett Publishing. Pg. 66.

72. Nietzsche, Friedrich (1997). Twilight of the Idols, Or How to Philosophize with the Hammer. Translated by Richard Polt. Cambridge: Hackett Publishing. Pg. 67.

73. Doleac, Miles (2014). In the Footsteps of Alexander: The King Who Conquered the Ancient World. NYC: Metro Books. Pg. 149.

74. Doleac, Miles (2014). In the Footsteps of Alexander: The King Who Conquered the Ancient World. NYC: Metro Books. Pg. 149.

75. Everitt, Anthony (2019). Alexander the Great: His Life and His Mysterious Death. NYC: Random House. Pg. 329.

76. Bose, Partha (2004). Alexander the Great's Art of Strategy: The Timeless Lessons of History's Greatest Empire Builder. NYC: Gotham Books. Pg. 216.

77. Worthington, Ian (2014). By the Spear : Philip II, Alexander the Great, and the Rise and Fall of the Macedonian Empire. Oxford: Oxford University Press. Pg. 242.

78. Everitt, Anthony (2019). Alexander the Great: His Life and His Mysterious Death. NYC: Random House. Pg. 353.

79. Arrian, Flavius (1884). The Anabasis of Alexander; or, The history of the Wars and Conquests of Alexander the Great. E.J. Chinnock (Translator). London: Hodder and Stoughton. 6.24.3

80. Everitt, Anthony (2019). Alexander the Great: His Life and His Mysterious Death. NYC: Random House. Pg. 353.

81. Everitt, Anthony (2019). Alexander the Great: His Life and His Mysterious Death. NYC: Random House. Pg. 354.

82. Everitt, Anthony (2019). Alexander the Great: His Life and His Mysterious Death. NYC: Random House. Pg. 422.

83. Covey, Stephen (1990). The Seven Habits of Highly Effective People: Powerful Lessons in Personal Change. NYC: Simon and Schuster. Pg. 107.

84. Earhart, Amelia (1933, September). "My Husband." Redbook Magazine. **See also:** Lovell, Mary S. (1989). The Sound of Wings: The Life of Amelia Earhart. NYC: St. Martin's Press. Pg. 101.

85. Covey, Stephen (2004). The 8th Habit: From Effectiveness to Greatness. NYC: Free Press. Pg. 40. Emphasis added.

86. Cartledge, Paul (2004). Alexander the Great. NYC: Vintage Books. Pg. 248.

87. Cartledge, Paul (2004). Alexander the Great. NYC: Vintage Books. Pg. 248.

88. Garvey, Patrick (2016, May 2). "Alexander the Great's 3 Heroes." Ancient Heroes. http://ancientheroes.net/blog/alexander-the-greats-3-heroes

89. Cartledge, Paul (2004). Alexander the Great. NYC: Vintage Books. Pg. 248.

90. Garvey, Patrick (2016, May 2). "Alexander the Great's 3 Heroes." Ancient Heroes. http://ancientheroes.net/blog/alexander-the-greats-3-heroes

91. Kets de Vries, Manfred & Engellau, Elisabet (2004). Are Leaders Born or Are They Made?: The Case of Alexander the Great. Karnac Books. Pg. 65.

92. Everitt, Anthony (2019). Alexander the Great: His Life and His Mysterious Death. NYC: Random House. Pg. 330.

93. Everitt, Anthony (2019). Alexander the Great: His Life and His Mysterious Death. NYC: Random House. Pg. 330.

94. Everitt, Anthony (2019). Alexander the Great: His Life and His Mysterious Death. NYC: Random House. Pg. 330.

95. Doleac, Miles (2014). In the Footsteps of Alexander: The King Who Conquered the Ancient World. NYC: Metro Books. Pg. 148.

96. Everitt, Anthony (2019). Alexander the Great: His Life and His Mysterious Death. NYC: Random House. Pg. 330.

97. Arrian, Flavius (1884). The Anabasis of Alexander; or, The history of the Wars and Conquests of Alexander the Great. E.J. Chinnock (Translator). London: Hodder and Stoughton. Pg. 294.

98. "Beginnings" (2021). All About History Book of Alexander the Great, Third Edition. San Francisco: Future Publishing Limited. Pg. 3.

99. Bowden, Hugh (2014). Alexander the Great: A Very Short Introduction. Oxford: Oxford University Press. Pg. 78.

100. Bowden, Hugh (2014). Alexander the Great: A Very Short Introduction. Oxford: Oxford University Press. Pg. 78.

101. Bowden, Hugh (2014). Alexander the Great: A Very Short Introduction. Oxford: Oxford University Press. Pg. 78.

102. Bowden, Hugh (2014). Alexander the Great: A Very Short Introduction. Oxford: Oxford University Press. Pg. 78.

103. Johnson, Paul (2009). Heroes: From Alexander the Great and Julius Caesar to Churchill and De Gaulle. NYC: HarperCollins. Pg. 38

104. Johnson, Paul (2009). Heroes: From Alexander the Great and Julius Caesar to Churchill and De Gaulle. NYC: HarperCollins. Pg. 27

105. Cartledge, Paul (2004). Alexander the Great. NYC: Vintage Books. Pg. 221.

106. Cartledge, Paul (2004). Alexander the Great. NYC: Vintage Books. Pg. 221.

107. Gracián, Baltasar (1892). Jacobs, Joseph (Translator). The Art of Worldly Wisdom. London: MacMillan and Co. Pg. 75.

108. Gracián, Baltasar (1892). Jacobs, Joseph (Translator). The Art of Worldly Wisdom. London: MacMillan and Co. Pg. 75.

109. Colvin, Geoffrey (2006, October 30). "What It Takes to Be Great." Fortune Magazine, Volume 154, Number 9. Pg. 206.

|7|

Spy Swiftly New Breakthroughs and Innovations to Advance: Rothschild's Run on Wellington's Win at Waterloo

1. Brandenburger, Adam (2020). "Strategy Needs Creativity." Chapter 8 in HBR Guide to Setting Your Strategy. Cambridge: Harvard Business Review Press. Pg. 66. See Also: https://hbr.org/2019/03/strategy-needs-creativity

2. Schom, Alan (1997). Napoleon Bonaparte. NYC: HarperCollins. Pg. 690.

3. Brezosky, Lynn (2005, December 11). "Pigeon Fanciers Breed for Speed." The Oklahoman. https://oklahoman.com/article/2923247/pigeon-fanciers-breed-for-speed

4. Bremmer, Ian and Keat, Preston (2010). Fat Tail: The Power of Political Knowledge in an Uncertain World. Oxford: Oxford University Press. Pg. 43.

5. Bremmer, Ian and Keat, Preston (2010). Fat Tail: The Power of Political Knowledge in an Uncertain World. Oxford: Oxford University Press. Pg. 43.

6. Knighton, Andrew (2016, March 14). "5 Ways Napoleon Made Himself into the New Charlemagne." War History Online. Irving, TX: Timera.

7. Ferguson, Niall (2008). The Ascent of Money: A Financial History of the World. NYC: Penguin. Pg. 80.

8. Morton, Frederic (2014). The Rothschilds: A Family Portrait. NYC: Diversion Books. Pg. 38.

9. Morton, Frederic (2014). The Rothschilds: A Family Portrait. NYC: Diversion Books. Pg. 38.

10. Morton, Frederic (2014). The Rothschilds: A Family Portrait. NYC: Diversion Books. Pg. 38.

11. Morton, Frederic (2014). The Rothschilds: A Family Portrait. NYC: Diversion Books. Pg. 38.

12. Morton, Frederic (2014). The Rothschilds: A Family Portrait. NYC: Diversion Books. Pg. 38.

13. Brown, Andrew (Editor)(2014). "Money: Top 5 Facts. Nathan Mayer Rothschild." All About History, Issue 10. Bournemouth: Imagine Publishing Ltd. Pg. 26.

14. Brown, Andrew (Editor)(2014). "Money: Top 5 Facts. Nathan Mayer Rothschild." All About History, Issue 10. Bournemouth: Imagine Publishing Ltd. Pg. 26.

15. Mansel, Philip (2014, September). "Power of the Court." History Today, Volume 64, Issue 9. London: History Today, Ltd. Pg. 27.

16. Staff Writer (2009, August 13). "Early Tools Were Born from Fire: Ancient humans were burning stones at least 70,000 years ago." Science. Washington, D.C.: American Association for the Advancement of Science (AAAS). https://www.science.org/content/article/early-tools-were-born-fire

17. Andrews, Evan (2021, February 18). "11 Innovations That Changed History." History. A&E Television Networks, LLC.

18. Wischkaemper, Jay (2001). "A Tribute to Perseverance: The Beginning of Flight." SW Aviator Magazine. Albuquerque: Southwest Regional Publishing, Inc.

19. Lipton, Bruce and Bhaerman, Steve (2009). Spontaneous Evolution: Our Positive Future (and a Way to Get There from Here). Carlsbad, CA: Hay House, Inc. Pg. 204.

20. Schoemaker, Paul J. H.; Krupp, Steve; and Howland, Samantha (2019). "Strategic Leadership: The Essential Skills." Chapter 1 in HBR Guide to Thinking Strategically. Boston: Harvard Business Review Press. Pg. 341.

21. Bowman, Nina (2020). "Spotting Trends and Patterns that Affect Your Business." In HBR Guides to Building Your Strategic Skills. Harvard Business School Publishing. Pg. 371.

22. Lynch, Lt. General (Ret.) Rick (2013). Adapt or Die: Leadership Principles from an American General. Grand Rapids: Baker Books. Pg. 197.

23. Day, Spencer (2018). "Genghis Khan: The Nomadic Pauper Who Nearly Conquered the World." History Revealed, Issue 61. Bristol: Immediate Media Company. Pg. 33.

24. Mustermann, Erik (2018, June 10). "The Stirrup: Genghis Khan's Deadliest Weapon." War History Online. https://www.warhistoryonline.com/war-articles/the-stirrup-genghis-khans-deadliest-weapon.html

25. White, Lynn (1964). Medieval Technology and Social Change. London: Oxford University Press. Pg. 38.

26. Staff Writer (2021, March 20) "History of Equestrian Stirrups." American Equus. https://americanequus.com/history-of-stirrups/

27. Mustermann, Erik (2018, June 10). "The Stirrup: Genghis Khan's Deadliest Weapon." War History Online. https://www.warhistoryonline.com/war-articles/the-stirrup-genghis-khans-deadliest-weapon.html

28. Day, Spencer (2018). "Genghis Khan: The Nomadic Pauper Who Nearly Conquered the World." History Revealed, Issue 61. Bristol: Immediate Media Company. Pg. 33.

29. Bouguet, Cyril; Barsoux, Jean-Louis; Wade, Michael (2022, Spring). "Stop Sabotaging Your Ability to Innovate." Harvard Business Review, On Point. Pg. 10.

30. Bouguet, Cyril; Barsoux, Jean-Louis; Wade, Michael (2022, Spring). "Stop Sabotaging Your Ability to Innovate." Harvard Business Review, On Point. Pg. 10.

31. Barron, Robber (2015, December 9). "Carnegie Steel: Building a Modern America." MBA Student Perspectives, Harvard Business School. Cambridge: Harvard Business School Publishing. https://digital.hbs.edu/platform-rctom/submission/carnegie-steel-building-a-modern-america/

32. Barron, Robber (2015, December 9). "Carnegie Steel: Building a Modern America." MBA Student Perspectives, Harvard Business School. Cambridge: Harvard Business School Publishing. https://digital.hbs.edu/platform-rctom/submission/carnegie-steel-building-a-modern-america/

33. Grosse, Karl "Charlemagne: Warrior. Innovator. King." (2013) [Documentary, Season 1, Episode 1] Germany: Taglicht Media.

34. Gilmont, Jean-Francois (2003). "Protestant Reformations and Reading." Chapter in A History of Reading in the West (Edited by Guglielmo Cavallo and Roger Chartier. Boston: University of Massachusetts Press. Pg. 213.

35. Hanley, Wayne (2005). The Genesis of Napoleonic Propaganda 1796—1799. NYC: Columbia University Press. Chapter 3. http://www.gutenberg-e.org/haw01/frames/fhaw03.html

36. Negrete, Miles (2021). "Was Hitler's grand conquest doomed to fail from the start?" Quora. https://www.quora.com/Was-Hitlers-grand-conquest-doomed-to-fail-from-the-start See Also: Back, George I. and Thompson, George Raynor (2023, Last Accessed) "World War II and After." Britannica. https://www.britannica.com/technology/military-communication/World-War-II-and-after

37. Chiles, James R. (2016, April). "Lyndon Johnson's Campaign by Helicopter: In 1948, "All the Way with LBJ" meant scooting around Texas in a Bell 47D." Air & Space Magazine. https://www.airspacemag.com/history-of-flight/campaign-by-helicopter-180958436/

38. Reeves, Martin and Haanaes, Knut (2015). Your Strategy Needs a Strategy: How to Choose and Execute the Right Approach. Cambridge: Harvard Business Review Press. Pg. 89.

39. Note: Strategy experts usually recommend the inclusion of several factors in the external environment. This is commonly referred to as a PESTEL analysis, an acronym that includes the following key environmental factors: Political, Economic, Socio-cultural, Technological, Environmental, and Legal. Depending on your area or field, not every one of these will be equally important. Nevertheless, the development of a new technology, process, or innovation could come in any one of these areas.

40. Bowman, Nina (2020). "Spotting Trends and Patterns that Affect Your Business." In HBR Guides to Building Your Strategic Skills. Harvard Business School Publishing. Pg. 371.

41. Linkow, Peter (1999, July). "What Gifted Strategic Thinkers Do Study Identifies Key Competencies of Strategic Thinking." Training & Development. https://cdn.ymaws.com/www.sahra.org/resource/resmgr/imported/what_gifted_strategic_thinkers_do_article_edited_cpk_nov_2010.pdf

42. HBR Analytic Services (2014). "The Digital Dividend: First-Mover Advantage: A Report by Harvard Business Review Analytic Services. Harvard Business School Publishing. https://hbr.org/resources/pdfs/comm/verizon/18832_HBR_Verizon_Report_IT_rev3_webview.pdf

43. HBR Analytic Services (2014). "The Digital Dividend: First-Mover Advantage: A Report by Harvard Business Review Analytic Services. Harvard Business School Publishing. https://hbr.org/resources/pdfs/comm/verizon/18832_HBR_Verizon_Report_IT_rev3_webview.pdf

44. Bradenburger, Adam (2022, Spring). "To Change the Way You Think, Change the Way You See." Harvard Business Review, On Point. Pg. 33.

45. Duhigg, Charles (2016). Smarter, Faster, Better: The Secrets of Being Productive in Life and Business. NYC: Random House. Pg. 278.

46. Duhigg, Charles (2016). Smarter, Faster, Better: The Secrets of Being Productive in Life and Business. NYC: Random House. Pg. 151.

47. Duhigg, Charles (2016). Smarter, Faster, Better: The Secrets of Being Productive in Life and Business. NYC: Random House. Pg. 153.

48. Duhigg, Charles (2016). Smarter, Faster, Better: The Secrets of Being Productive in Life and Business. NYC: Random House. Pg. 151.

49. Duhigg, Charles (2016). Smarter, Faster, Better: The Secrets of Being Productive in Life and Business. NYC: Random House. Pg. 151.

50. Duhigg, Charles (2016). Smarter, Faster, Better: The Secrets of Being Productive in Life and Business. NYC: Random House. Pgs. 151-152.

51. Tracy, Brian (2004). Getting Rich Your Own Way: Achieve All Your Financial Goals Faster than You Ever Thought Possible. NYC: John Wiley and Sons, Inc. Pg. 245.

52. Bouguet, Cyril; Barsoux, Jean-Louis; Wade, Michael (2022, Spring). "Stop Sabotaging Your Ability to Innovate." Harvard Business Review, On Point. Pg. 12.

53. Kennedy, Robert F. (1969). Thirteen Days: A Memoir of the Cuban Missile Crisis. NYC: Penguin Books. Pg. 112. See Also: Janis, Irving (1983). Groupthink: Psychological Studies of Policy Decisions and Fiascoes, 2nd Edition. Boston: Houghton Mifflin Company.

54. Duhigg, Charles (2016). Smarter, Faster, Better: The Secrets of Being Productive in Life and Business. NYC: Random House. Pg. 271.

55. Duhigg, Charles (2016). Smarter, Faster, Better: The Secrets of Being Productive in Life and Business. NYC: Random House. Pgs. 272-273.

56. Moon, Youngme (2005, May). "Break Free from the Product Life Cycle." Harvard Business Review. https://hbr.org/2005/05/break-free-from-the-product-life-cycle

57. Brandenburger, Adam (2020). "Strategy Needs Creativity." Chapter 8 in HBR Guide to Setting Your Strategy. Cambridge: Harvard Business Review Press. Pg. 66.

58. Brandenburger, Adam (2020). "Strategy Needs Creativity." Chapter 8 in HBR Guide to Setting Your Strategy. Cambridge: Harvard Business Review Press. Pg. 66.

59. Bradenburger, Adam (2022, Spring). "To Change the Way You Think, Change the Way You See." Harvard Business Review, On Point. Pg. 34.

60. Bradenburger, Adam (2022, Spring). "To Change the Way You Think, Change the Way You See." Harvard Business Review, On Point. Pg. 34.

61. Khan, Yasmin (2018, February). "Gandhi in Britain." BBC History Magazine. Bristol: Immediate Media Co. https://www.historyextra.com/period/20th-century/gandhi-in-britain/

62. Khan, Yasmin (2018, February). "Gandhi in Britain." BBC History Magazine. Bristol: Immediate Media Co. https://www.historyextra.com/period/20th-century/gandhi-in-britain/

63. Gandhi, Rajmohan (2007). Mohandas: A True Story of a Man, His People and An Empire. NYC: Penguin. Pg. 59.

64. Khan, Yasmin (2018, February). "Gandhi in Britain." BBC History Magazine. Bristol: Immediate Media Co. https://www.historyextra.com/period/20th-century/gandhi-in-britain/

65. Gandhi, M.K. (1993). An Autobiography: The Story of My Experiments with Truth. Bombay: Navajivan Publishing House. Pg. 114.

66. Khan, Yasmin (2018, February). "Gandhi in Britain." BBC History Magazine. Bristol: Immediate Media Co. https://www.historyextra.com/period/20th-century/gandhi-in-britain/

67. Khan, Yasmin (2018, February). "Gandhi in Britain." BBC History Magazine. Bristol: Immediate Media Co. https://www.historyextra.com/period/20th-century/gandhi-in-britain/

68. Khan, Yasmin (2018, February). "Gandhi in Britain." BBC History Magazine. Bristol: Immediate Media Co. https://www.historyextra.com/period/20th-century/gandhi-in-britain/

69. Khan, Yasmin (2018, February). "Gandhi in Britain." BBC History Magazine. Bristol: Immediate Media Co. https://www.historyextra.com/period/20th-century/gandhi-in-britain/

70. Duhigg, Charles (2016). Smarter, Faster, Better: The Secrets of Being Productive in Life and Business. NYC: Random House. Pg. 253.

71. Duhigg, Charles (2016). Smarter, Faster, Better: The Secrets of Being Productive in Life and Business. NYC: Random House. Pg. 252.

72. Hargadon, Andrew and Sutton, Robert I. (1997, December). "Technology Brokering and Innovation in a Product Development Firm." Administrative Science Quarterly, Volume 42, Number 4. Pg. 716. https://www.researchgate.net/publication/23402 1560_Technology_Brokering_and_Innovation_in_ a_Product_Design_Firm See Also: .Duhigg, Charles (2016). Smarter, Faster, Better: The Secrets of Being Productive in Life and Business. NYC: Random House. Pg. 252

73. Duhigg, Charles (2016). Smarter, Faster, Better: The Secrets of Being Productive in Life and Business. NYC: Random House. Pg. 250.

74. Hargadon, Andrew and Sutton, Robert I. (1997, December). "Technology Brokering and Innovation in a Product Development Firm." Administrative Science Quarterly, Volume 42, Number 4. Pg. 748. https://www.researchgate.net/publication/23402 1560_Technology_Brokering_and_Innovation_in_ a_Product_Design_Firm

75. Hall, Bruce (Producer). (2018). "The Pope who founded modern diplomacy." Pope: The Most Powerful Man in History. CNN Original Series. [Documentary Film]. United States: Glass Entertainment Group. https://www.cnn.com/videos/world/2018/03/19/pop e-price-of-renaissance-progress-2.cnn

76. Hall, Bruce (Producer). (2018). Pope: The Most Powerful Man in History. CNN Original Series. [Documentary Film]. United States: Glass Entertainment Group. https://www.cnn.com/shows/pope

77. Hall, Bruce (Producer). (2018). Pope: The Most Powerful Man in History. CNN Original Series. [Documentary Film]. United States: Glass Entertainment Group. https://www.cnn.com/shows/pope

78. Duhigg, Charles (2016). Smarter, Faster, Better: The Secrets of Being Productive in Life and Business. NYC: Random House. Pg. 253.

79. Duhigg, Charles (2016). Smarter, Faster, Better: The Secrets of Being Productive in Life and Business. NYC: Random House. Pg. 263.

80. Duhigg, Charles (2016). Smarter, Faster, Better: The Secrets of Being Productive in Life and Business. NYC: Random House. Pg. 263.

81. Duhigg, Charles (2016). Smarter, Faster, Better: The Secrets of Being Productive in Life and Business. NYC: Random House. Pg. 250.

82. Duhigg, Charles (2016). Smarter, Faster, Better: The Secrets of Being Productive in Life and Business. NYC: Random House. Pg. 252.

83. Brandenburger, Adam (2020). "Strategy Needs Creativity." Chapter 8 in HBR Guide to Setting Your Strategy. Cambridge: Harvard Business Review Press. Pg. 66.

84. Maloney, Nancy (2018, February 23). "Five traits of a stand-out strategist." VSA Partners. https://www.vsapartners.com/news-ideas/five-traits-of-a-stand-out-strategist/

85. Maloney, Nancy (2018, February 23). "Five traits of a stand-out strategist." VSA Partners. https://www.vsapartners.com/news-ideas/five-traits-of-a-stand-out-strategist/

86. McNamara, Robert. (2020, August 27). "The Bessemer Steel Process." ThoughtCo.com. https://www.thoughtco.com/bessemer-steel-process-definition-1773300

87. Strathern, Paul (2016). The Medici: Power, Money, and Ambition in the Italian Renaissance. Oakland: Pegasus Books. Pg. 43.

88. Strathern, Paul (2016). The Medici: Power, Money, and Ambition in the Italian Renaissance. Oakland: Pegasus Books. Pg. 43.

89 . Tracy, Brian (2002). Victory! Applying the Proven Principles of Military Strategy to Achieve Success in Your Business and Personal Life. NYC: AMACOM. Pgs. 278-279.

90. Blakemore, Erin (2019, June 21). "Who were the Mongols? Under Genghis Khan, the Mongol army became a technologically advanced force and created the second-largest kingdom in history." National Geographic. https://www.nationalgeographic.com/culture/article/mongols

91. Gates, Bill (2007, December 14). "Bill Gates: The Skills You Need to Succeed." BBC News. http://news.bbc.co.uk/2/hi/business/7142073.stm

92. Gavetti, Giovanni and Rivkin, Jan W. (2005, April). "How Strategists Really Think: Tapping the Power of Analogy." Harvard Business Review. https://hbr.org/2005/04/how-strategists-really-think-tapping-the-power-of-analogy

93. Morgan, Gareth (1980). "Paradigms, Metaphors, and Problem Solving in Organization Theory." Administrative Science Quarterly. Volume 25, Number 4. Pg. 611.

94. Oswick, Cliff; Keenoy, Tom & Grant, David (2002). "Metaphor and Analogical Reasoning in Organization Theory: Beyond Orthodoxy." The Academy of Management Review. Volume 27, Number 2. Pg. 295.

95. Lakoff, George (1995). "Metaphor, Morality, and Politics, Or, Why Conservatives Have Left Liberals in the Dust." Social Research. Volume 62, Number 2. Pg. 177.

96. Marquis De Noailles (Editor)(1923). The Life and Memoirs of Count Molé (1781-1855), Volume 1 (1804-1815). London: Hutchinson & Co. Pg. 90.

97. Roberts, Andrew (2014). Napoleon: A Life. NYC: Viking. Pg. 107.

98. Gavetti, Giovanni and Rivkin, Jan W. (2005, April). "How Strategists Really Think: Tapping the Power of Analogy." Harvard Business Review. https://hbr.org/2005/04/how-strategists-really-think-tapping-the-power-of-analogy

99. Gavetti, Giovanni and Rivkin, Jan W. (2005, April). "How Strategists Really Think: Tapping the Power of Analogy." Harvard Business Review. https://hbr.org/2005/04/how-strategists-really-think-tapping-the-power-of-analogy

100. Gavetti, Giovanni and Rivkin, Jan W. (2005, April). "How Strategists Really Think: Tapping the Power of Analogy." Harvard Business Review. https://hbr.org/2005/04/how-strategists-really-think-tapping-the-power-of-analogy

101. Gavetti, Giovanni and Rivkin, Jan W. (2005, April). "How Strategists Really Think: Tapping the Power of Analogy." Harvard Business Review. https://hbr.org/2005/04/how-strategists-really-think-tapping-the-power-of-analogy

102. Gavetti, Giovanni and Rivkin, Jan W. (2005, April). "How Strategists Really Think: Tapping the Power of Analogy." Harvard Business Review. https://hbr.org/2005/04/how-strategists-really-think-tapping-the-power-of-analogy

103. Gavetti, Giovanni and Rivkin, Jan W. (2005, April). "How Strategists Really Think: Tapping the Power of Analogy." Harvard Business Review. https://hbr.org/2005/04/how-strategists-really-think-tapping-the-power-of-analogy

104. Gavetti, Giovanni and Rivkin, Jan W. (2005, April). "How Strategists Really Think: Tapping the Power of Analogy." Harvard Business Review. https://hbr.org/2005/04/how-strategists-really-think-tapping-the-power-of-analogy

105. This topic is covered in greater detail in Chapter 6, Section 3, Subsection 2, which focuses on using analogies from history. While the idea here is to use analogies as a conceptual tool for strategic, creative and innovative thinking, in order to make the best use of the power and avoid the pitfalls of analogy, involves following a similar, slightly overlapping set of steps:

(A.) Identify the Analogies. Because analogies are an inherent part of how we think, it is easy to use them without being consciously aware of it. Thus, the first step to using analogies or analogical reasoning effectively is to become more aware of the analogies we are using, and the potential analogies available. As Gavetti and Rivkin write, leaders "who pay attention to their own analogical thinking will make better strategic decisions and fewer mistakes." Source: Gavetti, Giovanni and Rivkin, Jan W. (2005, April). "How Strategists Really Think: Tapping the Power of Analogy." Harvard Business Review. https://hbr.org/2005/04/how-strategists-really-think-tapping-the-power-of-analogy

(B.) Resist Superficial Similarities and Common Cognitive Biases. Greater awareness can also help with the second key step, looking beyond the superficial similarities. Naturally, the most obvious similarities are likely to come to our attention first. But what is obvious can also be superficial and, thus, a poor analogy. Be careful to avoid superficial similarities—which research shows is surprisingly common. "In laboratory experiments conducted by psychologists, subjects—even well-educated subjects—are readily seduced by similarities they should know to be superficial." Source: Gavetti, Giovanni and Rivkin, Jan W. (2005, April). "How Strategists Really Think: Tapping the Power of Analogy." Harvard Business Review. https://hbr.org/2005/04/how-strategists-really-think-tapping-the-power-of-analogy

Gavetti and Rivkin also warn strategists to watch out for anchoring (i.e. the first analogy to gain even a minor foothold or early momentum tends to leave a lasting influence), and confirmation bias (i.e. the tendency to search for information to confirm our initial interpretations or existing beliefs).HBRStrategistsAnalogy0 A few simple questions can go a long way toward avoiding these biases. Start by questioning the analogy and challenging the assumptions behind it. Where does it break down, and why? And what does that break say about the differences? Are the differences important? What are the implications of these differences? Be careful not to disregard information that conflicts with your initial judgment. What are the implications of adopting this analogy? If you do begin to rely on it, how will it effect the future?

(C.) Search for Additional Analogies. Rather than getting tied down to one analogy, why not sit with the tension between two analogies? Analogies are really just frames for thinking through situations, but there is no need to limit yourself to just one frame. In fact, having a few useful, but perhaps slightly conflicting, analogies may help to give you a better handle on the options and potential pitfalls you face, and how you might best move ahead. Alternatively, if you need to chose one dominant analogy in order to move forward, see if you can't use the other analogy as a check on specific strategies or tactics, or perhaps start with a pilot project in different areas or at different times.

(D.) Take Action and Test. Finally, based on appropriate adaptations or customized calibrations of the analogy, map out a course of action for moving forward, but be prepared to revisit the analogy later, altering your course as needed. This leads directly to the sixth and final approach to help spur creative thinking and generate innovative ideas.

106. "Tesla Says Edison Was an Empiricist; Electrical Technician Declares Persistent Trials Attested Inventor's Vigor. 'His Method Inefficient' A Little Theory Would Have Saved Him 90% of Labor, Ex-Aide Asserts—Praises His Great Genius." The NYC Times (1931, October 19). Pg. 25.

107. "Tesla Says Edison Was an Empiricist; Electrical Technician Declares Persistent Trials Attested Inventor's Vigor. 'His Method Inefficient' A Little Theory Would Have Saved Him 90% of Labor, Ex-Aide Asserts—Praises His Great Genius." The NYC Times (1931, October 19). Pg. 25.

108. Thomke, Stefan & Reinertsen, Donald (2013). "Six Myths of Product Development." HBR's 10 Must Reads on Innovation. Boston: Harvard Business Review Press. Pg. 99.

109. Emerson, Ralph Waldo (1911). Journals of Ralph Waldo Emerson: With Annotations, Vol. 6. Boston: Houghton Mifflin Company. Pg. 302.

110. Bouguet, Cyril; Barsoux, Jean-Louis; Wade, Michael (2022, Spring). "Stop Sabotaging Your Ability to Innovate." Harvard Business Review, On Point. Pg. 15.

111. Bouguet, Cyril; Barsoux, Jean-Louis; Wade, Michael (2022, Spring). "Stop Sabotaging Your Ability to Innovate." Harvard Business Review, On Point. Pg. 15.

112. Cuban, Mark (2011) How to Win at the Sport of Business: If I Can Do It, You Can Do It. Pg. 41.

113. Grant, Adam (2021). Think Again: The Power of Knowing What You Don't Know. NYC: Viking. Pg. 28.

114. Grant, Adam (2021). Think Again: The Power of Knowing What You Don't Know. NYC: Viking. Pg. 29.

115. Spina, Chiara; Camuffo, Arnaldo; and Gambardella, Alfonso (2020, November 18). "Founders, Apply the Scientific Method to Your Startup." Harvard Business Review. https://hbr.org/2020/11/founders-apply-the-scientific-method-to-your-startup

116. Duhigg, Charles (2016). Smarter, Faster, Better: The Secrets of Being Productive in Life and Business. NYC: Random House. Pg. 278-279

117. Duhigg, Charles (2016). Smarter, Faster, Better: The Secrets of Being Productive in Life and Business. NYC: Random House. Pg. 279

118. Forbes, B.C. (1921). "Why Do So Many Men Never Amount to Anything? Thomas A. Edison, the Great Inventor, Answers this Pointed Question." American Magazine, Volume 91. Pg. 89.

119. Forbes, B.C. (1921). "Why Do So Many Men Never Amount to Anything? Thomas A. Edison, the Great Inventor, Answers this Pointed Question." American Magazine, Volume 91. Pg. 89.

120. Forbes, B.C. (1921). "Why Do So Many Men Never Amount to Anything? Thomas A. Edison, the Great Inventor, Answers this Pointed Question." American Magazine, Volume 91. Pg. 89.

121. Gates, Bill (2013, October 8). "America's Greatest Inventor." GatesNotes: The Blog of Bill Gates. https://www.gatesnotes.com/about-bill-gates/americas-greatest-inventor See also: the "Foreword" of Leonard DeGraaf's Edison and the Rise of Innovation (2013) NYC: Sterling Signature Publishing.

122. Schoemaker, Paul J. H.; Krupp, Steve; and Howland, Samantha (2019). "Strategic Leadership: The Essential Skills." Chapter 1 in HBR Guide to Thinking Strategically. Boston: Harvard Business Review Press. Pg. 13.

123. Schoemaker, Paul J. H.; Krupp, Steve; and Howland, Samantha (2019). "Strategic Leadership: The Essential Skills." Chapter 1 in HBR Guide to Thinking Strategically. Boston: Harvard Business Review Press. Pg. 340.

124. Chandler, David G. (Editor)(2015). Napoleon's Military Maxims. Cheltenham, England: The History Press. Pg. 16.

125. Chandler, David (2016). "General Introduction." In Cairnes, William E. (Editor)(2016). The Military Maxims of Napoleon. NYC: Skyhorse Publishing. Pg. 25.

126. Roberts, Andrew (2015, June). "Why We'd Be Better Off if Napoleon Never Lost at Waterloo." Smithsonian Magazine. Washington, D.C.: Smithsonian Institution. https://www.smithsonianmag.com/history/we-better-off-napoleon-never-lost-waterloo-180955298/

127. Chandler, David G. (Editor)(2015). Napoleon's Military Maxims. Cheltenham, England: The History Press. Pg. 16.

128. Dietrich, William (2015). Napoleon's Rules: Life and Career Lessons from Bonaparte. Burrows Publishing. Pg. 77.

129. Petre, Francis Loraine (1984). Napoleon at War. NYC: Hippocrene Books. Pg. 9.

130. Chandler, David G. (1979). Dictionary of the Napoleonic Wars. Arms and Armour Press. Pg. 18.

131. Petre, Francis Loraine (1984). Napoleon at War. NYC: Hippocrene Books. Pg. 9.

132. Chandler, David G. (1979). Dictionary of the Napoleonic Wars. Arms and Armour Press. Pg. 18.

|8|

To Unlock Unparalleled Power, Target Your Peak Leverage Points: The Legend of Lady Godiva

1. Kiyosaki, Robert T. and Lechter, Sharon (2012). Rich Dad's Retire Young, Retire Rich: How to Get Rich Quickly and Stay Rich Forever! Scottsdale: Plata Publishing, LLC. Pg. 48.

2. Donoghue, Daniel (2003). Lady Godiva: A Literary History of the Legend. Malden, MA: Blackwell Publishing. Pg. 27

3. Donoghue, Daniel (2003). Lady Godiva: A Literary History of the Legend. Malden, MA: Blackwell Publishing. Pg. 27.

4. Donoghue, Daniel (2003). Lady Godiva: A Literary History of the Legend. Malden, MA: Blackwell Publishing. Pg. 28.

5. Donoghue, Daniel (2003). Lady Godiva: A Literary History of the Legend. Malden, MA: Blackwell Publishing. Pg. 28.

6. Donoghue, Daniel (2003). Lady Godiva: A Literary History of the Legend. Malden, MA: Blackwell Publishing. Pg. 28.

7. Donoghue, Daniel (2003). Lady Godiva: A Literary History of the Legend. Malden, MA: Blackwell Publishing. Pg. 28.

8. Donoghue, Daniel (2003). Lady Godiva: A Literary History of the Legend. Malden, MA: Blackwell Publishing. Pg. 28.

9. Donoghue, Daniel (2003). Lady Godiva: A Literary History of the Legend. Malden, MA: Blackwell Publishing. Pg. 28.

10. Donoghue, Daniel (2003). Lady Godiva: A Literary History of the Legend. Malden, MA: Blackwell Publishing. Pg. 27.

11. Donoghue, Daniel (2003). Lady Godiva: A Literary History of the Legend. Malden, MA: Blackwell Publishing. Pg. 27.

12. Donoghue, Daniel (2003). Lady Godiva: A Literary History of the Legend. Malden, MA: Blackwell Publishing. Pg. 27.

13. Coe, Charles (2003, July-August). "Lady Godiva: The Naked Truth." Harvard Magazine. Cambridge: Harvard Magazine, Inc. https://harvardmagazine.com/2003/07/lady-godiva-the-naked-tr.html

14. Holmes, Oliver Wendell (1892). *The Works of Oliver Wendell Holmes in Thirteen Volumes*, Volume V. Boston: Houghton, Mifflin and Company. Pg. 221. Professor Holmes in a letter to Mr. Langdon.

15. Tracy, Brian (2000). The 100 Absolutely Unbreakable Laws of Business Success. San Francisco: Berrett-Koehler Publishers, Inc. Pg. 331.

16. Tracy, Brian (2000). The 100 Absolutely Unbreakable Laws of Business Success. San Francisco: Berrett-Koehler Publishers, Inc. Pgs. 331-332.

17. Kiyosaki, Robert (2012). Retire Young Retire Rich: How to Get Rich Quickly and Stay Rich Forever! NYC: Warner Business Books. Pg. xiii.

18. Covey, Sean; McChesney, Chris; and Huling, Jim (2012). The 4 Disciplines of Execution: Achieving Your Wildly Important Goals. NYC: Simon and Schuster. Pg. 41.

19. Covey, Sean; McChesney, Chris; and Huling, Jim (2012). The 4 Disciplines of Execution: Achieving Your Wildly Important Goals. NYC: Simon and Schuster. Pg. 41.

20. Senge, Peter M. (1990). The Fifth Discipline: The Art and Practice of the Learning Organization. NYC: Doubleday. Pg. 64.

21. Note: The rudder of the RMS Queen Mary weighs 160 tons, equal to the entire tonnage of the Mayflower.

22. Farrell (1972, February). "Playboy Interview: A Candid Conversation with the Visionary Architect, Inventor, Philosopher R. Buckminster Fuller." Playboy, Volume 19, Number 2. Pg. 59. See Buckminster Fuller Institute: https://www.bfi.org/sites/default/files/attachments/pages/CandidConversation-Playboy.pdf

23. Senge, Peter M. (1990). The Fifth Discipline: The Art and Practice of the Learning Organization. NYC: Doubleday. Pg. 64.

24. Abraham, Jay (2023 L.A.). "Leverage Marketing." Abraham Group. https://www.abraham.com/topic/leverage-marketing/ See also: https://s3-us-west-2.amazonaws.com/jayabrahamassets/Joseph/LeverageMarketingExtract.mp3 (Quote Starts @ 1:28). See also: https://www.tonyrobbins.com/career-business/the-power-of-leverage/

25. Senge, Peter M. (1990). The Fifth Discipline: The Art and Practice of the Learning Organization. NYC: Doubleday. Pg. 64.

26. Robbins, Anthony (2023, March L.A.) "The Power of Leverage: Get Ahead with Time, Achievements, Connections, and More." The Tony Robbins Blog: Career and Business. https://www.tonyrobbins.com/career-business/the-power-of-leverage/

27. Tracy, Brian (2000). The 100 Absolutely Unbreakable Laws of Business Success. San Francisco: Berrett-Koehler Publishers, Inc. Pg. 333.

28. Cardone, Grant (2023, January 29). "A self-made millionaire shares 8 money secrets rich people know that 'most of us don't.'" CNBC. https://www.cnbc.com/2023/01/29/self-made-millionaire-shares-what-rich-people-do-differently-that-make-them-ultra-wealthy.html

29. Ferriss, Timothy (2009). The 4-Hour Workweek: Escape 9-5, Live Anywhere, and Join the New Rich. NYC: Random House. Pg. 34.

30. Ferriss, Timothy (2009). The 4-Hour Workweek: Escape 9-5, Live Anywhere, and Join the New Rich. NYC: Random House. Pg. 34.

31. Butler-Bowdon, Tom (2008). *50 Prosperity Classics: Attract It, Create It, Manage It, Share It. Wisdom from the Best Books on Wealth Creation and Abundance.* London: Nicholas Brealey Publishing. Pg. 143.

32. Butler-Bowdon, Tom (2008). *50 Prosperity Classics: Attract It, Create It, Manage It, Share It. Wisdom from the Best Books on Wealth Creation and Abundance.* London: Nicholas Brealey Publishing. Pg. 144.

33. Axelrod, Alan (2013). Catherine the Great CEO: 7 Principles to Guide and Inspire Modern Leaders. NYC: Sterling. Pg. 10.

34. Meadows, Donella (2008). Thinking in Systems: A Primer. London: Earthscan. Pg. 145.

35. Meadows, Donella (1999). "Leverage Points: Places to Intervene in a System." The Donella Meadows Project: Academy for Systems Change. Hartland, VT: The Sustainability Institute. https://donellameadows.org/wp-content/userfiles/Leverage_Points.pdf

36. One of the best models for thinking about where to intervene was first developed by former MIT system analyst and environmental scientist Donella Meadows, which she elaborated in her book, *Thinking in Systems* (2008). Building on the work of Meadows and others, another quality resource here is the work of MIT's Peter Senge, including parts of his books, *The Fifth Discipline* (2006), *The Fifth Discipline Fieldbook*, and *The Dance of Change*.

37. Senge, Peter M. (1990). The Fifth Discipline: The Art and Practice of the Learning Organization. NYC: Doubleday. Pg. 65.

38. Senge, Peter M. (1990). The Fifth Discipline: The Art and Practice of the Learning Organization. NYC: Doubleday. Pg. 44.

39. Senge, Peter M. (1990). The Fifth Discipline: The Art and Practice of the Learning Organization. NYC: Doubleday. Pg. 44.

40. Senge, Peter M. (1990). The Fifth Discipline: The Art and Practice of the Learning Organization. NYC: Doubleday. Pg. 40.

41. Meadows, Donella (2008). Thinking in Systems: A Primer. London: Earthscan. Pg. 161.

42. Meadows, Donella (2008). Thinking in Systems: A Primer. London: Earthscan. Pg. 162.

43. Meadows, Donella (2008). Thinking in Systems: A Primer. London: Earthscan. Pg. 162.

44. Meadows, Donella (2008). Thinking in Systems: A Primer. London: Earthscan. Pg. 162.

45. Brain, Jessica (2022, May 12). "Harthacnut." Historic UK: History UK. Devon: Historic UK Ltd. https://www.historic-uk.com/HistoryUK/HistoryofEngland/Harthacnut/

|9|

Profit from the Supremacy of Strategic Surprise: The Triumph of the Vikings—The Sons of Ragnar Lothbrok, Oleg, Rollo, Canute the Great, and Other Seafaring War Wolves of the Viking Age

1. Bonaparte, Napoleon (1845). Military Maxims of Napoleon. Translated by J. Akerly. NYC: Wiley and Putnam. Pg. 95.

2. Ross, Steven T. (1988). "Napoleon and Maneuver Warfare." In Borowski, Harry (Editor) The Harmon Memorial Lectures in Military History, 1959—1987: A Collection of the First Thirty Harmon Lectures Given at the United States Air Force Academy. Washington, D.C.: Office of Air Force History. Pg. 310.

3. Hastein Ragnarsson is typically known as simply Hastein, but some historians refer to him as Anstign, Astignus, Halfdan, or Hasting.

4. Ragnar's last name is sometimes spelled as Lodbrok. Hastein may have claimed to be the son of Ragnar for prestige, but historians have been unable to say definitively either way.

5. Jones, Gwyn (1968). A History of the Vikings. NYC: Oxford University Press. Pg. 216.

6. Bartlett, W. B. (2019). Vikings: A History of the Northmen. Gloucestershire: Amberley Publishing. Pg. 137.

7. Bartlett, W. B. (2019). Vikings: A History of the Northmen. Gloucestershire: Amberley Publishing. Pg. 137.

8. Logan, F. Donald (1991). The Vikings in History, 2nd Edition. London: Routledge. Pg. 126.

9. Jones, Gwyn (1968). A History of the Vikings. NYC: Oxford University Press. Pg. 216.

10. Price, Neil (2020). Children of Ash and Elm: A History of the Vikings. NYC: Basic Books. Pg. 437.

11. Jones, Gwyn (1968). A History of the Vikings. NYC: Oxford University Press. Pg. 217

12. Jones, Gwyn (1968). A History of the Vikings. NYC: Oxford University Press. Pg. 217

13. Bartlett, W. B. (2019). Vikings: A History of the Northmen. Gloucestershire: Amberley Publishing. Pg. 181

14. Jones, Gwyn (1968). A History of the Vikings. NYC: Oxford University Press. Pg. 217

15. Bartlett, W. B. (2019). Vikings: A History of the Northmen. Gloucestershire: Amberley Publishing. Pg. 137

16. Bartlett, W. B. (2019). Vikings: A History of the Northmen. Gloucestershire: Amberley Publishing. Pg. 137

17. Bartlett, W. B. (2019). Vikings: A History of the Northmen. Gloucestershire: Amberley Publishing. Pgs. 137-138.

18. Thon, Jan Ingar (2022). "Did They Try to Plunder Rome? The Vikings Attacked Both London and Paris, But According to the Chronicles of Norman Historian Dudo of Saint-Quentin, They Also Tried to Invade Rome." Insider History Collection: Vikings. Kolbotn, Norway: Bonnier Publications International AS. Pg. 40.

19. Thon, Jan Ingar (2022). "Did They Try to Plunder Rome? The Vikings Attacked Both London and Paris, But...Also Tried to Invade Rome." Insider History Collection: Vikings. Kolbotn, Norway: Bonnier Publications International AS. Pg. 41.

20. Bartlett, W. B. (2019). Vikings: A History of the Northmen. Gloucestershire: Amberley Publishing. Pg. 138

21. Thon, Jan Ingar (2022). "Did They Try to Plunder Rome? The Vikings Attacked Both London and Paris, But...Also Tried to Invade Rome." Insider History Collection: Vikings. Kolbotn, Norway: Bonnier Publications International AS. Pg. 40.

22. Thon, Jan Ingar (2022). "Did They Try to Plunder Rome? The Vikings Attacked Both London and Paris, But...Also Tried to Invade Rome." Insider History Collection: Vikings. Kolbotn, Norway: Bonnier Publications International AS. Pg. 41.

23. Thon, Jan Ingar (2022). "Did They Try to Plunder Rome? The Vikings Attacked Both London and Paris, But...Also Tried to Invade Rome." Insider History Collection: Vikings. Kolbotn, Norway: Bonnier Publications International AS. Pg. 41.

24. Whaley, Barton (2007). Stratagem: Deception and Surprise in War. Norwood, MA: Artech House. Pg. 64.

25. Ridgley, Stanley K. (2012). Strategic Thinking Skills: The Great Courses. The Great Courses. Chantilly, Virginia: The Teaching Company, LLC. Lecture 4 (22:07).

26. Griffith, Paddy (1995). The Viking Art of War. London: Greenhill Books. Pg. 272.

27. Daniel, Donald and Herbig, Katherine (1981). Strategic Military Deception. NYC: Pergamon Press. Pg. 179.

28. Daniel, Donald and Herbig, Katherine (1981). Strategic Military Deception. NYC: Pergamon Press. Pg. 189.

29. Daniel, Donald and Herbig, Katherine (1981). Strategic Military Deception. NYC: Pergamon Press. Pg. 189.

30. Erfurth, Waldemar (1943). Surprise. Harrisburg, PA: Military Service Company. Pg. 385.

31. Livio, Mario (2017). Why: What Makes Us Curious. NYC: Simon & Schuster. Pg. 46.

32. Livio, Mario (2017). Why: What Makes Us Curious. NYC: Simon & Schuster. Pg. 45.

33. Bonaparte, Napoleon (1845). Military Maxims of Napoleon. Translated by J. Akerly. NYC: Wiley and Putnam. Pg. 95.

34. Wilson, Robert Thomas (1860). Narrative of Events During the Invasion of Russia by Napoleon Bonaparte, and the Retreat of the French Army, 1812. London: John Murray. Pgs. 14-15.

35. Bonaparte, Napoleon; Tarbell, Ida M. (Editor)(1897). Napoleon's Addresses: Selections from the Proclamations, Speeches and Correspondence of Napoleon Bonaparte. Boston: Joseph Knight Company. Pg. 122.

36. Timofeychev, Alexey (2018, February 22). "Surprised by Russia: 5 things that bewildered Napoleon in 1812." Russia Beyond. https://www.rbth.com/history/327666-surprised-by-russia-napoleon

37. Timofeychev, Alexey (2018, February 22). "Surprised by Russia: 5 things that bewildered Napoleon in 1812." Russia Beyond. https://www.rbth.com/history/327666-surprised-by-russia-napoleon

38. Bonaparte, Napoleon; Tarbell, Ida M. (Editor)(1897). Napoleon's Addresses: Selections from the Proclamations, Speeches and Correspondence of Napoleon Bonaparte. Boston: Joseph Knight Company. Pg. 122.

39. Sun Tzu (2008). The Art of War. Translated by Lionel Giles. Radford, VA: Wilder Publications. Pg. 62.

40. Bartlett, W. B. (2019). Vikings: A History of the Northmen. Gloucestershire: Amberley Publishing. Pg. 55.

41. Jones, Gwyn (1968). A History of the Vikings. NYC: Oxford University Press. Pg. 194.

42. Roesdahl, Else (1998). The Vikings, 2nd Edition. London: Penguin Books. Pg. 234.

43. William of Normandy ordered a false retreat to lure the English from the hill. The trick worked and his forces easily surrounded and destroyed the English. The Normans used a similar tactical surprise at Arques in 1053, Messina in 1060, and, later, in the Battle of Cassel in 1071. See: Bradbury, Jim (2004). The Routledge Companion to Medieval Warfare. NY: Routledge. Pgs. 160-161.

44. Bartlett, W. B. (2019). Vikings: A History of the Northmen. Gloucestershire: Amberley Publishing. Pg. 55.

45. Bartlett, W. B. (2019). Vikings: A History of the Northmen. Gloucestershire: Amberley Publishing. Pgs. 79-80.

46. Jones, Gwyn (1968). A History of the Vikings. NYC: Oxford University Press. Pg. 214.

47. Brownworth, Lars (2014). The Sea-Wolves: A History of the Vikings. UK: Crux Publishing. Pg. 40.

48. Sawyer, P.H. (1982). Kings and Vikings: Scandinavia and Europe A.D. 700—1100. London: Routledge. Pg. 94.

49. Hadley, Sawn and Richards, Julian (2021). The Viking Great Army and the Making of England. Thames and Hudson. Pg. 47.

50. Head, Tom (2017). World History 101: From Ancient Mesopotamia and the Viking Conquests to Nato and Wikileaks, an Essential Primer on World History. Avon, MA: Adams Media. Pg. 103.

51. Jones, Gwyn (1968). A History of the Vikings. NYC: Oxford University Press. Pg. 194.

52. Jones, Gwyn (1968). A History of the Vikings. NYC: Oxford University Press. Pgs. 194-195.

53. Price, Neil (2020). Children of Ash and Elm: A History of the Vikings. NYC: Basic Books. Pg. 335.

54. Bartlett, W. B. (2019). Vikings: A History of the Northmen. Gloucestershire: Amberley Publishing. Pg. 56.

55. Sawyer, Peter (1997). The Oxford Illustrated History of the Vikings. NYC: Oxford University Press. Pg. 251.

56. Haywood, John (2015). Northmen: The Viking Saga, 793-1241 AD. London: Head of Zeus, Ltd. Pg. 174.

57. Barraclough, Eleanor Rosamund (2016). Beyond the Northlands: Viking Voyages and the Old Norse Sagas. Oxford: Oxford University Press. Pg. 321.

58. Haywood, John (2015). Northmen: The Viking Saga, 793-1241 AD. London: Head of Zeus, Ltd. Pg. 266

59. Bartlett, W. B. (2019). Vikings: A History of the Northmen. Gloucestershire: Amberley Publishing. Pg. 136

60. Bartlett, W. B. (2019). Vikings: A History of the Northmen. Gloucestershire: Amberley Publishing. Pg. 136

61. Ries, Al and Trout, Jack (2002). "The Law of the Category." In The 22 Immutable Laws of Marketing. NYC: HarperCollins. Pg. 15.

62. Jones, Gwyn (1968). A History of the Vikings. NYC: Oxford University Press. Pg. 211.

63. Haywood, John (2015). Northmen: The Viking Saga, 793-1241 AD. London: Head of Zeus, Ltd. Pg. 97

64. Jones, Gwyn (1968). A History of the Vikings. NYC: Oxford University Press. Pg. 211.

65. Winroth, Anders (2014). The Age of the Vikings. Princeton: Princeton University Press. Pg. 19.

66. Jones, Gwyn (1968). A History of the Vikings. NYC: Oxford University Press. Pg. 211.

67. Ferguson, Robert (2009). The Vikings: A History. NYC: Viking. 182.

68. Haywood, John (2015). Northmen: The Viking Saga, 793-1241 AD. London: Head of Zeus, Ltd. Pg. 97

69. Jones, Gwyn (1968). A History of the Vikings. NYC: Oxford University Press. Pg. 211.

70. Jones, Gwyn (1968). A History of the Vikings. NYC: Oxford University Press. Pg. 211.

71. Haywood, John (2015). Northmen: The Viking Saga, 793-1241 AD. London: Head of Zeus, Ltd. Pg. 60.

72. Williams, Gareth (2014, March). "How the Vikings Ruled the Waves." BBC History Magazine. Bristol: Immediate Media Co. Pg. 26.

73. Harl, Kenneth (2013). The Vikings. The Great Courses. Chantilly, Virginia: The Teaching Company, LLC. Lecture 10.

74. Jones, Gwyn (1968). A History of the Vikings. NYC: Oxford University Press. Pg. 223.

75. Brownworth, Lars (2014). The Sea-Wolves: A History of the Vikings. UK: Crux Publishing. Pg. 79-80.

76. Brownworth, Lars (2014). The Sea-Wolves: A History of the Vikings. UK: Crux Publishing. Pg. 80.

77. Brownworth, Lars (2014). The Sea-Wolves: A History of the Vikings. UK: Crux Publishing. Pg. 80.

78. Haywood, John (2015). Northmen: The Viking Saga, 793-1241 AD. London: Head of Zeus, Ltd. Pg. 137.

79. Ferguson, Robert (2009). The Vikings: A History. NYC: Viking. 667.

80. Winroth, Anders (2014). The Age of the Vikings. Princeton: Princeton University Press. Pg. 247.

81. Winroth, Anders (2014). The Age of the Vikings. Princeton: Princeton University Press. Pg. 18.

82. Winroth, Anders (2014). The Age of the Vikings. Princeton: Princeton University Press. Pg. 72.

83. Winroth, Anders (2014). The Age of the Vikings. Princeton: Princeton University Press. Pg. 71.

84. Winroth, Anders (2014). The Age of the Vikings. Princeton: Princeton University Press. Pg. 71.

85. Winroth, Anders (2014). The Age of the Vikings. Princeton: Princeton University Press. Pg. 71.
86. Winroth, Anders (2014). The Age of the Vikings. Princeton: Princeton University Press. Pg. 18.
87. Erfurth, Waldemar (1943). Surprise. Harrisburg, PA: Military Service Company. Pg. 393.
88. Erfurth, Waldemar (1943). Surprise. Harrisburg, PA: Military Service Company. Pg. 393.
89. Ferguson, Robert (2009). The Vikings: A History. NYC: Viking. 83.
90. Brownworth, Lars (2014). The Sea-Wolves: A History of the Vikings. UK: Crux Publishing. Pg. 66.
91. Haywood, John (2015). Northmen: The Viking Saga, 793-1241 AD. London: Head of Zeus, Ltd. Pg. 60.
92. Haywood, John (2015). Northmen: The Viking Saga, 793-1241 AD. London: Head of Zeus, Ltd. Pg. 60.
93. Brownworth, Lars (2014). The Sea-Wolves: A History of the Vikings. UK: Crux Publishing. Pg. 66.
94. Haywood, John (2015). Northmen: The Viking Saga, 793-1241 AD. London: Head of Zeus, Ltd. Pg. 60.
95. Brownworth, Lars (2014). The Sea-Wolves: A History of the Vikings. UK: Crux Publishing. Pg. 66.
96. Adams, Max (2018). The Viking Wars: War and Peace in King Alfred's Britain, 789–955. NYC: Pegasus Books. Pg. 115.
97. Brownworth, Lars (2014). The Sea-Wolves: A History of the Vikings. UK: Crux Publishing. Pg. 66.
98. Brownworth, Lars (2014). The Sea-Wolves: A History of the Vikings. UK: Crux Publishing. Pg. 66.
99. Mueller-Vollmer, Tristan and Wolf, Kirsten (2022). Vikings: An Encyclopedia of Conflict, Invasions, and Raids. Santa Barbara: ABC-CLIO. Pg. 126.
100. Sprague, Martina (2007). Norse warfare: The Unconventional Battle Strategies of the Ancient Vikings. NYC: Hippocrene Books, Inc. Pg. 233. See Also: Jones, Gwyn (1968). A History of the Vikings. NYC: Oxford University Press. Pg. 219.
101. Jones, Gwyn (1968). A History of the Vikings. NYC: Oxford University Press. Pg. 219.
102. Sprague, Martina (2007). Norse warfare: The Unconventional Battle Strategies of the Ancient Vikings. NYC: Hippocrene Books, Inc. Pg. 233.
103. Dougherty, Martin J. (2014). Vikings: A History of the Norse People. London: Amber Books Ltd. Pg. 112.
104. Logan, F. Donald (1991). The Vikings in History, 2nd Edition. London: Routledge. Pg. 143.
105. Brownworth, Lars (2014). The Sea-Wolves: A History of the Vikings. UK: Crux Publishing. Pg. 66.
106. Brownworth, Lars (2014). The Sea-Wolves: A History of the Vikings. UK: Crux Publishing. Pg. 67.
107. Brownworth, Lars (2014). The Sea-Wolves: A History of the Vikings. UK: Crux Publishing. Pg. 67.
108. Brownworth, Lars (2014). The Sea-Wolves: A History of the Vikings. UK: Crux Publishing. Pg. 67.
109. Brownworth, Lars (2014). The Sea-Wolves: A History of the Vikings. UK: Crux Publishing. Pg. 67.
110. Brownworth, Lars (2014). The Sea-Wolves: A History of the Vikings. UK: Crux Publishing. Pg. 66.
111. Bartlett, W. B. (2019). Vikings: A History of the Northmen. Gloucestershire: Amberley Publishing. Pg. 150.
112. Jarman, Cat (2021). River Kings: A New History of the Vikings from Scandinavia to the Silk Road. London: William Collins. Pgs. 22-23.
113. Brink, Stefan & Price, Neil (2008). The Viking World. NYC: Routledge. Pg. 342.
114. Logan, F. Donald (1991). The Vikings in History, 2nd Edition. London: Routledge. Pg. 151.
115. Price, Neil (2020). Children of Ash and Elm: A History of the Vikings. NYC: Basic Books. Pg. 408.
116. Jones, Gwyn (1968). A History of the Vikings. NYC: Oxford University Press. Pg. 221.
117. Adams, Max (2018). The Viking Wars: War and Peace in King Alfred's Britain, 789–955. NYC: Pegasus Books. Pg. 117.
118. Jones, Gwyn (1968). A History of the Vikings. NYC: Oxford University Press. Pg. 219.
119. Hjardar, Kim & Vike, Vegard (2016). Vikings at War. Oxford: Casemate Publishers. Pg. 546. Note: Strangely, a number of historians cite the 350 ships figure, which would put the number of Vikings well north of 10,000 Viking warriors. Also, it's not clear if Hjardar's figure excludes the extent to which their ships were used as supply depots. Nevertheless, as time went on, these numbers changed. "In the 9th century, especially from 840 on, the size and scale of Viking attacks go up significantly. And certainly by the end of the 9th century, these small contingents of Vikings who might represent fleets of 10, 15, 20 ships can very easily assemble into larger groups of a 100 vessels, 120 vessels, and all of a sudden you have 5,000 or 10,000 very seasoned and well-trained warriors. And this is the only way to account for the remarkable success the Vikings had in England, particularly between 865 and 878, or the kinds of attacks they can wage in the Carolingian empire, where they could put Paris under siege, and, really during the Carolingian monarchy [where the Vikings bring it] to its knees." Source: Harl, Kenneth (2013). The Vikings, The Great Courses. Chantilly, Virginia: The Teaching Company, LLC. Lecture 10.
120. Jones, Gwyn (1968). A History of the Vikings. NYC: Oxford University Press. Pg. 219.
121. Bartlett, W. B. (2019). Vikings: A History of the Northmen. Gloucestershire: Amberley Publishing. Pg. 151.
122. Winroth, Anders (2014). The Age of the Vikings. Princeton: Princeton University Press. Pg. 18.
123. Bartlett, W. B. (2019). Vikings: A History of the Northmen. Gloucestershire: Amberley Publishing. Pg. 151.
124. Edoardo, Albert (2018, January 11). "Alfred the Great's Viking Wars: Inside the Anglo-Saxon Fight to Save England." History of War. https://www.historyanswers.co.uk/history-of-war/alfred-the-greats-viking-wars-inside-the-anglo-saxon-fight-to-save-england/
125. Bartlett, W. B. (2019). Vikings: A History of the Northmen. Gloucestershire: Amberley Publishing. Pg. 151.
126. Dougherty, Martin J. (2014). Vikings: A History of the Norse People. London: Amber Books Ltd. Pg. 222.
127. Hall, Richard (2017) "The Viking Capture of York." The Jorvik Viking Centre. Coppergate, York: York Archaeological Trust. https://www.jorvikvikingcentre.co.uk/wp-content/uploads/2017/01/The-Viking-Capture-of-York.pdf
128. Brownworth, Lars (2014). The Sea-Wolves: A History of the Vikings. UK: Crux Publishing. Pg. 68
129. Dougherty, Martin J. (2014). Vikings: A History of the Norse People. London: Amber Books Ltd. Pg. 112.

130. Dougherty, Martin J. (2014). Vikings: A History of the Norse People. London: Amber Books Ltd. Pg. 222.

131. Dougherty, Martin J. (2014). Vikings: A History of the Norse People. London: Amber Books Ltd. Pg. 112.

132. Harl, Kenneth (2013). The Vikings, The Great Courses. Chantilly, Virginia: The Teaching Company, LLC. Lecture 10.

133. Hjardar, Kim & Vike, Vegard (2016). Vikings at War. Oxford: Casemate Publishers. Pg. 225.

134. Hjardar, Kim & Vike, Vegard (2016). Vikings at War. Oxford: Casemate Publishers. Pg. 225.

135. Hadley, Sawn and Richards, Julian (2021). The Viking Great Army and the Making of England. Thames and Hudson. Pg. 251-252.

136. Mueller-Vollmer, Tristan and Wolf, Kirsten (2022). Vikings: An Encyclopedia of Conflict, Invasions, and Raids. Santa Barbara: ABC-CLIO. Pg. 265.

137. Mueller-Vollmer, Tristan and Wolf, Kirsten (2022). Vikings: An Encyclopedia of Conflict, Invasions, and Raids. Santa Barbara: ABC-CLIO. Pg. 265.

138. Brownworth, Lars (2014). The Sea-Wolves: A History of the Vikings. UK: Crux Publishing. Pg. 68.

139. Mueller-Vollmer, Tristan and Wolf, Kirsten (2022). Vikings: An Encyclopedia of Conflict, Invasions, and Raids. Santa Barbara: ABC-CLIO. Pg. 265.

140. Roller, Sarah (2018, October 10). "3 Key Battles in the Viking Invasions of England." History Hit. https://www.historyhit.com/key-battles-of-the-viking-invasions-of-england/.

141. Bartlett, W. B. (2019). Vikings: A History of the Northmen. Gloucestershire: Amberley Publishing. Pg. 152.

142. Bartlett, W. B. (2019). Vikings: A History of the Northmen. Gloucestershire: Amberley Publishing. Pg. 152.

143. Giles, J.A. (1912). The Anglo-Saxon Chronicle. London: G. Bell and Sons. Pg. 49.

144. Sawyer, P.H. (1982). Kings and Vikings: Scandinavia and Europe A.D. 700—1100. London: Routledge. Pg. 91.

145. Hjardar, Kim & Vike, Vegard (2016). Vikings at War. Oxford: Casemate Publishers. Pg. 549.

146. Brownworth, Lars (2014). The Sea-Wolves: A History of the Vikings. UK: Crux Publishing. Pg. 68.

147. Ferguson, Robert (2010). The Hammer and the Cross: A New History of the Vikings. NYC: Penguin Books. Pg. 346.

148. James, Edward (2011, March 29). "Overview: The Vikings, 800 to 1066." BBC. https://www.bbc.co.uk/history/ancient/vikings/overview_vikings_01.shtml

149. Dougherty, Martin J. (2014). Vikings: A History of the Norse People. London: Amber Books Ltd. Pg. 115.

150. Lapidge, Michael et al (Editor)(2014). The Wiley Blackwell Encyclopedia of Anglo-Saxon England, Second Edition. West Sussex: John Wiley & Sons, Ltd. Pg. 526.

151. Blanchard, Keith (Editorial Director)(2022). Warriors of the Ancient World. USA: a360media. Pg. 9.

152. Dougherty, Martin J. (2014). Vikings: A History of the Norse People. London: Amber Books Ltd. Pg. 223.

153. Price, Neil (2020). Children of Ash and Elm: A History of the Vikings. NYC: Basic Books. Pg. 407.

154. Abels, Richard P. (2013). Alfred the Great: War, Culture and Kingship in Anglo-Saxon England. London: Routledge. Pgs. 137, 138.

155. Harl, Kenneth (2013). The Vikings, The Great Courses. Chantilly, Virginia: The Teaching Company, LLC. Handout Pg. 78.

156. Harl, Kenneth (2013). The Vikings, The Great Courses. Chantilly, Virginia: The Teaching Company, LLC. Handout Pg. 79.

157. Abels, Richard P. (2013). Alfred the Great: War, Culture and Kingship in Anglo-Saxon England. London: Routledge. Pg. 147. Note: The Vikings gained control of Mercia in 874.

158. Note: The Vikings gained control of Northumbria (York) in 867, then all of Northumbria in 876.

159. Harl, Kenneth (2013). The Vikings, The Great Courses. Chantilly, Virginia: The Teaching Company, LLC. Handout Pg. 79.

160. Abels, Richard P. (2013). Alfred the Great: War, Culture and Kingship in Anglo-Saxon England. London: Routledge. Pg. 140.

161. Abels, Richard P. (2013). Alfred the Great: War, Culture and Kingship in Anglo-Saxon England. London: Routledge. Pg. 148.

162. Abels, Richard P. (2013). Alfred the Great: War, Culture and Kingship in Anglo-Saxon England. London: Routledge. Pg. 148.

163. Abels, Richard P. (2013). Alfred the Great: War, Culture and Kingship in Anglo-Saxon England. London: Routledge. Pg. 148.

164. Abels, Richard P. (2013). Alfred the Great: War, Culture and Kingship in Anglo-Saxon England. London: Routledge. Pg. 148.

165. Parker, Philip (2014). The Northmen's Fury: A History of the Viking World. London: Random House. Pg. 99.

166. Parker, Philip (2014). The Northmen's Fury: A History of the Viking World. London: Random House. Pg. 99.

167. Haywood, John (2015). Northmen: The Viking Saga, 793-1241 AD. London: Head of Zeus, Ltd. Pg. 68.

168. Abels, Richard P. (2013). Alfred the Great: War, Culture and Kingship in Anglo-Saxon England. London: Routledge. Pg. 148.

169. Abels, Richard P. (2013). Alfred the Great: War, Culture and Kingship in Anglo-Saxon England. London: Routledge. Pg. 149.

170. Haywood, John (2015). Northmen: The Viking Saga, 793-1241 AD. London: Head of Zeus, Ltd. Pg. 68.

171. Haywood, John (2015). Northmen: The Viking Saga, 793-1241 AD. London: Head of Zeus, Ltd. Pg. 68.

172. Haywood, John (2015). Northmen: The Viking Saga, 793-1241 AD. London: Head of Zeus, Ltd. Pg. 68.

173. Haywood, John (2015). Northmen: The Viking Saga, 793-1241 AD. London: Head of Zeus, Ltd. Pg. 68.

174. Brownworth, Lars (2014). The Sea-Wolves: A History of the Vikings. UK: Crux Publishing. Pg. 79.

175. Brownworth, Lars (2014). The Sea-Wolves: A History of the Vikings. UK: Crux Publishing. Pg. 79.

176. Parker, Philip (2014). The Northmen's Fury: A History of the Viking World. London: Random House. Pg. 99.

177. Abels, Richard P. (2013). Alfred the Great: War, Culture and Kingship in Anglo-Saxon England. London: Routledge. Pg. 137-138.

178. Giles, J.A. (1912). The Anglo-Saxon Chronicle. London: G. Bell and Sons. Pg. 60.

179. Brownworth, Lars (2014). The Sea-Wolves: A History of the Vikings. UK: Crux Publishing. Pg. 79.

180. Brownworth, Lars (2014). The Sea-Wolves: A History of the Vikings. UK: Crux Publishing. Pg. 79.

181. Brownworth, Lars (2014). The Sea-Wolves: A History of the Vikings. UK: Crux Publishing. Pg. 79.

182. Parker, Philip (2014). The Northmen's Fury: A History of the Viking World. London: Random House. Pg. 99.

183. Harl, Kenneth (2013). The Vikings, The Great Courses. Chantilly, Virginia: The Teaching Company, LLC. Lecture 10.

184. Harl, Kenneth (2013). The Vikings, The Great Courses. Chantilly, Virginia: The Teaching Company, LLC. Lecture 10.

185. Harl, Kenneth (2013). The Vikings, The Great Courses. Chantilly, Virginia: The Teaching Company, LLC. Lecture 10.

186. Price, Neil (2020). Children of Ash and Elm: A History of the Vikings. NYC: Basic Books. Pg. 395.

187. Dougherty, Martin J. (2014). Vikings: A History of the Norse People. London: Amber Books Ltd. Pg. 226.

188. Bartlett, W. B. (2019). Vikings: A History of the Northmen. Gloucestershire: Amberley Publishing. Pg. 181.

189. Haywood, John (2015). Northmen: The Viking Saga, 793-1241 AD. London: Head of Zeus, Ltd. Pg. 68. Quote: "The Danes did not regard oaths sworn to Christians as binding."

190. Parker, Philip (2014). The Northmen's Fury: A History of the Viking World. London: Random House. Pg. 99.

191. Ferguson, Robert (2010). The Hammer and the Cross: A New History of the Vikings. NYC: Penguin Books. Pg. 138.

192. Shaw, Alan (2018, September 30). "On this day, 1938: Peace for our time was a hollow boast by Neville Chamberlain." The Sunday Post. Dundee, Scotland: DC Thomson Co. Ltd. https://www.sundaypost.com/fp/on-this-day-1938-peace-for-our-time-was-a-hollow-boast-by-neville-chamberlain/

193. Lindsay, James M. (2015, April 30). "The Vietnam War in Forty Quotes." Council on Foreign Relations. https://www.cfr.org/blog/vietnam-war-forty-quotes See also: Burr, William and Kimball, Jeffrey (2006, July 31). "Nixon White House Considered Nuclear Options Against North Vietnam, Declassified Documents Reveal." The National Security Archive. https://nsarchive2.gwu.edu/NSAEBB/NSAEBB195/#4 See also: Mueller, John E. (1980, December). "The Search for the 'Breaking Point' in Vietnam." International Studies Quarterly, Volume 24, Number 4. Pg. 497.

194. Grubin, David (Producer) (2000). Napoleon: Episode I: To Destiny. [Documentary Film]. Empires (Series). United States: PBS. http://www.pbs.org/empires/napoleon/n_about/resources/page_1.html

195. Grubin, David (Producer) (2000). Napoleon: Episode I: To Destiny. [Documentary Film]. Empires (Series). United States: PBS. http://www.pbs.org/empires/napoleon/n_about/resources/page_1.html

196. Grubin, David (Producer) (2000). Napoleon: Episode I: To Destiny. [Documentary Film]. Empires (Series). United States: PBS. http://www.pbs.org/empires/napoleon/n_about/resources/page_1.html

197. Grubin, David (Producer) (2000). Napoleon: Episode I: To Destiny. [Documentary Film]. Empires (Series). United States: PBS.

http://www.pbs.org/empires/napoleon/n_about/resources/page_1.html

198. Lapidge, Michael et al (Editor)(2014). The Wiley Blackwell Encyclopedia of Anglo-Saxon England, Second Edition. West Sussex: John Wiley & Sons, Ltd. Pg. 124.

199. Ferguson, Robert (2010). The Hammer and the Cross: A New History of the Vikings. NYC: Penguin Books. Pg. 148.

200. Ferguson, Robert (2010). The Hammer and the Cross: A New History of the Vikings. NYC: Penguin Books. Pg. 148.

201. Ferguson, Robert (2010). The Hammer and the Cross: A New History of the Vikings. NYC: Penguin Books. Pg. 148.

202. Bartlett, Wayne (2020). "Emperor of the North" All About History Book of Vikings, 14th Edition. San Francisco: Future Publishing Limited. Pg. 50.

203. Bartlett, Wayne (2020). "Emperor of the North" All About History Book of Vikings, 14th Edition. San Francisco: Future Publishing Limited. Pg. 50.

204. Mueller-Vollmer, Tristan and Wolf, Kirsten (2022). Vikings: An Encyclopedia of Conflict, Invasions, and Raids. Santa Barbara: ABC-CLIO. Pg. 83.

205. Note: The Byzantines was the name later given to the Greeks and Romans living in Constantinople, the capital of the Byzantine Empire (i.e. Eastern Roman Empire)].

206. Note: If he was honest with himself, Leo knew why this was happening. Known by Leo and the Byzantines as Varangians (a term referring to all those Vikings, conquerors, traders and settlers who originated in Sweden or greater Scandinavia), the Vikings' early contacts with Constantinople had been peaceful, largely centered around trade.RiverKings202 It was only after the Byzantines had helped one of the regional tribes block a disputed section of the river, an important stretch in the Vikings' trade route, that their anger was aroused. By the early 10th century, these river king raiders were intent on expanding their trade networks.

207. Plummer III, Comer (2006, June 12). "Ancient History: Walls of Constantinople." Military History. History Net. https://www.historynet.com/ancient-history-walls-of-constantinople/

208. Logan, F. Donald (1991). The Vikings in History, 2nd Edition. London: Routledge. Pg. 189.

209. Harl, Kenneth (2013). The Vikings, The Great Courses. Chantilly, Virginia: The Teaching Company, LLC. Handout Pg. 129. Note: "Far from serving as a deterrent, Constantinople's formidable reputation seemed to attract enemies. As the capital of a mighty empire, and at the crossroads of two continents, Constantinople represented to the early medieval world what Rome and Athens had meant to classical times," Comer writes in Military History. "The 'Queen of Cities,' she was a magnet for pilgrim, trader, and conqueror alike. None were wanting. The citadel turned back besieging armies 17 times in the course of a millennium. With each succeeding onslaught, Constantinople became ever more the final stronghold of Greek civilization." Source: Plummer III, Comer (2006, June 12). "Ancient History: Walls of Constantinople." Military History. History Net. https://www.historynet.com/ancient-history-walls-of-constantinople/

Like most of the Vikings who settled in Novgorod (today's Russia) and other areas along the river routes between the Baltic and Black seas, Oleg was one of the Northmen who originated in Scandinavia. Source: Logan, F. Donald (1991). The Vikings in History, 2nd Edition. London: Routledge. Pg. 188.

In Eastern Europe, these Northmen or Scandinavian Vikings, mostly from Sweden, were known as Rus ("the men who row"), and they came to rule over a multitude of subjected peoples throughout this region—in at least one case, according to Saint Nestor's Russian Primary Chronicle, by invitation. This is how Oleg's cousin, Rurik (the Viking who led the 860 attack on Constantinople), came to rule over the many diverse peoples of Novgorod. Source: Bauer, Susan Wise (2010). The History of the Medieval World: From the Conversion of Constantine to the First Crusade. New York: W.W. Norton. Pg. 721.

When Oleg came to power, his great Viking fleet of multiethnic pagans, Nestor the Chronicler reports, was "stuffed with men from twelve different nations." Source: Bauer, Susan Wise (2010). The History of the Medieval World: From the Conversion of Constantine to the First Crusade. New York: W.W. Norton. Pg. 721.

With this great multitude of tribes, "Oleg sallied forth by horse and by ship, and the number of his vessels was two thousand." Source: Saint Nestor the Chronicler (c. 1113 A.D.). The Russian Primary Chronicle. Cross, Samuel Hazzard and Sherbowitz-Wetzor, Olgerd (Editors). Cambridge, MA: The Mediaeval Academy of America. Pg. 64.

210. Albert, Daniel (2021, November 11). "Miklagard: When the Vikings Reached Constantinople." Life in Norway. https://www.lifeinnorway.net/miklagard-vikings-constantinople/

211. Harl, Kenneth (2013). The Vikings, The Great Courses. Chantilly, Virginia: The Teaching Company, LLC. Handout, Pg. 129.

212. Albert, Daniel (2021, November 11). "Miklagard: When the Vikings Reached Constantinople." Life in Norway. https://www.lifeinnorway.net/miklagard-vikings-constantinople/

213. Saint Nestor the Chronicler (c. 1113 A.D.). The Russian Primary Chronicle. Cross, Samuel Hazzard and Sherbowitz-Wetzor, Olgerd (Editors). Cambridge, MA: The Mediaeval Academy of America. Pg. 64.

214. Jarman, Cat (2021). River Kings: A New History of the Vikings from Scandinavia to the Silk Road. London: William Collins. Pg. 204. See Also: Saint Nestor the Chronicler (c. 1113 A.D.). The Russian Primary Chronicle. Cross, Samuel Hazzard and Sherbowitz-Wetzor, Olgerd (Editors). Cambridge, MA: The Mediaeval Academy of America. Pg. 64.

215. Saint Nestor the Chronicler (c. 1113 A.D.). The Russian Primary Chronicle. Cross, Samuel Hazzard and Sherbowitz-Wetzor, Olgerd (Editors). Cambridge, MA: The Mediaeval Academy of America. Pg. 64

216. Saint Nestor the Chronicler (c. 1113 A.D.). The Russian Primary Chronicle. Cross, Samuel Hazzard and Sherbowitz-Wetzor, Olgerd (Editors). Cambridge, MA: The Mediaeval Academy of America. Pg. 64.

217. Jarman, Cat (2021). River Kings: A New History of the Vikings from Scandinavia to the Silk Road. London: William Collins. Pg. 204.

218. Saint Nestor the Chronicler (c. 1113 A.D.). The Russian Primary Chronicle. Cross, Samuel Hazzard and Sherbowitz-Wetzor, Olgerd (Editors). Cambridge, MA: The Mediaeval Academy of America. Pg. 64

219. Note: While some historians doubt the veracity of this colorful account, there is nothing especially difficult about attaching a flat bottomed ship to a wheeled cart. In fact, there are a number of historical instances—including the Romans, Spartans, Avars, and the Vikings themselves, in their assault on Paris—in which armies moved ships across land as part of their assault on a city, often over much greater distances than the three or so miles Oleg's Viking fleet required. Furthermore, the Ottomans created a track to move ships across land in this same general area—from the Bosporus Strait to the Golden Horn—when they conquered Constantinople in 1453. More still, in the Book of the Golden Hall Master (c. 550 A.D.), the Daoist scholar and crown prince Xiao Yi describes a "wind-driven carriage" that had a mast and sails and could carry up to 30 people over land. Regardless of the feasibility of such an assault, perhaps the most convincing factor of this particular case is the result: The Rus-Byzantine commercial treaty of 911-912 which established exceptionally favorable terms for the Vikings. Source: Jones, Gwyn (1968). A History of the Vikings. NYC: Oxford University Press. Pg. 259. As Ferguson writes in The Vikings: A History, "Byzantine written sources contain no direct reference to this raid of 907, a fact which has led some to doubt that it ever took place at all. But the terms of the peace and trade treaty which followed the attack, and which are given in some detail in the Russian Primary Chronicle, show Constantinople, in the persons of the emperors Leo and Alexander, ceding trading terms to the Rus so favorable as to be unthinkable other than as the result of military defeat or the threat of such." Source: Ferguson, Robert (2009). The Vikings: A History. NYC: Viking. Pg. 228.

220. Bauer, Susan Wise (2010). The History of the Medieval World: From the Conversion of Constantine to the First Crusade. New York: W.W. Norton. Pg. 722.

221. Breemer, Jan S. (2000, December). War As We Knew It: The Real Revolution in Military Affairs/Understanding Paralysis in Military Operations. Maxwell Air Force Base, Alabama: Center for Strategy and Technology. Pg. 16.

222. Michaelson, Gerald (2003). Sun Tzu for Success: How to Use The Art of War to Master Challenges and Accomplish the Important Goals in Your Life. Avon, MA: Adams Media Corporation. Pg. 101.

223. Saint Nestor the Chronicler (c. 1113 A.D.). The Russian Primary Chronicle. Cross, Samuel Hazzard and Sherbowitz-Wetzor, Olgerd (Editors). Cambridge, MA: The Mediaeval Academy of America. Pg. 64

224. Jarman, Cat (2021). River Kings: A New History of the Vikings from Scandinavia to the Silk Road. London: William Collins. Pg. 204.

225. Harl, Kenneth (2013). The Vikings, The Great Courses. Chantilly, Virginia: The Teaching Company, LLC. Handout, Pg. 129.

226. Ferguson, Robert (2010). The Hammer and the Cross: A New History of the Vikings. NYC: Penguin Books. Pg. 119.

227. Ferguson, Robert (2010). The Hammer and the Cross: A New History of the Vikings. NYC: Penguin Books. Pg. 119.

228. Brownworth, Lars (2014). The Sea-Wolves: A History of the Vikings. UK: Crux Publishing. Pgs. 39-40.

229. Williams, Gareth (2014, March). "How the Vikings Ruled the Waves." BBC History Magazine. Bristol: Immediate Media Co. Pg. 26.

230. Williams, Gareth (2014, March). "How the Vikings Ruled the Waves." BBC History Magazine. Bristol: Immediate Media Co. Pg. 26.

231. Williams, Gareth (2014, March). "How the Vikings Ruled the Waves." BBC History Magazine. Bristol: Immediate Media Co. Pg. 26.

232. Christensen, Elise (2022). "Longships Went Everywhere: Viking ships made Scandinavians invincible." Insider History Collection: Vikings. Kolbotn, Norway: Bonnier Publications International AS. Pg. 52.

233. Winroth, Anders (2014). The Age of the Vikings. Princeton: Princeton University Press. Pg. 18

234. Christensen, Elise (2022). "Longships Went Everywhere: Viking ships made Scandinavians invincible." Insider History Collection: Vikings. Kolbotn, Norway: Bonnier Publications International AS. Pg. 49.

235. Brownworth, Lars (2014). The Sea-Wolves: A History of the Vikings. UK: Crux Publishing. Pg. 40

236. Jarman, Cat (2021). River Kings: A New History of the Vikings from Scandinavia to the Silk Road. London: William Collins. Pg. 63.

237. Brownworth, Lars (2014). The Sea-Wolves: A History of the Vikings. UK: Crux Publishing. Pg. 39.

238. Brownworth, Lars (2014). The Sea-Wolves: A History of the Vikings. UK: Crux Publishing. Pg. 39.

239. Brownworth, Lars (2014). The Sea-Wolves: A History of the Vikings. UK: Crux Publishing. Pg. 40.

240. Brownworth, Lars (2014). The Sea-Wolves: A History of the Vikings. UK: Crux Publishing. Pg. 40.

241. Christensen, Elise (2022). "Longships Went Everywhere: Viking ships made Scandinavians invincible." Insider History Collection: Vikings. Kolbotn, Norway: Bonnier Publications International AS. Pg. 49.

242. Christensen, Elise (2022). "Longships Went Everywhere: Viking ships made Scandinavians invincible." Insider History Collection: Vikings. Kolbotn, Norway: Bonnier Publications International AS. Pg. 48-49.

243. Brownworth, Lars (2014). The Sea-Wolves: A History of the Vikings. UK: Crux Publishing. Pg. 39.

244. Christensen, Elise (2022). "Longships Went Everywhere: Viking ships made Scandinavians invincible." Insider History Collection: Vikings. Kolbotn, Norway: Bonnier Publications International AS. Pg. 52.

245. Christensen, Elise (2022). "Longships Went Everywhere: Viking ships made Scandinavians invincible." Insider History Collection: Vikings. Kolbotn, Norway: Bonnier Publications International AS. Pg. 52.

246. Brownworth, Lars (2014). The Sea-Wolves: A History of the Vikings. UK: Crux Publishing. Pg. 40.

247. Jarman, Cat (2021). River Kings: A New History of the Vikings from Scandinavia to the Silk Road. London: William Collins. Pg. 63.

248. Bartlett, W. B. (2019). Vikings: A History of the Northmen. Gloucestershire: Amberley Publishing. Pg. 83.

249. Jarman, Cat (2021). River Kings: A New History of the Vikings from Scandinavia to the Silk Road. London: William Collins. Pg. 66.

250. Christensen, Elise (2022). "Longships Went Everywhere: Viking ships made Scandinavians invincible." Insider History Collection: Vikings. Kolbotn, Norway: Bonnier Publications International AS. Pg. 55.

251. Christensen, Elise (2022). "Longships Went Everywhere: Viking ships made Scandinavians invincible." Insider History Collection: Vikings. Kolbotn, Norway: Bonnier Publications International AS. Pg. 48.

252. Harl, Kenneth (2013). The Vikings, The Great Courses. Chantilly, Virginia: The Teaching Company, LLC. Lecture9

253. Christensen, Elise (2022). "Longships Went Everywhere: Viking ships made Scandinavians invincible." Insider History Collection: Vikings. Kolbotn, Norway: Bonnier Publications International AS. Pg. 48.

254. Harl, Kenneth (2013). The Vikings, The Great Courses. Chantilly, Virginia: The Teaching Company, LLC. Lecture9.

255. Harl, Kenneth (2013). The Vikings, The Great Courses. Chantilly, Virginia: The Teaching Company, LLC. Lecture9

256. Harl, Kenneth (2013). The Vikings, The Great Courses. Chantilly, Virginia: The Teaching Company, LLC. Lecture9

257. Bartlett, W. B. (2019). Vikings: A History of the Northmen. Gloucestershire: Amberley Publishing. Pg. 124.

258 Brindza, Paul (2023, March 12 L.A.) "Who Invented Magnets?" Jefferson Lab. Thomas Jefferson National Accelerator Facility - Office of Science Education. Newport News, VA. https://education.jlab.org/qa/historymag_01.html

259. Davis, Matt (2019, March 22). "Vikings unwittingly made their swords stronger by trying to imbue them with spirits." Big Think. https://bigthink.com/hard-science/norse-rituals/

260. Harl, Kenneth (2013). The Vikings, The Great Courses. Chantilly, Virginia: The Teaching Company, LLC. Handout, Pg. 129.

261. Albert, Daniel (2021, November 11). "Miklagard: When the Vikings Reached Constantinople." Life in Norway. https://www.lifeinnorway.net/miklagard-vikings-constantinople/ .

262. Ferguson, Robert (2010). The Hammer and the Cross: A New History of the Vikings. NYC: Penguin Books. Pg. 182.

263. Bauer, Susan Wise (2010). The History of the Medieval World: From the Conversion of Constantine to the First Crusade. New York: W.W. Norton. 733.

264. Bauer, Susan Wise (2010). The History of the Medieval World: From the Conversion of Constantine to the First Crusade. New York: W.W. Norton. 733.

265. Kipling, Rudyard (1940). "Dane-Geld." Rudyard Kipling's Verse. Garden City, NY: Doubleday. Pgs. 716-717.

266. Kipling (1940), Pgs. 716-717.

267. Kipling (1940), Pgs. 716-717.

268. Harl, Kenneth (2013). The Vikings, The Great Courses. Chantilly, Virginia: The Teaching Company, LLC. Handout, Pg. 71.

269. Harl, Kenneth (2013). The Vikings, The Great Courses. Chantilly, Virginia: The Teaching Company, LLC. Lecture 14.

270. Harl (2013), Lecture 14.

271. Ferguson, Robert (2010). The Hammer and the Cross: A New History of the Vikings. NYC: Penguin Books. Pg. 182.

272. Ferguson, Robert (2010). The Hammer and the Cross: A New History of the Vikings. NYC: Penguin Books. Pg. 182.

273. Harl (2013), Lecture 14.

274. Harl (2013), Lecture 14.

275. Harl (2013), Lecture 14.

276. Harl, Kenneth (2013). The Vikings, The Great Courses. Chantilly, Virginia: The Teaching Company, LLC. Handout, Pg. 72.

277. Harl (2013), Lecture 14.

278. Harl (2013), Lecture 14.

279. Harl, Kenneth (2013). The Vikings, The Great Courses. Chantilly, Virginia: The Teaching Company, LLC. Handout, Pg. 70.

280. Harl (2013), Lecture 14.

281. Harl (2013), Lecture 14.

282. Harl (2013), Lecture 14.

283. Van Houts, Elizabeth (Editor and Translator) (2000). The Normans in Europe. Oxford: Manchester University Press. Pg. 37.

284. Van Houts, Elizabeth (Editor and Translator) (2000). The Normans in Europe. Oxford: Manchester University Press. Pg. 37

285. Harl, Kenneth (2013). The Vikings, The Great Courses. Chantilly, Virginia: The Teaching Company, LLC. Handout, Pg. 73

286. Harl, Kenneth (2013). The Vikings, The Great Courses. Chantilly, Virginia: The Teaching Company, LLC. Lecture14

287. Harl, Kenneth (2013). The Vikings, The Great Courses. Chantilly, Virginia: The Teaching Company, LLC. Lecture14

288. Harl, Kenneth (2013). The Vikings, The Great Courses. Chantilly, Virginia: The Teaching Company, LLC. Handout, Pg. 73

289. Harl, Kenneth (2013). The Vikings, The Great Courses. Chantilly, Virginia: The Teaching Company, LLC. Lecture14

290. Harl, Kenneth (2013). The Vikings, The Great Courses. Chantilly, Virginia: The Teaching Company, LLC. Handout, Pg. 72

291. Harl, Kenneth (2013). The Vikings, The Great Courses. Chantilly, Virginia: The Teaching Company, LLC. Lecture14.

292. Harl, Kenneth (2013). The Vikings, The Great Courses. Chantilly, Virginia: The Teaching Company, LLC. Lecture14.

293. Van Houts, Elizabeth (Editor and Translator) (2000). The Normans in Europe. Oxford: Manchester University Press. Pg. 38

294. Harl, Kenneth (2013). The Vikings, The Great Courses. Chantilly, Virginia: The Teaching Company, LLC. Handout, Pgs. 72-73.

295. Harl, Kenneth (2013). The Vikings, The Great Courses. Chantilly, Virginia: The Teaching Company, LLC. Handout, Pg. 73.

296. Bartlett, W.B. (2016). "England's Viking Overlord." Interview. History of Royals, Issue 6. Imagine Publishing Ltd. Pg. 95.

297. Roesdahl, Else (1998). The Vikings, 2nd Edition. London: Penguin Books. Pg. 234.

298. Harl, Kenneth (2013). The Vikings, The Great Courses. Chantilly, Virginia: The Teaching Company, LLC. Lecture11.

299. Harl, Kenneth (2013). The Vikings, The Great Courses. Chantilly, Virginia: The Teaching Company, LLC. Lecture11.

300. Bartlett, W. B. (2019). Vikings: A History of the Northmen. Gloucestershire: Amberley Publishing. Pg. 169.

301. Bartlett, W. B. (2019). Vikings: A History of the Northmen. Gloucestershire: Amberley Publishing. Pg. 169.

302. Bartlett, W. B. (2019). Vikings: A History of the Northmen. Gloucestershire: Amberley Publishing. Pg. 186.

303. Haywood, John (2015). Northmen: The Viking Saga, 793-1241 AD. London: Head of Zeus, Ltd. Pg. 64.

304. Haywood, John (2015). Northmen: The Viking Saga, 793-1241 AD. London: Head of Zeus, Ltd. Pg. 61.

305. Bartlett, W. B. (2019). Vikings: A History of the Northmen. Gloucestershire: Amberley Publishing. Pg. 151.

306. Hjardar, Kim & Vike, Vegard (2016). Vikings at War. Oxford: Casemate Publishers. Pg. 547.

307. Bartlett, W. B. (2019). Vikings: A History of the Northmen. Gloucestershire: Amberley Publishing. Pg. 151.

308. Price, Neil (2020). Children of Ash and Elm: A History of the Vikings. NYC: Basic Books. Pg. 408.

309. Harl, Kenneth (2013). The Vikings, The Great Courses. Chantilly, Virginia: The Teaching Company, LLC. Lecture 10.

310. Hjardar, Kim & Vike, Vegard (2016). Vikings at War. Oxford: Casemate Publishers. Pg. 225.

311. Hjardar, Kim & Vike, Vegard (2016). Vikings at War. Oxford: Casemate Publishers. Pg. 225.

312. Brownworth, Lars (2014). The Sea-Wolves: A History of the Vikings. UK: Crux Publishing. Pg. 39.

313. Brownworth, Lars (2014). The Sea-Wolves: A History of the Vikings. UK: Crux Publishing. Pg. 39.

314. Jarman, Cat (2021). River Kings: A New History of the Vikings from Scandinavia to the Silk Road. London: William Collins. Pgs. 66-67.

315. Harl, Kenneth (2013). The Vikings, The Great Courses. Chantilly, Virginia: The Teaching Company, LLC. Lecture9.

316. Roesdahl, Else (1998). The Vikings, 2nd Edition. London: Penguin Books. Pg. 118.

317. Harl, Kenneth (2013). The Vikings, The Great Courses. Chantilly, Virginia: The Teaching Company, LLC. Lecture 9.

318. Roesdahl, Else (1998). The Vikings, 2nd Edition. London: Penguin Books. Pg. 119.

319. Roesdahl, Else (1998). The Vikings, 2nd Edition. London: Penguin Books. Pg. 119.

320. Pruitt, Sarah (2018, September 4). "6 Things We Owe to the Vikings." History. A&E Television Networks, LLC. https://www.history.com/news/6-things-we-owe-to-the-vikings

321. Note: Sweyn Forkbeard, the father of Canute, is often cited as the first king of England, but this point is highly disputed. "Sveinn was never formally elected king although there is some suggestion that the witan, the Anglo-Saxon council, was due to meet him in York and formalize his claim to the throne within two weeks of his death. Sveinn's son Cnut was with him when he expired."VikingNorthmen329 He had himself declared King of England on December 25, 1013, but then died

February 3, 1014 (5 weeks later and 2 weeks before the witan was supposed to vote).

322. Bartlett, W. B. (2019). Vikings: A History of the Northmen. Gloucestershire: Amberley Publishing. Pg. 331.

323. Brownworth, Lars (2014). The Sea-Wolves: A History of the Vikings. UK: Crux Publishing. Pg. 180.

324. Brownworth, Lars (2014). The Sea-Wolves: A History of the Vikings. UK: Crux Publishing. Pg. 181.

325. Bartlett, W. B. (2019). Vikings: A History of the Northmen. Gloucestershire: Amberley Publishing. Pg. 342.

326. Jones, Gwyn (1968). A History of the Vikings. NYC: Oxford University Press. Pg. 370.

327. Brownworth, Lars (2014). The Sea-Wolves: A History of the Vikings. UK: Crux Publishing. Pg. 181.

328. Jones, Gwyn (1968). A History of the Vikings. NYC: Oxford University Press. Pg. 371.

329. Brownworth, Lars (2014). The Sea-Wolves: A History of the Vikings. UK: Crux Publishing. Pg. 181.

330. Huntingdon, Henry (1853). The Chronicle of Henry of Huntingdon: Comprising the History of England, from the Invasion of Julius Caesar to the Accession of Henry II. Forester, Thomas (Translator). London: Henry G. Bohn. Pg. 196.

331. Note: Canute was the first undisputed Viking king of England. In Alison Weir's authoritative text, Britain's Royal Families: The Complete Genealogy, she writes of Forkbeard, "he usurped the throne of England in the autumn of 1013, having defeated and deposed Ethelred II; he claimed the throne by right of conquest, but had no dynastic claim to it. He was never crowned." Weir, Alison (2008). Britain's Royal Families: The Complete Genealogy. London: Vintage. Pg. 37.

332. Brownworth, Lars (2014). The Sea-Wolves: A History of the Vikings. UK: Crux Publishing. Pg. 182.

333. Ferguson, Robert (2010). The Hammer and the Cross: A New History of the Vikings. NYC: Penguin Books. Pg. 346.

334. Ferguson, Robert (2010). The Hammer and the Cross: A New History of the Vikings. NYC: Penguin Books. Pg. 346.

335. Ferguson, Robert (2010). The Hammer and the Cross: A New History of the Vikings. NYC: Penguin Books. Pg. 346.

336. Ferguson, Robert (2010). The Hammer and the Cross: A New History of the Vikings. NYC: Penguin Books. Pgs. 345-346.

337. Brownworth, Lars (2014). The Sea-Wolves: A History of the Vikings. UK: Crux Publishing. Pg. 182.

338. Larson, Laurence Marcellus (1912). Canute the Great: 995 (circ)—1035: And the Rise of Danish Imperialsim During the Viking Age. NYC: G.P. Putnam's Sons. Pg. 123.

339. Huntingdon, Henry (1853). The Chronicle of Henry of Huntingdon: Comprising the History of England, from the Invasion of Julius Caesar to the Accession of Henry II. Forester, Thomas (Translator). London: Henry G. Bohn. Pg. 196.

340. Huntingdon, Henry (1853). The Chronicle of Henry of Huntingdon: Comprising the History of England, from the Invasion of Julius Caesar to the Accession of Henry II. Forester, Thomas (Translator). London: Henry G. Bohn. Pg. 196.

341. Brownworth, Lars (2014). The Sea-Wolves: A History of the Vikings. UK: Crux Publishing. Pg. 184.

342. Whitelock, Dorothy (2022, September 20). "Canute I." Encyclopedia Britannica. https://www.britannica.com/biography/Canute-I

343. Jarman, Cat (2021, November). "Emma of Normandy: not just a two-time queen consort of England." History Extra. https://www.historyextra.com/period/anglo-saxon/emma-normandy-queen-life-marriages-children-death-buried/

344. Brownworth, Lars (2014). The Normans: From Raiders to Kings. UK: Crux Publishing. Pg. 58.

345. Brownworth, Lars (2014). The Sea-Wolves: A History of the Vikings. UK: Crux Publishing. Pg. 183.

346. Brownworth, Lars (2014). The Normans: From Raiders to Kings. UK: Crux Publishing. Pgs. 58-59.

347. Somerville, Angus and McDonald, R. Andrew (2014). The Viking Age: A Reader, 2nd Edition. Toronto: University of Toronto Press. Pg. 435.

348. Bartlett, Wayne (2020). "Emperor of the North" All About History Book of Vikings, 14th Edition. San Francisco: Future Publishing Limited. Pg. 52.

349. Somerville, Angus and McDonald, R. Andrew (2014). The Viking Age: A Reader, 2nd Edition. Toronto: University of Toronto Press. Pg. 435.

350. Brownworth, Lars (2014). The Sea-Wolves: A History of the Vikings. UK: Crux Publishing. Pg. 184

351. Bartlett, Wayne (2020). "Emperor of the North" All About History Book of Vikings, 14th Edition. San Francisco: Future Publishing Limited. Pg. 51.

352. Bartlett, W.B. (2016). "England's Viking Overlord." Interview. History of Royals, Issue 6. Imagine Publishing Ltd. Pg. 95.

353. Brownworth, Lars (2014). The Sea-Wolves: A History of the Vikings. UK: Crux Publishing. Pg. 184.

354. Brownworth, Lars (2014). The Sea-Wolves: A History of the Vikings. UK: Crux Publishing. Pg. 184.

355. Brownworth, Lars (2014). The Sea-Wolves: A History of the Vikings. UK: Crux Publishing. Pg. 184.

356. Bartlett, Wayne (2020). "Emperor of the North" All About History Book of Vikings, 14th Edition. San Francisco: Future Publishing Limited. Pg. 50.

357. Haywood, John (2015). Northmen: The Viking Saga, 793-1241 AD. London: Head of Zeus, Ltd. Pg. 97.

358. Jones, Gwyn (1968). A History of the Vikings. NYC: Oxford University Press. Pg. 211.

359. Haywood, John (2015). Northmen: The Viking Saga, 793-1241 AD. London: Head of Zeus, Ltd. Pg. 97.

360. Harl, Kenneth (2013). The Vikings, The Great Courses. Chantilly, Virginia: The Teaching Company, LLC. Handout, Pg. 71-72.

361. Jones, Gwyn (1968). A History of the Vikings. NYC: Oxford University Press. Pg. 394.

362. Jones, Gwyn (1968). A History of the Vikings. NYC: Oxford University Press. Pg. 394.

363. Bartlett, W. B. (2019). Vikings: A History of the Northmen. Gloucestershire: Amberley Publishing. Pg. 183.

364. Bartlett, W. B. (2019). Vikings: A History of the Northmen. Gloucestershire: Amberley Publishing. Pg. 183.

|10|

Exploit the Unexpected Genius of Simplicity:
Alexander the Great Fulfills the Prophecy
of the Gordian Knot

1. Pietersen, Willie (2016, February 12). "Von Clausewitz on War: Six Lessons for the Modern Strategist." Strategy: Ideas at Work. Columbia Business School. https://www8.gsb.columbia.edu/articles/ideas-work/von-clausewitz-war-six-lessons-modern-strategist
2. Pietersen, Willie (2016, February 12). "Von Clausewitz on War: Six Lessons for the Modern Strategist." Strategy: Ideas at Work. Columbia Business School. https://www8.gsb.columbia.edu/articles/ideas-work/von-clausewitz-war-six-lessons-modern-strategist
3. Bennett, William J. (2001). Virtues of Leadership. Nashville, TN: Thomas Nelson, Inc. Pg. 29.
4. Lonsdale, David J. (2007). Alexander the Great: Lessons in Strategy. London: Routledge. Pg. 157.
5. Lonsdale, David J. (2007). Alexander the Great: Lessons in Strategy. London: Routledge. Pg. 157.
6. Clausewitz, Carl von (2008). On War. Translated by Michael Eliot Howard and Peter Paret. Princeton: Princeton University Press. Pg. 119.
7. Clausewitz, Carl von (2008). On War. Translated by Michael Eliot Howard and Peter Paret. Princeton: Princeton University Press. Pg. 119.
8. Lonsdale, David J. (2007). Alexander the Great: Lessons in Strategy. London: Routledge. Pg. 157.
9. Freedman, Lawrence (2014, October 14). "The Master Strategist is Still a Myth." War on the Rocks. Texas National Security Review. https://warontherocks.com/2014/10/the-master-strategist-is-still-a-myth/
10. Maxwell, John C. (2018). Developing the Leader Within You 2.0 Workbook. NYC: HarperCollins. Pg. 112.
11. Leigh, Andrew (2011). Charisma: The Secrets of Making a Lasting Impression. London: Prentice Hall. Pg. 42.
12. Lonsdale, David J. (2007). Alexander the Great: Lessons in Strategy. London: Routledge. Pg. 108. Note: "The nine principles are mass, objective, offensive, surprise, economy of force, maneuver, unity of command, security and simplicity."
13. Cohen, William A. (2004). The Art of the Strategist: 10 Essential Principles for Leading Your Company to Victory. NYC: AMACOM. Pg. 101.
14. Cohen, William A. (2004). The Art of the Strategist: 10 Essential Principles for Leading Your Company to Victory. NYC: AMACOM. Pg. 101.
15. Robbins, Anthony (2014). Money: Master the Game. 7 Simple Steps to Financial Freedom. NYC: Simon and Schuster. Pg. 41.
16. Breeden, Alice and Howe, Adam (2021). "Why Simplicity is the Key to Accelerating Performance: Companies that excel at simplicity throughout their organizations continuously and repeatedly seek to kill complexity in four key areas: strategy, operating model, culture, and activity." Heidrick & Struggles. https://www.heidrick.com/en/insights/organizational-effectiveness/why_simplicity_is_the_key_to_accelerating_performance
17. Breeden, Alice and Howe, Adam (2021). "Why Simplicity is the Key to Accelerating Performance: Companies that excel at simplicity throughout their organizations continuously and repeatedly seek to kill complexity in four key areas: strategy, operating model, culture, and activity." Heidrick & Struggles. https://www.heidrick.com/en/insights/organizational-effectiveness/why_simplicity_is_the_key_to_accelerating_performance
18. Emerson, Ralph Waldo (1897). Works of Ralph Waldo Emerson. London: George Routledge and Sons, Limited. Pg. 583.
19. Koch, Richard and Lockwood, Greg (2016). Simplify: How the Best Businesses in the World Succeed. London: Entrepreneur Press. Pg. 3-4.
20. Koch, Richard and Lockwood, Greg (2016). Simplify: How the Best Businesses in the World Succeed. London: Entrepreneur Press.Pgs. xxiii-xxiv.
21. Koch, Richard and Lockwood, Greg (2016). Simplify: How the Best Businesses in the World Succeed. London: Entrepreneur Press.4
22. Koch, Richard and Lockwood, Greg (2016). Simplify: How the Best Businesses in the World Succeed. London: Entrepreneur Press.6
23. Krugman, Paul; Wells, Robin; Olney, Martha (2007). Essentials of Economics. NYC: Worth Publishers. Pg. 325.
24. Duggan, William (2003). The Art of What Works. NYC: McGraw-Hill. Pg. x.
25. Duggan, William (2003). The Art of What Works. NYC: McGraw-Hill. Pg. x.
26. Tichy, Noel and Charan, Ram (1989, September-October, Updated March 2, 2020). "Speed, Simplicity, Self-Confidence: An Interview with Jack Welch." Harvard Business Review. https://hbr.org/1989/09/speed-simplicity-self-confidence-an-interview-with-jack-welch
27. Tsouras, Peter G. (2020). The Greenhill Dictionary of Military Quotations. Yorkshire: Greenhill Books. Pg. 200.
28. Chesterton, G.K. (1986). The Quotable Chesterton: A Topical Compilation of the Wit, Wisdom and Satire of G.K. Chesterton. San Francisco: Ignatius Press. Pg. 324.
29. Kinsella, Warren (2007). The War Room: Strategies from the Political Trenches on How to Win. Toronto: The Dundurn Group. Pg. 93.
30. Zinsser, William (2012). On Writing Well: An Informal Guide to Writing Nonfiction. NYC: HarperCollins. Pg. 15.
31. Tichy, Noel and Charan, Ram (1989, September-October, Updated March 2, 2020). "Speed, Simplicity, Self-Confidence: An Interview with Jack Welch." Harvard Business Review. https://hbr.org/1989/09/speed-simplicity-self-confidence-an-interview-with-jack-welch
32. Tichy, Noel and Charan, Ram (1989, September-October, Updated March 2, 2020). "Speed, Simplicity, Self-Confidence: An Interview with Jack Welch." Harvard Business Review. https://hbr.org/1989/09/speed-simplicity-self-confidence-an-interview-with-jack-welch
33. Tichy, Noel and Charan, Ram (1989, September-October, Updated March 2, 2020). "Speed, Simplicity, Self-Confidence: An Interview with Jack Welch." Harvard Business Review.

https://hbr.org/1989/09/speed-simplicity-self-confidence-an-interview-with-jack-welch

34. Tichy, Noel and Charan, Ram (1989, September-October, Updated March 2, 2020). "Speed, Simplicity, Self-Confidence: An Interview with Jack Welch." Harvard Business Review. https://hbr.org/1989/09/speed-simplicity-self-confidence-an-interview-with-jack-welch

35. Eckhart, Peter (2020). Simplicity for Success in Business. U.S. Simplifier, Inc. Pg. 105.

36. Gallo, Carmine (2016). The Storyteller's Secret: From TED Speakers to Business Legends, Why Some Ideas Catch On and Others Don't. NY: St. Martin's Press. Pg. 114.

37. Lonsdale, David J. (2007). Alexander the Great: Lessons in Strategy. London: Routledge. Pg. 8.

38. Tichy, Noel and Charan, Ram (1989, September-October, Updated March 2, 2020). "Speed, Simplicity, Self-Confidence: An Interview with Jack Welch." Harvard Business Review. https://hbr.org/1989/09/speed-simplicity-self-confidence-an-interview-with-jack-welch

39. Collinson, Simon and Melvin, Jay (2012). From Complexity to Simplicity: Unleash Your Organizations Potential. NYC: St. Martin's Press. Pg. 149.

40. Cohen, William A. (2004). The Art of the Strategist: 10 Essential Principles for Leading Your Company to Victory. NYC: AMACOM. Pg. 102.

41. Cohen, William A. (2004). The Art of the Strategist: 10 Essential Principles for Leading Your Company to Victory. NYC: AMACOM. Pg. 102.

42. Collinson, Simon and Melvin, Jay (2012). From Complexity to Simplicity: Unleash Your Organizations Potential. NYC: St. Martin's Press. Pg. 149.

43. Cohen, William A. (2004). The Art of the Strategist: 10 Essential Principles for Leading Your Company to Victory. NYC: AMACOM. Pg. 102.

44. Cohen, William A. (2004). The Art of the Strategist: 10 Essential Principles for Leading Your Company to Victory. NYC: AMACOM. Pg. 102.

45. Tracy, Brian (2002). Victory! Applying the Proven Principles of Military Strategy to Achieve Success in Your Business and Personal Life. NYC: AMACOM. Pg. 168.

46. Clausewitz, Carl von (2007). On War. Translated by Michael Eliot Howard and Peter Paret. Oxford: Oxford University Press. Pg. 146.

47. Tracy, Brian (2002). Victory! Applying the Proven Principles of Military Strategy to Achieve Success in Your Business and Personal Life. NYC: AMACOM. Pg. 168.

48. Newton, Isaac (1994). Treatise on the Apocalypse. Maurizio Mamiani (Translator). Turin, Italy: Bollati Boringhieri. Pg. 28.

49. Koch, Richard and Lockwood, Greg (2016). Simplify: How the Best Businesses in the World Succeed. London: Entrepreneur Press.Pg. xxii.

50. Koch, Richard and Lockwood, Greg (2016). Simplify: How the Best Businesses in the World Succeed. London: Entrepreneur Press.Pg. xxii

51. Tracy, Brian (2002). Victory! Applying the Proven Principles of Military Strategy to Achieve Success in Your Business and Personal Life. NYC: AMACOM. Pg. 168.

52. Churchill, Winston (1931, June 27). "Unlucky Alfonso" Collier's, Column 2, P. F. Collier and Son, NYC. Pg. 49.

53. Staff Writer (2021). "Edward Everett, the Other (Much Longer) Speaker at Gettysburg." New England Historical Society. https://newenglandhistoricalsociety.com/edward-everett-reminds-nation-still-one-people/

54. Leigh, Andrew (2011). Charisma: The Secrets of Making a Lasting Impression. London: Prentice Hall. Pg. 42.

55. Editorial Board (2013, November 14). "Retraction for our 1863 editorial calling Gettysburg Address 'silly remarks': Editorial." PennLive. https://www.pennlive.com/opinion/2013/11/a_patriot-news_editorial_retraction_the_gettysburg_address.html

56. Opinion (1986, July 24). "Lincoln Had a Tough Act to Follow." The NYC Times. https://www.nytimes.com/1986/07/24/opinion/l-lincoln-had-a-tough-act-to-follow-159186.html

57. Sandburg, Carl (1954). Abraham Lincoln: The Prairie Years and the War Years. Harcourt, Brace & World. Pg. 445.

58. Everett, Edward (1863, November 20). "Edward Everett Letter to Abraham Lincoln," in Collected Works of Abraham Lincoln. Volume 7. Pg. 25. See also: https://hd.housedivided.dickinson.edu/node/41268

59. Eckhart, Peter (2020). Simplicity for Success in Business. U.S. Simplifier, Inc. Pg. 35.

60. Slater, Robert (2004). Jack Welch on Leadership. NYC: McGraw Hill. Pg. 82.

61. Tichy, Noel and Sherman, Stratford (2018). Control Your Destiny or Someone Else Will: How Jack Welch Created $400 Billion of Value by Transforming GE. NYC: Doubleday.

62. Tichy, Noel and Charan, Ram (1989, September-October, Updated March 2, 2020). "Speed, Simplicity, Self-Confidence: An Interview with Jack Welch." Harvard Business Review. https://hbr.org/1989/09/speed-simplicity-self-confidence-an-interview-with-jack-welch

63. Schumacher, E.F. (1973, August). "Small is Beautiful." The Radical Humanist, Vol. 37, No. 5. Pg. 22.

64. Eckhart, Peter (2020). Simplicity for Success in Business. U.S. Simplifier, Inc. Pg. 51.

65. Eckhart, Peter (2020). Simplicity for Success in Business. U.S. Simplifier, Inc. Pg. 52.

66. Norman, Donald A. (2011). Living with Complexity. Cambridge: MIT Press. See also: https://fs.blog/complexity-bias/

67. Big Think (2021, June 2). "Want to tap into the power of simplicity? You must first define." Big Think. Freethink Media, Inc. https://bigthink.com/plus/want-to-tap-into-the-power-of-simplicity-you-must-first-define/

68. Rich, Ben R. (1995). "Clarence Leonard (Kelly) Johnson: February 27, 1910—December 21, 1990." Biographical Memoirs, Volume 67. National Academy of Sciences. Washington, D.C.: National Academy Press. Pg. 221.

69. Rich, Ben R. (1995). "Clarence Leonard (Kelly) Johnson: February 27, 1910—December 21, 1990." Biographical Memoirs, Volume 67. National Academy of Sciences. Washington, D.C.: National Academy Press. Pg. 231.

70. Rich, Ben R. (1995). "Clarence Leonard (Kelly) Johnson: February 27, 1910—December 21, 1990." Biographical Memoirs, Volume 67. National Academy of Sciences. Washington, D.C.: National Academy Press. Pg. 231.

71. Lonsdale, David J. (2007). Alexander the Great: Lessons in Strategy. London: Routledge. Pg. 157.

72. Eckhart, Peter (2020). Simplicity for Success in Business. U.S. Simplifier, Inc. Pg. 20.

73. Lonsdale, David J. (2007). Alexander the Great: Lessons in Strategy. London: Routledge. Pg. 157.

74. Lonsdale, David J. (2007). Alexander the Great: Lessons in Strategy. London: Routledge. Pg. 157.

75. Denny, Lonna (2019). "Sifting the Essential from the Non-Essential." Farnum Street. https://fs.blog/albert-einstein-simplicity/ See also: https://sfchiro.org/albert-einstein-on-sifting-the-essential-from-the-non-essential/

76. Lombardi Jr., Vince (2001). What It Takes to Be #1: Vince Lombardi on Leadership. NYC: McGraw-Hill. Pg. 187.

77. Lombardi Jr., Vince (2001). What It Takes to Be #1: Vince Lombardi on Leadership. NYC: McGraw-Hill. Pg. 187.

78. Lombardi Jr., Vince (2001). What It Takes to Be #1: Vince Lombardi on Leadership. NYC: McGraw-Hill. Pg. 187.

79. Lombardi Jr., Vince (2001). What It Takes to Be #1: Vince Lombardi on Leadership. NYC: McGraw-Hill. Pg. 185.

80. Lombardi Jr., Vince (2001). What It Takes to Be #1: Vince Lombardi on Leadership. NYC: McGraw-Hill. Pg. 185.

81. Gordon, Jon (2021, November 15, last accessed). "Lead with Your Strengths." The Jon Gordon Companies. https://jongordon.com/blog/lead-your-strengths/

82. Gordon, Jon (2021, November 15, last accessed). "Lead with Your Strengths." The Jon Gordon Companies. https://jongordon.com/blog/lead-your-strengths/

83. Segall, Ken (2016). Think Simple: How Smart Leaders Defeat Complexity. NY: Penguin. Pg. 220.

84. Gordon, Jon (2021, November 15, last accessed). "Lead with Your Strengths." The Jon Gordon Companies. https://jongordon.com/blog/lead-your-strengths/

85. Eckhart, Peter (2020). Simplicity for Success in Business. U.S. Simplifier, Inc. Pg. 23.

86. Clausewitz, Carl von (2008). On War. Translated by Michael Eliot Howard and Peter Paret. Princeton: Princeton University Press. Pg. 146.

87. Greene, Robert (1998). The 48 Laws of Power. NYC: Penguin Books. Pg. xxi.

88. Porter, Michael (2008). On Competition, Updated and Expanded Edition. Boston: Harvard Business School Publishing. Pg. 57.

89. Denny, Lonna (2019). "Sifting the Essential from the Non-Essential." Farnum Street. https://fs.blog/albert-einstein-simplicity/ See also: https://sfchiro.org/albert-einstein-on-sifting-the-essential-from-the-non-essential/

90. Denny, Lonna (2019). "Sifting the Essential from the Non-Essential." Farnum Street. https://fs.blog/albert-einstein-simplicity/ See also: https://sfchiro.org/albert-einstein-on-sifting-the-essential-from-the-non-essential/

91. Wheeler, John Archibald (1980). Albert Einstein 1879—1955, A Biographical Memoir. Washington D.C.: National Academy of Sciences. http://www.nasonline.org/publications/biographical-memoirs/memoir-pdfs/einstein-albert.pdf Pg. 102.

92. English, Fenwick (Editor)(2022). The Palgrave Handbook of Educational Leadership and Management Discourse. Cham, Switzerland: Palgrave MacMillan. Pg. 138.

93. Wheeler, John Archibald (1980). Albert Einstein 1879—1955, A Biographical Memoir. Washington D.C.: National Academy of Sciences. http://www.nasonline.org/publications/biographical-memoirs/memoir-pdfs/einstein-albert.pdf Pg. 103.

94. Wheeler, John Archibald (1980). Albert Einstein 1879—1955, A Biographical Memoir. Washington D.C.: National Academy of Sciences. http://www.nasonline.org/publications/biographical-memoirs/memoir-pdfs/einstein-albert.pdf Pg. 102.

95. Wheeler, John Archibald (1980). Albert Einstein 1879—1955, A Biographical Memoir. Washington D.C.: National Academy of Sciences. http://www.nasonline.org/publications/biographical-memoirs/memoir-pdfs/einstein-albert.pdf Pg. 106.

96. Wheeler, John Archibald (1980). Albert Einstein 1879—1955, A Biographical Memoir. Washington D.C.: National Academy of Sciences. http://www.nasonline.org/publications/biographical-memoirs/memoir-pdfs/einstein-albert.pdf Pgs. 105-106.

97. Eckhart, Peter (2020). *Simplicity for Success in Business.* U.S. Simplifier, inc. Pg. 114.

98. Thiel, Peter (2014). Zero to One: Notes on Startups, or How to Build the Future. NYC: Crown Business. Pg. 65.

99. Thiel, Peter (2014). Zero to One: Notes on Startups, or How to Build the Future. NYC: Crown Business. Pg. 65.

100. Denny, Lonna (2019). "Sifting the Essential from the Non-Essential." Farnum Street. https://fs.blog/albert-einstein-simplicity/ See also: https://sfchiro.org/albert-einstein-on-sifting-the-essential-from-the-non-essential/

101. Covey, Stephen (1990). The Seven Habits of Highly Effective People: Powerful Lessons in Personal Change. NYC: Simon and Schuster.

102. Covey, Stephen (1990). The Seven Habits of Highly Effective People: Powerful Lessons in Personal Change. NYC: Simon and Schuster.

103. Covey, Stephen (1990). The Seven Habits of Highly Effective People: Powerful Lessons in Personal Change. NYC: Simon and Schuster.

104. Lonsdale, David J. (2007). Alexander the Great: Lessons in Strategy. London: Routledge. Pg. 157.

105. Lonsdale, David J. (2007). Alexander the Great: Lessons in Strategy. London: Routledge. Pg. 157.

106. Gordon, Jon (2021, November 15, last accessed). "Lead with Your Strengths." The Jon Gordon Companies. https://jongordon.com/blog/lead-your-strengths/

107. Pietersen, Willie (2016, February 12). "Von Clausewitz on War: Six Lessons for the Modern Strategist." Strategy: Ideas at Work. Columbia Business School. https://www8.gsb.columbia.edu/articles/ideas-work/von-clausewitz-war-six-lessons-modern-strategist

|11|

Focus Your Forces, Amass Your Resources, Concentrate on Just One Thing: Cleopatra Regains and Sustains Her Egyptian Reign

1. Emerson, Ralph Waldo (1866). The Complete Works of Ralph Waldo Emerson: Comprising His Essays, Lectures, Poems, and Orations. Volume II. "The

Conduct of Life." London: William Clowes & Sons. Pg. 339.

2. Marden, Orison Swett (1911). Pushing to the Front. Petersburg, NY: The Success Company's. Pg. 164.

3. McDermott, Bridget (2013). "The Last Pharaoh and the Fall of Egypt." All About History. Issue 2. Bournemouth: Imagine Publishing, Ltd. Pg. 68.

4. McDermott, Bridget (2013). "The Last Pharaoh and the Fall of Egypt." All About History. Issue 2. Bournemouth: Imagine Publishing, Ltd. Pg. 68.

5. Goldsworthy, Adrian (2010). Antony and Cleopatra. New Haven: Yale University Press. Pg. 319.

6. White, Frances (2016). "Serpent of the Nile: Cleopatra." All About History, Issue 46. Bournemouth: Imagine Publishing, Ltd. Pg. 34.

7. Preston, Diana (2009). Cleopatra and Antony: Power, Love, and Politics in the Ancient World. Pg. 213.

8. Preston, Diana (2009). Cleopatra and Antony: Power, Love, and Politics in the Ancient World. Pg. 213.

9. Preston, Diana (2009). Cleopatra and Antony: Power, Love, and Politics in the Ancient World. Pg. 213.

10. Preston, Diana (2009). Cleopatra and Antony: Power, Love, and Politics in the Ancient World. Pgs. 211-212.

11. Redonet, Fernando Lillo (2015, October-November). "Antony and Cleopatra." National Geographic History. Washington, D.C.: National Geographic Society. Pg. 21.

12. Preston, Diana (2009). Cleopatra and Antony: Power, Love, and Politics in the Ancient World. Pgs. 213-214.

13. Preston, Diana (2009). Cleopatra and Antony: Power, Love, and Politics in the Ancient World. Pg. 214.

14. Goldsworthy, Adrian (2010). Antony and Cleopatra. New Haven: Yale University Press. Pg. 319.

15. Goldsworthy, Adrian (2010). Antony and Cleopatra. New Haven: Yale University Press. Pg. 319.

16. Preston, Diana (2009). Cleopatra and Antony: Power, Love, and Politics in the Ancient World. Pg. 211.

17. Preston, Diana (2009). Cleopatra and Antony: Power, Love, and Politics in the Ancient World. Pg. 211.

18. Goldsworthy, Adrian (2010). Antony and Cleopatra. New Haven: Yale University Press. Pg. 319.

19. Redonet, Fernando Lillo (2015, October-November). "Antony and Cleopatra." National Geographic History. Washington, D.C.: National Geographic Society. Pgs. 21,25.

20. Plutarch (1965 [c. 75 A.D.]). Makers of Rome. Ian Scott-Kilvert (Translator) NYC: Penguin. Pg. 293. https://classics.domains.skidmore.edu/lit-campus-only/primary/translations/Plutarch%20Ant.pdf

21. Plutarch (1965 [c. 75 A.D.]). Makers of Rome. Ian Scott-Kilvert (Translator) NYC: Penguin. Pg. 293. https://classics.domains.skidmore.edu/lit-campus-only/primary/translations/Plutarch%20Ant.pdf

22. Redonet, Fernando Lillo (2015, October-November). "Antony and Cleopatra." National Geographic History. Washington, D.C.: National Geographic Society. Pgs. 21,25.

23. McDermott, Bridget (2013). "The Last Pharaoh and the Fall of Egypt." All About History. Issue 2. Bournemouth: Imagine Publishing, Ltd. Pg. 68.

24. Preston, Diana (2009). Cleopatra and Antony: Power, Love, and Politics in the Ancient World. Pg. 215.

25. Preston, Diana (2009). Cleopatra and Antony: Power, Love, and Politics in the Ancient World. Pg. 215.

26. Greene, Robert (2001). The Art of Seduction. NYC: Penguin. Pg. 208.

27. Goldsworthy, Adrian (2010). Antony and Cleopatra. New Haven: Yale University Press. Pgs. 320-321.

28. McDermott, Bridget (2013). "The Last Pharaoh and the Fall of Egypt." All About History. Issue 2. Bournemouth: Imagine Publishing, Ltd. Pg. 68.

29. Greene, Robert (2001). The Art of Seduction. NYC: Penguin. Pg. 208.

30. Goldsworthy, Adrian (2010). Antony and Cleopatra. New Haven: Yale University Press. Pg. 321.

31. Goldfinch, Lottie (2014, November). "Cleopatra: Queen at Any Cost." History Revealed. Bristol: Immediate Media Company. Pg. 86.

32. Goldfinch, Lottie (2014, November). "Cleopatra: Queen at Any Cost." History Revealed. Bristol: Immediate Media Company. Pg. 86.

33. Schiff, Stacy (2010, December). "Rehabilitating Cleopatra." Smithsonian Magazine. https://www.smithsonianmag.com/history/rehabilitating-cleopatra-70613486/

34. Schiff, Stacy (2010, December). "Rehabilitating Cleopatra." Smithsonian Magazine. https://www.smithsonianmag.com/history/rehabilitating-cleopatra-70613486/

35. White, Frances (2016). "Serpent of the Nile: Cleopatra." All About History, Issue 46. Bournemouth: Imagine Publishing, Ltd. Pg. 38.

36. White, Frances (2016). "Serpent of the Nile: Cleopatra." All About History, Issue 46. Bournemouth: Imagine Publishing, Ltd. Pg. 38.

37. White, Frances (2016). "Serpent of the Nile: Cleopatra." All About History, Issue 46. Bournemouth: Imagine Publishing, Ltd. Pg. 38.

38. White, Frances (2016). "Serpent of the Nile: Cleopatra." All About History, Issue 46. Bournemouth: Imagine Publishing, Ltd. Pg. 38.

39. Berthezène, Pierre (1855). Souvenirs Militaires de la République et de l'Empire, 2. Paris. Pg. 309. See also: Brands, Hal (2023). The New Makers of Modern Strategy. Princeton: Princeton University Press. Pg. 327.

40. Cohen, William A. (2004). The Art of the Strategist: 10 Essential Principles for Leading Your Company to Victory. NYC: AMACOM. Pg. 62.

41. Rumelt, Richard (2011). Good Strategy, Bad Strategy. London: Profile Books Ltd. Pg. 102.

42. Cohen, William A. (2004). The Art of the Strategist: 10 Essential Principles for Leading Your Company to Victory. NYC: AMACOM. Pg. 61

43. Hart, B.H. Liddell (1991). Strategy, Second Revised Edition. NYC: Meridian. Pg. 334.

44. Ridgley, Stanley K. (2012). Strategic Thinking Skills: The Great Courses Course Guidebook. The Great Courses. Chantilly, Virginia: The Teaching Company, LLC. Pg. 22.

45. Clausewitz, Carl von (2007). On War. Translated by Michael Eliot Howard and Peter Paret. Oxford: Oxford University Press. Pgs. 147-148.

46. Rumelt, Richard (2011). Good Strategy, Bad Strategy. London: Profile Books Ltd. Pg. 143.

47. Tracy, Brian (2002). Victory! Applying the Proven Principles of Military Strategy to Achieve Success in Your Business and Personal Life. NYC: AMACOM. Pg. 60.

48. Carlyle, Thomas (1894). Life of Friedrich Schiller. London: George Routledge and Sons, Limited. Pg. 44.

49. Tracy, Brian (2002). Victory! Applying the Proven Principles of Military Strategy to Achieve Success in

Your Business and Personal Life. NYC: AMACOM. Pg. 75.

50. Tracy, Brian (2002). Victory! Applying the Proven Principles of Military Strategy to Achieve Success in Your Business and Personal Life. NYC: AMACOM. Pg. 69.

51. Marden, Orison Swett (1911). Pushing to the Front. Petersburg, NY: The Success Company's. Pg. 155.

52. Churchill, Winston (1946, March 5). "The Sinews of Peace ('Iron Curtain Speech')." International Churchill Society. https://winstonchurchill.org/resources/speeches/1946-1963-elder-statesman/the-sinews-of-peace/

53. Churchill, Winston (1946, March 5). "The Sinews of Peace ('Iron Curtain Speech')." International Churchill Society. https://winstonchurchill.org/resources/speeches/1946-1963-elder-statesman/the-sinews-of-peace/

54. Humes, James C. (2012). Churchill: The Prophetic Statesman. Regnery History. Pg. 21.

55. "Winston Churchill and the Cold War." America's National Churchill Museum, Westminster College, Fulton, Missouri. https://www.nationalchurchillmuseum.org/winston-churchill-and-the-cold-war.html

56. Bramley, Chris (Editor)(2018). "Before Apollo." The Apollo Story. Sky at Night Magazine, BBC. Bristol: Immediate Media Co. Pg. 9.

57. Bizony, Piers (2014, August). "The Space Race." History Revealed, Issue 6. Bristol: Immediate Media Company. Pg. 36.

58. Bizony, Piers (2014, August). "The Space Race." History Revealed, Issue 6. Bristol: Immediate Media Company. Pg. 36.

59. Bizony, Piers (2014, August). "The Space Race." History Revealed, Issue 6. Bristol: Immediate Media Company. Pg. 36.

60. Das, Saswato R. (2009, July 16). "The Moon Landing through Soviet Eyes: A Q&A with Sergei Khrushchev, son of former premier Nikita Khrushchev." Scientific American. https://www.scientificamerican.com/article/apollo-moon-khrushchev/

61. Bizony, Piers (2014, August). "The Space Race." History Revealed, Issue 6. Bristol: Immediate Media Company. Pg. 36.

62. Das, Saswato R. (2009, July 16). "The Moon Landing through Soviet Eyes: A Q&A with Sergei Khrushchev, son of former premier Nikita Khrushchev." Scientific American. https://www.scientificamerican.com/article/apollo-moon-khrushchev/

63. Yegorov, Oleg (2017, August 9). "Why the USSR Failed to Send an Astronaut to the Moon?" Russia Beyond. Moscow: RT. https://www.rbth.com/why_russia/2017/08/09/why-the-ussr-failed-to-send-an-astronaut-to-the-moon_819736

64. Yegorov, Oleg (2017, August 9). "Why the USSR Failed to Send an Astronaut to the Moon?" Russia Beyond. Moscow: RT. https://www.rbth.com/why_russia/2017/08/09/why-the-ussr-failed-to-send-an-astronaut-to-the-moon_819736

65. Yegorov, Oleg (2017, August 9). "Why the USSR Failed to Send an Astronaut to the Moon?" Russia Beyond. Moscow: RT. https://www.rbth.com/why_russia/2017/08/09/why-the-ussr-failed-to-send-an-astronaut-to-the-moon_819736

66. Mandino, Og (1988). The Greatest Salesman in the World: Part II The End of the Story. NYC: Bantam. Pg. 112.

67. Emerson, Ralph Waldo (1866). The Complete Works of Ralph Waldo Emerson: Comprising His Essays, Lectures, Poems, and Orations. Volume II. "The Conduct of Life." London: William Clowes and Sons. Pg. 339.

68. Emerson, Ralph Waldo (1866). The Complete Works of Ralph Waldo Emerson: Comprising His Essays, Lectures, Poems, and Orations. Volume II. "The Conduct of Life." London: William Clowes and Sons. Pg. 338.

69. Note: Moving freely amongst the most aristocratic circles, Casanova was acquainted with European royalty, popes and cardinals, a number of political luminaries—including Catherine the Great, Louis XV, George III, Benjamin Franklin, and Pope Benedict XIV—as well as a great many of the important thinkers and celebrities of the day, including Goethe, Mozart, Rousseau and Voltaire.

70. Cohen, William A. (2004). The Art of the Strategist: 10 Essential Principles for Leading Your Company to Victory. NYC: AMACOM. Pg. 69.

71. Greene, Robert (2001). The Art of Seduction. NYC: Penguin. Pgs. 32-33.

72. Greene, Robert (1998). The 48 Laws of Power. NYC: Penguin Books. Pg. 233.

73. Greene, Robert (1998). The 48 Laws of Power. NYC: Penguin Books. Pg. 233.

74. Greene, Robert (1998). The 48 Laws of Power. NYC: Penguin Books. Pg. 233. See Also: . Greene, Robert (2001). The Art of Seduction. NYC: Penguin. Pgs. 32-33.

75. Cohen, William A. (2004). The Art of the Strategist: 10 Essential Principles for Leading Your Company to Victory. NYC: AMACOM. Pg. 69.

76. Cohen, William A. (2004). The Art of the Strategist: 10 Essential Principles for Leading Your Company to Victory. NYC: AMACOM. Pg. 69.

77. Greene, Robert (1998). The 48 Laws of Power. NYC: Penguin Books. Pg. 175.

78. Mapletoft, John (1707). Select Proverbs, Italian, Spanish, French, English, Scotish, British, &c. Chiefly Moral. London: Star, St. Paul's Church-yard. Pg. 53.

79. Greene, Robert (1998). The 48 Laws of Power. NYC: Penguin Books. Pg. 175.

80. The Holy Bible, New Testament for Everyone (NTE) (2011). Philippians 3:13. Biblegateway.com. Biblica, Inc. https://www.biblegateway.com/passage/?search=Philippians+3%3A13&version=NTE

81. Carnegie, Andrew (1885, June 23). "The Road to Business Success." Commencement Address, Curry Commercial College in Pittsburgh, Pennsylvania.

82. Ries, Al (1996). Focus: The Future of Your Company Depends On It. NYC: HarperCollins. Pg. 128.

83. Ries, Al (1996). Focus: The Future of Your Company Depends On It. NYC: HarperCollins. Pg. 287.

84. Frakes, Jonathan (2001). "Jonathan Frakes—The Next Generation's Number One, Will Riker, and Trek director." BBC.

85. Ries, Al (1996). Focus: The Future of Your Company Depends On It. NYC: HarperCollins. Pg. 146.

86. Ries, Al (1996). Focus: The Future of Your Company Depends On It. NYC: HarperCollins. Pg. 146.

87. Ries, Al (1996). Focus: The Future of Your Company Depends On It. NYC: HarperCollins. Pgs. 146-147.

88. Ries, Al (1996). Focus: The Future of Your Company Depends On It. NYC: HarperCollins. Pgs. 146-147.

89. Ries, Al (1996). Focus: The Future of Your Company Depends On It. NYC: HarperCollins. Pg. 139.

90. Ries, Al (1996). Focus: The Future of Your Company Depends On It. NYC: HarperCollins. Pg. 148.

91. Cohen, William A. (2004). The Art of the Strategist: 10 Essential Principles for Leading Your Company to Victory. NYC: AMACOM. Pg. 27.

92. Covey, Sean; McChesney, Chris; and Huling, Jim (2012). The 4 Disciplines of Execution: Achieving Your Wildly Important Goals. NYC: Simon and Schuster. Pg. 40.

93. Marden, Orison Swett (1911). Pushing to the Front. Petersburg, NY: The Success Company's. Pg. 162.

94. Marden, Orison Swett (1911). Pushing to the Front. Petersburg, NY: The Success Company's. Pg. 157.

95. Asprey, Robert (2000). The Rise of Napoleon Bonaparte. NYC: Basic Books. Pg. 532.

96. Asprey, Robert (2000). The Rise of Napoleon Bonaparte. NYC: Basic Books. Pg. 532.

97. Asprey, Robert (2000). The Rise of Napoleon Bonaparte. NYC: Basic Books. Pg. 532.

98. Asprey, Robert (2000). The Rise of Napoleon Bonaparte. NYC: Basic Books. Pg. 533.

99. Clayton, Tim (2020). "Trafalgar: The Battle." The Story of the Napoleonic Wars, Collector's Edition. BBC History Magazine. Bristol: Immediate Media Company. Pg. 31.

100. Clayton, Tim (2020). "Trafalgar: The Battle." The Story of the Napoleonic Wars, Collector's Edition. BBC History Magazine. Bristol: Immediate Media Company. Pg. 31.

101. White, Frances (2022). "Nelson and the Battle of Trafalgar." History of War, Naval Warfare, 2nd Edition. Bath: Future Publishing Limited. Pg. 62.

102. Africa got lost in a storm, but was slowly approaching the battle.

103. White, Frances (2022). "Nelson and the Battle of Trafalgar." History of War, Naval Warfare, 2nd Edition. Bath: Future Publishing Limited. Pg. 58.

104. Asprey, Robert (2000). The Rise of Napoleon Bonaparte. NYC: Basic Books. Pg. 533.

105. Wilson, Andrew R. (2012). Masters of War: History's Greatest Strategic Thinkers. The Great Courses. Chantilly, Virginia: The Teaching Company, LLC. Actual Quote: "He was using a new signal system that allowed him to coordinate his preparations much better than the French."

106. Roberts, Andrew (2014). Napoleon: A Life. NYC: Viking. Pg. 263.

107. Clayton, Tim (2020). "Trafalgar: The Battle." The Story of the Napoleonic Wars, Collector's Edition. BBC History Magazine. Bristol: Immediate Media Company. Pg. 30.

108. Roberts, Andrew (2014). Napoleon: A Life. NYC: Viking. Pg. 263.

109. Roberts, Andrew (2014). Napoleon: A Life. NYC: Viking. Pg. 263.

110. Keller, Gary (2013). The ONE Thing: The Surprisingly Simple Truth Behind Extraordinary Results. Austin: Bard Press. Pgs. 4-5.

111. Pietersen, Willie (2016, February 12). "Von Clausewitz on War: Six Lessons for the Modern Strategist." Strategy: Ideas at Work. Columbia Business School. https://www8.gsb.columbia.edu/articles/ideas-work/von-clausewitz-war-six-lessons-modern-strategist

112. Ridgley, Stanley K. (2012). Strategic Thinking Skills: The Great Courses Course Guidebook. The Great Courses. Chantilly, Virginia: The Teaching Company, LLC. Pg. 23.

113. Ridgley, Stanley K. (2012). Strategic Thinking Skills: The Great Courses Course Guidebook. The Great Courses. Chantilly, Virginia: The Teaching Company, LLC. Pg. 22.

114. Rumelt, Richard (2011). Good Strategy, Bad Strategy. London: Profile Books Ltd. Pg. 142.

115. Mahan, Alfred Thayer (1911). Naval Strategy Compared and Contrasted with the Principles and Practices of Military Operations on Land. Boston: Little, Brown, and Company. Pg. 127.

116. Robinson, C.W. et al (1914). Wars of the 19th Century. London: The Encyclopedia Britannica Company, Ltd. Pg. 29.

117. Clausewitz, Carl von (2008). On War. Translated by Michael Eliot Howard and Peter Paret. Princeton: Princeton University Press. Pg. 597.

118. Diesen, Glenn (2021). Russian Conservatism: Managing Change Under Permanent Revolution. Lanham: Rowman & Littlefield. Pg. 188.

119. Clausewitz, Carl von (2008). On War. Translated by Michael Eliot Howard and Peter Paret. Princeton: Princeton University Press. Pgs. 595-596.

120. Clausewitz, Carl von (2008). On War. Translated by Michael Eliot Howard and Peter Paret. Princeton: Princeton University Press. Pg. 596.

121. Freedman, Lawrence (2013). Strategy: A History. Oxford: Oxford University Press. Pg. 91.

122. Freedman, Lawrence (2013). Strategy: A History. Oxford: Oxford University Press. Pg. 92

123. Stephens, Alan and Baker, Nicola (2006). Making Sense of War: Strategy of the 21st Century. NYC. Pg. 7.

124. Stephens, Alan and Baker, Nicola (2006). Making Sense of War: Strategy of the 21st Century. NYC. Pgs. 7-8.

125. Cohen, William A. (2004). The Art of the Strategist: 10 Essential Principles for Leading Your Company to Victory. NYC: AMACOM. Pg. 62.

126. Cohen, William A. (2004). The Art of the Strategist: 10 Essential Principles for Leading Your Company to Victory. NYC: AMACOM. Pg. 62. [Emphasis Added]

127. Tracy, Brian (2002). Victory! Applying the Proven Principles of Military Strategy to Achieve Success in Your Business and Personal Life. NYC: AMACOM. Pg. 60.

128. Uffindell, Andrew (2003). Great Generals of the Napoleonic Wars. Kent: Spellmount Ltd. Pg. 19.

129. Tracy, Brian (2002). Victory! Applying the Proven Principles of Military Strategy to Achieve Success in Your Business and Personal Life. NYC: AMACOM. Pg. 63.

130. Tracy, Brian (2002). Victory! Applying the Proven Principles of Military Strategy to Achieve Success in Your Business and Personal Life. NYC: AMACOM. Pg. 63.

131. Uffindell, Andrew (2003). Great Generals of the Napoleonic Wars. Kent: Spellmount Ltd. Pg. 21.
132. Tracy, Brian (2002). Victory! Applying the Proven Principles of Military Strategy to Achieve Success in Your Business and Personal Life. NYC: AMACOM. Pg. 63.
133. Tracy, Brian (2002). Victory! Applying the Proven Principles of Military Strategy to Achieve Success in Your Business and Personal Life. NYC: AMACOM. Pg. 63.
134. Tracy, Brian (2002). Victory! Applying the Proven Principles of Military Strategy to Achieve Success in Your Business and Personal Life. NYC: AMACOM. Pg. 64.
135. Cohen, William A. (2004). The Art of the Strategist: 10 Essential Principles for Leading Your Company to Victory. NYC: AMACOM. Pg. 62.
136. Tracy, Brian (2002). Victory! Applying the Proven Principles of Military Strategy to Achieve Success in Your Business and Personal Life. NYC: AMACOM. Pg. 60.
137. Cohen, William A. (2004). The Art of the Strategist: 10 Essential Principles for Leading Your Company to Victory. NYC: AMACOM. Pg. 62.
138. Cohen, William A. (2004). The Art of the Strategist: 10 Essential Principles for Leading Your Company to Victory. NYC: AMACOM. Pg. 59.
139. Lambert, Andrew (2020). "Trafalgar: The Consequences." The Story of the Napoleonic Wars, Collector's Edition. BBC History Magazine. Bristol: Immediate Media Company. Pg. 37.
140. Brigden, James (2022). "Why the Battle of Trafalgar was so important for Britain." History. United Kingdom: A&E Networks. https://www.history.co.uk/articles/why-the-battle-of-trafalgar-was-so-important-for-britain
141. Brigden, James (2022). "Why the Battle of Trafalgar was so important for Britain." History. United Kingdom: A&E Networks. https://www.history.co.uk/articles/why-the-battle-of-trafalgar-was-so-important-for-britain
142. Brigden, James (2022). "Why the Battle of Trafalgar was so important for Britain." History. United Kingdom: A&E Networks. https://www.history.co.uk/articles/why-the-battle-of-trafalgar-was-so-important-for-britain
143. Brigden, James (2022). "Why the Battle of Trafalgar was so important for Britain." History. United Kingdom: A&E Networks. https://www.history.co.uk/articles/why-the-battle-of-trafalgar-was-so-important-for-britain
144. Asprey, Robert (2000). The Rise of Napoleon Bonaparte. NYC: Basic Books. Pg. 533.
145. Roberts, Andrew (2014). Napoleon: A Life. NYC: Viking. Pg. 263.
146. Aitchison, Neville (2009). "The Tramp of Marching Feet." Guardian Political Review, Issue 57. Christchurch, New Zealand. Pg. 5. See Also: Mitchell, W.A. (1918). "Use of the General Reserve in Grand Tactic Maneuvers as Illustrated in the Russo-Japanese War." Professional Memoirs: Corps of Engineers, United States Army and Engineer Department at Large, Volume X, Numbers 49 to 54. Pg. 57.
147. Casanova, Giacomo (2007). History of My Life. NYC: Alfred A. Knopf. Pg. 15.
148. Casanova, Giacomo (1804). The Memoirs of Jacques Casanova de Seingalt, 1725-1798, Complete. Arthur Machen (Translator). NYC: G.P. Putnam's Sons. Pg. 793.
149. Rumelt, Richard (2011). Good Strategy, Bad Strategy. London: Profile Books Ltd. Pg. 142
150. Hart, B.H. Liddell (1991). Strategy, Second Revised Edition. NYC: Meridian. Pg. 334.
151. White, Frances (2014). "The Ruthless Rise to Power of Cleopatra." All About History, Issue 18. Bournemouth: Imagine Publishing, Ltd. Pg. 74.
152. Kluth, Andreas (2011). Hannibal and Me: What History's Greatest Military Strategist Can Teach Us About Success and Failure. NYC: Riverhead Books. Pg. 134.
153. Goldfinch, Lottie (2014, November). "Cleopatra: Queen at Any Cost." History Revealed. Bristol: Immediate Media Company. Pg. 85.
154. Greene, Robert (2001). The Art of Seduction. NYC: Penguin. Pg. 7.
155. Greene, Robert (2001). The Art of Seduction. NYC: Penguin. Pg. 7.
156. Greene, Robert (1998). The 48 Laws of Power. NYC: Penguin Books. Pg. 207.
157. Greene, Robert (1998). The 48 Laws of Power. NYC: Penguin Books. Pg. 207.
158. Kluth, Andreas (2011). Hannibal and Me: What History's Greatest Military Strategist Can Teach Us About Success and Failure. NYC: Riverhead Books. Pg. 134.
159. Goldfinch, Lottie (2014, November). "Cleopatra: Queen at Any Cost." History Revealed. Bristol: Immediate Media Company. Pg. 84.
160. White, Frances (2014). "The Ruthless Rise to Power of Cleopatra." All About History, Issue 18. Bournemouth: Imagine Publishing, Ltd. Pg. 74.
161. Goldfinch, Lottie (2014, November). "Cleopatra: Queen at Any Cost." History Revealed. Bristol: Immediate Media Company. Pg. 85.
162. Cohen, William A. (2004). The Art of the Strategist: 10 Essential Principles for Leading Your Company to Victory. NYC: AMACOM. Pg. 69.
163. Cohen, William A. (2004). The Art of the Strategist: 10 Essential Principles for Leading Your Company to Victory. NYC: AMACOM. Pg. 69.
164. Casanova, Giacomo (2007). History of My Life. NYC: Alfred A. Knopf. Pg. 526.
165. Casanova, Giacomo (2007). History of My Life. NYC: Alfred A. Knopf. Pg. 506.
166. Casanova, Giacomo (2007). History of My Life. NYC: Alfred A. Knopf. Pg. 497.
167. Casanova, Giacomo (2007). History of My Life. NYC: Alfred A. Knopf. Pg. 496.
168. Casanova, Giacomo (2007). History of My Life. NYC: Alfred A. Knopf. Pg. 495.
169. Casanova, Giacomo (2007). History of My Life. NYC: Alfred A. Knopf. Pg. 496.
170. Casanova, Giacomo (2007). History of My Life. NYC: Alfred A. Knopf. Pg. 495.
171. Casanova, Giacomo (2007). History of My Life. NYC: Alfred A. Knopf. Pg. 501.
172. Casanova, Giacomo (2007). History of My Life. NYC: Alfred A. Knopf. Pg. 501.
173. Casanova, Giacomo (2007). History of My Life. NYC: Alfred A. Knopf. Pg. 501.

174. Casanova, Giacomo (2007). History of My Life. NYC: Alfred A. Knopf. Pg. 502.
175. Casanova, Giacomo (2007). History of My Life. NYC: Alfred A. Knopf. Pg. 511.
176. Casanova, Giacomo (2007). History of My Life. NYC: Alfred A. Knopf. Pg. 511.
177. Cohen, William A. (2004). The Art of the Strategist: 10 Essential Principles for Leading Your Company to Victory. NYC: AMACOM. Pg. 69.
178. Cohen, William A. (2004). The Art of the Strategist: 10 Essential Principles for Leading Your Company to Victory. NYC: AMACOM. Pg. 69.
179. Casanova, Giacomo (1804). *The Memoirs of Jacques Casanova de Seingalt, 1725-1798, Complete.* Arthur Machen (Translator). NYC: G.P. Putnam's Sons. Pg. 1370.
180. Ridgley, Stanley K. (2012). Strategic Thinking Skills: The Great Courses Course Guidebook. The Great Courses. Chantilly, Virginia: The Teaching Company, LLC. Pg. 23.
181. Goldsworthy, Adrian (2010). Antony and Cleopatra. New Haven: Yale University Press. Pg. 319.
182. Beevor, Antony (2022, July). "Russia's Doomed Revolution." Rob Attar Interview with Antony Beevor. BBC History Magazine. Pg. 57.
183. Beevor, Antony (2022, July). "Russia's Doomed Revolution." Rob Attar Interview with Antony Beevor. BBC History Magazine. Pg. 57.
184. Beevor, Antony (2022, July). "Russia's Doomed Revolution." Rob Attar Interview with Antony Beevor. BBC History Magazine. Pg. 57.
185. Beevor, Antony (2022, July). "Russia's Doomed Revolution." Rob Attar Interview with Antony Beevor. BBC History Magazine. Pg. 57.
186. McPherson, James M. (2009, January). "Lincoln as Commander in Chief: A self-taught strategist with no combat experience, Abraham Lincoln saw the path to victory more clearly than his generals." Smithsonian Magazine. https://www.smithsonianmag.com/history/
187. McPherson, James M. (2009, January). "Lincoln as Commander in Chief: A self-taught strategist with no combat experience, Abraham Lincoln saw the path to victory more clearly than his generals." Smithsonian Magazine. https://www.smithsonianmag.com/history/
188. McPherson, James M. (2009, January). "Lincoln as Commander in Chief: A self-taught strategist with no combat experience, Abraham Lincoln saw the path to victory more clearly than his generals." Smithsonian Magazine. https://www.smithsonianmag.com/history/
189. McPherson, James M. (2009, January). "Lincoln as Commander in Chief: A self-taught strategist with no combat experience, Abraham Lincoln saw the path to victory more clearly than his generals." Smithsonian Magazine. https://www.smithsonianmag.com/history/
190. McPherson, James M. (2009, January). "Lincoln as Commander in Chief: A self-taught strategist with no combat experience, Abraham Lincoln saw the path to victory more clearly than his generals." Smithsonian Magazine. https://www.smithsonianmag.com/history/
191. Badash, Lawrence (1996, February). "The Discovery of Radioactivity." Physics Today, Volume 49, 2, 21. American Institute of Physics. Pg. 25.
192 Margaritondo, G. (2010, March). "From Becquerel to Nanotechnology: One Century of Decline of Scientific Dissemination, Publishing and Technology Transfer." Modern Physics Letters B, Volume 24, No. 12. World Scientific Publishing Company. Pgs.1155-1156. See also: Thompson, Silvanus P. (1896). "On Hyperphosphorescence." Phil. Mag. Volume 42, Pgs. 103-107. See also: Reid, Robert (1974). Marie Curie. NYC: Saturday Review Press/E.P. Dutton & Co., Inc. Pgs. 76-79, 83.
193. Casanova, Giacomo (2007). History of My Life. NYC: Alfred A. Knopf. Pg. 539.
194. Casanova, Giacomo (2007). History of My Life. NYC: Alfred A. Knopf. Pg. 539.
195. Casanova, Giacomo (2007). History of My Life. NYC: Alfred A. Knopf. Pg. 539.
196. Hoefer, Richard (2019). Advocacy Practice for Social Justice, 4th Edition. Oxford: Oxford University Press. Pg. 87.
197. Hart, B.H. Liddell (1991). Strategy, Second Revised Edition. NYC: Meridian. Pg. 336.
198. Ridgley, Stanley K. (2012). Strategic Thinking Skills: The Great Courses. Chantilly, Virginia: The Teaching Company, LLC. Lecture 1.
199. Ridgley, Stanley K. (2012). Strategic Thinking Skills: The Great Courses. Chantilly, Virginia: The Teaching Company, LLC. Lecture 1.
200. Curie, Eve (1937). Madame Curie: A Biography by Eve Curie. NYC: Doubleday. Pgs. 186-187.
201. Reid, Robert (1974). Marie Curie. NYC: Saturday Review Press/E.P. Dutton & Co., Inc. Pg. 86.
202. Reid, Robert (1974). Marie Curie. NYC: Saturday Review Press/E.P. Dutton & Co., Inc. Pg. 86.
203. Reid, Robert (1974). Marie Curie. NYC: Saturday Review Press/E.P. Dutton & Co., Inc. Pg. 87.
204. Reid, Robert (1974). Marie Curie. NYC: Saturday Review Press/E.P. Dutton & Co., Inc. Pg. 87.
205. Reid, Robert (1974). Marie Curie. NYC: Saturday Review Press/E.P. Dutton & Co., Inc. Pg. 87.
206. Curie, Eve (1937). Madame Curie: A Biography by Eve Curie. NYC: Doubleday. Pg. 196.
207. Curie, Eve (1937). Madame Curie: A Biography by Eve Curie. NYC: Doubleday. Pg. 196.
208. Curie, Eve (1937). Madame Curie: A Biography by Eve Curie. NYC: Doubleday. Pg. 196.
209. Curie, Eve (1937). Madame Curie: A Biography by Eve Curie. NYC: Doubleday. Pg. 196.
210 . Curie, Eve (1937). Madame Curie: A Biography by Eve Curie. NYC: Doubleday. Pgs. 196-197.
211. Curie, Eve (1937). Madame Curie: A Biography by Eve Curie. NYC: Doubleday. Pg. 187.
212. Curie, Eve (1937). Madame Curie: A Biography by Eve Curie. NYC: Doubleday. Pg. 187.
213. Curie, Eve (1937). Madame Curie: A Biography by Eve Curie. NYC: Doubleday. Pg. 197.
214. Reid, Robert (1974). Marie Curie. NYC: Saturday Review Press/E.P. Dutton & Co., Inc. Pg. 83.
215. Curie, Eve (1937). Madame Curie: A Biography by Eve Curie. NYC: Doubleday. Pg. 196.
216. Curie, Eve (1937). Madame Curie: A Biography by Eve Curie. NYC: Doubleday. Pg. 189.
217. Reid, Robert (1974). Marie Curie. NYC: Saturday Review Press/E.P. Dutton & Co., Inc. Pg. 92.
218. Goldsmith, Barbara (2005). Obsessive Genius: The Inner World of Marie Curie. NYC: Atlas Books. Pg. 128.
219. Goldsmith, Barbara (2005). Obsessive Genius: The Inner World of Marie Curie. NYC: Atlas Books. Pg. 128.
220. Redness, Lauren (2015). Radioactive: Marie & Pierre Curie: A Tale of Love and Fallout. NYC: HarperCollins.
221. Fröman, Nanny (1996, February 28). "Marie and Pierre Curie and the discovery of polonium and radium"

(Lecture). Royal Swedish Academy of Sciences. Stockholm, Sweden The Nobel Prize. https://www.nobelprize.org/prizes/themes/marie-and-pierre-curie-and-the-discovery-of-polonium-and-radium/

222. Reid, Robert (1974). Marie Curie. NYC: Saturday Review Press/E.P. Dutton & Co., Inc. Pg. 25.

223. Curie, Eve (1937). Madame Curie: A Biography by Eve Curie. NYC: Doubleday. Pg. 185.

224. Reid, Robert (1974). Marie Curie. NYC: Saturday Review Press/E.P. Dutton & Co., Inc. Pg. 75.

225. Curie, Marie (1923). Pierre Curie. Charlotte and Vernon Kellogg (Translators). NYC: The Macmillan Company. Pg. 167.

226. Curie, Marie (1923). Pierre Curie. Charlotte and Vernon Kellogg (Translators). NYC: The Macmillan Company. Pg. 186.

227. Fröman, Nanny (1996, February 28). "Marie and Pierre Curie and the discovery of polonium and radium" (Lecture). Royal Swedish Academy of Sciences. Stockholm, Sweden The Nobel Prize. https://www.nobelprize.org/prizes/themes/marie-and-pierre-curie-and-the-discovery-of-polonium-and-radium/

228. Curie, Marie (1923). Pierre Curie. Charlotte and Vernon Kellogg (Translators). NYC: The Macmillan Company. Pg. 186-187.

229. Curie, Marie (1923). Pierre Curie. Charlotte and Vernon Kellogg (Translators). NYC: The Macmillan Company. Pg. 186.

230. Curie, Marie (1923). Pierre Curie. Charlotte and Vernon Kellogg (Translators). NYC: The Macmillan Company. Pg. 107.

231. Curie, Marie (1923). Pierre Curie. Charlotte and Vernon Kellogg (Translators). NYC: The Macmillan Company. Pg. 109.

232. Curie, Marie (1923). Pierre Curie. Charlotte and Vernon Kellogg (Translators). NYC: The Macmillan Company. Pg. 188.

233. Redness, Lauren (2015). Radioactive: Marie & Pierre Curie: A Tale of Love and Fallout. NYC: HarperCollins.

234. "Marie Curie: Unlikely Revolutionary." (2015). Oregon Public Broadcasting United States: Moreno/Lyons Productions LLC. http://www.mysteryofmatter.net/Curie.html

235. Curie, Marie (1923). Pierre Curie. Charlotte and Vernon Kellogg (Translators). NYC: The Macmillan Company. Pg. 188.

236. Curie, Marie (1923). Pierre Curie. Charlotte and Vernon Kellogg (Translators). NYC: The Macmillan Company. Pg. 189.

237. Curie, Marie (1923). Pierre Curie. Charlotte and Vernon Kellogg (Translators). NYC: The Macmillan Company. Pg. 188.

238. Curie, Marie (1923). Pierre Curie. Charlotte and Vernon Kellogg (Translators). NYC: The Macmillan Company. Pg. 190.

239. Curie, Marie (1923). Pierre Curie. Charlotte and Vernon Kellogg (Translators). NYC: The Macmillan Company. Pg. 190.

240. Fröman, Nanny (1996, February 28). "Marie and Pierre Curie and the discovery of polonium and radium" (Lecture). Royal Swedish Academy of Sciences. Stockholm, Sweden The Nobel Prize. https://www.nobelprize.org/prizes/themes/marie-

and-pierre-curie-and-the-discovery-of-polonium-and-radium/

241. Fröman, Nanny (1996, February 28). "Marie and Pierre Curie and the discovery of polonium and radium" (Lecture). Royal Swedish Academy of Sciences. Stockholm, Sweden The Nobel Prize. https://www.nobelprize.org/prizes/themes/marie-and-pierre-curie-and-the-discovery-of-polonium-and-radium/

242. Reid, Robert (1974). Marie Curie. NYC: Saturday Review Press/E.P. Dutton & Co., Inc. Pg. 89.

243. Rumelt, Richard (2011). Good Strategy, Bad Strategy. London: Profile Books Ltd. Pg. 103.

244. Rumelt, Richard (2011). Good Strategy, Bad Strategy. London: Profile Books Ltd. Pg. 103.

245. Rumelt, Richard (2011). Good Strategy, Bad Strategy. London: Profile Books Ltd. Pg. 103.

246. Note: Other experts argue it's as few as 3 or as many as 20 impressions, but it is also believed to be determined by the effectiveness of the ad and, even more importantly, by social proof.

247. Rumelt, Richard (2011). Good Strategy, Bad Strategy. London: Profile Books Ltd. Pg. 103.

248. Rumelt, Richard (2011). Good Strategy, Bad Strategy. London: Profile Books Ltd. Pg. 103.

249. Rumelt, Richard (2011). Good Strategy, Bad Strategy. London: Profile Books Ltd. Pg. 103.

250. Fröman, Nanny (1996, February 28). "Marie and Pierre Curie and the discovery of polonium and radium" (Lecture). Royal Swedish Academy of Sciences. Stockholm, Sweden The Nobel Prize. https://www.nobelprize.org/prizes/themes/marie-and-pierre-curie-and-the-discovery-of-polonium-and-radium/

251. Curie, Marie (1923). Pierre Curie. Charlotte and Vernon Kellogg (Translators). NYC: The Macmillan Company. Pg. 191-192.

252. "Marie Curie: Nobel Prize in Physics 1903, Nobel Prize in Chemistry 1911." Women Who Changed Science. The Nobel Prize. Nobel Media https://www.nobelprize.org/womenwhochangedscience/stories/marie-curie

253. "Marie Curie: Nobel Prize in Physics 1903, Nobel Prize in Chemistry 1911." Women Who Changed Science. The Nobel Prize. Nobel Media https://www.nobelprize.org/womenwhochangedscience/stories/marie-curie

254. "Marie Curie: Nobel Prize in Physics 1903, Nobel Prize in Chemistry 1911." Women Who Changed Science. The Nobel Prize. Nobel Media https://www.nobelprize.org/womenwhochangedscience/stories/marie-curie

255. Goldsworthy, Adrian (2010). Antony and Cleopatra. New Haven: Yale University Press. Pg. 320.

256. Goldsworthy, Adrian (2010). Antony and Cleopatra. New Haven: Yale University Press. Pg. 321.

257. Goldsworthy, Adrian (2010). Antony and Cleopatra. New Haven: Yale University Press. Pgs. 320-321.

258. Goldsworthy, Adrian (2010). Antony and Cleopatra. New Haven: Yale University Press. Pg. 322.

259. Schiff, Stacy (2010, December). "Rehabilitating Cleopatra." Smithsonian Magazine. https://www.smithsonianmag.com/history/rehabilitating-cleopatra-70613486/

260. Schiff, Stacy (2010, December). "Rehabilitating Cleopatra." Smithsonian Magazine.

https://www.smithsonianmag.com/history/rehabil
itating-cleopatra-70613486/

261. Schiff, Stacy (2010, December). "Rehabilitating
Cleopatra." Smithsonian Magazine.
https://www.smithsonianmag.com/history/rehabil
itating-cleopatra-70613486/

262. Schiff, Stacy (2010, December). "Rehabilitating
Cleopatra." Smithsonian Magazine.
https://www.smithsonianmag.com/history/rehabil
itating-cleopatra-70613486/

263. Tracy, Brian (2002). Victory! Applying the Proven
Principles of Military Strategy to Achieve Success in
Your Business and Personal Life. NYC: AMACOM. Pg.
76.

264. Tracy, Brian (2002). Victory! Applying the Proven
Principles of Military Strategy to Achieve Success in
Your Business and Personal Life. NYC: AMACOM. Pg.
76.

265. Tracy, Brian (2002). Victory! Applying the Proven
Principles of Military Strategy to Achieve Success in
Your Business and Personal Life. NYC: AMACOM. Pg.
76.

266. Keller, Gary (2013). The ONE Thing: The Surprisingly
Simple Truth Behind Extraordinary Results. Austin:
Bard Press. Pg. 24.

267. Mandino, Og (1988). The Greatest Salesman in the
World: Part II The End of the Story. NYC: Bantam. Pg.
112. See also: Keller, Gary (2013). The ONE Thing: The
Surprisingly Simple Truth Behind Extraordinary Results.
Austin: Bard Press. Pg. 19.

268. Tracy, Brian (2002). Victory! Applying the Proven
Principles of Military Strategy to Achieve Success in Your
Business and Personal Life. NYC: AMACOM. Pg. 76.

|12|

Catapult and Shield Your Power
through Mutually Assured Success:
The Rothschilds vs. the Republic of Pirates

1. Hoffman, Reid (2012, November 6). "Why
Relationships Matter: I-to-the-We." LinkedIn.
https://www.linkedin.com/pulse/2012110619341
2-1213-why-relationships-matter-i-to-the-we

2. Plutarch (1878 [circa 100 A.D.]). Sayings of Kings and
Commanders. In Plutarch's Moralia. E. Hinton of
Witney [Translator]. Pg. 174.
http://www.attalus.org/old/sayings1.html

3. Plutarch (1878 []). Sayings of Kings and Commanders.
E. Hinton of Witney [Translator]. Pg. 174.
http://www.attalus.org/old/sayings1.html

4. Hieronymus Osius (1574). "Agricola et Filii." Phryx
Aesopus Habitu Poetico.
http://aesopus.pbworks.com/w/page/1472440/osius
http://aesopus.pbworks.com/w/page/1472490/osius0
53

5. Aesop (1968 [6th century B.C.]), "The Bundle of Sticks"
or "The Father and His Quarreling Sons." Aesop's
Fables, Translated by George Fyler Townsend. NYC:
International Collector's Library.

6. Ferguson, Niall (1999). The House of Rothschild: The
World's Banker, 1849–1999, Volume 2. Pg. 26.

7. Ferguson, Niall (1999). The House of Rothschild:
Money's prophets, 1798–1848, Volume 1. Pg. 42.

8. Muson, Howard (2002, April 1). "Money's Prophets."
Campden FB Magazine.

http://www.campdenfb.com/article/money%E2%80%
99s-prophets

9. Mizen (Day), Spencer (2018, November). "Genghis
Khan: the Mongol warlord who almost conquered the
world." BBC History Revealed. Immediate Media
Company Ltd. Pg. 32.

10. Johnson, Paul (2004). A History of the Jews. London:
Harper. Pg. 317.

11. Muson, Howard (2002, April 1). "Money's Prophets."
Campden FB Magazine.
http://www.campdenfb.com/article/money%E2%80%
99s-prophets

12. Muson, Howard (2002, April 1). "Money's Prophets."
Campden FB Magazine.
http://www.campdenfb.com/article/money%E2%80%
99s-prophets

13. Muson, Howard (2002, April 1). "Money's Prophets."
Campden FB Magazine.
http://www.campdenfb.com/article/money%E2%80%
99s-prophets

14. The Holy Bible, New International Version (2011)(NIV).
Proverbs 24:6. Biblica, Inc.
https://www.biblegateway.com/passage/?search=Pro
verbs+24%3A6+&version=NIV

15. Hoffman, Reid (2012, November 6). "Why
Relationships Matter: I-to-the-We." LinkedIn.
https://www.linkedin.com/pulse/2012110619341
2-1213-why-relationships-matter-i-to-the-we

16. Freedman, Lawrence (2013). Strategy: A History.
Oxford: Oxford University Press. Pg. 91

17. Freedman, Lawrence (2013). Strategy: A History.
Oxford: Oxford University Press. Pg. 115

18. Ghyczy, Tiha von; Oetinger, Bolko von; and Bassford,
Christopher (2001). Clausewitz on Strategy: Inspiration
and Insight from a Master Strategist. NYC: John Wiley
& Sons, Inc. Pg. 143.

19. Freedman, Lawrence (2013). Strategy: A History.
Oxford: Oxford University Press. Pg. 30

20. The Holy Bible, New Living Translation (NLT)(2015).
Ecclesiastes 4:9-12. Bible Gateway. Carol Stream,
Illinois: Tyndale House Foundation.
https://www.biblegateway.com/passage/?search=Eccl
esiastes%204%3A9-12&version=NLT

21. Mirvis, Philip & Googins, Bradley (2022). Sustainability
to Social Change: Lead Your Company from Managing
Risks to Creating Social Value. UK: Kogan Page. Pg. 196.

22. Hare, Brian and Woods, Vanessa (2020). Survival of the
Friendliest: Understanding Our Origins and
Rediscovering Our Common Humanity. NYC: Random
House. Pg. xviiii-xxvii.

23. Hare, Brian and Woods, Vanessa (2020). Survival of the
Friendliest: Understanding Our Origins and
Rediscovering Our Common Humanity. NYC: Random
House. Pg. xxiv.

24. Hare, Brian and Woods, Vanessa (2020). Survival of the
Friendliest: Understanding Our Origins and
Rediscovering Our Common Humanity. NYC: Random
House. Pg. xxiv-xxv.

25. Hare, Brian and Woods, Vanessa (2020). Survival of the
Friendliest: Understanding Our Origins and
Rediscovering Our Common Humanity. NYC: Random
House. Pg. xxv.

26. Hare, Brian and Woods, Vanessa (2020). Survival of the
Friendliest: Understanding Our Origins and
Rediscovering Our Common Humanity. NYC: Random
House. Pg. xxv.

27. Hare, Brian and Woods, Vanessa (2020). Survival of the Friendliest: Understanding Our Origins and Rediscovering Our Common Humanity. NYC: Random House. Pg. xxv.

28. Donne, John. (1988). No Man Is an Island. UK: Souvenir Press Limited.

29. Kouzes, James and Posner, Barry (2012). The Leadership Challenge: How to Make Extraordinary Things Happen in Organizations, 5th Edition. San Francisco: Wiley. Pg. 21.

30. Aron, Paul (2009). We Hold These Truths...and Other Words that Made America. Lanham: Rowman & Littlefield Publishers, Inc. Pg. 52. Note: Ben Franklin allegedly said this to John Hancock, the president of the Continental Congress. Hancock initially said, after signing the Declaration of Independence ,"There must be no pulling different ways. We must all hang together." In response, Franklin said, "Yes, we must, indeed, all hang together, or most assuredly we shall all hang separately." Some historians are skeptical that Franklin actually said this, but, as Paul Aron writes, "Still, it sure sounds like Franklin, who loved to pun and who saw in the most somber of moments an opportunity for a punch line." Pg. 52.

31. Simon, Rebecca (2021, April 21). "'It cannot be helped': on facing death as calmly as a pirate." Psyche. Aeon Media Group Ltd. https://psyche.co/ideas/it-cannot-be-helped-on-facing-death-as-calmly-as-a-pirate

32. Simon, Rebecca (2021, April 21). "'It cannot be helped': on facing death as calmly as a pirate." Psyche. Aeon Media Group Ltd. https://psyche.co/ideas/it-cannot-be-helped-on-facing-death-as-calmly-as-a-pirate

33. Woodard, Colin (2007). The Republic of Pirates: Being the True and Surprising Story of the Caribbean Pirates and the Man Who Brought Them Down. Boston: Mariner Books. Pgs. 14-15.

34. Woodard, Colin (2007, April 29). "Life in 'The Republic of Pirates.'" NPR. https://www.npr.org/templates/story/story.php?storyId=9903589

35. Rediker, Marcus (1981, April). "'Under the Banner of King Death': The Social World of Anglo-American Pirates, 1716 to 1726." The William and Mary Quarterly, Volume 38, Number 2. https://www.jstor.org/stable/1918775 Pg. 206.

36. Dryden, Robert Gordon (2000). "Successful Pirates and Capitalist Fantasies: Charting Fictional Representations of Eighteenth-And Early Nineteenth-Century English Fortune Hunters." LSU Historical Dissertations and Theses. Louisiana State University. Pgs. 42-43. https://digitalcommons.lsu.edu/gradschool_disstheses/7191

37. Woodard, Colin (2007). The Republic of Pirates: Being the True and Surprising Story of the Caribbean Pirates and the Man Who Brought Them Down. Boston: Mariner Books. Pg. 20.

38. Andrews, Evan (2015, September 4). "The Most Successful Pirate You've Never Heard Of." History. A&E Networks, LLC. https://www.history.com/news/henry-everys-bloody-pirate-raid-320-years-ago

39. Andrews, Evan (2015, September 4). "The Most Successful Pirate You've Never Heard Of." History. A&E Networks, LLC. https://www.history.com/news/henry-everys-bloody-pirate-raid-320-years-ago

40. Woodard, Colin (2007). The Republic of Pirates: Being the True and Surprising Story of the Caribbean Pirates and the Man Who Brought Them Down. Boston: Mariner Books. Pg. 27.

41. Rediker, Marcus (2004). Villains of All Nations: Atlantic Pirates in the Golden Age. Boston: Beacon Press. Pg. 43.

42. Simon, Rebecca (2021, April 21). "'It cannot be helped': on facing death as calmly as a pirate." Psyche. Aeon Media Group Ltd. https://psyche.co/ideas/it-cannot-be-helped-on-facing-death-as-calmly-as-a-pirate

43. Kinkor, Kenneth J. (2001). "Black Men Under the Black Flag." in Pennell, C.R.'s Bandits at Sea: A Pirates Reader. NYC: NYC University Press. Pg. 200.

44. Rediker, Marcus (1981, April). "'Under the Banner of King Death': The Social World of Anglo-American Pirates, 1716 to 1726." The William and Mary Quarterly, Volume 38, Number 2. https://www.jstor.org/stable/1918775 Pg. 208.

45. Simon, Rebecca (2021, April 21). "'It cannot be helped': on facing death as calmly as a pirate." Psyche. Aeon Media Group Ltd. https://psyche.co/ideas/it-cannot-be-helped-on-facing-death-as-calmly-as-a-pirate_&_JollyRoger0

46. Rediker, Marcus (1981, April). "'Under the Banner of King Death': The Social World of Anglo-American Pirates, 1716 to 1726." The William and Mary Quarterly, Volume 38, Number 2. https://www.jstor.org/stable/1918775 Pg. 210

47. Rediker, Marcus (1981, April). "'Under the Banner of King Death': The Social World of Anglo-American Pirates, 1716 to 1726." The William and Mary Quarterly, Volume 38, Number 2. https://www.jstor.org/stable/1918775 Pg. 210

48. Rediker, Marcus (1981, April). "'Under the Banner of King Death': The Social World of Anglo-American Pirates, 1716 to 1726." The William and Mary Quarterly, Volume 38, Number 2. https://www.jstor.org/stable/1918775 Pg. 210

49. Rediker, Marcus (1981, April). "'Under the Banner of King Death': The Social World of Anglo-American Pirates, 1716 to 1726." The William and Mary Quarterly, Volume 38, Number 2. https://www.jstor.org/stable/1918775 Pg. 210

50. Woodard, Colin (2007). The Republic of Pirates: Being the True and Surprising Story of the Caribbean Pirates and the Man Who Brought Them Down. Boston: Mariner Books. Pg. 2

51. Rediker, Marcus (1981, April). "'Under the Banner of King Death': The Social World of Anglo-American Pirates, 1716 to 1726." The William and Mary Quarterly, Volume 38, Number 2. https://www.jstor.org/stable/1918775 Pg. 210

52. Rediker, Marcus (1981, April). "'Under the Banner of King Death': The Social World of Anglo-American Pirates, 1716 to 1726." The William and Mary Quarterly, Volume 38, Number 2. https://www.jstor.org/stable/1918775 Pg. 210

53. Woodard, Colin (2007). The Republic of Pirates: Being the True and Surprising Story of the Caribbean Pirates and the Man Who Brought Them Down. Boston: Mariner Books. Pg. 2

54. Woodard, Colin (2007, April 29). "Life in 'The Republic of Pirates.'" NPR. https://www.npr.org/templates/story/story.php?storyId=9903589

55. Toussaint, Kristin (2022, June 7). "Many CEOs are now making 670 times more than their company's media-

wage workers: At 49 publicly traded companies, the gap between what CEOs and median-wage workers earn is a 1,000-to-1 ratio." Fast Company. https://www.fastcompany.com/90758765/many-ceos-are-now-making-670-times-more-than-their-companys-average-workers See also: Anderson, Sarah et al (2022). "Executive Excess 2022." Institute for Policy Studies. https://ips-dc.org/report-executive-excess-2022/

56. Rediker, Marcus (1981, April). "'Under the Banner of King Death': The Social World of Anglo-American Pirates, 1716 to 1726." The William and Mary Quarterly, Volume 38, Number 2. https://www.jstor.org/stable/1918775 Pg. 211.

57. Rediker, Marcus (1981, April). "'Under the Banner of King Death': The Social World of Anglo-American Pirates, 1716 to 1726." The William and Mary Quarterly, Volume 38, Number 2. https://www.jstor.org/stable/1918775 Pg. 219.

58. Rediker, Marcus (1981, April). "'Under the Banner of King Death': The Social World of Anglo-American Pirates, 1716 to 1726." The William and Mary Quarterly, Volume 38, Number 2. https://www.jstor.org/stable/1918775 Pg. 219.

59. D'Costa, Krystal (2014, September 19). "Why Did Pirates Fly the Jolly Roger?" Scientific American. Nature America, Inc. https://blogs.scientificamerican.com/anthropology-in-practice/why-did-pirates-fly-the-jolly-roger/

60. Woodard, Colin (2007). The Republic of Pirates: Being the True and Surprising Story of the Caribbean Pirates and the Man Who Brought Them Down. Boston: Mariner Books. Pg. 2

61. Woodard, Colin (2007). The Republic of Pirates: Being the True and Surprising Story of the Caribbean Pirates and the Man Who Brought Them Down. Boston: Mariner Books. Pg. 3

62. Woodard, Colin (2007). The Republic of Pirates: Being the True and Surprising Story of the Caribbean Pirates and the Man Who Brought Them Down. Boston: Mariner Books. Pg. 3

63. Kinkor, Kenneth J. (2001). "Black Men Under the Black Flag." in Pennell, C.R.'s Bandits at Sea: A Pirates Reader. NYC: NYC University Press. Pg. 200.

64. Rediker, Marcus (1997). "Hydrarchy and Libertalia: The Utopian Dimensions of Atlantic Piracy in the Early Eighteenth Century." in David J. Starkey et al Pirates and Privateers: New Perspectives on the War on Trade in the Eighteenth and Nineteenth Centuries. Exeter: University of Exeter Press. Pg. 34.

65. Simon, Rebecca (2021, April 21). "'It cannot be helped': on facing death as calmly as a pirate." Psyche. Aeon Media Group Ltd. https://psyche.co/ideas/it-cannot-be-helped-on-facing-death-as-calmly-as-a-pirate

66. Simon, Rebecca (2021, April 21). "'It cannot be helped': on facing death as calmly as a pirate." Psyche. Aeon Media Group Ltd. https://psyche.co/ideas/it-cannot-be-helped-on-facing-death-as-calmly-as-a-pirate

67. Hewitt, D.G. (2018, March 1). "Female Pirates Who Were Every Bit as Fearsome as Blackbeard." History Collection. Spike Media Property. https://historycollection.com/women-pirates-every-bit-fearsome-blackbeard/10/

68. Hewitt, D.G. (2018, March 1). "Female Pirates Who Were Every Bit as Fearsome as Blackbeard." History Collection. Spike Media Property.

https://historycollection.com/women-pirates-every-bit-fearsome-blackbeard/10/

69. D'Costa, Krystal (2014, September 19). "Why Did Pirates Fly the Jolly Roger?" Scientific American. Nature America, Inc. https://blogs.scientificamerican.com/anthropology-in-practice/why-did-pirates-fly-the-jolly-roger/

70. Kuhn, Gabriel (2010). Life Under the Jolly Roger: Reflections on Golden Age Piracy. Oakland: PM Press. Pgs. 28-29.

71. Woodard, Colin (2007). The Republic of Pirates: Being the True and Surprising Story of the Caribbean Pirates and the Man Who Brought Them Down. Boston: Mariner Books. Pgs. 1-2, 7.

72. Woodard, Colin (2007, April 29). "Life in 'The Republic of Pirates.'" NPR. https://www.npr.org/templates/story/story.php?storyId=9903589

73. Woodard, Colin (2007). The Republic of Pirates: Being the True and Surprising Story of the Caribbean Pirates and the Man Who Brought Them Down. Boston: Mariner Books. Pg. 8

74. Cialdini, Robert (2001). Influence: Science and Practice, 4th Edition. Boston: Allyn and Bacon. Pg. 150.

75. "New Study Finds Our Desire for 'Like-Minded Others' is Hard-Wired." (2016, February 23). Wellesley College. https://www.wellesley.edu/news/2016/february/node/83586 See also: Bahns, Angela; Crandall, Christian; Gillath, Omri; and Preacher, Kristopher (2017, February). "Similarity in Relationships as Niche Construction: Choice, Stability, and Influence Within Dyads in a Free Choice Environment." Journal of Personality and Social Psychology, Volume 112, Number 2. Pgs. 329-355. https://pubmed.ncbi.nlm.nih.gov/26828831/

76. "New Study Finds Our Desire for 'Like-Minded Others' is Hard-Wired." (2016, February 23). Wellesley College. https://www.wellesley.edu/news/2016/february/node/83586 See also: Bahns, Angela; Crandall, Christian; Gillath, Omri; and Preacher, Kristopher (2017, February). "Similarity in Relationships as Niche Construction: Choice, Stability, and Influence Within Dyads in a Free Choice Environment." Journal of Personality and Social Psychology, Volume 112, Number 2. Pgs. 329-355. https://pubmed.ncbi.nlm.nih.gov/26828831/

77. Montoya, R. Matthew; Horton, Robert S.; Kirchner, Jeffrey (2008, December 1). "Is actual similarity necessary for attraction? A meta-analysis of actual and perceived similarity." Journal of Social and Personal Relationships, Volume 25, Number 6. Pgs. 889-922. https://www.researchgate.net/publication/249719130_Is_Actual_Similarity_Necessary_for_Attraction_A_Meta-Analysis_of_Actual_and_Perceived_Similarity

78. Woodard, Colin (2007). The Republic of Pirates: Being the True and Surprising Story of the Caribbean Pirates and the Man Who Brought Them Down. Boston: Mariner Books. Pg. 1.

79. Woodard, Colin (2007). The Republic of Pirates: Being the True and Surprising Story of the Caribbean Pirates and the Man Who Brought Them Down. Boston: Mariner Books. Pg. 4.

80. Woodard, Colin (2007). The Republic of Pirates: Being the True and Surprising Story of the Caribbean Pirates and the Man Who Brought Them Down. Boston: Mariner Books. Pg. 4.

81. Woodard, Colin (2007, April 29). "Life in 'The Republic of Pirates.'" NPR. https://www.npr.org/templates/story/story.php?storyId=9903589

82. Woodard, Colin (2007). The Republic of Pirates: Being the True and Surprising Story of the Caribbean Pirates and the Man Who Brought Them Down. Boston: Mariner Books. Pg. 4.

83. Woodard, Colin (2007). The Republic of Pirates: Being the True and Surprising Story of the Caribbean Pirates and the Man Who Brought Them Down. Boston: Mariner Books. Pg. 4.

84. Williams, Emma Slattery (2021, December). "Hunting Pirates: how piracy's golden age came to an end." BBC History Revealed, Issue 101. https://www.historyextra.com/period/stuart/pirate-hunters-trials-execution-gallows/ Pg. 53.

85. McCarthy, Kevin M. (1994). Twenty Florida Pirates. Sarasota: Pineapple Press, Inc. Pg. 45.

86. Rediker, Marcus (1981, April). "'Under the Banner of King Death': The Social World of Anglo-American Pirates, 1716 to 1726." The William and Mary Quarterly, Volume 38, Number 2. https://www.jstor.org/stable/1918775 Pg. 225

87. Williams, Emma Slattery (2021, December). "Hunting Pirates: how piracy's golden age came to an end." BBC History Revealed, Issue 101. https://www.historyextra.com/period/stuart/pirate-hunters-trials-execution-gallows/ Pg. 52.

88. Coyle, Daniel (2018). The Culture Code: The Secrets of Highly Successful Groups. NY: Bantam. Pg. 169.

89. Rediker, Marcus (1981, April). "'Under the Banner of King Death': The Social World of Anglo-American Pirates, 1716 to 1726." The William and Mary Quarterly, Volume 38, Number 2. https://www.jstor.org/stable/1918775 Pg. 226.

90. Rediker, Marcus (1981, April). "'Under the Banner of King Death': The Social World of Anglo-American Pirates, 1716 to 1726." The William and Mary Quarterly, Volume 38, Number 2. https://www.jstor.org/stable/1918775 Pg. 226.

91. Konstam, Angus (2022). "The Lost Pirate Republic." All About History Annual, Volume 9. London: Future Publishing Limited. Pg. 99.

92. Rediker, Marcus (1981, April). "'Under the Banner of King Death': The Social World of Anglo-American Pirates, 1716 to 1726." The William and Mary Quarterly, Volume 38, Number 2. https://www.jstor.org/stable/1918775 Pg. 226.

93. Rediker, Marcus (1981, April). "'Under the Banner of King Death': The Social World of Anglo-American Pirates, 1716 to 1726." The William and Mary Quarterly, Volume 38, Number 2. https://www.jstor.org/stable/1918775 Pg. 226.

94. Aron, Paul (2009). We Hold These Truths...and Other Words that Made America. Lanham: Rowman & Littlefield Publishers, Inc. Pg. 52.

95. Lincoln, Abraham (1858, June 16). "Proceedings of the Republican state convention." Springfield, Illinois: Bailhache & Baker. See Also: The Holy Bible, New International Version (NIV)(2011). Matthew 12:25 Biblegateway.com. Biblica, Inc. https://www.biblegateway.com: "Jesus knew their thoughts and said to them, "Every kingdom divided against itself will be ruined, and every city or household divided against itself will not stand."

96. Ridgley, Stanley K. (2012). Strategic Thinking Skills: The Great Courses. Chantilly, Virginia: The Teaching Company, LLC. Lecture 1.

97. Harrington, Ann (1999, November 22). "The Big Ideas Ever since Frederick Taylor pulled out his stopwatch, big thinkers have been coming up with new--though not always better--ways to manage people and business." Fortune. http://archive.fortune.com/magazines/fortune/fortune_archive/1999/11/22/269065/index.htm

98. Pearce, Craig L. and Ensley, Michael D. (2004). "A reciprocal and longitudinal investigation of the innovation process: the central role of shared vision in product and process innovation teams (PPITs)." Journal of Organizational Behavior. Volume 25. Pg. 260.

99. Senge, Peter M. (1990). The Fifth Discipline: The Art and Practice of the Learning Organization. NYC: Doubleday. Pg. 206

100. Ferguson, Niall (1999). The House of Rothschild: The World's Banker, 1849–1999, Volume 2. Pg. 26.

101. Ziglar, Z. (2019). The Goals Program: How to Stay Motivated Series, Book 2. Issaquah, WA: Made for Success Publishing.

102. Ferguson, Niall (1999). The House of Rothschild: Money's prophets, 1798–1848, Volume 1. Pg. 76.

103. Ferguson, Niall (1999). The House of Rothschild: Money's prophets, 1798–1848, Volume 1. Pg. 76.

104. Ferguson, Niall (1999). The House of Rothschild: Money's prophets, 1798–1848, Volume 1. Pg. 76.

105. Ferguson, Niall (1999). The House of Rothschild: Money's prophets, 1798–1848, Volume 1. Pg. 76.

106. Ferguson, Niall (1999). The House of Rothschild: Money's prophets, 1798–1848, Volume 1. Pg. 76.

107. Ferguson, Niall (1999). The House of Rothschild: Money's prophets, 1798–1848, Volume 1. Pg. 76. Emphasis Added.

108. Ferguson, Niall (1999). The House of Rothschild: Money's prophets, 1798–1848, Volume 1. Pg. 76.

109. Ferguson, Niall (1999). The House of Rothschild: Money's prophets, 1798–1848, Volume 1. Pg. 76.

110. Ferguson, Niall (1999). The House of Rothschild: Money's prophets, 1798–1848, Volume 1. Pg. 76.

111. Note: Studies on charismatic leadership, transformational leadership, and visionary leadership all bear this out. In fact, so long as they believe it, all other things being equal, the more inspiring the vision the harder people will work to realize it.

112. Coyle, Daniel (2018). The Culture Code: The Secrets of Highly Successful Groups. NY: Bantam. Pg. 171.

113. Coyle, Daniel (2018). The Culture Code: The Secrets of Highly Successful Groups. NY: Bantam. Pgs. 224-225.

114. Coyle, Daniel (2018). The Culture Code: The Secrets of Highly Successful Groups. NY: Bantam. Pg. 225.

115. Carnegie, Andrew (1899, October 15). "Carnegie on How to Get Rich: The Retired Steel King Furnishes Some Sound Advice." St. Louis Globe-Democrat. Pg. 36. https://www.newspapers.com/clip/84452036/carnegieadvice/

116. Weick, K. E. (1979). The Social Psychology of Organizing (2nd ed.). Reading, MA: Addison-Wesley. Pg. 193.

117. Rock, David and Grant, Heidi (2016, November 04)."Why Diverse Teams Are Smarter." Harvard

Business Review. https://hbr.org/2016/11/why-diverse-teams-are-smarter

118. Paraphrased from Darwin, Charles (1859). The Origin of Species. Author unknown.

119. Matthias, Meg (2023, March 13 L.A.). "Why Have So Many World Leaders Married Their Cousins?" Encyclopedia Britannica https://www.britannica.com/story/why-have-so-many-world-leaders-married-their-cousins **Note:** Rothschild gave his descendants little choice, writes Britannica, "by refusing to allow his female descendants to inherit his wealth, banking great Mayer Amschel Rothschild guaranteed that for his daughters and granddaughters to find wealthy, suitable husbands, they would have to look among their cousins. (And so they did: four pairs of Rothschild cousins, as well as one uncle-niece pairing, were wed.)." Fact-checked by The Editors of Encyclopedia Britannica.

120. Note: Competence is especially important in regard to each individual's clearly defined roles and responsibilities, but also with respect to collaboration itself. Collaboration is not just an attitude or a mindset. Collaboration is also a skill that can be developed.

121. Muson, Howard (2002, April 1). "Money's Prophets." Campden FB Magazine. http://www.campdenfb.com/article/money%E2%80%99s-prophets

122. Muson, Howard (2002, April 1). "Money's Prophets." Campden FB Magazine. http://www.campdenfb.com/article/money%E2%80%99s-prophets

123. Boller, Paul F. (1991). Congressional Anecdotes. NYC: Oxford University Press. Pg. 299.

124. Rediker, Marcus (2004). Villains of All Nations: Atlantic Pirates in the Golden Age. Boston: Beacon Press. Pg. 42

125. HBO has a comedy series that's loosely based off of Stede Bonnet's leadership as a pirate captain called Our Flag Means Death—94% on Rotten Tomatoes.

126. Woodard, Colin (2007). The Republic of Pirates: Being the True and Surprising Story of the Caribbean Pirates and the Man Who Brought Them Down. Boston: Mariner Books. Pg. 132.

127. Rediker, Marcus (2004). Villains of All Nations: Atlantic Pirates in the Golden Age. Boston: Beacon Press. Pg. 41.

128. Rediker, Marcus (2004). Villains of All Nations: Atlantic Pirates in the Golden Age. Boston: Beacon Press. Pg. 41.

129. Rediker, Marcus (2004). Villains of All Nations: Atlantic Pirates in the Golden Age. Boston: Beacon Press. Pg. 41.

130. Rediker, Marcus (2004). Villains of All Nations: Atlantic Pirates in the Golden Age. Boston: Beacon Press. Pg. 42.

131. Johnson, Captain Charles (1927 [1724]). A General History Of The Robberies And Murders Of The Most Notorious Pirates, From Their First Rise And Settlement In The Island Of Providence To The Present Year. London: Routledge.232.

132. Dolin, Eric Jay (2018). Black Flags, Blue Waters: The Epic History of America's Most Notorious Pirates. NYC: W.W. Norton & Co. Pg. 163.

133. Johnson, Captain Charles (1927 [1724]). A General History Of The Robberies And Murders Of The Most Notorious Pirates, From Their First Rise And Settlement In The Island Of Providence To The Present Year. London: Routledge.352.

134. Johnson, Captain Charles (1927 [1724]). A General History Of The Robberies And Murders Of The Most Notorious Pirates, From Their First Rise And Settlement In The Island Of Providence To The Present Year. London: Routledge.231.

135. Johnson, Captain Charles (1927 [1724]). A General History Of The Robberies And Murders Of The Most Notorious Pirates, From Their First Rise And Settlement In The Island Of Providence To The Present Year. London: Routledge.232.

136. Ferguson, Niall (1999). The House of Rothschild: The World's Banker, 1849–1999, Volume 2. NYC: Penguin.

137. Cooper, Richard N. (2000, March/April). "The House of Rothschild: The World's Banker, 1849-1999." Foreign Affairs. https://www.foreignaffairs.com/reviews/capsule-review/2000-03-01/house-rothschild-worlds-banker-1849-1999. Note: As of 2022, on the Forbes list of billionaires, which includes more than 2500 billionaires from all around the world, not a single member of the Rothschild family is on the list. The Walton family, of Wal-Mart, in contrast currently has 7 family members on the list. https://www.forbes.com/real-time-billionaires/#50fbcd2f3d78)

138. Staff Writer (2011, October 6). "A Byte Out of History" A Most Helpful Ostrich: Using Ultra Intelligence in World War II." U.S. Federal Bureau of Investigation. https://www.fbi.gov/news/stories/byte-out-of-history-using-ultra-intelligence-in-world-war-ii

139. Wells, Anthony R. (2020). Between Five Eyes: Fifty Years Inside the Intelligence Community. Oxford: Casemate. Pg. viii.

140. "Winston Churchill and the Cold War." America's National Churchill Museum, Westminster College, Fulton, Missouri. https://www.nationalchurchillmuseum.org/winston-churchill-and-the-cold-war.html

141. Corera, Gordon (2021, March 5). "Diary Reveals Birth of Secret UK-US Spy Pact that Grew into Five Eyes." BBC News. https://www.bbc.com/news/uk-56284453

142. Vucetic, Srdjan (2020, January 2). "CANZUK anyone?" Diplomat & International Canada. https://diplomatonline.com/mag/2020/01/canzuk-anyone/

143. Brown, Andrew (Editor)(2014). "Money: Top 5 Facts. Nathan Mayer Rothschild." All About History, Issue 10. Bournemouth: Imagine Publishing Ltd. Pg. 26.

144. Johnson, Captain Charles (1927 [1724]). A General History Of The Robberies And Murders Of The Most Notorious Pirates, From Their First Rise And Settlement In The Island Of Providence To The Present Year. London: Routledge. Pg. 398.

145. Ferguson, Niall (1999). The House of Rothschild: Money's prophets, 1798–1848, Volume 1. Pg. 77.

146. Ferguson, Niall (1999). The House of Rothschild: Money's prophets, 1798–1848, Volume 1. Pg. 77.

147. Ferguson, Niall (1999). The House of Rothschild: Money's prophets, 1798–1848, Volume 1. Pg. 77.

148. Ferguson, Niall (1999). The House of Rothschild: Money's prophets, 1798–1848, Volume 1. Pg. 76.

149. Ferguson, Niall (1999). The House of Rothschild: Money's prophets, 1798–1848, Volume 1. Pg. 77.

150. Ferguson, Niall (1999). The House of Rothschild: Money's prophets, 1798–1848, Volume 1. Pg. 77.

151. Staff Writer (2023, March 5: Last Accessed). "Five Arrows: The five arrows remain an enduring symbol of the Rothschild name." The Rothschild Archive. https://www.rothschildarchive.org/family/the_rothschild_name_and_arms/five_arrows

152. Rediker, Marcus (1981, April). "'Under the Banner of King Death': The Social World of Anglo-American Pirates, 1716 to 1726." The William and Mary Quarterly, Volume 38, Number 2. https://www.jstor.org/stable/1918775 Pg. 220.

153. Rediker, Marcus (1981, April). "'Under the Banner of King Death': The Social World of Anglo-American Pirates, 1716 to 1726." The William and Mary Quarterly, Volume 38, Number 2. https://www.jstor.org/stable/1918775 Pg. 220.

154. Rediker, Marcus (1981, April). "'Under the Banner of King Death': The Social World of Anglo-American Pirates, 1716 to 1726." The William and Mary Quarterly, Volume 38, Number 2. https://www.jstor.org/stable/1918775 Pg. 221.

155. Rediker, Marcus (1981, April). "'Under the Banner of King Death': The Social World of Anglo-American Pirates, 1716 to 1726." The William and Mary Quarterly, Volume 38, Number 2. Pg. 222. https://www.jstor.org/stable/1918775

   Popular pirate phrases include words such as: ahoy (hello), aye (yes), avast (pay attention), blimey (expression of disbelief), booty (treasure), chase gun (main cannon at the bow), clap of thunder (strong drink), dead men tell no tales (no survivors), hearties (good friends), hornswaggle (cheat), jack (flag), jolly roger (pirate flag), keelhaul (torture involving being dragged under the ship across the barnacles), landlubber (novice or clumsy person, no sailing skills), parley (to conference with the opposition), prize (captured ship), savvy? (do you understand?), scallywag (rookie pirate or noob), scupper (throw overboard), scuttle (sink ship), seadog (veteran or old sailor or pirate), shiver me timbers (expression of surprise, originally when the wood or "timbers" of the ship were hit or splintered), three sheets to the wind (very drunk), weigh anchor (let's go or getting moving), yellow flag (used to indicate diseased crew, sometimes used as a trick to avoid being boarded), yo ho ho! (cheerful expression to get attention).

156. Rediker, Marcus (1981, April). "'Under the Banner of King Death': The Social World of Anglo-American Pirates, 1716 to 1726." The William and Mary Quarterly, Volume 38, Number 2. https://www.jstor.org/stable/1918775 Pg. 222.

157. Rediker, Marcus (1981, April). "'Under the Banner of King Death': The Social World of Anglo-American Pirates, 1716 to 1726." The William and Mary Quarterly, Volume 38, Number 2. https://www.jstor.org/stable/1918775 Pg. 222.

|13|

Believe Absolutely to Inspire Absolute Belief: Joan of Arc Turns the Tide of the Hundred Years' War

1. Marden, Orison Swett (1974). Success Unlimited Magazine, Volume 21, Issues 7-12. Success Unlimited, Inc. Pg. 49.

2. Trask, Willard Ropes (1961). Joan of Arc: Self-Portrait. Springfield, Ohio: Collier Books. Pg. 13.

3. Twain, Mark (2007 [1896]). *Joan of Arc: Personal Recollections of Joan of Arc by The Sieur Louis de Conte (Her Page and Secretary)*. San Francisco: Ignatius Press. Pg. 86. Note: This book was written by Mark Twain from the perspective of Sieur Louis de Conte (it was not actually written by Conte).

4. Twain, Mark (2007 [1896]). Joan of Arc: Personal Recollections of Joan of Arc by The Sieur Louis de Conte (Her Page and Secretary). San Francisco: Ignatius Press. Pg. 86.

5. Twain, Mark (2007 [1896]). Joan of Arc: Personal Recollections of Joan of Arc by The Sieur Louis de Conte (Her Page and Secretary). San Francisco: Ignatius Press. Pg. 86.

6. Barker, Juliet (2012). Conquest: The English Kingdom of France 1417-1450. Cambridge: Harvard University Press. Pg. 107.

7. Hill, Napoleon (1971). You Can Work Your Own Miracles. NYC: The Random House Publishing Group. Pg. 144.

8. Thoreau, Henry David (1873). A Week on the Concord and Merrimack Rivers. Boston: James R. Osgood & Co., Publishers. Pg. 149.

9. Greene, Robert (1998). The 48 Laws of Power. NYC: Penguin Books. Pg. 221.

10. Kennedy, Dan and Kessler, Chip (2010). Making Them Believe: The 21 Principles and Lost Secrets of Dr. J.R. Brinkley-Style Marketing. Garden City, NY: Glazer-Kennedy Publishing. Pg. 93.

11. White, Richard D. (2006). Kingfish: The Reign of Huey P. Long. NYC: Random House. Pg. 5.

12. White, Richard D. (2006). Kingfish: The Reign of Huey P. Long. NYC: Random House. Pg. 5.

13. Maxwell, John (2007). Talent is Never Enough Workbook. Nashville: Thomas Nelson. Pg. 6.

14. Pernoud, Regine (1982). Joan of Arc: By Herself and Her Witnesses. NYC: Scarborough House. Pg. 35.

15. Stead, William Thomas (Editor)(1893). Borderland: A Quarterly Review and Index, Volume 1. Princeton: Princeton University Press. Pg. 32. **See Also:** Murray, T. Douglas (1902). Jeanne D'Arc: Maid of Orleans: Being the Story of her Life, her Achievements, and her Death, as attested on Oath and Set forth in the Original Documents. NYC: McClure, Phillips & Co. Pg. 223.

16. Castor, Helen (2014). Joan of Arc: A History. London: Faber & Faber. Pg. 205. **Note:** But was it belief in herself or in God? What's interesting about Joan of Arc is that while she was perceived by outsiders to be a living illustration of a young woman with remarkable self-confidence and self-belief, Joan herself explained her actions and behaviors as being entirely dependent on her faith. As she once said, "Although I would rather have remained spinning [wool] at my mother's side ... yet I must go and I must do this thing, for my Lord wills that I do so." In other words, regardless of the perceptions of others, Joan's belief in her ability to save France was based exclusively on her faith in God and the belief that it was God's will for her to save France. That is, it was God, not herself, that led to her striking boldness and courage. Nevertheless, it was still her unshakeable faith, and, moreover, she evidently believed that she was worthy of being a vessel of God. What's more, with regard to the practical effects, it would be difficult to make the case that putting your faith in Providence is in any way an inferior approach, provided you believe in a loving, faithful, and

omnipotent God. In fact, among believers, one could make the case that faith supersedes self-belief. As the Spanish mystic and Roman Catholic saint Teresa of Avila put it, "God plus one equals an army."

17. Jackson, Curtis and Greene, Robert (2009). The 50th Law. NYC: HarperCollins. Pg. 260.

18. Jackson, Curtis and Greene, Robert (2009). The 50th Law. NYC: HarperCollins. Pg. 260.

19. Reifsnyder, Richard W. (2019, June 3). "The Practical Faith of Theodore Roosevelt: Presbyterian and Paternal Influences. Presbyterian Historical Society, The National Archives of the PCUSA. https://www.history.pcusa.org/blog/2019/06/practical -faith-theodore-roosevelt-presbyterian-and-paternal-influences See Also: Marschall, Rick (2010). "A True Christian American President." https://www1.cbn.com/churchandministry/a-true-christian-american-president Christian Broadcasting Network, Inc.

20. Rosenberg, Michelle. (2019). Warriors and Wenches: Sex and Power in Women's History. Yorkshire: Pen & Sword Books. Pg. 28.

21. Sun Tzu (1996 [circa 5th century B.C.]) The Complete Art of War. Ralph D. Sawyer (Translator). NYC: Westview Press. Pg. 108.

22. Robbins, Anthony (1991). Awaken the Giant Within: How to Take Immediate Control of Your Mental, Emotional, Physical and Financial Destiny. NYC: Simon and Schuster. Pg. 301.

23. Robbins, Anthony (1991). Awaken the Giant Within: How to Take Immediate Control of Your Mental, Emotional, Physical and Financial Destiny. NYC: Simon and Schuster. Pg. 7.

24. Schmidt, Todd (2008, May-June). "Reforming the Madrasah: A Disregarded Dimension in the War on Terrorism." Military Review. Pg. 29.

25. Dickson, Gary (2012). "Charisma, Medieval and Modern." Religions, Volume 3, Issue 3. Pg. 766.

26. Dickson, Gary (2012). "Charisma, Medieval and Modern." Religions, Volume 3, Issue 3. Pg. 766.

27. Dickson, Gary (2012). "Charisma, Medieval and Modern." Religions, Volume 3, Issue 3. Pg. 766.

28. Grafton, Philippa (Editor)(2021). "Behind the Legend of Joan of Arc." History of War: Book of the Hundred Years' War, 4th Edition. Bournemouth: Future Publishing Limited. Pg. 119.

29. Garlow, James L. (2002). The 21 Irrefutable Laws of Leadership Tested by Time. Nashville: Thomas Nelson Publishers. Pg. 188.

30. Grafton, Philippa (Editor)(2021). "Behind the Legend of Joan of Arc." History of War: Book of the Hundred Years' War, 4th Edition. Bournemouth: Future Publishing Limited. Pgs. 114-115.

31. Pernoud, Regine and Clin, Marie-Veronique (1999). Joan of Arc: Her Story. NYC: St. Martin's Press. Pg. 20.

32. Luntz, Frank (2011). Win: The Key Principles to Take Your Business from Ordinary to Extraordinary. NYC: Hyperion. Pg. 208.

33. Dombowsky, Don (2014). Nietzsche and Napoleon: The Dionysian Conspiracy (Political Philosophy Now). Pg. 71.

34. Luntz, Frank (2011). Win: The Key Principles to Take Your Business from Ordinary to Extraordinary. NYC: Hyperion. Pg. 208.

35. Luntz, Frank (2011). Win: The Key Principles to Take Your Business from Ordinary to Extraordinary. NYC: Hyperion. Pg. 208.

36. Luntz, Frank (2011). Win: The Key Principles to Take Your Business from Ordinary to Extraordinary. NYC: Hyperion. Pg. 208.

37. Caddy, Florence (1886). Footsteps of Jeanne D'Arc: A Pilgrimage. London: Hurst and Blackett. Pg. 123.

38. Grafton, Philippa (Editor)(2021). "Behind the Legend of Joan of Arc." History of War: Book of the Hundred Years' War, 4th Edition. Bournemouth: Future Publishing Limited. Pg. 115.

39. Murray, T. Douglas (1902). Jeanne D'Arc: Maid of Orleans: Being the Story of her Life, her Achievements, and her Death, as attested on Oath and Set forth in the Original Documents. NYC: McClure, Phillips & Co. Pg. 234.

40. Hollway, Don (2020, January 3). "Joan of Arc and the Siege of Orléans." Warfare History Network. https://warfarehistorynetwork.com/2020/01/03/j oan-of-arc-siege-of-orleans/

41. Hollway, Don (2020, January 3). "Joan of Arc and the Siege of Orléans." Warfare History Network. https://warfarehistorynetwork.com/2020/01/03/j oan-of-arc-siege-of-orleans/

42. Hollway, Don (2020, January 3). "Joan of Arc and the Siege of Orléans." Warfare History Network. https://warfarehistorynetwork.com/2020/01/03/j oan-of-arc-siege-of-orleans/

43. Hollway, Don (2020, January 3). "Joan of Arc and the Siege of Orléans." Warfare History Network. https://warfarehistorynetwork.com/2020/01/03/j oan-of-arc-siege-of-orleans/

44. Robbins, Anthony (1991). Awaken the Giant Within: How to Take Immediate Control of Your Mental, Emotional, Physical and Financial Destiny. NYC: Simon and Schuster. Pg. 57.

45. Robbins, Anthony (1991). Awaken the Giant Within: How to Take Immediate Control of Your Mental, Emotional, Physical and Financial Destiny. NYC: Simon and Schuster. Pg. 48.

46. Tarcher, Jeremy P. (Ed.)(2007). The Prosperity Bible: The Greatest Writings of All Time on the Secrets to Wealth and Prosperity. NYC: Penguin. Pg. 111.

47. Tarcher, Jeremy P. (Ed.)(2007). The Prosperity Bible: The Greatest Writings of All Time on the Secrets to Wealth and Prosperity. NYC: Penguin. Pg. 111.

48. Twain, Mark (2007 [1896]). Joan of Arc: Personal Recollections of Joan of Arc by The Sieur Louis de Conte (Her Page and Secretary). San Francisco: Ignatius Press. Pg. 86.

49. Twain, Mark (2007 [1896]). Joan of Arc: Personal Recollections of Joan of Arc by The Sieur Louis de Conte (Her Page and Secretary). San Francisco: Ignatius Press. Pg. 86.

50. Stead, William Thomas (Editor)(1893). Borderland: A Quarterly Review and Index, Volume 1. Princeton: Princeton University Press. Pg. 32. See also: Twain, Mark (2007 [1896]). Joan of Arc: Personal Recollections of Joan of Arc by The Sieur Louis de Conte (Her Page and Secretary). San Francisco: Ignatius Press. Pg. 97. See also: Murray, T. Douglas (1902). Jeanne D'Arc: Maid of Orleans: Being the Story of her Life, her Achievements, and her Death, as attested on Oath and Set forth in the Original Documents. NYC: McClure, Phillips & Co. Pg. 223

51. Twain, Mark (2007 [1896]). Joan of Arc: Personal Recollections of Joan of Arc by The Sieur Louis de Conte (Her Page and Secretary). San Francisco: Ignatius Press. Pg. 89.

52. Twain, Mark (2007 [1896]). Joan of Arc: Personal Recollections of Joan of Arc by The Sieur Louis de Conte (Her Page and Secretary). San Francisco: Ignatius Press. Pg. 89.

53. Hollway, Don (2020, January 3). "Joan of Arc and the Siege of Orléans." Warfare History Network. https://warfarehistorynetwork.com/2020/01/03/joan-of-arc-siege-of-orleans/

54. Robbins, Anthony (1991). Awaken the Giant Within: How to Take Immediate Control of Your Mental, Emotional, Physical and Financial Destiny. NYC: Simon and Schuster. Pg. 49.

55. Heller, Erich (1975). The Disinherited Mind: Essays in Modern German Literature. NYC: Harper. Pg. 26.

56. Robbins, Anthony (1991). Awaken the Giant Within: How to Take Immediate Control of Your Mental, Emotional, Physical and Financial Destiny. NYC: Simon and Schuster. Pg. 51.

57. Robbins, Anthony (1991). Awaken the Giant Within: How to Take Immediate Control of Your Mental, Emotional, Physical and Financial Destiny. NYC: Simon and Schuster. Pg. 51.

58. Robbins, Anthony (1991). Awaken the Giant Within: How to Take Immediate Control of Your Mental, Emotional, Physical and Financial Destiny. NYC: Simon and Schuster. Pg. 51.

59. Robbins, Anthony (1991). Awaken the Giant Within: How to Take Immediate Control of Your Mental, Emotional, Physical and Financial Destiny. NYC: Simon and Schuster. Pg. 51.

60. Robbins, Anthony (1991). Awaken the Giant Within: How to Take Immediate Control of Your Mental, Emotional, Physical and Financial Destiny. NYC: Simon and Schuster. Pg. 51.

61. Robbins, Anthony (1991). Awaken the Giant Within: How to Take Immediate Control of Your Mental, Emotional, Physical and Financial Destiny. NYC: Simon and Schuster. Pg. 49.

62. Robbins, Anthony (1991). Awaken the Giant Within: How to Take Immediate Control of Your Mental, Emotional, Physical and Financial Destiny. NYC: Simon and Schuster. Pg. 49.

63. Saint Joan of Arc (1996). Joan of Arc: In Her Own Words. Willard Ropes Trask (Translator). NYC: Turtle Point Press. Pg. 27.

64. Note: This also helps to explain why leading by example is one of the most powerful practices a leader can employ to maintain morale and win people over. Walking the talk can be one of the most powerful parts of the process of delivering on the promise. Take the example of the Desert Fox. Anytime an army is far away in a foreign land, struggling with adequate supplies, morale is at risk. During World War II, for example, Adolf Hitler was forced to open up a third major front to deal with the Allied forces in North Africa. It was here where the mythical status of the Desert Fox was born (pg. 51). It was here where German general Erwin Rommel became a living legend among his men. "The German and Italian soldiers noticed how their general was always in the thick of the action on the front line. He lived, sweated, slept and ate like his men. Several times, while driving close to the front in his command car, he met British patrols and only escaped by luck. Such courage won the respect of his troops. Rommel called the soldiers his 'Africans,'" writes Danielsen, "and they affectionately referred to him as Erwin. They shared a sense of being far from home and almost forgotten by the rest of the German Army. The men knew full well that North Africa was not the priority when it came to distributing tanks, petrol and new supplies between the many fronts of Nazi Germany. But they endured the privations, because," Danielsen continues, "they had the invincible Erwin. 'Always there is this strange magic strength that this soldier radiates to his troops, right down to the last rifleman,' wrote war correspondent Baron von Esebeck about Rommel's effect on combat morale." Danielsen, Hanne-Luise (Editor)(2022). "Desert Fox: Rommel Outwitted the British in the Sahara." *Bringing History to Life: 3rd Reich at War*. Norway: Bonnier Publications International. Pgs. 50-51.

65. Hollway, Don (2020, January 3). "Joan of Arc and the Siege of Orléans." Warfare History Network. https://warfarehistorynetwork.com/2020/01/03/joan-of-arc-siege-of-orleans/

66. Hollway, Don (2020, January 3). "Joan of Arc and the Siege of Orléans." Warfare History Network. https://warfarehistorynetwork.com/2020/01/03/joan-of-arc-siege-of-orleans/

67. Hollway, Don (2020, January 3). "Joan of Arc and the Siege of Orléans." Warfare History Network. https://warfarehistorynetwork.com/2020/01/03/joan-of-arc-siege-of-orleans/

68. Hollway, Don (2020, January 3). "Joan of Arc and the Siege of Orléans." Warfare History Network. https://warfarehistorynetwork.com/2020/01/03/joan-of-arc-siege-of-orleans/

69. Hollway, Don (2020, January 3). "Joan of Arc and the Siege of Orléans." Warfare History Network. https://warfarehistorynetwork.com/2020/01/03/joan-of-arc-siege-of-orleans/

70. Murray, T. Douglas (1902). Jeanne D'Arc: Maid of Orleans: Being the Story of her Life, her Achievements, and her Death, as attested on Oath and set forth in the Original Documents. NYC: McClure, Phillips & Co. Pg. 236.

71. Murray, T. Douglas (1902). Jeanne D'Arc: Maid of Orleans: Being the Story of her Life, her Achievements, and her Death, as attested on Oath and Set forth in the Original Documents. NYC: McClure, Phillips & Co. Pg. 236.

72. Hollway, Don (2020, January 3). "Joan of Arc and the Siege of Orléans." Warfare History Network. https://warfarehistorynetwork.com/2020/01/03/joan-of-arc-siege-of-orleans/

73. Hollway, Don (2020, January 3). "Joan of Arc and the Siege of Orléans." Warfare History Network. https://warfarehistorynetwork.com/2020/01/03/joan-of-arc-siege-of-orleans/

74. Hollway, Don (2020, January 3). "Joan of Arc and the Siege of Orléans." Warfare History Network. https://warfarehistorynetwork.com/2020/01/03/joan-of-arc-siege-of-orleans/

75. Grafton, Philippa (Editor)(2021). "Behind the Legend of Joan of Arc." History of War: Book of the Hundred

Years' War, 4th Edition. Bournemouth: Future
Publishing Limited. Pg. 116.

76. Garlow, James L. (2002). The 21 Irrefutable Laws of
Leadership Tested by Time. Nashville: Thomas Nelson
Publishers. Pg. 187.

77. Garlow, James L. (2002). The 21 Irrefutable Laws of
Leadership Tested by Time. Nashville: Thomas Nelson
Publishers. Pg. 188.

78. Garlow, James L. (2002). The 21 Irrefutable Laws of
Leadership Tested by Time. Nashville: Thomas Nelson
Publishers. Pg. 188.

79. Manning, Scott (2010, January 6). "Joan of Arc's
Military Successes and Failures." Historian on the
Warpath. https://scottmanning.com/content/joan-of-
arc-military-successes-and-failures/

80. Twain, Mark (1899). Joan of Arc: Personal
Recollections of Joan of Arc by The Sieur Louis de
Conte (Her Page and Secretary), Volume II. NYC:
Harper & Brothers. Pgs. 34-35.

81. Twain, Mark (2007 [1896]). Joan of Arc: Personal
Recollections of Joan of Arc by The Sieur Louis de
Conte (Her Page and Secretary). San Francisco: Ignatius
Press. Pg. 290.

82. Twain, Mark (2007 [1896]). Joan of Arc: Personal
Recollections of Joan of Arc by The Sieur Louis de
Conte (Her Page and Secretary). San Francisco: Ignatius
Press. Pg. 292.

83. Collier, Robert (2007). "The Secret of the Ages," In The
Prosperity Bible: The Greatest Writings of All Time on
the Secrets to Wealth and Prosperity. Tarcher, Jeremy
P. (Editor) NYC: Penguin. Pg. 870.

84. Garlow, James L. (2002). The 21 Irrefutable Laws of
Leadership Tested by Time. Nashville: Thomas Nelson
Publishers. Pg. 185.

85. Churchill, Winston (2015 [1956]). History of the
English-Speaking Peoples, Volume 1: The Birth of
Britain. London: Bloomsbury. Pg. 260.

86. Hatful, Jonathan (2014). "Heroes and Villains: Joan of
Arc." All About History, Issue 10. Bournemouth:
Imagine Publishing Ltd. Pg. 29.

87. Tarcher, Jeremy P. (Ed.)(2007). The Prosperity Bible:
The Greatest Writings of All Time on the Secrets to
Wealth and Prosperity. NYC: Penguin. Pg. 42.

88. Tarcher, Jeremy P. (Ed.)(2007). The Prosperity Bible:
The Greatest Writings of All Time on the Secrets to
Wealth and Prosperity. NYC: Penguin. Pg. 43.

89. Lipton, Bruce H. (2008). The Biology of Belief:
Unleashing the Power of Consciousness, Matter and
Miracles. Carlsbad, CA: Hay House, Inc. Pg. 117.

90. Shakespeare, W. (2001) Julius Caesar. Edited by R. Gill.
Oxford: Oxford University Press. Act 1, Scene 2, 145.

91. Cohen, Jennie (2020, January 3). "7 Surprising Facts
About Joan of Arc: Explore seven surprising facts about
Joan of Arc, the courageous teenager who rose from
obscurity to lead the French army." History Channel.
https://www.history.com/news/7-surprising-facts-
about-joan-of-arc

92. Pickels, Dwayne (2002). Joan of Arc. NY: Chelsea House
Publishers. Pg. 79.

93. Harrison, Kathryn (2012, January 5). "Joan of Arc:
Enduring Power." The NYC Times.
https://www.nytimes.com/2012/01/06/opinion/joan-
of-arc-enduring-power.html

94. Harrison, Kathryn (2012, January 5). "Joan of Arc:
Enduring Power." The NYC Times.

95. Twain, Mark (2007 [1896]). Joan of Arc: Personal
Recollections of Joan of Arc by The Sieur Louis de
Conte (Her Page and Secretary). San Francisco: Ignatius
Press. Comment on the cover of Twain's book.

96. Twain, Mark (2007 [1896]). Joan of Arc: Personal
Recollections of Joan of Arc by The Sieur Louis de
Conte (Her Page and Secretary). San Francisco: Ignatius
Press. Pg. 20. See also: Garlow, James L. (2002). The 21
Irrefutable Laws of Leadership Tested by Time.
Nashville: Thomas Nelson Publishers. Pg. 188-190.

|14|

Model the Masters of Strategic Agility; Engineer the Flexibility and Mobility to Quickly and Cleverly Adapt: Genghis Khan and His Savage Slayers Conquer the Islamic World

1. Duggan, William (2002). Napoleon's Glance: The Secret
of Strategy. Pg. 19. "The fact was that I was not a
master of my actions because I was not so insane as to
attempt to bend events to conform to my policies. On
the contrary, I bent my policies to accord with the
unforeseen shape of the events."

2. Albustani, Hareth (2021). "Crushing Khwarezmia: The
Mongols' First Campaign Against the Muslim World Set
a Precedent: Surrender or Die." All About History:
Genghis Khan and the Mongol Empire. Bournemouth:
Imagine Publishing, Ltd. Pg. 57.

3. Albustani, Hareth (2021). "Crushing Khwarezmia: The
Mongols' First Campaign Against the Muslim World Set
a Precedent: Surrender or Die." All About History:
Genghis Khan and the Mongol Empire. Bournemouth:
Imagine Publishing, Ltd. Pg. 57.

4. Ratchnevsky, Paul. Genghis Khan: His Life and Legacy.
Pg. 120.

5. Turnbull, Stephen (2003). Genghis Khan and the
Mongol Conquests 1190—1400. Oxford: Osprey
Publishing Ltd. Pg. 20.

6. McLynn, Frank (2015). Genghis Khan: His Conquests,
His Empire, His Legacy. Boston: Da Capo Press. Pg. 257.

7. McLynn, Frank (2015). Genghis Khan: His Conquests,
His Empire, His Legacy. Boston: Da Capo Press. Pg. 258.

8. Weatherford, Jack (2005). Genghis Khan and the
Making of the Modern World. NYC: Three Rivers Press.
Pg. 84.

9. Weatherford, Jack (2005). Genghis Khan and the
Making of the Modern World. NYC: Three Rivers Press.
Pg. 84.

10. Peers, Chris (2015). Genghis Khan and the Mongol War
Machine. South Yorkshire: Pen and Sword Books Ltd.
Pg. 120.

11. Weatherford, Jack (2005). Genghis Khan and the
Making of the Modern World. NYC: Three Rivers Press.
Pg. 86.

12. Weatherford, Jack (2005). Genghis Khan and the
Making of the Modern World. NYC: Three Rivers Press.
Pg. 86.

13. Weatherford, Jack (2005). Genghis Khan and the
Making of the Modern World. NYC: Three Rivers Press.
Pg. 84.

14. McLynn, Frank (2015). Genghis Khan: His Conquests,
His Empire, His Legacy. Boston: Da Capo Press. Pg. 259.

15. Stephens, Alan and Baker, Nicola (2006). Making Sense
of War: Strategy of the 21st Century. NYC. Pg. 8.

16. Albustani, Hareth (2021). "Crushing Khwarezmia: The Mongols' First Campaign Against the Muslim World Set a Precedent: Surrender or Die." All About History: Genghis Khan and the Mongol Empire. Bournemouth: Imagine Publishing, Ltd. Pg. 57.

17. Albustani, Hareth (2021). "Crushing Khwarezmia: The Mongols' First Campaign Against the Muslim World Set a Precedent: Surrender or Die." All About History: Genghis Khan and the Mongol Empire. Bournemouth: Imagine Publishing, Ltd. Pg. 58.

18. McLynn, Frank (2015). Genghis Khan: His Conquests, His Empire, His Legacy. Boston: Da Capo Press. Pg. 261.

19. Albustani, Hareth (2021). "Crushing Khwarezmia: The Mongols' First Campaign Against the Muslim World Set a Precedent: Surrender or Die." All About History: Genghis Khan and the Mongol Empire. Bournemouth: Imagine Publishing, Ltd. Pg. 58.

20. Albustani, Hareth (2021). "Crushing Khwarezmia: The Mongols' First Campaign Against the Muslim World Set a Precedent: Surrender or Die." All About History: Genghis Khan and the Mongol Empire. Bournemouth: Imagine Publishing, Ltd. Pg. 58.

21. McLynn, Frank (2015). Genghis Khan: His Conquests, His Empire, His Legacy. Boston: Da Capo Press. Pg. 261.

22. McLynn, Frank (2015). Genghis Khan: His Conquests, His Empire, His Legacy. Boston: Da Capo Press. Pg. 262.

23. McLynn, Frank (2015). Genghis Khan: His Conquests, His Empire, His Legacy. Boston: Da Capo Press. Pg. 263.

24. Hart, Captain B.H. Liddell (1927). Great Captains Unveiled. London: William Blackwood & Sons Ltd. Pg. 12.

25. McLynn, Frank (2015). Genghis Khan: His Conquests, His Empire, His Legacy. Boston: Da Capo Press. Pg. 271.

26. Weatherford, Jack (2005). Genghis Khan and the Making of the Modern World. NYC: Three Rivers Press. Pg. 74.

27. Sloan, Julia (2006). Learning to Think Strategically. San Diego: Butterworth-Heinemann. Pg. 42.

28. McLynn, Frank (2015). Genghis Khan: His Conquests, His Empire, His Legacy. Boston: Da Capo Press. Pg. 271.

29. McLynn, Frank (2015). Genghis Khan: His Conquests, His Empire, His Legacy. Boston: Da Capo Press. Pg. 259.

30. McLynn, Frank (2015). Genghis Khan: His Conquests, His Empire, His Legacy. Boston: Da Capo Press. Pg. 263.

31. Man, John (2014). The Mongol Empire: Genghis Khan, His Heirs and the Founding of Modern China. NYC: Bantam Press. Pg. 101.

32. McLynn, Frank (2015). Genghis Khan: His Conquests, His Empire, His Legacy. Boston: Da Capo Press. Pg. 261.

33. McLynn, Frank (2015). Genghis Khan: His Conquests, His Empire, His Legacy. Boston: Da Capo Press. Pg. 259.

34. McLynn, Frank (2015). Genghis Khan: His Conquests, His Empire, His Legacy. Boston: Da Capo Press. Pg. 271.

35. McLynn, Frank (2015). Genghis Khan: His Conquests, His Empire, His Legacy. Boston: Da Capo Press. Pg. 271.

36. McLynn, Frank (2015). Genghis Khan: His Conquests, His Empire, His Legacy. Boston: Da Capo Press. Pg. 271.

37. McLynn, Frank (2015). Genghis Khan: His Conquests, His Empire, His Legacy. Boston: Da Capo Press. Pg. 271.

38. McLynn, Frank (2015). Genghis Khan: His Conquests, His Empire, His Legacy. Boston: Da Capo Press. Pg. 272.

39. Albustani, Hareth (2021). "Crushing Khwarezmia: The Mongols' First Campaign Against the Muslim World Set a Precedent: Surrender or Die." All About History: Genghis Khan and the Mongol Empire. Bournemouth: Imagine Publishing, Ltd. Pg. 58.

40. McLynn, Frank (2015). Genghis Khan: His Conquests, His Empire, His Legacy. Boston: Da Capo Press. Pg. 271.

41. Albustani, Hareth (2021). "Crushing Khwarezmia: The Mongols' First Campaign Against the Muslim World Set a Precedent: Surrender or Die." All About History: Genghis Khan and the Mongol Empire. Bournemouth: Imagine Publishing, Ltd. Pg. 58.

42. Peers, Chris (2015). Genghis Khan and the Mongol War Machine. South Yorkshire: Pen and Sword Books Ltd. Pg. 119-120.

43. McLynn, Frank (2015). Genghis Khan: His Conquests, His Empire, His Legacy. Boston: Da Capo Press. Pg. 269.

44. Peers, Chris (2015). Genghis Khan and the Mongol War Machine. South Yorkshire: Pen & Sword Books Ltd. Pg. 120.

45. Note: At first glance, this may appear to be the opposite of the approach detailed in Chapter 11 on concentrating your forces. However, there are two points worth mentioning: First, splitting your forces to travel to a destination or in order to approach the strategic focus point (i.e. "center of gravity") from two different directions simultaneously, is still consistent with the principle of concentration. Concentration requires amassing your resources at the strategic focus point (i.e. the point of impact), not before you get to that point (though it does increase the risk that your enemy's strategic focus point will be one of your temporarily less concentrated parts). Second, concentrating your forces does not necessarily mean concentrating all the forces or resources at your disposal. It means concentrating sufficient resources to ensure a decisive victory. If that requires the great bulk of your resources, as is often the case (e.g. Napoleon's forces at Toulon), so be it. If, however, only one-third of your resources is sufficient to ensure a decisive victory at the strategic focus point because your opponent is either badly outnumbered or broadly dispersed (i.e. the opposite of concentration), all the better.

46. McLynn, Frank (2015). Genghis Khan: His Conquests, His Empire, His Legacy. Boston: Da Capo Press. Pg. 268.

47. Albustani, Hareth (2021). "Crushing Khwarezmia: The Mongols' First Campaign Against the Muslim World Set a Precedent: Surrender or Die." All About History: Genghis Khan and the Mongol Empire. Bournemouth: Imagine Publishing, Ltd. Pg. 58.

48. McLynn, Frank (2015). Genghis Khan: His Conquests, His Empire, His Legacy. Boston: Da Capo Press. Pg. 272.

49. Peers, Chris (2015). Genghis Khan and the Mongol War Machine. South Yorkshire: Pen and Sword Books Ltd. Pg. 125.

50. Hart, Captain B.H. Liddell (1927). Great Captains Unveiled. London: William Blackwood & Sons Ltd. Pg. 15.

51. Hart, Captain B.H. Liddell (1927). Great Captains Unveiled. London: William Blackwood & Sons Ltd. Pg. 15.

52. Peers, Chris (2015). Genghis Khan and the Mongol War Machine. South Yorkshire: Pen and Sword Books Ltd. Pg. 38.

53. Albustani, Hareth (2021). "Crushing Khwarezmia: The Mongols' First Campaign Against the Muslim World Set a Precedent: Surrender or Die." All About History: Genghis Khan and the Mongol Empire. Bournemouth: Imagine Publishing, Ltd. Pg. 58.

54. McLynn, Frank (2015). Genghis Khan: His Conquests, His Empire, His Legacy. Boston: Da Capo Press. Pg. 273.

55. Hart, Captain B.H. Liddell (1972). History of the First World War. London: Pan Books Ltd. Pg. 396.
56. McLynn, Frank (2015). Genghis Khan: His Conquests, His Empire, His Legacy. Boston: Da Capo Press. Pg. 274.
57. McLynn, Frank (2015). Genghis Khan: His Conquests, His Empire, His Legacy. Boston: Da Capo Press. Pg. 274.
58. McLynn, Frank (2015). Genghis Khan: His Conquests, His Empire, His Legacy. Boston: Da Capo Press. Pg. 274.
59. Hart, Captain B.H. Liddell (1927). Great Captains Unveiled. London: William Blackwood & Sons Ltd. Pg. 15.
60. Hart, Captain B.H. Liddell (1927). Great Captains Unveiled. London: William Blackwood & Sons Ltd. Pg. 15.
61. McLynn, Frank (2015). Genghis Khan: His Conquests, His Empire, His Legacy. Boston: Da Capo Press. Pg. 274.
62. McLynn, Frank (2015). Genghis Khan: His Conquests, His Empire, His Legacy. Boston: Da Capo Press. Pg. 274.
63. Albustani, Hareth (2021). "Crushing Khwarezmia: The Mongols' First Campaign Against the Muslim World Set a Precedent: Surrender or Die." All About History: Genghis Khan and the Mongol Empire. Bournemouth: Imagine Publishing, Ltd. Pg. 58.
64. McLynn, Frank (2015). Genghis Khan: His Conquests, His Empire, His Legacy. Boston: Da Capo Press. Pg. 274.
65. McLynn, Frank (2015). Genghis Khan: His Conquests, His Empire, His Legacy. Boston: Da Capo Press. Pg. 275.
66. McLynn, Frank (2015). Genghis Khan: His Conquests, His Empire, His Legacy. Boston: Da Capo Press. Pg. 275.
67. McLynn, Frank (2015). Genghis Khan: His Conquests, His Empire, His Legacy. Boston: Da Capo Press. Pg. 278.
68. Weatherford, Jack (2005). Genghis Khan and the Making of the Modern World. NYC: Three Rivers Press. Pg. 74.
69. McLynn, Frank (2015). Genghis Khan: His Conquests, His Empire, His Legacy. Boston: Da Capo Press. Pg. 275.
70. McLynn, Frank (2015). Genghis Khan: His Conquests, His Empire, His Legacy. Boston: Da Capo Press. Pg. 275.
71. Turnbull, Stephen (2003). Genghis Khan and the Mongol Conquests 1190—1400. Oxford: Osprey Publishing Ltd. Pg. 20.
72. McLynn, Frank (2015). Genghis Khan: His Conquests, His Empire, His Legacy. Boston: Da Capo Press. Pg. 278.
73. Turnbull, Stephen (2003). Genghis Khan and the Mongol Conquests 1190—1400. Oxford: Osprey Publishing Ltd. Pg. 20.
74. McLynn, Frank (2015). Genghis Khan: His Conquests, His Empire, His Legacy. Boston: Da Capo Press. Pg. 278.
75. Turnbull, Stephen (2003). Genghis Khan and the Mongol Conquests 1190—1400. Oxford: Osprey Publishing Ltd. Pg. 20.
76. Man, John (2014). The Mongol Empire: Genghis Khan, His Heirs and the Founding of Modern China. NYC: Bantam Press. Pg. 103.
77. Peers, Chris (2015). Genghis Khan and the Mongol War Machine. South Yorkshire: Pen and Sword Books Ltd. Pg. 126.
78. Albustani, Hareth (2021). "Crushing Khwarezmia: The Mongols' First Campaign Against the Muslim World Set a Precedent: Surrender or Die." All About History: Genghis Khan and the Mongol Empire. Bournemouth: Imagine Publishing, Ltd. Pg. 58-60.
79. McLynn, Frank (2015). Genghis Khan: His Conquests, His Empire, His Legacy. Boston: Da Capo Press. Pg. 278.
80. McLynn, Frank (2015). Genghis Khan: His Conquests, His Empire, His Legacy. Boston: Da Capo Press. Pg. 277.
81. Peers, Chris (2015). Genghis Khan and the Mongol War Machine. South Yorkshire: Pen and Sword Books Ltd. Pg. 125.
82. Peers, Chris (2015). Genghis Khan and the Mongol War Machine. South Yorkshire: Pen and Sword Books Ltd. Pg. 127.
83. Weatherford, Jack (2005). Genghis Khan and the Making of the Modern World. NYC: Three Rivers Press. Pg. 75.
84. McLynn, Frank (2015). Genghis Khan: His Conquests, His Empire, His Legacy. Boston: Da Capo Press. Pg. 277
85. Man, John (2014). The Mongol Empire: Genghis Khan, His Heirs and the Founding of Modern China. NYC: Bantam Press. Pg. 82(eBook109)
86. Peers, Chris (2015). Genghis Khan and the Mongol War Machine. South Yorkshire: Pen and Sword Books Ltd. Pg. 127.
87. Man, John (2014). The Mongol Empire: Genghis Khan, His Heirs and the Founding of Modern China. NYC: Bantam Press. Pg. 82(eBook109)
88. Weatherford, Jack (2005). Genghis Khan and the Making of the Modern World. NYC: Three Rivers Press. Pg. 88.
89. Weatherford, Jack (2005). Genghis Khan and the Making of the Modern World. NYC: Three Rivers Press. Pg. 88.
90. Weatherford, Jack (2005). Genghis Khan and the Making of the Modern World. NYC: Three Rivers Press. Pg. 86.
91. Weatherford, Jack (2005). Genghis Khan and the Making of the Modern World. NYC: Three Rivers Press. Pg. 86.
92. McLynn, Frank (2015). Genghis Khan: His Conquests, His Empire, His Legacy. Boston: Da Capo Press. Pg. 261.
93. McLynn, Frank (2015). Genghis Khan: His Conquests, His Empire, His Legacy. Boston: Da Capo Press. Pg. 261.
94. McLynn, Frank (2015). Genghis Khan: His Conquests, His Empire, His Legacy. Boston: Da Capo Press. Pg. 261-262.
95. Albustani, Hareth (2021). "Crushing Khwarezmia: The Mongols' First Campaign Against the Muslim World Set a Precedent: Surrender or Die." All About History: Genghis Khan and the Mongol Empire. Bournemouth: Imagine Publishing, Ltd. Pg. 60.
96. Peers, Chris (2015). Genghis Khan and the Mongol War Machine. South Yorkshire: Pen and Sword Books Ltd. Pg. 127.
97. Man, John (2014). The Mongol Empire: Genghis Khan, His Heirs and the Founding of Modern China. NYC: Bantam Press. Pg. 82. (eBook109)
98. Peers, Chris (2015). Genghis Khan and the Mongol War Machine. South Yorkshire: Pen and Sword Books Ltd. Pg. 127.
99. Albustani, Hareth (2021). "Crushing Khwarezmia: The Mongols' First Campaign Against the Muslim World Set a Precedent: Surrender or Die." All About History: Genghis Khan and the Mongol Empire. Bournemouth: Imagine Publishing, Ltd. Pg. 60.
100. Peers, Chris (2015). Genghis Khan and the Mongol War Machine. South Yorkshire: Pen and Sword Books Ltd. Pg. 127.
101. Peers, Chris (2015). Genghis Khan and the Mongol War Machine. South Yorkshire: Pen and Sword Books Ltd. Pg. 113.

102. Covey, Stephen (1990). The Seven Habits of Highly Effective People: Powerful Lessons in Personal Change. NYC: Simon and Schuster. Pg. 18.

103. Coleman, John (2023, Spring). "The Best Strategic Leaders Balance Agility and Consistency." Harvard Business Review, Special Issue: How to Think More Strategically. Cambridge: Harvard Business Publishing. Pg. 26.

104. Aurelius, Marcus (2002 [Circa 170-180 A.D.]). The Meditations. NYC: Random House, Inc. Note: This quote is, according to philosophy professor Dirk Baltzly, a "highly creative" paraphrase or translation of the following much longer, less eloquent: "But among the principles readiest to thine hand, upon which thou shalt pore, let there be these two. One, that objective things do not lay hold of the soul, but stand quiescent without; while disturbances are but the outcome of that opinion which is within us. A second, that all this visible world changes in a moment, and will be no more; and continually bethink thee to the changes of how many things thou hast already been a witness. 'The Universe—mutation: Life—opinion.'" See also: O'Rourke, Ciara (2019, September 26). "No, Marcus Aurelius didn't say this about opinions and facts." PolitiFact. https://www.politifact.com/factchecks/2019/sep/26/viral-image/no-marcus-aurelius-didnt-say-about-opinions-and-fa/ As O'Rourke writes, "Marcus Aurelius's view wasn't that there are no facts. Rather, he believed there are facts but that properly understood, none of the facts of the external world should disturb us. [...] "'Everyone has a limited perspective on it,'" Baltzly said.

105. Thoreau, Henry David (1851, August 5). The Writings of Henry David Thoreau, Volume 8 of 20, Journal II: 1850—September 15, 1851. Bradford Torrey (Editor). Project Gutenberg. Pg. 373. https://www.gutenberg.org/files/59031/59031-h/59031-h.htm#Page_373 See also: Richardson Jr., Richard D. (1986). Henry Thoreau: A Life of the Mind. San Francisco: University of California Press. Pg. 171. Richardson wrote the quotation oft misattributed to Thoreau: "It's not what you look at that matters, it's what you see."

106. Robson, David (2022). The Expectation Effect: How Your Mindset Can Change Your World. Edinburgh: Canongate. Pg. 17.

107. Crum, Alia (2018, January). World Economic Forum. Davos, Switzerland. https://mbl.stanford.edu/news/world-economic-forum-2018 See also: https://www.youtube.com/watch?v=vTDYtwqKBI8

108. Heller, Erich (1975). The Disinherited Mind: Essays in Modern German Literature. NYC: Harper. Pg. 26. Quote: "Be careful how you interpret the world; it is like that." Emphasis in the original.

109. Shakespeare, William (1973). The Merry Wives of Windsor. Harmondsworth Baltimore: Penguin.

110. Henley, William Ernest (1875). "Invictus." In Book of Verses, Life and Death (Echoes). NYC: Scribner & Welford Pg. 57.

111. Crum, Alia (2018, January). World Economic Forum. Davos, Switzerland. https://mbl.stanford.edu/news/world-economic-forum-2018 See also: https://www.youtube.com/watch?v=vTDYtwqKBI8

112. Crum, Alia (2018, January). World Economic Forum. Davos, Switzerland. https://mbl.stanford.edu/news/world-economic-forum-2018 See also: https://www.youtube.com/watch?v=vTDYtwqKBI8

113. Schoemaker, Paul; et al (2023, Spring). "Strategic Leadership: The Essential Skills." Harvard Business Review, Special Issue: How to Think More Strategically. Cambridge: Harvard Business Publishing. Pg. 122.

114. Sloan, Julia (2006). Learning to Think Strategically. San Diego: Butterworth-Heinemann. Pg. 42.

115. Sloan, Julia (2006). Learning to Think Strategically. San Diego: Butterworth-Heinemann. Pg. 42.

116. Montgomery, Cynthia (2012). The Strategist: Be the Leader Your Business Needs. NYC: Harper. Pg. 19.

117. Ridgley, Stanley K. (2012). Strategic Thinking Skills: The Great Courses. Chantilly, Virginia: The Teaching Company, LLC. Lecture 1 (12:30).

118. Rigby, Darrell; Elk, Sarah; and Berez, Steve (2020, May-June). "The Agile C-Suite: A New Approach to Leadership for the Team at the Top." Harvard Business Review. Pg. 71.

119. Sun Tzu (2008). The Art of War. Lionel Giles (Translator). Radford, VA: Wilder Publications. X. Terrain, #31. See also: http://classics.mit.edu/Tzu/artwar.html

120. The Holy Bible, New International Version (2011). Book of Numbers 13:1-2, 17-20. Biblegateway.com. Biblica, Inc. https://www.biblegateway.com/passage/?search=Numbers+13%3A17-20&version=NIV

121. Tracy, Brian (2002). Victory! Applying the Proven Principles of Military Strategy to Achieve Success in Your Business and Personal Life. NYC: AMACOM. Pg. 111.

122. Tracy, Brian (2002). Victory! Applying the Proven Principles of Military Strategy to Achieve Success in Your Business and Personal Life. NYC: AMACOM. Pg. 112.

123. Tracy, Brian (2002). Victory! Applying the Proven Principles of Military Strategy to Achieve Success in Your Business and Personal Life. NYC: AMACOM. Pgs. 111-112.

124. Tracy, Brian (2002). Victory! Applying the Proven Principles of Military Strategy to Achieve Success in Your Business and Personal Life. NYC: AMACOM. Pg. 111.

125. Hart, Captain B.H. Liddell (1927). Great Captains Unveiled. London: William Blackwood & Sons Ltd. Pg. 11-12.

126. Tracy, Brian (2002). Victory! Applying the Proven Principles of Military Strategy to Achieve Success in Your Business and Personal Life. NYC: AMACOM. Pgs. 112-113.

127. McManus, John C. (2004). The Americans at D-Day: The American Experience at the Normandy Invasion. NYC: Forge Books. Pg. 87.

128. Manchester, William (1978). American Caesar: Douglas MacArthur 1880—1964. NYC: Back Bay Books. Pg. 348.

129. Wilson, Woodrow (1926). The New Democracy: Presidential Messages, Addresses, and Other Papers (1913-1917), Volume I of II. NYC: Harper & Brothers Publishers. Pg. 95.

130. Patton, General George S. (1947). War as I Knew It. NYC: Houghton Mifflin Company. Pg. 116.

131. Hart, Michael H. (1992). The 100: A Ranking of the Most Influential Persons in History. NYC: Citadel Press. Pg. 145.
132. Kovacs, Peter (2018). "Famous People In History: Genghis Khan." The Thinking Gentleman. https://www.thethinkinggentleman.com/2018/07/18/famous-people-in-history-genghis-khan/amp/
133. Peers, Chris (2015). Genghis Khan and the Mongol War Machine. South Yorkshire: Pen and Sword Books Ltd. Pg. 121.
134. Peers, Chris (2015). Genghis Khan and the Mongol War Machine. South Yorkshire: Pen and Sword Books Ltd. Pg. 121.
135. Staff Writer (2021, March 20) "History of Equestrian Stirrups." American Equus. https://americanequus.com/history-of-stirrups/
136. Mustermann, Erik (2018, June 10). "The Stirrup: Genghis Khan's Deadliest Weapon." War History Online. https://www.warhistoryonline.com/war-articles/the-stirrup-genghis-khans-deadliest-weapon.html
137. Mustermann, Erik (2018, June 10). "The Stirrup: Genghis Khan's Deadliest Weapon." War History Online. https://www.warhistoryonline.com/war-articles/the-stirrup-genghis-khans-deadliest-weapon.html
138. Smith, David (2021). "Military Might of the Mongols." All About History: Genghis Khan and the Mongol Empire. Bournemouth: Imagine Publishing, Ltd. Pg. 36.
139. Boyle, David et al (1999). Micropedia: People Who Shaped History. Bath: Dempsey Parr. Pg. 177.
140. McLynn, Frank (2015). Genghis Khan: His Conquests, His Empire, His Legacy. Boston: Da Capo Press. Pg. 264-265.
141. Weatherford, Jack (2005). Genghis Khan and the Making of the Modern World. NYC: Three Rivers Press. Pg. 77.
142. Pelegero, Borja (2015, August-September). "Genghis Khan: Conqueror of Empires." National Geographic History, Volume 1, Number 3. Washington, D.C.: National Geographic Partners, LLC. Pg. 75.
143. Pelegero, Borja (2015, August-September). "Genghis Khan: Conqueror of Empires." National Geographic History, Volume 1, Number 3. Washington, D.C.: National Geographic Partners, LLC. Pg. 75.
144. Bawden, Charles R. "Genghis Khan: Mongol Ruler." Encyclopedia Britannica. https://www.britannica.com/biography/Genghis-Khan
145. Leberecht, Tim (2016, October 31). "Make Your Strategy More Agile." Harvard Business Review. https://hbr.org/2016/10/make-your-strategy-more-agile
146. Emerson, Ralph Waldo (1841). Self-Reliance. White Plains: Peter Pauper Press.
147. Grant, Adam (2021). Think Again: The Power of Knowing What You Don't Know. NYC: Viking. Pg. 24.
148. Grant, Adam (2021). Think Again: The Power of Knowing What You Don't Know. NYC: Viking. Pg. 24.
149. Aghina, Wouter; De Smet, Aaron; and Weerda, Kirsten (2015). "Agility: It rhymes with stability." McKinsey Insights. McKinsey & Company. https://www.mckinsey.com/business-functions/organization/our-insights/agility-it-rhymes-with-stability
150. Aghina, Wouter; De Smet, Aaron; and Weerda, Kirsten (2015). "Agility: It rhymes with stability." McKinsey Insights. McKinsey & Company. https://www.mckinsey.com/business-functions/organization/our-insights/agility-it-rhymes-with-stability
151. Johnson, Chalmers (2004). "From Political Scientist to Public Intellectual," Chalmers Johnson Interview. Conversations with History; Institute of International Studies, University of California at Berkeley. http://globetrotter.berkeley.edu/people4/CJohnson/cjohnson-con1.html
152. Grant, Adam (2021). Think Again: The Power of Knowing What You Don't Know. NYC: Viking. Pg. 24.
153. Grant, Adam (2021). Think Again: The Power of Knowing What You Don't Know. NYC: Viking. Pg. 24.
154. Emerson, Ralph Waldo (1908 [1841]). The Essay on Self-Reliance. NYC: Roycrofters. Pg. 23.
155. Von Moltke, Helmuth (1871). Moltke's Military Works: II. Activity as Chief of the Army General Staff in Peacetime. "About Strategy," An Essay from the Year 1871. Berlin, Germany: Ernst Siegfried Mittler und Sohn. Pg. 291.
156. Weatherford, Jack (2005). Genghis Khan and the Making of the Modern World. NYC: Three Rivers Press. Pg. 74.
157. Dunford, Chauney (Editor)(2019). Leaders Who Changed History. NYC: DK Publishing. Pg. 54.
158. Weatherford, Jack (2005). Genghis Khan and the Making of the Modern World. NYC: Three Rivers Press.
159. Peers, Chris (2015). Genghis Khan and the Mongol War Machine. South Yorkshire: Pen and Sword Books Ltd. Pg. 82.
160. Smith, David (2021). "Military Might of the Mongols." All About History: Genghis Khan and the Mongol Empire. Bournemouth: Imagine Publishing, Ltd. Pg. 34.
161. Smith, David (2021). "Military Might of the Mongols." All About History: Genghis Khan and the Mongol Empire. Bournemouth: Imagine Publishing, Ltd. Pg. 34.
162. Freedman, Lawrence (2022, July/August). "Why War Fails: Russia's Invasion of Ukraine and the Limits of Military Power." Foreign Affairs, Volume 101, Number 4. Pg. 22.
163. Freedman, Lawrence (2022, July/August). "Why War Fails: Russia's Invasion of Ukraine and the Limits of Military Power." Foreign Affairs, Volume 101, Number 4. Pg. 13.
164. Bannister, Nicholas and Barrie, Chris (1999, July 1). "Murdoch's Spin on the Web." The Guardian. https://www.theguardian.com/uk/1999/jul/02/3
165. Sun Tzu (2007). Sun Tzu's The Art of War. Gary Gagliardi (Translator). Seattle, WA: Clearbridge Publishing. X. Terrain, Pg. 121.
166. Kotter, John & Cohen, D. S. (2015). Successful Organizational Change: The Kotter-Cohen Collection. Boston: Harvard Business Review Press. Pg. 78.
167. Brooke, Connor (2013, August 1). "Three Agile Business Lessons from Genghis Khan." London: Business2Community. https://www.business2community.com/strategy/three-agile-business-lessons-from-genghis-khan-0571671
168. Kovacs, Peter (2018). "Famous People In History: Genghis Khan." The Thinking Gentleman. https://www.thethinkinggentleman.com/2018/07/18/famous-people-in-history-genghis-khan/amp/
169. Hart, Captain B.H. Liddell (1927). Great Captains Unveiled. London: William Blackwood & Sons Ltd. Pg. 10.

170. Hart, Captain B.H. Liddell (1927). Great Captains Unveiled. London: William Blackwood & Sons Ltd. Pg. 9.

171. Wilkes, Jonny (2015, September). "Genghis Khan: Conqueror of the World." History Revealed, Issue 20. Bristol: Immediate Media Company. Pg. 80.

172. Aghina, Wouter; Ahlback, Karin; De Smet, Aaron; Lackey, Gerald; Lurie, Michael; Murarka, Monica; and Handscomb, Christopher (2018, January 22). "The Five Trademarks of Agile Organizations." McKinsey & Company. https://www.mckinsey.com/business-functions/people-and-organizational-performance/our-insights/the-five-trademarks-of-agile-organizations

173. Aghina, Wouter; Ahlback, Karin; De Smet, Aaron; Lackey, Gerald; Lurie, Michael; Murarka, Monica; and Handscomb, Christopher (2018, January 22). "The Five Trademarks of Agile Organizations." McKinsey & Company. https://www.mckinsey.com/business-functions/people-and-organizational-performance/our-insights/the-five-trademarks-of-agile-organizations

174. Dunford, Chauney (Editor)(2019). Leaders Who Changed History. NYC: DK Publishing. Pg. 54.

175. Smith, David (2021). "Military Might of the Mongols." All About History: Genghis Khan and the Mongol Empire. Bournemouth: Imagine Publishing, Ltd. Pg. 36.

176. Chandler, David G. (1966). The Campaigns of Napoleon: The Mind and Method of History's Greatest Soldier. NYC: Scribner. Pg. 148.

177. Wasson, James, United States Army. "The Development of The Corps D'Armée And Its Impact on Napoleonic Warfare." The Napoleon Series. The Waterloo Association. https://www.napoleon-series.org/military-info/organization/c_armycorps.html#1

178. Wasson, James, United States Army. "The Development of The Corps D'Armée And Its Impact on Napoleonic Warfare." The Napoleon Series. The Waterloo Association. https://www.napoleon-series.org/military-info/organization/c_armycorps.html#1

179. Duggan, William (2003). The Art of What Works. NYC: McGraw-Hill. Pg. 18.

180. Duggan, William (2003). The Art of What Works. NYC: McGraw-Hill. Pg. 18.

181. Duggan, William (2003). The Art of What Works. NYC: McGraw-Hill. Pg. 22.

182. Duggan, William (2003). The Art of What Works. NYC: McGraw-Hill. Pg. 18.

183. Strauss, Barry (2012). Masters of Command: Alexander, Hannibal, Caesar, and the Genius of Leadership. NYC: Simon & Schuster. Pg. 31.

184. Strauss, Barry (2012). Masters of Command: Alexander, Hannibal, Caesar, and the Genius of Leadership. NYC: Simon & Schuster. Pg. 31.

185. Lynch, Lt. General (Ret.) Rick (2013). Adapt or Die: Leadership Principles from an American General. Grand Rapids: Baker Books. Pg. 197.

186. Pelegero, Borja (2015, August-September). "Genghis Khan: Conqueror of Empires." National Geographic History, Volume 1, Number 3. Washington, D.C.: National Geographic Partners, LLC. Pg. 72.

187. Pelegero, Borja (2015, August-September). "Genghis Khan: Conqueror of Empires." National Geographic History, Volume 1, Number 3. Washington, D.C.: National Geographic Partners, LLC. Pg. 72.

188. Pelegero, Borja (2015, August-September). "Genghis Khan: Conqueror of Empires." National Geographic History, Volume 1, Number 3. Washington, D.C.: National Geographic Partners, LLC. Pg. 72.

189. Pelegero, Borja (2015, August-September). "Genghis Khan: Conqueror of Empires." National Geographic History, Volume 1, Number 3. Washington, D.C.: National Geographic Partners, LLC. Pg. 72.

190. Pelegero, Borja (2015, August-September). "Genghis Khan: Conqueror of Empires." National Geographic History, Volume 1, Number 3. Washington, D.C.: National Geographic Partners, LLC. Pg. 72.

191. Pelegero, Borja (2015, August-September). "Genghis Khan: Conqueror of Empires." National Geographic History, Volume 1, Number 3. Washington, D.C.: National Geographic Partners, LLC. Pg. 72.

192. Pelegero, Borja (2015, August-September). "Genghis Khan: Conqueror of Empires." National Geographic History, Volume 1, Number 3. Washington, D.C.: National Geographic Partners, LLC. Pg. 72.

193. Wilkes, Jonny (2015, September). "Genghis Khan: Conqueror of the World." History Revealed, Issue 20. Bristol: Immediate Media Company. Pg. 80.

194. Wilkes, Jonny (2015, September). "Genghis Khan: Conqueror of the World." History Revealed, Issue 20. Bristol: Immediate Media Company. Pg. 80.

195. Blanchard, Keith (Editorial Director)(2022). Warriors of the Ancient World. USA: a360media. Pg. 13.

196. Blanchard, Keith (Editorial Director)(2022). Warriors of the Ancient World. USA: a360media. Pg. 15.

197. Smith, David (2021). "Military Might of the Mongols." All About History: Genghis Khan and the Mongol Empire. Bournemouth: Imagine Publishing, Ltd. Pg. 34.

198. Cartwright, Mark (2019, October 10). "Mongol Warfare." World History Encyclopedia. https://www.worldhistory.org/Mongol_Warfare/

199. Cartwright, Mark (2019, October 10). "Mongol Warfare." World History Encyclopedia. https://www.worldhistory.org/Mongol_Warfare/

200. Smith, David (2021). "Military Might of the Mongols." All About History: Genghis Khan and the Mongol Empire. Bournemouth: Imagine Publishing, Ltd. Pg. 34.

201. Pistorius, Dr. Micki (2020, February). "Did History Get the Story Wrong? Qin Shi Huang, Genghis Khan, Attila the Hun." Ancient Origins, Issue 18. Pg. 68.

202. Dunford, Chauney (Editor)(2019). Leaders Who Changed History. NYC: DK Publishing. Pg. 54.

203. Pelegero, Borja (2015, August-September). "Genghis Khan: Conqueror of Empires." National Geographic History, Volume 1, Number 3. Washington, D.C.: National Geographic Partners, LLC. Pg. 66.

204. Pelegero, Borja (2015, August-September). "Genghis Khan: Conqueror of Empires." National Geographic History, Volume 1, Number 3. Washington, D.C.: National Geographic Partners, LLC. Pg. 68.

205. Brooke, Connor (2013, August 1). "Three Agile Business Lessons from Genghis Khan." London: Business2Community. https://www.business2community.com/strategy/three-agile-business-lessons-from-genghis-khan-0571671

206. Pistorius, Dr. Micki (2020, February). "Did History Get the Story Wrong? Qin Shi Huang, Genghis Khan, Attila the Hun." Ancient Origins, Issue 18. Pg. 68.

207. Greene, Robert (1998). The 48 Laws of Power. NYC: Penguin Books. Pg. 422.
208. Horton, James (2021) "Conquering China." All About History: Genghis Khan and the Mongol Empire. Bournemouth: Imagine Publishing, Ltd. Pg. 51.
209. Blanchard, Keith (Editorial Director)(2022). Warriors of the Ancient World. USA: a360media. Pg. 15.
210. Weatherford, Jack (2005). Genghis Khan and the Making of the Modern World. NYC: Three Rivers Press. Pg. 75.
211. Weatherford, Jack (2005). Genghis Khan and the Making of the Modern World. NYC: Three Rivers Press. Pg. 76.
212. Strauss, Barry (2012). Masters of Command: Alexander, Hannibal, Caesar, and the Genius of Leadership. NYC: Simon & Schuster. Pg. 31.
213. Strauss, Barry (2012). Masters of Command: Alexander, Hannibal, Caesar, and the Genius of Leadership. NYC: Simon & Schuster. Pg. 31.
214. Strauss, Barry (2012). Masters of Command: Alexander, Hannibal, Caesar, and the Genius of Leadership. NYC: Simon & Schuster. Pg. 31.
215. Chandler, David G. (Editor)(2015). Napoleon's Military Maxims. Cheltenham, England: The History Press. Pg. 57.
216. Chandler, David G. (Editor)(2015). Napoleon's Military Maxims. Cheltenham, England: The History Press. Pg. 57.

|15|

Wield Power with Wisdom, Get Both in and Out of the Game: Martin Luther King Jr. Assumes Leadership, Becomes the Symbol of the Civil Rights Movement

1. Sobel, Andrew and Panas, Jerold (2012). Power Questions: Build Relationships, Win New Business, and Influence Others. NYC: John Wiley & Sons. Pg. 81.
2. Bruns, Roger (2006). Martin Luther King, Jr.: A Biography. Westport, CT: Greenwood Press. Pgs. 41-42. Quote: "In some ways it was the most important hour of his life. His own home had just been bombed, his wife and baby could have been killed; this was the first deep test of his Christian principles and his theories of nonviolence."
3. Oates, Stephen B. (1982). Let the Trumpet Sound: A Life of Martin Luther King Jr. NYC: HarperCollins Publishers, Inc. Pgs. 89-90.
4. Bruns, Roger (2006). Martin Luther King, Jr.: A Biography. Westport, CT: Greenwood Press. Pg. 41.
5. King, Martin Luther (2010 [1958]). Stride Toward Freedom: The Montgomery Story. Boston: Beacon Press. Pgs. 43,54.
6. Menand, Louis (2018, April 4). "When Martin Luther King, Jr., Became a Leader." The NYCer. https://www.newyorker.com/news/daily-comment/when-martin-luther-king-jr-became-a-leader
7. King, Martin Luther (1998). The Autobiography of Martin Luther King, Jr. NYC: Warner Books. Pg. 44.
8. Menand, Louis (2018, April 4). "When Martin Luther King, Jr., Became a Leader." The NYCer. https://www.newyorker.com/news/daily-comment/when-martin-luther-king-jr-became-a-leader
9. Oates, Stephen B. (1982). Let the Trumpet Sound: A Life of Martin Luther King Jr. NYC: HarperCollins Publishers, Inc. Pgs. 65, 90.
10. Gardner, Howard (1995). Leading Minds: An Anatomy of Leadership. NYC: Basic Books. Pg. 219.
11. King, Dr. Martin Luther (1967, November). The Trumpet of Conscience.
12. Menand, Louis (2018, April 4). "When Martin Luther King, Jr., Became a Leader." The NYCer. https://www.newyorker.com/news/daily-comment/when-martin-luther-king-jr-became-a-leader
13. Menand, Louis (2018, April 4). "When Martin Luther King, Jr., Became a Leader." The NYCer. https://www.newyorker.com/news/daily-comment/when-martin-luther-king-jr-became-a-leader
14. King, Martin Luther (1998). The Autobiography of Martin Luther King, Jr. NYC: Warner Books. Pg. 44
15. Payne, Charles (2005, December 2). "Unsung Heroes of the Montgomery Bus Boycott." [Interview.] NPR. https://www.npr.org/templates/story/story.php?storyId=5035704 **See Also:** Finkleman, Paul (2009). Encyclopedia of African American History, 1896 to the Present. Oxford University Press. Pg. 360.
16. King, Martin Luther (1998). The Autobiography of Martin Luther King, Jr. NYC: Warner Books. Pg. 44
17. King, Martin Luther (1998). The Autobiography of Martin Luther King, Jr. NYC: Warner Books. Pg. 44
18. Menand, Louis (2018, April 4). "When Martin Luther King, Jr., Became a Leader." The NYCer. https://www.newyorker.com/news/daily-comment/when-martin-luther-king-jr-became-a-leader
19. King, Martin Luther (1998). The Autobiography of Martin Luther King, Jr. NYC: Warner Books. Pg. 45
20. King, Martin Luther (1998). The Autobiography of Martin Luther King, Jr. NYC: Warner Books. Pg. 45
21. King, Martin Luther (1998). The Autobiography of Martin Luther King, Jr. NYC: Warner Books. Pg. 45
22. Bruns, Roger (2006). Martin Luther King, Jr.: A Biography. Westport, CT: Greenwood Press. Pg. 40.
23. King, Martin Luther (1998). The Autobiography of Martin Luther King, Jr. NYC: Warner Books. Pg. 45
24. King, Martin Luther (2010 [1958]). Stride Toward Freedom: The Montgomery Story. Boston: Beacon Press. Pg. 48.
25. King, Martin Luther (2010 [1958]). Stride Toward Freedom: The Montgomery Story. Boston: Beacon Press. Pg. 48.
26. Menand, Louis (2018, April 4). "When Martin Luther King, Jr., Became a Leader." The NYCer. https://www.newyorker.com/news/daily-comment/when-martin-luther-king-jr-became-a-leader
27. Phillips, Donald T. (1998). Martin Luther King, Jr. On Leadership: Inspiration & Wisdom for Challenging Times. NYC: Warner Books. Pg. 38.
28. Oates, Stephen B. (1982). Let the Trumpet Sound: A Life of Martin Luther King Jr. NYC: HarperCollins Publishers, Inc. Pg. 66.
29. Tassell, Nige (2016, March). "Martin Luther King and the March on Washington." History Revealed, Issue 27. Pg. 29.
30. Gardner, Howard (1995). Leading Minds: An Anatomy of Leadership. NYC: Basic Books. Pg. 207.

31. McCullough, David (2001). Mornings on Horseback: The Story of an Extraordinary Family, a Vanished Way of Life, and the Unique Child Who Became Theodore Roosevelt. NYC: Simon and Schuster. Pg. 30.

32. Robbins, Anthony (2023, March 14). "The 20 Best Motivational Quotes." TonyRobbins.com San Diego, CA: Robbins Research International, Inc. https://www.tonyrobbins.com/tony-robbins-quotes/inspirational-quotes/

33. MacKellar, Pamela H. (2008). The Accidental Librarian. Medford: Information Today, Inc. Pg. 75.

34. Greene, Robert (2018). The Laws of Human Nature. NYC: Viking. Pg. 22

35. Greene, Robert (2018). The Laws of Human Nature. NYC: Viking. Pg. 22

36. Greene, Robert (2018). The Laws of Human Nature. NYC: Viking. Pg. 13

37. Greene, Robert (2018). The Laws of Human Nature. NYC: Viking. Pg. 22

38. Greene, Robert (2018). The Laws of Human Nature. NYC: Viking. Pg. 184.

39. Heifetz, Ronald A. (1994). Leadership Without Easy Answers. Cambridge, MA: Harvard University Press. Pg. 252.

40. King Jr., Martin Luther (1963). Strength to Love. Boston: Beacon Press. Pg. 2. Quote: "Let us consider, first, the need for a tough mind, characterized by incisive thinking, realistic appraisal, and decisive judgment. The tough mind is sharp and penetrating, breaking through the crust of legends and myths and sifting the true from the false. The tough-minded individual is astute and discerning. He has a strong, austere quality that makes for firmness of purpose and solidness of commitment. Who doubts that this toughness of mind is one of man's greatest needs? Rarely do we find men who willingly engage in hard, solid thinking. There is an almost universal quest for easy answers and half-baked solutions. Nothing pains some people more than having to think."

41. Greene, Robert (2006). The 33 Strategies of War. NYC: Penguin Books. Pg. 19.

42. Heifetz, Ronald A. (1994). Leadership Without Easy Answers. Cambridge, MA: Harvard University Press. Pg. 252.

43. Greene, Robert (2021). The Daily Laws: 366 Meditations on Power, Seduction, Mastery, Strategy, and Human Nature. NYC: Viking. Pg. 308.

44. Greene, Robert (2006). The 33 Strategies of War. NYC: Penguin Books. Pg. 19.

45. Gergen, David (2001). Eyewitness to Power: The Essence of Leadership Nixon to Clinton. NYC: Simon & Schuster. Pg. 42.

46. Sobel, Andrew and Panas, Jerold (2012). Power Questions: Build Relationships, Win New Business, and Influence Others. NYC: John Wiley & Sons. Pg. 81.

47. Heifetz, Ronald A. (1994). Leadership Without Easy Answers. Cambridge, MA: Harvard University Press. Pg. 252.

48. Thoreau, Henry David (1910). Walden. NYC: Thomas Y. Crowell & Co. Pgs. 427. Quote: "I went to the woods because I wished to live deliberately," Thoreau later wrote, "to front only the essential facts of life, and see if I could not learn what it had to teach, and not, when I came to die, discover that I had not lived."

49. Martin, Lerone (2023, Last Accessed). "Martin Luther King Jr.: Arrests." The Martin Luther King, Jr. Research and Education Institute. Stanford University. https://kinginstitute.stanford.edu/mlk-topic/martin-luther-king-jr-arrests

50. King Jr., Martin Luther (1963). "Letter from a Birmingham Jail." In Why We Can't Wait, ed. Martin Luther King, Jr., Pgs. 77-100.

51. Twain, Mark (1961). Twain: Wit and Wisecracks. White Plains, NYC: Peter Pauper Press. Pg. 7.

52. Borton, Terry (1970). "Applying the Process Approach" Chapter 8 in Reach, Touch and Teach. NYC: McGraw-Hill.

53. Other useful reflection tools include the following:
   After Action Review (AAR)—One useful tool which originated with the U.S. Army is known as the After Action Review or AAR. This frameworks has four questions which, ideally, are asked by a skilled facilitator rather than the team leader: (1.) What was expected to happen? (2.) What really happened? (3.) What went wrong and why? (4.) And what went well and why? Whether the outcome was better or worse than expected, the focus is on a careful diagnosis of the gap between what was supposed to happen and what actually happened. Dweck, Buckingham, Gino, Francesca, Zenger, John (2021). HBRs 10 Must Reads on Lifelong Learning. Harvard Business School Publishing. Pg. 151
   The 5R Framework—This framework has five stages of reflection: reporting (what happened), responding (what are your thoughts, feelings, and observations about what happened?), relating (how does this connect to your knowledge, skills, and experience or lack thereof?), reasoning (what ideas or theories do you have that can help to explain what happened or how or why it happened?), reconstructing (how will this impact your practice of future actions in the future?).
   Sentence Completion Exercises—Sentence completions are another useful tool for facilitating deeper thinking, as well as self-understanding and personal growth. The procedure basically involves beginning with an incomplete sentence, a "sentence stem," that you would like to have an answer to. One you have a stem or perhaps a few different stems, then you proceed to complete that stem between 6 and 10 different times with different endings. The three key rules are: (1.) do not stop writing, (2.) there are no wrong answers, and (3.) each ending must be a grammatically correct completion of the sentence.

54. Gardner, Howard (1995). Leading Minds: An Anatomy of Leadership. NYC: Basic Books. Pg. 210.

55. Gardner, Howard (1995). Leading Minds: An Anatomy of Leadership. NYC: Basic Books. Pg. 210.

56. Gardner, Howard (1995). Leading Minds: An Anatomy of Leadership. NYC: Basic Books. Pg. 212.

57. Greene, Robert (2018). The Laws of Human Nature. NYC: Viking. Pg. 21

58. Greene, Robert (2018). The Laws of Human Nature. NYC: Viking. Pg. 21

59. Oates, Stephen B. (1982). Let the Trumpet Sound: A Life of Martin Luther King Jr. NYC: HarperCollins Publishers, Inc. Pgs. 89-90.

60. Oates, Stephen B. (1982). Let the Trumpet Sound: A Life of Martin Luther King Jr. NYC: HarperCollins Publishers, Inc. Pgs. 89-90.

61. Bruns, Roger (2006). Martin Luther King, Jr.: A Biography. Westport, CT: Greenwood Press. Pg. 42.

62. Bennett, William J. (2001). Virtues of Leadership. Nashville, TN: Thomas Nelson, Inc. Pg. vii.
63. Bennett, William J. (2001). Virtues of Leadership. Nashville, TN: Thomas Nelson, Inc. Pg. vii.

|16|

Execute from the Vital Center of the Action. Master the Secrets of Strategy Execution at the Front: Captain Henry Morgan Outwits the Spanish Armada

1. Covey, Sean; McChesney, Chris; and Huling, Jim (2012). The 4 Disciplines of Execution: Achieving Your Wildly Important Goals. NYC: Simon and Schuster. Pg. 27.
2. Robbins, Tony (2014). Money: Master the Game: 7 Steps to Financial Freedom. NYC: Simon & Schuster. Pg. 65. **See also:** Robbins, Tony (2017). Unshakeable. NYC: Simon & Schuster.Pg. 10.
3. Sherry, Frank (1986). Raiders and Rebels: A History of the Golden Age of Piracy. NYC: HarperCollins. Pg. 58.
4. Piatt, Walter E. (1998). The Attack on Panama City By Henry Morgan. Masters Thesis, Fort Leavenworth: U.S. Army Command and General Staff College. https://apps.dtic.mil/sti/pdfs/ADA350055.pdf Pgs. 32-33.
5. Talty, Stephan (2007). Empire of Blue Water: Captain Morgan's Great Pirate Army, the Epic Battle for the Americas, and the Catastrophe that Ended the Outlaws' Bloody Reign. NYC: Crown Publishing. Pg. 179.
6. Talty, Stephan (2007). Empire of Blue Water: Captain Morgan's Great Pirate Army, the Epic Battle for the Americas, and the Catastrophe that Ended the Outlaws' Bloody Reign. NYC: Crown Publishing. Pg. 180.
7. Talty, Stephan (2007). Empire of Blue Water: Captain Morgan's Great Pirate Army, the Epic Battle for the Americas, and the Catastrophe that Ended the Outlaws' Bloody Reign. NYC: Crown Publishing. Pg. 180.
8. Talty, Stephan (2007). Empire of Blue Water: Captain Morgan's Great Pirate Army, the Epic Battle for the Americas, and the Catastrophe that Ended the Outlaws' Bloody Reign. NYC: Crown Publishing. Pg. 180-181.
9. Talty, Stephan (2007). Empire of Blue Water: Captain Morgan's Great Pirate Army, the Epic Battle for the Americas, and the Catastrophe that Ended the Outlaws' Bloody Reign. NYC: Crown Publishing. Pg. 180.
10. Talty, Stephan (2007). Empire of Blue Water: Captain Morgan's Great Pirate Army, the Epic Battle for the Americas, and the Catastrophe that Ended the Outlaws' Bloody Reign. NYC: Crown Publishing. Pg. 86. (ebook103)
11. Talty, Stephan (2007). Empire of Blue Water: Captain Morgan's Great Pirate Army, the Epic Battle for the Americas, and the Catastrophe that Ended the Outlaws' Bloody Reign. NYC: Crown Publishing. Pg. 180.
12. Thomas, Graham A. (2015). The Pirate King: The Incredible Story of the Real Captain Morgan. NYC: Skyhorse Publishing. Pg. 85.
13. Konstam, Angus (2007). Scourge of the Seas: Buccaneers, Pirates, and Privateers. Oxford: Osprey Publishing Ltd. Pg. 40.
14. Konstam, Angus (2007). Scourge of the Seas: Buccaneers, Pirates, and Privateers. Oxford: Osprey Publishing Ltd. Pg. 40.
15. Konstam, Angus (2018). The Pirate World: A History of the Most Notorious Sea Robbers. Oxford: Osprey Publishing. Pg. 109.
16. Konstam, Angus (2018). The Pirate World: A History of the Most Notorious Sea Robbers. Oxford: Osprey Publishing. Pg. 109.
17. Iggulden, Conn and Iggulden, David (2010). The Dangerous Book of Heroes. NYC: William Morrow. Pg. 215.
18. The Holy Bible, Jubilee Bible (JUB)(2020). Judges 3:28. Ransom Press International. Bible Gateway. https://www.biblegateway.com/passage/?search=Judges+3%3A28&version=JUB
19. Talty, Stephan (2007). Empire of Blue Water: Captain Morgan's Great Pirate Army, the Epic Battle for the Americas, and the Catastrophe that Ended the Outlaws' Bloody Reign. NYC: Crown Publishing. Pg. 168. Note: Captain Morgan's lieutenant was a French pirate captain who had served under the notoriously vicious pirate captain François "The Bane of Spain" l'Olonnais "in his glory days."
20. Thomas, Graham A. (2015). The Pirate King: The Incredible Story of the Real Captain Morgan. NYC: Skyhorse Publishing. Pg. 89.
21. Little, Benerson (2010). How History's Greatest Pirates Pillaged, Plundered, and Got Away with It: The Stories, Techniques, and Tactics of the Most Feared Sea Rovers from 1500-1800. Beverly, MA: Fair Winds Press. Pg. 88.
22. Thomas, Graham A. (2015). The Pirate King: The Incredible Story of the Real Captain Morgan. NYC: Skyhorse Publishing. Pg. 89.
23. Thomas, Graham A. (2015). The Pirate King: The Incredible Story of the Real Captain Morgan. NYC: Skyhorse Publishing. Pg. 90.
24. Talty, Stephan (2007). Empire of Blue Water: Captain Morgan's Great Pirate Army, the Epic Battle for the Americas, and the Catastrophe that Ended the Outlaws' Bloody Reign. NYC: Crown Publishing. Pg. 171.
25. Talty, Stephan (2007). Empire of Blue Water: Captain Morgan's Great Pirate Army, the Epic Battle for the Americas, and the Catastrophe that Ended the Outlaws' Bloody Reign. NYC: Crown Publishing. Pg. 179.
26. Little, Benerson (2010). How History's Greatest Pirates Pillaged, Plundered, and Got Away with It: The Stories, Techniques, and Tactics of the Most Feared Sea Rovers from 1500-1800. Beverly, MA: Fair Winds Press. Pg. 101.
27. Exquemelin, Alexandre Olivier (1853). The History of the Buccaneers of America: Containing Detailed Accounts of those Bold and Daring Freebooters Chiefly Along the Spanish Main, in the West Indies and in the Great South Sea, Succeeding the Civil Wars in England. Boston: Benjamin B. Mussey & Co. Pg. 174.
28. Exquemelin, Alexandre Olivier (1853). The History of the Buccaneers of America: Containing Detailed Accounts of those Bold and Daring Freebooters Chiefly Along the Spanish Main, in the West Indies and in the Great South Sea, Succeeding the Civil Wars in England. Boston: Benjamin B. Mussey & Co. Pg. 118. See also: Thomas, Graham A. (2015). The Pirate King: The Incredible Story of the Real Captain Morgan. NYC: Skyhorse Publishing. Pg. 102.
29. Thomas, Graham A. (2015). The Pirate King: The Incredible Story of the Real Captain Morgan. NYC: Skyhorse Publishing. Pg. 103.
30. Talty, Stephan (2007). Empire of Blue Water: Captain Morgan's Great Pirate Army, the Epic Battle for the Americas, and the Catastrophe that Ended the Outlaws' Bloody Reign. NYC: Crown Publishing. Pg. 181.

31. Thomas, Graham A. (2015). The Pirate King: The Incredible Story of the Real Captain Morgan. NYC: Skyhorse Publishing. Pg. 100.
32. Exquemelin (1853), Pg. 118.
33. Thomas, Graham A. (2015). The Pirate King: The Incredible Story of the Real Captain Morgan. NYC: Skyhorse Publishing. Pg. 100.
34. Exquemelin (1853), Pg. 118.
35. Exquemelin (1853), Pg. 119.
36. Thomas, Graham A. (2015). The Pirate King: The Incredible Story of the Real Captain Morgan. NYC: Skyhorse Publishing. Pg. 104.
37. Little, Benerson (2010). How History's Greatest Pirates Pillaged, Plundered, and Got Away with It: The Stories, Techniques, and Tactics of the Most Feared Sea Rovers from 1500-1800. Beverly, MA: Fair Winds Press. Pg. 99.
38. Thomas, Graham A. (2015). The Pirate King: The Incredible Story of the Real Captain Morgan. NYC: Skyhorse Publishing. Pg. 105.
39. Exquemelin (1853), Pg. 121.
40. Exquemelin (1853), Pg. 176.
41. Thomas, Graham A. (2015). The Pirate King: The Incredible Story of the Real Captain Morgan. NYC: Skyhorse Publishing. Pg. 105.
42. Thomas, Graham A. (2015). The Pirate King: The Incredible Story of the Real Captain Morgan. NYC: Skyhorse Publishing. Pg. 106.
43. Little, Benerson (2010). How History's Greatest Pirates Pillaged, Plundered, and Got Away with It: The Stories, Techniques, and Tactics of the Most Feared Sea Rovers from 1500-1800. Beverly, MA: Fair Winds Press. Pg. 99. See also: Schultz, Angela Michelle (2019, November 7). "Captain Henry Morgan and the Maracaibo Raid." Owlcation. Maven Media Brands, LLC.
44. Little, Benerson (2010). How History's Greatest Pirates Pillaged, Plundered, and Got Away with It: The Stories, Techniques, and Tactics of the Most Feared Sea Rovers from 1500-1800. Beverly, MA: Fair Winds Press. Pg. 99.
45. Thomas, Graham A. (2015). The Pirate King: The Incredible Story of the Real Captain Morgan. NYC: Skyhorse Publishing. Pg. 87-88. (ebook104-105) See also: Exquemelin (1853), Pg. 120.
46. Exquemelin (1853), Pg. 177.
47. Thomas, Graham A. (2015). The Pirate King: The Incredible Story of the Real Captain Morgan. NYC: Skyhorse Publishing. Pg. 106.
48. Thomas, Graham A. (2015). The Pirate King: The Incredible Story of the Real Captain Morgan. NYC: Skyhorse Publishing. Pg. 106.
49. Little, Benerson (2010). How History's Greatest Pirates Pillaged, Plundered, and Got Away with It: The Stories, Techniques, and Tactics of the Most Feared Sea Rovers from 1500-1800. Beverly, MA: Fair Winds Press. Pg. 99.
50. Thomas, Graham A. (2015). The Pirate King: The Incredible Story of the Real Captain Morgan. NYC: Skyhorse Publishing. Pg. 106.
51. Exquemelin (1853), Pg. 121.
52. Exquemelin (1853), Pg. 121.
53. Thomas, Graham A. (2015). The Pirate King: The Incredible Story of the Real Captain Morgan. NYC: Skyhorse Publishing. Pg. 107.
54. Little, Benerson (2010). How History's Greatest Pirates Pillaged, Plundered, and Got Away with It: The Stories, Techniques, and Tactics of the Most Feared Sea Rovers from 1500-1800. Beverly, MA: Fair Winds Press. Pg. 99-100.
55. Exquemelin (1853), Pg. 122.
56. Ambrose, Stephen (1997). Americans at War. Jackson: University Press of Mississippi. Pg. 128.
57. Little, Benerson (2010). How History's Greatest Pirates Pillaged, Plundered, and Got Away with It: The Stories, Techniques, and Tactics of the Most Feared Sea Rovers from 1500-1800. Beverly, MA: Fair Winds Press. Pg. 100.
58. Thomas, Graham A. (2015). The Pirate King: The Incredible Story of the Real Captain Morgan. NYC: Skyhorse Publishing. Pg. 110.
59. Thomas, Graham A. (2015). The Pirate King: The Incredible Story of the Real Captain Morgan. NYC: Skyhorse Publishing. Pg. 110.
60. Thomas, Graham A. (2015). The Pirate King: The Incredible Story of the Real Captain Morgan. NYC: Skyhorse Publishing. Pg. 108.
61. Thomas, Graham A. (2015). The Pirate King: The Incredible Story of the Real Captain Morgan. NYC: Skyhorse Publishing. Pg. 110.
62. Little, Benerson (2010). How History's Greatest Pirates Pillaged, Plundered, and Got Away with It: The Stories, Techniques, and Tactics of the Most Feared Sea Rovers from 1500-1800. Beverly, MA: Fair Winds Press. Pg. 100.
63. Thomas, Graham A. (2015). The Pirate King: The Incredible Story of the Real Captain Morgan. NYC: Skyhorse Publishing. Pg. 113.
64. Thomas, Graham A. (2015). The Pirate King: The Incredible Story of the Real Captain Morgan. NYC: Skyhorse Publishing. Pg. 113.
65. Thomas, Graham A. (2015). The Pirate King: The Incredible Story of the Real Captain Morgan. NYC: Skyhorse Publishing. Pg. 114.
66. Note: The military proverb that "generals always fight the last war," which has come to mean "murderous folly," is based on the idea that, as important as it is to learn from the last war, something might be different this time that could change everything. In other words, you clearly do not want to repeat the mistakes made last time, but you can't assume that everything will be the same either. Of course, it would be foolish not to prepare to avoid the mistakes made last time, especially given that there may be many similarities. The problem is when generals (but also entrepreneurs, executives, politicians, etc.) become too rigid in their thinking and planning for the next war, based on their experience in the last one.
67. Thomas, Graham A. (2015). The Pirate King: The Incredible Story of the Real Captain Morgan. NYC: Skyhorse Publishing. Pg. 113.
68. Exquemelin (1853), Pg. 126.
69. Zahedieh, Nuala (2004). "Morgan, Sir Henry (c.1635–1688)." Oxford Dictionary of National Biography. Oxford University Press.
70. Zahedieh, Nuala (2004). "Morgan, Sir Henry (c.1635–1688)." Oxford Dictionary of National Biography. Oxford University Press.
71. Little, Benerson (2010). How History's Greatest Pirates Pillaged, Plundered, and Got Away with It: The Stories, Techniques, and Tactics of the Most Feared Sea Rovers from 1500-1800. Beverly, MA: Fair Winds Press. Pg. 99-100.
72. Exquemelin (1853), Pg. 126.
73. Exquemelin (1853), Pg. 126.
74. Little, Benerson (2010). How History's Greatest Pirates Pillaged, Plundered, and Got Away with It: The Stories,

Techniques, and Tactics of the Most Feared Sea Rovers from 1500-1800. Beverly, MA: Fair Winds Press. Pg. 101.

75. Iggulden, Conn and Iggulden, David (2010). The Dangerous Book of Heroes. NYC: William Morrow. Pg. 214.

76. Thomas, Graham A. (2015). The Pirate King: The Incredible Story of the Real Captain Morgan. NYC: Skyhorse Publishing. Pg. 117.

77. Iggulden, Conn and Iggulden, David (2010). The Dangerous Book of Heroes. NYC: William Morrow. Pg. 214.

78. Little, Benerson (2010). How History's Greatest Pirates Pillaged, Plundered, and Got Away with It: The Stories, Techniques, and Tactics of the Most Feared Sea Rovers from 1500-1800. Beverly, MA: Fair Winds Press. Pg. 101.

79. Piatt, Walter E. (1998). The Attack on Panama City By Henry Morgan. Masters Thesis, Fort Leavenworth: U.S. Army Command and General Staff College. https://apps.dtic.mil/sti/pdfs/ADA350055.pdf Pgs. 65.

80. Piatt, Walter E. (1998). The Attack on Panama City By Henry Morgan. Masters Thesis, Fort Leavenworth: U.S. Army Command and General Staff College. https://apps.dtic.mil/sti/pdfs/ADA350055.pdf Pgs. 65.

81. Zahedieh, Nuala (2004). "Morgan, Sir Henry (c.1635–1688)." Oxford Dictionary of National Biography. Oxford University Press.

82. Bossidy, Larry and Charan, Ram (2002). Execution: The Discipline of Getting Things Done. NYC: Crown Business. Pg. 6.

83. Powell, Colin (2006). "A Leadership Primer, Part II." United States, Department of the Army. Washington, D.C.: Homeland Security Digital Library. https://www.hsdl.org/?view&did=467329 PowerPoint slide #5, Lesson #5..

84. Von Moltke, Helmuth (1871). Moltke's Military Works: II. Activity as Chief of the Army General Staff in Peacetime. "About Strategy," An Essay from the Year 1871. Berlin, Germany: Ernst Siegfried Mittler und Sohn. Pg. 291.

85. Iodice, Emilio F. (2022, January). "Lessons from History: The Astonishing Rise to Leadership and Power of Napoleon Bonaparte." The Journal of Values-Based Leadership, Volume 15, Issue 1. Pg. 3. https://scholar.valpo.edu/cgi/viewcontent.cgi?article=1389&context=jvbl

86. Duggan, William (2002). Napoleon's Glance: The Secret of Strategy. NYC: Thunder's Mouth Press. Pg. 17.

87. Lyons, Justin D. (2023, Spring). "Challenging Poseidon: Alexander the Great's 332 BCE Siege of Tyre was won ...daring strategy..." Military History Quarterly. Pg. 76.

88. Sloan, Julia (2006). Learning to Think Strategically. San Diego: Butterworth-Heinemann. Pg. 28. See also A's copy, pg. 6.

89. Sloan, Julia (2006). Learning to Think Strategically. San Diego: Butterworth-Heinemann. Pg. 6.

90. Cohen, William A. (2006). Secrets of Special Ops Leadership: Dare the Impossible—Achieve the Extraordinary. NYC: AMACOM. Pg. 76.

91. Gardner, Mark Lee (2016). Rough Riders: Theodore Roosevelt, His Cowboy Regiment, and the Immortal Charge Up San Juan Hill. NYC: HarperCollins. Pg. 153.

92. Gardner, Mark Lee (2016). Rough Riders: Theodore Roosevelt, His Cowboy Regiment, and the Immortal Charge Up San Juan Hill. NYC: HarperCollins. Pg. 154.

93. Roosevelt, Theodore (1922). Theodore Roosevelt: An Autobiography. NYC: Charles Scribner's Sons. Pg. 106.

94. Gardner, Mark Lee (2016). Rough Riders: Theodore Roosevelt, His Cowboy Regiment, and the Immortal Charge Up San Juan Hill. NYC: HarperCollins. Pg. 157.

95. Gardner, Mark Lee (2016). Rough Riders: Theodore Roosevelt, His Cowboy Regiment, and the Immortal Charge Up San Juan Hill. NYC: HarperCollins. Pg. 158.

96. Roosevelt, Theodore (1922). Theodore Roosevelt: An Autobiography. NYC: Charles Scribner's Sons. Pg. 124.

97. Morris, Edmund (1979). The Rise of Theodore Roosevelt. NYC: Random House. Pg. 685. See also: Roosevelt, Theodore (1922). Theodore Roosevelt: An Autobiography. NYC: Charles Scribner's Sons. Pg. 124.

98. Goodwin, Doris Kearns (2014). The Bully Pulpit: Theodore Roosevelt, William Howard Taft, and the Golden Age of Journalism. NYC: Simon and Schuster. Pg. 230.

99. Roosevelt, Theodore (1899). The Rough Riders. NYC: Charles Scribner's Sons. Pg. 123.

100. Roosevelt, Theodore (1899). The Rough Riders. NYC: Charles Scribner's Sons. Pg. 127.

101. Roosevelt, Theodore (1922). Theodore Roosevelt: An Autobiography. NYC: Charles Scribner's Sons. Pg. 106.

102. Cohen, William A. (2006). Secrets of Special Ops Leadership: Dare the Impossible—Achieve the Extraordinary. NYC: AMACOM. Pg. 76.

103. Danielsen, Hanne-Luise (Editor)(2022). "Desert Fox: Rommel Outwitted the British in the Sahara." Bringing History to Life: 3rd Reich at War. Norway: Bonnier Publications International. Pg. 46.

104. Danielsen, Hanne-Luise (Editor)(2022). "Desert Fox: Rommel Outwitted the British in the Sahara." Bringing History to Life: 3rd Reich at War. Norway: Bonnier Publications International. Pg. 50.

105. Danielsen, Hanne-Luise (Editor)(2022). "Desert Fox: Rommel Outwitted the British in the Sahara." Bringing History to Life: 3rd Reich at War. Norway: Bonnier Publications International. Pg. 50.

106. Sides, Hampton (2019, November 11). "Douglas MacArthur Is One of America's Most Famous Generals. He's Also the Most Overrated." Time. https://time.com/5724009/douglas-macarthur-is-one-of-americas-most-famous-generals-hes-also-the-most-overrated/

107. Dagle, Robbin M. (2020, September 8). "Liberator or 'Dugout Doug'?: MacArthur's legacy in the Philippines revisited." CNN. https://www.cnnphilippines.com/life/culture/2020/9/8/douglas-macarthur-history-controversy.html

108. Halberstam, David (2007). The Coldest Winter: America and the Korean War. NYC: Hyperion. Pg. 543.

109. Halberstam, David (2007). The Coldest Winter: America and the Korean War. NYC: Hyperion. Pg. 543.

110. Halberstam, David (2007). The Coldest Winter: America and the Korean War. NYC: Hyperion. Pg. 543.

111. Freedman, Lawrence (2022). Command: The Politics of Military Operations from Korea to Ukraine. Oxford: Oxford University Press. Pg. 40.

112. Halberstam, David (2007). The Coldest Winter: America and the Korean War. NYC: Hyperion. Pg. 543.

113. Brunson, Robert O. (7 April 2003). "The Inchon Landing: An Example of Brilliant Generalship". Strategy Research Project. U.S. Army War College.

114. Covey, Sean; McChesney, Chris; and Huling, Jim (2012). The 4 Disciplines of Execution: Achieving Your Wildly Important Goals. NYC: Simon and Schuster. Pg. 35.

115. Bossidy, Larry and Charan, Ram (2002). Execution: The Discipline of Getting Things Done. NYC: Crown Business. Pg. 185.

116. Gamble, Paul & Blackwell, John (2004). Knowledge Management: A State of the Art Guide. London: Kogan Page. Pg. 84.

117. Dietrich, William (2015). Napoleon's Rules: Life and Career Lessons from Bonaparte. Burrows Publishing. Pg. 85.

118. Machiavelli, Niccolò (1921 [1532]). The Prince. Ricci, Luigi (Translator). London: Oxford University Press. Pg. 47.

119. Neilson, Gary; Martin, Karla; & Powers, Elizabeth (2008, June). "The Secrets to Successful Strategy Execution." Harvard Business Review. https://hbr.org/2008/06/the-secrets-to-successful-strategy-execution See also: https://www.forbes.com/sites/forbescoachescouncil/2021/07/28/strategy-execution-is-critical-yet-often-ignored/

120. Bossidy, L. & Charan, R. (2002). Execution: The Discipline of Getting Things Done. NYC: Crown Business. Pg. 234.

121. Collins, Jim (2001). Good to Great: Why Some Companies Make the Leap...and Others Don't. NYC: Random House.

122. Collins, Jim (2001). Good to Great: Why Some Companies Make the Leap...and Others Don't. NYC: Random House.

123. Bossidy, Larry and Charan, Ram (2002). Execution: The Discipline of Getting Things Done. NYC: Crown Business. Pg. 109.

124. Bossidy, Larry and Charan, Ram (2002). Execution: The Discipline of Getting Things Done. NYC: Crown Business. Pg. 110.

125. Bossidy, Larry and Charan, Ram (2002). Execution: The Discipline of Getting Things Done. NYC: Crown Business. Pg. 7.

126. Little, Benerson (2010). How History's Greatest Pirates Pillaged, Plundered, and Got Away with It: The Stories, Techniques, and Tactics of the Most Feared Sea Rovers from 1500-1800. Beverly, MA: Fair Winds Press. Pg. 88.

127. Reeves, Richard (1993). President Kennedy: Profile of Power. NYC: Simon & Schuster. Pg. 45.

128. Roosevelt, Theodore (1910, April 23). "Citizenship in a Republic." Public Address at the Sorbonne. Paris, France.

129. McNeilly, Mark R. (1996). Sun Tzu and the Art of Business: Six Strategic Principles for Managers. NYC: Oxford University Press. Pg. 59.

130. Covey, Stephen (2006). The Speed of Trust: The One Thing that Changes Everything. NYC: Free Press. Pg. 34.

131. Williamson, Tim (Editor-in-Chief)(2021). "Operation Barbarossa." History of War, Issue 95. Bath: Future PLC. P. 25.

132. Royde-Smith, John Graham (2022, December 28, Last Accessed). "Operation Barbarossa." Encyclopedia Britannica. https://www.britannica.com/event/Operation-Barbarossa

133. Faligot, Roger (2019). Chinese Spies: From Chairman Mao to Xi Jinping. Translated by Lehrer, Natasha. London: C. Hurst and Co. Publishers Ltd. Pg. 38.

134. Murbach, Gregor (Producer); Jones, Julian (Director)(2022). "Barbarossa." The Rise of the Nazis. [Documentary Film]. PBS. Season 2, Episode 1. https://www.pbs.org/show/rise-nazis/

135. Garner, Tom (2021). "Stalin Brought Barbarossa On Himself." History of War, Issue 95. Bath: Future PLC. Pg. 29.

136. Williamson, Tim (Editor-in-Chief)(2021). "Operation Barbarossa." History of War, Issue 95. Bath: Future PLC. P. 25.

137. Glantz, David (2011). Operation Barbarossa: Hitler's Invasion of Russia 1941. The History Press. Pg. 287.

138. Note: Paranoia is one of the most dangerous of mental diseases for leaders. When you no longer trust your own inner circle, the people trying to help you the most, your days are numbered. For further reading, see: Kets De Vries, Manfred F.R. (2005). Lessons On Leadership By Terror: Finding Shaka Zulu In The Attic (New Horizons in Leadership Studies). Edward Elgar Publisher.

139. Royde-Smith, John Graham (2022, December 28, Last Accessed). "Operation Barbarossa." Encyclopedia Britannica. https://www.britannica.com/event/Operation-Barbarossa

140. Garner, Tom (2021). "Stalin Brought Barbarossa On Himself." History of War, Issue 95. Bath: Future PLC. Pg. 33.

141. Garner, Tom (2021). "Stalin Brought Barbarossa On Himself." History of War, Issue 95. Bath: Future PLC. Pg. 29.

142. Williamson, Tim (Editor-in-Chief)(2021). "Operation Barbarossa." History of War, Issue 95. Bath: Future PLC. Pg. 25.

143. Garner, Tom (2021). "Stalin Brought Barbarossa On Himself." History of War, Issue 95. Bath: Future PLC. Pg. 29.

144. Garner, Tom (2021). "Stalin Brought Barbarossa On Himself." History of War, Issue 95. Bath: Future PLC. Pg. 29.

145. Garner, Tom (2021). "Stalin Brought Barbarossa On Himself." History of War, Issue 95. Bath: Future PLC. Pg. 29.

146. Covey, Sean; McChesney, Chris; and Huling, Jim (2012). The 4 Disciplines of Execution: Achieving Your Wildly Important Goals. NYC: Simon and Schuster. Pg. 35.

147. Covey, Sean; McChesney, Chris; and Huling, Jim (2012). The 4 Disciplines of Execution: Achieving Your Wildly Important Goals. NYC: Simon and Schuster. Pg. 35.

148. Covey, Sean; McChesney, Chris; and Huling, Jim (2012). The 4 Disciplines of Execution: Achieving Your Wildly Important Goals. NYC: Simon and Schuster. Pg. 35.

149. Cote, Catherine (2020, November 17). "5 Keys to Successful Strategy Execution." Harvard Business Review. https://online.hbs.edu/blog/post/strategy-execution

150. Cote, Catherine (2020, November 17). "5 Keys to Successful Strategy Execution." Harvard Business Review. https://online.hbs.edu/blog/post/strategy-execution

151. Note: Monitoring might include some sort of simple, but compelling scorecard, task management software, or a more detailed performance management system, but the key is that it is easily understood, measures what it says it measures, and helps the team stay focused on the vision, strategy, and goals. Unfortunately, this is apparently a tall order. According to the 2020 Gartner Execution Gap Survey, "58% of organizations believe their performance management systems are insufficient for monitoring the performance of strategy." StrategyExPillars0 One straightforward tool strategists often use to monitor changes in the landscape or situation, including both the internal and external environment, is known as a PESTEL analysis. PESTEL is an acronym which stands for political, economic, social, technological, environmental, legal.

152. Brown, Paul B. (2005). Fast Company: The Rules of Business: 55 Essential Ideas to Help Smart People (and Organizations) Perform at Their Best. NYC: Doubleday. Pg. 63.

153. Thomas, Graham A. (2015). The Pirate King: The Incredible Story of the Real Captain Morgan. NYC: Skyhorse Publishing. Pg. 113.
154. Covey, Sean; McChesney, Chris; and Huling, Jim (2012). The 4 Disciplines of Execution: Achieving Your Wildly Important Goals. NYC: Simon and Schuster. Pgs. 35-36.
155. Covey, Sean; McChesney, Chris; and Huling, Jim (2012). The 4 Disciplines of Execution: Achieving Your Wildly Important Goals. NYC: Simon and Schuster. Pgs. 35-36.
156. Konstam, Angus (2007). Scourge of the Seas: Buccaneers, Pirates, and Privateers. Oxford: Osprey Publishing Ltd. Pg. 146.
157. Sherry, Frank (1986). Raiders and Rebels: A History of the Golden Age of Piracy. NYC: HarperCollins. Pg. 121
158. Seitz, Don C. (1925). Under the Black Flag. NYC: The Dial Press. Pg. 195.
159. Seitz, Don C. (1925). Under the Black Flag. NYC: The Dial Press. Pg. 216.
160. Seitz, Don C. (1925). Under the Black Flag. NYC: The Dial Press. Pg. 216.
161. D'Costa, Krystal (2014, September 19). "Why Did Pirates Fly the Jolly Roger?" Scientific American. Nature America, Inc. https://blogs.scientificamerican.com/anthropology-in-practice/why-did-pirates-fly-the-jolly-roger/
162. Staff Writer (2022, June 22). "Mastermind Groups: Everything You Need to Know." Ramsey Solutions. Lampo Licensing, LLC.https://www.ramseysolutions.com/business/master mind-group
163. Duhigg, Charles (2012). The Power of Habit: Why We Do What We Do in Life and Business. NYC: Random House. Pgs. 92-93.
164. Tjan, Anthony K.; Harrington, Richard J.; and Hsieh, Tsun-Yan (2012). Heart, Smarts, Guts and Luck: What It Takes to be an Entrepreneur and Build a Great Business. Cambridge, MA: Harvard Business Review Press. Pg. 92.
165. Greene, Robert (2012). Mastery. NYC: Viking. Pg. 201.
166. McAuliffe, Kenneth J. (2012, January 11). "The story of the NUTS! reply." U.S. Army. Washington, D.C.: Public Affairs Media Relations Division, U.S. Dept. of Defense. https://www.army.mil/article/92856/the_story_of_the_ nuts_reply
167. McAuliffe, Kenneth J. (2012, January 11). "The story of the NUTS! reply." U.S. Army. Washington, D.C.: Public Affairs Media Relations Division, U.S. Dept. of Defense. https://www.army.mil/article/92856/the_story_of_the_ nuts_reply
168. McAuliffe, Kenneth J. (2012, January 11). "The story of the NUTS! reply." U.S. Army. Washington, D.C.: Public Affairs Media Relations Division, U.S. Dept. of Defense. https://www.army.mil/article/92856/the_story_of_the_ nuts_reply
169. McAuliffe, Kenneth J. (2012, January 11). "The story of the NUTS! reply." U.S. Army. Washington, D.C.: Public Affairs Media Relations Division, U.S. Dept. of Defense. https://www.army.mil/article/92856/the_story_of_the_ nuts_reply
170. McAuliffe, Kenneth J. (2012, January 11). "The story of the NUTS! reply." U.S. Army. Washington, D.C.: Public Affairs Media Relations Division, U.S. Dept. of Defense. https://www.army.mil/article/92856/the_story_of_the_ nuts_reply
171. McAuliffe, Kenneth J. (2012, January 11). "The story of the NUTS! reply." U.S. Army. Washington, D.C.: Public Affairs Media Relations Division, U.S. Dept. of Defense.
https://www.army.mil/article/92856/the_story_of_the_ nuts_reply
172. Weatherford, Jack (2005). Genghis Khan and the Making of the Modern World. NYC: Three Rivers Press. Pg. 92. Weatherford paraphrases Genghis Khan as saying "There is no good in anything until it is finished."
173. Lamb, Harold (1927). Genghis Khan: The Emperor of All Men. Garden City, NY: Garden City Publishing. Pg. 66.
174. Cohen, William A. (2006). Secrets of Special Ops Leadership: Dare the Impossible—Achieve the Extraordinary. NYC: AMACOM. Pg. 191.
175. Dietrich, William (2015). Napoleon's Rules: Life and Career Lessons from Bonaparte. Burrows Publishing. Pg. 13.
176. Tracy, Brian (2002). Victory! Applying the Proven Principles of Military Strategy to Achieve Success in Your Business and Personal Life. NYC: AMACOM. Pg. 263.
177. Maxwell, J. C. (2011). Beyond Talent: Become Someone Who Gets Extraordinary Results. Nashville: Thomas Nelson. Pg. 131.
178. Bossidy, Larry and Charan, Ram (2002). Execution: The Discipline of Getting Things Done. NYC: Crown Business. Pg. 128.
179. Cohen, William A. (2006). Secrets of Special Ops Leadership: Dare the Impossible—Achieve the Extraordinary. NYC: AMACOM. Pg. 195.
180. Tracy, Brian (2002). Victory! Applying the Proven Principles of Military Strategy to Achieve Success in Your Business and Personal Life. NYC: AMACOM. Pg. 265.
181. Bossidy, Larry and Charan, Ram (2002). Execution: The Discipline of Getting Things Done. NYC: Crown Business. Pg. 127.
182. Tracy, Brian (2002). Victory! Applying the Proven Principles of Military Strategy to Achieve Success in Your Business and Personal Life. NYC: AMACOM. Pg. 283.
183. Roosevelt, Theodore (1900, March 31). "Character and Success." The Outlook, 64. Pgs. 725-727. http://www.foundationsmag.com/tr-character.html
184. Churchill, Winston and Gilbert, Martin (2001). The Churchill War Papers: The Ever-Widening War, Volume 3, 1941. NYC: W. W. Norton & Company. Pg. xlvii.
185. Stewart, Matthew (2009). The Management Myth: Debunking Modern Business Philosophy. NYC: W.W. Norton & Company. Pg. 174.
186. Dennis, Felix (2006). How to Get Rich: One of the World's Greatest Entrepreneurs Shares His Secrets. NYC: Portfolio. Pg. 70.
187. Bradt, George; Check, Jayme; & Lawler, John (2022). The New Leader's 100-Day Action Plan: Take Charge, Build Your Team, and Deliver Better Results Faster. NYC: Wiley. Pg. 118.
188. Brown, Paul B. (2005). Fast Company: The Rules of Business: 55 Essential Ideas to Help Smart People (and Organizations) Perform at Their Best. NYC: Doubleday. Pg. 62.
189. Thomas, Graham A. (2015). The Pirate King: The Incredible Story of the Real Captain Morgan. NYC: Skyhorse Publishing. Pg. 112.
190. Little, Benerson (2010). How History's Greatest Pirates Pillaged, Plundered, and Got Away with It: The Stories, Techniques, and Tactics of the Most Feared Sea Rovers from 1500-1800. Beverly, MA: Fair Winds Press. Pg. 101.
191. Sherry, Frank (1986). Raiders and Rebels: A History of the Golden Age of Piracy. NYC: HarperCollins. Pg. 371.

Made in the USA
Las Vegas, NV
20 January 2024

84632834R00314